*In grateful appreciation of
your participation in the*

75th Annual

Hanukkah Dinner and Convocation

of Yeshiva University

Sunday, December 12, 1999
3 Teves 5760

*In honor of Dr. Norman Lamm, this gift has been
graciously underwritten by the Jesselson Family.*

The
Religious Thought of
Hasidism

Text and Commentary

BOOKS BY NORMAN LAMM

A Hedge of Roses: Jewish Insights into Marriage and Married Life

The Royal Reach: Discourses on the Jewish Tradition and the World Today

The Good Society: Jewish Ethics in Action

Faith and Doubt: Studies in Traditional Jewish Thought

Torah Lishmah: Torah for Torah's Sake, in the Works of Rabbi Hayyim of Volozhin and his Contemporaries

Torah Umadda: The Encounter of Religious Learning and Worldly Knowledge in the Jewish Tradition

Halakhot ve'Halikhot (Hebrew): Jewish Law and the Legacy of Judaism: Essays and Inquiries in Jewish Law

The Shema: Spirituality and Law in Judaism: As Exemplified in the Shema, the Most Important Passage in the Torah

Yeshiva University gratefully acknowledges the support of Michael and Fiona Scharf towards the publication of this volume

Sources and Studies in
Kabbalah, Hasidism, and Jewish Thought

Volume IV
The Religious Thought of Hasidism
Text and Commentary

Edited by Norman Lamm
President and Jakob and Erna Michael
Professor of Jewish Philosophy
Yeshiva University, New York

Associate Editor: Yaakov Elman
Associate Professor of Judaic Studies
Yeshiva University, New York

The
Religious Thought of
Hasidism

Text and Commentary

NORMAN LAMM

with contributions by
Allan Brill and Shalom Carmy

The Michael Scharf Publication Trust of
Yeshiva University Press

© Copyright 1999
NORMAN LAMM

Library of Congress Cataloging-in-Publication Data

The religious thought of Hasidism : text and commentary / [translated
and edited by] Norman Lamm.
    p.   c.m – – (Sources and studies in Kabbalah, Hasidism, and
Jewish thought : v. 4)
  Includes bibliographical references and index.
  ISBN 0-88125-501-7. – – ISBN 0-88125-440-1 (pb)
  1. Hasidism– –Doctrines.   2. Hasidism– –Translations into English.
3. Ethics, Jewish.   I. Lamm, Norman.   II. Series.
BM198.2.R45   1999
296.8'332– –DC21   98-52553
                                                                   CIP

Manufactured in the United States of America

Distributed by
KTAV Publishing House, Inc.
900 Jefferson Street
Hoboken, NJ 07030

This volume is dedicated to

the memory of two sainted hasidic masters

in whose modest synagogues I prayed in my youth,
and from whom I learned the wonders, the charm, the
mystery, and the teaching of Hasidism

Rabbi David Yitzchak Isaac Rabinowitz

The Skolier Rebbe

descendant of the Baal Shem Tob

and

Rabbi Yisrael Elazar Hopstein

The Kozhnitzer Rebbe

descendant of the Maggid of Kozhnitz

may the memory of the righteous be blessed

Contents

CONTENTS

10. HUMILITY AND SADNESS. R. Elimelekh of Lizhensk.
Source: Noam Elimelekh to Bamidbar, s.v. o yomar va-yedaber

11. JOY AND FREEDOM. R. Nahman of Bratslav.
Source: Likkutei Etzot, Simḥah, nos. 7, 10, 26, 27

12. DANCE, SONG, AND HUMOR. R. Nahman of Bratslav.
Source: Likkutei Etzot, Simḥah, nos. 12, 14, 15, 29

CHAPTER TWELVE, PART B, SMALLNESS AND GREATNESS   403

Introduction

1. DEFINING *KATNUT* AND *GADLUT*. Besht.
Source: Zava'at ha-Rivash, no. 129.

2. *DEVEKUT* IN "SMALLNESS." Besht.
Source: Zava'at ha-Rivash, no. 67

3. *DEVEKUT* IN "SMALLNESS" (continued). Besht.
Source: Zava'at ha-Rivash, no. 137

4. SMALLNESS AS A PREPARATION FOR GREATNESS. R. Moshe Hayyim Ephraim of Sudlikov.
Source: Degel Maḥaneh Ephraim to Vayetzei, beginning

5. SMALLNESS AS THE EXPERIENCE OF GOD'S ABSENCE. R. Yaakov Yosef of Polennoye.
Source: Ketonet Passim, Shemini, p. 11a

6. LEVITY LEADS TO GREATNESS. Besht.
Source: Keter Shem Tov, p. 2

7. GREATNESS AND SMALLNESS IN THE RATIONAL AND DEVOTIONAL REALMS. R. Dov Ber, the Maggid of Mezeritch.
Source: Maggid Devarav le-Yaakov, no. 205

8. HOLDING ON TO GOD DURING GREATNESS. R. Elimelekh of Lizhensk.
Source: Noam Elimelekh to Emor, s.v. be-inyan

9. YOUTHFULNESS AND MATURITY. R. Levi Yitzhak of Berdichev.
Source: Kedushat Levi to Yitro, s.v. o yevo'ar anokhi

CHAPTER THIRTEEN, PEACE   413

Introduction

Love of Fellow Man and Peacefulness

1. THE LOVE OF MAN. R. Elimelekh of Lizhensk.
Source: Noam Elimelekh, Hanhagot ha-Adam, no. 8

2. THE PROPER ATTITUDE. R. Elimelekh of Lizhensk.
Source: Tefillah Kodem ha-Tefillah

3. PEACE AMONG OPPOSITES. R. Nahman of Bratslav.
Source: Likkutei Etzot, Shalom, no. 10

4. IDENTIFYING WITH THE OTHER. R. Menahem Mendel of Vitebsk.
Source: Peri ha-Aretz u-Peri ha-Etz to Shofetim

5. THE LIMBS OF ONE BODY. R. Shneur Zalman of Liady.
Source: Iggeret ha-Kodesh, chap. 22

Preface

This volume on the religious thought of Hasidism as revealed in the words of its founders and early leaders intends to fulfill two purposes: first, to acquaint the reader with the intellectual and spiritual foundations of Hasidism and, second, to correct certain misconceptions about it that are part of the popular wisdom concerning this movement which has, in our own day, shown a remarkable resiliency.

The academic study of Hasidism has in comparatively recent years begun to take seriously the primary sources of the movement, especially the books, essays, and other literature of its major exponents. Much like the popular views of Hasidism—which both romanticized and demonized it beyond recognition, identifying it with the "shtetl" experience which it either glamorized or scorned—too many students of religion have fallen prey to reductionist tendencies. Thus, some have seen Hasidism as essentially a folk religion, its essence preserved in stories, anecdotes, and folklore, while others have regarded it as but another albeit less esoteric brand of Jewish mysticism. Some— whether admiringly or critically—have considered Hasidism to be a complete break with the rabbinic tradition that held sway for millennia, holding on to a number of externals of language and appearance but intrinsically constituting a new and bold theology; others— whether apologetically or disparagingly—viewed it as the old tradition in a new dress with no fundamental points of friction between them.

Whatever their views, too many have failed to appreciate the intellectual power and theological importance of the leaders of the movement over the last two centuries and more. These have been overlooked partially because of the reductionist inclination mentioned above and partially because of a language problem: some hasidic thinkers created their own vocabulary; others were regrettably inarticulate; while others delivered their discourses orally, generally on the late afternoon of the Sabbath (at the Third Meal), and their acolytes who later wrote them down were often distinguished by their lack of literary grace.

Another element of importance in gaining a more realistic and correct insight into the nature of Hasidism, one which has suffered from neglect in the past, is the array of significant if sometimes subtle differences in the thinking of the leading expositors of Hasidism. While there certainly is a coherent set of principles that is common to all the major hasidic thinkers, the points of contention among them on the great issues of religious thought are surely worthy of exploration.

This volume does not propose to cover the entire gamut of hasidic life and thought; indeed, that would be both presumptuous and foolhardy. The reader must know at the outset what the limitations of this book are.

First, while the oral traditions, tales of the masters, miracle stories, songs and melodies, piquant and often far-fetched interpretations of biblical verses and talmudic or midrashic passages, are surely of importance in understanding Hasidism, they have received relatively adequate treatment elsewhere, and the time has come to restore the balance. Much of the hasidic spirit pulsates through the stories, the music, and the *bon mots* of the hasidic masters, but there is much more of solidly intellectual-theological importance that is more explicit than implicit and that has not received sufficient notice in the past. It is true that it is often difficult to tell whether a certain interpretation is a charming "gut vort" (*bon mot*) or a subtle insight of theological and intellectual significance. In such cases I have sinned on the side of generosity and assumed that it belongs in this volume. Moreover, so very much of serious hasidic thought is offered by way of exegesis, which may sound quite convoluted to the modern sensibilities of the uninitiated reader, that it would have been impossible to omit such passages without doing violence to the aspirations of the book. (The tendency of hasidic writers to interlace their ideological statements with "words of Torah" is so pronounced and prevalent, that much of the material in the notes is dedicated to guiding the reader through some of the homiletic exercises and then clarifying the essential message.) Yet, for the greatest part I have opted for the written over the oral and the cogitative or theological over the simply exegetical.

Second, I have confined myself largely to the first three generations of the movement: the Besht (the accepted acronym for R. Israel Baal Shem Tov, the founder) and his contemporaries; his immediate disciples, especially R. Dov Ber (the Maggid of Mezeritch) and R. Yaakov Yosef of Polennoye; and the many distinguished disciples of the former. Despite these chronological limitations, I have permitted myself an occasional foray into later generations, especially the radical and fascinating great-grandson of the Besht, R. Nahman of Bratslav; certain of the eminent thinkers of the Habad school; the prolific antimodernist R. Zevi Elimelekh Shapira of Dinov; the profound R. Zadok ha-Kohen Rabinowitz of Lublin (which brings us to the edge of the twentieth century); and a few others whose significance as thinkers commended themselves, if sometimes arbitrarily, to the author.

This book has had an extraordinarily long period of gestation. It began in my childhood. My paternal grandfather, whom I knew but slightly, had been a follower—one of many thousands—of the Rebbe of Belz. My maternal grandfather, with whom I studied Talmud and whom I admired endlessly, was a "hasidischer rav," an eminently scholarly rabbi of the classical mode who had profound ties with the hasidic giants of his generation, particularly those of the Sanzer dynasty. The atmosphere of my parents' home was observant but not hasidic in practice, yet it was filled with the lore and love of Hasidism.

As an undergraduate, I recall starting to write a term paper on the conflict between the hasidic "courts" of the Sanzer and the Sadigorer, but aborting the effort because I was so dismayed by the degradation that the lofty ideas of the founders of Hasidism suffered at the hands of some of their less distinguished followers. The subservience of noble ideals to personal vendettas, the unthinking and occasionally destructive loyalties, and the rank intolerance were, I felt, a desecration of what the masters of Hasidism had to teach to us. In time, and with a bit more maturity, I learned to weigh the good against the bad, valuing the former and rejecting the latter—especially in its various contemporary revivals.

My interest in Hasidism rekindled, but now with the benefit of a more critical stance, I chose as my doctoral thesis the work of the most important critic of the movement, the eminent rabbinic authority of Russian Jewry in the latter part of the eighteenth century, R. Hayyim of Volozhin who, following his teacher R. Elijah the Gaon of

Vilna, became the leading theoretician of the mitnaggedic world. (This dissertation was later published in Hebrew and then in English under the title *Torah Lishmah: Torah for Torah's Sake in the Works of Rabbi Hayyim of Volozhin and His Contemporaries*.)

Viewing Hasidism in its encounter with the classical rabbinic world gave me additional opportunity to acquaint myself not only with the lore but with the serious concepts with which hasidic masters were struggling.

This book proper began as a course in hasidic thought and literature at Yeshiva University's Erna Michael College (now Isaac Breuer College) in the mid '60s, and continued with similar courses and additional development at Yeshiva's Stern College for Women and the Graduate School of City University of New York. Over the years, many learned friends and learned colleagues were of inestimable value to me. I am especially indebted to Rabbi Israel Schepansky for his vast erudition in rabbinic literature, and to Rabbi Alter B. Metzger of Stern College for Women for his generous assistance in providing references to Habad writings. To them, to others whom I have inadvertently failed to mention—too many for me to acknowledge with any pretense of comprehensiveness—and to my students in these courses, I offer genuine thanks.

Yet I cannot use this as an excuse for failing to mention those whose special contributions and assistance in the past year or two have made me particularly indebted to them, especially because I am mindful of the talmudic teaching that "a good deed is ascribed to the one who completes it." Rabbi Shalom Carmy, with whom I team-taught a course in Hasidism at Yeshiva, has written a number of the introductions to individual chapters of this volume as well as the general introduction. Dr. Alan Brill of Yeshiva University's Yeshiva College and Bernard Revel Graduate School, a young but already seasoned scholar, contributed the chapter on the role of women in Hasidism. Dr. Yaakov Elman, a man of most impressive versatility in many areas of Jewish scholarship, edited this volume with great care not only in his capacity as the co-editor of the series of which it is part, but equally or more so as a labor of love for the subject. His virtuosity as well as his virtue will always remain dear to me. Mr. Bernard Scharfstein of KTAV Publishing has for many years continued to insist that I put aside time to prepare this book for publication. But for his encouragement, persistence, and personal friendship, this book would still be gathering dust in unmarked and unremarkable folders in some unreachable place in my filing cabinet. The Memorial

Foundation for Jewish Culture, in the person of Dr. Jerry Hochbaum, encouraged my wavering determination to finish and publish this book by providing a generous grant a number of years ago. I would be remiss were I to omit mention of officials and staff members of two libraries who were of inestimable help in the preparation of this volume. One is the staff of the Mendel Gottesman Library of Yeshiva University and, in particular, Mrs. Leah Adler, and Messrs. Zvi Erenyi and Zalman Alpert. The second is the Library of Agudas Chassidei Chabad Ohel Yosef Yitzchak Lubavitch, its director, Rabbi S. D. Levin, and Rabbi Y. Y. Keller. I acknowledge with most sincere thanks Rabbi Yehudah Krinsky, of Agudas Chassidei Chabad, who generously gave permission for the use of Habad's superb English translations of R. Shneur Zalman of Liady's *Tanya*. Though the reader will find that I have altered it in places, and added and modified notes and annotations, its availability saved me a good deal of unnecessary toil. The friendship and cooperation of all the above place me in their debt. My gratitude to them is unstinting. I would like to thank Robert J. Milch and Deena Stillerman for their technical skill and work beyond the call of duty.

It is my hope that all these efforts, both mine and others', will prove vindicated by the appearance of this volume and its use either as a text in formal classes or as an instrument for personal edification by readers intrigued by one of the most vital movements in the multi-millennial history of Judaism.

May this book make some contribution, no matter how modest, to the renaissance of Judaism in our times and especially to the greater practice of spirituality, concentration, and love—as taught by the great masters of Hasidism—in our religious life.

NORMAN LAMM
New York City
August 26, 1998
4 Ellul, 5738

Note to the Reader

This anthology has been composed with two types of readers in mind. One is the person who wishes to gain a general view of hasidic thought, and has the time to read it from cover to cover; the other is a reader who is interested in certain topics, perhaps from a cross-cultural or interdisciplinary perspective. Thus, while I encourage everyone to read the book in its entirety (even if inclined to skip some footnotes!), I have designed the book for the "skip-and-dip" reader as well.

For example, three or four selections, because they relate to various topics, are repeated in order to give the reader a more comprehensive view of an entire topic without the bother of leafing back and forth. Given the size of the book, I thought it better to repeat those few selections rather than force the reader to refer back to the selection's earlier appearance. The result is, I hope, a more rather than less readable book.

The reader should be aware of the style and circumstances in which the originals were written. As mentioned above, most hasidic homilies were not written down by their "authors" but rather by designated listeners who, after the Sabbath, would record in their somewhat defective Hebrew what they had heard in the original Yiddish. This accounts not only for the lack of fluency and the deficiencies in grammar and syntax of the original, but also their cumbersome structure. In part this reflects the difference between a written text, which should be to the point, and oral homilies—especially traditional forms of Jewish preaching which usually worked by indirection. The preacher (classically) begins with a verse or talmudic statement which apparently has nothing to do with the topic at hand, thus creating a certain suspenseful attention and expectation on the part of his audience, and eventually works his way around to the point, often digressing in order to inform and even entertain. Were the original speaker to record his own thoughts, he would almost certainly eliminate the digressions. A good illustration is a comparison of two of our most prominent authors, the great Maggid of Mezeritch and one of his most influential disciples, R. Levi Yitzhak of Berdichev. R. Levi Yitzhak was assigned the task of editing his master's homilies, and produced the classic *Maggid Devarav le-Yaakov*, which is often brief to the point of obscurity, never prolix or verbose. R. Levi Yitzhak was less lucky in his own case; the editors of *his* talks preserved much of the original tenor and style of the original talks, and thus emerge both prolix and verbose. The style of hasidic writing in general is often obscure, although I have tried to render it more accessible to the contemporary reader, and when it appears to be simple, it is quite sophisticated and not at all simplistic.

In the case of the very foundation of hasidic writing, the first hasidic work every printed, the *Toledot Yaakov Yosef* of R. Yaakov Yosef of Polennoye, we have a different problem. Here R. Yaakov Yosef, one of the most celebrated preachers of his time (even before he "converted" to Hasidism), shows himself a master of the genre of eighteenth century Jewish preaching. Unfortunately, that style ill befits the modern temper. Though I have made some "cuts" in our translations, the text that remains may still seem a bit intimidating for some readers. I hereby encourage readers to persevere, and assure them that the gain is well worth the effort, especially since these digressions are often as important—or even more important: than the main topic. Indeed, in some cases I have chosen to translate *just* the digressions.

Another word of caution: chapters vary in length as well as difficulty. Some are very long and some are quite difficult—indeed, some are both. Given the complexity of *all* religious thought regarding God and His relation to the world, not least of all Jewish philosophical and mystical thought on this topic, we must expect the same from hasidic thinkers—and that is what we get. It is, therefore, with some trepidation that I open the book with a chapter on that topic, but I would not be true to my sources or to the immanent progression of the ideas were I not to do so. However, the reader should not allow him or herself to get bogged down in that opening chapter. For some readers, indeed, the better part of wisdom would be save it for last.

Finally, while much effort has gone into ensuring that transliterations, etc., are consistent, this has not been done mechanically; my primary concern has been readability. Thus, while the Hebrew letter *tsadi* has ordinarily been transliterated with a "tz," we thought "zaddik" more comfortable for the reader than "tzaddik." *Het* was generally not dotted, except in cases where an exact transliteration was thought necessary. In all these decisions, the reader's comfort has been my primary concern.

Finally, please note the Glossary and biographical sketches at the back of the book.

General Introduction

This book offers a corrective to the popular impression that early Hasidism was incorrigibly, blithely, and profoundly unintellectual by presenting annotated translations of selected passages, arranged according to topic. The introductory sections provide an overview and a context for the subject matter of each chapter. This General Introduction aims to do the same for the entire volume, sketching the historical background of the early hasidic movement and charting the central ideas in their intellectual context. We must also consider the nature of the hasidic literature itself, in order to evaluate the significance for Hasidism and for the history of Jewish thought in general, of the texts and ideas in this book. Our discussion will furthermore make explicit some of the reasons underlying the choice of passages included here in the light of current scholarship.

ORIGINS: THE BESHT AND HIS APPEAL

Of the founder of the hasidic movement, R. Israel Baal Shem Tov (usually referred to by the acronym "the Besht"), little is known. Even the authenticity of the few letters ascribed to him is debated. The most reliable is his letter to R. Gershon Kutover; see the preface to chapter 17, selection 22. The scanty information at our disposal testifies to a youth during which his spiritual powers were concealed, followed by a revealed stage, beginning in his late thirties, during which he was active at various sites in Eastern Europe (primarily in present-day Ukraine) until his death (1760) in his early sixties. His disciples, to whom we are indebted for the transmission of his teaching, were no doubt overwhelmed by his personality; yet his contemporaries did not, so far as we know, refer to him in their written works by name. Posthumous reports make it possible to reconstruct his ideas, and suggest what books were important to him. Yet the original intent of the movement, like the biography of its charismatic founder, remains shrouded in mystery.

Among several phenomena proposed by historians as major factors in the rise of Hasidism, with a continued effect on its ideology, two deserve our attention. The first is the Sabbatean debacle of 1666. The late Professor Gershom Scholem, in particular, insisted on the pervasive impact of this episode. The belief in the messianic claims made on behalf of Shabbetai Zevi swept the Jewish world. The Sabbatean fervor was accompanied by kabbalistic views tinged with antinomianism, the conviction that under eschatological conditions, traditional halakhic imperatives no longer held. When the candidate, scheduled to inaugurate the final redemption, was converted to Islam, a profound disillusionment set in among most Jews.

At the same time, Sabbatean tenets survived in certain mystical circles. This was obvious with respect to the Donmeh, Turkish disciples who followed Shabbetai into apostasy, and the Frankists in mid-eighteenth-century Eastern Europe. The latter group struggled for recognition, in the eyes of Gentile authority, as a legitimate Judeo-Christian sect; according to legend, the Besht, in his old age, confounded them in debate, and otherwise labored mightily against them. But others hid their Sabbatean leanings in public, although they entertained the discredited views in private. The atmosphere of suspicion was dramatically illustrated through the 1750s, when the eminent R. Jacob Emden of Altona accused the at least equally distinguished chief rabbi of Prague, R. Jonathan Eyebeschutz, of subscribing to the Sabbatean heresy, setting off a controversy that pitted the highest authorities against each other.

How did this situation affect Hasidism? Fear of antinomianism indisputably contributed to the distrust with which Hasidism was regarded in the late eighteenth and early nineteenth centuries. Hasidic practices, particularly during prayer, that appeared to take lightly standard halakhic strictures, overridden for the sake of greater emotional realization, took on an ominous quality; any activity that segregated hasidim from others could not fail to arouse suspicion. In Scholem's view, however, the ideological influences on Sabbateanism on Hasidism went far beyond this. Here we must note two interrelated but distinct effects, both of which are open to question.

1. Scholem postulated substantial Sabbatean influence on hasidic thought. He maintained that there was a significant continuity between the early hasidim and the underground currents of heresy. When hasidic practice seems to deviate from the established Halakhah, whenever hasidic masters throw out antinomian hints, such as the notion that sin may serve to bring man closer to God, we are, according to Scholem, coming into contact with the dark, rebellious spirit of heresy, albeit in an attenuated form, capable of surviving in the hostile post-Sabbatean environment.

Scholem's history, by arguing for Sabbatean influence on Hasidism, thus magnifies the discontinuity between Hasidism and conventional Jewish piety oriented to halakhic norms. This depiction of the background to Hasidism can be challenged in two ways. One would demonstrate that the radical elements in Hasidism may be less prominent than one might initially assume. To take the most conspicuous example: the Sabbateans held that sin could serve as a vehicle of redemption. Hasidic writers, too, speak of *yeridah le-tzorekh aliyah* ("descent for the purpose of ascent") and the like. The hasidic masters, however, do not advocate the prospective justification of transgression: the "sanctification of sin" is generally applied retrospectively and limited in scope—to sins committed in thought rather than in action, to sins resulting from the decision of the saintly individual to become involved with the masses, and so forth. This is a far cry from the radical antinomianism of the Sabbateans.

The other challenge to Scholem's theory draws on the impressive research of Mendel Piekarz. Piekarz submits that the presence of unconventional themes detected in the early hasidic literature implies, not contact with Sabbateanism, but continuity with pre-Sabbatean ideas amply documented in popular mainstream works like *Shnei Luhot ha-Berit,* by the sixteenth-century kabbalist R. Isaiah Horowitz, as well as a number of unpublished texts. If these concepts attract attention and criticism when mouthed by hasidim, it is because their employment by Sabbateans rendered them improper rather that because of any substantive theological impropriety. In any event, contemporary scholarship has become skeptical of Scholem's appeal to pan-Sabbatean causation in this area.

2. Scholem spoke of Hasidism as the "neutralization" of the Messianic impulse. This means that Hasidism internalized and spiritualized the external political goals that are inseparable from tradi-

tional eschatology: the messianic redemption is realized, if only partially, when the individual existence becomes a redeemed one. The idea of a hasidic "neutralization" of eschatology promised an improvement of Jewish morale, which had first been crushed by persecution and hardship, and then inflamed to fever pitch by the speculation that resulted in Sabbateanism. This transformation of Judaism's historical-political ideals inhibits the advent of another false messiah.

Indeed, much has been made of the hasidic movement as a response to the low morale engendered by the social and educational structure of the Jewish community in Eastern Europe during the first half of the eighteenth century. In this account, the rabbinic establishment basks in its intellectual elitism, oblivious to their disenfranchised brethren; one recalls the anecdotes about R. Gershon of Kutov's initial contempt for his "ignorant" brother-in-law who is, of course, none other than the Besht. Scholars like Dubnow in the early twentieth century, who are fond of castigating the elitist rabbinic attitude, tend to identify it with halakhic stringency and existential gloominess.

Surely many passages in the hasidic literature express a vigorous resentment of rabbinic learning when it is detached from genuine piety; R. Yaakov Yosef of Polennoye frequently calls such scholars *shedin yehuda'in* ("Jewish demons"). The Besht's predilection for teaching by parable and anecdote enabled him to reach a larger audience than a more formal approach, though there was no lack of itinerant preachers who addressed the broader community throughout his lifetime. The propensity of hasidic thinkers to utilize kabbalistic theosophical categories to shed light on man's spiritual psychology points to a "democratic" concern for existential relevance. And the hasidic proclivity to "serve God in joy" was remarkable enough to attract the arrows of their opponents, who accused them of various excesses.

Yet some features of this picture need to be modified. Jacob Katz has argued that the standards of rabbinic training in this period were in decline, so that the gap between scholar and layman was narrowing, making it more difficult for the people to accept their authority. True, Hasidism championed broad involvement in Jewish mystical literature, and devoted a great deal of time to prayer and other nonintellectual manifestations of service to God. But this did not imply a rejection of conventional Torah study, with its focus on Halakhah. Even less was Hasidism consistent with a relaxed attitude to the scrupulous observance of halakhic law.

Katz suggested that Hasidism initially attracted an intellectually engaged segment of the community, though not the elite leadership—what has come to be called the "secondary elite" by those who study intellectual history. The typical hasidic disciple was thus likely to come from the ranks of the schoolteachers and ritual slaughterers. And Weiss identified the Maggidim —the itinerant preachers—as the emerging leaders of the movement. It is such men who formed the original constituency for the discourses excerpted and presented in this book.

SUCCESSOR GENERATIONS: THE PROBLEM OF TRANSMISSION

The second generation of hasidic leaders was dominated by the Besht's two major disciples, R. Yaakov Yosef of Polennoye and R. Dov Ber ("the Maggid") of Mezeritch. R. Yaakov Yosef is best known today for his four volumes of discourses on the Torah. The *Toledot Yaakov Yosef*, which he published during his lifetime (1781), was the first hasidic book to see print. Like most subsequent hasidic texts, the *Toledot*, despite the atypical involvement of the author in the publication and the complex structure of many of the discourses, is a book less composed than compiled. The source for the material is clearly oral, presumably words spoken at the Sabbath table. The written version is thus derived from the face-to-face encounter.

It was the Maggid, by contrast, who nurtured the third generation of hasidic masters, including such titans as R. Levi Yitzhak of Berdichev, R. Elimelekh of Lizhensk, and R. Shneur Zalman of Liady, the founder of Habad Hasidism. Less robust than the Besht, he did not travel; instead, his followers regularly visited him at his "court" in Mezeritch, thus instituting what became the prevalent pattern of hasidic leadership. His doctrines, far more ascetic than the usual portrayal of Hasidism, assumed permanent form only through the efforts of his disciples.

These two major figures of the second generation, among others, conveyed many aphorisms and insights of the Besht. By the 1780s the Besht's growing reputation justified the marketing of anthologies of his sayings, such as the *Keter Shem Tov*. The number of adherents to Hasidism was also growing, and the movement's expansion itself became a challenge to hasidic ideals and were a spur for the development of new ideas and modes of communication.

One major shift involved the role of the hasidic zaddik or rebbe. In the tradition of the Besht, each Jew was intended to aspire to the level and attainments of the outstanding individual. Now this goal was no longer viewed as realistic. The rebbe became the primary conduit of divine benefaction, and the individual participated in the higher spiritual life insofar as he attached himself to the rebbe. This move, initially inspired and theologically justified by R. Yaakov Yosef, is associated with R. Elimelekh of Lizhensk, who established Hasidism in Galicia (roughly covering the southern Poland of today). It is often bemoaned as a symptom of decline or even corruption of the original hasidic enterprise, in which individual striving is replaced by the cult of their charismatic leader and, eventually, the rebbe's hereditary successors. In extenuation, we should note that the aggrandizement of the zaddik offers a solution, though not necessarily a happy one, to an unavoidable problem, namely, the apparent inability of the ordinary Jew to attain the heights of spirituality of God-awareness.

The question of how to educate a far-flung community also affected the intellectual and organizational development of Habad. As the spearhead of Hasidism in Lithuania and Belarus, R. Shneur Zalman confronted an entrenched opposition to Hasidism. The controversy was associated with the illustrious name of R. Elijah, the Vilna Gaon, talmudic sage and kabbalist par excellence of his era. So brightly burned the antagonism between the camps that hasidim were accused, based on a misunderstanding, of calculating the Gaon's death on Sukkot 1795, and some mitnaggedim ("opponents"—the sobriquet that clung to non-hasidic Lithuanians) were responsible for R. Shneur Zalman's arrest by the Russian authorities on charges that ranged from suspicion of heterodox theosophy to channeling funds to Russia's enemies. (The latter referred to the hasidim who had ascended to the Holy Land, where Napoleon had recently waged war, and who depended on contributions from their peers.)

R. Shneur Zalman, as the principal exemplar and advocate of traditional talmudic learning among the first several generations of hasidic leadership, was admirably suited to carry the message of Hasidism into the Lithuanian citadels of Torah learning. But his vigorous authorship was not exhausted by the composition of a major halakhic code. He struck his most powerful blow for hasidic ideas by producing a new kind of hasidic book, the *Tanya*. The book was a methodical exposition of hasidic doctrine presented by R. Shneur Zalman (albeit less esoterically than in his other hasidic works), rather than an unsystematic record of oral discourses. This "intellectual" approach to Hasidism made direct personal contact with the rebbe less urgent. And, in fact, the Habad court was so arranged as to maximize the time devoted by the rebbe to new recruits, while encouraging veteran hasidim to fend for themselves. The choice of the systematic treatise in addition to the Torah aperçu as a mode of literary expression is the hallmark of later Habad hasidim as well, as is the desire to spread the tent of Habad Hasidism as widely as possible. The reader of this book will soon note the orderly character of the sections from *Tanya* as compared with the impressionist quality of the selections from other hasidic texts.

This book focuses almost entirely on the first three generations of the hasidic movement, up to R. Shneur Zalman's death while fleeing the French invasion of Russia in 1812. The two main exceptions are R. Zevi Elimelekh of Dinov (the *Benei Yisaskhar*), who was still a young man at the time, and the seminal R. Zadok ha-Kohen Rabinowitz of Lublin, who lived to the end of the nineteenth century. R. Zadok is the highly creative representative of a significant trend in nineteenth-century Polish hasidic intellectual life. This tradition is most often associated with R. Simha Bunem of Parshis'kha and R. Menahem Mendel of Kotzk, whose period of greatest impact began in the late 1820s.

This hasidic approach is generally identified with a streak of radical individualism and a ruthless stripping away of false motivations. It was the fate of the enigmatic Kotzker, who left no writings, to attract about his name a rich collection of sharp anecdotes and aphorisms. An apparent crisis in his life, precipitating his withdrawal from the active leadership of his hasidim (c. 1840), became the subject of fascinated and horrified speculation. To some writers on Hasidism, such as Buber, the furious quest for integrity appeared like a desperate effort to regain the authenticity of the hasidic movement, compromised by the ineluctable process of routinization and the abdication of individual responsibility engendered by the cult of the zaddik.

Now the Kotzker's extant statements, like those of R. Simha Bunem, put enormous emphasis on conventional Torah study. The Kotzker's closest disciples, his son-in-law R. Abraham Borenstein of Sochachov (the *Avnei Nezer*) and R. Yitzhak Meir of Gur (*Hiddushei ha-Rim*), are best known for their halakhic works. Their descendants and heirs continued to pursue a full integration of talmudic training and hasidic originality. From one point of view, that which is indifferent to the traditional as the centerpiece of Jewish spiritual and intellectual life, this development is irrelevant to the hasidic message, perhaps even another symptom of routinization. From another perspective, forcefully articulated by R. Abraham Isaac Kook, this tendency, like the intellectual orientation of Habad, bespeaks a higher synthesis of Hasidism and "mainstream" rabbinic Judaism. If that is the case, then the Kotzker imparted the insight that no authentic religious community can long abide on devotional power alone; the intellectual gesture, specifically the intellectual energy generated by Torah study, is essential for the perpetuation of genuine religious passion in Judaism.

R. Zadok of Lublin, in any event, was a disciple of the Izhbitzer, who had begun his teaching career as a student of the Kotzker. While he took from the Izhbitzer a propensity to deterministic psychological and historical analysis somewhat out of keeping with the Kotzker legacy, his remarkable posthumous writings need to be viewed in the light of the developments outline above.

THE CENTRALITY OF THE WRITTEN WORD

For the past century and longer, most Western readers have become familiar with Hasidism through collections of tales about the founders of the movement, some of which, e.g. Buber's and Elie Wiesel's, have attained wide circulation. This is not the place to discuss the provenance of various stories, their content, and the problems of utilizing them as historical sources, let alone a detailed analysis of the manner in which the compilers of the tales shaped the material in the light of their own preoccupations. Naturally, such an analysis would support our reliance on early written works as a source for the first three generations of hasidic masters, if only because the reported tales are much further removed, chronologically, from the figures portrayed.

But what is at stake in our desire to know hasidic ideas through the recorded thoughts of the founders is more than merely the historian's congenital preference for what is primitive over what comes after. For an emphasis on hasidic thought and exegesis arrives at a somewhat different Hasidism than that arising from the later narratives alone. Where Buber, for example, could downplay the centrality of traditional study and commitment to performance of the mitzvot in favor of a stress on the communal values that Buber himself preached, the early hasidic texts themselves testify to a much more traditional community, both in its commitment to Halakhah and in its intellectual life. Furthermore, the primary hasidic texts also depict a community engrossed in the language and concepts of Kabbalah, thus confirming another strong continuity between the ideas of the hasidic movement and prevailing currents in pre-hasidic Judaism.

The difference in perspectives between the literary and the narrative orientations to hasidic intellectual history has implications for several focal concepts discussed in this book. Take the notions of *devekut* (attachment to God) or *avodah be-gashmiyut* (worship through corporeal activities). From the Buberian standpoint, buttressed by his retelling of hasidic stories, the idea that man can serve God and become closer to God through everyday activities amounts to the assertion that the sanctification of everyday actions and human relationships is the true and ultimate goal of hasidic teaching. But, as Scholem argues, the literature supports a very different reading, according to which involvement in worldly activities is not the end of hasidic fulfillment, but rather a means toward an otherworldly religious consummation.

Is the picture of Hasidism presented in this book truly representative of the movement and its contribution? One can easily imagine some disappointed reader insisting that our version of Hasidism is not radical enough, that, by relying on the hasidic "classics," it makes too much of the continuities between Hasidism and its "Orthodox" opponents, that it encourages the reader to assimilate what is new and astonishing in Hasidism into "mainstream" Judaism (and insinuating, *ad hominem*, that all this reflects a bias of the author!).

Several points can be made in response. As noted above, the selections in this volume are taken from the literature that is closest to the source; one can hardly expect to get a better picture from largely legendary material recorded and compiled at a much later date. Moreover, by confining the selections almost entirely to the first three generations, we are confronting Hasidism in its most radical period, before the softening effects of routinization and assimilation to more mainstream rabbinic currents could erode its unique characteristics. If even this period exhibits continuity with "perennial" Judaism, this would, presumably, say a great deal about the place of Hasidism in the history of Jewish thought.

At the same time, it is important to recognize that the process of toning down the radical elements of Hasidism may have already begun in the early stages of the literature. This significant sociological point has already been urged vigorously in recent years by Zeev Gries. Gries maintains that a writer speaking for an embattled group is more likely to put its more moderate foot forward than to arouse antagonism by flaunting controversial positions. For example, the pseudigraphic *Zavaat ha-Rivash* (testament of the Besht), emanating from the Maggid's circle, inculcates ethical principles that are virtually indistinguishable from those of any number of non-hasidic works. Its purpose, therefore, may not have been to spread the tenets of Hasidism as much as to reassure outsiders that Hasidism was not, in fact, the deviant movement they suspected it of being. If that is the case, then we must proceed with caution; the earliest documentary evidence at our disposal would give a true picture only of how hasidic authors wished to be perceived externally, beneath which the esoteric currents would remain hidden and impenetrable.

As noted above, the arrangement of the selections is topical. Brief biographies of the hasidic masters are found in the Appendix. The more fundamental, hence weightier, subjects appear in the earlier chapters. Much of the kabbalistic terminology introduced in these chapters (especially in "God and Providence," "The Soul," and "Devekut") plays a significant role throughout the book. Nevertheless, there are readers who will get a better feel for hasidic thought by starting with other, less abstract, and less systematic themes. In some chapters, the unique contribution of Hasidism will be noticeable; in others, hasidic ideas will appear conventional to students of Jewish thought.

Careful readers will already have intuited that hasidic thought is not monolithic. The hasidic rubric accommodates a variety of positions and attitudes on the rationality of faith, on the nature of *devekut*, on the relationship between hasid and rebbe, on the nature and relative importance of prayer and Torah study, on the tension between joy and the affirmation of worldly pleasures and self-respect on one hand, and the gravity of repentance and the ascetic gesture on the other hand. Many of the selections in this book invite the reader to ponder the dialogue within hasidic literature on these subjects.

Much secondary literature on Hasidism effects an elegiac tone. This is quite natural, given that the integral Eastern European culture that originally nurtured hasidic culture is irretrievably gone, its heirs murdered and physically uprooted in a catastrophe unparalleled in the dark history of the human race. The nostalgic mood is well suited to a society wistfully alienated from the religious universe of Hasidism, its fundamental beliefs, commitments, and goals. Thus Gershon Scholem concludes his magisterial *Major Trends in Jewish Mysticism* with the story of the Baal Shem Tov:

> When [he] had a difficult task before him, he would go to a certain place in the woods, light a fire and mediate in prayer—and what he had set out to perform was done. When a generation later the "Maggid" of

Mezeritch was faced with the same task he would go to the same place in
the woods and say: We can no longer light the fire, but we can still speak
the prayers—and what he wanted done became reality. Again a generation
later Rabbi Moshe Leib of Sassov had to perform this task. And he too
went into the woods and said: We can no longer light a fire, nor do we
know the secret meditations belonging to the prayer, but we do know the
place in the woods to which it all belongs—and that must be sufficient;
and sufficient it was. But when another generation had passed and Rabbi
Israel of Rizhin was called upon to perform the task, he sat down on his
golden chair in his castle and said: We cannot light the fire, we cannot
speak the prayers, we do not know the place, but we can tell the story of
how it was done. And, the story-teller adds, the story which he told had
the same effect as the actions of the other three.

Traditional Torah learning knows neither the detachment of the
academician nor the romantic sadness of the sentimentalist. In the
Bet Midrash the dead masters of discourse are thought of, with no
self-consciousness, in the present tense: "The Rambam *says*; the
Raavad *asks*; R. Hayyim *explains*." For Jewish thought to become alive
to us, it is necessary that we learn how to think ourselves back into
contemporaneity with the past Sages. With respect to hasidic
thought, the volume in your hand is a modest beginning. There are
exciting issues that appear but peripherally in these pages, such as
how hasidic literature reads the Bible and how hasidic masters probe
the structure of the festivals and special occasions of the Jewish year.
And if the later writers are not, by and large, as radical as the earlier
generations, their insights are no less creative and relevant. Most
important, in becoming contemporary with the past, the past can also
inspire our own thinking, and contribute to our own creativity, sometimes in ways that the subjects of this study may never have anticipated.

The
Religious Thought of
Hasidism

Text and Commentary

1

God and Providence

Theism, the belief in a personal God, requires the assertion of two apparently contradictory propositions about God and the resolution of the dialectical tension between them. These two themes are the immanence and the transcendence of God.

An analogy to human personality might be helpful. We express our personality in relationship to others, and that is a function of distance. My friend must not be too far, too remote for me to interact with him. If he is too distant from me—spatially, intellectually, socially, spiritually, or whatever—relationship becomes impossible, and where there is no human relationship there can be no human personality. Similarly, for me to relate to my friend as a personality, it is necessary not only that he not be too remote from me, but equally that he not be too close to me, i.e., identical with me. If he is so close to me in essence that he is indeed me, then I am not relating to another at all. Personality and relationship thus require that the other be far but not too far, close but not too close.

Similarly (but by no means identically), the ascription of personality to God requires that He be transcendent, that He be the Other, different ("far") from the created order in essence, in substance, in nature, so that we are aware of a Presence to which or to Whom we can attempt to relate. However, if this transcendence or beyondness is taken alone, the distance is infinite and there is no way to cross the

1

chasm between man and God, created and Creator. One can posit such a God—endlessly remote, infinitely different from man and utterly indifferent to him. This, essentially, is the doctrine of deism. Unmitigated transcendence leads to deism, and undoes theism by making relationship with God impossible, thus robbing Him of any attributes of personality.

The other side of the coin is immanence, the closeness of God to man, or, more accurately, the "withinness" of God in the world. God's inherence in the cosmos ensures that He is close enough to be related to, to be experienced, to be loved and feared, to assume the aspects of personality. But if transcendence is eliminated altogether, and immanence is taken alone, we again lose hold of personality, except that this time we emerge not with a God Who is infinitely remote and other, and therefore incommunicado, but one Who is so deeply within us, so closely identified with nature, that there is no Other to relate to. Here we have again destroyed theism, this time arriving at pantheism, the belief that all is God, i.e., that He is defined as the principle of Nature, identified with the world itself, and coextensive with it. Such a God may inspire certain religious emotions, but not the whole range of them. And neither deism nor pantheism can provide for relation or revelation.

It is only theism that can allow for a God Who creates and reveals, Who communicates and knows, Who loves and commands and challenges and rewards and punishes. But in order to do this, theism must embrace these two opposite notions, immanence and transcendence, and allow for the tension between them to be played out both in the history of God's relationship with mankind and in the individual's religious experience and consciousness. It is for this reason that Judaism, as the preeminent monotheistic faith, has always embraced both immanence and transcendence in its conception of God. While it is possible to incline to one or the other of the two poles, both must always be retained if the fundamental Jewish approach to the understanding of the divine is to remain intact.

The tension between immanence and transcendence remained fairly stable throughout the history of Rabbinic Judaism, until the end of the eighteenth century and the emergence of Beshtian Hasidism. For reasons both internal and external, the result of organic development and of historic circumstance, a new balance between immanence and transcendence was established by the founders of Hasidism. While the belief in divine transcendence was most certainly retained, the greatest emphasis was now placed upon divine immanence, and a host of

consequences flowed therefrom. The greater role played by immanence and the nearness of the Creator went hand in hand with the
emotional trajectory of the young hasidic movement. Because God
was so close, it became possible to make greater demands upon the
hasid's consciousness of God at all times. The classical doctrine of
devekut, attachment to or communion with God, was thus given a
new emotional twist and raised to new levels of significance.
Accompanying this development was the emphasis on *simhah*, joy, as
a fundamental of Hasidism. And so too for many other ideas with
which we shall deal in the course of this work.

It is a moot question for the historian of ideas as to which came
first and which exercised the greater influence—external societal and
other historical pressures or internal ideological and intellectual development. In all probability, "real life" creates new challenges—economic, political, cultural—and as a result, whole new ways of thinking emerge in response. Yet, this does not mean that ideas are merely
disguised instinctual reactions with no life of their own. Ideas may
have their genesis as reactions to specific stimuli, but they in turn
assume the role of stimuli and give rise to other ideas and concepts,
and thus become intellectually creative and, to a large extent,
autonomous.

The same holds true for the emergence and development of the
immanentist emphasis in hasidic thought. Conditions in Eastern
Europe in the late eighteenth century may well have evoked the need
for more uninhibited religious emotionalism, for a greater stress on
feeling over intellect, for a tilt toward engaging the mass of Jews in
revivalist religious life as opposed to the austerity of the scholarly
elite, for internality over behaviorist expression, for a romantic rather
than a rationalistic bent. But once the ideas so generated were
absorbed by the most creative of the hasidic masters, they took on a
life of their own and kept on changing and growing. While the great
majority of hasidic teachers were not systematic thinkers—indeed,
they are distinguished by their almost total lack of organization and
systematic exposition, a sure mark of a genuinely romantic movement—the basic ideas of the movement immanently crystallized into
discernible patterns and structures.

Hasidism did not presume to innovate. Its leaders were not conscious of changing anything in Judaism. They sought not to *create* but
to *recover* religious truths. They accepted the totality of the inherited
Jewish tradition—biblical, talmudic, kabbalistic; and if, in the process
of carrying it on, they gave greater prominence to an idea here and

muted an idea there, they did so in the confidence that they were expressing the original intent of their forebears and the will of the Holy One. Thus they were located fully within the classical Rabbinic Jewish tradition, and yet, because they sang the same lyrics to a slightly new tune, they succeeded, almost despite themselves, in creating a powerful mass movement, a new constellation of the same ideas in new relationships with each other, and a rearrangement of received values.

In this new pattern of thought, the doctrine of divine immanence is the fundamental concept from which most other hasidic religious concepts are derivable and, at the least, with which they are compatible.

In searching for precedents for the new emphasis on divine immanence, Hasidism found both biblical and kabbalistic sources aplenty. Isaiah 6:3 ("the whole world is full of His glory") and *Tikkunei Zohar* 57 ("there is no place that is empty of Him") became the most popular sources for the doctrine of divine immanence, repeated again and again by the foremost teachers of Hasidism. For the hasidic masters, the idea of immanence issued naturally from the concept of God's unity as expressed in the Shema, the biblical verse recited thrice daily by religious Jews, "Hear, O Israel, the Lord is our God, the Lord is One" (Deut. 6:4). Thus, in selection 1, R. Pinhas of Koretz, a colleague of the Besht, deduces the all-pervasive presence of God from His unity, and from the verse just cited.

While for most hasidic thinkers the concept of immanence means just what it seems to mean, that God is within all that exists, the passage from R. Pinhas of Koretz anticipates a radical twist that some subsequent hasidic masters were to give to the principle, one that further developed the theme of immanence and concluded with the doctrine of acosmism or illusionism. One of the most seminal thinkers of Hasidism, the Habad leader R. Menahem Mendel, wrote of three successive interpretations of the unity of God. The first and most obvious is that there exist no other gods. His oneness excludes other deities—the simplest expression of monotheism. The medieval Jewish philosophers took this a step further and interpreted God's unity as uniqueness, a difference in quality as well as in number; He is utterly incomparable and hence in essence unknowable. The third stage was reached by the Besht and his students, especially the Great Maggid, R. Dov Ber of Mezeritch, and was most elaborately developed by R. Shneur Zalman of Liady, founder of the Habad school of Hasidism. This interpretation holds that God is not only one and not only unique but He is utterly alone; *nothing* exists other than God, all else is illusion. There is, in reality, no cosmos, no world, nothing at all but God.[1] The idea is powerful but did not win unanimous acceptance. One of the hasidic opponents of this radical immanentism, R. Zevi Hirsch of Zidachov, will be cited in the course of this chapter (see selection 4).[2]

As important as it held the principle of immanence to be, Hasidism never yielded on its awareness of divine transcendence. Some early historians of Hasidism, particularly during the Haskalah period, insisted upon terming the hasidic doctrine pantheistic, which, in fact, it would have been had the principle of divine transcendence been abandoned. But this clearly did not occur (and one wonders whether there was an ulterior ideological motive behind the happy discovery by exponents of the Haskalah that Hasidism was really heretical). A more felicitous and accurate description of the hasidic doctrine would be the one coined, in a different context and for a different purpose, by Prof. Charles Hartshorne: panentheism, i.e., that all is within God. If God's immanence in the cosmos exhausts the divine existence, if there remains nothing of God that transcends the world, then we are left with pantheism, and we are outside the pale of Judaism. But if the belief in immanence—that all exists by virtue of God, and that He infuses all that exists—does not deny that He also transcends the mundane sphere, then it is proper to assert that the world exists within God, and hence the all-pervasive immanence advocated by Hasidism does not result in pantheism but in panentheism, which, indeed, has no less than midrashic warrant: "He is the place of the world, and the world is not His place" (Genesis Rabbah 68:9; and see below, chap. 5, selection 1).

The coexistence of immanence and transcendence in hasidic thought, despite the heavy emphasis on the former, requires elaboration as to their relationship, and this is the theme of several selections in this chapter. Among them are extended excerpts from R. Shneur Zalman, founder of Habad (selection 12), and from his grandson and the third head of the movement, R. Menahem Mendel of Lubavitch (selection 13). Both men are highly sophisticated thinkers and tend to be arcane. The excerpts presented here are difficult and characteristically complex, but they are significant (the notes accompanying the selections should make them more comprehensible).

---

1. For more on this, see L. Jacobs, *Seeker of Unity*, esp. pp. 69–70, also my *The Shema: Spirituality and Law in Judaism*, ch. 7.
2. See Additional Note *1.

Hasidism's conceptual subtlety carried with it important auxiliary ideas and significant practical implications. Selection 12 is a critical instance: R. Shneur Zalman identifies Torah with the domain of immanence, inasmuch as it pertains to the judgment of states of affairs in this world, while the service of God through the commandments brings man into relation with the sphere of transcendence, which is undifferentiated and hence inaccessible to categorization. Since the transcendent sphere is ultimately more pure than the immanent sphere, the result is to elevate the value of mitzvot relative to Torah, without demoting the latter.[3]

The remaining selections are not much easier, dealing, as they do, with certain important kabbalistic doctrines. Like other strands in Jewish thought (including the system of the Gaon of Vilna, the most prominent of its ideological intellectual adversaries), Hasidism subscribes to the vocabulary and world-picture of Kabbalah. Hence some familiarity with the kabbalistic orientation is required in reading hasidic texts. The specific contours of hasidic teachings on the unity of God and creation are dependent on these elements. Much of the hasidic emphasis on the immanence of God flows from kabbalistic formulations. There are implications, as well, for hasidic views of Torah study and the worship of God.

How does one God, Who cannot possibly have anything in common with the world, create that world, in all its multiplicity? How can particular beings exist distinct from God, Who is the Source of all being? Is His presence uniform, extending even to evil events and things? These are perennial philosophical questions. Kabbalah formulates its answers about these matters by means of the sefirot and the idea of *tzimtzum*, God's "self-limitation" in order to allow room for creation. The Ein-Sof (= the Infinite) is beyond any categorization. Creation, however, occurs by a descent of the divine light of the Ein-Sof which takes place through ten sefirot (or "vessels" emanated from the Ein-Sof) representing a hierarchy of aspects of God. Man's service of God, and the raising of the world to its original state of unity, involves the inversion of the process of emanation. The worshiper puts himself in relation to the lowest sefirah, Malkhut ("Kingship"), and then seeks to ascend ever higher, uniting each sefirah in turn to those about it. The sefirot also serve to categorize different aspects of man's experience of God and to generate a complex network of correspondences, as it were, between the divine sphere and the world (e.g.,

---

3. For the practical implications, see below, chaps. 6 and 7.

the lower seven sefirot correspond to the three patriarchs, David and Solomon, Moses and Aaron), thus providing a focus for man's contemplation of God. Particularly in Habad, the ten sefirot are internalized and become a template for character traits. None of this, however, is permitted to compromise the basic tenet of divine unity.

The idea of *tzimtzum* ("contraction"), so important in the mystical system of R. Isaac Luria (known as the Ari) in the sixteenth century, implies that God "withdrew" His Presence in order to "make room" for the world. R. Isaac Luria taught that the Ein-Sof—God in His innermost, most ineffable, unknowable, and absolute essence—contracted within Himself (the act of *tzimtzum*), thus leaving a *ḥalal*, or vacuum, in the divine Being. Into this vacuum He radiated a "line" or "thread" of Light, which turned into ten "vessels" (a synonym for the ten sefirot), which were inactive, merely the potential for the divine self-revelation but not yet a reality. The Ein-Sof then poured some of its own essence into these vessels, thus vitalizing them. However, this encounter between the infinitude of the Ein-Sof's Light and the limited nature of the ten sefirot resulted in a cosmic "accident" or catastrophe, the Breaking of the Vessels, which were unable to contain the infinite plenitude of the Ein-Sof. The overflow of "sparks" fell into a variety of *kelipot*, or "shells"—symbols of mundane denseness, the nondivine, the potential for evil—where they were "captured" and await redemption, or liberation, by man by means of his service of the Lord, especially the performance of the mitzvot, the study of Torah, and kabbalistic meditations. When all the divine sparks resulting from the Breaking of the Vessels have been redeemed from their servitude to base matter, they will have been "elevated to their Source," the Messiah will come, and Israel and the world will be redeemed.

The emphasis on contraction avoids the danger of pantheism, the view that God and the world are identical. At the same time, kabbalists are reluctant to speak of God as totally transcendent, which would imply that He is absent or uninvolved in the world. It is likewise out of the question to infer that the process of *tzimtzum*, emanating through the sefirot, allows for "change" in God. How to do justice to the inherent tensions in this conceptual framework and how to explain them is clearly no simple matter, and some of the variations proffered by hasidic thinkers may be found in the selections below.

In hasidic literature, the message about God is richer than the interplay of kabbalistic theosophical categories outlined above. There is a poetry to the hasidic discussion, a sustained effort not only to talk *about* God, but also to capture the quality of the religious experience itself. Frequently, this is done by means of parables; even more often, by bringing to life the world of the biblical text in a novel and quite elastic fashion. And often the cumulative attempts appear contradictory, because the religious experience, from the limited human perspective, is contradictory and paradoxical: God is available to different individuals, and to the same individual at different times, in a variety of ways. Hasidism is remarkably sensitive to human reality—man's nobility and his foibles, his promise and his perils, his strengths and his weaknesses, and above all his vulnerabilities and the vagaries of inescapable inconsistencies and instabilities.

A good example of how important insights are expressed, and embedded in elaborate and often convoluted homiletics, is provided by selection 5, from the writings of R. Yaakov Yosef.

Hasidic literature abounds in insights on religious existence. The reader should bear in mind the intimate relation between colorful and evocative material of this kind and the fundamental versions of kabbalistic doctrine that underlie the hasidic masters' homiletic and poetic creativity.

In some ways the selections in this chapter are the most difficult in the book. Those who find them forbidding are advised to make do with this introduction for the time being and go on to the rest of the book, perhaps returning to them at the end.

1. GOD IS EVERYWHERE
Source: R. Pinhas of Koretz, Likkutei Amarim, p. 14d, cited in Sefer Besht to Va'ethanan, no. 13

Hear, O Israel, the Lord is our God, the Lord is One (Deut. 6:4).
    The term ehad ("one") in the reading of the Shema, which proclaims the unity of God, [requires us to] state that there is nothing in the whole world other than the Holy One, Who fills the whole earth with His glory.[4] The principal intention [of the commandment to recite the Shema] is that we should consider ourselves null and void, and [understand] that there is nothing to us but the soul within us, which is part of God above. Hence there is nothing in the whole world except the One God.[5]

---

4. "The whole world is full of His glory" (Isa. 6:3). This verse, the foundation for the hasidic doctrine of divine immanence, is constantly referred to in hasidic literature.
5. R. Pinhas seems to be hinting here at the contention of some hasidic thinkers, especially of the Habad school, that the whole material world is merely an illusion. Divine immanence is seen as the other side of the coin of acosmism, the unreality of the world. See Additional Notes *5 and *6.

Our principal thought when reciting the word *eḥad* should be that the whole earth is full of His glory and there is nothing[6] [in the universe] devoid of Him.

2. GOD UNCHANGED BY CREATION
Source: R. Shneur Zalman of Liady, Tanya, Likkutei Amarim, chaps. 20–21

Concerning the essential theme of the unity of the Holy One: He is called One and Unique, and "all believe that He is all alone,"[7] exactly as He was before the world was created, when He was all alone, as it is written, "Thou wast the same before the world was created; Thou hast been the same since the world was created."[8] This means exactly the same, without any change, as it is written, *For I the Lord have not changed* (Mal. 3:6).

Neither this world nor the supernal worlds effect any change in God's unity by their having been created *ex nihilo*. Just as He was all alone, single and unique, before they were created, so He is One and Alone, single and unique, now that they have been created, since beside Him everything is as nothing, absolutely null and void. For the coming into being of all the upper and lower worlds out of nonbeing, the vital power that sustains them [and prevents them] from reverting to their previous state of nonexistence and nothingness, is but the word of God and the breath of His mouth[9] that is clothed[10] in them. The nature of the divine order is not like that of a creature of flesh and blood.[11] When man utters a word, the breath emitted in speaking is something that can be sensed and perceived as a thing apart from him, separate from its source, i.e., the ten faculties of the soul.

However, the speech of the Holy One is not, heaven forbid, separated from Him, for there is nothing outside of Him and there is no place devoid of Him.[12] . . . God's speech and thoughts are absolutely at

---

6. The zoharic statement, often quoted by hasidim, that "there is *no place* empty of Him" (*Tikkunei Zohar* 57) is cited here as "there is *nothing* empty of Him," perhaps as a continuation of the preceding statement, which applies this thoroughgoing immanentism to man, and holds that the only part of humankind which has reality is the soul, which is a "part" of God.

7. Mahzor of Rosh Hashanah and Yom Kippur.

8. Shaharit service. See Yalkut, Va-Ethannan 835, citing Jerusalem Talmud.

9. Paraphrasing Ps. 33:6.

10. In hasidic works, the term *levush* ("clothing, garment") is a code-word for divine immanence, especially in the writings of R. Shneur Zalman (see below, n. 72).

11. Berakhot 40a.

12. *Tikkunei Zohar*, tikkun 57, p. 91b.

one with His essence and being, even after His speech has been actualized in the creation of the worlds, just as it was united with Him before the worlds were created. Thus there is no change at all in His self, but only for the created beings which receive their life-force from His word.

3. THE UPPER AND LOWER UNITY
Source: R. Shneur Zalman of Liady, Tanya, Sha'ar ha-Yiḥud veha-Emunah, chap. 7

Introduction

In the sixth chapter of Sha'ar ha-Yiḥud, R. Shneur Zalman deals with a central problem for his immanentist-acosmic view: if God is all there is, and what we see as the solid, real, substantial world is but an illusion, how does this illusion arise? If, because of God's all-pervasive omnipresence, the cosmos is unreal, why does it seem real? What role does it play given the overwhelming reality of the Divine Presence? How does the illusion relate to the reality?

His answer, basic to the whole Habad theology, is propounded in chapter 7, part of which is excerpted here. It involves two significant points. First, there is a distinction between the two major Names of God. The Tetragrammaton, the ineffable four-lettered Hebrew "proper" Name, represents the divine quality of Hesed, or "love," in the sense of the generation of existence. This Name (formally translated in English as "the Lord") infuses and thus sustains the whole creation. Because God is infinite, this creative function is infinite, and tends to create infinitely. But a truly infinite creation is, by its utter limitlessness, so all-suffusing that it overshoots its mark and results in a world-which-is-no-world. An analogy: if the sun's rays were infinite, they would not warm and sustain terrestrial life but would destroy it by incinerating it. Hence, there is a countermotion in the divine realm, and that is the sphere of Gevurah ("strength"), or withdrawal, that which curbs and limits the light. This is represented by the divine Name Elohim ("God"), which, in dialectic tension with the infinite generation of the Tetragrammaton, results in a limited and hence viable creation. The overpowering divine grace (shefa Elohi) of God's creativity is neutralized by the overwhelming restraint, and the result is a "real" world.

Second, the perception of a "real" world is not the full, true vision of things. For man, the cosmos appears separate from God. But this is not the divine view. For the Ein-Sof, only the Tetragrammaton is real; i.e., the cosmos is a divinely conjured illusion, for *only* God truly exists. From this ultimate perspective, the light *is* infinite: only those who stand in the shadow of Elohim, which curbs and limits the light, are deluded into thinking that the world they sense is real in that it has an existence separate from Ein-Sof.[13] R. Shneur Zalman continues this theme in the excerpt below as he analyzes the Zohar's treatment of the two principal verses of the daily prayers, the Shema ("Hear, O Israel, the Lord is our God, the Lord is One"), and the *Barukh Shem* ("Blessed be His Name, Whose glorious kingdom is for ever and ever").

*

How we may understand the Zohar's statement that the verse *Shema Yisrael* ("Hear, O Israel") is the upper unity and *Barukh Shem* ("Blessed be His Name") is the lower unity.[14] For *va'ed* ("Blessed . . . Whose kingdom is *va'ed* [for ever and ever]") is *eḥad* ("Hear, O Israel . . . is *eḥad* [One]") through the substitution of letters.[15]

The cause of the contraction and concealment whereby the Holy One obscured the life-force of the world, thus making the world appear as an independent entity, is this:

As is well known, the world was created for the sake of the revelation of His kingdom, since "there is no king without a nation."[16] The word *am* ("nation") is related to the word *omemot* ("dimmed" or "subdued"),[17] inasmuch as they [the people of the nation] are separate entities, and thus estranged and remote from the level of the king. For

---

13. On the correspondence of the divine names and the kabbalistic sefirot, see M. Hallamish, *Mavo la-Kabbalah*, pp. 114–116.

14. Zohar I, 18b. (Cf. below, selection 4, for a different interpretation of this statement.) See also my *Halakhot ve-Halikhot*, chap. 3, and *The Shema*, pp. 47–59.

15. Zohar II, 134a. The rules of Hebrew grammar divide the letters of the alefbet into groups according to their source in the organs of speech, and the letters in each group are considered interchangeable. Since *alef, heh, vav,* and *yud* fall into one group, *alef* may be interchanged with *vav*. Since *alef, bet, heh,* and *ayin* fall into another phonetic category, *bet* may be interchanged with *ayin*. Hence, *eḥad* becomes *va'ed*; on the use of letter-symbols to explain the divine unity and immanence, see below, nn. 25 and 28.

16. This phrase, which is very popular in rabbinic literature, has no direct source in Talmud or Midrash. However, see Pirkei de-R. Eliezer, chap. 3, where the revelation of His Kingdom is mentioned as one of the purposes of creation.

17. As in *geḥalim omemot* (Berakhot 53b), "coals which have become dim." Cf. Rashi to Judg. 5:14, s.v. *aḥarekha*.

even if the king had very many sons, the name "kingdom" would not apply to them; nor would it apply to nobles alone. Only *in the multitude of people is the glory of the king* (Prov. 14:28).

The divine Name which indicates the attribute of God's kingdom (Malkhut) is the name Adnut ("Lordship"),[18] for He is *the Lord of the whole earth* (Josh. 3:11, 13). Hence, this attribute and this Name bring the world into existence and sustain it, so that it is what it is now, a completely independent and separate entity, rather than utterly nullified. Were this attribute and this Name to be withdrawn, God forbid, the world would revert to its source in the Word of God and the breath of His mouth, and would be completely nullified there, so that it could not even be called a world.

The term "world" may be applied only to that which possesses the dimensions of space and time—"space" referring to east, west, north, and south, above and below; and "time" to past, present, and future. None of these dimensions has any relationship to the holy supernal attributes.[19] Only concerning His attribute of Malkhut is it possible to say that He is King above without end and below without limit, and likewise in all four directions. The same is true regarding the dimension of time: "The Lord reigns, the Lord reigned, and the Lord will reign."[20] Thus, the vitality of space and the vitality of time, their coming into being from nothingness[21] and their continued existence for as long as they will last, come from His attribute of Malkhut and Adnut.

Since God's Kingship is perfectly united with His essence, space and time are also completely nullified in relation to His essence, even as the light of the sun is nullified in the sun.[22]

---

18. This refers to the Name *Adonay*, lit. "my Lord," which should not be confused with the Tetragrammaton, although the latter is pronounced as if it were the former. *Adon* is a "master" or "lord." For the purposes of this discourse, Elohim, Malkhut, and Adnut are equally indicative of the lower unity.

19. The nine higher sefirot, not including Malkhut, the tenth and lowest.

20. From the Shaharit service, combining verses from Ps. 93:1, Ps. 10:16, and Exod. 15:18.

21. Maimonides, *Guide of the Perplexed* 2:13, holds that time too is a creation *ex nihilo*, for it depends on the motion of created things. For a contrary opinion, see Additional Note *4.

22. Since time and space exist only in the realm of Malkhut, and the latter, like all the sefirot, is indivisibly part of the Ein-Sof, time and space do not have a "real," independent existence. The analogy is to the sun's rays, which have no existence separate from their source, the sun. See chap. 8 of R. Shneur Zalman's work.

This explains the intertwining of the two Names, Adnut and the Tetragrammaton.[23] The Tetragrammaton, which indicates that "He was, He is, and He will be," teaches us that God is beyond time, as explained [in *Raya Mehemna* on the portion of Pinhas].[24] He is likewise beyond space, for He continually brings all the dimensions of space into existence, everywhere from the uppermost to the lowermost region and in the four directions.[25]

Although God is beyond space and time, He is nevertheless also found below, in space and time; i.e., He unites with His attribute of Malkhut, from which space and time are derived and come into existence. This is the lower unity,[26] His essence and being, which is called by the name Ein-Sof; [it] completely fills the whole earth temporally and spatially. In the heavens above and on the earth below and in the four directions, all is equally permeated with the light of the Ein-Sof, since He is on the earth below exactly as in the heavens above. For everything within the dimensions of space is completely nullified in the light of the Ein-Sof, which clothes itself in it through the attribute of Malkhut that is part of His unity. But Kingship is the way of contraction (*tzimtzum*) and concealment, serving to curb the light of the Ein-Sof; otherwise the existence of time and space would be completely nullified, and there would be no dimension of time and space whatsoever even for the lower worlds.[27]

---

23. *ADNY* and *YHVH* (the Tetragrammaton) appear together over 290 times in Scripture. Their letters are often interdigitated in the Kabbalah to produce other Names. This is done in one of two ways. The intertwining of *Adnut* in the Tetragrammaton implies that the interdigitation begins with the latter, hence: *YAHD-VNHY*. The intertwining of the Tetragrammaton in *Adnut* implies the other alternative: *AYDHNVYH*. For the difference between the two, see Additional Notes, *2.
24. Zohar III, 257b.
25. Because the Tetragrammaton predominates in the conjunction of the two Names, *YAHDVNHY*, indicating that time and space are nullified in relation to Him. This is the upper unity affirmed in the Shema.
26. In the letter-combination *AYDHNVYH*, the Name *ADNY*, implying rulership and relationship, prevails. This, then, is the meaning of the Zohar's statement that *Barukh Shem* denotes the lower unity. Malkhut implies finite, material existence which is nevertheless filled with God's essence. On this unification, see further in Elijah de Vidas, *Reshit Ḥokhmah*, Sha'ar ha-Ahavah, chap. 9, cited also in *Shelah*, Sha'ar ha-Otiot I, p. 44a. Cf. G. Scholem, *On the Kabbalah and Its Symbolism*, pp. 104–109, and Jacobs, *Hasidic Prayer*, p. 142.
27. In this further elaboration, R. Shneur Zalman wants to safeguard the concept of divine immanence even within the realm of the lower unity, where the world's existence is affirmed. In this realm too, he asserts, the Ein-Sof infuses all, expressing itself through the tenth and lowest of the ten sefirot, Malkhut. It is Malkhut that curbs the

4. UNITY WORKS BOTH WAYS
Source: R. Zevi Hirsch of Zhidachov, Ketav Yosher Divrei Emet, beginning (in Sur me-Ra va-Aseh Tov, end)

Introduction

This selection is excerpted from a lengthy essay which forms an excursus to R. Zevi Hirsch's main work, *Sur me-Ra va-Aseh Tov*. It is, simultaneously, an elaboration of his hasidic-kabbalistic theory of the oneness of God, and a polemic against the philosophical tradition in Judaism, which he condemns as an alien Greek graft and a destruction of "true wisdom," i.e., the Kabbalah. R. Zevi Hirsch did not stand alone in his opposition to medieval Jewish philosophy; it was widespread not only among hasidic leaders but among their opponents, the mitnaggedim. Mainstream rabbinic tradition never completely made its peace with the philosophic vein, despite such luminaries as Maimonides, who were equally preeminent in both disciplines. R. Shneur Zalman, who often cites Maimonides' *Guide*, is in this respect an exception (see below, chap. 3, introduction).

R. Zevi Hirsch, however, does not even mention Maimonides. He is far more troubled by another medieval representative of the integration of the two traditions, the eleventh-century rabbinic judge, poet, and philosopher, Rabbenu Bahya b. Joseph Ibn Pakuda. R. Bahya was the author of *Hovot ha-Levavot* ("The Duties of the Heart"), most of which is an elaboration of the need for inwardness, proper religious motivation, and spiritual integrity. The *Hovot ha-Levavot* became enormously popular over the ages, and the author was lovingly referred to as *he-hasid* ("the pious one" or "the saint"). Hasidim were especially fond of the work, although others too respected it. But one "gate," or section, of this opus (which otherwise deals exclusively with moral-spiritual problems) was usually skipped, or skimmed over lightly, because it was blatantly "philosophical," and that was *Sha'ar ha-Yihud*, "The Gate of Unity." In this section, Bahya, writing under Neoplatonic influence, offers seven proofs of the divine unity.

Bahya was a problem to hasidic writers like R. Zevi Hirsch for two reasons. First, as indicated, he was able to combine unques-

---

light of the Ein-Sof, which, in its infinity, threatens to overwhelm everything else and reduce it to nothingness as it absorbs everything. Yet even in the arena of Malkhut, the Ein-Sof is all-pervasive.

tioned piety with "Greek" philosophizing. And second, his approach to such fundamental issues as the unity of God was philosophic rather than kabbalistic. R. Zevi Hirsch is profoundly disturbed by Bahya's statement that one may ask, in the course of analyzing the doctrine of divine unity, whether God exists and whether He is one. "How harsh are the words," writes R. Zevi Hirsch, "Ah, Lord God! Look and see, my brothers, that this pious man says things, without proof, against the Torah."

R. Zevi Hirsch's solution is ingenious, if not unique. He reinterprets R. Bahya's *Sha'ar ha-Yihud* as Kabbalah disguised as philosophy. Underneath the speculative terminology lies concealed the "true," i.e., kabbalistic, way. (The term "true" is often a code-word for Kabbalah, hence the "true unity" in the first sentence in this selection.) It is obvious, he concedes, that R. Bahya was influenced by R. Saadia Gaon; this was in fact so, and Bahya quotes R. Saadia by name. But instead of concluding from this that R. Bahya wrote philosophy, R. Zevi Hirsch arrives at the opposite conclusion: "The geonim certainly were mystics, and all their words were part of the Kabbalah," or "received by tradition," which in this context is the same thing. "All the words of this pious man [i.e., R. Bahya] are based upon investigations of the true unity," i.e., the divine unity according to the Kabbalah. (R. Saadia's work was often interpreted as mystical in nature, and the Besht was reputed to be a transmigration of Saadia. See below, chap. 8, introduction.) R. Zevi Hirsch now directs his attention to the true unity, and his conclusions, as we shall see later, are not consonant with R. Shneur Zalman's position as recorded in the preceding selection.

*

Understanding God's true unity posed insurmountable problems for [some] early thinkers until, in their wearying search, they found it necessary to study Greek philosophy. . . . Other thinkers regretted this, protesting against those who occupied themselves with Greek philosophy. . . .

[The subject is dealt with at length in R. Bahya's *Hovot ha-Levavot*, chap. 4 of *Sha'ar ha-Yihud*.]

All the words of this pious man [i.e., Bahya] are based upon investigations of the true unity, in fulfillment of the commandment to unify God wholeheartedly, as stated in the portion of Shema Yisrael,[28]

28. Deut. 6:4–5, where, after the Shema ("Hear, O Israel, the Lord is our God, the Lord is One"), it is stated: "And thou shalt love the Lord thy God with all thy heart."

and as it was transmitted to us by our venerable patriarch Jacob, who together with his unblemished sons proclaimed the unity of God when his soul was ready to ascend to heaven.[29] The search in the *Ḥovot ha-Levavot* is concentrated on defining God's Oneness in a true sense and not merely as an imaginary term, as is customary among the common people.

Now, my brother, the awesome ways of the unification[30] of God were transmitted to us through the sacred Zohar and by the Ari [R. Isaac Luria] in his book *Peri Etz Ḥayyim*. According to this doctrine, the unification is effected by proceeding from below to above, through the channels of all the worlds in readiness to offer up one's soul and be martyred for God's sake and for the sanctification of His name. Whoever thus unifies the truthful God is ready to give his life in loving communion with all Jews in their totality, as exemplified by Jacob and his sons before his soul departed.

Every intelligent person ought to commune with the souls of the righteous as they ascend level after level, through the world of the sefirot, until they reach the level of the Ein-Sof. For they unify God's blessed Names with powerful devotion, to the point that their souls are consumed, truly unifying by means of the word *eḥad* until they reach the level of the Ein-Sof, the First Cause and the Cause of all causes such that there is none higher than Him up above and none lower down below, and likewise on every side. "He fills all the worlds and surrounds all the world."[31] Hence, just as the world evolved by His will from above to below, from cause to effect at the time of Creation, so do we unify His great Name, from below to above, from effect to cause—all the way up to the Cause of all causes, the One.[32]

---

29. See Pesahim 56a: "When the sons gathered around Jacob's deathbed, Jacob wanted to reveal to them the end of days [i.e., the time of the messianic redemption]. But the Shekhinah departed from him, and Jacob worried: 'Perhaps there is a blemish in my family, God forbid, just as there was in the family of [my grandfather] Abraham, who begot Ishmael, and of my father Isaac, who begot Esau.' So his sons said to him: 'Hear, O Israel [Jacob was also named Israel], the Lord is our God, the Lord is One'; just as you believe only in the One, so are we united in the belief in the One God."

30. *Yiḥud ha-Shem*, the "unification" rather than the "unity" of God, i.e., how man perceives and expresses his faith in the divine unity. In mystical contexts, the term has another meaning: man's role in "repairing," primarily by means of meditations, the rift in God's primordial unity.

31. Zohar (*Raya Mehemna*) III, 225a. For a more elaborate definition of *memallei kol almin* and *sovev kol almin*, see below, selection 12.

32. The meditation in the recitation of the Shema must proceed in the reverse direction from that of creation: the creation came from above-to-below, and the medita-

This is the purpose of our service—in reading the Shema, in prayer, and especially in the service of sacrifices. . . .

The Jerusalem Targum in its translation of *In the beginning God created* (Gen. 1:1) adds the comment, "with wisdom," meaning with the sefirah of Hokhmah. According to the Zohar to Genesis,[33] the word *Elohim* signifies the sefirah of Binah ("Understanding"), from which were evolved heaven and earth, which represent, respectively, the sefirot of Tiferet ("Beauty") and Malkhut.[34] We indeed unify all the sefirot, all the way up to the First Cause, namely, the Ein-Sof. Thus, by the power of His actions, He emanates and renews the Creation daily, from the abundant light of His concealed glory, until He fills all the worlds. Were He to withdraw from them, everything—even

---

tion on divine unity is from below-to-above. (These terms must be understood symbolically, not spatially: "above-to-below" means cause-to-effect, and "below-to-above" denotes inferring from effect-to-cause.) Since the natural world is the result of a long chain of development consisting of descents from spiritual world to spiritual world, beginning with the Ein-Sof until the emergence of the natural world, the appropriate meditation which seeks out the utter and absolute unity of God must reach beyond the multiplicity of mundane and supramundane phenomena, through the ten divine sefirot, to the Ein-Sof. Thus, its "direction" is from below-to-above. The references to the need to be prepared to offer up one's soul, even to the point of being killed, apply not only to martyrdom (loving God to the extent of suffering martyrdom for His sake is talmudically mandated in Berakhot 54a), but to its spiritual analogue: the ascent to the Ein-Sof, who consumes all in the process of absorbing it. Because this meditation is so difficult, R. Zevi Hirsch recommends the contemplative company of the souls of the righteous who can more easily perform the adventure of elevating the mind to God.

33. Zohar I, 31b.

34. The divine Names, according to the Zohar, represent the various sefirot. "In the beginning" is taken as "by means of the beginning," this term being applied to Hokhmah, the first sefirah after Keter which, because of its proximity to the Ein-Sof, is not included in the actual creative process, which requires sefirot of a higher degree of differentiation; hence, lower down on the scale. "God," or Elohim, is Binah. When Hokhmah and Binah dialectically encounter each other (and "In the beginning God created" becomes, according to Zohar symbolism, "By means of Hokhmah and Binah [the Ein-Sof] created"), "heaven and earth" result. "Heaven" is Tiferet, which represents the upper sefirot from Keter through Yesod. "Earth" is Malkhut. "Heaven and earth" therefore implies the entire ensemble of sefirot.

The point, according to the kabbalistic view of Creation, is that the process begins with Ein-Sof and goes down the scale of sefirot to Malkhut, the lowest. The divine grace (*shefa*), which grants existence to the divine (sefirotic) structures as well as to the natural order, proceeds from the Ein-Sof and descends downward. Therefore, meditations on the divine unity must proceed in the opposite direction, from below to above, from Malkhut to Ein-Sof, endeavoring to transcend the realms of multiplicity as we reach for the utterly One.

including all the sacred Names—would remain lifeless, like bodies without souls.[35] Consider what the prophet Elijah said at the beginning of *Tikkunei ha-Zohar*: "Thou art wise, but Thou art not known through wisdom," meaning that even when His force expands through any of the sefirot, such as Hokhmah, we have no knowledge of His quality, substance, essence, or purpose.

This, then, is the true meaning of the commandment to read the Shema: to unify all the worlds, i.e., sefirot, and all souls into the totality of the soul of Israel [reaching] unto the Ein-Sof by means of the willingness to offer up one's soul to the Lord. Thereby, we draw down power from the light of His essence. For we elevate the worlds to their original root, to the Ein-Sof, by virtue of Torah study and the performance of mitzvot. From thence is drawn His will to increase and renew life in all the worlds.[36]

One may ask: What is the purpose of this service for us and for our children? The answer is: This is precisely what God willed, so that everything would be accomplished by an awakening-from-below, through the study of Torah and the performance of the mitzvot which He has given to the holy offspring, the people of the Lord, the nation of the God of Jacob. . . .

Thus I will very briefly explain to you, my brother, the secret of the Zohar's statement that *Shema Yisrael* is the upper unity of the Tetragrammaton, and *Barukh Shem Kevod* is the lower unity, that of the Name *Elohim*, which is related to the Tetragrammaton as a specific to the general.[37]

In the unification of *Shema Yisrael* we elevate the female waters by offering up our souls to the Tetragrammaton,[38] and we include our-

---

35. The sefirot (or divine Names) have no existence apart from the Ein-Sof.

36. When man succeeds in ascending to the Ein-Sof, the latter releases new and augmented grace (*shefa*), reanimating the sefirot and the natural world. The motion from below-to-above begets the reverse motion—and its blessings for the world. Hence, the cosmic importance of Torah, mitzvot, and the proper meditations.

37. Zohar III, 264a; I, 18b.

38. "Female waters" is the kabbalistic term for the below-to-above motion, equivalent to another term widely used, "the awakening from below." The converse is "male waters," or "the awakening from above." The former denotes human initiative and endeavor, the latter, divine grace and effluence (*shefa*). One evokes the other. R. Zevi Hirsch holds that the human initiative, man's attempt to overcome the fragmentation of the world and reach out for the Ein-Sof, is the definition of the Zohar's upper unity, which is the essence of the first verse, *Shema Yisrael*. The second verse, *Barukh Shem Kevod*, is the lower unity, and represents God's response, His emanation of *shefa* and hence felicity to the worlds below.

selves with all the souls and worlds for the purpose of ascending to the One Who is the Cause of all causes, "Who is One, but not like a number."[39] In this way the name *Elohim*, which denotes specific actions in all the worlds, is unified with the Tetragrammaton, the apex of all levels, and the two are unified with each other and included in each other, until the *ehad*, the First Cause, is reached. This is called the upper unity, the ascent of all worlds to the highest of heights, the Ein-Sof.

After achieving the elevation and ascent [to the Ein-Sof] and communion (*devekut*) with Him Who is truly One, we draw down, by means of the unification of *Barukh Shem*, etc., His effluent will, the channels of His overflowing blessing, from *ehad* ("one"). These are the male waters, providing additional blessings and the extension of His lovingkindness to all the worlds from the root of the Tetragrammaton.[40] This is called the lower unity, whereby the uppermost is united with the lowermost.[41]

Afterword

The views expressed by R. Shneur Zalman (see selection 3) and R. Zevi Hirsch differ greatly. For R. Shneur Zalman, the Zohar's upper unity is an affirmation of the world's nonexistence; nothing exists but God. The lower unity reflects man's perception; man perceives himself and his world as real, and hence in relationship with God, Who is immanent in the "real" world. Clearly, R. Shneur Zalman sees the upper unity as dominant, for which reason it is the essence of the Shema verse rather than the Barukh Shem. Man is condemned to live within a divine illusion and act as if it were ultimately real, but he believes and knows and affirms that it is only an illusion.

---

39. A quotation from the Elijah passage at the beginning of *Tikkunei Ha-Zohar*. God's unity is so beyond the "one" of the number system that "two" and "three," etc., are unimaginable. His oneness is absolute and incomparable.

40. The lower unity, says R. Zevi Hirsch in part of the passage omitted in this selection, unites the upper spheres, identified with the Tetragrammaton, with the world of Malkhut, which is highlighted in the *Barukh Shem* verse: "Blessed be His Name Whose glorious *Kingdom* is forever and ever." The unity of the Tetragrammaton is the "generalization," in the sense that fissures and fragmentations are overcome, whereas the realm of Malkhut is the "specific," for this is the realm that is real for man; tangible, finite, palpable.

41. See Additional Note *3 for the author's own gloss at this point.

For R. Zevi Hirsch, the question of acosmism or illusionism does not arise. He completely avoids what may seem to be a dangerously close brush with pantheism. His interpretation of the Zohar's two unities is based solely upon the doctrine of *hishtalshelut* ("declensions"), the innumerable series of worlds that mediate between the Ein-Sof and the mundane realm, the latter being the end product of a long series of emanations of cause and effect, losing in holiness but gaining in definition, finiteness, multiplicity, complexity, and denseness as the distance from the utterly simple, pure, and unique Ein-Sof grows. The upper unity of the Shema is an act of elevation—meditation leading from the multiplicity and complexity of the sensate world to its ultimate Cause in the pure and simple One. The lower unity, that of *Barukh Shem*, is the descent of divine grace from the First Cause, the Ein-Sof, through the original channels of descent, to our world of multiplicity and fragmentation. It is the upper unity, the human act of elevation, that R. Zevi Hirsch celebrates as clearly superior. There is no theory of acosmism in his interpretation of the Zohar. The affirmation of a unity that transcends all plurality and multiplicity does not, for him, entail a doctrine of illusionism that negates the world of experience. Moreover, whereas for R. Shneur Zalman the *Barukh Shem* is a metaphysical meditation, for R. Zevi Hirsch it is a prayer.

5. "THE PLACE THAT WASN'T"
Source: R. Yaakov Yosef of Polennoye, Ben Porat Yosef, p. 140[42]

Let us explain the verse *The Lord is nigh unto all that call upon Him, to all that call upon Him in truth (be-emet)* (Ps. 145:18). Let us understand what is meant by *in truth*.

The answer, it seems to me, is as follows: According to *Tikkunei Zohar*, "R. Elazar said, 'Is it not written, *For I the Lord change not* (Mal. 3:6)?' They answered, 'Certainly He does not change . . . and does not hide Himself. But toward sinners, the Holy One changes and hides Himself. Thus is it written, *I will hide My face from them* (Deut. 32:20),'" etc.[43]

---

42. This passage is a good example of hasidic *derush*, especially the *derashot* ("homilies") of R. Yaakov Yosef. A series of questions is posed, and answers are suggested in reverse order, so that the whole issue is clarified by the time the first question is resolved.
43. Tikkun 26, p. 71b.

To understand this, we must turn to the Zohar (e.g., II, 146b), which says that the gates of the *hekhalot* ("palaces, halls") of prayer are one above the other, and the angels receive the prayers and transfer them upward to the Throne of Glory; there is one angel whose height is a five hundred years' journey, and so on.

Now this must be understood: do we not know of God, blessed be His Name, that *the whole earth is full of His glory* (Isa. 6:3),[44] and that "there is no place empty of Him"?[45] If so, then His blessed glory is found wherever anyone prays. In that case, why is it necessary for our prayers to be received by angels who go and transmit them from *hekhal* ("palace") to *hekhal*?[46]

It seems to me that the answer follows upon...a parable that my teacher, the Besht, once told before the sounding of the shofar on Rosh Hashanah. There was once a great and wise king who magically created the illusion of walls and towers and gates. He commanded his people to come to him by way of these gates and towers, and had treasures from the royal treasury displayed at every gate. There were some who went as far as the first gate and then returned, laden with treasure. Others proceeded to gates deeper within the palace and closer to the king; but none reached the king himself. At last, the king's son made a great effort to go to his father, the king. Then he saw that there was really no barrier separating him from his father, for it was all an illusion.[47] The point of the parable is obvious—and "the words of a wise man's mouth are gracious."[48]

...I heard from my teacher [the Besht] of blessed memory on the verse *all the workers of iniquity shall be scattered* (Ps. 92:10): by means of man's knowledge that *the whole earth is full of His glory* (Isa. 6:3), and

---

44. This verse is the *locus classicus* for the hasidic doctrine of divine immanence.
45. *Tikkunei Zohar* 57; this statement is likewise used consistently by hasidim to express the concept of divine omnipresence and immanence.
46. R. Yaakov Yosef is here trying to reconcile hasidic immanentism with the notion of the *hekhalot* so prominent in Merkabah mysticism, which conceived of God in His transcendence, with angels composing magniloquent hymns for His solemnity. See G. Scholem, *Major Trends in Jewish Mysticism*, second lecture, and esp. pp. 55 and 62.
47. This famous Beshtian parable is often taken as an illustration of hasidic denial of the world's reality. When hasidic immanentism is given a radical twist, it tends toward illusionism or acosmism, a doctrine especially elaborated in the Habad system. The parable of the illusory palace seems to bear this out, and most scholars, beginning with Zweifel, have so interpreted the parable. (The assertion by some writers, that the parable is a disguised pantheism, is invalid.) See Additional Note *4.
48. Eccl. 10:12; a traditional expression of approval.

that every motion and thought, everything, comes from Him—by this very knowledge are all the workers of iniquity scattered.[49] Hence, all the angels and the *hekhalot* were created and made, as it were, from His essence, like the snail whose shell is formed of itself.[50] So, by means of this knowledge, there is no longer any barrier or sundering curtain between man and God.

Now you are able to understand the words of the *Tikkunei Zohar*, mentioned above, about the verse *For I the Lord change not*. The passage concludes, *but for those who rely on Him and His Shekhinah, He never changes*. Understand this.[51]

This enables us to understand the verse *the Lord is nigh unto them that call upon Him in truth (be-emet)*. In other words, all who call upon Him in *emet*—beginning, middle, and end[52]—know that *the earth is full of His glory*, and that *there is no place empty of Him*." Thus, by means of *emet*, He is "nigh unto them that call upon Him in *emet*." Understand this.

6. FROM SPIRIT TO MATTER TO SPIRIT
Source: R. Shelomoh of Lutzk, second introduction to *Maggid Devarav le-Yaakov* by R. Dov Ber, the Maggid of Mezeritch

First of all, it is important to know that *the whole earth is full of His glory* (Isa. 6:3) and *there is no place that is empty of Him*,[53] and that He is

---

49. This Beshtian interpretation is consistent with the hasidic belief in the nonreality, or privative nature, of evil.
50. A well-known illustration often cited in hasidic literature to teach that all is in God. It first appears in Genesis Rabbah 21:5, but in a totally different context pertaining to how Adam's skin, which was made of a nail-like substance that protected him from cuts and bruises, was replaced by "garments of skins." Our finger and toenails are but remnants of what we have lost.
51. That is, those who possess this true intuition into the allness of God and the illusory nature of the cosmos will know that He does not change, and that evil is nonexistent.
52. The word *emet* ("truth"), consisting of *alef* (the first letter of the Hebrew alphabet), *mem* (a middle letter), and *tav* (the final letter), implies totality. Cf. J.T. Sanhedrin 1:1, Shabbat 104a.
53. *Tikkunei Zohar*, tikkun 57. The principle of divine immanence is crucial to the rest of the passage, which dwells upon contemplating the world as reflecting in some way the higher reality of the Divine Presence. After emanating from its undifferentiated origin in the Ein-Sof, the world assumes various specific forms. R. Shelomoh explains immanence by means of the kabbalistic sefirot, or "worlds," whereas R. Shneur Zalman (in *Sha'ar ha-Yiḥud ve-ha-Emunah*, below, selection 9) uses letter-symbolism as a medium for structuring divine immanence.

in all the worlds, etc. This idea can be sensed in everything, for the life-force of the Creator is everywhere. Everything possesses taste, odor, appearance, or love; i.e., it is beloved or feared or considered beautiful, and so on for all other attributes. When we abstract this quality from its corporeality and contemplate only its spirituality,[54] such as taste or odor, and the like, in and of itself, it will be obvious to us that the taste or odor, etc., is intangible and invisible, and can only be apprehended conceptually by man's life-force and soul.[55] Therefore, it is certainly a spiritual thing: a life-force of the Creator that dwells in this material object, as the soul does in the body. So it is with every thing and with every motion, for as *Hovot ha-Levavot* says, "all your motions are tied to the will of the Creator."[56] In all of them there exist sparks of vitality drawn from the Creator, Who is the Bond of Life and the Light of Life and the Source of Life and the Life of Life; from Him is drawn the life-force for every object, from the highest heights to the lowest depths.

That is what we mean when we say that He contracted[57] His Shekhinah in order to dwell in the lower worlds. Every spark is derived from its own world. For instance, an object of love: the love within it derives from the world of love; i.e., there certainly must be a source and root from which love is derived for everything that entails love. In order better to understand the idea of this root, let us think of the spirituality of the root of love itself, as mentioned above. Obviously, it is only the undifferentiated life-force of the Creator which contracted itself, as it were, so that it could be perceived as the quality of love. There is, as well, a vitality and spirituality that cannot

---

54. The term "spiritual" is used here as a synonym for "abstract."

55. Note the similarity to the Platonic Ideas.

56. *Hovot ha-Levavot*, Sha'ar ha-Behinah. Actually, R. Bahya was referring more to providence in its transcendental form than to the immanentist conception intended here.

57. Heb. *tzimtzem*, related to *tzimtzum*, the "contraction" of divinity. The term first appears in Exodus Rabbah 34:1, where God says that He will "contract" His presence (Shekhinah) so as to dwell in the Tabernacle. Whereas in the Midrash *tzimtzum* implies the contraction of God's infinite presence *into* a finite, circumscribed area, R. Isaac Luria says that the Ein-Sof moved into Himself *away* from a central point, thus leaving "place" for the worlds. R. Shelomoh uses the term in its midrashic rather than its Lurianic sense. The contractions take place *after* the primordial act of Lurianic *tzimtzum*. The divine grace (*shefa*) is undifferentiated and is "contracted" into various worlds which it animates, and each world, in turn, endows the *shefa* with finite attributes.

be perceived as love, but only in some other category, such as fear or beauty or one of the other attributes. All of them are the divine life-force and spirituality, as mentioned, but none of them can be perceived in the same way as the others, for each was contracted by means of a different contraction, leading to a different form or perception. But in their inner essence all are alike, for they are all [divine] life-force and spirituality, as mentioned, because all derive from the same root, where there is no differentiation whatsoever. This is what is meant by the statement in *Tikkunei Zohar* that "in Ein-Sof are seen all the supernal forms," i.e., through the contraction of perception, as mentioned. For it is in the category of the female, relating to what is above it, for it receives from the Root of Roots.[58] The intelligent will understand this.[59]

The loci of these attributes are called worlds (*olamot*) because the life-force of the Creator is concealed (*mit'alem*)[60] and contracted in the particular perception of each quality. They are also called measures (*middot*) because they are perceived and understood according to a specific size and measure, and no other.[61] In truth, each of them is constituted of all the others.[62] . . .

Let us return to our subject.[63] As mentioned, there is nothing that does not have a root up above. That is why the holy tongue [Hebrew] has a source and active and passive forms; i.e., the source is the root

---

58. In the Ein-Sof, the "Root of Roots," all is One, and there is no distinction or differentiation. After the divine light flows away from the realm of the Ein-Sof, the contractions bring multiplicity into being. The divine grace issues undifferentiated from the Ein-Sof, which, as the active Source, is considered the male principle; the realm outside it, where *tzimtzum* occurs, receives the flow and, as the passive recipient, is termed female (perhaps because it is in the womb that the differentiation of the organs takes place).

59. Alluding to the esoteric nature of his kabbalistic references. R. Shelomoh's metaphysics is highly Platonic, as is so much of Lurianic mysticism. Perhaps the reason for this lengthy metaphysical-kabbalistic excursus is to prepare the way for the concept of *devekut* in the religiously "neutral" realm where the Halakhah offers no judgment. See below, chap. 5.

60. The root of both words is *ayin-lamed-mem*. Hence, the "worlds" (i.e., the sefirot) are disguises for the Ein-Sof, Who is "concealed" in them.

61. The undifferentiated grace from the Ein-Sof is divided into different qualities in the sefirot. "Size" and "measure" are not to be taken literally, but symbolize finite properties which make them specific and cognizable.

62. The *olamot* or *middot* (synonyms for the sefirot) interpenetrate one other, so that each sefirah is composed of ten sefirot.

63. A brief excursus on Lurianic Kabbalah has been omitted.

of a thing, as mentioned.[64] The active agent is the man who acts and draws from the source and the root. The passive is the quality drawn from the source and the root.

Take happiness, for instance. There is a world of happiness, as mentioned above, by which I mean the life-force of the Creator which is perceived through the quality of happiness. That is the source. A happy person is active and draws down upon himself the divine grace of happiness from the world of happiness, at the specific time that he is happy, but not before then, for before then he was not happy. The man's happiness itself is passive. When man is in a hearty state, and uses his reason, it may be that the spark which he sees through his physical eyes is small in size, but when he abstracts it from the corporeality in which it is clothed, and reflects that it is the life-force of Godliness derived from the supernal root, then its light and vitality will be endlessly great and mighty,[65] because through its spirituality and life-force it is connected to the source.

We must see the supernal root and source in everything. . . . In every matter we must always contemplate our essential attributes, whether those of love or fear or anything else, and also our speech and our voice and our thought, discerning that they are, in essence, divine life-force and spirituality. For surely every one of them is derived from its supernal root and source, i.e., it is the root of love from which love is drawn to all creatures and substances of love; the same holds for the root of fear and the other attributes. So too the root of the world of speech, from which words are drawn to all who speak—and indeed to all creatures, for in all of them there exist the words of the Holy One; for His life-force is like a voice, and the garments in which His life-force is contracted are like speech, which encompasses and contracts the voice. The intelligent will understand this. Similarly, there is the root of the world of thought, as mentioned.

---

64. Linguistic analogies were a favorite theme of kabbalists and kabbalistically influenced hasidic writers. *Makor*, usually translated as "source," is also the term for the infinitive in Hebrew grammar. It can be conjugated in the active voice (*pa'al*) or the passive (*nif'al*), among others. (R. Shelomoh equates the infinitive [*makor*, "source"] with the root [*shoresh*] of the word, treating the two terms as synonyms.) Thus, Hebrew's grammatical and spiritual "roots" are related.

65. By means of this contemplation, man reverses the process of descent or flow from the Ein-Sof. This return, whereby man "reveals" the (hidden) immanence of God in any object, quality, or experience, leads him on to joy and rapture.

When we contemplate this and understand it, we will surely be overwhelmed by great awe and shame before Him who dwells within us in all our movements, as is written in *Hovot ha-Levavot*, "Do not rebel against your Master, for He sees you, and how can He cause His power and His life-force, may He be blessed, to act against His own will?"[66]

We must always cleave to God in wondrous *devekut*.[67] We have to know that by serving the Creator, and by *devekut* to Him, we can elevate all the worlds, because since every one of our attributes and statements and thoughts cleaves to the root from which it is drawn to all creatures, certainly all creatures will cleave to us, and we cleave to the Creator.[68]

This enables us to understand the dictum, "All the world rests on one pillar, and its name is 'righteous' [*zaddik*]."[69]

7. GOD'S GARMENTS
Source: R. Pinhas of Koretz, *Likkutim Yekarim*, p. 17c, cited in *Sefer ha-Besht*, Bereshit, no. 15

The whole earth is full of His glory (Isa. 6:3). *His glory (kevodo)* should be understood in the sense of "His garment," i.e., that God is enclothed, so to speak, in the corporeal. Hence, *the whole earth is full of His glory* implies [that God fills] all corporeality. Thus "God's glory" refers to His clothing.[70]

---

66. I have not been able to locate the source of this quotation. A similar thought may be found in Cordovero's *Tomer Devorah*, 1:1.

67. *Devekut* is communion, or the act of "cleaving" to God, which in Hasidism became an ecstatic experience (see below, chap. 5). For R. Shelomoh, it entails contemplation of the divine immanence, which leads to the return of a quality to its abstraction in its source-world, and thence to its *tzimtzum*-source in the Root of Roots, i.e., the Ein-Sof.

68. By means of this contemplation, man not only achieves his personal *devekut* but contributes to a cosmic *devekut*, drawing to himself all the physical and emotional properties that he shares with the rest of the natural order and leading them back to the root, or Ein-Sof.

69. Hagigah 12b. In causing the world's cosmic elevation, the righteous man becomes central to all creation, which explains why the Talmud describes him as the pillar of the world. Hasidic writers often used the term *zaddik* both in its traditional sense of a righteous person and with the more specific meaning of a charismatic (hasidic) leader (see below, introduction to chap. 8).

70. A straightforward statement of hasidic immanentism: the world is God's garment; just as the body fills a garment, so God indwells in the world. The identification of "glory" with clothing probably derives from the talmudic interpretation of Isa. 10:16. R. Yohanan, we are told, referred to his clothing as "my glory" (Shabbat 113b). See too Prov. 25:2, "It is the glory of God to conceal a thing."

8. PERPETUAL IMMANENCE
Source: Besht, Keter Shem Tov II, p. 2b

The Creator is found in every act of physical movement. It is impossible to make any motion or to utter any word without the power of the Creator. That is the meaning of *the whole earth is full of His glory* (Isa. 6:3).

9. SOUL IN THE INANIMATE
Source: R. Shneur Zalman of Liady, Tanya, Sha'ar ha-Yiḥud veha-Emunah, chap. 1

Know this day, and ponder in thy heart, that the Lord, He is God in heaven above and upon the earth beneath (Deut. 4:39).

It is necessary to understand [this verse]. Is it even conceivable that there is a god who is immersed in the waters beneath the earth, so that [Scripture] has to warn so strongly: *and ponder in thy heart?*[71]

Now, it is written, *For ever O Lord, Thy word standeth fast in heaven* (Ps. 119:89). The Besht, of blessed memory, explained: *Thy word* [refers to] God's saying, *Let there be a firmament in the midst of the waters* (Gen. 1:6). These words and letters are what *stand forever* in the firmament of the heavens, clothed[72] in all the firmaments forever, in order to give them life; as it is written, *But the word of our God shall stand forever* (Isa. 40:8), and His words live and exist everlastingly.[73] For were the letters to be withdrawn even for a moment, heaven forbid, and returned to

---

71. The reference to "waters beneath the earth" may pertain to the commandment against making a graven image "of anything that is in heaven above . . . or *in the water under the earth*" (Exod. 20:4, Deut. 5:8). Earlier in the same discourse, Moses warns against fashioning images, including images of "any fish that is in the waters under the earth" (Deut. 4:18).

72. In hasidic works generally, and especially in the writings of R. Shneur Zalman, *levush* ("clothing, garment") is a code-word for the concept of immanence. Divinity indwelling or enwrapped in nature is said to be "clothed" in the "garment" of matter. See above, selection 7 and selection 2.

73. In the Kabbalah, the letters of the Hebrew alphabet, wherewith the Creator commanded the world and its parts to come into being, as recorded in Genesis, are themselves the vehicles of God's creative energy. All that exists is the externalization of concealed divine language. This is true not only of the initial act of Creation, but equally of God's sustaining of the cosmos; the world continues to exist by virtue of the divine letters and words that first brought it into being. R. Shneur Zalman, following the Besht, sees the concept of immanence in the roles of the letters and words that sustain existence.

their source, all the heavens would become null and void, and it would be as if they had never existed, and they would be as nonexistent as [they were] before the divine saying, *Let there be a firmament*, etc.

So is it with all the created things in all the worlds, higher and lower, and even in this material earth, even in the actual category of the inanimate. Were the letters of the Ten Utterances[74] by which the world was created during the first six days of Creation to be withdrawn from them for but an instant, heaven forbid, they would return to a state of nullity and emptiness, as they were before the six days of Creation.

R. Isaac Luria, of blessed memory, said that even in what is completely inanimate, such as stones and earth and water, there exist soul and spiritual vitality—the enclothing of the letters of the appropriate word from the Ten Utterances—which animate and quicken the inanimate, so that it can come into being from the null and void that prevailed before the six days of Creation. Although the word "stone" is not mentioned in the Ten Utterances in the Torah, nevertheless vitality, i.e., existence, is drawn to stone by means of the permutations and commutations of the letters which are transposed back and forth through the 231 gates,[75] as is mentioned in the *Sefer Yetzirah*,[76] until the proper combination for the word "stone" develops and derives from the Ten Utterances, and it is this which is the life of that stone. So it is with regard to everything in the created world: the names by which they are designated in the holy tongue (Hebrew) are composed of the very letters of the words that descend level to level, from the Ten Utterances of the Torah, by means of the transpositions and substitutions of the letters, through the 231 gates, until they reach and are enclothed in that specific creation, in order to animate it. Specific created things cannot receive their vitality directly from the Ten Utterances, for the vitality flowing directly from the Ten Utterances is too great for the class of individual creations. They have the capacity to receive vitality only after it has descended and been progres-

---

74. Avot 5:1. The word *amar*, "said" or "uttered," referring to God's commands in the act of Creation, occurs nine times in the Creation narrative in Genesis, and *bereshit* ("in the beginning") is itself considered an utterance.

75. This refers to the number of ways that the twenty-two letters of the Hebrew alphabet can be interchanged or permutated to each other. For a detailed explanation, see below, chap. 7, n. 94.

76. "The Book of Creation," one of the earliest and most influential kabbalistic works. See Scholem, *Major Trends in Jewish Mysticism*, pp. 75 ff. et passim.

sively diminished, from one level to the level below, by means of transpositions and substitutions of the letters and of the *gematriot* which are their numerical values; at that point they can be condensed and enclothed and realized in a particular creation.[77] This name, by which it is designated in the holy tongue, is the vessel for the vitality concentrated in the letters of the name, descended from the Ten Utterances of the Torah, which have the power and vitality to create *ex nihilo*, and to give it life forever; for the Torah and the Holy One are all one.[78]

10. GOD IS IN ROME
Source: R. Nahman of Bratslav, Likkutei Moharan, I, no. 33, b

It is necessary to know that *the whole earth is full of His glory* (Isa. 6:3), and that "there is no place empty of Him,"[79] and that "He fills all the worlds and surrounds all the worlds."[80]

Therefore, even if you are engaged in doing business with pagans, you cannot offer an excuse for yourself by saying that it is impossible to serve God because of the grossness and corporeality that befall you as a result of your continual business dealings with them. For our Sages long ago revealed to us that Godliness may be found in all material things, and in all the pagan languages,[81] because without the presence of His Godliness, they would have no life or existence whatsoever, as it is written, *And Thou givest them all life* (Neh. 9:6). It is only that this vitality and Godliness are there in diluted form, after many contractions, just sufficient to keep them alive and no more. For the Holy One contracted His Godliness with many and varied contractions,

---

77. Thus the principle of letter-mysticism is applied even to objects too trivial to be mentioned in the Creation account in Genesis; at the same time, the point is made that God's immanence is not uniform in the world, but is differentiated in accordance with the significance of the various objects.

78. Zohar III, 93b, and with modifications, Zohar II, 60a; III, 73a; and elsewhere. In this passage, the unity of God and Torah is evident from the scheme of creation and sustenance of the world just developed: God's creative energy is implemented via the very words of the Torah; see Additional Note *5.

79. *Tikkunei Zohar*, tikkun 70.

80. Zohar (*Raya Mehemna*), III, 225a.

81. A somewhat less immanentist position was earlier propounded by R. Isaiah Halevi Horowitz (ca. 1555–1628) in his *Shenei Luḥot ha-Berit* (ed. Jerusalem, 1963, Masekhet Shavuot 36a). He asserts the sanctity of the names of pagan deities written in Scripture, by virtue of the inherent Godliness of all of creation. See my *Torah Lishmah*, p. 98, n. 136.

from His first thought to the very core of the corporeal world, the abode of the *kelipot*. The longer the chain of descending gradations, and the greater the contractions as it descends, the more is His Godliness clothed in many garments. This is what our Sages revealed to us when they gave us access to understanding, so that the intelligent man may know that Godliness and the life-force inhere in everything material. As our Sages said: *tot* in Coptic means "two," and *fot* in the language of Africa means "two."[82] Thereby they sought to inform us that His Godliness exists even in all the pagan languages, giving them life.[83]

Now we can understand what the Jerusalem Talmud means when it teaches: "If someone asks you, 'Where is your God?' say to him, 'In the great city of Rome,' as it is said, *One calleth to me out of Seir* (Isa. 21:11)."[84] The person who asks "Where is your God?" is immersed in the abode of the *kelipot*, for he has taken himself out of the community[85] and denied the fundamental principle of Judaism by saying, "Where is your God?" imagining that God is not present where he is. Therefore, say to him: "Even in your place, immersed as you are in the abode of the *kelipot*, there too you will be able to find His Godliness, for He gives life to all, as it is written, *and Thou givest them all life* (Neh. 9:6).[86] Even from there you can cleave to Him and return to Him in complete repentance. For *it is not far off* (Deut. 30:11); it is only that where you are, [Godliness] is wrapped in many garments."

The more man rises from level to level, the closer he draws to God, knowing Him with greater understanding. For the higher the level, the fewer the garments and the smaller the contractions. Then he is closer to God and can love God with great love.[87]

---

82. Menahot 34b. The Talmud suggests that the biblical word for "phylacteries," *totafot* (Deut. 6:8), derives from two pagan languages. Two plus two are four, the number of passages written on the parchment of the head phylactery.

83. R. Nahman here seems to be aiming at the idea of worship through corporeality (see below, chap. 9), and grounds it in the concept of immanence.

84. Ta'anit 1:1, with minor changes. For the Sages, Seir and Esau are symbols of Rome.

85. A euphemism for heresy. Cf. the wicked son in the Passover Haggadah.

86. R. Nahman regards the questioner as a heretic because he implicitly denies the immanence of God. He identifies him with heathen Rome, and responds that God dwells even where the heretic is, as symbolized by "Rome," the token of physicality and spiritual denseness.

87. See Additional Note *6.

11. IMMANENCE EVEN IN EVIL
Source: R. Mosheh Hayyim Ephraim, Degel Mahaneh Ephraim to Emor, p. 128

These are the commandments which, if a man do, he shall live by them; I am the Lord (Lev. 18:5).[88]

There is a profound way [of interpreting] this, but I am afraid to explain it, for my heart hesitates lest I err in my vision,[89] heaven forbid. Therefore, I shall only give a slight hint, and if the Lord grants me the privilege of understanding the matter thoroughly, I shall explain further.

I heard from [the Besht] my Master, my grandfather of blessed memory, that the Chief of the World (*alufo shel olam*) is concealed within sin.[90] *The words of a wise man's mouth are gracious* (Eccl. 10:12).

The meaning of this is that the *alef* is not revealed, it is not recognized in the pronunciation [of the word]. And similarly with the word "impure";[91] here too the *alef* is swallowed at the end [of the word].

To understand this: when a man commits a sin, heaven forbid, then his wisdom departs from him, as the Sages said, "No man commits a sin unless the spirit of madness enters in him."[92] At such a time he thinks that certainly *the Lord hath forsaken the land* (Ezek. 8:12, 9:9) and is no longer concerned with it. For if he knew and believed that all his actions are [done] in the presence of the Lord, Who exercises providence over all his activities, certainly he would never have committed this sin. In truth, [what the sinner thinks] is an utter lie; for His blessed providence is present even there [in the sinful act].[93]

---

88. The quotation is somewhat inaccurate. It should read, "Ye shall therefore keep My statutes and My ordinances, which if a man do . . ." The change does not affect the discourse.

89. Paraphrase of Isa. 28:7.

90. The Hebrew word for "sin," *het*, consists of three letters, *het, tet,* and *alef;* the first two are pronounced, but the third, *alef,* is silent. As the first letter of the alphabet, *alef* often assumes special significance and, because it has the numerical value of one, sometimes stands for God (*Otiot de-R. Akiva,* B, *alef*). In the Besht's interpretation, *alef* also stands for God, but not because of its numerical value; instead, it is revocalized from *alef* to *aluf,* a "chief," as in Gen. 36:15–19, Exod. 15:15, and elsewhere. The concept expressed by locating *alef-aluf* in sin (*Het*) is quite radical: the immanence of God even in evil. Hence, the author's hesitation. See below, n.93.

91. *Tamei,* spelled *tet, mem, alef.*

92. Sotah 3a.

93. The phrase "His blessed providence" instead of "the Holy One, blessed be He," is intended to soften the view propounded. The author's sensitivity to the possible antinomian consequences of this idea, all too reminiscent of Sabbateanism, is also evident in the apologies at the beginning and end of the discourse.

Imagine, if you can, that His providence was absent from [the sinner] even for but a moment; [if that were to happen, the sinner] would immediately die at that instant and would be unable to do anything whatsoever. Therefore, the Holy One is surely present—but in great hiddenness and concealment.

This is alluded to by the concealment of the *alef*, which stands for the *aluf* ("chief") of the world, at the end [of the word]. Now surely, when a man betakes himself to commit a sin, heaven forbid, but refrains from doing it because of [his awareness of] the Holy One, or when he performs a mitzvah because of his fear and love of the Holy One, this is termed the aspect of *alef*. [When a man acts virtuously, this comes under] the category of *I am the first* (Isa. 44:6), and when, heaven forbid, [he succumbs to sin], that is called *I am the last* (ibid.).[94] Of course, *I*—that is, *I* as *the last*—yearn to arrive at the level of *I* [am] *the first*, for [the sake of] its [own] life; for every [spiritual] descent in level is termed "death"; and when there is a [spiritual] ascent, as when one performs a mitzvah or restrains oneself from doing a sin, or repents from the [evil] one has already done, then the *I am the last* is brought to life by *I am the first*. Then the divine light emanates from above to below,[95] and it becomes *I am the first, and I am the last, and beside Me there is no God*, for certainly the Lord has not forsaken the world, but He watches with open eyes over every particular of what is done in His world and in all the worlds, and He grants life to all of them.

This is what is alluded to in *which if a man shall do, he shall live by them; I am the Lord*. That is, if a man obeys the ordinances and commandments, *I am the last* becomes *I am the first*, so that *I am the first, and I am the last, and beside Me there is no other God*, as was mentioned.[96]

---

94. Now that *alef* has been identified as symbolizing God, the verse indicates that God's position in our lives depends upon our conduct. When man indulges in sin (*Het-tet-alef*) or in immoral acts that render him impure (*tet-mem-alef*), the *alef* comes concealed at the end; "I am the last." But when, despite temptation, man performs a good deed or resists sin or repents, then "I am the first," for it is man's consciousness of God's omnipresence that dissuades him from evil or motivates him to do good.

95. In terms of this discourse, from "I am the first" to "I am the last." Thus spiritual ascent (from "last" to "first") is an increment of life, and spiritual descent (from "first" to "last"), which diminishes the divine vitality, may be termed "death."

96. The symbolism is now homiletically applied to the verse with which the discourse began. *Va-ḥai ba-hem* no longer means, as the plain reading of the text suggests, "and he [man] shall live by them [the commandments]," but rather, "and He [God's presence in the world] shall live [i.e., gain in the vitality of spiritual ascent] by them [by means of man performing the mitzvot]."

May the Lord forgive me if I have erred, and may He show me wonders in His holy Torah, the Torah of truth, for me and my descendants
forever, Amen.

12. IMMANENCE, TRANSCENDENCE, AND ESSENCE
Source: R. Shneur Zalman of Liady, Likkutei Torah to Re'eh, s.v. ani le-dodi,
pp. 33a–b

As is well known, [God relates to the world in two ways:] *memallei kol
almin* and *sovev kol almin*.[97] The meaning of *memallei kol almin* is that a
kind of divine illumination is drawn into all created things to bring
them to life, by means of the Ten Utterances,[98] [such as] *Let there be
light* (Gen. 1:3), etc., as it is written, *By the word of the Lord were the
heavens made* (Ps. 33:6). [This means] that it is enclothed within them,
in their very insides—drawn into them to become their life-force—
and is divided into [different] parts so as to animate "each one according to its own capacity."[99] Thus, for instance, in the material world of
mineral, vegetable, animal, and human,[100] the mineral, too, came into
being by means of the Ten Utterances, and divine vitality flows into
it by means of the [appropriate Utterance], even as the divine vitality
flows into the vegetable and the animal. Nevertheless, this [divine]
vitality is severely restricted [in the mineral kingdom], but the vegetable possesses more of it, the animal more than the vegetable, and
the human more than the others, and so on. According to this pattern,
in the spiritual worlds there is a corresponding differentiation into
many levels. Each receives a [degree of] vitality different and separate
from that received by any other. This [differentiation] derives from
the sphere of Malkhut, which is called *memallei kol almin*, for [as the
lowest of the sefirot] it is embedded deeply within the worlds.

However, the category of *sovev kol almin* is that of a divine influence
and illumination which is not drawn into and enclothed in the worlds
in revealed form, so that it can be perceived by [them in accordance
with] their understanding. Rather, it encompasses them from above.
It is called *sovev kol almin* because it surrounds (*sovev*) all [the worlds]
uniformly. It undergoes no differentiation, for it is not enclothed in a
revealed form [accessible to] understanding, so that it can be said,

---

97. Lit. "He who fills the worlds" and "He who surrounds the worlds," the zoharic
terms respectively indicating divine immanence and transcendence.
98. See above, n. 74.
99. *Zohar Ḥadash*, I, 103a.
100. The four prime divisions of the natural world, in ascending order of importance.

"Here it illuminates and is revealed to this degree, and there to another degree." Hence it is uniform, and everything is equal before it, etc. Concerning it does Scripture say, *Do I not fill heaven and earth?* (Jer. 23:24); i.e., by means of *sovev kol almin*, for "there is no place that is empty of Him."[101]

However, the verse *the whole earth is full of His glory* (Isa. 6:3) refers to *memallei kol almin*, for [God's immanence] is called "glory" (*kavod*). Now, the Rabbis said that *kavod* refers to the Torah.[102] That was because Torah derives from Hokhmah.[103] Thirty-two pathways issue from Hokhmah, comparable to the pathways and lanes that are used to go from place to place. So from the upper wisdom the [divine] grace (*shefa*) is drawn in differentiated form in order to become *memallei kol almin* until it is drawn into corporeality itself, according to all the details of the Torah, such as valid and invalid, etc., for [the Torah deals with] material things, such as offerings to the priests, tithes, etc., as is well known.[104] But by means of the mitzvot a revelation of light occurs in the category of *sovev kol almin*, which encompasses [from without].

The matter [may be explained] as follows: As is well known, Torah becomes food for the divine soul, as it is written, *Yea, Thy law (torah) is in my inmost parts* (Ps. 40:9). Just as food enters deep into a person and is transformed into life-force in his innards, so by means of Torah a revelation of the illumination of Hokhmah is drawn that can actu-

---

101. *Tikkunei Zohar* 57. What R. Shneur Zalman means is that the verse from Jeremiah, although it uses the verb *malei*, which implies immanence, comprehensively indicates uniformity—including both heaven and earth—and thus signifies *sovev*, or transcendence. However, "the whole earth is full of His glory" implies *memallei* because "glory" (*kavod*) is a synonym for Torah, which perforce is pluralistic and differentiated. See the next paragraph.
102. Avot 6:3.
103. *Zohar Hadash*, II, 121b, et passim.
104. Two things have been established: (1) that transcendence is unknowable and uniform, and (2) that immanence sustains existence in differentiation and is, by its very multiplicity, knowable in discrete conceptual units. R. Shneur Zalman now proceeds to show that immanence (*memallei kol almin*) and transcendence (*sovev kol almin*) are related, respectively, to Torah and the mitzvot (commandments). Torah, preeminently halakhic in nature, is judgmental: permitted or forbidden, valid or invalid, innocent or guilty. It is an expression of immanence by virtue of its plurality of values and norms, and because its mode is cognitive—study. Mitzvot, as is explained below, are a function of transcendence. The commandments are performed, not reasoned or studied; they summon a single-valued response of the will and obedience to the divine command. In the spiritual effects that follow, they are uniform and not amenable to rational understanding.

ally be grasped by the mind. So *I have put My words in thy mouth* (Isa. 51:16). This is the aspect of *memallei kol almin*, which enclothes itself in the worlds, actually within them. However, the mitzvot become garments for the divine soul [rather than food]. Just as a garment is on a man's body, on the outside, and does not enter within him, so the *shefa* drawn down by the mitzvot encompasses [the world] from without. It is in the category of *sovev kol almin*, which is beyond understanding.

That is why the garments are innately more precious than food, for they have a more exalted source.[105] . . .

Repentance is possible in this world, but not in the world-to-come. There you remain [forever] as you are, without the power to change from your present condition [except by an act of special divine grace]; but you yourself can do nothing [to change]. The reason is that in the world-to-come, as the Sages said, "[the righteous sit] and derive pleasure [from the radiance of the Shekhinah],"[106] for they apprehend divinity openly and with understanding. It is, therefore, in the class of *memallei kol almin*, which is manifested in revealed form, for, as mentioned, *memallei kol almin* is differentiated. If you are a member of one class, you cannot transpose yourself into another class, for they are differentiated and separated one from the other, and each is in its own

---

105. Since R. Shneur Zalman assigns to transcendence (clothing) a higher value than immanence (nourishment), one must assume that he assigns greater value to this world than to the next, for the next world is the realm where God is encountered in His immanence, whereas in this world He is encountered in His transcendence. What R. Shneur Zalman does not say, but is important as a "hidden agenda," is that the same reasoning would assign a higher value to performing mitzvot than to studying Torah, which is apparently consistent with the hasidic transvaluation of the hierarchy of Jewish values.

This should by no means be taken simplistically, for R. Shneur Zalman's scheme is enormously sophisticated and subtle. It is true that he assigns a higher spiritual status to transcendence, but *in effect* he makes immanence the religious person's major concern and experience, thus emphasizing the role of immanence for Hasidism without deprecating transcendence. He does this by identifying transcendence as uniform and, as such, beyond human comprehension and cognition. Immanence, expressed through the Torah's multivalued halakhic structure, is amenable to reason and understanding, and thus is the primary realm of religious activity and creativity.

To put it differently, man can *approach* God in His transcendence, but *relates* to Him in His immanence. Thus, while immanence may be subordinate to transcendence, it is religiously more relevant in human life, and Torah, which is identified with immanence, remains of immediate interest to man in his relations to God. See Additional Note *7.

106. Berakhot 17a.

place. However, in this world, there exists the category of illumination of *sovev kol almin*. Even though it is concealed, and cannot be comprehended, it is active here. Because it is *sovev kol almin*, which is uniform and everything is equal before it, then *If thou be righteous, what
givest thou Him?* (Job 35:7).[107] Hence, repentance is possible, for even if
you are now utterly wicked, at the very lowest level, you can transform yourself to become completely righteous, from the vantage of
the illumination of *sovev kol almin*.

Concerning repentance, when we pray, "Cause us to return to Thee
(*le-fanekha*) in perfect repentance,"[108] ["to Thee"] refers "to Thy interi-
or,"[109] which is even higher than the category of *sovev kol almin*. God is
called *sovev* ("surrounds") and *makkif* ("encompasses") only in relation
to the worlds, but His self and essence are beyond (*sovev kol almin*).[110]
By means of repentance, we draw upon ourselves a new light, through
the revelation of His essence, correcting all faults and removing all
defects, etc. But how can we effect an arousal in such very lofty
realms, in His essence, so as to draw down a new light from Him?
[The answer is] that this is what we pray for, "Cause us to return,"
etc. "Cause us to return to Thee"; pour down upon us a spirit from the
exalted heights, and cause great mercy to flow upon us from the
source of mercy . . . so that we will be able to repent.

The repentance must remove all defects, whether the defect is due
to a failure to perform mitzvot, thereby preventing and diminishing
the revelation of the light of *sovev kol almin* that is elicited by the
mitzvot, or whether it is created by [a failure to study] Torah, which
is the source of *memallei kol almin*.[111] Hence, "Cause us to return to
Thee in perfect repentance."

---

107. This means that from the standpoint of divine transcendence, all distinctions
vanish, for everything is uniform. Since from this persective there is no difference
between right and wrong, vice and virtue, the mechanism of repentance lies with
transcendence, for in its uniformity all past sins are obliterated and the sinner may
be transformed into a righteous person.
108. From the weekday Amidah.
109. *Le-fanekha*, "before Thee" or "to Thee," is a contraction of "to Thy *panim* (face),"
which can be read as *penim* ("interior, inwardness"). Hence, the conclusion that the
petition for repentance is directed to God's "interior," or absolute essence.
110. For R. Shneur Zalman, transcendence is itself an aspect of divine relatedness as
the counterpart to immanence; beyond that is the sphere of divine essence or
absoluteness, in which relation as such does not exist.
111. Repentance is effected in the realm of *sovev kol almin*, the metaphysical uniformity of which permits the passing of one state (guilt) into another (innocence).
However, the source and potency of repentance issue from the absoluteness of God's

13. IMMANENCE AND TRANSCENDENCE
Source: R. Menahem Mendel of Lubavitch, Derekh Mitzvotekha, Mitzvat Tzitzit, pp. 14b, 15a

The Creation of the world, and its coming into existence from nothing . . . by the power of the Creator who renews the world *ex nihilo*, takes place through two currents of life-force flowing from Him to the world. First is the life-force emanated into the interiority of existing things. By this I mean to say that [the things] apprehend [this life-force] with their vessels which are qualified to receive it,[112] such as reason, which is grasped in man's brain, or the power of motion, which is grasped in his organs of locomotion. This holds in the same way for all the higher beings, each according to its rank.

The [divine] light and life-force enclothed internally in the recipients are not sufficient to call [the recipients] into existence from nothingness, because the creation and renewal of substance *ex nihilo* cannot take place except by means of an unlimited power. But this life-force is enclothed in a receiving vessel which is limited, [and] how can [a finite vessel] contain this [infinite] force? Hence, the genesis and continued existence of all beings must primarily come about by means of the second emanation from Him. This [emanation] is not enclothed in the interior of all beings, i.e., [it is not accessible] to their wisdom and understanding and knowledge and other spiritual powers; these do not apprehend His essence and His existence as the brain apprehends reason, because [this flow] of power and life-force is unlimited. It is infinite (Ein-Sof), for it is light and life-force that illumine from the glow of His glory, and it is not within the capacity of finite beings to grasp and apprehend it. [This infinite emanation] animates them and brings them out of absolute nothingness into the existence they possess, and sustains them every hour and every moment. Although it is not apprehended by them internally, it exists in them and preserves them in life.

This [second type of emanation] is called *makkif* ("encompassing, surrounding") in the books of the Kabbalah. It is not enclothed in the

---

essence, which transcends His transcendence. Thus, forgiveness is assured not only for sins committed against the divine immanence (Torah), but also for transgressions against God's transcendence (mitzvot).

112. The degree and quality of immanence is contingent upon the absorptive capacity and nature of the substance or organ. Transcendence, however, is uniform with respect to all created things.

vessels of the recipients, each one according to his station, but nevertheless keeps [all things] alive. This [transcendence] is the main [flow]. The life-force that is enclothed inwardly is called the inner light. In the language of the Zohar and the *Raya Mehemna*, [these two emanations are] called *sovev* ("surrounding," equivalent to *makkif*; i.e., transcendence) and *memallei* ("filling, inhering"; i.e., immanence). . . .

The unlimited illumination from the glow of His glory preserves all the worlds in life *ex nihilo*, even though they do not apprehend it inwardly. This is infinitely and illimitably greater than the life-force enclothed internally, for the inner light, which is called *memallei*, contracts in accordance with the nature of the receiving vessel. . . . Thus, the life-force in this world, in its totality, is very constricted. [It is limited] to the four classes of mineral, vegetable, animal, and man. In the lower Garden of Eden, which is the spiritual [essence] of the world of Asiyah,[113] the life-force is in a state of greater revelation; for us, whose service [of God takes place] in this lowly world, the lower Garden of Eden [represents] the reward for our service, for there the revelation of the Shekhinah is greater than in this lowly world. . . .

There is no limit to the multitude of ascents that are possible in the form of enhanced perceptions of His blessed Godliness. All this [pertains to] the illumination of Godliness, which is enclothed inwardly, and which progressively constricts itself relative to the degree of the descent of the worlds. Accordingly, the ascents are from below to above.[114] In the language of the Kabbalah, this revelation is called *kav* ("line") and *ḥut* ("thread"), [and is] drawn from the Ein-Sof through Adam Kadmon and Atzilut, etc.[115] But the life-force, which is not enclothed within the beings but encompasses them, is [itself] uniform, and considers everything alike, from the beginning level to the last. It is as concealed from the choicest of beings as from the least of

---

113. The lowest of the four worlds that mediate between the Ein-Sof and the phenomenal world.

114. Spiritual growth is a function of immanence. Unlike transcendence, which is uniform, immanence is differentiated and suffers constriction and diminution until it reaches us. Hence, man's spiritual ascents take place in precisely the reverse order, gaining in perception as they rise toward God.

115. Adam Kadmon, or "Primordial Man," was the first configuration of divine light to flow into the primeval space created by the initial act of *tzimtzum*, God's withdrawal into Himself. A ray of the Ein-Sof, called the line or thread, penetrates through the first zone, Adam Kadmon, and then through the four worlds, beginning with Atzilut and ending with Asiyah. This emanation suffers diminution and constriction as it descends through the worlds, and is identified with *memallei*, or immanence.

them, for it is an aspect of Ein-Sof, before whom all that is, is as nothing. [The life-force] animates them in its capacity of *makkif*, as was explained above, and as *makkif* it can illuminate [even the very lowest level of creation, such as] the inanimate of the world of Asiyah.[116]....

That is why the soul descends into the body: in order to observe the Torah and the mitzvot, thereby evoking the revelation of His Godliness in both categories mentioned above, *sovev* and *memallei*. Although *sovev* encompasses [the creation] and is concealed, i.e., transcendent, it can be evoked by [observing] the commandments. But Torah is derived from Hokhmah[117] and is an aspect of the inner light, as mentioned above.[118] [However,] the commandments are [an expression of] the *Ratzon ha-Elyon* ("Supernal Will"),[119] in the category of *sovev*. . . .

The revelation that comes through the inner light, by means of Torah, is the mystery of the Garden of Eden.[120] But the revelation of the *Or Makkif* ("Encompassing Light") [will take place] only at the end of days, when the dead are resurrected, for [only] then will our eyes be able to behold the revelation of His unlimited and encompassing, i.e., transcendent, Godliness. . . .

The explanation of this is as follows: As we know, studying Torah is the main occupation in the Garden of Eden. . . . Of course, this does

---

116. Man can only perceive God's presence in the world as immanent; this is the "revealed" form, for the degrees of perception vary. Yet in the "concealed" form, i.e., because as undifferentiated emanation it is not directly accessible to human cognition, divine transcendence is uniformly present throughout the creation. In other words, the Ein-Sof *creates* the cosmos by means of transcendence, and *relates* to it by means of immanence.

117. Hokhmah, the highest of the ten sefirot in R. Shneur Zalman's system, is identified as the locus of Torah.

118. Thus Torah is an aspect of immanence, an identification reinforced by its halakhic nature—its multiplicity of value-judgments and distinctions—corresponding to the differentiated manner in which immanence is revealed in the world.

119. *Ratzon ha-Elyon* is identical with Keter, which is one level higher than Hokhmah. In R. Shneur Zalman's system (of which R. Menahem Mendel is a leading and original expositor), Hokhmah is the first of the ten sefirot, and Keter is assigned to the intermediate region between the absolute, self-contained Ein-Sof and the realm of the sefirot, God's self-revelation. By associating mitzvot with Keter, and Torah study with Hokhmah, R. Menahem Mendel relates the observance of the commandments to transcendence, and hence a higher spiritual level than Torah, which expresses divine immanence.

120. R. Menahem Mendel now proceeds to elaborate the eschatological consequences of the correspondence of Torah-immanence and mitzvot-transcendence.

not refer to studying Torah in its literal, i.e., exoteric, sense, for [in the Garden of Eden] there is no corporeality [and as a result the Halakhah, dealing as it does with the physical world, is irrelevant].[121] . . . But the world-to-come, which is the time of the resurrection of the dead, is the reward for observing the commandments. Thus, it is the revelation of the source of [all spiritual] pleasures, for these are His Will, in which is contained the essence of pleasure, infinitely higher than the radiance of pleasure in the wisdom of Torah.

14. TZIMTZUM: AN INFUSION OF LIGHT
Source: R. Shneur Zalman of Liady, Tanya, Sha'ar ha-Yiḥud veha-Emunah, chap. 7

Introduction

The doctrine of tzimtzum can be taken either literally or figuratively. Later kabbalists were divided on the question. R. Immanuel Hai Ricchi (1688–1743) was the leading advocate of the literalist interpretation, while R. Joseph Ergas (1685–1730), his contemporary, expounded the symbolist position. It is the latter view to which R. Shneur Zalman is deeply committed. His critical barb in this passage is generally taken to be directed at the Gaon of Vilna, the eminent leader of the mitnaggedic world.[122] Yet the Gaon's position on this question is unclear.

Teitelbaum has correctly demonstrated that the Gaon was not simply a literalist,[123] and others maintain that he was a symbolist (e.g., R. Abraham Simhah of Amstislaw, in a letter appended to Luzzatto's Derekh Tevunot [Jerusalem, 1880], ascribes R. Hayyim of Volozhin's advocacy of the figurative interpretation to the Gaon's teaching). In the Likkutei ha-Gra Zal appended to the Gaon's commentary on the Sifra di-Tzeniuta (Vilna, 1882), the term tzimtzum is applied not to the Ein-Sof itself but to the divine will and providence, even though they are removed and emanated from the Ein-Sof. This is a symbolist position. But whether or not the Gaon is indeed the literalist that R. Shneur Zalman makes him out to be (without here mentioning him by name), the end product of liter-

---

121. The mystical or kabbalistic interpretation of the Torah is its "inner meaning."
122. M. Teitelbaum, Ha-Rav mi-Ladi u-Mifleget ḤaBaD, vol. 1, p. 87; M. Wilensky, Ḥasidim u-Mitnaggedim, vol. 1, pp. 196 ff.
123. Teitelbaum, Ha-Rav mi-Ladi, pp. 87 ff.

alism on the *tzimtzum* issue is transcendentalism. As opposed to the immanentist view of Hasidism, this theory holds that God relates to the world not by infusing it but by governing it "from above," by means of a detached providence.

R. Shneur Zalman's symbolist interpretation of *tzimtzum*, however, leads to immanentism. For him, the *tzimtzum* reflects man's perception and not reality: no "contraction" *actually* occurred in the divine essence; rather, it was *made to appear* so, in order that the cosmos might exist, if only as an illusion. But if no *tzimtzum* occurred literally and actually, then nothing exists but God; and not only have we established immanence but also the radical twist given to it by R. Shneur Zalman, namely, acosmism.

*

From what has been said heretofore,[124] one may understand the error of some who consider themselves wise, may God forgive them, but erred and went astray in their study of the writings of the Ari [R. Isaac Luria]. They interpreted literally the [Ari's] doctrine of *tzimtzum*[125] as mentioned therein—that the Holy One withdrew Himself and His essence, heaven forbid, from this world, and only guides all the created beings in the heavens above and on the earth below with individual providence from above.

Now, aside from the fact that it is altogether impossible to interpret the matter of *tzimtzum* literally, for that would attribute corporeal events to the Holy One, Who is removed from them by many myriads of separations *ad infinitum*, they also do not speak wisely. Surely they believe, as befits "believers the sons of believers,"[126] that the Holy

---

124. Referring to the first part of his seventh chapter, most of which is included in selection 3 above.

125. As already explained (see end of section 3 and middle of section 4; also see section 15), the Kabbalah posits an essence of God, the Ein-Sof, that is totally without distinction or differentiation in its absolute perfection, unknowable and indescribable, and devoid of all attributes—even of volition. The turning outwards of the Ein-Sof takes place by means of the emanation of the ten sefirot, which are its self-expression. The problem, however, is that the Ein-Sof, by virtue of its very absoluteness, leaves no "space" for that-which-is-not-Ein-Sof; the existence of any object that is other than Ein-Sof constitutes an infringement of His infinity. Hence, Luria asserts that preceding the emanation of the sefirot an act of *tzimtzum* ("constriction" or self-limitation) took place, whereby the Ein-Sof entered into Himself, leaving "room" for the creative process to take place by the emanation of the sefirot into the *ḥalal* ("primordial space") which thus emerged.

126. Shabbat 97a, referring to the Jewish people, who are "knights of faith" by inheritance.

One knows all the created beings in this lowly world and exercises providence over them, and that His knowledge of them adds neither plurality nor novelty to Him, for He knows everything by knowing Himself.[127] His essence, being, and knowledge are, as it were, all one.[128]

That is why it says in *Tikkunim*, tikkun 57: "There is no place empty of Him, neither in the upper worlds nor in the lower worlds." Similarly it is written in *Raya Mehemna* on the portion of Pinhas: "He grasps all and none can grasp Him. . . . He surrounds all the worlds . . . . and no one escapes His domain; He fills all the worlds . . . He binds and unites a kind to its kind, upper with lower, and there is no connection among the four elements but through the Holy One, as He is within them."[129]

"None can grasp Him" means that not even one of the supernal intelligences[130] can grasp with his intellect the essence and being of the Holy One. As it says in the introduction to the *Tikkunei ha-Zohar*: "You are the Hidden One of all the hidden, and no thought whatsoever can grasp You." So it is in the lower worlds, where, although "He fills all the worlds," He is unlike the soul of man, which is enclosed within the body, affected and influenced by bodily changes, such as pain from blows or cold or the heat of fire, and so forth. The Holy One, however, is not affected by the changes in this world from summer to winter and from day to night, as it is written: *Even darkness is not dark for You, and night shines as day* (Ps. 139:12), for He is not the least bit encompassed within the worlds even though He fills them.

This is also the meaning of "He surrounds all worlds." For example, when man reflects upon an intellectual subject or thinks about a physical matter, his mind encompasses the subject whose image is formed in his mind, but does not embrace it in actual fact. The Holy One, however, of Whom it is written, *For My thoughts are not your thoughts* (Isa. 55:8), actually embraces each and every creature with

---

127. The source for this idea, often mentioned by R. Shneur Zalman, is Maimonides (Hilkhot Yesodei ha-Torah 2:10, *Guide* 1:68). Maimonides maintains that God and His knowledge are one and the same, based on the Aristotelian notion that with God, the cognizing subject, the cognized object, and the act of cognition are all one. God knows by knowing Himself, for everything else in the world is contingent upon Him.
128. Therefore it would be absurd to assert, as the literalists do, that God is absent from a place where His knowledge and providence function.
129. Zohar III, 225a. In ancient physics, fire, air, water, and dust are the four basic elements of which all created things are composed.
130. The angels, who according to Maimonides are incorporeal and are called intelligences because they differ from one another only in the extent and degree of their comprehension (*Guide* 1:49).

His thought and His knowledge of all created beings. For His knowledge is indeed its life-force and that which brings it into existence from nothingness into a being of actual reality.[131]

"He fills all worlds" refers to the life-force which clothes itself within the created being. It is powerfully contracted within [the created being], varying according to the being's intrinsic nature, which is finite and of limited quantity and quality, i.e., significance and importance. . . . The vitality which is instilled in them [in this manner] is greatly and mightily contracted, for it must undergo many powerful contractions until, from its power and light, created beings are brought into existence, as they are, finite and limited. The source of this life-force is "the breath of the Holy One's mouth," which clothes itself in the Ten Utterances of the Torah.[132] The breath of His mouth could have expanded endlessly and without limit, creating worlds infinite in quantity and quality, and giving them life forever, and thus this world would not have been created at all. . . . But the Holy One contracted the light and the vitality in order that the breath of His mouth could infuse and be invested in the combinations of the letters of the Ten Utterances and their complicated combinations, by substitutions and transpositions of the letters themselves and their numerical values and equivalents. For each substitution and transposition indicates the descent of light and vitality degree by degree, in order for it to be able to create and give life to creatures whose quality and significance are lower than the quality and significance of the creatures created from the letters and words of the Ten Utterances themselves, in which God in His glory and essence is clothed; for the Ten Utterances are His attributes. And the numerical value indicates the progressive diminution of the light and life-force until only its final level remains, which is the sum and number of the kinds of powers and grades contained in the light and life-force invested in a particular combination of a particular world.

(It is only after all these contractions and others like them, as God's wisdom has ordained, that the light and vitality could be invested even in the lower created things, such as inanimate stones and dust. . . . Through numerous and powerful contractions, degree by degree, there descended from it a life-force so thoroughly condensed that it

131. Transcendence, in other words, is the act of divine cognition, whereby God's knowledge of creation sustains it without being affected by it.
132. See selection 9, above, for a more elaborate explanation of R. Shneur Zalman's use of letter-mysticism to expound his doctrine of immanentism. (See too above, nn. 15 and 50.)

clothes itself in a stone. This is the soul of the inanimate being, which gives it life and brings it into existence *ex nihilo* at every instant. . . . This is the aspect of "He fills all worlds" as distinguished from the aspect of "He surrounds all worlds.")[133]

15. TZIMTZUM: AN ACT OF LOVE
Source: R. Dov Ber, the Maggid of Mezeritch, Maggid Devarav le-Yaakov, no. 1

"Why did God reveal the account of Creation to Israel? Because they said 'We will do' before 'and we will understand' (Exod. 24:7)."[134]

This may be understood in the light of what the Rabbis said: that God's first thought in Creation was to create Israel.[135] His earliest will was to create the world so that Israel would be righteous in every generation.

Therefore, God contracted (*tzimtzem*) His pure light, as it were, just as a father diminishes (*metzamtzem*) his intelligence and prattles for the sake of his young son. All sorts of other childish qualities are generated in the father, who loves these childish qualities, so that the son may enjoy them, and this is a source of joy to him.[136]

For the Holy One, past and future are the same, and thus the Holy One derived pleasure from the deeds of the righteous even before Creation, and so contracted (*tzimtzem*) Himself.[137]

God's self-contraction (*tzimtzum*) is called Hokhmah, for Wisdom is

---

133. The last paragraph is enclosed in parentheses in the text. "He surrounds all worlds" (*sovev kol almin*) denotes transcendence, while "He fills all worlds" (*memallei kol almin*) affirms immanence. R. Shneur Zalman's approach, as outlined here, establishes *tzimtzum* as a form of immanence, in contrast to those who hold that it brought about divine withdrawal and transcendence. Thus his symbolist approach to *tzimtzum* leads to the doctrine of immanentism (see the introduction to this selection).

134. Song of Songs Rabbah 1:2, s.v. *heviani ha-melekh. Nishma*, which is usually translated as "we shall obey," is interpreted as "we shall understand." Hence, Israel responded at Sinai, "We shall do as You wish even before we understand it."

135. Genesis Rabbah 1:4.

136. Just as the father subjects his intellect to *tzimtzum*, or contraction, in order to communicate pleasurably with his young child, so God undergoes *tzimtzum* in order to reveal Himself, especially to the righteous, from whom He derives and to whom He gives pleasure. The purpose of the contraction is emanation, revelation.

137. This explains how the Ein-Sof can undergo *tzimtzum* out of love for the righteous even though the righteous (and the world) have not yet been created. Since God is above time, He can view the future as present or past.

found as Ayin ("Nothingness"),[138] as it is written, *But hokhmah is found from ayin* (Job 28:12).[139]

The self-contraction was for Israel's sake, and love caused the self-contraction to take place. Thus it is written, *And these are the generations of Isaac, Abraham's son: Abraham begot Isaac* (Gen. 25:19).[140]

16. TZIMTZUM: THE DESCENT OF GOD AND THE ASCENT OF MAN
Source: R. Dov Ber, the Maggid of Mezeritch, Or ha-Emet, p. 4 11c

Who covereth the heaven with clouds, Who prepareth rain for the earth (Ps. 147:8).

There are two kinds of giving. One is when a rich man gives a gift to his friend [who is also rich], and the other when he gives to a poor

---

138. Hokhmah is here identified as the zone of nothingness. It is both the matrix of all subsequent emanations and the realm in which everything is annihilated and thus co-equal. By positing the divine self-contraction as equivalent to nothingness, the Maggid seems to be saying that it was an act of concealment. This is the opposite of the point made two paragraphs earlier, that the self-contraction was an act of revelation. In this, the Maggid follows R. Moses Cordovero's principle that "concealment is the cause of revelation, and revelation, the cause of concealment" (*Pardes Rimmonim,* shaar 1), i.e., the Ein-Sof has to conceal its light in order to accommodate it to the vessels so as to be revealed to the world. Thus *tzimtzum* has different significance for God (concealment) and for man (revelation). This dialectical reconciliation of withdrawal and emanation is in the general spirit of hasidic harmonization, which tried to play down the note of cosmic dissonance in Luria's catastrophe theory.
139. The standard translation is, "But wisdom, where shall it be found?" In the kabbalistic exegesis of this verse, Hokhmah derives from Ayin, which is identified with Keter. According to the Maggid, however, Ayin is identified with Hokhmah. See below, chap. 8, selection 14.
140. The point is typically obscure but significant. In a later passage in the same work (in *Maggid Devarav le-Yaakov,* ed. Shatz-Uffenheimer, p. 42 [end, no. 25], and cf. p. 112 [no. 67]), the Maggid uses the traditional kabbalistic symbolism for the three patriarchs. Abraham represents Hesed ("Love"); Isaac, Din ("Judgment," or as it is usually called, Gevurah, "Strength"); and Jacob, Rahamim ("Mercy"). (The last of these three is a variation for the third sefirah, usually identified as Beauty.) The Maggid's homiletic innovation is the translation of *et,* in *Avraham holid et Yitzhak* ("Abraham begot Isaac"), as "with," instead of leaving it untranslated as usual. Hence: "Abraham begot [Jacob] with Isaac." Transposing to the realm of the sefirot, Hesed and Din flow into, and are dialectically resolved in, Rahamim. The relevance to the present passage is clear. From God's point of view, the act of self-contraction is one of concealment, hence Din. From man's point of view, the *tzimtzum* is an act of revelation, hence Hesed. The two opposites are reconciled in Rahamim, an act of compassion. The harmonistic moment of Hasidism is thus revealed in the Maggid's treatment of the concept of *tzimtzum.*

man. The difference between them is that the rich recipient is not embarrassed to receive the gift, but the poor man is embarrassed. In order to spare the poor man embarrassment, the rich man acts as if he has nothing left but the gift he is giving him; and then there is no embarrassment.[141]

That is the meaning of *Who covereth the heaven with clouds*. For a parable is taught in *Raya Mehemna*: a tailor took a whole piece of cloth and cut it into strips. Someone who is not a tailor thinks that he has spoiled it. But someone who understands tailoring knows that the cloth is meant for a glove or some other garment, and in order for the garment to be sewn up, the services of an artisan are necessary.

Similarly, before the Creation, God was alone. He created the worlds so that they could acknowledge His greatness. *And the rich is not acknowledged before the poor* (Job 34:19);[142] before there was poverty, His lordship went unacknowledged. Therefore a breaking[143] was necessary so that the light could be acknowledged.

Now, everything was created through Hokhmah. *The Lord by ḥokhmah founded the earth* (Prov. 3:19). Hence, if I wish to raise the sparks,[144] *The fear of the Lord is the beginning of ḥokhmah* (Ps. 111:10).[145] When a man is seized with an alien thought,[146] he must bring himself to the attribute of fear, which is shame or embarrassment. He must be embarrassed before the Holy One, Who "dwells with the contrite"[147]— here with me, and I entertain such foolish thoughts! And so, upon attaining the attribute of fear, one should consider oneself as nothing,

---

141. The rich man acts as if he were poor, so there is no shame for the poor man in receiving the gift. Since they are "equals," the gift is a gift and not charity, and is in the same category as a gift given by one rich man to another.

142. In the biblical text, *lifnei* has the meaning of excess ("nor regardeth the rich man more than the poor") or physical presence ("nor regardeth the rich man in the presence of the poor"). The Maggid interprets the word in the sense of temporal priority: the rich man is not regarded or acknowledged *before* the poor.

143. The Breaking of the Vessels, the mystical notion of the catastrophe which culminated in the Creation.

144. After the shattering of the sefirot, sparks of the Ein-Sof were scattered, and it is they which sustain Creation. Man must redeem the sparks by elevating them back to their Source by means of mitzvot or by contemplation.

145. As the source of all creative existence, Hokhmah is the sphere to which everything must be raised.

146. Distractions, usually sexual, from his religious service or contemplation. See below, chap. 6.

147. Based on Isa. 57:15.

for Ayin comes from Hokhmah,[148] and in Hokhmah all was made lucid.[149]

Now we are able to understand the verse *Who covereth the heaven with clouds*. *Heaven* is the symbol of the intellect, and *clouds* symbolize corporeal objects;[150] thus, God "covereth the intellect with corporeal objects." *Who prepareth rain for the earth*: rain saturates the earth so that grain may grow. The Shekhinah, as it were, comes down to the lowest levels, so that what is on earth may rise up. . . . Those on the lowest levels are embarrassed to ascend by themselves; hence the Shekhinah comes to the lowest levels, like rain to the earth, to make the grain grow. This now is the meaning of *Who prepareth rain for the earth*, for *matar* ("rain") is symbolic of the Shekhinah, which is also called Matronita.

Afterword

This selection develops the same theme as the preceding one, but more as *derashah* than biblical commentary. Man's intellect or spiritual dimension is arrested by his corporeality, rendering him in a state of fear-shame. But the Shekhinah descends and enables him to rise—presumably back to Hokhmah.

The reader is expected to make the connection between the beginning and end of the discourse. When the poor man receives a gift from the rich man and is thereby made to recognize his own poverty, he is filled with shame and embarrassment. Similarly, man, incarcerated in corporeality, is embarrassed before God, Who dwells with him even though his mind is filled with foolishness. However, God desires man to raise the sparks and rise from fear-shame to a higher level. Therefore, the Shekhinah comes down to man—the equivalent of the rich man pretending to be poor, as if this were all he had to give. God divests Himself of His transcendent magnificence in order to communicate with man, who other-

---

148. The identification of Hokhmah and Ayin in the Maggid's thought is discussed in selection 15.

149. The chain of ideas proceeds as follows: in order to elevate the sparks, as when one is overcome with alien thoughts, one must restore the sparks to Hokhmah. Since "the beginning of Hokhmah is fear," and fear is the same as shame or embarrassment, the process of elevation begins with fear-embarrassment and concludes with Hokhmah-Ayin.

150. *Av* ("cloud") also means "thick, dense," and hence stands for physicality.

wise would be reluctant or unable to communicate with Him because of his awareness of his finitude and his moral limitations.

Thus far for the raising of the sparks, which the Maggid interprets as the return to Ayin-Hokhmah. How does the parable of the tailor fit into this scheme? The cutting of the whole cloth into strips is an obvious reference to the Lurianic Breaking of the Vessels. But the point the Maggid is making is that this is a catastrophe only from the point of view of those who do not understand what the tailor-God intends. In fact, there is nothing accidental or destructive about the act. The Breaking is a necessary and deliberate prelude to, and part of, orderly creation. There is nothing mythical about the process; it is a planned act, not a cosmic accident. It is only when heaven-intellect is "clouded" that man fails to understand this.

Why, then, was it necessary for the vessels, or sefirot, to be broken? The answer is in line with the classical hasidic notion, rooted in both Kabbalah and Midrash, that God's greatness, in order to qualify as greatness, had to be recognized as such, and for this it was necessary that He not be alone, but that creatures, necessarily inferior to ("poorer than") Him, be brought into being. The "poor" acknowledge the "rich"; the light is appreciated only after the Breaking.

However, God did not want man to remain in this state of spiritual poverty, and so—like the rich man who pretends to be poor in order to spare the recipient's feelings—He divested Himself, as it were, of all His possessions except for His gift of existence. Here is a parable of *tzimtzum*, the self-contraction of the Ein-Sof. Clearly, the Lurianic myth must not be taken literally, for God truly remains "rich." (The Maggid sides with R. Joseph Ergas and other disciples of Luria who insisted upon a metaphorical interpretation of *tzimtzum*, as against R. Immanuel Hai Ricchi, who accepted the doctrine literally.) It is, rather, a kind of ethically caused fiction, an "as-if" self-constriction, such that man *thinks* that God, as Ein-Sof, has withdrawn into Himself. From God's vantage, however, nothing has changed with regard to Himself.

The next step, as the Maggid cryptically implies, is man's rise in response to the Shekhinah's descent, or the self-constriction of the Ein-Sof. Just as recognizing the orderliness of the initial act of the Breaking requires the wisdom and knowledge of an artisan, so does the artisan proceed to "sew it up." The act of *tikkun*, the restoration of the harmony of the divine spheres, is man's response to the divine challenge. And this "sewing," or *tikkun*, is by means of a return to Hokhmah-Ayin, as explained above. It is an act undertaken for the sake of man's elevation and not as an act of compassion for God's shattered wholeness.

ADDITIONAL NOTES

*1   As we stated earlier, the doctrine of immanence is of the most fundamental importance in Hasidism and is one of its most characteristic ideas. I believe that there is not a single major hasidic thinker, other than possibly R. Zevi Hirsch of Zhidachov, who disagrees with this thesis. However, the late Prof. Abraham Joshua Heschel maintained that, in opposition to the Besht, there was one exception: R. Menahem Mendel of Kotzk, the profound, mysterious Polish zaddik of whom a great deal is reported but who never wrote down—or at least never published—any of his thinking.[151] The Kotzker, Heschel avers, was poignantly aware of man's alienation and estrangement from God and from the Truth, and therefore felt the disparity between the divine and the mundane. "He was profoundly opposed to the Baal Shem Tov's conception that the world was infused with the Divine. When asked where God dwelt, the Baal Shem answered, everywhere; the Kotzker, where He is allowed to enter . . ."

Heschel's theory is unacceptable. The very dearth of reliable written material from the master himself, or at least approved by him, makes verification of either thesis impossible. But Heschel is reduced to quoting a single aphorism of the Kotzker to prove his point that the Kotzker rejected the central doctrine of Hasidism as established by the Besht. Certainly the pervasive sadness and pessimism that plagued the Kotzker for most of his life would indicate that he experienced the transcendence rather than the immanence of God. But that does not yet mean that he abandoned the fundamental Beshtian emphasis on immanence and its central role in hasidic thinking. After all, the Kotzker may have been the most extreme example of melancholia, but many other leading Zaddikim suffered agonizing bouts of depression,[152] and yet intellectually they continued to espouse the immanentist views of the Besht and the Maggid and their colleagues. Most important, had the Kotzker truly rejected this cornerstone of hasidic religious ideology, his many opponents would not have remained silent about such a revolutionary turn, and we would not have had to wait for the mid-twentieth century to discover it. The argument *ex silencio* is critical in this case.

Similarly, there is reason to disagree with the late Joseph Weiss, who posits two polar opposites in the basic conception of God amongst hasidic thinkers.[153] The first, "mystic religion," is typified by the Maggid and Habad and, partially, by the Besht; the second, "faith religion," is represented by R. Nahman of Bratslav. The former is acosmic, possibly pantheistic, and tends toward an impersonal conception of God. The latter is voluntaristic, as opposed to the ontological bias of the Maggid and R. Shneur Zalman; it sees the will of God working itself out transcendentally in the encounter

151. Heschel, *A Passion for Truth*, pp. 32–33.
152. For a number of interesting examples, see Elie Wiesel's *Souls on Fire*.
153. Weiss, *Meḥkarim be-Ḥasidut Bratslav*, pp. 87–90.

between God and man, and is therefore highly personalistic. While the typology proposed by Weiss is a felicitous one, and allows us to categorize different thinkers according to this meaningful classification, it also tends toward overstatement. Habad is, of course, highly intellectual and more concerned with the world of emanation than God's Will, but that hardly means that we are justified in imputing to it pantheism (about which see further) or an impersonal conception of God. Even more, the fact that the Bratslaver is highly voluntaristic and cherishes faith more than reason, even more than kabbalistic intellection, hardly makes him an opponent of the immanence taught by his great-grandfather, the Besht. Indeed, we shall include one selection from the writings of the Bratslaver which clearly shows his advocacy of the principle of immanence, and shall comment on it further in our notes to that passage (see selection 11).

*2   The difference between the two is this: where the series of letters begins with the Y of the Tetragrammaton, that which is symbolized by this ineffable Name dominates Adnut or Malkhut, represented by *ADNY*. Hence, the cosmos is not viewed as separate from God, and the independence and hence existence of the world is denied, for only God exists. This is identical to the "Upper Unity" attributed to the verse *Shema Yisrael*. "Hear, O Israel, *YHVH* is our God, *YHVH* is One."

The other combined Name, beginning with the *A* of *ADNY* and establishing its dominance, is the "Lower Unity," implied in the second verse, *Barukh Shem*, "Blessed be His Name Whose glorious kingdom is for ever and ever." Under this aspect, the cosmos is affirmed, for God in His capacity as a "Lord" must have a "kingdom" over which to rule.

The Upper Unity is thus that vision of God and world in which the divine presence overwhelms and hence nullifies the world: only God exists, all else is mere illusion. This is the aspect of the Tetragrammaton. The Lower Unity, represented by the various other divine Names, depicts a relationship between king and subjects, i.e., between God and world, and hence confirms both. It is in this dimension that man's life is lived, his emotions felt, his environment experienced.

In a further refinement, Habad writers maintain that the Upper Unity marks the unity of Atzilut, the first of the four worlds, with the Ein-Sof, whereas the Lower Unity indicates the unity of the three lower worlds with the Ein-Sof. The difference is that in the former case, because Atzilut is essentially negative—being closest to the Ein-Sof it is a unity of that which never recognized itself as possessing an existence independent of the Ein-Sof; whereas in the latter case the unity is that of an existence which *experiences* separateness and perceives the (illusory) world as existent, but which acknowledges *intellectually* that it is null and void in the face of the Ein-Sof.

*3   Note: This [interpretation] is unlike the one published recently in a book by a great and famous contemporary scholar, who explained these terms in an essay he called *Shaar ha-Yihud*.

Believe me, my brother, that no light illuminates his ways, his unhelpful and ineffective speculations, and his analogies. I have already cautioned you above, my brother, to keep far away from this. For all his ways in this [subject] are perilous, and one who treasures his life will keep his distance from them. The Lord God knows and is witness that I do not say these things for my own glory, but only to keep my colleagues away from these ruminations which are contaminated by philosophical speculations. Enough said.[154]

---

154. "Enough said." It is generally assumed that this barb is aimed at R. Dov Ber, son

*4   J. G. Weiss, however, has challenged this conventional wisdom. He asserts that the parable is not a metaphysical statement at all, and that its subject is not the cosmos but the spiritual-experiential life of man (see his "Reshit Tzemiḥatah shel ha-Derekh ha-Ḥasidit," *Zion* 17 [1951]: 97–99). By analyzing the several versions of the Beshtian parable, he concludes that it is meant to teach the Besht's theory of *avodah be-gashmiyut* ("worship through corporeality"; see chap. 12). The point of the allegory is that the lesser individuals consider corporeality and physical pleasures as a distraction from divine service, expressed as sustained *devekut*, but the beloved son, symbol of the spiritually superior person, knows that physicality and distracting thoughts

---

and successor of R. Shneur Zalman, in his *Shaar ha-Yiḥud*. So, Louis Jacobs in *Seeker of Unity*, p. 86. My own inclination is to identify the object of R. Zevi Hirsch's animadversion as R. Shneur Zalman himself, whose *Shaar ha-Yiḥud veha-Emunah*, chap. 7, we excerpted and translated in the previous selection. In a private communication to me (Jan. 20, 1980), Dr. Jacobs supports his view by referring to the letter of R. Isaac Epstein, appended to *Seeker of Unity*, from which it appears that the charge of teaching "philosophy" rather than Hasidism was directed at R. Dov Ber. Second, R. Shneur Zalman's *Shaar ha-Yiḥud veha-Emunah* may still have been referred to as pt. II of *Tanya* (or *Likkutei Amarim*) rather than by its separate name. Third, R. Dov Ber's work is called *Shaar ha-Yiḥud* (without the *veha-Emunah*) and is indeed more "philosophical" than other Hasidic works. A number of other scholars whom I have consulted tend to agree that the intended victim is R. Dov Ber, because R. Zevi Hirsch would not have attacked so eminent a personage as the famous father, R. Shneur Zalman. Nevertheless, I maintain that a case can be made for an attack by R. Zevi Hirsch on R. Shneur Zalman himself. For one thing, the gloss or note which, in most editions of the book, is placed *before* the former's discussion of Upper and Lower Unity—and therefore might be understood as a general broadside against philosophical speculation by hasidic authors—is in one edition (Lublin, 1928) placed several paragraphs later, after a more elaborate exposition of the two forms of unification. This is appropriate because, as is evident, R. Shneur Zalman and R. Zevi Hirsch have different interpretations of the zoharic concepts of Upper Unity and Lower Unity. True, R. Zevi Hirsch mentions only *Shaar ha-Yiḥud*, but it could well be an abbreviation of the full title, *Shaar ha-Yiḥud veha-Emunah*, which name was already used in the first edition in 1797, alongside the other names, *Tanya* II and *Sefer Ḥinnukh Katan*. R. Dov Ber's work was first published in Kapust in 1820 as the second part of *Ner Mitzvah ve-Torah Or*. (R. Zevi Hirsch was born in 1763 and died in 1831. His *Sur me-Ra va-Aseh Tov* was published posthumously in 1833. There is no indication when the manuscript was completed; this awaits internal examination of the text. The one full biography, *Tzevi la-Tzaddik* [Jerusalem, 1931], is essentially hagiographic and offers no guidance on this question.) That our author was displeased with the view of R. Shneur Zalman is evident from another passage in this present work (Tel Aviv, 1969) in which R. Zevi Hirsch writes: "I saw what someone has written in the name of our master, R. Dov Ber [the 'Great' Maggid of Mezeritsch], in answer to our question, that time too was created, and in the beginning there was no time. In truth, I do not believe that this could have been said by this holy man [the Maggid], because. . ." The theory that time was created, and the attribution of this view to the Maggid, was made by R. Shneur Zalman in his edition of the prayerbook, in his comments to the

are not at all an obstacle, but can be used to enhance the service of God by uninter-rupted contemplation.

While Weiss makes a case for his interpretation on the basis of the variants of the parable itself, his evidence is not conclusive. It is more likely that the parable admits of both interpretations, but that here R. Yaakov Yosef, in seeking to resolve the con-flict between the *hekhalot* passage from the Zohar and "the whole earth is full of His glory," etc., is dealing with a metaphysical problem, and the solution is supplied by the illusionism yielded by the parable. The context strongly suggests that R. Yaakov Yosef himself interpreted the story as an allegory of acosmism. Other parts of the dis-course, such as the exegesis of *Tikkunei Zohar* referring to the sinners and God's muta-bility toward them, can be interpreted both ways—the sinner suffers ontological blindness in failing to perceive the exhaustive immanence of God, or the sinner fails to appreciate that his very sins can be transmuted into instruments of divine service. Later on in the same homily, R. Yaakov Yosef specifically refers to the *yetzer ha-ra* (Evil Urge) as convertible to a source of spiritual fecundity by the knowledge that "the whole world is full of His glory."

*5   Note that the concept of immanence which the author is propounding in the name of the Besht parallels, or possibly derives from, the Lurianic notion of "sparks." The concept of sparks is obviously one which leads to immanentism. However, the Lurianic concept of sparks leads to a kind of "normal" immanentism, by which is meant that the divine is within or infuses the real, corporeal universe; whereas the Beshtian-Habad idea of the word itself becoming reality, based on the older letter mysticism, leads to the radical immanentism of acosmism or illusionism, i.e., the cosmos is "unreal" or merely an illusion, because only God exists, nothing else. Even though the author quotes Luria, the differences are significant. The Lurianic sparks lead, as noted above, to immanentism, whereas the Habad idea is acosmic. The crucial difference is that for immanentism the divine infuses matter, which retains independent existence, whereas the acosmic idea is that this immanent divin-ity is the source of the existence of matter; hence, matter in itself and of itself has no existence and therefore is illusory.

It should be added that the Lurianic-Beshtian theory departs from the dominant approach in the history of Jewish thought. The prevailing opinion was that divine providence for individuals (*hashgaḥah peratit*) is limited only to humans; for all else, providence applies only to the species in general (*hashgaḥah kelalit*). Thus, the opin-ion of the Sages of the Talmud as summarized by Maimonides (*Guide* 3:17, 51); and see Nahmanides (commentary to Gen. 18:19) and *Sefer ha-Ḥinnukh* 169. The kabbal-ists were generally of the same opinion; see R. Joseph Ergas' *Shomer Emunim* II, no. 81. (That God does not exercise providence over the individuals of other species does not, however, mean that He does not *know* them and what occurs to them; R. Joseph Albo, *Ikkarim* 4:7.) By asserting that every created item, even in the animal world, possess-es a "soul," as Luria did, and certainly with the Besht's elaboration, attributing its con-tinued existence to its re-creation by virtue of divine immanence, individual provi-

Shema (*Sha'ar ha-Keriat Shema* [Kehot, 1965 ed.], pp. 150–51), and was first published in 1803. Now, in the gloss in question, our author refers to a *previous* comment he made in criticism of the same anonymous "philosophizer." I suggest that he is refer-ring to the passage on time which I have just cited, and therefore the object of his crit-icism in both notes is R. Shneur Zalman.

dence over the differentia of all nonhuman species is presupposed. Whether the converse is true, i.e., whether the many thinkers who deny individual providence for other species necessarily disagree with the Beshtian thesis of constant re-creation, is an open question; R. Menahem Mendel Schneersohn (the late Lubavitcher Rebbe and head of the Habad movement) inclines to the opinion that they would not disagree with the Beshtian idea; see his *Likkutei Sihot*, vol. 8, *Bemidbar* (Kehot, 1974), p. 283.

*6 This passage amply disproves the thesis of Joseph G. Weiss (*Meḥkarim be-Ḥasidut Bratslav*, chap. 4), who distinguishes two polar opposites in the basic conception of God among hasidic thinkers: the religion of mysticism, represented by the Maggid and R. Shneur Zalman, and already in some form by the Besht, which is acosmic and panentheistic if not pantheistic; and the religion of faith of R. Nahman of Bratslav, which is voluntaristic rather than ontological, and which emphasizes not the "vitality" of God in creation but the will of God working itself out transcendentally in the encounters between God and man. The present passage, which is not uncharacteristic of R. Nahman, certainly marks him as a hasidic immanentist. Whatever the differences in emphasis and doctrine between R. Nahman and other hasidic masters, he did not depart from them in asserting immanentism.

*7   This view of R. Shneur Zalman may be contrasted with that of the leading mitnaggedic theoretician, R. Hayyim of Volozhin, for whom immanence and transcendence are defined in exactly the opposite manner: immanence is uniform, hence unknowable and, as it were, expresses the divine view, while transcendence is differentiated and cognizable, and hence the exclusive means for man's approach to God. In effect, R. Shneur Zalman is the immanentist, R. Hayyim the transcendentalist. (See my *Torah Lishmah* [Eng ed.], pp. 81 ff.; my *Faith and Doubt*, chap. 2; and, in greater detail in my article, "The Phase of Dialogue and Reconciliation," in *Tolerance and Movements of Religious Dissent in Eastern Europe*, ed., Bela K. Kiraly [New York: Columbia University Press, 1975], esp. pp. 124–126.) One further point, somewhat elusive, should be brought to the reader's attention. For R. Shneur Zalman, the hasidic thinker, repentance (as we shall see in the paragraphs that follow) is effected in the realm of transcendence, which he identifies with the mitzvot rather than Torah. R. Hayyim holds that it is Torah, and the study of Torah, that is the source and origin of repentance (*Torah Lishmah* [Eng ed.], p. 87).

2

The Soul

INTRODUCTION

The language which Hasidism employs to describe the human soul is taken from the Kabbalah, so we must begin by examining the terminology of the kabbalists. Because the structure of the soul needs to be looked at systematically, this chapter draws heavily on the Tanya, the one work of early Hasidism that proposes an organized account of hasidic theology and anthropology.

Based on the synonyms appearing in the Bible, the Kabbalah distinguishes five levels of the soul in ascending order, *nefesh, ruah, neshamah, hayyah, yehidah*; of these, the first three are frequently discussed in the literature, and referred to by the acronym NaRaN. In selection 5, from R. Zadok ha-Kohen, we see how the three may be related to one another dialectically. Kabbalah also recognizes, in descending order, four spiritual "worlds" that mediate between the Ein-Sof (in His infinite transcendence) and our world: Atzilut ("Emanation"), Beriah ("Creation"), Yetzirah ("Formation"), and Asiyah ("Action"), of which the lowest (according to most kabbalists) corresponds to our own world. This structure, too, serves as the framework for distinctions between different realizations of the soul.

No less important is the further subdivision of the levels in accordance with the principle of the ten sefirot. This idea refers primarily to the kabbalistic doctrine of God. God Himself transcends human understanding, but in expounding upon God's relation to the world,

55

the kabbalists distinguished ten levels of emanation. Inevitably, the attempt to communicate these mysteries involves anthropomorphic language. Thus the first three sefirot, Hokhmah ("Wisdom"), Binah ("Understanding"), and Da'at ("Knowledge"), carry intellectual connotations.[1] The seven lower sefirot correspond to character traits: Hesed ("Mercy"), Gevurah ("Valor" or "Strength"), and so forth.

The reverse movement is to construct not a theology but an anthropology based on the doctrine of the sefirot. Here the kabbalistic account governs the statements we make about the structure of the soul. Allied to this approach is the kabbalistic identification of biblical figures with various sefirot: Abraham, Isaac, and Jacob with Hesed, Gevurah, and Tiferet, respectively; Joseph with Yesod. This kind of analysis treats the patriarchs as metaphysical figures and also applies these categories to the biblical narratives. It plays a significant role in all biblical interpretation inspired by Kabbalah, not least in hasidic texts.

The kabbalistic traditions taken over by Hasidism accord a substantial structure to evil. The *sitra ahara* is literally the "other side," an anti-world of sefirot parallel to the "holy side" (*sitra de-kedushah*). Likewise, the Tanya speaks of two souls within the Jew, the divine soul and the animal soul. And, the Tanya speaks as well, of the neutral zone of *kelipat nogah*, a realm that is not itself holy, but can be redeemed through proper service to God. This brings us to the subjects of elevating the sparks and serving Him through the corporeal discussed in other chapters (see chaps. 9, 11).

A reader confronting this mode of looking at human beings may well raise the following question: What are the implications of employing so highly schematized an account of the psyche, one that tends to reify human nature? Isn't there a danger that the categories can harden into a deterministic grid in which each component is locked in place? R. Zadok ha-Kohen, in a passage excerpted in this chapter (selection 5), speaks about the ascent of the individual through the various levels of soul, and insists upon an invariable path that must be traversed. Yet a more recent thinker like Rav Abraham Isaac Kook (1865–1935), who has strong affinities with R. Zadok, eschews the notion that the spiritual development of the individual cannot deviate from a specific prescribed progression.

---

1. See below, n. 18, on the question of enumeration.

1. THE JEWISH SOUL
Source: R. Shneur Zalman of Liady, Likkutei Amarim, Tanya, chaps. 1–2

R. Hayyim Vital [1542–1620] wrote . . . that every Jew, whether right-eous or wicked, possesses two souls, as it is written, *The souls which I have made* (Isa. 57:16), alluding to two souls.[2]

The first soul originates in the *kelipah* [impure shell] and the *sitra aḥara* [demonic realm], clothed in the blood of man [and] giving life to the body, as it is written: *For the life of the flesh is in the blood* (Lev. 17:11). All the evil characteristics stem from it, such as anger and pride, the lust for pleasure, frivolity, scoffing, boasting, and idle talk, sloth, and melancholy.[3]

From this soul stem also the good characteristics that are to be found in the innate nature of all Jews, such as mercy and benevolence. For in the case of Israel, the soul of the *kelipah* is derived from *kelipat nogah*, ("the shell of Venus") which also contains good, beacuse it originates in the mystical tree of knowledge of good and evil (Gen. 2:9).[4] . . .

The second Jewish soul is truly a part of God above,[5] as it is writ-ten: *And He breathed into his nostrils the breath of life* (Gen. 2:7),[6] and *Thou didst breathe the soul into me.*[7] And it is written in the Zohar: "He who exhales, exhales from within himself,"[8] i.e., from his core and his inwardness, for it is something of his internal and innermost vitality that man emits when exhaling forcefully.

---

2. This pertains only to the soul of a Jew. R. Shneur Zalman conceives of the soul of the non-Jew quite differently, but that part of his discussion has been omitted. For an analytical description of his ideas on the gentile soul, see M. Hallamish, "The Attitude of the Kabbalists to Non-Jews," in Hallamish and Kasher, *Filosophia Yisraelit*, pp. 49-71

3. R. Shneur Zalman subscribes to the idea that human characteristics derive from the four basic elements: fire, water, wind, and earth. The exact relationships have been deleted in our translation. The first soul, which he also refers to as the "vital" or "ani-mal" soul, has its locus in the blood; its function is to keep the body alive and nourish the "natural" character, both good and evil, mentioned in the text.

4. See below, selection 5.

5. The expression is based on Job 31:2. Further on, the second, superior soul is called the divine soul.

6. See Nahmanides' Commentary, ad loc.

7. Weekday Shaharit service; Berakhot 60b.

8. This statement, usually ascribed to the Zohar or to Nahmanides, is not found in the Zohar. The idea is that just as exhaled breath comes from the depths of one's self, so the divine soul is derived from the very essence of God.

By way of example, that is how the souls of Israel were conceived in His thought before He created them.[9] It is written, *My firstborn son, Israel* (Exod. 4:22), and *Ye are children unto the Lord your God* (Deut. 14:1); i.e., just as a child is derived from his father's brain, so the soul of every Jew is, as it were, derived from God's thought and wisdom.[10]

There are myriads of different gradations of souls *ad infinitum*; hence the superiority of the souls of the patriarchs and of our teacher Moses to the souls of our own generation, who live in the period preceding the coming of the Messiah, and who are, in reality, like the heels of the feet compared with the brain and head. Similarly, in every generation there are Israel's leaders, whose souls are like the head and brain in comparison with those of the masses and the ignorant. Likewise, all souls differ from one another, for every soul consists of *nefesh, ruah,* and *neshamah*.[11] Nevertheless, the root of every *nefesh*, from the highest rank of all to the lowest that is embodied within the illiterate and the most worthless, derives, so to speak, from the Supreme Mind, namely, the Supernal Wisdom.

This is analogous to the derivation of the son from his father's brain, to the extent that even his toenails issue from the very same drop of semen, by being in the mother's womb for nine months, descending degree by degree, changing continually, until even the nails are formed from it. Yet [after this process] it is still bound and united in a wonderful and essential unity with its original essence and being—the drop from the father's brain. And even now, in the son, the nails receive their nourishment and life from the brain, which is in the head. As is stated in the Talmud: "From the white of the

---

9. In Genesis Rabbah 1:4 and elsewhere. The plain meaning of the text is the midrashic idea that God was thinking about the souls of Israel even before He created the world. Here, however, the statement is given a typical kabbalistic twist: the origin of all Jewish souls is in the divine "thought," which is the equivalent of the first of the ten sefirot, Hokhmah. Similarly, since "brain" is the equivalent of Hokhmah, the exegesis of the two verses in the next sentence supports the idea that the souls of Israel derive from the sphere of divine wisdom.

10. The biology here originated in the writings of the Greek physicians and was adopted by the kabbalists early on: the child comes from the semen, which, in turn, derives from the father's brain. (We have deleted a brief reference to Maimonides' view on the nature of divine wisdom. Its import is to demonstrate that God's wisdom is identical with Himself, not superadded to His essence, and hence the divine soul is actually a part of God above.)

11. The tripartite division of the (divine) soul; see Zohar I, 206a; II, 141b. (The fourth and fifth souls are *hayyah* and *yehidah;* they are less frequently discussed because of their superior degree of transcendence.)

father's drop of semen are formed the veins, the bones, and the nails."[12]

Similarly, as it were, this holds true for the root of every *nefesh, ruah,* and *neshamah* in the totality of Israel on high. In descending degree by degree, through the descent of the worlds of Atzilut, Beriah, Yetzirah, and Asiyah from His blessed Hokhmah—as it is written: *Thou has made them all with wisdom* (Ps. 104:24)—the *nefesh, ruah,* and *neshamah* of the ignorant and unworthy come into being. They remain, nevertheless, bound and united in a wonderful and mighty unity with their original essence and entity, namely, the extension of Supernal Wisdom. For the nurturance and life of the *nefesh, ruah,* and *neshamah* of the ignorant are drawn from the *nefesh, ruah,* and *neshamah* of the saints and sages, the heads of Israel in their generations.[13]

This explains the comment of our Rabbis on the verse *and to cleave unto Him* (Deut. 30:20): "He who cleaves unto a [Torah] scholar is deemed by Scripture as if he has become attached to the very Shekhinah."[14] Through attachment to scholars, the *nefesh, ruah,* and *neshamah* of the ignorant are bound up and united with their original essences and their roots in the Supernal Wisdom, He and His wisdom being one, and "He is the knowledge."[15]

2. THE TEN SEFIROT OF THE JEWISH SOUL
Source: R. Shneur Zalman of Liady, Tanya, Likkutei Amarim, chap. 3

Each level of these three, *nefesh, ruah,* and *neshamah,* comprises ten faculties, corresponding to the supernal ten sefirot from which they were descended.[16] These ten sefirot are divided into two groups: the three

---

12. Niddah 31a.
13. This rather opaque passage begins by begging the question: If all souls derive from Hokhmah, and are thus a part of God above, how do we account for the differences among them? R. Shneur Zalman answers that there is an organic unity within the plurality. The hierarchy of souls form an organic whole by virtue of their common origin in God. At the end of the paragraph, a second dimension is added: In addition to the vertical connection of all Jewish souls in all eras with divine wisdom, they are horizontally bound up with each other. In every generation, there is a bond between hoi polloi ("heels") and the saints and sages ("brain"). We have here an allusion to the relationship between the zaddik and his people, a theme developed in chap. 32 of *Likkutei Amarim* (see below, chap. 13, selection 8, where this important discussion is translated). Our exegesis of this excerpt follows M. Hallamish in "Alim Rishonim," esp. pp. 69–76.
14. Ketubbot 111b. What for the Talmud is a metaphor is for R. Shneur Zalman a literal statement, expressing a kabbalistic truth.
15. The two dimensions mentioned in n. 13 are here blended.

mothers and the seven doubles.[17] The mothers are Hokhmah, Binah, and Da'at.[18] The seven . . . are Hesed, Gevurah, Tiferet, etc.

Similarly, in the human soul the ten aspects are divided into two groups: *sekhel* ("intellect") and *middot* ("affective attributes"). The intellect comprises Hokhmah, Binah, and Da'at; the affective attributes are love of God, fear and awe of God, glorification of God, etc.[19] The three components that constitute the intellect are called mothers, the source of the *middot*, for the latter are the "offspring" of HaBaD [the acronymn for *hokhmah-binah-da'at*].[20]

---

16. This is the central statement of the Habad interpretation of Hasidism. The Kabbalah tended to describe the divine structures in human terms. R. Shneur Zalman, for whom the kabbalistic doctrines were a given, reverses the order. He describes man's personality in terms of divine sefirot. Thus, whereas the Kabbalah elaborated an anthropological theology, he offers a theological anthropology, or kabbalistic psychology. By asserting the equivalents of the ten sefirot in each level of the soul—an idea which flows naturally from the preceding chapter of his work, where he posits that the soul issues from and is verily a part of God—R. Shneur Zalman opens up the possibility of attaining knowledge of God by probing the human soul.

17. By "mothers" he means that the seven lower aspects issue from these three. The term "doubles" implies the dualities suggested by the latter sefirot, such as love/fear (or might), etc.

18. There are two theories on the identification of the three highest sefirot. Most kabbalists list them as Keter, Hokhmah, and Binah. R. Shneur Zalman favors the view which counts Hokhmah as first, Binah as second, and Da'at as third, with Keter transitional between the Ein-Sof and the sefirot. As such, Keter transcends the completely emanated sefirot and cannot be included in the ten. My teacher, Rabbi Joseph B. Soloveitchik, of blessed memory, suggested to me that in excluding Keter, R. Shneur Zalman removed the study of the sefirot from the realm of secret wisdom, the teaching of which is circumscribed by tradition, and opened up the Kabbalah, in its hasidic version, for popular, exoteric study.

19. These are, respectively, the human or psychological correlatives of Hesed, Gevurah, and Tiferet.

20. The intellectual tone of Habad Hasidism is here clearly prefigured: affect issues from intellect. Moreover, the emotions are conditioned by the degree of one's cognitive faculties; the greater one's intellect, the more significant the objects of one's love and fear (see R. Shneur Zalman's *Iggeret ha-Kodesh* 15). Intellect and emotion are thus inseparable, and this connection is what makes Habad distinctive.

3. SOUL AND INTELLECT
Source: R. Shneur Zalman of Liady, Likkutei Torah to Vayikra, p. 4b

In the third chapter of *Likkutei Amarim*[21] it says that the soul has ten
aspects, corresponding to the ten sefirot, etc. But something is omitted: the explanation that even Hokhmah, the first of the ten, is only a
vessel for the soul's essence. Just as the physical brain is only a container for intellectual potency and the wisdom that devolves from the
soul, so, in turn, the soul's intellectual potency is only a vessel for its
essence.[22]

Man's intellect does not always function evenly. Sometimes his
mind is clear, other times it is not—so much so that he talks nonsense.
Since the intellect is always changing, we cannot say that it is the
essence of the soul, and that the soul's essence consists only of the ten
aspects comprising intellect and attributes,[23] or even that the soul is
one (indivisible) reality, to wit, intellect. Rather, the intellect is merely a vessel. Even will (*ratzon*), which stands higher than intellect, i.e.,
Hokhmah, in the soul, is also only a vessel. . . .

(That is why the mind has the capacity to grow. An infant has a
very small mind, and as he grows up, attains greater intellectual and
affective attributes. . . . Since the soul was in him from the very beginning, why was his mind undeveloped? The answer is that the soul
transcends intellect, and the latter is a force that emanates from the
former. In order for this force to expand overtly, there must be a vessel to contain it—a function filled by the brain, which becomes the
vessel for the light of the intellect. . . . Hence, in childhood, because of
the smallness of the brain, the intellect's illumination is limited. But
the soul itself is enclothed in it from the very beginning.)[24]

Now, the essence and substance of the soul are a part of God, who
is beyond the ten aspects, which are limited, but is rather "a simple,

---

21. R. Shneur Zalman here refers to his earlier work by one of its alternative names,
Sefer ha-Benonim, and adds that the same theme is repeated in chap. 12 of that work.
22. The analogy has two layers: the brain is the physical container for the intellect (or
mind); the mind, in turn, is the vessel for the soul or spirit. In contrast to this assertion of the nonidentity of mind and spirit, or of intellect and soul, the medieval rationalists regarded the two as the same.
23. The ten aspects of the soul, here posited as equivalent to the ten sefirot of the
divine emanations, are likewise composed of intellect (the first or upper three) and
attributes (the affective final seven). Yet soul cannot be identified with intellect, either
in part, as the upper three of the ten human sefirot, or in whole, as an indivisible
essence.
24. The whole passage appears in parentheses in the original.

indivisible light," etc. So, too, wrote the Gaon Rabbi Judah Loew of Prague [the Maharal; ca. 1525–1609] in the second preface to the book *Gevurot ha-Shem*: "If you were to ask, 'Since His substance is neither intellect nor corporeality' (heaven forbid that anyone say such a thing!), 'then what is He?' our reply would be: 'Can you really understand the soul in the human body?' Certainly, then, you cannot ask such questions about the Creator, of whom it is written: *for man shall not see Me and live* (Exod. 33:20)."[25] It is clear [from the Maharal's explanation] that the soul itself transcends intellect.

4. THE SOUL AND EVIL
Source: R. Shneur Zalman of Liady, Tanya, Likkutei Amarim, chap. 6

God hath made even the one as well as the other (Eccl. 7:14).[26] Just as the divine soul consists of ten holy sefirot and is clothed in three holy garments,[27] so the soul, which is derived from the *sitra aḥara* of the *kelipat nogah* ("shell of Venus"), which is clothed in man's blood, consists of ten crowns of impurity.[28] These are the seven evil attributes, which stem from the four evil elements mentioned above[29] and the intellect begetting them, which is subdivided into three, namely, wisdom, understanding, and knowledge [i.e., HaBaD, an acronym formed from the initial letters of these terms], the source of these attributes (*middot*). For the *middot* vary according to the quality of the intellect. Hence a child desires and loves petty things of little worth because his intellect is limited and too immature to appreciate things that are much more precious. Likewise, he is provoked to anger and vexation over trivial matters; so, too, with boasting and other attributes.

When a person meditates on these ten unclean categories, or speaks them, or acts by them, then the thought in his brain, the speech in his mouth, and the power of action in his hands and other limbs are called

---

25. Second preface, standard edition of Maharal's works, p. 10.
26. As understood by kabbalists, this means that good and evil are symmetrical: everything in the realm of the holy and the good has its counterpart in the forces of evil and the *kelipot* ("shells").
27. Thought, speech, and deed; see below.
28. See Zohar III, 41a. R. Shneur Zalman continues to exploit his analogy of the divine sefirotic structure with the human soul (see above, selection 2). Just as there is an evil underside to the ten sefirot of holiness in the divine order, so man has the capacity for virtue and saintliness, and also for evil and the demonic.
29. Anger and pride, lust, frivolity, sloth; see above, selection 1.

the impure garments of these ten unclean categories and enclothe them at the time of the action, speech, or thought. Together these constitute all the deeds that are done under the sun, which are all *vanity and striving after wind* (Eccl. 1:14), in the sense of "ruination of the spirit," as interpreted in the Zohar.[30]

This is true as well of all words and thoughts that are not directed toward God and His will and service. For this is the meaning of *sitra ahara*, i.e., not the side of holiness. The holy side is nothing but the indwelling and extension of the holiness of the Holy One, and He rests only on that which abnegates itself completely to Him, either actually, as in the case of the angels above, or potentially, as in the case of every Jew down below, [for every Jew] has the capacity to abnegate himself completely to the Holy One, through martyrdom for the sanctification of God.

That is why our Sages said that even "when a single individual sits and engages in the Torah, the Shekhinah rests on him,"[31] and that "the Shekhinah rests on every gathering of ten Jews."[32]

However, that which does not surrender itself to God, but is a separate thing by itself, does not receive its vitality from the holiness of the Holy One, i.e., from the inner essence and substance of the holiness itself. Instead, [it derives its sustenance] from "behind the back [of holiness],"[33] so to speak, descending degree by degree, through myriads of degrees with the lowering of the worlds, by way of cause-and-effect and many contractions. [The process continues] until the light and life are so diminished, through repeated diminutions, that they can be compressed and enclosed in a state of exile, so to speak, within the separated thing. Thereby it is endowed with vitality and existence *ex nihilo*, so that it does not revert to nothingness and nonexistence as it was before it was created.

Hence, this world and all it contains is called the world of *kelipah* and *sitra ahara*. Therefore, all mundane affairs are difficult and "evil," and wicked men prevail.[34]

---

30. The Zohar (II, 59a) reads *re'ut* ("striving") as *ra'ut* ("ruination), and understands *ruah* as "spirit" rather than "wind."
31. Avot 3:6.
32. Sanhedrin 39a.
33. *Ahorayim*, the underside, or "back," of holiness.
34. Note that "evil" too is part of creation. Hasidism rejects a dualistic notion of "evil." R. Shneur Zalman's thesis that "evil" is ultimately sustained by the Ein-Sof preserves the strong immanentism of Hasidism. (I have placed "evil" in quotation marks because of the Beshtian denial of its essential reality; see below chap. 15, introduction.)

5. DEFINING NEFESH, RUAH, AND NESHAMAH
Source: R. Zadok Ha-Kohen of Lublin, Zidkat ha-Zaddik, no. 227

All Israel has perfect faith in God's existence, unity, and providence, for Jews, as it is said, are "believers, the sons of believers."[35] This is called the *nefesh* of the holiness of Israel. But he who has greater merit is given *ruah*.[36] His heart is made so pure that he feels it in his heart; he emerges from the level of faith to the level of truth, which is clear and recognizable to the heart, as opposed to mere faith. When he is purified even further, he merits the *neshamah* of the mind, i.e., wisdom: to be wise in his perception of God.

It is impossible to attain *neshamah* before *ruah*, and anyone who feels he has achieved this may be sure that it most certainly is not divine wisdom that is being emanated to him through his *neshamah*.

First one must first merit the vital *ruah* in his heart, feeling the divine truth. *Neshamah* comes from the word *neshimah* ("breath"), the inhaling of *ruah* ("air") which one breathes into one's nostrils. The essence of vitality is *ruah*; but one constantly needs to breathe in new *ruah*. It is the function of the *neshamah* constantly to breathe new divine *ruah* into the heart by means of new insights of wisdom in the mind, always apprehending new, vital *ruah*.

Nefesh is a human power, as it is written, *the blood is the soul* (Lev. 17:14). *Nefesh* is found even in the ignorant, for it is the power to do, speak, and think what God wills, in accordance with one's knowledge, through one's faith, anchored in the heart, in the living God and eternal King.

Ruah, as in *the spirit (ruah) of God spoke to me* (2 Sam. 23:2), refers to students of Torah, because the word of God in their mouths awakens a feeling in the heart to recognize that there is a God and Creator of the world.

A Torah scholar who thinks creatively about the Torah merits *neshamah*, which is the breathing in of a drop of new life at every moment after the one in which God in His goodness renews the act of creation, daily and forever; i.e., the spirit of vitality that inheres in creatures and is part of the act of creation; for the *neshamah* is from the world of Beriah ("Creation"), as is known.[37]

---

35. Shabbat 97a, Tanhuma to Exodus 23.
36. Zohar II, 94b.
37. In this passage, R. Zadok offers a new interpretation of the tripartite division of the soul. *Nefesh* functions in accordance with faith. Even the ignorant, if they are

6. THE LOCUS OF MAN
Source: R. Nahman of Bratslav, Likkutei Etzot, Da'at, no. 9

Intellect and knowledge are the essence of man. Hence, where a man's thoughts are, that is where he is.[38] This means that we must truly flee from evil thoughts so that we do not establish our place there, God forbid. We must force ourselves to think good thoughts in order to merit knowing and conceiving divine knowledge. Thus, we will actually *be* there and be absorbed as part of God and merit eternal life and wholeness of knowledge. We will be saved from all want.

7. THE SOUL AS WIFE
Source: R. Elimelekh of Lizhensk, Noam Elimelekh to Vayishlah, s.v. va-yikah et shtei nashav

A man has two wives. One is the woman whom God commanded him to marry in order to *be fruitful and multiply* (Gen. 1:28). The second is his holy soul—the intellective soul—which God placed in man. The soul's sole desire is divine service; to ascend to its source, the supernal place from which it was hewn. This soul is called *a woman of valor*

---

pious, attain it. *Ruah* is a higher level, where faith rises to the level of truth—not mere belief, but conviction. Even if one is not a *talmid hakham*, one must study Torah to reach the level of *ruah*. However, *ruah* is a static state; a truth is perceived, and the epistemological process ends. *Neshamah*, on the other hand, requires creativity—dynamic growth from perception to clearer perception, from truth to greater truth, and is therefore attained by creative scholars of Torah who, through their *hiddushim* (novellae, or innovativeness), imitate God in His creative office. *Nefesh* and *ruah* are equivalent to states in the natural order, corresponding, respectively, to the worlds of Asiyah and Yetzirah. The creative intellect, however, is, as it were, supernatural; *neshamah* derives from the more transcendent world of Beriah. (Asiyah implies natural fact or action, Yetzirah is the change from one state of nature to another [*yesh mi-yesh*]; Beriah represents the truly creative act [*creatio ex nihilo*, or *yesh me-ayin*].)

38. A popular idea among hasidic thinkers. Since man is what he thinks, he is wherever his thoughts are. His body may be in the synagogue, but if his mind wanders to the marketplace or the gambling den, then that is where his "essence" is. Conversely, if he thinks good thoughts, he is spiritually transported to the highest realms until he achieves communion with God. A word of caution is needed here. The hasidic emphasis on mentation, as articulated here by R. Nahman, does not necessarily mean discursive, rational, analytic thought. "Intellect and knowledge are the essence of man" is not a restatement of the Cartesian *cogito ergo sum*. *Sekhel* and *da'at* here mean thought in its most comprehensive sense, including—and perhaps primarily—emotion. For a parallel distinction in Western philosophy between thinking and narrower reasoning processes, see H. Arendt, *The Life of the Mind*, vol. 1.

(Prov. 31:10), "a good wife—a good gift to her husband."[39] Because of her, man can attain the level of unending greatness. One who chooses genuine divine service is not interrupted in his service of God even by his human wife. On the contrary, she supports him, as it is written: *When a man's ways please the Lord, He maketh even his enemies to be at peace with him* (Prov. 16:7); "*his enemies*, this is his wife."[40] These are man's two wives.

Man also has two maidservants, the animal soul and the *yetzer ha-ra* ("evil urge"). Both of these interfere with his divine service. But when he hallows and purifies himself, and breaks his physical appetites and his *yetzer ha-ra*, then everything supports him. He extracts something precious from something cheap,[41] and even the evil urge becomes good. He now serves God with *both* impulses, the good and the evil.[42] The animal soul that induces his physical desires now supports him also, for he hallows himself even in that which is permitted—eating, drinking, and other acts.[43] Thus, he elevates everything to supreme holiness.

---

39. Yevamot 63b, quoting Ben-Sira 26:3.
40. Genesis Rabbah 54:1, paraphrasing Mic. 7:6; meaning that the enemy par excellence is the enemy who is part of one's household.
41. Paraphrasing Jer. 15:19.
42. See Mishnah, Berakhot 54a.
43. A reference to the hasidic doctrine of *avodah be-gashmiut*. See on this, below, chap. 9.

3

Faith

INTRODUCTION

The classical heritage of medieval Jewish philosophy, as represented by Saadia Gaon, Bahya Ibn Pakuda, and Maimonides, is closely associated with what Harry A. Wolfson called the "double faith theory." According to this approach, religious truths can be known in two ways: by prophetic revelation (and the tradition to which it gives birth) and by rational inquiry. Both are legitimate sources of truth, and both rely, in different degrees, on revelation. Whereas conviction brought about by independent rational inquiry partakes of a higher level of knowledge, and is recommended to everyone who is capable of pursuing it, Hasidism is routinely assigned to the opposite pole of the Jewish intellectual tradition: total reliance on faith, revelation, tradition, and firm repudiation of philosophical speculation.[1]

To some extent, this is because Hasidism has generally rejected organized secular education, which is associated with the prospect of religious rationalism. Partly, too, it is because the hasidic intellectual tradition seems alien to the content and style of rational religion. But hasidic thought, as revealed by the selections in this chapter, is neither monolithic nor simple-minded. The following analysis supplies a framework within which the various hasidic attitudes to rational

---

1. For a nuanced discussion of this point, see E. Shmueli, *Ba-Dor ha-Yehudi ha-Aḥaron be-Polin*, a memoir in which an Israeli philosopher describes his youth as the son of an Alexander hasid.

inquiry can be placed in context. It distinguishes four motives behind the religious critique of rational speculation.

1. *Logical (absolute)*. This position holds that reason is incapable of proving some, or all, of the beliefs that religion requires. Exponents of this view may promote rationalism with respect to some beliefs but reject it with respect to others (e.g., they may use reasoning to establish God's incorporeality, but not His existence or providence).[2]

2. *Logical (relative)*. This position holds that while reason is theoretically able to sustain religious dogma, it fails to do so in practice. When the failure is due to individual deficiencies, members of the intellectual and spiritual elite may seek fulfillment through speculation, but the failure may also derive from systemic factors. For example, the possibility of rational inquiry may have been withdrawn once Abraham founded the Jewish way to God. Rationalist thinkers like Saadia Gaon, aware of the intellectual limitations of the masses, stressed the need for faith based on revelation. Hasidic critics, however, maintained that a path to belief open only to the intellectual elite *must* be religiously inferior to a highway accessible to every Jew.[3]

3. *Metaphysical*. In this view, there is a qualitative difference between experience of God attained through reason and through simple faith or ancestral tradition. The philosophers gave a higher rank to the former, but some hasidic masters deprecated knowledge yielded by reason. They held that reason is less vital than simple faith; to seek enlightenment through the indirect inferential route of logical argumentation is to misunderstand, from the outset, the object of religious truth; truth discovered through reason is external to man's experience, whereas faith addresses his inner essence; reason is finite by its very nature (since it is derived from the finite human intellect), as opposed to traditional faith, which is rooted in the Jew's ontological status as a participant in God's covenant with Abraham. Connected to this family of criticisms, but not identical with it, is the doctrine that a proposition with theological significance cannot be known both by reason and by faith; the two are not only different ways of knowing, but mutually exclusive modes of cognition.

4. *Historical*. Adherents of this position argue that commitments engendered by simple, unquestioning faith are best able to stand up to the rigors of persecution and the temptation to apostasy. Hasidic

---

2. E.g., see selection 5, where R. Zevi Elimelekh seeks to impose this approach on Maimonides.
3. E.g., see selection 18.

opponents of philosophy like to quote the philippics of R. Yosef Ya'avetz, who popularized the idea that when Spanish Jewry was subjected to powerful conversionist pressures in the century before the expulsion, the sophisticated often succumbed, whereas the simple remained true to their faith.[4]

In order to understand how various hasidic teachers reacted to these themes, we must remember that Hasidism bears both a radical thrust and an ingrained conservative tendency. Hasidism prized living religious experience. Inasmuch as the independent intellectual venture (though not necessarily the search for proofs) leads to a vibrant, less routine spiritual existence, the quest for God through the natural world serves to enhance piety.[5] To the extent that a sophisticated emphasis on the rationally supported conception of God leads to a cold, desiccated religious experience, it is a threat to the ideals of Hasidism, and must be rejected in favor of the pure freshness of innocent faith. And insofar as Hasidism addresses both the spiritually ambitious and the less adventurous, stolid piety of the average Jew, its teachings must save both the former and the latter from the wrong approach.

The last paragraph presumes that the life of the mind is crucial to man's relationship with God. On that assumption, if man's capacity for rational theological thought is a mark of superiority, it is to be cultivated; if it is judged an inferior approach, it must be eschewed. Of course, there may be an alternative outlook: If religious experience is of the utmost importance, the nature and quality of belief, as a purely intellectual process, may be a matter of relative indifference. This would be the case if the principal avenue of religious experience were contemplative or ecstatic, as was the case for most of the early hasidic thinkers, including the Besht. Hence R. Nahman of Bratslav, for whom simple faith and trust are central, and for whom a vigorous and uncompromising assault on philosophical speculation takes on a singular fervor, appears to represent an extreme position among the early masters.[6] The harsh language of his younger contemporary R. Zevi Elimelekh of Dinov chastises a generation in which the inroads of the

---

4. On Ya'avetz, see G. Nigal, "The Literary Influence of R. Yosef Ya'avetz" and "De'otav shel R.Y. Ya'avetz al Filosofiya u-Mitpalesfim, Torah u-Mitzvot." On R. Zevi Elimelekh's use of these themes, see M. Pierkarz, "'Al Mah Avdah Galut Sefarad'—ke-Leqah kelapei ha-Haskalah be-Mizrah Eiropa."
5. See selection 2.
6. See J. Weiss, *Mehkarim be-Hasidut Bratslav*, pp. 87–95.

Haskalah in Poland already threaten Hasidism both intellectually and politically.[7]

The following anecdote about R. Pinhas Shapira of Koretz (d. 1791), a contemporary of the Besht, encapsulates a typical hasidic attitude toward the medieval philosophical legacy. A man asked R. Pinhas' son to lend him a book. The son gave him Maimonides' *Guide* and was chastised by his father, who said: "Having Rambam's books in the house introduces fear of heaven in a man's heart."[8] R.Pinhas had no use for "wisdom." Unlike the intellectualist Habad school, which quotes the *Guide* as readily as any work of Kabbalah,[9] he is not putting his copy of the *Guide* to scholarly use. Yet his statement appears to bestow upon the book an almost talismanic power to induce fear of heaven. This is a perspective beyond praise or blame, that bypasses the content of Maimonides' enterprise in order to sanctify his person.[10]

Belief in God's providence and the concomitant virtue of trust (*bittahon*) are especially important for the thinkers we are considering. The strength or weakness of faith, in this area, is dramatically manifested in the individual's prayer life and behavior. Trust also exhibits an element of self-fulfillment; both psychologically and metaphysically, it can be argued that God's providence for the individual stands in direct proportion to the individual's trust in God.[11] Thus, when hasidic masters speak of man's efforts to achieve faith, the focus

---

7. See Pierkarz, "'Al Mah Avedah Galut Sefarad,'" pp. 87—89.

8. Cited by J. Dienstag, "*Guide to the Perplexed* and *Sefer ha-Madda* in Hasidic Literature," pp. 312–313.

9. Ibid. Subsequent hasidic authors extended the integration of Maimonides' *Guide*. The outstanding exemplar, R. Joseph Rosin, the "Rogatchover" of Dvinsk, incorporates Maimonides' philosophical categories in his halakhic novellae. The Rogatchover, in turn, exercised great influence on R. Menachem Mendel Schneersohn, the late Lubavitcher Rebbe. See also my *Halakhot ve-Halikhot*, pp. 11-15.

10. Maimonides' *Guide* serves as a litmus test of attitudes toward the interaction of Torah and wisdom. This is partly because of his preeminent position in the Torah world, and partly because the *Guide* became the battleground on which the late medieval controversies about philosophy were fought. The role of Saadia's *Emunot ve-De'ot* for medieval German Jewry helped to assimilate it to the mystical tradition (Scholem, *Major Trends in Jewish Mysticism*, pp. 111–114), to the point where the Besht is regarded as Saadia's transmigration (Scholem, "The Historical Image of the Besht," p. 319). R. Bahya Ibn Pakuda's championship of philosophy could be correctly viewed as subservient to his moralistic goals. Maimonides remains the philosophical inquirer par excellence.

11. E.g., see selection 9.

invariably is less on the avoidance of atheism (hardly a major temptation for the average eighteenth-century hasid)[12] than on man's willingness, nay yearning, to trust absolutely and unconditionally in God.

Concentration on divine providence helps to explain why hasidic
thinkers like R. Nahman and R. Zevi Elimelekh of Dinov, when they
feel threatened by doubt, turn against rational investigation. This is
largely because scientific reasoning offers naturalistic explanations of
the phenomena of this world, not so much undermining religion as
supplanting God's exclusive causative power. To be sure, the two
causative orders can be correlated if the natural order is viewed as a
manifestation of God's will.[13] Yet on the experiential level, belief in scientific explanations presents a perpetual temptation to rely on human
initiative.

In the light of this, it should not come as a surprise that the Besht,
who frequently healed the sick by extrascientific means, fought a running battle with physicians.[14] It is still less surprising that R. Nahman,
even as he was dying of consumption, inveighed against the medical
profession.[15] His aim was not merely assent to the propositional truth
of Judaism; it was a struggle for the truth of simplicity against the
false glitter of cleverness.

1. FAITH AND KNOWLEDGE
Source: R. Yaakov Yosef of Polennoye, Ketonet Passim to Vayikra, p. 1a, first
uva-zeh yuvan

Knowledge of God's existence must be in addition to the tradition
received from our ancestors. As our Sages learned from the verse
Wisdom is good with inheritance (Eccl. 7:11): "Even if you have received
a Torah scroll from your fathers, it is a mitzvah to write one for yourself."[16]

*O, continue Thy lovingkindness unto them that know Thee, and Thy right-
eousness to the upright in heart. Let not the foot of pride overtake me* (Ps.
36:11–12). *Them that know Thee* are those who *know* and [strive intellectually to] understand [God] in addition to tradition. *The upright in
heart* are those who do not wish to *know* and understand God intel-

---

12. R. Nahman was unusual in that he spent a great deal of time with *maskilim*, the
enlightened antagonists of traditional Judaism.
13. See selection 25.
14. See E. Ben-Amos and J. Mintz, *In Praise of the Baal Shem Tov*, index, s.v. "Doctors."
15. See A. Green, *Tormented Master*, pp. 250–262.
16. Sanhedrin 21b; figuratively, faith should be based on received tradition *and* personal knowledge of God.

lectually, but instead rely on tradition [as the sole source of faith] because they are of upright heart and fear to enter into [philosophical] inquiry, saying, "Let not the foot of pride overtake me." They do not want to entertain doubts about the blessed Lord, heaven forbid, like the problem of the wicked who prosper.[17] Since their motivation is for the sake of heaven, [the psalmist prays] *and Thy righteousness to the upright in heart.*[18] So too the meaning of *Dwell in the land and cherish faith, so shalt thou delight thyself in the Lord, and He shall grant thee the petitions of thy heart* (Ps. 37:3). If you derive pleasure from [personal] knowledge of God in addition to faith by tradition, then He will grant your desires.

2. KNOWLEDGE OF GOD THROUGH HIS WONDROUS DEEDS
Source: R. Elimelekh of Lizhensk, Noam Elimelekh to Kedoshim, s.v. o yomar ve-khi tizbeḥu

The blessed Lord created worlds without end and without number, and they are all held together by His holy Name, the blessed Tetragrammaton. We know the world through God's wonderful and awesome deeds, and must bind the worlds [until we link them with] the blessed Ein-Sof. This [act] is the primary service of God. Do not tell yourself, "It is enough to believe in the one true Creator; I need not inquire into and seek God through His wondrous deeds." That is not the true path [to God]. Rather, you must know God through His acts, as Scripture states: *Know the God of your father and serve Him* (1 Chron. 28:9) through His wondrous deeds. The blessed Creator can only be known through His deeds, for He is not a body, nor does He resemble a physical being, nor can He be comprehended by corporeal means.[19]

3. FAITH BASED ON TRADITION, NOT INVESTIGATION
Source: R. Zevi Elimelekh of Dinov, Benei Yisaskhar, Adar 3, derush 2

The Jew is not permitted to reason on matters of faith. True service of

---

17. The problem of theodicy. Religious philosophy rationalizes God's ways. As a method, it is based on doubt, though the doubt may be only academic. Simple faith, however, does not entertain questions that could destroy the basis of faith.

18. The psalmist, says R. Yaakov Yosef, prays for those who, for good reason, do not wish to know God through rational analysis.

19. Cf. Maimonides, *Guide* 1.54, which teaches that man can speak positively about God only by speaking of His actions. See also the opening chapters of *Mishneh Torah*, Hilkhot Yesodei ha-Torah.

God is to have faith because of tradition. Our Creator said of Abraham: *For I have known him to the end that he may command his children . . . that they may keep the way of God* (Gen. 18:19). *I have known him* means that I have given him knowledge [of God] from which faith will proceed naturally to his descendants.[20] Similarly, David said to his son Solomon: *Know the God of your father* (1 Chron. 28:9). This alludes to faith based on ancestral tradition. David did not say: "[Know] God through your own personal process of reasoning."

Faith based on ratiocination is called sight, for intellectual conceptions are akin to physical perceptions. Our Sages said, "I see the words of Admon."[21] Thus there is faith through sight, so to speak. But faith based on tradition is likened to the sense of hearing with the ears.

R. Yosef Ya'avetz wrote that those who reasoned about matters of faith during the decrees in Spain changed their religion [lit. their honor] on the day of wrath.[22] The women and the "intellectual lightweights" whose faith was based on tradition, however, hallowed the glorious and awesome Name [of God], thereby passing the test of purification. We have explained the reason for this. Those who enter into the divine mysteries know that the Breaking [of the Vessels] is related to the category of eyes. The category of the ears, however, is related to the mystery of the perfect restoration.[23] Therefore, faith related to sight can be destroyed and nullified.[24] But faith related to hearing cannot be destroyed and nullified. This is what is meant by *Hear, and your soul shall live* (Isa. 55:3). Understand it.

Furthermore, faith by tradition is an inheritance from Abraham, of whom God said, *For I have known him*. God granted Abraham the power of knowledge. Since faith of this kind derives from the Ein-Sof,

---

20. Jews obtain faith by nature as an inheritance from Abraham, who, paradoxically (and see the next passage), obtained it directly through philosophical speculation.

21. Ketubbot 108b. This means: I agree with the words of Admon.

22. R. Zevi Elimelekh much admired R. Yosef Ya'avetz, a sixteenth-century opponent of philosophy, and wrote a commentary on his *Or ha-Ḥayyim* (see the excerpts from *Ma'ayan Gannim* in selections 4, 5, and 6 below). According to Ya'avetz, during the persecutions and forced baptisms in Spain in 1391, thousands of Jews who were philosophically inclined accepted Christianity instead of suffering martyrdom for the sanctification of God's Name.

23. The ultimate *tikkun* that will reunite and restore the mystical worlds to their primordial harmony.

24. Sight, for R. Zevi Elimelekh, connotes reasoning, while hearing symbolizes faith, especially faith based on tradition.

it is endless.[25] But faith attained through human reasoning comes from a finite being and therefore can, heaven forbid, be terminated. ...

Even if you are inclined to think about faith by rationally contemplating good and evil, i.e., [even if] you seek to achieve faith on the basis of evidence obtained by an intellective process and are not content with faith based upon tradition, this too is forbidden.[26] For Abraham's descendants, faith comes as an inheritance from Abraham. ...

Remember that you must believe absolutely, without doubts and without hidden complaints. Philosophical speculation is a disgrace for the Jew because faith comes naturally to the descendants of Abraham. If you are not content with faith based on tradition and want to engage in philosophical speculation, it is as if you were confessing, heaven forbid, that you are not a link in the genealogical chain of Abraham's descendants.

4. WHY PHILOSOPHICAL SPECULATION IS PROHIBITED
Source: R. Zevi Elimelekh of Dinov, Ma'ayan Gannim to Or ha-Hayyim, chap. 4, no. 20

The early generations trod the path of philosophical contemplation. None remained [believers] except some unique individuals in their respective generations, until our father Abraham came and was commanded to observe circumcision. He and his descendants were forbidden to engage in speculative reasoning. Instead, he was to trust in the Torah. Any intelligent person will wonder why our father Abraham merited so much honor, seeing that he himself reasoned about God's existence and unity. I shall, in passing, inform you what a crime and iniquity it is to reason even now. [For you might say:] We already have faith in God through tradition. Why would it be sinful to understand [this faith] through the intellect? Why has philosophical speculation been forbidden? ...

My friend, please let your spirit not be aghast at my words when you first read them. Delve into them twice or thrice, and then you will understand them thoroughly.

First point: God created the world *ex nihilo*. [That is,] He created what was absent. This is one of the principles of faith laid down in

---

25. Ein-Sof (literally "no end") is a term for the essence and absoluteness of God; faith derived from God is, like God, unending.
26. It is not only forbidden to replace tradition with reason as the source of one's faith; reason is even ruled out as a supplement to tradition.

the Torah. No one denies it except total apostates. As is well known, every skilled workman acts for a purpose and in order to provide something he was lacking before. But the Creator is perfect and lacks nothing. [Therefore, God,] as it were, acted as He did for the benefit of His creatures. . . .

As mentioned above, artisans work in order to obtain what they lack. An artisan who makes silver eating and drinking vessels, for instance, lacks a vessel with which to eat and drink, so he makes one in order to satisfy his need. If he makes the vessel in order to sell it at a profit, he puts himself before his craft, estimates first what he lacks, and produces enough vessels to fulfill that need. Thus he takes precedence over the act and the craft.

This is not the case with the Creator of all. He lacked nothing, for He is perfect with absolute perfection. He created all the worlds for the benefit of His creatures. God did not, as it were, put Himself first; but rather His creatures. They were in His thought [at the time of Creation], since He is absolutely perfect, and did not make His creatures in order to fulfill a deficiency of His, God forbid. No, He created [the world] for the benefit of His creatures.

Second point: The purpose of all created entities is the human race which is in this world. . . . All of them (i.e., all the different species) were created for man's needs. Thus, man is the primary end of Creation. Even the heavenly hosts were created for man's sake. As anyone can see, it says in the Torah that man is the goal of the universe's design, and all other creatures were created [to fulfill] his needs. This is because man was created in order to be capable of free choice and will. The higher creatures, such as angels, do not possess free will; [only] man was created capable of choice. Hence, when man chooses to do good, God delights in the work of His hands. Because of this [free will], God owes man reward or punishment depending on his deeds.

Third point: Since we know that all the creatures in the upper and lower [worlds] were created to serve man's needs, they are governed according to his [man's] deeds. Through his deeds, [such as studying] Torah and [observing the] commandments, man causes various actions in the upper [worlds], and causes great grace (shefa) to flow from world to world. The reverse is also true, in that man, through his [evil actions], prevents the shefa from flowing. It was the Creator's wish that everything that happens in the upper worlds should be caused by the awakening from below; [i.e.,] that man, by serving [God] through his prayers, Torah study, actions, and yihudim, should cause grace (*shefa'im*) in the upper lights through the awakening from below—from man the servant [of God]. The Creator commanded that everything was to be governed according to the deeds of man, who is the purpose of Creation, in order to please God. Since everything is governed by the awakening from below, we must understand that even the beginning of Creation was an awakening from below. For the branch always attests to the nature of the root.[27] But that is impossible in this case, for God created everything *ex nihilo*.[28]

Our Sages, the wise men of truth, taught us, from the verse *These were the potters and those that dwelt among plantations and hedges; there they dwelt occupied in the king's work* (1 Chron. 4:23), that God consulted the souls of the righteous.[29] Although these are profound words for the enlightened in knowledge, understand that this idea is one of the mysteries of Creation, as it were; namely, that God delights in the service of Israel, and that a certain righteous man at a certain time will serve Him with a specific service. Since past, present, and future are the same to God, it is as if this future event [i.e., the service of the zaddik] has already taken place. This event is like the awakening from below. Thus the righteous are truly the creators, those who sit at the hedges with the king in his work.

When a righteous man serves God by studying Torah and doing the commandments at the appointed time, God has already seen this acceptable act from the time of Creation. This act awakened God's thought to create the world in order to please Himself. Our Sages expounded upon the word *bereshit* (Gen. 1:1): "for the sake of Israel which is called *reshit*."[30] . . . The world was created only for Israel, because man is the purpose of Creation and was created to please God. Man was created to be capable of free choice and will, and Israel are the ones who choose good. Thus they [Israel] were God's intention and incentive for Creation. This was the meaning of our Sages' saying that "the thought of Israel preceded the thought of Creation."[31] In the

---

27. Since the worlds are sustained because of the awakening from below, it seems plausible that the world was created for this reason.
28. How can the world have been created for the sake of certain human actions if no humans existed at the time?
29. Genesis Rabbah 8:7.
30. Pesikta Zuta and Rashi on Gen. 1:1. *Bereshit* is the construct form, meaning "In the beginning of." There is no object attached to the preposition. The Sages interpreted "of" in the sense of "for" and completed the phrase with "Israel," based on Jer. 2:3, where Israel is called *reshit*.
31. Genesis Rabbah 1:4.

same vein, the word *Yisrael* ("Israel") is made up of the words *li* ("for me") and *resh* ("beginning").[32] Now, if you contemplate the matter you will come to realize that the source of the souls of Israel is still within the primordial thought known in the Torah as "utterances" (*ma'amarot*), "And God said . . . "[33]

Therefore, as far as the concept of God is concerned, the soul of the Jew, by its nature, does not need philosophical investigation, because his roots cleave to the primordial thought itself, the thought that engenders creation *ex nihilo*. . . . The other nations, however, inasmuch as their souls are not derived from the thought itself, but from the periphery of the thought, require philosophical investigation. They are *children in whom there is no faith* (Deut. 32:20). Now you can understand that any Jew who reasons about the concept of God loses his precious status. [By so doing] he testifies that he is not of the Jewish people, and that he is not subsumed in the primordial thought.

Fourth point: Our Sages said that *be-hibbaram* [i.e., *heaven and earth*] *were created* (Gen. 2:4) is equivalent to "for Abraham." The world was created because of Abraham's merit.[34] This means that Abraham's soul is the source of all the Jewish souls which were in the primordial thought and for which the worlds were created. Before Abraham's soul was uncovered [at the time of his birth], the generations deteriorated, for they followed [the path of] philosophical reasoning, which corrupted their human wisdom. Consequently they were drawn to evil lusts and were lost. This continued until the light of the east shined from the darkness, i.e., the birth of [Abraham, who is called] Ethan the Ezrahite.[35]

---

32. Meaning, "the beginning [of Creation] is for me [or, because of me.]"
33. See Avot 5:1.
34. Genesis Rabbah 12:9. The consonants of *be-hibbaram* and *Abraham* are the same.
35. See Ps. 89:1, 1 Kings 5:11, and Yalkut Shimoni at both places. A word-play on *Ezrah* and *mizrah* ("east"), both of which have the same root, *zrh* ("to shine"). As R. Zevi Elimelekh goes on to explain, Abraham, born in a generation of darkness, resorted to philosophical reasoning to perceive the existence of God. After he found God, however, "his soul returned to its roots"; and the knowledge he acquired should suffice for his descendants. All Jews know the existence of God by tradition as established by Abraham. Cf. above, selection 3, by the same author.

5. INVESTIGATING THE EXISTENCE AND UNITY OF GOD
Source: R. Zevi Elimelekh of Dinov, Ma'ayan Gannim to Or ha-Ḥayyim, chap. 10, 27a, nos. 3–4[36]

"If, nevertheless, you yearn for a proof of God's incorporeality, seek it in the Sefer ha-Yashar[37] and the Ḥovot ha-Levavot,[38] and thus you shall hear it from a pious teacher who has expertise in the art of philosophy. Do not delve too deeply, for the reward for faith is greater than the reward for speculative reasoning, as it is written: the righteous shall live by his faith (Hab. 2:4), not by his rational investigation."[39]

Note that the rabbi [i.e., R. Yosef Ya'avetz] spoke only of rejecting corporeality, which is equivalent to believing in the divine unity. From the words of Maimonides it is apparently a mitzvah to establish that God is not corporeal.[40] However, it seems to me that reasoning about the belief in God's existence is entirely forbidden.

Quite the contrary, one should believe in it with perfect faith. . . . Moreover, one should trust the words of this rabbi [R. Joseph Ya'avetz, who says] not to engage in philosophizing even on the subject of God's unity.[41] But if you feel a need to engage in philosophy, you may satisfy it by studying the books recommended by the rabbi.

6. "THE TREE OF KNOWLEDGE"
Source: R. Zevi Elimelekh of Dinov, Ma'ayan Gannim to Or ha-Ḥayyim, chap. 2, 8b, no. 5

And thou, Solomon my son, know thou the God of thy father and serve Him with a whole heart (1 Chron. 28:9). [At the beginning of the Amidah prayer] we say "Our God and the God of our fathers." "Our God" refers to the God whose divinity we have proven by way of wisdom and the intellect. "God of our fathers" refers to the aspect of His divin-

---

36. Or ha-Ḥayyim was written by R. Yosef Ya'avetz, one of the Spanish Jews expelled in 1492. See selection 3, above.
37. "Book of the Just," a work on ethics ascribed variously to the French tosafists R. Jacob Tam of Ramerupt and R. Jacob of Orleans (both 12th cent.). See Azulai, Shem ha-Gedolim, s.v. Sefer ha-Yashar.
38. "Duties of the Heart," an ethico-philosophic work by R. Bahya Ibn Pakuda (Spain, 11th cent.).
39. This concludes the citation from Or ha-Ḥayyim. Next comes the comment of R. Zevi Elimelekh in Ma'ayan Gannim, note 4.
40. See Mishneh Torah, Hilkhot Yesodei ha-Torah 1:6, 8.
41. Namely, God's incorporeality, which is a prerequisite to the belief in His unity; see Maimonides, Hilkhot Yesodei ha-Torah 1:7.

ity which we have received by way of tradition from our fathers—without intellectual reflection.

Remember, too, that philosophical contemplation of the divine is called *the tree of knowledge of good and evil* (Gen. 2:9).[42] This is because in order to exercise our cognitive faculties, we have to reflect on the good and its opposite, delving into all aspects of the contrary position. Thus, heart and mind incline both to the good and to its opposite. This is not the case with faith received through tradition, which is wholehearted, without the mind's inclination.

David said: "*Thou, my son Solomon*, are noted for wisdom of every kind and are able to use reason to derive proofs of faith; nevertheless, *know the God of thy father*, and do not seek proofs, but *serve Him with a whole heart*, for reasoning about proofs is not whole-hearted service, because it inclines the mind, even if only for the moment, to both the good and its opposite."[43]

7. "TASTING" FAITH AND "SEEING" IT
Source: R. Dov Ber, the Maggid of Mezeritch, Likkutim Yekarim, n. 199, p. 60b

The reason we say "Our God and the God of our fathers" is that there are two types of people who believe in God. Those of the first type believe in God because they follow in the ways of their ancient fathers. Their faith is strong. The second are those who attain religious faith as a result of philosophical reasoning. The difference is that those of the first type have an advantage in that they cannot be seduced [away from the faith] even if they are shown contrary proofs [against God's existence], for their faith is strong because of their ancestral tradition. Further, they have never investigated [God's existence]. However, they are also at a disadvantage in that their faith is by rote, lacking reason and knowledge. The second have an advantage because they recognize the Creator [by virtue of their own reasoning]; hence, their faith is as strong as their philosophical ability, attaining a complete faith and total love. But they too lack something, in that it is easy to seduce them [away from the faith]. If they are [merely] shown contradictory evidence, they will be seduced. But there is no one higher than the person who has both of these attributes. He strongly relies on his ancient fathers, and [faith] comes to him because

42. Maimonides, *Mishneh Torah*, Hilkhot Teshuvah 5:1, avers that the tree of the knowledge of good and evil indicates man's capacity to determine his belief "on his own, with his mind and thought."
43. See selections 2 and 3 above for a different reading of 1 Chron. 28:9.

he reasons [about it for himself]. This is complete and good faith. Because of this we say: "Our God and the God of our fathers."[44]

The verse *taste and see that the Lord is good* (Ps. 34:9) can be explained in a similar manner: *taste* through philosophical investigation, and *see* how our fathers acted.

8. BELIEVING IN CREATION AND IN INDIVIDUAL PROVIDENCE
Source: R. Shneur Zalman of Liady, Tanya, Sha'ar ha-Yiḥud veha-Emunah, chap. 2

Here is the answer to the heretics, exposing the basic error of those who deny individual providence and the signs and miracles recorded in the Torah. These people err by false analogy. They liken the actions of God, the Creator of heaven and earth, to the actions and schemes of man. When a vessel leaves the hands of the potter, it no longer needs what the potter does. The potter's hands have left the vessel, and the potter goes off to the market, but the vessel continues to exist in the same shape and form as when it left the potter's hands. That is how these fools imagine the Creation of heaven and earth. But their eyes are so blind that they do not see the great difference between man's actions and schemes, which constitute creation out of something and consist of mere changes in form and substance—like an ingot of silver which becomes a vessel—and the Creation of heaven and earth, which is creation out of nothing. The Creation of the world is a greater wonder than the splitting of the Red Sea. In the latter case, God drove back the sea by a strong east wind throughout the night, so that the waters were split and stood like a wall.[45] Had God momentarily stopped the wind, the waters would have returned and gravitated downwards as they naturally do; of course, they would no longer have stood up like a wall. This is true even though the natural state of water's gravitation is itself produced *ex nihilo*. In contrast, a wall of stones stands by itself and a wind is not needed to keep it up. The nature of water, however, is different. All the more so is this the case with creation *ex nihilo*, which is supernatural and certainly more wondrous than the splitting of the Red Sea. Surely if the power of the Creator were withdrawn from the created object, the object would return to absolute nothingness (its original state). The power of the Creator must *always* be in the created object in order to animate and sustain it.

---

44. See the preceding selection for a different understanding of "Our God and the God of our fathers."
45. See Exod. 14:21–22.

9. THE RECIPROCITY OF PURE FAITH
Source: *R. Menahem Mendel of Vitebsk, Peri Etz to Miketz*

Introduction

In this selection, R. Menahem Mendel seems to be expounding a form of progressive providence. In this view, divine providence is not uniform vis-à-vis humanity. God is more watchful over certain people than over others. The more one is under the watchful gaze of providence, the less one is susceptible to occurrences caused by blind chance. The converse is also true. This theory was first propounded by Maimonides (see *Guide* 3:18) seven hundred years before R. Menahem Mendel. Maimonides, of course, uses a totally different criterion as the standard for man's earning the share of his providence. Maimonides' conception is precisely the idea which R. Menahem Mendel strongly opposes: intellectual cognition of God, in the philosophical sense. The norm R. Menahem Mendel espouses is faith in divine providence itself. Needless to say, these differences are quite characteristic of the gene al views of the two thinkers.

*

One must believe in individual providence over everything in the world, big and small, and that nothing [occurs] without God's providence. Through this trust in God, namely, faith in His providence and that His acts are true and faithful (for the divine act is always good), man elevates this cause (Providence) and binds it with supernal wisdom. To the extent that man has faith and reflects upon providence, he draws God's providence upon himself. If one believes in God's individual providence, then one is cared for individually even to bruising a finger.[46] If man loses his faith in divine providence, he is placed under the [blind] laws of nature and is called an apostate.

10. PERCEIVING TRUTH WITHOUT KNOWLEDGE
Source: *R. Nahman of Bratslav, Likkutei Etzot, Emet ve-Emunah, sec. 4*

It is impossible to attain faith except through truth, for faith applies only to that which the intellect does not understand; faith is inap-

---

46. "Man does not bruise his finger below unless it was so decreed from on high" (Hullin 7b).

plicable when the intellect understands. If so, then when the intellect does not understand, how is one to attain faith in that which one should believe?[47] Hence, we must say that faith is dependent upon truth.[48] If you wish to know the real truth, you must understand, of your own accord, that you must maintain a holy belief in God and the real zaddikim and the holy Torah, even though it is impossible to know and understand these matters through our corporeal intellect.[49] Only by perceiving truth through the eyes of truth[50] can we understand, even if only dimly, that it is the truth. As these beliefs cannot be understood through the intellect, we must exclusively fortify our faith to perfection.[51]

11. TRUTH WHICH IS SUBORDINATE TO FAITH
Source: R. Gedaliah of Linitz, Teshuot Ḥen to Vaeira, p. 55a, s.v. ve-hifleti.

We are required to believe completely in divine providence, which is the source of everything even though the human intellect cannot comprehend it. Only after believing completely is it possible to understand the belief to a limited extent.[52] That is what "truth and faith"

---

47. If faith cannot be derived from a humanly comprehensible source, how can it be attained? Obviously we can only know that which we can know, but faith applies to that which we cannot know. How, then, can we attain faith?
48. Ordinarily truth applies precisely to a knowable and/or known entity. The truth spoken of here, however, is the kind that cannot be understood or analyzed. Since faith depends upon truth, and one who wishes to know the truth must believe in God, the zaddikim, and the Torah, faith is the basis as well as the goal of truth. This skirts the tautological, and tells us very little about truth other than to make it totally subservient to faith.
49. R. Nahman denies rationalism any role in the scheme of religion. Reason neither has nor can have a place in religion, for religion is rooted in faith, and faith does not apply to anything to which reason also applies. Thus faith and reason are never found in the same domain.
50. Truth, which here is a type of faith (see above n. 49), can only be attained through truth. One cannot attain faith through reason. Since the end is not subject to conscious thought, knowledge is irrelevant in attaining faith.
51. Cf. Likkutei Etzot, Emet va-Tzedek, sec. 33, where R. Nahman asserts that intellectual understanding is the result of strong (i.e., pious) faith. At the end, "matters which had to be taken before on pure faith . . . one is privileged to understand intellectually because of one's strong faith." Understanding does not lead to faith, but faith leads to understanding.
52. Meaning, by implication, that faith in God should be unconditional.
53. The two words recited immediately after the reading of the Shema every evening. R. Gedaliah understands them as nouns, but in context they are adjectives.

means.[53] Truth applies to what is comprehended by the intellect; the object of knowledge is clear. Faith, by definition, is something uncomprehended, [something] known to be so only by faith.

The verse *Thy faith in the nights* (Ps. 92:3) means that it is necessary to employ faith at times that can be likened to *the nights*, [i.e., times when] the object cannot be comprehended by the intellect.

In the morning we say "true and firm."[54] This is because, even after attaining comprehension through faith, we must return to faith, because it is impossible to understand the thing sufficiently by means of intellect alone. The most that we understand is only a minuscule part of the thing itself. Therefore we say "and firm," which is a synonym for faith. For the knowledge we have attained is often not called "truth" in and of itself, but is subordinate to faith, whose synonym is "firm." We must use both means, truth, i.e., human understanding, and faith, for we cannot conduct ourselves on the basis of truth alone. Those who wish to act only on the basis of truth, and refuse to do anything unless they have total understanding, are deluded. The correct way is faith in God planted in our hearts like a faithful peg, and afterwards we may seek to understand the truth.

12. FAITH DUE TO ANCESTRAL MERIT
Source: R. Yaakov Yosef of Polennoye, Toledot Yaakov Yosef to Yitro, end

Complete faith and trust in God is a wonderful attribute. Our father Abraham, upon meriting this attribute, considered it a great divine favor that God had brought him to this level. Thus it is written: *And he believed in the Lord, and he counted it for him for righteousness* (Gen. 15:6) [i.e., Abraham counted it for himself as a great favor].[55] Our teacher Moses said: *But they will not believe me* (Exod. 4:1). At that time Moses had failed to find some merit for which the Children of Israel could be deemed worthy of attaining complete faith. This was so until God answered him that faith is attained through ancestral merit. That is why [the people of] Israel are called "believers, the children of believers."[56]

---

54. The two words recited immediately following the morning Shema.
55. This deviates from Rashi's reading of the verse, i.e., that God accounted it to Abraham as righteousness. R. Yaakov Yosef, like Nahmanides, reverses the meaning of the two pronouns; he also understands *tzedakah* in the sense of "favor."
56. Shabbat 97a, Numbers Rabbah 7:5, Tanhuma Shemot 23.

13. SIMPLE FAITH IS NOT A MITZVAH
Source: R. Zadok ha-Kohen of Lublin, Zidkat ha-Zaddik, nos. 207 and 229

I am the Lord your God (Exod. 20:2) was not said in the imperative form, because this would go against the simple faith that is inherent in every Jew.[57] A mitzvah is not applicable to the condition of inherent faith,[58] for what point would there be in commanding someone who does not believe? Rather, Israel are "believers, the children of believers."[59]

14. SIMPLE FAITH IS MANDATORY FOR JEWS
Source: R. Zevi Elimelekh of Dinov, Benei Yisaskhar, Sivan, ma'amar 5, no. 19

For us, the children of Israel, the people of God, the purpose of all of our actions is faith, which is our inheritance and exists in us naturally, through the Torah. God forbid that we should engage in philosophical speculation! We are even required to believe in the words of the Sages without seeking rational proof. . . . We are obligated to believe through the sense of hearing as much as through the sense of sight, without distinction. Sight should make no more of an imprint or effect upon the heart than hearing.[60]

If we are obligated regarding the words of the Sages, all the more so regarding what is explicitly stated in the Torah, and specifically that which constitutes the principles of religion, namely, God's existence and unity, and reward and punishment. God forbid that anyone philosophize about these beliefs even in the fanciful notion that he is doing so for the sake of heaven; reasoning philosophically in order to prove these beliefs rationally is unthinkable [even if the motive] is to render oneself immune to violating the faith under duress. Such words should be ignored and not even mentioned. . . .

---

57. In the sense of casting aspersions upon the Jewish people, as if they needed a commandment in order to believe.

58. Faith is not subject to command. Note too the medieval dispute as to whether belief in the existence of God is one of the 613 commandments. Maimonides holds that it is, in *Sefer ha-Mitzvot*, positive commandment 1, as opposed to *Halakhot Gedolot*. See Nahmanides' notes to *Sefer ha-Mitzvot* and his commentary to Exod. 20:2.

59. See above, n. 56.

60. Sight, for R. Zevi Elimelekh, connotes reasoning, whereas hearing symbolizes faith, especially through tradition. See above, selection 3.

I call upon the testimony of the pious saint R. Yosef Ya'avetz, who noted that it was precisely the philosophical rationalists who converted to Christianity during the decrees in Spain and Portugal.[61] It was the "intellectual lightweights" and the women, whose faith springs only from tradition, who hallowed the glorious and awesome Name of God.

(Do not contradict me by citing the names of the holy ones who are in the land of the immortals—Saadia Gaon, in his *Emunot ve-De'ot*, the pious saint Bahya Ibn Pakuda in his *Ḥovot ha-Levavot*, and Maimonides. Herein lies a hidden secret.[62] They had to sustain the world during the fifth millennium, when it was in the category of darkness. This was a temporary injunction.)

15. THE DANGERS OF INTELLECTUAL SPECULATION
Source: *R. Avraham Katz of Kalisk, Iggerot Ba'al ha-Tanya, no. 59*

All questions concerning exalted matters . . . revolve around one point, namely, *Behold, the fear of the Lord, that is wisdom* (Job 28:28), which is not the case with the opposite: "the wise have no bread," i.e., the essentials of fear and faith.[63] Fear of God is the innermost point around which all the planets revolve and all the worlds are built. It is the first primary intellect and also the final one. And since we are not to move from this point, God commanded us regarding practical halakhic requirements (*halakhah le-ma`aseh*) and trust in the Sages, to keep us from turning away from true faith, so that we will then prosper. . . . Torah and intellectual pursuits on their own, without the background of fear of God, are isolated, perishable, and bring destruction to their possessor. This innermost point of fear of God is "the ulti-

---

61. As noted above, R. Zevi Elimelekh much admired R. Yosef Ya'avetz and wrote a commentary on his *Or ha-Ḥayyim* (see the excerpts from *Ma'ayan Gannim* in selections 4, 5, and 6). According to Ya'avetz, during the persecutions and forced baptisms in Spain in 1391, thousands of Jews who were inclined to philosophical speculation in religious matters accepted Christianity instead of suffering martyrdom for the sanctification of God's Name.

62. If philosophical speculation is so alien to Judaism, why did Saadia, Bahya, and Maimonides engage in it? The answer is a "secret" or "mystery," i.e., to be found in the realm of mysticism.

63. Quoting Eccl. 9:11. Fear of God leads to wisdom, not the other way around. Wisdom (i.e., philosophical reasoning) does not lead to fear of God, and men of intellect often lack the fear of God that leads to true wisdom.

mate reality set in the original thought."[64] Through it ascends and descends the source of blessings and good in store for the righteous. However, when one builds on reason alone, without the required deeply entrenched[65] fear, even though it is all good, judgments are nevertheless awakened. The broadening of intellect without limit [and untempered by fear of God may be the cause] of deep darkness, as is well known.

Hence it is unclear to me why books by some heavenly saints, whose written words on the paths of heaven are like coals of fire concerning exalted matters—not every mind can absorb this—were printed.[66] These works were written for those who have saintly souls[67] or who serve God out of love and have overcome the deficiencies of their nature. . . . However, now [that these works are in print] they are easily obtainable . . . endangering those who lack merit. . . . For the intellect develops[68] in accordance with our purification of body and soul; and commensurately with this does it attract our reason. . . . In my opinion, if I had the power, I would gather all these holy books [dealing with philosophical questions], which are presently scattered in the hands of novices, and would reserve them for the pure of soul. Beginners could then learn from them little by little as their intellects developed after great preparation. I would remove these books from the general market lest [those unprepared for philosophy] be overpowered by beasts of [unrestrained] intellect[69]—corporeal thinking, without absorptive capacity, dragging the mind along into a realm from which all who enter therein never return,[70] heaven forbid.[71] . . .

---

64. From the poem Lekha Dodi, recited at the inauguration of the Sabbath.

65. Quoting Eccl. 7:24, "deep, deep, who can find it?"

66. This apparently refers to the philosophical writings of Saadia Gaon, Bahya Ibn Pakuda, and Maimonides. However, it is not entirely clear who is being criticized, the three philosophers for putting their ideas in written form, or those who later printed their works, thus ensuring that they would be widely distributed and popularized.

67. Those whose souls have overpowered the corruptions and contaminations of the body, for in essence all souls are holy.

68. The translation is in accordance with the corrected reading of the text: nivneh, "is built" or "develops," and not nivzeh, which means "is disgraceful," an obvious misprint.

69. Paraphrasing Exod. 23:29–30.

70. Referring to "None that go into her return" (Prov. 2:19), which according to Avodah Zarah 17a means heresy (minut). In other words, a believer who turns to heresy finds it hard to revert to devout belief.

71. R. Avraham Kalisker, in this letter to R. Shneur Zalman of Liady, the founder of Habad, criticizes him for disseminating his esoteric philosophy to all who are ready to listen. Hence, the following is a direct admonishment to R. Shneur Zalman and his followers.

I feel it incumbent as a command and a duty to warn all transgressors with a great and awesome warning, so long as the fear of God still touches their hearts. Listen and your souls will live. *And in all things that I have said unto you take ye heed* (Exod. 23:13), for these are the same old words uttered by the mouth of the saintly Rabbi Menahem Mendel,[72] who wrote to you in a like vein and more. For one needs special urging in your land,[73] which is corrupted with coarseness,[74] and therefore I urge you to be less concerned with esoteric intellectual matters, because a cloud hides[75] true mystical knowledge, and intellectualism may be a cause for extinguishing the candle, heaven forbid. . . .

I seek your righteousness out of great love [and therefore wish to restore you to a simple faith], as it is written: *God made man upright, but they have sought out many inventions* (Eccl. 7:29). Before the sin Adam was in the category of the simple man (*tam*), as the Sages have written of Jacob, about whom it is said, *Jacob was a simple man* (Gen. 25:27), in the image of Adam.[76] Faith, which is overwhelmingly important, as mentioned, transcends intellectuality. But after the sin Adam fell into various intellectual traps, as it is written: *In the day ye eat thereof* the tree of knowledge, *then your eyes shall be opened and ye shall be as God, knowing good and evil* (Gen. 3:5); *And their eyes were opened, and they knew that they were naked* (Gen. 3:7). For the beginning of evil comes from the intellect's awakening of judgments. The righteous are accustomed in informal talk to point to the phrase *And the daughter of a priest if she profane herself by playing the harlot* (Lev. 21:9) [as indicating] that harlotry has its beginning in the intellect.[77] Many have been lost and turned heretic from overattention to matters of the intellect.

---

72. R. Avraham was one of the disciples of the Besht and the Maggid of Mezeritch who settled in Eretz Israel. A passage from the work of R. Menahem Mendel of Vitebsk, who was a leader of this group, appears above as selection 9.
73. Literally, "[the word] *tzav* ('command') is an expression of urging," a quotation from Rashi's commentary to Lev. 6:2.
74. *Meshubbeshet be-gasut*, a play on *meshubbeshet be-gayasot*, "entangled [i.e., infested] with raiders" (Yevamot 115a).
75. Alluding to Job 22:14.
76. Bava Batra 58a.
77. A word-play. The verse says *ki tehel liznot*. In the Eastern European (Ashkenazic) pronunciation of Hebrew, *sehel* ("shall begin") is a homonym for "intellect" (*sekhel*). Hence, homiletically, intellect (*sekhel*) leads to adultery or harlotry (*zenut*).

16. CAUSES OF DOUBT IN FAITH
Source: R. Yaakov Yosef of Polennoye, Tzafnat Pa'ane'aḥ to Yitro, s.v. ve-nir'eh de-shamati mi-mori, p. 64a

I heard from my teacher the Baal Shem Tov that it is related in the responsa of Maimonides (the Epistle on Resurrection) that some seventy-one people from a distant country signed a letter to him. "May our rabbi teach us," they wrote, "since the doctrine of the resurrection of the dead is not mentioned explicitly in the Torah, but is the subject of inquiry in the Talmud, where they found hints and expounded various proofs,[78] should not we ourselves also inquire into this and seek to derive proofs by considering both opposing views?"...

Maimonides did not want to respond to this question. He commanded his pupil, R. Judah Ibn Tibbon, to write the answer. The contents of the answer follow: "Because you entertain this doubt, I know that your souls do not come from Abraham, Isaac, and Jacob, but rather from the people of Sodom and Gomorrah.... For there are souls that derive from heaven and earth and the seven planets and the like. ...

"There is a basic problem in connection with the Creation of the world: Wasn't the entire act of creating the world produced 'according to its will,' as our Rabbis said?[79] Why, then, did earth not wish to be heaven? We must say that God did not permit the earth to be the heaven. The earth is only allowed to *wish* it was heaven. This is because there must also be an earth in the world, and the same applies to all the other created beings.[80] That is the meaning of 'they were created according to their natures.'[81]

"The same holds true for man. There must be wicked people,

---

78. Sanhedrin 90a—93a. See also Abarbanel's commentary to Leviticus, preface to Be-hukkotai. Maimonides' *Epistle on Resurrection* is a response to those who asked whether his infrequent mention of this doctrine indicated indifference to it. Maimonides affirms his belief in resurrection.

79. Rosh Hashanah 11a. The point is obscure. R. Yaakov Yosef is probably referring to the Talmud's statement that all creations were brought into being *le-da'atan*, which, according to Rashi (ad loc.) means that each species was asked if it wanted to be created, and all answered in the affirmative. Hence the question, why did the earth not wish to be the heaven?

80. That is, every entity must be itself, for that is the nature of the world.

81. The solution is that every individual entity, and not only the world in general, was created according to its nature.

mediocre people, and righteous people, for 'there is advantage to light over darkness.'[82] This means that there is also some advantage to be derived from darkness. [In the same vein, there is some advantage in the existence of wicked people, for] the virtues of the righteous are seen better when contrasted with the deeds of the wicked. Each group was created according to its nature and according to its will. One might ask: Given the aforementioned, does not the problem of free will versus divine foreknowledge arise?[83] Since you deny the expositions of the Sages, you do not understand the explanation of this problem.

"The soul of man is composed of blood, which is produced from extractions of foods. The digested food is separated into various [nutritional and excretional] components. First the bile secretes a fluid toward the food found in the intestines. The undesirable food is then separated, becomes excrement, and is expelled from the body. The second separation [comprises those liquids] which are discharged as urine. The third becomes sweat. The fourth becomes hair and nails. In the fifth separation, the blood is absorbed by the liver and spleen. The select and desirable blood enters the heart and, afterwards, the brain; the intellect and mind are produced from this.

"From your words it is clear that you deny the validity of the words of our Sages. Thus you have not avoided eating forbidden food and impure things. Hence your intellect has been produced from the blood of unfit and forbidden animals. Your intellect is naturally drawn toward that which is impure. How can you decide, then, against the talmudic Sages, whose intellectual capacity was broader than the sea? . . . Since you have entered into doubt and apostasy concerning the words of the Sages, know for sure that your punishment is imminent."

Indeed, so it happened. A king came upon them, and murdered and destroyed them. They wished to change their religion, but [the non-Jewish conquerors] refused to accept them because they denied the resurrection of the dead. Even non-Jews believe in the mystery of rein-

---

82. According to Eccl. 2:13, *Wisdom exceeded folly as light excels over darkness*. The word *min* ("over") is homiletically interpreted as a derivative. Hence light's advantage is more evident due to the existence of darkness.

83. See Maimonides, *Mishneh Torah*, Hilkhot Teshuvah 5:5. Maimonides deals with the question of how humankind can have free will when God foresees every future action, but R. Yaakov Yosef's problem goes beyond the issue of divine prescience, because he proposes a rigid determinism and predestination which excludes any free will at all!

carnation and resurrection of the dead; all the more so the philosophers [who certainly believe in these doctrines]. A few of these people heeded Maimonides' words and repented. This concludes [the story found in Maimonides' responsa].

It was the spirit of God that was speaking through Maimonides, for his prediction was fulfilled. The fact that punishment closely followed apostasy can be explained by the words of our Sages: "He who directs his heart to vain thoughts forfeits his life."[84] The pious Rabbi Yosef Ya'avetz wrote that he who clings to God is the object of His providence and is not subject to chance.[85] When he ceases to cling to God, providence ceases to apply to him. All the more is this true when *these evils come upon us because our God is not among us* (Deut. 31:17).

17. FAITH AND SPECULATION
Source: R. Nahman of Bratslav, Likkutei Moharan, II, 19

Our principal purpose and perfection lies in serving the Lord in complete simplicity, without any sophistication.

There are philosophers[86] who say that our principal purpose and reason for existence in the world-to-come is only to know everything as it is; for instance, to know a star as it is, to know its essence, and why it is located in such-and-such specific place. For there is the *intelligens*, the *intellectum*, and the *intellectus*; i.e., the quality of the thinker, the intellect itself, and that which is conceived by the intellect. They maintain that the goal of our existence in the world-to-come is that all three should become one, i.e., the *intelligens*, the *intellectum*, and the *intellectus*. Hence they spend their days in this world contemplating and mastering these concepts, regarding this as their purpose. In their opinion, this in itself is the world-to-come, except that in this world, where they are enclothed in bodies, they do not derive as much pleasure from [philosophical] speculation. But in the world-to-come, where they will be divested of their bodies, they will derive great pleasure from it. According to their evil opinion, our purpose is essentially attained by means of philosophical reasoning and secular sciences.

But truly, we hold that our purpose is fulfilled only through faith

---

84. Avot 3:4.
85. This idea was first proposed by Maimonides himself; see n. 47.
86. The Hebrew reads *meḥakkerim*, "philosophizers," which in this genre of literature means philosophers, with special emphasis on the Jewish rationalist tradition of the Middle Ages.

and the practical observances, serving the Lord by means of the Torah, simply and artlessly. By this means alone do we merit what we merit—*no eye has seen* . . . (Isa. 64:3).[87] So it is written, *The beginning of wisdom is the fear of the Lord* (Ps. 111:10)—the essential beginning of wisdom and prior to it is only the fear of the Lord; for one must give precedence to fear, i.e., piety, over wisdom.

Proof that their opinion is incorrect, heaven forbid, is that according to them only a very few people, the philosopher-intellectuals, would ever fulfill their purpose. But how are lesser people, the majority and mainstay of the world, to attain their purpose, seeing that they do not have sufficient intellect to engage in philosophical speculation and to grasp these ideas? In truth, we fulfill our purpose only and specifically by means of simplicity, i.e., the fear of the Lord and the practical observances, in utter artlessness.

This is what is meant by *The end of the matter, all having been heard: fear God, and keep His commandments; for this is the whole of man* (Eccl. 12:13). King Solomon teaches us that the fulfillment of our purpose, i.e., "the end of the matter,"[88] comes about only by means of simplicity, fearing the Lord and observing His commandments artlessly. Hence *the end of the matter, all having been heard: fear God, and keep His commandments*, alluding to the quality of simplicity and artlessness, fearing the Lord and keeping His commandments, etc. That is why the verse concludes, *for this is the whole of man*, i.e., it is possible for every man[89] to observe this and to attain his purpose thereby, since the essence of all is *fear God*, etc., There every man can attain his purpose.

In truth, it is a very great transgression to philosophize, heaven forbid, and to study books of secular knowledge, heaven forbid. Only the very great zaddik is permitted to do this, to study the seven sciences.[90]

---

87. This verse is traditionally interpreted as stating that no human eye can behold the fullness of the reward in the world-to-come (Berakhot 34b).

88. The word here translated as "purpose" is *takhlit*, which has the dual meaning of "purpose" and "conclusion," as does the English word "end." Hence the author's interpretation of *sof*, "the end, or conclusion, of the matter," as *takhlit*, "purpose." See too *Likkutei Moharan* I, 18a.

89. The scriptural text reads, "For this is *kol ha-adam*." The Hebrew word *kol* means both "all" or "whole" and "every." The plain meaning of the verse is "for this is the whole of man." R. Yaakov Yosef, however, prefers the second, implying that if piety rather than philosophical knowledge is the ultimate good, then it is attainable by "every" man. The elitist nature of the philosophical enterprise is in itself proof of its invalidity.

90. In the Middle Ages, all knowledge was divided into seven branches of wisdom. See also Prov. 9:1.

For one who enters into these sciences, heaven forbid, can stumble there. In each science there is a stumbling block in the category of Amalek, and because of this stumbling block one tends to fall, heaven forbid. Amalek was a philosopher and inquirer, and denied the foundations of the faith, as it is written, *And he* [Amalek] *feared not God* (Deut. 25:18), i.e., he conducted himself only by means of reason, but had no fear, i.e., piety, whatsoever.[91] But the tzaddik, when he enters into the seven sciences, strengthens himself and remains on his firm basis, by means of faith, as in *the righteous liveth by his faith* (Hab. 2:4). . . . Thus it is written, concerning our master Moses on the occasion of the war with Amalek, *And his hands were steady* (Exod. 17:12),[92] for by means of faith (*emunah*) he weakened Amalek, i.e., science and philosophical reasoning, as mentioned above. Thus *and his hands were faithful* (*emunah*); *his hands* refers to the practical commandments,[93] for they are the expressions of faith (*emunah*), as it is written, *All Thy commandments are emunah (faithful)* (Ps. 119:86), for by means of faith and the practical commandments, which are the opposite of the category of Amalek, he weakened Amalek. . . .

The philosophers and the heretics interpret the Torah in accordance with their sciences and heresy, [maintaining] that the whole Torah, including the practical commandments written in the Torah, is to be explained by means of form and intelligence.[94]

18. THE RESTORATION OF FAITH
Source: *R. Nahman of Bratslav, Emet va-Zeddek; Emunah, no. 40*

The restoration of fallen faith is something marvelous. It is difficult to understand rationally how someone's faith can be restored by means of a suggestion,[95] since if the person in question lacks faith, he will not

---

91. In the traditional literature Amalek is the personification of heresy and skepticism. In gematria, the numerical value of the name Amalek, 240, is equal to that of *safek* ("doubt").

92. *Emunah* usually means "faith," but in this text it means "faithful" in the sense of "steady" or "steadfast." The author interprets the text for his own purposes by referring to the more popular usage.

93. The reference to hands is interpreted as implying those observances which are carried out by the body, practically, rather than by the mind, intellectually.

94. These philosophical terms were often used by the medieval rationalists. Allegorization of the commandments as symbols of matter and form is frequently condemned in the antiphilosophical literature.

95. That is, by advice as to some technique or device by which faith can be reestablished.

have faith in the suggestion, heaven forbid. Thus, for instance, we recommended above[96] that in order to attain the proper faith in the Sages, one should make vows.[97] Elsewhere it was explained that the best advice for attaining faith in general is by studying the decisors[98] and by discussing matters of faith. Here too one must first believe in the suggestion. But how can one who is still far from faith do so?

Indeed, someone who has completely fallen away from faith, heaven forbid, such as an idol worshipper or a person who is learned in secular studies, will certainly not be helped by any of the above-mentioned suggestions. Since he does not believe at all, and is not searching for faith, he does not believe in the suggestions about how to attain faith. The same is true for faith in the Sages. However, Israel is a holy people; they are "believers, the sons of believers,"[99] and their origin is in faith. Hence, when a Jew falls away from his faith, heaven forbid, there certainly remains some "dot" of faith within him. The very fact that he feels pain at having fallen away from faith, and seeks good advice on how to restore and strengthen his faith, this in itself is an act of faith. For in the innermost parts of his heart, he truly believes in God and in the holy zaddikim. However, he does not feel this faith openly and fully, for to him faith is in the category of smallness[100] and brokenness. That is why advice will be effective for him, because as soon as he is offered a good suggestion for the enhancement of his faith, he grabs hold of it as if it were a precious stone, for a bit of faith still exists deep within him, and he truly yearns to perfect and elevate his fallen, broken faith. Therefore he can gather several good bits from the broken fragments of his faith and thereby make it whole.

This is equivalent to the category of "the tablets and the broken remnants of the tablets lay together in the ark."[101] By the very fact

---

96. In *Emet va-Tzeddek*, no. 37.

97. The hasid who is confused by the claims of competing zaddikim and wishes to accept the true zaddik and avoid the inauthentic ones, says R. Nahman, should make and immediately fulfill ascetic vows. By learning in this way to do without this-worldly pleasures, he will sensitize himself to the true zaddik, who, in contrast to the inauthentic ones, has only contempt for worldly desires and pleasures.

98. The *posekim*—the great codifiers and respondents of the Halakhah who offered practical halakhic decisions on questions of Jewish law.

99. Shabbat 97a, Numbers Rabbah 7:5, Tanhuma Shemot 23.

100. Heb. *katnut*; a hasidic term for the lack of inspiration and vitality. See below, chap. 12; chap. 5, selection 8; and chap. 8, selection 11.

101. Even the broken shards of the tablets brought down by Moses from Sinai were accorded a place of honor in the ark (Berakhot 8b). The Talmud applies this to the law that respect must be shown to an elderly scholar who has forgotten his learning.

that he sees his broken faith as corresponding to the category of the broken tablets, by this alone is it restored. His faith is thus perfected anew, in the category of the whole tablets. By virtue of the fact that a "dot" of his broken faith remained within him, he responded to the suggestions of the Sages, in whom his faith had been broken, and thereby returns to restore his faith, which act is in the category of the acceptance of the tablets the second time,[102] for faith is the foundation of the whole Torah.

19. RENEWAL AS A COROLLARY OF FAITH
Source: R. Moshe Hayyim Ephraim, Degel Maḥaneh Ephraim to Ekev, beginning

An important principle in the service of the Creator is that faith is of its essence. My grandfather the Besht emphasized that it is the basis of the entire Torah and divine service. King David said, All Your commandments are rooted in faith (Ps. 119:86),[103] because the essence of the commandments is belief in God. Only he who believes that God renews the act of Creation every day can pray every day;[104] for as he becomes a new creature each day, and the worlds are newly created, he must pray and give praise and thanks to Him who created everything, including himself. Likewise he must pray for himself, for his wife and children, for his daily sustenance, and for all appropriate things. If you do not believe with complete faith that God renews the act of Creation each day, then you will see prayer and the mitzvot as hackneyed and commonplace, and you will scorn the recitation of the same words every day.[105]

My grandfather spoke in this vein when he commented on the verse Do not cast me off in old age (Ps. 71:9). This means that prayers should not be considered old by the supplicant. Just as old age causes weakness in man's limbs, because of the diminishing powers, juices, and circulation of the blood that keeps man alive, so it is with matters of the spirit. That which is old [i.e., prayer by rote] gives man neither

---

102. The second time Moses received the tablets of the Decalogue at Sinai.
103. Lit. "All your commandments are faithful."
104. The belief in the constant renewal of Creation is mentioned in the daily Shaharit service.
105. Without faith, the prayers become rote formulas rather than living, meaningful words.

great pleasure nor vitality. This is not the case with something new [i.e., prayer in which the worshiper believes and senses immediate relevance]. This is the meaning of "Consider them—the words of the Torah—each day as new,"[106] for *they are new every morning; great is Thy faithfulness* (Lam. 3:23).[107] *They are new every morning* refers to God renewing the act of Creation daily, and because of this, *great is Thy faithfulness*.[108] Thus faith is the foundation of prayer and the commandments.

20. THE BITTER WATERS OF TORAH
Source: R. Yitzhak Yehudah Yehiel of Komarno, Netiv Mitzvotekha, p. 109

My brother and friend! In truth, how bitter are the bitter waters of Torah that pass over us![109] For in the beginning the Torah itself is bitter. The reason is so that we can distinguish between one who has a true Jewish soul and one whose soul issues from the multitude that accompanied Israel out of Egypt. For "no stranger shall approach thereto,"[110] and the Torah's initial bitterness will discourage those who are disqualified from tasting of the precious sweetness of the light of Torah that appears afterwards.

It is written in the *Berit Menuhah*[111] that a scholar who denies the Torah and becomes a heretic, heaven forbid, does so because some of the bitter waters passed over him and he drank from them and was unable to bear it, and therefore he studied and rejected.[112]

It is unnecessary to state that at the beginning, when one first undertakes to serve God and accept the yoke of Torah, one tastes of the bitterness of death. Even a completely righteous person must submit to these bitter pains every day and every time and every hour, in order to enter into the light of life and the way of the righteous.

---

106. Pesikta Zutrata, Va-Ethannan 6:6. In the biblical context, *they* refers to God's mercies; here it is understood to mean the created things.
107. In the biblical context, *Thy faithfulness* refers to God. The phrase is understood here as referring to man's faith in God. Thus there is a link between prayer, which avers that God renews the act of creation daily, and faith, which affirms that credo.
108. See n. 107.
109. Paraphrasing Exod. 15:23—25; i.e., law is given at a place of bitter waters which must be sweetened.
110. Paraphrasing Num. 17:5.
111. A kabbalistic work attributed to R. Abraham b. Isaac of Granada (14th cent.).
112. Alluding to Avot 1:11, and paraphrasing *Berit Menuhah*, chap. 1.

Therefore, accept all this bitterness upon yourself, and the Almighty in His great compassion will let you taste of the pleasantness of the world-to-come while you are still in this world. In this manner all the bitterness will be transformed into sweetness, into light for the soul.

But above all, my brother, keep silent, keep silent. Accept all this in love. Then the light of the King of all life will shine upon you.

21. TRUST BY THE MANY AND THE FEW
Source: R. Yaakov Yosef of Polennoye, Toledot Yaakov Yosef to Noah, sec. 3

There are scholars and righteous persons who are in the category of the Sabbath because they do not wish to occupy themselves with the pursuit of worldly goods. They depend on their trust in God to satisfy their material needs. However, not everyone merits such trust in God. . . . "Many have done as R. Simon bar Yohai did but have not succeeded,"[113] so I have heard, means that they did not attain the same level of trust in God as R. Simon did. "For I have seen the elite, but they are few."[114] Therefore most people must engage in worldly pursuits and trust in God's help to complete their efforts.

22. GOD'S GRACE IS STOPPED BY WEAKENING FAITH
Source: R. Elimelekh of Lizhensk, Noam Elimelekh to Be-Har, s.v. ve-khi tomru mah nokhel

When God created the world, He engendered channels overflowing with abundance (*shefa*) in order to satisfy man's needs. This flow, by its nature, cannot be interrupted. However, when man falls from his level and loses trust in God, Who is the true provider Who feeds and sustains the world with prosperity and without interruption, then man, with his unclean thoughts, produces a blemish in the upper worlds, God forfend, and weakens the power of the upper realm. At such a time the flow of grace (*shefa*) ceases. In order for it to reappear, God must command it to flow anew, as at the beginning of Creation.[115]

---

113. Prov. 16:15, Berakhot 35a; R. Simon devoted himself totally to Torah and did not seek the worldly means to support himself.

114. Sukkah 45b. R. Simon bar Yohai was the author of this statement.

115. Thus man's faith in God has cosmic consequences. R. Elimelekh expresses a similar thought in his comment to Be-shallah, s.v. *va-yomer Hashem el Mosheh.*

23. RELIANCE ON GOD IS NOT LIMITED TO THE MERITORIOUS
Source: R. Naḥman of Bratslav, Likkutei Etzot, Bitaḥon 4

The essence of true trust in God is simply to trust God and to do good, as it is written: *Trust in the Lord and do good* (Ps. 37:4). This means that you should not let material concerns distract you from Torah study and service of God. Instead, occupy yourself with Torah and divine service, and trust God to sustain you throughout the days of your life. If, however, you lack this type of trust, by means of which you can totally divest yourself of worldly cares, and you wish to engage in business or labor, at least set aside time for Torah study and pray at the appointed times. . . . In this case, too, do not worry or become confused because of your concern about making a living; but trust in God. Furthermore, trust God to provide material compensation for expenses incurred in order to do a mitzvah, make interest-free loans, and give charity. Because of your faith, God will bless you. Even those who know that their deeds are not of the highest order should not falter in their trust and say: Who am I to trust in and depend upon God, for my deeds have been evil? They too should trust in God's never-ending kindnesses and mercies, and trust God to have mercy upon them and to feed and sustain them, for *the Lord is good to all* (Ps. 145:9).

24. TRUSTING GOD DIRECTLY
Source: R. Mosheh Hayyim Ephraim, Degel Maḥaneh Ephraim to Beshallah, p. 95b, s.v. vayomru

My grandfather the Baal Shem Tov said, on *Blessed is the man that trusts (bataḥ) in the Lord, and whose security (mivtaḥ) is the Lord* (Jer. 17:7), that there is one who trusts, one who promises, and a cause which secures the fulfillment of the promise.[116] An illustration: God assures us that He will provide our needs if we follow the ways of God. We trust this assurance. The agency through which we attain trust is the means through which God will provide us with sustenance; for example, trade or some other means. However, at this point we have not yet attained true faith. True faith is attained when we realize that God

---

116. The plain meaning of the verse is a promise, "If man secures himself in God, God will become his security." The text follows the exposition given by R. Mosheh Hayyim Ephraim in the name of the Besht.

exists alone and there is none other than He; therefore no intermediary agent or cause is needed to sustain us. The reason is that God is the Source of all causes; even if we should take no initiative in obtaining a livelihood for ourselves, God, in His great kindness, will provide for us.

This is the meaning of *Blessed is the man that trusteth in the Lord and whose security is the Lord*: God should be our security, only God and no other cause to provide for us. God assures us that we need take no initiative in worldly matters which is an agent for sustenance. Everything is from God. Even if we gain the object because of an intermediary agent, we must believe fully that it is directly from God, Who wished to sustain us in this way. We must not think that the object was necessarily derived from the agent, but should trust in God.

4

Love and Fear

The love and the fear of God are the two major poles of religious experience. They are, of course, ancient concepts. At the very beginning of the Torah we are introduced to the fear of God: "And [Adam] said, I heard Thy voice in the garden, and I was afraid because I was naked, and I hid myself" (Gen. 3:10). Fear of God thus pervades the human condition and, moreover, is somehow tied in with the experience of shame, a theme which did not elude the Zohar and the many Hasidic writers who drew on the kabbalistic tradition (and which is reflected in a number of the selections presented in this chapter.) In Deuteronomy Moses constantly exhorts us to love and fear the Lord with all our heart and soul and might.

Love and fear should not, of course, be understood in the way they are used in everyday life. When applied to God and to religious experience, love and fear are qualitatively different from "I'm afraid of catching the flu" or "I love chocolate ice cream"—or, more to the point, fear of a mugger and love of a friend or a spouse. Fear, in a religious context, more often means awe or reverence rather than the apprehension of harm from some malevolent force. Love designates an outpouring of religious sentiment and religious passion unrelated either to the sentiment or the sexuality which so often characterizes human love. And yet, the very fact that these terms are used at all to describe quite different religious phenomena clearly implies that there is a core of common meaning that binds the specifically spiritual dimensions they designate and the ordinary emotions the terms represent. Normal fear must be present, to some extent and in some way, in the fear of God, and normal affection, with its pains and pleasures, must similarly apply to the rare and beautiful experience of the love of God. Indeed, a number of the hasidic thinkers whose writings on this theme are excerpted in this chapter treat this problem both directly and indirectly.

The love and fear of God have been subjected to analysis by thinkers and philosophers in all traditions of the historical religions. In Judaism, the classic account is probably that offered by Maimonides in the beginning of his halakhic opus, the *Mishneh Torah*. Maimonides is, of course, the great rationalist, and yet when he speaks of the love of God he waxes rhapsodic—a poetic "lapse" which in no way curtails his analytic prowess. Thus he writes in the second chapter of the Laws of Foundations of the Torah, after codifying the mitzvah of the love and fear of God:

> What is the way to love Him and fear Him? When a man contemplates His great and marvelous deeds and creations, and sees in them His incomparable and infinite wisdom, he immediately loves and praises and exalts and experiences an overwhelming desire to know the Great Name. As David said, "My soul thirsteth for God, the living God."
>
> And when he thinks about these very things, he immediately recoils and is afraid and knows that he is a small, dark, lowly creature standing with diminutive and insignificant intelligence before the One Who is perfect in knowledge; as David said, "When I see Thy heavens, the work of Thy fingers, what is man that Thou takest cognizance of him?"
>
> According to this do I explain great principles of the work of the Master of the Worlds that they might enable an intelligent person to love the Name, as the sages taught concerning love, that "as a result [of contemplating Nature] you will come to acknowledge Him Who created the world by His word."

This is not the place to undertake an exegesis of Maimonides' statements on the themes of love and fear of God, but it is worth noting a number of interesting items: both love and fear issue from contemplation of the same natural phenomena; one is a reaction of reaching out and wishing to know more, the other a reaction of recoil and retreat and worthlessness; and both reactions are immediate and instantaneous—he "immediately" loves and fears God. We shall meet some of these same themes in the writings of the hasidic masters whom we shall cite.[1]

With the emergence of Hasidism, in the late eighteenth century, as a movement which valued ecstasy over intellect, inwardness over outwardness, and spirituality over external behavior, it was inevitable that love and fear of God would play a new and more prominent role, especially for those many pious Jews who had become alienated from the scholarly classes. Indeed, that was so, and while it would be erroneous, and even silly, to say that these elemental religious emotions were dormant until the rise of Hasidism, it is true that the movement talked and wrote about it more often and more openly and that it refined the interpretations of these polar religious experiences in accordance with its ideological needs.

The contemporary reader who expects what he or she is probably conditioned to expect—that, as a romantic movement seeking to engage the masses and to emphasize heart over mind, Hasidism gave greater weight to love than to fear—will be disappointed. Hasidism was a highly sensitive and spiritually sophisticated movement, and despite the caricatures of it by its critics, did not offer the kind of naive bromides that so many of us moderns take for granted, viz., that love is "good" and fear is "bad." Most hasidic masters may have written poorly or not at all, they may have been unsystematic and even disorganized in their thoughts, and they may have spoken to their followers in tales and parables, but that by no means indicates that they were spiritual or even intellectual simpletons. And the calculus of love and fear as the principal religious experiences of Judaism, as they taught it, bears no resemblance to the moral and spiritual ingenuousness often attributed to them.

In perusing or studying this chapter, the reader will notice both the basic continuity of Hasidism with traditional Judaism in treating of these major themes and, as well, the innovative nuances, emphases, and analyses that, together, gave impetus and coherence to the new movement. Religious experience is, for the hasidic thinker, of special moment because he is both a highly subjective participant and an objective analyst. When the hasidic masters write, either descriptive-

---

1. It is instructive to note in passing the similarities between Maimonides' analysis of love and fear and those of the early-twentieth-century theologian Rudolf Otto, who, like Maimonides seven hundred years earlier, described the religious experiences of fascination and terror in much the same way that Maimonides analyzed love and fear. See his *The Idea of the Holy*, translated by John N. Harvey, New York, 1923. For more on this theme, see my *The Shema*.

ly or normatively, of love and fear, we sense that we have before us not a disembodied phenomenological or psychology-of-religion analysis by a scholar of comparative religion (necessary as such detachment may be for academic purposes), but nothing less than a thinly disguised form of spiritual autobiography.

Note, in reviewing these selections, that the hasidic masters dealt with such problems as authentic and spurious forms of love and fear of God; the relation of such religious experience to religious behavior, i.e., the mitzvot; how love and fear relate to the sefirot, which is another way of asking how the inner life of man reflects the inner life of God; how religious experience relates to the intellectual aspects of Judaism; love and fear and the reaction to Nature (these last two continue the discussion in the citation above from Maimonides); are these exquisite experiences the result of conscious striving or are they gifts of divine grace; how do they relate to each other, and which— and which form—is superior; how, as emotions, can they be commanded in the Torah; what do they share, as homonyms, with the ordinary everyday varieties of love and fear; the relation of love of God to other loves; the love of God amidst a plethora of material pleasures; and so on.

1. THE SOURCE OF LOVE AND FEAR
Source: R. Shneur Zalman of Liady, Tanya, Likkutei Amarim, chap. 3

The intellect, which is [located] in the intellectual soul and which comprehends everything, is called "Wisdom" (Hokhmah), "the power of everything."[2] "Understanding" (Binah) is the actualizing of this potential through intellectual reflection upon a certain concept in order to understand it thoroughly and in depth.[3] These two [Wisdom and Understanding] are the "father" and "mother" from which love and fear of God are born. Fear of God is born of the intellect's deep reflection upon God's greatness: how He fills all worlds and encompasses all worlds and the fact that everything is as naught before Him.[4] Through this "exalted fear" (*yirat ha-romemut*)[5] fear is awakened

---

2. A word-play on *hokhmah* ("wisdom"), breaking it up into *ko'ah* ("the potential of") and *mah* ("what is"). See Zohar III, 28a and 34a.

3. Zohar III, 225a. Binah ("Understanding") is the actualization of the potential (Hokhmah, or "Wisdom").

4. See Isa. 40:17 and Zohar I, 111b.

5. The sense of awe that results from the contemplation of God's grandeur.

in man's mind and thought.[6] Man fears and is humbled by God's infinite greatness.

This fear will in turn inflame man's heart with "strong love," as with flashes of fire, passionately, yearningly, and longing for the greatness of the blessed Ein-Sof. This is the "yearning of the soul," as it is written: *My soul yearneth, yea, even pineth, for the courts of the Lord* (Ps. 84:3); *My soul thirsteth for God* (ibid. 63:2). This "thirst" derives from the element of fire which is in the divine soul, as the natural philosophers have stated.[7] It is similarly stated in *Etz Ḥayyim* [by R. Hayyim Vital] that the element of fire is in the heart, and the source of water and moisture is the mind; so is it stated in *Etz Ḥayyim*, gate 50, that [water] is associated with Wisdom (Hokhmah), which is therefore called "the water of the divine soul."[8] The rest of the attributes (*middot*) are all derived from love and fear and their derivations. . . .

Da'at (Knowledge) [the third sefirah], is derived from *And Adam knew (yada) Eve* (Gen. 4:1) and implies attachment and union.[9] One binds his intellect, through very strong and mighty bonds, with the greatness of the Ein-Sof. Otherwise, not true fear and love result, but rather false imaginations.[10] Hence, knowledge is the [source of] the existence and sustenance of the moral attributes and [the sefirah of Tiferet] includes Hesed [the sefirah of Love] and Gevurah, which is to say love and its derivatives, and fear and its derivatives.[11]

---

6. This is R. Shneur Zalman's basic thesis. The seven moral attributes (*middot*) can only be attained through the three primary intellectual virtues. Fear and love, which correspond to the left and right sides of the kabbalistic description of God (and hence of man's divine soul), are derivatives of knowledge. Thus, the intellectual attributes are the foundations from which fear and love (the affective attributes) spring. There is neither love nor fear without understanding. Though this idea seems out of consonance with the general emotionalism of Hasidism, it is based on R. Shneur Zalman's understanding of kabbalistic theosophy. This doctrine underscores the fact that Habad Hasidism, the school of R. Shneur Zalman and his successor Lubavitch rebbes, is less radical than other hasidic groups in its emphasis on the moral attributes or elements in religious life.

7. I.e, one of the four elements, earth, air, fire and water. See *Tanya*, chap. 1.

8. Water descends from high places to low, and thus symbolizes Wisdom (Hokhmah), the highest of the ten sefirot, and also Love (Hesed), the first of the attributes (*middot*), for the divine grace (*shefa*) descends from them to the lower sefirot.

9. As carnal "knowledge" implies the joining together of two separate bodies, so does intellectual knowledge connote the attachment of cognizer and cognized object.

10. Fear and love not born of intellectual comprehension are not fear and love at all, but poor imitations.

11. Hesed is associated with the "right side" of the affective elements, and hence with love, while Gevurah is associated with the "left side," and hence fear.

2. THE POSITIVE AND NEGATIVE PRECEPTS REPRESENT LOVE AND FEAR
Source: R. Shneur Zalman of Liady, Tanya, Likkutei Amarim, chap. 4

Love is the root of the 248 positive precepts. They derive from it, and without it they have no true existence, for he who observes them sincerely is the one who loves God and wants to cleave to Him truly. It is impossible to cling to Him without the observance of the 248 positive precepts, which are, so to speak, the 248 limbs of the King.[12] . . .

Fear is the root of the 365 negative precepts. [This is a manifestation of] the fear one has in rebelling against the King of Kings, the Holy One.[13] [A more superior type of fear] is the inward type in which man is ashamed to disobey God and to do evil in His eyes, because of His greatness, namely, *any abomination which God hates* (Deut. 12:31), [for these] are the *kelipot* and the *sitra aḥara*, whose source is man. Their manifestation is in the 365 negative precepts.[14]

3. THE MITZVOT AS SOURCES OF LOVE AND FEAR
Source: R. Shneur Zalman of Liady, Tanya, Likkutei Amarim, chap. 42

The essence of fear of a human king is of his inner self and vitality and not fear of his physical self,[15] since one does not fear him when he is

12. The explanation of this idea is found in *Likkutei Amarim*, chap. 23. Just as the physical limbs are the outer garment to the soul, so the commandments are the outer garment to the internal Divine Will. Thus the 248 precepts are the "limbs" of God.

13. The idea that the positive mitzvot represent love of God and the negative mitzvot fear of Him was earlier developed by Nahmanides to Exod. 20:8.

14. It is interesting to note that R. Shneur Zalman finds it impossible to cling to God without the 248 positive precepts. That is, only through the Torah's norms can one achieve *devekut*. This, of course, is in full accord with the traditional Jewish approach emphasizing Halakhah. See, for example, Sifrei to Deut. 6:6 (quoted in Rashi). This comment emphasizes the educational aspect of the mitzvot, an aspect which I believe would be shared by the author. But note that R. Eliahu Mizrahi (supercommentary to Rashi) opposes this position to that of Maimonides, which emphasizes the study of nature as a means to love and fear. Not all hasidic thinkers agree on this point. Some felt that one can attain *devekut* without the mitzvot; in fact this approach is more common than the one utilizing mitzvot. See selections chap. 5 (Devekut), selections 9—11 and 16, among others.

15. In modern terms, one fears the "mind" of the human being, which is the potential of power, rather than the physical limbs, which can do nothing if not directed to do so by the mind.

asleep.[16] [Likewise is it with the fear of God.] God's internal essence and vitality are unknown to the physical senses but are known intellectually. By physical perception of physical phenomena (lit. "body and garments") one *knows* that God's vitality is enveloped within them. Precisely in this way should one fear God by physically perceiving the heaven, the earth, and all their hosts in which is enveloped the light of the Ein-Sof in order to animate them.

4. UNINDUCED LOVE AND FEAR
Source: R. Pinhas of Koretz, Likkutim Yekarim, p. 3a

There is one who prays in sadness because of his state of melancholy (lit. "black bile") and imagines that he prays with great fear. Likewise, there is one who imagines that he prays with great love and this is because of his state of euphoria (lit. "red bile"). However, when one is in a state of [true] love of God, and shame thereby descends upon him and he wants to praise God and triumph over the evil impulse for His sake, that is good. For man is only called a servant of God through fear and love.

He must see to it that fear should descend upon him [from Above] and not inspire it in himself.[17] True fear occurs when shuddering and trembling descend upon him such that because of the fear one does not know where he is, his thoughts have become purified, and his tears roll down of their own accord. But when this is not the case, then even if it appears that one loves God, that certainly is not so. For this is the *gate to the Lord* (Ps. 118:20): Fear is the gate to love, and if one does not enter the gate, which is fear, how can he attain love? When one is in the above state [i.e., self-generated melancholy or euphoria], he is not even a "servant," and is certainly not capable of having fear descend upon him. This is not the proper service for a Jew; it is simply a service by rote. One [who is in this state] imagines that he actually serves God in joy, but it is nothing more than foolish joy. Therefore, let him return to God with all his heart and all his soul.[18]

---

16. When one sleeps he has no power to direct action outside of himself. Thus, in Jewish sources, one who is sleeping is likened to a corpse in that both are considered to have lost their souls, whose function is to animate the body.
17. That is, man's efforts should be directed toward making himself worthy of the experience of religious fear, a divine gift, rather than creating the experience for himself.
18. R. Pinhas of Koretz distinguishes here between the spiritual and the emotional. There is a difference between states of authentic religious ecstasy and merely psych-

5. FEAR A BURDEN, LOVE A GIFT
Source: R. Zevi Elimelekh of Dinov, Benei Yisaskhar, Nisan, ma'amar 3, no. 9

The soul constantly longs to serve its Creator out of love, as do the angels (*mighty in strength that fulfill His word, hearkening unto the voice of His word* [Ps. 103:20]). In serving God, the angels long for a reward—that they should be granted an additional way to serve God, for they long for divine service, constantly. . . .

  Service as burden (Num. 4:47)[19] can be explained as service out of fear [or: dread] [of God]. Man does not receive pleasure from this toil; rather, he carries the yoke of service as a burden because of the dread [of God]. *Service as gift* (Num. 18:6)[20] is service out of love. Man receives pleasure from toiling in this type of service. [This type of service] is truly a gift from God, as it is written: "You shall see your world in your lifetime"[21]—you shall receive the pleasures of Eden [i.e., the eternal world] in this world [i.e., in your lifetime].[22]

---

logical conditions which are sham. The latter were present in the person prior to his immersion in prayer and religious devotion, and his ecstatic worship is therefore nothing more than an outlet for his original affective energies. In order for the religious experience to be considered genuine, it must be theocentric, not anthropocentric; it must be selfless and not merely a projection of his prior inner feeling. R. Pinhas is emphatic about this: the fear and the love are a gift from God, the object of fear and love, and cannot be acquired *directly* through human effort.

19. The Bible uses this term to denote the service rendered by those Levites who bore the parts of the Sanctuary during the journeys in the wilderness (see Num. 4:47). The author, of course, uses the term with a wholly different meaning.

20. This too is based on the biblical description of the Levites as "given" to God. The author again uses the term in an entirely different sense.

21. Berakhot 17a.

22. The meaning of "gift" in "service as gift" is a double one. On the one hand, man gives of himself in serving God totally and unconditionally; what he wants is God, not His reward. On the other hand, R. Zevi Elimelekh was apparently aware of the almost insurmountable psychological difficulty in offering oneself totally without any thought of self-interest. Therefore this type of service is attained only with divine aid as a gift. No amount of human effort by itself suffices to attain this idea. It *can* be attained, but only through God's grace. The topic of the ideal form of divine service is, of course, a major theme in hasidic theology, especially because purity of motive is an essential concept in the psychology of the divine servant.

6. FEAR AND THE DIVINE WILL
Source: R. Menahem Mendel of Vitebsk, Peri ha-Aretz to Noah

Fear regarding a mitzvah may occur when one considers that the act of the mitzvah is a divine matter. When one begins to perform the mitzvah by means of his physical limbs, and the paraphernalia of the mitzvah which are also material [e.g., tefillin, tzitzit], one's spirit is depressed and agitated in that he is reducing divinity to the level of the physical. Is, then, God corporeal, heaven forbid? Even though man experiences this anxiety from time to time, he is strengthened in his faith in God [through performance of the mitzvah]. This is so because the mitzvah binds [him to God], for the words of the living God [issue] from the Supernal Will that spoke them, and His will is effected down to the very end of the end [of the chain] of spiritual descent, the lowest level.[23] He understands that the Shekhinah is enveloped in the mitzvah for, as is known, every mitzvah concerns the Shekhinah, and the Shekhinah is invested in physical objects by virtue of the mitzvah in which his limbs are involved. They are bound together through the descent of the attributes [i.e., the lower seven attributes of the ten sefirot] and the understanding [the upper three, or "intellectual," sefirot] from their sources in the Ein-Sof. . . .

How does this binding take place? The word *mitzvah* [which means "commandment"] also implies binding.[24] This binding occurs by means of intellect and the understanding which one infuses into the mitzvah because of the fear and trembling with which one is gripped lest he reduce divinity to mere physicality. This fear, however, does not cause him to lose his faith, for he draws love and joy—which are derived from the attributes and the contemplation of God's greatness and His great mercies—from the blessed effluence (*shefa*) of the Ein-Sof and the Supernal Will, as the Shekhinah is enclothed in the lowliest of existence [i.e., the physical realm] to bind and unite it with Himself, so that they become one in complete *devekut*.

However, this can only be achieved after [experiencing] the preliminary fear. This is so because the [pleasurable] traits and the joy which one brings upon oneself, in the belief that He wills it so, are not true [or: authentic] ones, and it is only in his imagination that they can be compared [to genuine joy, etc.], unless fear of God precedes

---

23. Man is thus connected to God by means of the mitzvah.
24. The Hebrew root *tz-v-h* means "command," and in Aramaic, *tz-v-t* means "bind" or "be together."

them, thereby strengthening his faith. Thereafter, the love or joy or any other such quality which derived from [this] faith, is true [authentic], for this is what constitutes the Holy Spirit. For this reason it is mentioned several times in the Zohar and also the Talmud (Shabbat 31b) that fear must precede [the performance of a mitzvah]; if it does not, [the act] is meaningless, and not [of] the Holy Spirit.[25]

7. PERFECT FEAR RESULTS IN LOVE
Source: *Besht, Keter Shem Tov, pt. II, secs. 390—391*

The purpose of everything is fear [of God], for if there is no fear, wisdom is totally without importance.[26] The purpose of wisdom is fear. Even though one should serve God in love *and* in fear, one need only attain fear, and then the love of God will rest upon him of itself, for "it is in the nature of the man to pursue the woman."[27]

Man can verify for himself whether he has attained the perfect degree of fear of God. Let us take an illustration. One of the king's officers stands before the king. The object of the officer's great lust is passed in front of him. Had he not been standing in the presence of the king, the officer would surely want to fulfill this lust. Nevertheless, because he stands in the presence of the king, the lust for the object departs from him, and that is because the fear of being in the king's presence is so overpowering, that he no longer sees himself within the context of his traits [i.e., his likes and dislikes]. They have been nullified and are no longer in existence in the presence[28] of the fear of the king.[29]

Apropos of this, our rabbis said: "To what is a righteous man likened in the presence of God? To a candle in the presence of a

---

25. Zohar, introduction 11.
26. The author quotes as his source Avot 3:21, "If there is no fear, there is no wisdom."
27. Kiddushin 2b. Love is symbolized by "man," and fear by "woman." Man indicates the bestowing of divine abundance, and women its passive receipt. The association of fear with the female is explained in *Zidkat ha-Zaddik*, sec. 212: Fear is one's state upon recognition of a lack (i.e., of the grace [*shefa*] it is yet to receive). Therefore man's first effort following the recognition of a void must be directed toward fear, not love; the latter will then surely follow the former.
28. The personal desires of the officer become naught when he is in the mental state of awe for the king.
29. For a strikingly similar thought on the power of fear to destroy lust, see R. Joseph Dov Soloveichik, *Bet Halevi* (Warsaw, 1894), Parashat Yitro, s.v. *lo tahmod*. It is a psychological truth which can be confirmed by anyone who has had such an experience.

torch."[30] As a candle lit in the daytime offers no benefit,[31] and has no effect, so the desires of the righteous ones are capable of no action, because these desires are nullified out of existence because of the fear of God.[32]

8. LOVE LEADS TO FEAR
Source: R. Elimelekh of Lizhensk, Noam Elimelekh, Vayigash, s.v. vayigash

Even according to Thy fear so is Thy wrath (Ps. 90:11). Now, the term *fear* is irrelevant to God.[33] However, the term may be applied to Him in the sense that He loves man so much that He fears lest man sin (and therefore deny Him the opportunity to do good), for it is God's wont to do good to man.

Thus, God's fear is a "fear out of love," and the punishment that He metes out to man is also out of love, for He thereby ensures that it will be good for him in the end. By purifying man in this world through suffering, man receives his reward in the next world. This is the meaning of the verse *even according to Thy fear so is Thy wrath:* Just as God's fear issues from love of man,[34] so His wrath—the punishment he metes out to man—issues from His love of man. . . .

A person must cleave to the divine attributes. Hence, just as God fears out of His love [of man], so must man fear God out of love of God. He must be seized with fear lest he sin and thereby remove him-

---

30. Pesahim 8a.
31. One's sight in the daytime is unaffected by the presence of a candle. Cf. Shabbat 63a, "A candle in daylight is a useless thing."
32. The Sages advise the following: "Make His will as your will . . . [and] nullify your will in favor of His will" (Avot 2:4). This is a prescriptive statement that asks man to act or to refrain from acting in accordance with the divine will with as much enthusiasm as one fulfills the wishes of his heart. The Baal Shem Tov here describes the righteous man not as one who voluntarily assumes the divine will as his own, but rather as one who is incapable of fulfilling his own personal desires, simply because they no longer exist for him. The awe of God is so overwhelming that man loses all personal desires and can think of nothing other than fulfilling the divine will. Entertainment of any conflicting desires is a psychological impossibility based upon the righteous man's mental state—the simple and yet all-encompassing fear of God.
33. The author's interpretation of the verse is rather subtle. "According to Thy fear" is taken by the commentators to mean the fear owed to God by man. However, on a purely literal basis, one can conceivably translate the verse as "according to Thy fear," i.e., God's experience of fear. This is the meaning the author asserts in order to develop his major idea. See also selection 17 below.
34. That is, fear that man, through sin, will forfeit his share in the next world.

self from God's love. For the principle is this: Fear applies only to what the eyes see. What one does not see, he does not fear. But love is a matter of the heart, and the heart can imagine even that which is invisible. Now, the Creator is the One Who "sees but is not seen." A person must therefore imagine, in his heart, God's awesomeness and wonders and the greatness of His kingdom, and thus achieve "great love" for the Creator in his heart. Because thought itself is infinite, man can, by means of thought, attain great ideas without end.

Hence, man must bind himself [to God] with bonds of love, and from this love he will learn to fear sin, lest he thereby lose his love.[35]

9. THE RELATIONSHIP OF LOVE AND FEAR
Source: R. Elimelekh of Lizhensk, Noam Elimelekh to Vayehi, s.v. yehudah

In the blessing "With a great love hast Thou loved us,"[36] we say, "and unify our heart to love and fear Thy Name." This is apparently in contradiction to the principle that fear leads to love.

However, both [statements] are correct, for there are two kinds of fear.[37] There is a "lower fear," which is called "Lower Mother," and this is what leads to [that form of] love which is termed "brother," for it is not yet a perfect love.[38] This [inferior] category of love leads to perfect love, which is called "Father." This [superior] category of love leads to "higher fear," known as "[Higher] Mother."[39] Thus, it is writ-

---

35. R. Elimelekh's opinion here is quite clear: Fear is superior to love, for which reason love precedes fear. See, however, the next selection, where this is placed in a more comprehensive framework after analysis of both fear and love. From that discourse it will be seen that in this passage the author intends what he elsewhere calls "higher fear"; it is only this form of fear that may be attributed to God.
36. This is the blessing immediately preceding the Shema during the morning service.
37. These are "lower fear" and "higher fear." The former, for R. Elimelekh, is probably identical to fear of punishment, while the latter is synonymous with "fear [which is] exaltation." The two kinds of love are described by the author elsewhere in the same work (Noah, s.v. va-yoled noah): The lower form is imperfect in that it is tainted with self-interest because it coexists with profane "loves," such as love of money and love of women. Perfect love is one which not only is totally selfless, but in which these external, profane loves have been "elevated" or sublimated to the love of God.
38. The symbol "brother" is chosen by R. Elimelekh for the sake of his hasidic-kabbalistic exegesis of another verse, elsewhere in this discourse. Its signification is, simply, the lower or imperfect form of love of God.
39. The terms used by R. Elimelekh are taken from the classical Kabbalah, but it is difficult to tell to which sefirot he assigns each of these varieties of love and fear. See Y. Tishby, Mishnat ha-Zohar II (Mosad Bialik, 1961), pp. 293 ff. In the Zohar, "Lower Mother" refers to Malkhut ("Kingdom") and "Higher Mother" to Binah

ten, *Ye shall fear every man his mother and his father* (Lev. 19:3). This refers to the "lower fear," [for which reason] "mother" precedes "father." But with regard to honor,[40] which is love, "father" precedes "mother."[41]

10. LOVE AND FEAR
Source: R. Zevi Elimelekh of Dinov, *Benei Yisaskhar, Hodesh Nisan*, 4:2, p. 41c

It is well known that *depart from evil* (Ps. 34:15) is achieved by means of fear [of God], and *do good* (ibid.) by means of love, as our rabbis taught. Each of these is double, i.e., there are two levels of fear and two levels of love, as we know from the Holy Zohar and the Tikkunim.[42]

The disciples of the Besht wrote that man's major efforts must be directed toward attaining fear; love of God he will achieve as a result of divine assistance. The reason for this is that fear is considered a feminine category, and love is masculine,[43] and "it is in the nature of the man to pursue the woman, and not the nature of the woman to pursue the man."[44]

Maimonides writes: "It is a commandment to love and to fear the great, powerful, and awesome God."[45] Note that he places love before

---

("Understanding"). The term "Father" (Abba), however, is usually reserved for Hokhmah ("Wisdom"). So too in Lurianic Kabbalah, Hokhmah ("Wisdom") is the *partzuf* ("physiognomy") of Abba, and Binah that of Imma ("Mother"). In both systems Father is considered superior to Mother, in that Hokhmah precedes Binah in the emanation of the sefirot. Yet for R. Elimelekh, Father is clearly on a lower level than "Higher Mother." It is thus unclear how R. Elimelekh interprets the kabbalistic symbols which he uses in his analysis of love and fear.

40. "Honor" is taken by the author to be synonymous with love—not an untenable thesis. See Gerald Blidstein, *Honor Thy Father and Thy Mother*, New York, 1976, p. xii.

41. "Honor thy father and thy mother" (Exod. 20:12). Thus, love leads to "higher fear." The schema of R. Elimelekh is thus: Lower fear (Lower Mother) leads to imperfect love (Brother), which leads to perfect love (Father), which leads to higher fear (Higher Mother).

42. Zohar I, 11b, 12a; *Tikkunei Zohar*, tikkun 30, 33.

43. "Masculine" is the symbol of the active, "feminine" of the passive. See above, selection 7.

44. Kiddushin 2b. Thus, man must "pursue" fear, in the sense of deliberate exertion to attain this spiritual quality, whereas he must undertake no such efforts to attain love. The latter will pursue him, in that it comes to man of itself, as a gift from heaven.

45. Hilkhot Yesodei ha-Torah 2:1. The actual reading of the text of Maimonides is "the awesome and revered (*nikhbad*) God," but the change does not affect the point the author is making.

fear. This is so because, even though fear comes first, it is love which is the purpose of all; it is the desideratum, as expressed in *and do good*.

11. INWARD FEAR THE REMEDY FOR EXTERNAL FEAR
Source: R. Yaakov Yosef of Polennoye, Tzafnat Pa'ane'aḥ p. 49c—d

The commandment of fear refers to inward fear; through this, external fear is destroyed.

I heard the explanation of the philosopher's question from my teacher, the Baal Shem Tov: Since God is called awesome, why does the Torah need to command man to fear Him? Surely [the fear] will come of itself, as the fear of a human king is instilled in the subject of itself without a command.

The Baal Shem Tov explained: Fear refers to the lack of something: honor, wealth, life, etc. After the lack ceases to exist, there is no more fear. If one dies, he no longer fears the lack of life. The same is true of wealth. This type of fear is the external fear characteristic of all creatures. The mouse fears the cat; the cat fears the dog; the dog fears the wolf; and one man fears his neighbor.

Inward fear is a higher type of fear. This is [real] fear of the Creator.[46] However, even external fear which overcomes man is meant to arouse him to internal fear. This is because of divine grace. God's right hand is outstretched to man, and it bids man to bestir himself to [true] fear of God, through this [external fear].

Here, then, the philosopher's question about the need for a commandment to fear God, disappears. The meaning of *Israel, what does the Lord your God require of you except to fear God?* (Deut. 10:12) is as follows: Since the attribute of fear is found in all creatures, it is fitting for man to have the additional quality of arousing himself to internal fear *through* external fear, inasmuch as man knows that God's hand is outstretched to urge man to this.

If man understands that God's love is manifested in that He grants man external fear in order to bestir him to internal fear, then the fear is transformed into love, because man lovingly accepts external fear and thereby loses this type of fear. However, if man consciously intends to lose his external fear by accepting it lovingly, it is of no

---

46. "Fear of the Creator" is an expression which implies the fear of God—that is, awe of God as creator, and not fear of punishment or the like. The feeling of "creatureliness" leads to the worship of the Creator without the intrusion of elements which engender mundane fears of one kind or another.

avail. This is why the Torah warned *You shall love the Lord your God with all your heart* (Deut. 6:6), that man be whole-hearted when external fear occurs, *with all your soul and all your might* (ibid.), that he may have the right motivation.[47]

12. TWO TYPES OF LOWER FEAR
Source: R. Shneur Zalman of Liady, Tanya, Likkutei Amarim, chap. 43

"If there is no fear, there is no wisdom"[48] refers to the lower type of fear which motivates man to observe the divine commandments, both positive and negative. There is a lesser type [of the low type of fear]—one of "smallness"—and a superior type—one of "greatness."[49]

When one attains fear through contemplation of the greatness of God Who fills all of the worlds, this fear is the gateway to observance of the Torah and the commandments, but nevertheless it is external and inferior because it issues from [a contemplation of] the worlds, which are but a disguise of the Holy One, the King.

The higher type of fear is a self-effacing awe of God and internal reverence which is drawn from the divinity that inheres in the worlds. Our Sages said about this type of fear, "If there is no wisdom, there is no fear."[50]

13. TWO TYPES OF FEAR
Source: R. Shneur Zalman of Liady, Tanya, Likkutei Amarim, chap. 41

Fear is the source of *forsake evil* (Ps. 34:15), and love is the source of *do good* (ibid.) Yet it is inadequate to simply stimulate the attribute of love to *do good*. Before that one must at least arouse the natural fear, concealed in the heart of every Jew, not to rebel against the King of Kings, the Holy One, blessed be He. One's thought should concentrate upon the greatness of the Ein-Sof and upon His sovereignty. One should reflect profoundly upon this, depending upon one's men-

---

47. That is, the idea of external fear arousing one's preexistent internal fear, thus turning the (external) fear into love, must be embraced sincerely and practiced without ulterior motive in order to be effective. It does not work if it is used merely as a psychological ploy to ward off one's stressful fears or anxieties. The Baal Shem Tov is affirming a *spiritual* insight, not a therapeutic pyschological technique.
48. Avot 3:17.
49. Religious experience based upon the divinity immanent within nature is superior to that which issues from the contemplation of nature itself.
50. For a definition of these terms, see Selection 1.

tal powers and the time available to him, prior to studying Torah or fulfilling a mitzvah. Then, even if one is not seized by fear emotionally, nevertheless this service is considered a "perfect service" as the service of the kind a servant renders his master and king—insofar as he accepts upon himself the divine sovereignty, and experiences the fear of God intellectually and volitionally. This acceptance [of the fear of God] is undoubtedly genuine, since it is the nature of the souls of Israel not to rebel against the Holy King. However, one who studies Torah or performs a mitzvah simply through love in order to cling to God through Torah and mitzvot, does not come under the category of the service which a servant performs.[51]

Even he who, in his mind, does not feel fear or shame because of the low state of his own soul, originating in the lower degrees of the ten sefirot of Asiyah, but does intend to *serve* the King through his service, is considered as one who performs a complete service. This is because "fear" and "service" are accounted as two separate mitzvot of the 613, and it is possible to fulfill the one without the other.[52]

Moreover, one indeed observes the mitzvah of fear by intellectually experiencing fear of God, for at that moment his fear of God is no less than his fear of a human being.[53] This fear, however, is of the lower type, the fear of sin which precedes wisdom. The higher type is a humble feeling of awe [in the presence of God], etc. However, without fear at all, love alone will not do, much as a bird cannot fly with but one wing.

14. FEAR OF PUNISHMENT AN INITIAL STEP
Source: R. Menahem Mendel of Vitebsk, Peri ha-Aretz to Beshallah

The cry of the Children of Israel to God [when they were in Egypt] was because of the fear of physical destruction. This is fear of punishment, which is the lowest and least valuable type of fear. There are many types of fear, as the Zohar states, the highest of which is self-effacing awe [in the presence] of the Source and Root of all the worlds, so that the might and glory of God be made manifest to all even in this lowly world.[54]

---

51. I.e., it is not "perfect service."
52. In this case, one observes the precept of serving God but not fear of God.
53. Cf. Berakhot 28b.
54. Zohar, introduction, 11b.

Nevertheless, the first step and the beginning of one's [spiritual] development is fear of punishment or physical destruction, for then man cries out to God, in which case, in any event, he believes in Him [and knows] that his trouble comes from Him, and he believes that God has power to save him and hear his cry.

15. EXTERNAL FEAR: A PREPARATORY STATE TO HEAVENLY FEAR
Source: R. Menahem Nahum of Chernobyl, Me'or Einayim to Yitro, s.v. ve-da

On the verse *God hath so made it that men should fear before Him* (Eccles. 3:14), our rabbis said, "[Even] the thunder was created solely to straighten out the crookedness of the heart."[55] This was explained in the name of the Baal Shem Tov: God desires that all of Israel fear Him. He who has sense fears God because He is the Master, Sovereign, Source, and Root of all the worlds;[56] were God to withdraw His animating Presence even momentarily, all the worlds would vanish. Therefore man fears God to the extent that all his limbs tremble in fear of God and His majestic splendor[57] (unlike those fools who consider true fear as simply depression, and all that is necessary [for a pious person] is but a bit of fear. That is nonsense and ought not to be mentioned. For in truth it is necessary that one be overwhelmed by great fear and terror so that all his limbs tremble, but let us return to our subject.) This applies to those who have sense.

He, however, who is not sensible enough to fear God, God, nevertheless, desires his fear and therefore overawes him with something which will make him tremble and be frightened, such as the sound of thunder, which [even] his diminished sensibility can perceive as fearsome. God's intention is that man should proceed from this inferior type of fear to the superior type by reasoning as follows: Since thunder is but one of the manifestations of God's might [and induces fear], surely one should fear God Himself!

The same applies to other outward forms of fear. Fear of authority and fear of losing one's children, for instance, are instilled in man in order that he should proceed from these to the superior type of fear of

---

55. Berakhot 59a. The heart is treated here metaphorically; in the Bible it often connotes something equivalent to our mind.
56. Zohar, introduction, 11b, states that real fear is fear of God as Ruler of the universe.
57. Following Ps. 35:10.

God, which is attained when one fears God and nothing else. For this superior type of fear is that true fear of divinity itself which, in constricted form, inheres in these [worldly] matters which arouse fear in man because of his limited intelligence.

16. FEAR OF EVIL ITSELF
Source: R. Menahem Mendel of Vitebsk, Peri ha-Aretz to Nitzavim

There are various types of fear, the lowest of which is fear of punishment, which is [universal, in that it is] felt at all places and all times, even among the nations of the world; as it is written, *He that feared the word of the Lord among the servants of Pharaoh evacuated his servants and his cattle into the houses* (Exod. 9:20). Thus, even the Egyptians knew fear of punishment. Not for naught did God create fear of punishment, for the world is in need of it. The process of repentance begins with it, for man, upon violating God's command, becomes fleshly [i.e., gross, unspiritual] and is unable to attain the fear of exaltation (*yirat ha-romemut*)[58] because his heart lacks this power. Therefore, one regrets [the sin] and begins [the process of repentance through fear of punishment] and concludes likewise.

We already stated that repentance can only begin with physical fear—as material as ourselves at the time we committed the sin—such as the fear of death and [all kinds of suffering] upon which we need not elaborate. One also concludes with it,[59] but in a somewhat different manner, and that is the fear of evil, which is the cause of death and punishments. Since [sin consists of] adding power to the destructive force of evil, repentance must begin with a sense of horror at his clinging to evil, submitting to it such that he is forced to offend God. . . . Thus did the sages say: "The Evil Impulse judges the wicked,"[60] meaning that [the wicked] are forced to obey the will [of the Evil Impulse].

So has it been said that there is nothing in the world which is not a horse to its rider who rules and directs it, [for everything is caused by] that which animates and moves it, by deed, or speech or thought. [Similarly] the most subtle of thoughts that the mind is capable of perceiving must have something beyond it which illuminates it and is immanent in it. That [something] is "the good in the way of life"—

---

58. A state of awe, of exaltation or inspiration.
59. That is, with a form of fear located in the physical realm.
60. Berakhot 61b.

for the goal of joy and understanding is called "life," and that which inheres in it and animates it is called "good."

The good is that which is hidden [within life] as it is said, *How great is the good which You have hidden for those who fear You* (Ps. 31:20). It is also written, *God saw the light that it was good and He separated the light from the darkness* (Gen. 1:4), upon which the rabbis commented: "He hid it away for the righteous for the future."[61] Thus *See, I place before you today life,* true understanding, *and good* (Deut. 30:15), the inner light which animates it.

But *God also has set the one over against the other* (Eccles. 7:14).[62] There is death, which is curses and punishments, and evil, which is the cause of these punishments. With the absence of spiritual evil in messianic times, death will be eternally destroyed, for evil is the cause of destruction.

Evil is lust and resistance to God, even if only in improper word or thought, as it is written: *Beware of any evil thing* (Deut. 23:10), which the Sages interpreted as "Beware of any evil speech,"[63] for there is evil which reigns over speech and thought, which directs the sinner and rules him, making the sin attractive in his eyes. Without evil, all lusts and opposition to Torah would vanish and turn to naught; and why should man pursue that which is naught? Rather, it is the clinging of evil to him and what is in him, [that causes man's woes].

The greatness of one who fears sin lies in that he fears the sin itself, the attachment to evil, which is greater than the fears of all the punishments in the world. God will hear his anguished cry because of the evil which causes death and destruction. *From the belly of death I have cried to you* (Jon. 2:3) is applicable to him.

You animate all of them (Neh. 9:6); even evil is animated by holiness.[64]

---

61. Hagigah 12a.
62. A verse widely cited in kabbalistic and hasidic literature as the source for the principle of symmetry in the universe; God created sets of opposites in His world: good and evil, holy and profane, pure and impure, etc. Thus, just as there is life and good, there is death and evil.
63. Ketubbot 46a.
64. Here R. Menahem Mendel proceeds to discuss a certain kabbalistic doctrine in somewhat technical terms. The doctrine states that ever since the Breaking of the Vessels, the mystical cataclysm attendant upon creation, good and evil are mixed throughout. Thus all evil actions and entities contain a spark of holiness without which they could not exist. R. Menahem Mendel is amazed that God, who grants strength to man, does not deny him His power even when man is about to do an evil act—through the very God-given power of holiness. (This theme goes back at least to

17. FEAR OF PUNISHMENT AND FEAR OF SIN
Source: Besht, cited in Or Torah to Ekev, s.v. ve-attah yisrael mah and Etz ha-Da'at Tov, Likkutei Shir ha-Shirim

What does the Lord your God require of you except to fear the Lord your God (Deut. 10:12) can be explained by means of a parable.

To fear the Lord your God means that your fear should be similar to the fear [experienced by] the Lord your God. The fear of common people is fear of punishment; but God's fear for man is fear of sin. As a father fears that his son will become physically or spiritually ill, so God, because of His great mercy for man, always fears, as it were, that he will sin.[65] This is the meaning of *what does the Lord your God require of you*, that your fear too should be fear of sin, as is God's fear;[66] man's fear should be equivalent to God's fear.

Now as to the parable: A father cautioned his son against walking barefoot lest a thorn enter his foot. The young and immature son, however, did not heed his father's warning; he walked barefoot and a thorn entered his foot. Even though the thorn was not painful, the father feared the foot would swell and therefore took an awl and tore the skin around the thorn and removed it from the foot. When the father did this, the child suffered and cried out, but the father knew that the pain was in the best interests of the lad and thus ignored his weeping and forcibly removed the thorn. Later, the child again wanted to go barefoot but his father scolded him and exaggerated, saying: "Don't you remember the pain and suffering which you had when the thorn was removed from your foot? Therefore, take care not to go barefoot again lest you be hurt again by the removal of the thorn."[67] Now the father does not emphasize to the child that a thorn will pierce his foot, for the child is not concerned about this possibility; his main experience of pain was that caused by the removal of the thorn. The father therefore cautions the child against the pain he recognizes. Even though the father's concern and fear is the thorn penetrating the

the sixteenth-century R. Moses Cordovero in his *Tamar Devorah*.) When one analyzes what he has done (i.e., to animate evil through the power of the good), one feels remorseful and desires to return to God. Thus "fear" refers to fear of the evil which animates a sin and which thus is the root cause of human suffering.

65. Cf. selection 8 above.

66. See Berakhot 5a.

67. That is, the father, accommodating himself to the child's immature view, emphasized the pain of the cure, removal of the thorn or splinter, rather than the real cause for concern—the fear of infection.

body, he stresses to his young and immature child the removal of the thorn, in order to impress upon the child that he shouldn't walk bare-foot.

As the father's fear differs from that of the child, so man fears only the punishment, not the sin itself. However, the Holy One, as it were, fears and worries lest man sin, but he is not fearful concerning man's punishment which follows upon sin. On the contrary, [the punishment] is a manifestation of God's mercy, for it is God's medicine; He punishes man in order to purify him from his sins.[68]

This is the meaning of *what does the Lord your God require of you*: that your fear should be similar to His fear.

18. FEAR AND JOY
Source: R. Levi Yitzhak of Berdichev, Kedushat Levi, Bereshit, s.v. u-ve'ofan aḥer

By means of our love and fear and our good deeds, we arouse the supernal sefirot as well as the heavenly worlds out of which were cre-ated heaven and earth and which were emanated and created before heaven and earth, as we explained earlier. It is these sefirot which we activate by our good deeds; as is well known, "the deed below evokes the deed above."[69]

The Lord, being merciful and kind, taught us the good attributes which man should adopt, in order to stimulate supernal sefirot.[70] This is the explanation of *And all the earth was unformed and void* (Gen. 1:2): All earthly desires should be considered in man's eyes as nothing. *And the earth*—the earthly and material desires—*was unformed and void*; they must be *unformed and void* [i.e., meaningless and empty].

The verse continues: *And darkness was upon the face of the deep; and the spirit of God hovered over the face of the waters* (Gen. 1:2). The Lord instructed us in righteous qualities, that we may thereby evoke the supernal, radiant sefirot and thus naturally experience [the precept of] "where there is rejoicing there must [also] be trembling."[71] We explained this earlier: When a great king displays his hidden treasures,

---

68. Berakhot 5a.
69. A concept widely mentioned throughout the Zohar.
70. In the text, both human character qualities and divine sefirot are referred to as *middot* ("attributes"), thus emphasizing the effect of the former on the latter.
71. The interpretation by the Talmud (Berakhot 30b) of Ps. 2:11, "Serve the Lord with fear and rejoice with trembling."

his dominion, his power, and his palaces, with their locked secret chambers, the servant rejoices in that he recognizes that he serves such a great king. But he also trembles [in fear]: for how can he [a mere servant] serve such a great king? Certainly if he should, heaven forfend, violate the king's commandments—he is gripped by great fear and trembling. This is what is meant by "where there is rejoicing there must [also] be trembling."

So it is when one reflects upon the greatness of the Creator, and perceives how all the worlds, angels, and *hekhalot* (the mystical "palaces" of the divine realm) sing His praises, and are filled with fear and trembling [for the Lord]—the Lord illuminates man's mind with these thoughts, who thereby attains great joy, for he is serving the supreme God. But upon contemplating this [very] greatness of God, he trembles: Whom does he serve? Before whom does he speak? Before whom does he sit? Then his words and prayers [come forth] in fear, dread, and embarrassment.

19. FEAR OF TORAH SCHOLARS: AN INTERMEDIARY STAGE
Source: R. Mosheh Elyakim Beri'ah, son of the Maggid of Koznitz, Kehillat Mosheh to Ekev, cited in Sefer Baal Shem Tov, no. 192.[72]

I heard it said in the name of the saintly R. Israel Baal Shem Tov: The Zohar refers to various types of fear—fear of exaltation and fear of punishment, whereby one fears the Holy One because He may punish him.[73] This fear of punishment is akin to worshipping [someone or something] other than God, as it is stated in *Hovot ha-Levavot*.[74] The preferred type of fear is fear of exaltation, in which one fears God as Master and Ruler of the universe. In this, one only fears "heaven," for fear and punishment are inapplicable to heaven. Therefore, the Sages said "Let the fear of heaven be upon you."[75]

He who practices fear of punishment is far from attaining fear of exaltation. The median point between these two types is a new type of fear—fear of the scholar, as it has been said: *"The Lord your God you shall fear* (Deut. 10:20); this includes scholars."[76] He who has attained

---

72. See also R. Yaakov Yosef, *Ben-Porat Yosef*, p.50.
73. Introduction 11b; also *Likkutei Zohar, Tikkun* 30 and 39.
74. *Shaar Yihud ha-Ma'ase*, chap. 4.
75. Avot 1:3. Note the novel explanation of the common term "fear of heaven."
76. Bava Kama 41b. "Fear" in this case means reverence or awe in the presence of scholars of Torah, and therefore is midway between piety that issues from the fear of divine retribution and that which derives from the experience of exaltation attendant upon contemplating the majesty of God.

the level of fear of a scholar is not far from the level of fear of exaltation.

20. DELIGHTFUL LOVE
Source: R. Shneur Zalman of Liady, Tanya, Likkutei Amarim, chap. 9

The divine soul and the animal soul which comes from the shells are at war with each other over the body and limbs.[77] The divine soul desires that only it shall rule and lead the body and that all of the limbs should follow its discipline and be fully subjected to its authority.[78] [The divine soul further wishes that the body] should be a chariot for it and that its ten categories and three compartments (*nefesh, ruah, neshamah*) should be clothed by the bodily limbs. The body should be full of them and them only. That is: The three capacities of the head should be filled by the wisdom, understanding and knowledge (Hokhmah, Binah, Da'at = HaBaD) of the divine soul. Habad is: divine wisdom *and* its understanding—to reflect upon God's infinite greatness and, *through* knowledge, to create fear in the mind and heart and love of God. This love should be as a burning fire in one's heart and as sparks of a flame. One's soul should long and yearn to cling to the Ein-Sof with strong desire and passion. This feeling should be felt with all of one's heart, soul and being—from the depths of the heart in the right ventricle.[79] One's innards should be full of love to the point that it should extend even to the left ventricle, which is a manifestation of the *sitra ahara*. It is related to the element of water, which is evil, for it is the source of lust and is derived from the shell of *nogah*. But [the aforementioned] love should convert this evil organ from worldly pleasures to divine love, as it is written, *"You shall love the Lord your God with all your heart* (Deut. 6:7); with both your impulses."[80] That is, one should ascend to and reach the level of *great love*, which surpasses the level of *strong love*, that is comparable to burning coals. This love is known in Scripture as *love of delights* (Song of Songs 7:7), pleasure in God as in the next world. This pleasure

---

77. On the two "souls," see *Tanya*, chaps. 1—2, and see above, chap. 2 section 1.
78. This is a hasidic doctrine. A physical limb, by doing a mitzvah, becomes a vehicle (*merkavah*) for spirituality. Just as the chariot served as the means for Ezekiel's vision of the divine beings (Ezek. 1), so a mitzvah serves as a means for a human being to become a divine being.
79. The right side represents good, as the left side does evil.
80. Berakhot 54a.

takes place in the mind, wisdom, and intellect which delight in the knowledge of God according to its comprehension and its wisdom.

21. THE QUALITY OF LOVE OF THE BENONI[81]
Source: R. Shneur Zalman of Liady, Tanya, Likkutei Amarim, chap. 13

The divine soul is unable to rule over the animal soul in the *benoni* except when love of God is uncovered in one's heart at specific times, such as the hour of prayer. Even at this time, [the divine soul] only rules over [the animal soul], as it is written: *one nation shall prevail over the other* (Gen. 25:23).[82] When one rises the other falls, and vice versa. Thus when the divine soul gains strength and ascendancy over the animal soul in the source of power (*gevurot*) which is understanding (*binah*),[83] this understanding is manifested through reflection upon God, the blessed Ein-Sof. Through this understanding, a strong love of God, like sparks of fire, is born in the right ventricle of the heart. Then, the *sitra ahara* of the left ventricle is subordinated [to the love of God]. However, the *sitra ahara* is not destroyed fully in the *benoni*; it is destroyed completely only in the zaddik.

The type of love attained by the *benoni* during prayer, viz. elevating the divine soul over the animal soul, is not called true love as far as the zaddik is concerned. This is so because this state of love is temporary and it passes following prayer, as it is written: *The lip of truth shall be established forever, but a lying tongue is only for a moment* (Prov. 12:19). Nevertheless, for the level of the *benoni*, this type of love is called complete and true love.

22. SIMPLE, INSTINCTIVE LOVE
Source: R. Shneur Zalman of Liady, Tanya, Likkutei Amarim, chap. 18

It is important to know that even he who is limited in his knowledge

---

81.The person who has only attained an "intermediate" spiritual level, i.e., though he may lead an entirely blameless life, he has not yet subdued his entire nature to God's Will, and therefore is motivated by both his good and evil inclinations. See next note.
82. This refers to the prediction that Jacob will be mightier than Esau. In our context Jacob represents the divine soul and Esau represents the animal soul, according to R. Shneur Zalman. On the two levels of *benoni* and zaddik, see *Tanya*, chap. 1.
83. Understanding (Binah) is the third cognitive attribute in the kabbalistic description of God, and it is situated at the head of the left side. Thus, it is the source of might (*gevurot*), which is a collective term for the left side of the moral attributes. However, according to R. Shneur Zalman's "HaBaD" system, Binah is the *second* cognitive attribute and is situated on the *right* side. This divergence invites further study.

of God and lacks understanding of the greatness of the blessed Ein-Sof, through which [and only through which] fear and love of God can be generated, nevertheless *the word is very nigh unto thee* (Deut. 30:14). That is, to keep and do all of the Torah's precepts "and the study of Torah, [which] is equivalent to them all."[84] [It must be] in one's mouth and one's heart—in the depths of the heart and in with true sincerity with fear and love. This is the *love* concealed in the heart of the community of Israel, which is an inheritance to us from our fathers. . . .

Therefore, even the most worthless and the transgressors of Israel, in the majority of cases, sacrifice their lives for the sanctity of God's unity, even if they are boors and ignoramuses and do not know God's greatness. For whatever little knowledge they do possess, they do not reflect upon it at all, and so they sacrifice their lives not because of knowledge or contemplation. It is [to them] as if it were simply impossible to deny God's unity under any circumstance. This is because the one God illuminates and animates the entire soul, through being clothed under the aspect of Wisdom (*ḥokhmah*), which is beyond any graspable knowledge or intelligence.

23. "GREAT LOVE" AND "EVERLASTING LOVE"
Source: R. Shneur Zalman of Liady, Tanya, Likkutei Amarim, chap. 43

There are two levels of love—great love and everlasting love.[85] Great love is love of delights, and it is a flame which ascends of itself. It is considered a gift from above and is granted to him who is perfect in his fear, as is known from a saying of our Sages, "it is the nature of the man to pursue the woman."[86] Love is associated with man and the masculine, as it is written: *He hath remembered His loving kindness* (Ps. 98:3).[87] Woman is associated with fear of God (Prov. 31:30). . . . It is impossible to reach great love without first attaining fear. . . .

Everlasting fear is attained through reflection and knowledge of the greatness of the Ein-Sof, which fills all worlds and transcends all worlds, and compared to which everything is as naught. Through this

---

84. Peah 1:1.
85. The benediction preceding the morning Shema begins with the words *ahavah rabbah* ("great love"); that preceding the evening Shema is preceded by *ahavat olam* ("everlasting love").
86. Kiddushin 2b.
87. A word-play on the Hebrew verb *zakhar* ("remembered"), which can be read as the noun *zakhar* ("male").

reflection, the attribute of love is extended throughout the soul....
The soul loves God only and desires nothing further. . . . This type of
love can conceivably precede fear, according to the intellectual level
from which the love springs.[88] It is thus possible for a wicked sinner
to repent through love borne of the heart as he remembers the Lord,
his God. Nevertheless, fear is also present in him, albeit in a minor
and concealed degree. This fear is fear of sin, is a rebellion against
God. Love is in a state of revelation in the heart and mind. But this
path is a temporary and spontaneous occurrence which is granted by
the divine Providence as the occasion requires. This was the case with
Rabbi Eliezer ben Dordaya.[89]

The usual service, however, which hinges upon human free choice,
must be preceded by the observance of Torah and the precepts
through the lower fear in its smallness, at least to *depart from evil and
do good* (Ps. 34:15). One must illuminate his divine soul with the light
of the Torah, and *then* the light of love will shine upon his soul.

24. THE GREATEST LOVE OF ALL
Source: R. Shneur Zalman of Liady, Tanya, Likkutei Amarim, chap. 44

Each of the two levels of love—the great love and the everlasting
love[90]—is subdivided into many shades and gradations *ad infinitum*, in
each individual according to his capacity. . . . Yet there is one love
which incorporates both great love and everlasting love, and belongs
equally in every Israelite soul, as an inheritance from our patriarchs.
This is the meaning of what the Zohar says on the verse *Thou art my
soul; I desire Thee in the night* (Isa. 26:9), that "one should love God with
a love of the soul and spirit, as these are attached to the body and the
body loves them."[91] . . .

This is implied in the verse *My soul, I desire Thee*, which means,
"Since Thou art my true soul and life, *therefore* do I desire Thee." That

---

88. See above, selection 8.
89. Avodah Zarah 17a. He was a compulsive frequenter of prostitutes who repented
suddenly and intensely to the point of death. He is here entitled as the paradigm of
instantaneous, radical repentance.
90. Referring to the variation of terms used in the Shema benedictions at the morning and evening prayers, *ahavah rabbah* ("great love") and *ahavat olam* ("everlasting
love"). Cf. the preceding selection and the excerpt from *Zidkat ha-Zaddik* in selection
26.
91. Zohar III, 67a. This implies that the love of God is equated to the love of life itself.

is, when he is weak and exhausted he longs and yearns for his soul to revive in him; and when he goes to sleep he longs and yearns that his soul be restored to him when he awakens from his sleep. So do I long and yearn to draw the light of the blessed Ein-Sof, the life of true life, within me through occupation in the Torah. . . .

A great and more intense love than that—one which is likewise concealed in every Israelite soul as an inheritance from our ancestors—is that which is defined in *Raya Mehemna*: Like a son who strives for the sake of his father and mother whom he loves even more than his own body, soul, and spirit, for *have we not all one father?* (Mal. 2:1)."[92]

And although [one may ask]: who is the man and where is he who dares presume in his heart to approach and attain even a thousandth part of the degree of love of [Moses] the faithful shepherd? Nevertheless a minute portion and particle of his great goodness and light illumines the community of Israel in each generation, as is stated in the *Tikkunim* that "an emanation from him is present in every generation—to illuminate them."[93] Only, this glow is in a manner of great obscurity and concealment in the souls of all Israel.

25. THREE LOVES
Source: R. Zadok ha-Kohen of Lublin, Zidkat ha-Zaddik, no. 196

There are three loves: the love of Torah, the love of the Holy One, and the love of Israel. They are all one, as we know from the Zohar;[93a] one without the others is inadequate. The love of God is the source of all. For love of Israel alone, without love of God, [might be construed as simply] the love of fellowship and companionship. This was the nature of the generation that built the Tower of Babel (Gen. 11:1—9); they too loved companionship.[94] (I have heard that it is because of this that Boaz legislated the practice of greeting one's fellow man with the Name of the Lord.[95] Boaz liked fellowship very much and feared that his love was for fellow humans only, without loving God. Therefore

---

92. Zohar III, 281a.
93. *Tikkun* 69, pp. 112a, 114a, and see Zohar III, 216b, 273a.
93a. That is, God, Torah, and Israel constitute a unity.
94. Nahmanides on Gen. 11:2, citing Radak to 11:4.
95. Thus Boaz's greeting to the reapers, "The Lord be with you," and their response, "The Lord bless thee" (Ruth 2:4). See Berakhot 54a.

his opening remarks in company and his greetings were always in the name of God in order to demonstrate that he desired human companionship only so that he might thereby enhance the glory of heaven.)[96]

The love of Torah without love of God is but love of wisdom. This was [characteristic of] the generation of the Flood [in the days of Noah] (Gen. 6—8), about whom it is written in the Zohar that they were worthy of receiving the Torah because they loved learning so much.[97] (This is the reason that the *sons of God,* i.e., angels, came to the *daughters of men* [Gen. 6:2], for it is known that the female symbolizes desire and the male fulfillment. The angels possess wisdom and perception, but they do not have the Evil Urge and lust, as stated in the *Midrash ha-Ne'elam.*[98] Desire for the words of Torah too requires having an Evil Urge. Man has desire but lacks perception. Then the two are united[99]—but this is not the proper place to discuss this.) But without love of God, the love of wisdom leads to immorality.[100]

The Children of Israel, descendants of *Abraham who loved Me* (Isa. 41:8), have implanted in them from their very conception and birth the love of God. This love of God is the source of the other loves and corresponds to the sefirah of Keter ("Crown"), which is beyond man's perception. Hokhmah ("Wisdom") and Binah ("Understanding") represent the love of Torah and the love of Israel, for Binah is associated with the heart, and the heart is the locus of the love of human beings, as it is written, *As in water face answereth to face, so the heart of man to man* (Prov. 27:19).[101] (Every sefirah is a complete structure. The above

---

96. This passage appears in parentheses in the source. This holds as well for the other two parenthetical remarks in this excerpt. They were added by R. Zadok in later years.
97. Zohar III, 216.
98. Zohar I, 138a. The statement is also found in Genesis Rabbah 48:11.
99. That is, the marriage of the angels with the "daughters of men" symbolizes the combination of desire for knowledge with the knowledge itself. The latter without the former is inadequate for the true comprehension of Torah.
100. That is, the intellectual quest, without a religious foundation, leads to immorality. The generation of the Flood was guilty of immoral acts.
101. The author here structures the three loves according to the three highest sefirot. The love of God is equivalent to Keter, the transcendent source of all the other sefirot. The love of Torah is identified, obviously, with Hokhmah (Wisdom). Binah ("Understanding") is declared by the author as the sefirotic equivalent of love of man (or Israel) because in the kabbalistic structure of the sefirot as a macro-anthropos, Binah is identified with the heart, and the heart is the seat of emotions, hence love of fellow man. On his proof-text from Proverbs, see Rashi *ad loc.,* and see Tosafot Pesahim 113b, s.v. *she-ra'ah.*

are the first three within the sefirah of Hesed ["Love"]; the lower seven ones represent the expansion of their potencies.)[102]

Now these [i.e., the loves that correspond to the three highest sefirot] are the powers of *nefesh, ruah,* and *neshamah.*[103] The connection between one Israelite and another is the aspect of *nefesh.* One's connection to Torah is the aspect of *ruah.* And the connection to God is the aspect of *neshamah,* which comes from under the Divine Throne.

It is for this reason that [the Sages ordained that in our daily prayers] we say: "My God, the *neshamah* which Thou hast placed within me is pure." For no corruption prevails [in the region of the Divine Throne, locus of the *neshamah*], because it is a part of God,[104] and the love of God is never shaken. There did the Sages say that God says, "Would that they forsook Me but observed My Torah."[105] For He cannot, as it were, be forsaken by the Children of Israel, as in the verse *Surely with a mighty hand and with an outstretched arm and with fury poured out will I be king over you* (Ezek. 20:33).[106] Even if one increases his sins in order to provoke [God], he does not sever the root of the love of God, which corresponds to the sefirah of Keter, which is the concealed source of thought. "Even though one sins, he remains a Jew."[107]

26. THREE ADDITIONAL TYPES OF LOVE
Source: R. Zadok ha-Kohen of Lublin, Zidkat ha-Zaddik, no. 200

There are three types of love; minor love and great love are mentioned

---

102. This parenthetic remark qualifies the previous assertion. Every one of the ten sefirot is a "complete structure," hence it is itself composed of ten sefirot. The three highest sefirot, which represent the three loves, are all within the sefirah of Hesed ("Love"), and the lower seven sefirot within Hesed are the spelling out of the implications of the three loves symbolized by the first three sefirot.
103. In Kabbalah and Hasidism, the "soul" comprises several parts or layers. The three most basic of the five elements are, in ascending order, *nefesh,* the quality of biological vitality; *ruah,* the power of speech and intellect; and *neshamah,* the most spiritual and partly transcendent aspect of the soul that links man, ultimately, to God. See chap. 2 above.
104. As the most transcendent of the three souls, or levels of the soul, *neshamah* partakes of divine immutability, hence it is always pure. For the same reason the love of God, which our author identifies as equivalent to or emanating from *neshamah,* is unimpeachable.
105. *Petihta* to Lamentations Rabbah, beginning.
106. Hence, "Would that they forsook Me" is not to be taken literally but rhetorically, since it is impossible for the bond between God and Israel to be severed.
107. Sanhedrin 44a.

in the Zohar.[108] Great love and everlasting love are mentioned in the
blessings of the recitation of the Shema.[109] These three types characterize God's love of Israel as well as Israel's love of God, for they are
parallel; measure for measure.

Minor love is called in Scripture *concealed love* (Prov. 27:5):[110] the
kind of love whose actions are revealed in one's heart; it does not burn
with fiery flames. The *open reproof* (ibid.) where one chastises his heart
because of its distance from God, is the attribute of fear. Fear of God
is better than the aforementioned type of love, even though love is
generally better than fear. [Love is better than fear] when it is overt
and enthusiastic. This is called great love. [Great love] is a divine gift
which cannot be attained by human effort, as opposed to fear, which
can be attained by self-reproof. Concerning this [the rabbis] said:
"Everything is in the hands of heaven except the fear of heaven."[111]

Our father Abraham, the first (*rosh*, lit. "head") to strive [in this
direction],[112] was privileged to attain the attribute of love, which is
truly a divine gift not subject to human effort. Isaac, who was the
first to be born in holiness and it was promised before his birth that
he would be of God's seed,[113] was privileged [to attain] the attribute of
fear, which is attained through human effort. For such is God's measure: to show everyone the opposite,[114] in order that they should know
that the divine had done it all.

In reality, all types of love were present in all [of the patriarchs].
However, in the case of Isaac, the attributes of concealed love—or
small love—and fear were present in a stronger degree.

The [main] attribute of our father Jacob was the attribute of everlasting love, which is all-encompassing, true, eternal, and not subject
to destruction. As it is stated, "Our father Jacob did not die."[115]

---

108. Zohar to Pekudei, II, 254b.
109. Berakhot 11a.
110. "Open reproof is better than concealed love." The following paragraph elaborates
on the meaning of this passage.
111. Berakhot 33b.
112. The context here and in the next sentence indicates that *rosh* is better translated
as "first" than as the usual "head."
113. I.e., born Jewish, without the need to convert, as his father had to.
114. Abraham, who exerted effort, was rewarded with a divine gift. Isaac, who was
born through God's grace to his father Abraham, attained his level solely through his
own efforts.
115. Ta'anit 5b.

[Ordinarily,] love, [far from being an eternal attribute,] is a temporary manifestation, after which it disappears. Also, man is sometimes
joyful, in which case love is his dominant feeling. But when he is troubled, fear [overtakes him]. In reality, [though,] love is required
whether one is in a good mood or whether he is in a troubled mood.
This is written in the introduction to the Zohar[116] and is expounded
upon in the Talmud: *"With all your might* (Deut. 6:5); with *every*
attribute that He measures out to you."[117] This is associated with
Jacob our father, in whom both attributes were always present, as it
is written, "I had fear through my joy, and I rejoiced through my
fear."[118]

Therefore, in the evening service we say "great love," which is associated with Jacob, who established the evening prayer.[119] It was Jacob's
attribute to have an indestructible love [for God] even during the
night and the darkness of troubles. In the morning service, which was
established by Abraham,[120] we say "great love," which is related to
Abraham's attribute. For when the light of the day shines forth and
enters the hearts of the Children of Israel, their hearts become
enflamed with great love for God. Because God's love is parallel to
Israel's love, we say, "You have loved us with great love."

However, one version prescribes "everlasting love" to be said even in
the daytime.[121] The reasoning behind this is that now, when we are in
exile, we must arouse the attribute of everlasting love in times of trouble [evening] as well as in the daytime. The attribute of great love is
hidden, for if it were revealed in the hearts of the Children of Israel,
God, on His part, would have to respond with a corresponding love
which even *great waters* [representing the nations] *would not be able to
extinguish* (Song of Songs 8:7). The nations would then fall under
Israel. However, this love, with its proper enthusiasm, has disappeared
since the day on which the Temple was destroyed. [On that day,] the
fire upon the altar which enabled the fire of enthusiasm for God to

---

116. 12a.
117. Berakhot 54a.
118. Tana de-Vei Eliyahu Rabbah, chap. 3, beginning.
119. Berakhot 26b.
120. Ibid.
121. Berakhot 11b. According to the Sephardic ritual, which was later partially adopted by the Hasidim, "everlasting love" is recited in the morning too.

grow, was destroyed.[122] Even though this type of love appears from time to time, it is only a superficial appearance and does not come from the depths of the heart. Concerning this I heard, regarding *God is not in the fire* (1 Kings 19:12),[123] that one must thoroughly examine himself to be sure that his love is strong enough to the point of reaching *devekut* with God, at which time God is actually within oneself.[124]

27. GOD'S SUBSTANCE WITHIN MAN: THE SOURCE OF HIS LOVE
Source: R. Menahem Mendel of Vitebsk, Peri Etz to Shofetim

Worship of God is in place only after arranging praise of God[125] [on the one hand], and, [on the other hand,] the reminder to oneself of his virtual lack of self-worth and loneliness. [That is,] that man is formed from murky physical substance, dust from the earth. He cannot [even] see through his eyes or hear through his ears or understand through his heart, except that God [gave man this ability on the day of creation, and] *He that planted the ear, shall He not hear?* (Ps. 94:9).[126] Man does not even have the power of speech except [to speak] the word of God, as it is written: *O God, open my lips* (Ps. 51:17). Even the love and fear that man has for God, is this not God? For who loves if not the living God Who is extended throughout man's soul? And who is beloved by God and what is the love?[127] [Certainly] these must be hewn from the essence of God which is extended through and bound and united with the mundane world, and which is condensed in man, the microcosm. In every place where man stands, God also stands, for God is the place of man,[128] "God transcends all worlds and fills all worlds."[129] When the attribute of love overpowers man,[130] this feeling

---

122. The relation of the fire and love, apart from the fact that one becomes "burned up" with love, is exhibited in the fact that the altar's fire was never to be quenched nor was it quenched. See Lev. 6:13 and Avot 5:7. The fire, like the love, was everlasting.

123. God is not manifest through the love which is likened to a fire, i.e., everlasting.

124. But this is really impossible in our days, as was indicated earlier in the passage.

125. Berakhot 32a.

126. Lit. "on the day that 'He who planted the ear, shall He not hear?'"

127. That is, is it not so that the subject who loves, the object of the love, and the love itself are all really God? The reason for this is as follows.

128. "God is the place of the world, but the world is not His place" (Genesis Rabbah 68:10). As the world is contained in God, so is man contained in God.

129. *Tikkunei Zohar, tikkun* 57. See also Zohar III, 225a.

130. The style of the author is important here. Love enters man from without. Literally, it "attacks" man. Man is the object of God's grace; God gives His love to the

knows no end in man—all wealth becomes contemptible and everything is as naught before it,[131] because [the love itself] is from God. The
more he becomes enflamed [with the love of God], the more his heart
comprehends [divine] truths that are not a product of man's own soul.
For what can he accomplish when his body is of murky corporeality
[and from this one cannot attain the love of God]. But the spirit of
God speaks within man, His word is on his tongue, and his love is a
brand snatched from God's fire. [Only because of this can] man
become enflamed greatly without end [in the love of God], with an
endlessly resounding voice, so that the parchment is not [broad]
enough, nor are days sufficient to explain the absolute greatness of the
heart of the true lover [of God].

28. LOVING GOD MEANS READINESS TO SERVE HIM
Source: Kitvei Kodesh of Besht and the Maggid, p. 17b

Man's love of God is not directed toward God's selfhood. Rather, it is
aimed at the service and the glory of God. [This is like] a villager, who
certainly would not say "I love the king," for who is he to serve the
king? Rather he would boast that he loves to serve the king with awe.

29. FROM MATERIAL TO HEAVENLY LOVE
Source: R. Menahem Nahum of Chernobyl, Me'or Einayim, cited in Derash
Tov, Inyan Ahavah

It is easy to attain love while occupied in worldly pleasures, such as
eating and drinking. This is stated by the Baal Shem Tov as well as the
Talmud on the verse *How beautiful and how pleasant is the love of delights*
(Song of Songs 7:7).[132] The superior type of love is attainable through
awakening it in the delight that is in his nature. In this way it is easy
to attain love of God. Without this it is difficult to begin to love God.
    He who desires something should know that the desire comes from
the source of superior love. This desire is the result of divine aid, as

human being. This follows from the premise that the spirit of God is in man. It is not
man qua physical being which loves God. Love being a gift of God, no room is left for
religious snobbery. The reason X loves God and Y does not is that the former received
the gift, whereas the latter did not. (See the rest of the passage in *Peri Etz.*)
131. This phrase usually refers to God. However, the author uses it to mean that man,
when enflamed with love of God, cares for nothing but the object of his love.
132. There is nothing in the Talmud on this verse. The closest source is Eliyahu
Rabbah 5.

God is aware that without the natural desire it is impossible to awaken the superior love. When man lacks the knowledge [that the natural desire is sent by God in order to attain true love], and he pursues the desire for its own sake, he draws down the attribute of love [rather than returning it to its divine source].

5

Devekut

INTRODUCTION

In chapter 4, we saw how the theme of love and fear of God, already treated in classical rabbinical and theological literature, was further developed by Hasidism. This was in keeping with Hasidism's emphasis on the emotional element in Judaism and its preoccupation with the experiential life of the Jew. Nevertheless, there is no noticeable shift in interpretation or conceptualization that makes Hasidism's understanding of love and fear in any way radical or qualitatively different from what had been done before it arrived on the scene.

However, that is not true of *devekut*. Here, although we notice clear developmental signs and regular progress in the definitions of the theme, we arrive at a peculiarly hasidic stamp on the nature and quality of *devekut*. Indeed, if immanentism is its major metaphysical underpinning, *devekut* is Hasidism's chief and most characteristic religious value.

The essential idea of *devekut* is biblical in origin. The root *d-b-k*, to "cleave" or "cling" or "be attached," is common throughout the Bible. In five places in the Pentateuch, all in Deuteronomy, it is used specifically to designate the *devekut* of man with God. In the first of these passages (Deut. 4:4), Israel is described as "cleaving unto [lit. in *devekut* with] the Lord your God." The other four are phrased as, or imply, commandments. We are instructed to serve God and cleave to Him (ibid. 10:20 and 13:5), to walk in all His ways and cleave to Him (ibid. 11:22), and to obey Him and cleave to Him (ibid. 30:20).

The Sages were intrigued by the idea of cleaving to God. Is it possible, they asked, to adhere to One Who is described as a consuming fire? In other words, isn't there something absurd in speaking about so intimate an attachment between mortal man and the Infinite Source of all existence? Their answers take a number of forms. One might be termed the moral interpretation, based upon *imitatio Dei*: *devekut* is not with God Himself, but with His ways. As He visits the sick, consoles the mourner, buries the dead, and clothes the naked, so must we.[1] Another answer is the social one: consort with those who fear Him. Thus, help the scholar to earn his living, seek to marry into his family, etc. Neither of these connects *devekut* with religious experience as such.

Another classical interpretation of *devekut*, one which goes back to the Middle Ages and received great support from the leading mitnaggedic ideologist of the early nineteenth century, R. Hayyim of Volozhin, also seeks the object of *devekut* in something other than God Himself—in this case, Torah, which is the will and word of God. Being engrossed in the study of Torah is by its very nature a case of being in *devekut* with God, and no special consciousness or emotion need be present.

It is primarily in the mystical schools, beginning in the thirteenth century, that we find a more literal interpretation of *devekut* as communion with God. However, the exponents of this view faced the same problem as the talmudic Sages, and could not conceive of *devekut* with the Ein-Sof. They solved the problem, and retained God as the object of *devekut*, by focusing on the sefirot as the locus of communion. Most kabbalists regarded *devekut* as the last stage of man's ascent to God, which is brought about by means of meditations (*kavvanot*) on the Names of God—another term for the sefirot. These *devekut* meditations were to take place in seclusion, protected from the distractions and turbulence of the prosaic world.

Most important for an understanding of how the idea and practice of *devekut* developed, leading to the characteristic hasidic innovations, is the commentary of the renowned halakhist-mystic R. Moses Nahmanides (Ramban) to Deut. 11:22:

> Included in *devekut* is remembering God and loving Him constantly, your thoughts never leaving Him when you walk, when you lie down, when you rise; so much so, that when you talk with others, it is only with

---

1. Shabbat 133b, Berakhot 34b, Sanhedrin 99a, 111a; see Sanhedrin 92a.

your mouth and tongue [that you talk], but your heart is not in it, for [the heart] is in the presence of God. It is likely that those who have attained this [high] rank partake of eternal life even during their earthly sojourn, for they themselves [thus] become an abode of the Shekhinah, as was alluded to [by R. Yehudah Halevi] in the *Kuzari*.

This comment by Nahmanides is strongly reminiscent of a similar statement by Maimonides in his *Guide of the Perplexed* (3:51–52).[2] Nahmanides seems to imply that *devekut* is a commandment binding upon all but, as with many other mitzvot, open to gradations depending upon one's spiritual capacity; for Ibn Ezra, it is more a promise than a commandment. (The specific locus of *devekut* for Nahmanides is the last of the sefirot, which is united with Tiferet, representing the nine upper sefirot, thus in effect making *devekut* a communion with all the sefirot.)[3]

What is especially noteworthy is Nahmanides' understanding of *devekut* as taking place not in seclusion but in the course of day-to-day life. The theme is repeated and elaborated by R. Isaiah Horowitz several centuries later in his *Shenei Luḥot ha-Berit*: *devekut* is to be practiced in conjunction with one's profane activities.[4] Hence, we have before us two divergent views on the practice of *devekut*: Nahmanides and R. Isaiah Horowitz recommending it as desirable in the course of daily life, and the kabbalists, for whom it is achieved privately, in seclusion and isolation.

Coming closer to the hasidic period, we find further development in what Joseph G. Weiss has called the pre-hasidic circle of pneumatics.[5] In discussing *devekut*, Weiss offers the following morphology: One tradition of interpretation, identified most closely with the kabbalists, is that of *devekut* taking place outside the course of normal life, in mystical isolation. The second is that of contemplation within the world and society. This category may be subdivided into two classes: the dualistic and the monistic, or unified. In the first, the *devekut* indeed takes place in the course of one's regular activities, but has no contact or relationship with them. In the monistic form of *devekut*, the contemplation of communion merges with the profane work in which one is occupied.

---

2. See on this, and on hasidic *devekut* in general, G. Scholem's "Devekut, or Communion with God."
3. See H. Hanokh, *Nahmanides as Thinker and Kabbalist*, pp. 244–245.
4. See J. G. Weiss, "A Circle of Pneumatics in Pre-Hasidism."
5. In idem., "Reshit Tzemiḥataḥ."

In the pre-hasidic circle of pneumatics, one of the leading contemplatives was R. Nahman Kossover, whose view of *devekut* was dualistic. He held that one ought to engage in *devekut* (though R. Nahman does not use this term) without interruption even while part of one's mind is occupied with the prosaic pursuits of daily secular life. The content of the *devekut* meditation for R. Nahman Kossover is the visualization of the Tetragrammaton, the four-letter ineffable Name, which comes to man quite "naturally" if he voids his mind of all other thoughts.[6]

Since the sacred and the profane remain separate in R. Nahman's scheme, it is likely that his view of *devekut* would not have led to the hasidic idea of worship through corporeality (*avodah be-gashmiyut*).[7]

The Besht at first accepted R. Nahman Kossover's dualistic notion, but later proposed an innovative monistic method of *devekut*, whereby *devekut* meditation and the profane activity in which one is engaged come into contact with each other.

For the Besht, *devekut* was, as it was for Nahmanides and R. Nahman Kossover, a full-time activity. So important was *devekut* for the Besht that he regarded any distraction from its constancy as tantamount to idolatry. While he does not negate the element of meditative contemplation so cherished by the classical kabbalists, he emphasizes *devekut* as a state of heightened emotion, ecstatic and rhapsodic. *Devekut* was not to be a privilege of the spiritual-intellectual elite, but a goal for the common man. Moreover, *devekut* was not, as among the kabbalists, the end-goal of spiritual struggle, but its starting point, the first rung on the ladder leading to God. As an emotional experience that marks the initiation into religious experience, *devekut* now comes into the purview of the ordinary Jew as the focal point of his religious life—a development that introduced, as well, the possibility of externalization, such as the use of liquor and other artificial stimulants, to induce the necessary emotions. Nevertheless, while antagonists of Hasidism made much of such vulgarizations, and while any attempt to popularize spiritual practices necessarily entails risks, it is clear that the Beshtian notion of *devekut* had enormously positive consequences in the life of its adherents and ultimately for the spread of Hasidism among the masses of Jews in Eastern Europe.

---

6. This idea was known before R. Nahman Kossover; see *Me'irat Enayim* by R. Isaac of Acre, one of the prominent Gerona kabbalists, ed. H.A. Erlanger, Jerusalem, 5735, 278b-279a.

7. See below, chap. 9.

Scholars discern three stages in the Besht's development of *devekut*: (1) before he came into contact with the ideas propounded by R. Nahman Kossover, he held that *devekut* should be practiced in isolation from society; (2) under the influence of R. Nahman Kossover, he held that *devekut* should be achieved simultaneously with, but separately from, social or business activity (in some sources, the Besht is said to attribute this doctrine to his "teacher," the prophet Ahijah of Shiloh); and (3) when he advanced to the next stage, he held, not only that *devekut* must be simultaneous with social or physical activity, but that they must relate to each other and interpenetrate. Since *devekut* of this order acts to raise the sparks of the mundane activity, the dualism implicit in R. Nahman's vision is effectively dissolved. Note, in selection 25, the encounter of these two theories—R. Nahman Kossover's dualistic view, and the Besht's monistic one—in the homiletical interpretation by the author of *Sefat Emet* of Jacob's meeting with Joseph.

It is the third stage in the Besht's method of *devekut* that leads to *avodah be-gashmiyut*. Like everything else in the universe, *devekut* comes in two forms: *gadlut* ("greatness") and *katnut* ("smallness").[8] The major mode of *devekut* is spiritual service (*avodah be-ruhaniyut*), and its minor mode is corporeal service (*avodah be-gashmiyut*). *Devekut* in *gadlut* includes, especially, the emotional communion with God that occurs during prayer and Torah study by means of binding oneself to the spiritual element (the Light of the Ein-Sof) inherent in the words of prayer or Torah. This means concentrating not on the figures of speech or even the ideas, but on the spirit that animates them, thus yielding what Weiss calls the atomization of *devekut*. This created an approach to prayer and study, especially the latter, that brought Hasidism into conflict with the mitnaggedim, who considered it a distortion of the cardinal Jewish precept of Torah study.[9] (As mentioned above, *devekut* in its minor form, as *katnut*, leads to corporeal service, one of the more remarkable contributions of Hasidism.)

The general groundwork for the hasidic view of *devekut* is provided in the first three selections. In the three selections that follow, it is dealt with as an expression of *yihud*, "union" or "unification," a concept the content of which is difficult to define. Sometimes *yihud* means concentration of one's mind and thoughts, in the process of

8. See below, chap. 12.
9. We shall have more to say about this in chapter 7.

devekut, on the focal point.[10] Sometimes it implies simply the acknowledgment of divine unity. For the Besht it usually signifies binding one's thought to the "root of the Torah," breaking down the barriers between man and the high spirituality immanent in Torah, and effecting an organic whole (unification) of what seemed a collection of separate, isolated, and disparate elements. For the Maggid, who was one of the Besht's students, *yiḥud* implies the "need" of God and man for each other, and usually requires going from the *ani* ("I," selfhood, autonomy) to *ayin* ("nothing"; in the Hebrew, both words consist of the same three consonants, *a-n-y* and *a-y-n*, respectively); note especially selection 4. The union represented by *yiḥud* must not be confused with pantheistic obliteration of the self, which would go against the Jewish personalistic view of man. Even after *yiḥud* via *devekut*, man still remains man, or, perhaps, has first begun to become man in wholeness.

The last point constitutes a strong argument against Martin Buber, who saw in Hasidism what he called "pan-sacramentalism," the hallowing of all life in its here-and-now concreteness. This view, Buber holds, is in contrast to rabbinic "cultic sacramentalism." Buber's unflattering epithet characterizes the halakhic way as fragmenting life into the separate realms of the sacred and the profane, which leads, in his opinion, to spiritual stagnation. The hasidic view, however, is creative and redemptive; unfortunately, he continues, Hasidism eventually sold out to rabbinism because of the pressure of its mitnaggedic critics, and institutionalized cultic sacramentalism instead of effecting a true renewal by means of pan-sacramentalism. Thus, Hasidism degenerated into mere "religion."

The passage from the Maggid in selection 5 refutes Buber's reading of the hasidic sources. The Maggid certainly represents the movement at its apex of early growth, before any reconciliation or submission to the mitnaggedim could be said to have taken place, and yet it clearly speaks of the spiritualization of the world and not of the hallowing of the world's concreteness. The reader may refer, as well, to the introduction to the Maggid's magnum opus by his student, R. Shelomoh of Lutzk (see above, chap. 1, selection 6). Buber is reading his personal version of existentialism and his distaste for the Halakhah into the hasidic soul. Hasidism did not find redemptive power in the holiness

---

10. In hasidic parlance, "thought" and "reason" are used in a loose sense; they do not always connote intellection, and may indicate any intentional act of the soul, including will and emotion. See Scholem, "Devekut."

of the natural world, thus implying acceptance and fulfillment of its concreteness. Rather, it discovered the world's spiritual element—the immanence of the divine, whether through the sefirot or the Light of the Ein-Sof—and not, as it were, the divinity of the world that was the object of its *devekut*. Shatz-Uffenheimer, following Scholem, is quite correct in holding that, "the doctrine of *devekut* advocated the erasure of the Ego and its nullification in order for one to become repeatedly involved in the infinite reality of the Godhead to the limits of the possible."[11]

The chapter continues with three selections that deal with the varieties of *devekut* in Hasidism, although without going into great detail, followed by seven selections dealing with the techniques for achieving *devekut*. The first four deal with Torah and prayer, because the attempt to reach God through His immanence in the words of Torah and prayer is a major form of *devekut*, as mentioned above. The next three sections present the methods of attaining this special religious experience. The reader may wish to consult chap. 9, selection 2, which is relevant to this discussion.

Eight excerpts from hasidic literature are then devoted to two related problems: (1) the basic absurdity of *devekut*, already mentioned above in discussing the talmudic view, in that it seeks to enable man, a lowly and mortal speck in the created galaxies, to commune with the holy and pure Creator; (2) in a more practical vein, the question of how Hasidism can demand that its followers strive for uninterrupted *devekut* when, after all, they have to work for a living and tend to their daily and prosaic material needs—a problem already addressed, as mentioned, by both R. Nahman Kossover and the Besht. It may be worthwhile for the reader to turn to chap. 9, selection 3, in conjunction with these selections.

We conclude with two passages that deal specifically with the role of the zaddik in the practice of *devekut*, touching on two questions: How does the zaddik reconcile his obligations to his flock and their mundane needs with his own ambitions for constant *devekut*? As to whether *devekut* is for the common man, or only for the spiritual elite—this is taken up in chap. 9, selection 6, to which the reader is referred.

---

11. R. Shatz-Uffenheimer, *Hasidism as Mysticism*, pp. 240–241.

Devekut
A Story

A rabbi was once on a journey to visit the renowned zaddik, R. Hayyim of Sanz. On the way, he met a distinguished scholar who was a mitnagged. The latter asked him: "Why do you go to so much trouble to visit the zaddik? Why don't people come to see me?"

The rabbi answered: "The zaddik of Sanz knows all the thoughts that people have, and I, too, know some of them."

"In that case," said the scholar, "tell me what I am thinking about."

The rabbi answered: "You are thinking about the greatness of the blessed Creator and that He is present everywhere in the world."

The scholar triumphantly declared, "I can swear to you that I was not thinking about that, neither now nor at any time in the past."

"And that," the rabbi answered, "is why I and others travel to the zaddik of Sanz and not to you, for I can call heaven and earth as witness that he is in constant *devekut* with God, every single moment."

1. CONSTANT DEVEKUT
Source: Besht, Keter Shem Tov, I, sec. 169

It is a great achievement to keep in mind always that you are close to the Creator and that He surrounds you on all sides, as it is written, *Happy is the man who, when he thinks not of God, [this is attributed] to him as a sin* (Ps. 32:2).[12] This means that the instant you stop thinking about your attachment (*devekut*) to God, you incur a sin.

Our *devekut* to God should be such that we need not make a special mental effort each time to be aware of a feeling of nearness to Him. We should perceive the Creator intellectually as the Place of the world;[13] and man as a microcosm.[14] Thus we fulfill the verse *I have set the Lord always before me* (Ps. 16:8), as stated in *Shulḥan Arukh, Oraḥ Ḥayyim*, chap. 1.

---

12. The usual translation is: "Happy is the man unto whom the Lord counteth not iniquity" (*ashrei adam lo yaḥashov ha-Shem lo avon*). In this rendering, *yaḥashov* means "count," its subject is "the Lord," and the object is *avon*, "iniquity." The Besht, with a characteristic homiletical twist, understands *yaḥashov* as "will think" or "meditate," its subject as "man," and the object as "the Lord." With a comma inserted before the last two words (*lo avon*), the verse now yields: "Happy is the man who is so constantly involved in meditating upon the divine nearness that if he should for one moment be distracted from this thought, it would be considered a sin for him, relative to his normally high attainment."

13. Genesis Rabbah 68:10, "He is the Place of the world, but the world is not His place," i.e., the cosmos is contained within God, but He is not limited to the cosmos.

Afterword

The Besht's theory of *devekut* differs from the early kabbalistic view. The kabbalists see *devekut* as the ultimate achievement in man's spiritual struggle. The Besht perceived it as the very first rung on the ladder. Thus the opening statement of the *Shulḥan Arukh*, based on the verse "I have set the Lord always before me," is an all-important prerequisite in serving God. It is so important that even momentarily falling away from the state of *devekut* is considered a sin, as stated here.

2. THE EXTENT OF DEVEKUT
Source: *Besht, Keter Shem Tov, I sec. 200*

Devekut should be of the kind in which one focuses principally on the Creator, and not the kind wherein one concentrates mainly on the world and [only] incidentally on its Creator. For we cannot make any move whatsoever without His grace (*shefa*) and animating power.

3. DEVEKUT AND EXILE
Source: *R. Dov Ber, the Maggid of Mezeritch, Maggid Devarav le-Yaakov, no. 49, p. 70*

"Keep far away from a bad neighbor."[15]
    Nowadays, in the time of exile, attaining the holy spirit (*ruaḥ ha-kodesh*) is easier than it was when the Temple still existed.[16] This may be compared to a king who is much more difficult to approach in his

---

In Rabbinic Hebrew, God is often called *ha-Makom*, "the Place," and the preceding midrash is an explanation of the term. (For references to the term's origin, see E. E. Urbach, *The Sages*, chap. 4. and my *Torah Lishmah*, p. 98, n. 131.) For the Besht, this dictum is warrant for immanentism. Indeed, the statement is remarkably panentheistic, i.e., it supports the belief that the universe is *within* God—neither identical with Him (pantheism) nor wholly separate from Him (deism, or a more transcendental theism).

14. Since God is the Place of the world, and man is a miniature world (microcosm), God is the Place of man, i.e., man is in a natural state of *devekut* with Him. This is the intellectual or theological underpinning or stimulus for the *devekut* experience.

15. Avot 1:7. The passage that follows is typical "hasidic Torah"; here, an idea presented as a commentary on a text, in this case a mishnaic dictum.

16. The theme that religious experience is easier in the Diaspora than in the land of Israel is often found in the Maggid's works. With the official trappings of Temple and priestly service no longer in existence, there is an "informal" atmosphere in which it is easier to encounter the Divine Presence.

royal palace than on the road. When he is abroad, anyone who wishes may draw near to him. Even a villager who is unfit to visit the king
in his palace may approach and speak with him in an inn. Similarly
today, in exile, when you concentrate on *devekut* with God, His presence immediately rests upon you and dwells with you.

Therefore keep yourself far away from passions and alien thoughts,
so that you are not separated from God, and do everything only for
the sake of His Name.

That is what is meant by the passage: "Keep all that is bad far away
from the One Who dwells with you as a neighbor."[17]

4. DEVEKUT AND YIḤUD
Source: R. Shneur Zalman of Liady, Tanya, Likkutei Amarim, chap. 45

[In addition to fearing God and loving God,] there is another direct
road available to us: occupying ourselves with Torah study and the
performance of mitzvot for their own sake through the attribute of
our father Jacob, peace be unto him, namely, the attribute of mercy.[18]
Let us arouse in our minds great compassion before God for the divine
spark that animates our souls and descended from its source, the Life
of life, the blessed Ein-Sof.[19] . . .

---

17. In exile, with its "informal" religious structure, God may be encountered by means
of *devekut*. The Shekhinah (Divine Presence) exists passively within us; *devekut* actual-
izes its presence so long as we are ready to rid ourselves of base passions and alien (i.e.,
lustful) thoughts. The *derash*, or homiletic interpretation, of the Avot passage quoted
at the beginning of the selection rests on a word-play and a restructuring of the syntax of the three-word dictum. *Shakhen* ("a neighbor") is interpreted as the etymologically related *shekhinah* (the divine "presence" or "indwelling"). And the last Hebrew
word, *ra* ("bad"), is taken, not as an adjective modifying the second word, but as the
object of the first: "Keep far away from the Shekhinah all that is bad."
18. *Pardes Rimonim*, gate 23, chap. 10. In kabbalistic symbolism, Abraham represents
love, equivalent to the sphere of Hesed; Isaac, represents fear (restraint), or Gevurah:
and Jacob, Rahamim (mercy), which often substitutes for Tiferet as the sixth of the
sefirot.
19. As is made clear in several sentences omitted in the selection, R. Shneur Zalman is
alluding to the exile of the Shekhinah. In this alternative to straightforward fear and
love, the worshiper has compassion for the spark of divinity trapped in the corporeal
world and suffering because of its distance from its pure source. God's immanence,
while indispensable for the existence and functioning of the material world, is an
object of compassion, and this compassion for the violence wrought on man's sublime
spiritual dimension, his divine spark, leads the worshiper to renewed contact with
God.

That is what is meant by the verse *And Jacob kissed Rachel and raised his voice and wept* (Gen. 29:11). Rachel represents the congregation of Israel, the source of all souls.[20] And Jacob, with his supernal attribute of mercy (in *atzilut*), is the one who arouses great compassion for her.

And he raised his voice upwards to the source of higher mercies, called the Father of Mercies and their source.

And he wept to awaken and draw down an abundance of compassion upon all the souls, and their source in the congregation of Israel, to lift them up from their exile and unite them in the Higher Unity with the light of the Ein-Sof. This is achieved by kisses,[21] which means the attachment of spirit with spirit, as it is written, *Let Him kiss me with the kisses of His mouth* (Song of Songs 1:2), which means the union of the man's word with God's word, namely the Halakhah.[22] So, too, thought is coupled with thought, and deed with deed, the latter referring to the active observance of mitzvot, in particular the act of charity and loving-kindness (*ḥesed*). For *ḥesed* is the divine right arm,[23] which is an aspect of a real embrace, as it is written, *And his right arm did embrace me* (Song of Songs 2:6); while occupation in the Torah by word and in concentrated thought is an aspect of real kisses.[24]

---

20. See Genesis Rabbah 71:3, 82:11. Rachel symbolizes the collectivity of all Jewish souls of all time. The homily interprets the scriptural tale of Jacob's love for Rachel as a parable of *devekut* and *yiḥud*. For a somewhat different interpretation, see chap. 11, selection 8, especially n. 41.

21. The implication that *devekut* (the communion symbolized by kisses) is the basis of *yiḥud* has its source in the writings of the Besht and the Maggid. In his letter to R. Gershon of Kutov, the Besht says: "With every single utterance and all that comes out of your mouth during the time of your prayer and your study, intend to unify a Name. For in every single letter there are worlds and soul and divinity, and [these] ascend and bind up with each other and unite with each other. Afterwards, the letters bind up and unite with each other and a word is formed, and they unite in a true unity with God" (for a full translation of the letter, see below, chap. 17). Similarly, the Maggid extols the ideal of *yiḥud* achieved by *devekut* in a homily on *ḥatzotzerot* (see selection 5). For more on the interconnection of *devekut* and *yiḥud*, see the notes to selections 5 and 6.

22. Jacob's love for Rachel (or more accurately, in light of the theme of this text, his compassion for Rachel) is symbolic of *devekut* in that kisses are oral (thus the proof-text on "the kisses of His mouth") and stand for forms of communion that are intellectual or verbal, i.e., Torah study; embraces, involving physical action, stand for the (physical) mitzvot. Thus Halakhah, the principal form of Torah study, is the medium for *devekut*.

23. *Tikkunei Zohar*, introduction p. 17a; *gevurah* ("strength, restraint") is the left arm.

24. An entirely different interpretation of "And Jacob kissed Rachel" is given by R. Levi Yitzhak (see below, chap. 11, selection 8).

In this way one is able to attain the distinction of *ahavah rabbah* ("great love")[25] in the revelation of his heart, as is written: *Of Jacob, who redeemed Abraham* (Isa. 29:22), as has been explained elsewhere.[26]

5. DEVEKUT AND YIHUD (CONTINUED)
Source: R. Dov Ber, the Maggid of Mezeritch, Maggid Devarav le-Yaakov, no. 24, pp. 38 f.

Make two trumpets (ḥatzotzerot) of silver (Num. 10:2). That is, two *ḥatzi-tzurot* ("half-forms").[27] This is in accordance with the verse *and upon the likeness of the throne was a likeness as the appearance of a man (adam) upon it above* (Ezek. 1:26).[28] For *adam* ("man") by himself is only *dam* ("blood");[29] and the Word rests upon him.[30] Only when he is in *devekut* with the Holy One,[31] who is the *Alef* of the world, does he become [fully] an *adam*.[32]

---

25. On this term, see above, chap. 4, selection 23.

26. *Tanya, Likkutei Amarim*, chap. 32, end. Jacob, as stated, represents mercy (Rahamim) while Abraham symbolizes love (Hesed, equivalent to Ahavah). Hence, "Jacob redeems Abraham"; mercy, as compassion, arouses and inspires love.

27. A play on words. God and man, alone, are each only half a form, but when they meet and complement each other in the unification of *yiḥud*, they constitute the full gestalt of a man, as in the verse from Ezekiel that will now be expounded.

28. This verse is part of the description of the divine chariot in Ezekiel's prophetic vision. Focusing on the word for "man" in the verse, R. Shneur Zalman shows how it requires the participation of both man and God.

29. The first letter, *alef*, represents God's Unity, as will be explained. The other letters, *dalet* and *mem*, spell *dam*, "blood," which represents man's biological nature, since blood is the "life" of living creatures (Lev. 17:11).

30. This expression is equivalent to "the Shekhinah rests upon him," for in kabbalistic symbolism "word" stands for the lowest of the ten sefirot, Malkhut, which is identified with the Shekhinah, or Divine Presence. Even in his "merely" biological state, man is capable of having the Shekhinah dwell with him. But Kabbalah requires that man assist in the reunification of the Shekhinah (the feminine element) with the Holy One (the male element, representing the upper sefirot). In this state, therefore, man is still unfulfilled, for the Shekhinah, the aspect of God that accompanies him, is unconnected to the Holy One.

31. A frequent homiletic wordplay identifies *alef*, the first letter of the Hebrew alphabet, with God (in this case, "the Holy One"). *Alef* is numerically equal to one, and God is One. Moreover, *alef* is related to *aluf*, "chief," and God is called the *"Aluf* of the world" (see Hagigah 16a).

32. Only in a state of *devekut* with God (*A*) does man (*DaM*) achieve the metaphysical fulfillment of *ADaM*. Like other Jewish mystics, the Maggid does not preach the actual *unio mystica* of God and man. Man is the *bearer* of the Shekhinah, "the Word [which] rests upon him," to *its* union with the Holy One (see n. 30 above).

The Holy One performed many contractions (*tzimtzumim*) through many worlds in order to be united with man, who otherwise would be unable to bear His luminosity.[33]

A man must completely separate himself from corporeality in order to ascend through all the worlds and be in unity with the Holy One, until he is nullified from existence; and then he is called *adam* ("man").[34] . . .

Hence, *a great cloud, with a fire flashing up* (Ezek. 1:4). *A great cloud*, for at the beginning, darkness settles over man so that he cannot pray in ecstasy. Afterwards, *a fire flashing up*—ecstatic prayer.[35]

6. DEVEKUT AS RECIPROCAL LOVE
Source: R. Shneur Zalman of Liady, Tanya, Likkutei Amarim, chap. 46

Introduction

R. Shneur Zalman maintains that it is natural to love God, but that our love is concealed and must be aroused in order to be fully and freely expressed. The arousal can be effected by contemplating God's love for us. The divine love for man is so great that it elicits a reciprocal love. The two loves meet in the act of *devekut*.

*

There is yet another righteous way,[36] available to all and easily accessible, to arouse and kindle the light of love for God that is implanted and concealed in our hearts, so that it can shine forth like a burning fire; intensely and openly in heart and mind, to the point that we are prepared to offer up soul, heart, and might to the Lord, totally and completely, from the depths of our heart, in absolute truthfulness—and especially when reciting the Shema and its blessings.

---

33. In order for this *yiḥud* to take place, the Ein-Sof had to undergo successive contractions in order not to overwhelm man and jeopardize his existence. Similarly, as is pointed out in the next paragraph, man must respond to God's descent (contractions) by his own ascent, achieved by transcending his corporeality and physical needs and desires. God and man must reach out for each other in order to achieve fulfillment.
34. This too is from Ezekiel's vision of the divine chariot.
35. Before striving to attain *yiḥud* with God by means of *devekut*, man is "under a cloud," in spiritual darkness, his inner spiritual powers stilled. Only when he makes the great effort to reach out for God and complete himself are these inner potencies aroused, and then, in his prayer, he attains the gift of ecstasy, the "flashing fires."
36. In addition to fearing and loving God and having compassion for the divine spark ensconced in matter. See selection 4, above.

This way is by taking to heart the meaning of the verse *As in water face answereth to face, so does the heart of man to man* (Prov. 27:19). In other words, just as the likeness and features of the face we present to the water are reflected back to us by the water, so does our love for a loyal comrade awaken love for us in our friend's heart, thus reciprocally developing the true love that each of us has for the other, especially as we each see our friend's love for us.

This pattern of response comes naturally to all men even when they are of equal status. How much more so when a great and mighty king shows great and intense love for a commoner who is despised and alone among men, a disgraceful creature cast on the dunghill—yet the king comes down to him from the place of his glory, together with all his retinue, raising him from the dunghill and bringing him into his royal palace and into the innermost chamber, a place where neither servant nor prince may enter, and there shares the closest union and true companionship with him, with embraces, kisses, and spiritual attachment,[37] with all his heart and soul. How much more so will love for the king be aroused, of itself and in doubled intensity, in the heart of this most common and humble individual, with a true attachment of spirit, heart, and soul, and with endless sincerity. Even if his heart were like stone, it would surely melt and become water, and his soul would pour itself out like water with intensely soulful longing for the king's love.

In an exactly corresponding manner, but to an infinitely greater degree, has our God dealt with us. For His greatness is beyond comprehension, and He fills all the worlds and surrounds all the worlds.[38] We know from the holy Zohar and from the Ari [=R. Isaac Luria] about the infinite multitude of *hekhalot* ("palaces") and worlds; and about the countless myriads of angels in each world and *hekhal*. The Talmud states: "It is written, *Is there any numbering of His hosts?* (Job 25:3); yet it is also written, *A thousand thousands minister unto Him, and ten thousand times ten thousand stand before Him* (Dan. 7:10)." The discrepancy is explained by the answer: "*A thousand thousands* is the complement of one troop, but His troops are innumerable."[39] Yet before

---

37. "Embraces" refers to the performance of mitzvot requiring actions; "kisses," to mitzvot fulfilled orally, such as Torah study and prayer; "spiritual attachment" means meditation and contemplation—in short, *devekut* by thought, word, and deed. This is more elaborately stated in selection 4.

38. Designating, respectively, divine immanence and divine transcendence.

39. Hagigah 13b.

God, all of them are nothing at all, and their very existence is nullified, just as a single word is truly nothing compared to the essence and being of the one who uttered it, while the utterance was still a matter of thought or will and desire of the heart.

The angels all ask: "Where is the place of His glory?" and they answer: *The whole earth is full of His glory* (Isa. 6:3), i.e., His people Israel. For the Holy One forsook the higher and lower creatures, choosing none of them save His people Israel whom He brought out of Egypt, *the obscenity of the earth* (Gen. 42:9), the place of filth and impurity. "Not through the agency of an angel, nor of a seraph . . . but the Holy One, blessed be He, Himself in His glory,"[40] descended there, as is written, *And I am come down to deliver them* (Exod. 3:8). He did this in order to bring them near to Him in true closeness and unity, with a truly soulful attachment on the level of kisses of mouth to mouth by means of speaking the word of God, namely the Halakhah,[41] and the fusion of spirit to spirit, that is to say, comprehending the Torah and knowing His will and wisdom, all of which are truly one. He also draws them to Him with a form of embrace, the fulfillment of the 248 positive commandments, which symbolize the 248 organs of the King.[42] These are generally divided into three categories, right, left, and center, namely, Hesed ("Love"), Din ("Stern Justice"), and Rahamim ("Mercy")—the two arms and the body, and so forth.[43]

This clarifies the meaning of "Who has sanctified us by His commandments."[44] It is like one who betrothes[45] a wife so as to unite her with him in a perfect bond, as it is written, *And he shall cleave to his wife, and they shall be one flesh* (Gen. 2:24). Exactly similar, and even infinitely surpassing, is the union of the divine soul that is occupied in Torah and mitzvot—and of the animating soul and their garments—with the light of the Ein-Sof. Solomon, in the Song of Songs, com-

40. Passover Haggadah.
41. See selection 4. This is a description of *devekut* via the study of Torah.
42. See above, chap. 3, selection 2. The text here means *devekut* through the performance of the mitzvot.
43. The sefirotic triad of Hesed, Gevurah (often called Din), and Tiferet (sometimes called Rahamim) is symbolized graphically as, respectively, the right and left arms and the trunk of the body. *Tikkunei Zohar*, Introduction.
44. From the text of the berakhah recited before performing a positive commandment.
45. Since *kiddushin* is the term for a betrothal, *kiddeshanu* ("Who sanctified us") may be rendered as "Who betrothed us."

pared this union with the union of bridegroom and bride in attachment, desire, and pleasure, embrace and kissing.[46]

7. THE SIGN OF DEVEKUT
Source: Besht, Keter Shem Tov, I, sec. 192

As for the matter of *devekut*: some hold that [the sign that you have] achieved *devekut* is when you utter a single word during prayer and linger over it for a long time, because you are unable to separate yourself from it as a result of your *devekut*. Others say that *devekut* is achieved when you perform a mitzvah or study Torah in a way that turns your body into a "seat" for your *nefesh*, and the *nefesh* into one for the *ruaḥ*, and the *ruaḥ* into one for the *neshamah*,[47] and the *neshamah* becomes a seat to the light of the Shekhinah [hovering] above your head; and you feel as if this light were spreading all around you, with you sitting in its center, trembling with joy, and the heavens a dome above you.[48]

8. GREATNESS AND SMALLNESS
Source: Besht, Zava'at ha-Rivash, p. 25b, no. 137

Bear in mind that when you contemplate the Shekhinah's presence beside you in the same way that you contemplate material things, this is called *avodah be-katnut*.[49] In this state you may occasionally dis-

---

46. See above, n. 21, on the Besht's and the Maggid's views on the role of *devekut* in achieving *yiḥud* between man and the Ein-Sof. Note the use of erotic imagery. In prophetic and kabbalistic writings, this is the most potent source of similes and metaphors for the *devekut* experience. Moreover, as in this passage, literary similarities often enhance the imagery; e.g., "cleave" (*davak*) in "and he shall cleave to his wife" is the past participle of *devekut*. The end of the verse, "and they shall become one (*eḥad*) flesh," begs the allusion to *yiḥud*.

47. These three souls are discussed in the introduction to chap. 2.

48. It is difficult to tell whether the Besht is prescribing the means of attaining *devekut* or describing the signs of having achieved it. Style and context both point to the latter, so I have translated the passage accordingly. The first view of how to tell when *devekut* has been attained is more prosaic and less dramatic, but it is genuinely Beshtian (see too *Zava'at ha-Rivash*, p. 11a, n. 70). The second is a far more emotional, ecstatic experience: the ascent internally from lower soul to higher soul and finally to the divine light, in which man feels himself immersed, trembling in joy as the light seems to form a heavenly sphere around him.

49. The Besht's concept of greatness and smallness, or major and minor states, originated in Lurianic Kabbalah. It is discussed in much greater detail in chap. 12; see too, chap. 4, selection 13. Briefly, the two terms describe two states of man and are

cern many spherical heavens encircling you while you stand on a
point of this small planet earth;[50] the whole world is as nothing in
comparison to the Creator, who is the Ein-Sof who performed the
tzimtzum and made space within Himself to create the worlds. Even if
you understand this intellectually, you are unable to ascend to the
upper worlds, as implied by *from afar the Lord appeared unto me* (Jer.
31:2), because we see God only from a distance.

But by worshiping God with greatness you strengthen yourself
with great force and soar in your thought,[51] splitting through all the
heavens at once, rising beyond the angels and the ophanim and the
seraphim. This is the perfect service.[52]

9. DEVEKUT AND THE INTELLECT
*Source: R. Dov Baer, the Maggid of Mezeritch, Maggid Devarav le-Yaakov,
no. 79, pp. 137 f.*

When you attach yourself to God intensely, all the worlds will likewise draw closer and become attached to their Source, experiencing an
ascent. It is known that the more you rise upwards, the more intellect
and clarity you develop.[53] This will explain the case of R. Pinhas ben
Yair's donkey, which had enough intelligence to distinguish between
tithed and untithed produce.[54] The reason is that R. Pinhas ben Yair

---

universal. With regard to worship, smallness is a state of imperfection, whereas greatness is full development to the highest state. *Avodah be-katnut*, or worship during
smallness, contains an element of compulsion, and not the high qualities of fear and
love that characterize greatness. (See Scholem, "Devekut, or Communion With God,"
pp. 219 ff.). Even with regard to *devekut*, as this passage makes clear, smallness indicates a mechanical, emotionally thin quality, whereas greatness denotes fullness,
ecstasy, inspiration. *Devekut* in smallness is "seeing God from a distance," whereas
greatness implies a rhapsodic charge to the very heavens. In this first sentence, the
Besht describes the *intellectual* contemplation of God's omnipresence. He refers to it as
smallness because it is merely intellectual, no more than analogous to man's cogitation on secular matters.
50. Note the sensation of literal smallness, i.e., being dwarfed by the enormousness of
the cosmos.
51. *Mahshavah*, here translated as "thought," should not be narrowly construed as discursive, intellectual thought. It more pertinently applies to the totality of one's churn-
ing internal forces. Perhaps "spirit" would be more accurate.
52. That is, service in greatness.
53. This refers to the well-known medieval principle, based upon Aristotle and
Ptolemaic astronomy, according to which the outer edges of the universe (the translu-
nar regions), are more spiritual and less grossly material in substance.
54. Hullin 7a.

was so attached to God in perfect *devekut* that he elevated his corpo-reality along with himself,[55] inculcating it with intellect.

10. DEVEKUT THROUGH PRAYER AND TORAH
Source: Besht, Keter Shem Tov I, sec. 84, p. 11c

But you that cleave unto the Lord your God are alive every one of you this day (Deut. 4:4). This means that *devekut* is the cause of true life. When you have *devekut* with God, the Life of Life, you are alive in essence.[56] When you interrupt your *devekut*, you are alive only by accident. Just as heat is of the essence of fire, but is only accidental to water, so that the heat does not endure when the water is removed from the flame, [so it is with *devekut*].[57]

Regarding *devekut*, the Sages remarked on the verse *and to cleave unto Him* (Deut. 11:22): "How can one cleave to Him? Is not God *a devouring fire* (ibid. 4:24)? But it means to cleave to His attributes."[58] This means cleaving to Him through the Torah. The Besht also said: Surely when you are occupied with prayer and Torah, which is wholly composed of God's Name,[59] you ought to be in a state of strong *devekut*; and when performing your mundane activities the rest of the day, you should still have some *devekut*, fulfilling the commandment *I have set the Lord always before me* (Ps. 16:8).[60]

---

55. Interpreting the word for "ass," *ḥamor*, as *ḥomer*, "matter." The idea that *devekut* is not an abandonment of material existence, but its elevation, leads to the idea of *avodah be-gashmiyut*, the service of God by means of the body. See below, chap. 9.
56. As opposed to being alive by accident. See further.
57. Someone in *devekut* with God, to whom life is of His essence, is alive in essence; but without *devekut* his life is contingent, a mere accident.
58. Sifre Deut. 11:22. Cf. Sotah 14a
59. See Nahmanides' commentary on the Torah, introduction. The entire Pentateuch is mystically regarded as one Name of God when the spaces between words and portions are eliminated.
60. The verse is significant. *Devekut* is achieved, both during Torah study and prayer and during mundane activities, by meditating on the Tetragrammaton, based on the verse, "I have set the Lord (the Tetragrammaton) always before me." In this the Besht may have been influenced by R. Nahman Kossover, the leading protagonist of contin-ual *devekut* in the pre-hasidic circle of pneumatics, who based his concept of *devekut* on the visualization of the Tetragrammaton, hinted at in this verse (see *Shivḥei ha-Besht*, Hebrew ed., p. 92; English ed., p. 228; cf. J. G. Weiss, "Reshit Tzemiḥatah shel ha-Derekh ha-Ḥasidit," p. 60). According to this doctrine, constant attachment or con-templation means uninterrupted *devekut*, even while part of the mind is engaged in secular work (Weiss, p. 62). R. Yaakov Yosef relates that R. Nahman Kossover used to reproach people for not adequately fulfilling the requirement to meditate on the

To what may this be compared? To a candle or a burning coal. As long as there is still a living spark in it, the flame can be revived. If not even a spark is left, however, the fire must be produced anew.[61]

This, then, is the meaning of *you that cleave unto the Lord . . . are alive . . . this day*: cleaving to God (*devekut*) is not only a guarantee for attaining eternal life in the world-to-come, but it also ensures life in this world, which is called *this day*.[62]

Instruments of *Devekut*

11. DEVEKUT AND THE SECRETS OF THE TORAH
Source: R. Yaakov Yosef of Polennoye, Toledot Yaakov Yosef to Vayetzei, sec. 10, p. 89a

I learned from my teacher [the Besht] that the main purpose of engaging in Torah study and prayer is to attach oneself to the inner spirituality of the light of the Ein-Sof that inheres in the letters of the Torah and the prayers. This is called studying [Torah] for its own sake (*lishmah*), and it is what R. Meir meant when he said: "Whosoever engages in the Torah for its own sake (*lishmah*) merits many things . . . and the secrets of the Torah are revealed to him."[63] This means that he will know the future and all its happenings from the Torah.[64] He will also learn how to conduct himself when studying Torah and when serving God, in addition to his ability to perceive the upper worlds.[65]

Tetragrammaton even while doing business. He argued: "If it is possible to think about merchandise and business during prayer, then the reverse is likewise possible" (*Toledot Yaakov Yosef*, p. 20d).

61. *Devekut* during mundane activities is a prerequisite for maintaining proper *devekut* during prayer and Torah study. The maintenance of continual *devekut* is imperative to keep the spark alive, for it may be difficult to relight the flame of *devekut* once the fire has been extinguished.

62. *Devekut* assures us of being "alive, every one of you" if we are also in *devekut* "this day," in our mundane diurnal affairs.

63. Avot 6:1.

64. Because Torah is the repository of the light of the Ein-Sof, one who studies it with *devekut* (rather than as a discursive, intellectual discipline) may attain mystical illumination and prophecy.

65. See Additional Note *1.

12. WITHIN THE LETTERS OF THE TORAH
Source: R. Yaakov Yosef of Polennoye, Ben Porat Yosef, p. 59d

The way to attain *devekut* with God is through the letters of the Torah and the prayers, by attaching your thought and inwardness to the inner spirituality of the letters. This is the mystery of *Let Him kiss me with the kisses of His mouth* (Song of Songs 1:2)—a cleaving of spirit to spirit.[66]

13. INTO THE VERY WORDS OF TORAH
Source: R. Levi Yitzhak of Berdichev, Kedushat Levi ha-Shalem, Likkutim, beginning 105b, s.v. uve-ofen aḥer

When you speak any sacred words of prayer or Torah, wrap yourself in the letters that you utter.[67] If the word you pronounce is the Tetragrammaton, enshroud yourself in its letters, and then it will be pronounced as written.[68] However, in lands outside of Eretz Israel,

---

66. A kiss on the mouth is an "adhesion" of the lips during which two persons exchange breath. The Hebrew word for "breath" is *ruaḥ*, which also means "spirit." Since Solomon's Song of Songs is taken as a parable of the love between God and Israel—and, for Kabbalah and Hasidism, especially of the love between God and the individual worshiper—the verse refers to an intimate exchange of *penimiyut*, or inwardness. In his innermost heart, the worshiper, in *devekut*, cleaves to the innermost and hence divine essence that inheres in the words of Torah and prayer. Cf. R. Bahya b. Asher's Commentary to Leviticus 21.

67. In the kabbalistic-hasidic view, divine spirituality inheres with special force in the letters of the Torah. One form of *devekut*, therefore, has the worshiper reach out to God via the sacred letters.

68. The Talmud (Kiddushin 71a), based on Exod. 3:15, says regarding the Tetragrammaton: "Not the way I am written am I pronounced. I am written with *yod heh*, and I am uttered with *alef dalet*." That is, the Tetragrammaton is not pronounced phonetically, but is read it as if it were written *ADoNaY*, "the Lord" (as in most English translations of the Bible). Elsewhere (Pesahim 50a) the Talmud maintains that this holds only for the present ("this world"), but in the world-to-come, the Name will be read as written. In the part preceding this excerpt, R. Levi Yitzhak suggests that love of God is a greater virtue than fear of God, but one cannot attain the former without having first experienced the latter. The Tetragrammaton stands for love, and "the Lord" for fear. Hence, in this world we pronounce the Tetragrammaton as "the Lord" (= fear), but in the days of the Messiah we will read it as written (= love). He now asserts that one who is able to "garb himself" in the letters of the Name would be permitted to pronounce the Tetragrammaton as written, as did the high priest when he entered the Holy of Holies on Yom Kippur. As becomes clear later on, this is meant as a dispensation to pronounce the ineffable Name, and is a "natural" outcome after one attains a state of having shed his corporeality, for then the Shekhinah utters the words from his throat.

which are considered defiled,[69] achieving this state is very difficult, since it requires the shedding of corporeality. But in the [messianic] future, when *the earth shall be full of the knowledge of the Lord* (Isa. 11:9), and every Jew will possess great [spiritual] clarity, the Tetragrammaton will be uttered as written.

This will enable us to understand the verse *In every place where I mention My name, I will come unto thee and bless thee* (Exod. 20:21). Seemingly it would be more proper to say: "where *you* mention my Name."[70] But the intended meaning of the verse is as follows: You have to enfold yourself in these words when you pronounce them until you succeed in shedding your corporeality and annihilating your ego, and then you can achieve *devekut* with the letters. In this state, when corporeality has been annihilated, it is the Shekhinah that speaks from man's throat.[71]

This, then, is the meaning of *In every place where I will mention My Name*, etc., namely, I Myself; i.e., when you have divested yourself of corporeality and nullified your physical existence, then the Shekhinah Herself will utter the Name from your throat. Hence, uttering the ineffable Name as written is not permitted, because doing so requires that one be garbed in the letters [i.e., shed one's corporeality], and this exalted state is hard to come by in foreign lands, because they are defiled.[72]

---

69. All lands outside the Land of Israel are ritually impure by virtue of rabbinic enactment (see Shabbat 14b). The author apparently considers this world as identical to exile, "outside Eretz Israel."

70. The question that serves as a pretext for the interpretation is based on a literal reading of the verse. Most translations render, "where I cause My name to be mentioned," and this follows Rashi, who explains, "Where I will give you permission to mention my Name explicitly as written, there I will come to you and bless you," meaning "there I will cause My Shekhinah to dwell upon you," which is intended to teach us that only in the Temple, the final and permanent dwelling of the Shekhinah, were priests permitted to utter the Tetragrammaton explicitly.

71. "The Shekhinah speaks from his throat" is an often-quoted phrase describing Moses' prophecy, but it appears neither in the Talmud nor the Midrash. For the earliest analogue in the Zohar literature, see Zohar III, 232a (and thus correct R. J. Z. Werblowsky, *Joseph Karo*, p. 269 n. 2.). The phenomenon of automatic speech is displayed in the Maggid of R. Joseph Karo, best described in Werblowsky's book, chap. 12.

72. R. Levi Yitzhak continues: The incapacity to utter the Tetragrammaton, which symbolizes love, does not apply to the Name *ADoNaY*, because it represents fear of God, and that can be attained outside the Land of Israel. Nowadays, therefore, one *reads* the Tetragrammaton but *recites* it as *ADoNaY*, because the element of love is concealed and cannot be attained except by the rare act of divesting oneself of corporeality; but the element of fear of God is revealed and attainable even here in exile. The act

14. ASCENDING IN STAGES
Source: Besht, Likkutim Yekarim, p. 9b, no. 49

When you wish to ascend to a high state [of *devekut*],[73] you must do so in stages, from level to level.[74] At the beginning, plan only to ascend to the first heaven, which is at a distance of a five-hundred-year journey.[75] Then expand the heaven mentally in all directions, so that it does not seem low and small to you, but extends in every direction.[76] Once you are standing there, mentally fortify yourself to move on higher, and then still higher. But you cannot ascend all seven heavens at once; you must do so in stages. While praying, however, if you begin with the proper *devekut*, you are able to ascend to all seven heavens at one time.[77]

When ascending from level to level, beware of two things when you reach the first heaven: first, not to fall back down, and second, to continue moving ever upward. After your thoughts have securely settled you in the first heaven, move upward until you ascend to the world of the angels[78] and thence to the world of the Divine Throne,[79]

---

of shedding corporeality and enfolding oneself in the letters of Torah must await the messianic future. This interpretation differs from that of the classical commentators. Rashi and Ibn Ezra limit the articulation of the Tetragrammaton not only to the Temple period, but to the priests during the Temple service. R. Levi Yitzhak, however, would permit it to be said by priests or ordinary Jews, in or out of the Temple, provided that the state of *devekut* with the letters and the divesting of corporeality is achieved.

73. This passage contains both a descriptive and a prescriptive analysis of *devekut*. Note the attempt to describe the sensation of ascent by using the metaphor of climbing through the heavens: the sense of precariousness and vertigo as the dizziness of height threatens a greater fall; the visions of angels and seraphim, men and dogs; the experience of incorporeality (weightlessness?); and the ultimate achievement, probably extremely rare and limited to the spiritual elite, of foretelling the future.

74. At the outset, one's spiritual expectations must be modest. The ascent is gradual, although, as we shall later see, when one is fully in the midst of the experience (preferably during prayer), it is possible to leap beyond the intermediate stages to the pinnacle.

75. Pesahim 94b. According to tradition, there are seven heavens.

76. Breadth as well as height is a necessary dimension of the *devekut* experience.

77. This is probably the kind of *devekut* achieved in *avodah be-gadlut*, which is able to split through all the heavens at once. See selection 8.

78. Moving from the world of Asiyah ("action" or "making") to the next of the four worlds, Yetzirah ("formation"), the chief domain of the angels.

79. The World of Beriah ("creation"), also called the Throne or the *Merkavah*, is the domain of the highest angels. Cf. Scholem, *Major Trends in Jewish Mysticism*, p. 272.

and thereafter to the world of Emanation (Atzilut), where you remain with your mind attached to the Creator.

When you decide to ascend [to the upper worlds], you will first see what seems to be the image of a man and the images of dogs; these are the *kelipot*[80] that exist throughout the world of Asiyah. Be strong and do not fear.

At times, in this exalted state, you will be able to speak with your soul, without [using] your body,[81] for you will have separated yourself from your own body. This is the state of the divestiture of corporeality, whereby you have no sensation of your body and no thought of this world, but only of the upper worlds, i.e., the angels and seraphim. Afterwards, when you reach the world of Atzilut, you sense only the thinnest of the thin,[82] namely, His blessed emanation. This is where you will know the future.[83] Occasionally, however, you may come to know future events in the lower worlds, through proclamations originating there.[84]

---

80. Lit., "shells," the kabbalistic symbol of evil. These visions are frightening, as we read in the next sentence, but should not deter the adept from continuing the experience.

81. A form of automatic speech. Like all authentically mystical automatic experiences, such as audition or vision, automatic speech requires that the mind be in a state of deep absorption without conscious awareness of the physical self or environment (E. Underhill, *Mysticism*, p. 275). In the passage immediately following (*Likkutim Yekarim*, p. 10a, no. 50), we read more explicitly: "R. Israel Baal Shem Tov said about this, 'When I attach my thought to the Creator, I let my mouth speak what it wishes, for then I link these words with their supernal root in the Creator, for every word has its root above, in the sefirot.'"

82. In this highest and most abstract of all states, the contemplative sees no visions, hears no voices, speaks no words. He is on the level of utter silence, closest to the Source, the Ein-Sof. The term may also indicate the high-altitude sensation of reduced atmosphere.

83. In addition to automatic speech, there comes the experience of automatic hearing conveying messages about the future. In the passage immediately preceding (ibid. no. 48), we read that such prophetic utterances may be reliable: "If, when speaking [words of prayer, etc.] while in *devekut* in the upper world, and having no alien thought, a prophetic kind of thought occurs to you, it will certainly come true, because of the proclamations announced up above concerning this." That is, since the provenance of destiny is the upper worlds, "proclamations" heard while in communion with the upper spheres may be regarded as reliable. Of equal interest is the conclusion of the passage: "Sometimes you will hear a kind of voice speaking, in order that you merge the supernal voice with the voice of your prayer and your Torah [study], and [thus] you will hear a kind of voice foretelling the future." The auditory phenomenon is accepted as genuine not merely because it is paranormal, but because it has merged with the adept's own spiritual strivings.

84. It is not clear whether "there" refers to the lower worlds or the more supernal domain.

15. ASCENT TO THE UPPER WORLDS
Source: Besht, Likkutim Yekarim, no. 175

When you seek to achieve *devekut*, you must first traverse the world of Asiyah.[85] Then, in thought, you must soar much higher, and still higher, to the world of the angels and ophanim, and after this to the world of Beriah ("Creation"), until you feel that your thoughts have soared as high as the world of Atzilut. In the Zohar this is called "thought in which there is no action."[86]

Take care not to fall from your very elevated thoughts in the upper worlds and descend.[87] Strengthen yourself with all your might so that your thoughts remain high. That is why it is written, *Be ye not as the horse or as the mule, which have no understanding, whose mouth must be held in with bit and bridle, that they come not near unto thee* (Ps. 32:9); make a fence, as it were, so that you do not fall.[88]

When you are firmly in *devekut*, you will be able to strengthen yourself and resist any distracting thought that falls into your mind, because you are in *devekut* with God, and all things come from Him.[89]

Be strong of mind, so that your thought can ascend high into God's upper worlds. Like a man who strolls from room to room, so should your thoughts traverse the upper worlds.[90]

---

85. The lowest of the four worlds that mediate between our mundane sphere and the Ein-Sof. As in the immediately preceding selection, *devekut* begins in the physical world (Asiyah), and moves from there toward the uppermost and holiest of worlds, Atzilut ("Emanation").

86. Implied in Zohar II, 226b. The uppermost world is the most distant from the world of Asiyah. Note the cognitive-contemplative nature of *devekut* in this excerpt: there is no mention of ecstasy in any form. But while this indicates that the view of *devekut* expounded here has not yet developed into its "mature" hasidic form and is moored in kabbalistic meditations, the absence of the usual intricate and technical kabbalistic meditations is significant.

87. Having reached the highest level of *devekut*—contemplation that reaches into the world of Atzilut—man is in a most precarious position; his very height presents him with the danger of precipitous descent.

88. The prooftext is meant more for literary than exegetical purposes. Man *should*, like an animal, restrain himself with the spiritual-intellectual equivalent of bit and bridle, so as not to fall—a kind of mental boundary below which he will not allow himself to retreat.

89. The alien thought can be neutralized by contemplating that it too comes from God, in keeping with Hasidism's immanentist doctrine, and therefore it need not be a distraction from *devekut*. On alien thoughts (*maḥshavot zarot*), see the introductions to chap. 5 and chap. 11.

90. Having achieved the sense of having climbed upward from world to world, the adept arrives at a plateau where there is a feeling of movement and discovery, though no longer the experience of ascent. Throughout, *devekut* remains active and dynamic.

Let no one else be with you in the house when you seek *devekut*, for just as the chirping of birds can be a distraction, so the thoughts of another person [nearby] can be distracting.[91]

16. VISUALIZING THE DIVINE NAME
Source: R. Yaakov Yosef of Polennoye, Toledot Yaakov Yosef to Hayyei Sarah, sec. 2

I have set the Lord always before me (Ps. 16:8).[92]

I heard from R. Nahman[93] that this means that we must not force ourselves to visualize the ineffable Name [the Tetragrammaton] when it does not come to mind of its own accord, for that is called "taking the princess captive."[94] Rather, we should have God constantly in mind, sometimes as His Name appears in one verse and we contemplate it deeply, and sometimes as in another verse; until finally the Tetragrammaton appears by itself, visualized before us, etc. R. Nahman probably received this as a tradition from his teachers. *The words of a wise man's mouth are gracious!* (Eccl. 10:12).

I believe that this explains the verse, *When thou goest forth to battle against thine enemies, and the Lord thy God delivereth them into thy hands, and thou carriest them away captive, and thou seest among the captives a woman of goodly form, and thou hast a desire unto her, and wouldst take her to thee to wife* (Deut. 21:10–11). The Sages interpreted this verse as

---

91. A remarkable example of a belief in mental telepathy whereby one person may intrude on the thinking process of another. The requirement for seclusion when attempting to attain *devekut* marks this passage as of very early hasidic provenance, possibly pre-Beshtian. A similar report, almost verbatim, may be found in *Keter Shem Tov* (p. 28a, no. 216). However, a different opinion in the name of the Besht (*Zava'at ha-Rivash*, p. 10b, no 63) cautions against complete solitude as dangerous, and recommends that two persons be present in the room, "each one being alone with the Creator." The passage continues that when one is in *devekut*, this alone-with-God state can be achieved even when many others are present. The passage from *Zava'at ha-Rivash*, with its preference for community over solitude, probably marks a later stage in hasidic thinking on *devekut*.
92. The discourse that follows is based on two words in the biblical text. The first, usually translated as "the Lord," is the Tetragrammaton. The second, *le-negdi*, means not only "before me" but also "opposite me" or "against me."
93. R. Nahman Kossover, one of the most important members of the earliest hasidic circle, advocated visualization of the divine Name as a means of sustaining *devekut*.
94. Proper *devekut* does not permit a forced concentration on and visualization of the Tetragrammaton; the Name must emerge into one's consciousness by itself. The meaning of the metaphor becomes clear in the next paragraph.

referring to a permitted war (i.e., a war that is not obligatory).[95] . . .
Scripture is speaking of a war of thoughts, not actions. That is why it
cannot be referring to an obligatory war, which would mean a war to
rid the mind of prohibited thoughts, such as thoughts of immorality
and idolatry; but a permissible war, for we wish to sanctify our
thoughts, fulfilling the verse *I have set the Lord always before me* (Ps.
16:8), and removing all *permissible* thoughts about the vanities of this
world.[96] For if we force ourselves specifically to visualize the
Tetragrammaton at all times, that is the same as *thou carriest them
away captive*, taking the princess [i.e., the Tetragrammaton] into captivity. . . .

So, do not try to take Him by force, for that is the same as *thou carriest them away captive*. Instead, *thou hast a desire unto her*,[97] and probably she has a desire for you . . . and then *take her to thee to wife*.
Understand this.[98]

This, then, is the meaning of *I have set the Lord*, i.e., the
Tetragrammaton, *always before me* (*le-negdi*—"opposite me"), as if He
were always opposite me, preventing me from setting Him before me.
It is only proper to meditate on the Tetragrammaton when it presents
itself before me of its own accord.

17. TO AND FRO
Source: R. Yaakov Yosef of Polennoye, Toledot Yaakov Yosef to Tazria, sec. 2

I heard from my teacher [the Besht] an explanation of the verse *And*

---

95. The Halakhah categorizes Joshua's conquest of Canaan and battles for self-defense
as obligatory wars, and other military campaigns as permissible wars (see Mishnah
Sotah 8:7). The Sages limited the law of the captive wife to permissible wars (see Sifre
to Deut. 21:10).
96. Having spiritualized the biblical "battle," the author continues with the talmudic
dictum, interpreting obligatory war as the obligation to make war against forbidden
thoughts, and permissible war as a higher form of spiritual struggle, the attempt to
achieve uninterrupted *devekut* by voiding the mind of all mundane thoughts, even permitted ones. Allied with this is a further homiletic note: permissible war is not simply
a war against permitted (profane) thoughts, but a war conducted in a permissible, or
noncoercive, manner, i.e., one cannot forcibly conjure up the image of the
Tetragrammaton.
97. "Her" now referring to the Tetragrammaton, the "captive princess."
98. R. Yaakov Yosef is cautioning against the use of visualization as a form of thaumaturgy or magic, and is insisting on genuinely religious contemplation.

the living creatures ran and returned (Ezek. 1:14).[99] The soul, having been hewn from a holy place, ought always to yearn for its origin. However, lest its existence be annihilated [as a result of reabsorption into its spiritual source], it was ensconced in matter, so that it could also engage in material acts, such as eating and drinking and business and the like, so that it would not constantly be aflame in the service of God. This is in keeping with the mystery of *tikkun* and the maintenance of the body with the soul.

18. DEVEKUT THROUGH SUFFERING
Source: R. Yaakov Yosef of Polennoye, Toledot Yaakov Yosef to Vayigash, sec. 1

The only thing that is truly good is *devekut* with God, as it is written, *But as for me, the nearness of God is my good* (Ps. 73:28). However, *devekut* with the Shekhinah cannot be achieved unless we suppress our material nature and *yetzer ha-ra*, and this comes about through suffering. It is the opposite [of a life of pleasure], as it is written, *But Jeshurun waxed fat and kicked* (Deut. 32:15). This [pleasure-seeking] becomes a dividing screen severing the *devekut* between us and our Creator. . . . Only when the *yetzer ha-ra* is subdued through suffering is true *devekut* achieved.

This explains the verse *I adjure you, O daughter of Jerusalem, if ye find my beloved, what will ye tell him? That I am lovesick* (Song of Songs 5:8), meaning, even the sickness and pain that I suffered were for me acts of love, because through them I attained *devekut*.[100]

19. DEVEKUT NO MIRACLE
Source: R. Yaakov Yosef of Polennoye, Ben Porat Yosef, introduction, p. 9b

---

99. The "living creatures" that run to and fro (*ratzo va-shov*) in Ezekiel's famous vision of the divine chariot have generally been interpreted by mystics as the principle of alternation and dialectical tension. The Besht here applies the metaphor to his ambivalent conception of corporeality. The spiritual realms are obviously superior to the physical world, yet the soul must be connected to the body lest an exaggerated spiritualism defeat the function of *tikkun*. The soul thus runs to and fro between its supernal origin and its material abode.

100. The words *ḥolat ahavah ani* ("I am lovesick") are interpreted as "My sickness and suffering I accept with love, because they brought me nearer to the One I love [God], through *devekut*." *Devekut* is a heavenly reward for suffering accepted ungrudgingly and with no complaints, and not a refuge used by the sufferer to alleviate or sweeten the pain.

Introduction

The relation between an all-spiritual Creator and a material universe is a problem that has occupied the attention of theologians and mystics since antiquity. In Judaism, it takes on the added difficulty of God's commanding man to perform physical acts (mitzvot) as a way of carrying out His will: what interest can the Absolute have in mundane deeds, and how can material things be thought to affect a completely spiritual God? In Hasidism, the problem takes on yet a different hue: man's highest religious vocation is *devekut*, the attempt to commune with God, but how can this be expected of mere mortals, ensconced in flesh and blood?[101] It is this question that R. Yaakov Yosef begins with, suggesting that *devekut* is indeed a miracle, then showing that it cannot be so, for if Judaism is to be effective and normative, it must be based on something more "material" than the miraculous.

*

To connect form [which is spiritual] with matter [which is physical] is a marvel, as the Rema [R. Moses Isserles] wrote:[102] "And He works wondrously,"[103] in that He keeps man's spirit in his body, thus binding the spiritual to the corporeal.

However, the possibility of binding the spiritual to the physical is made more plausible by means of the following. If this were humanly impossible except for divine miracles, as the Rema stated, it would present a difficulty [regarding *devekut*]. The Bible says, for example, *Thou shalt know the God of thy father* (1 Chron. 28:9), and knowledge of God is *devekut*, even as belief in God is *devekut*, *And they believed in the Lord* (Exod. 14:31). According to Rema, however, how can man, who is corporeal, cleave to Him Who is the Spirit of the spiritual and the Life of life? Even more difficult is the explicit commandment, *And unto Him shall ye cleave* (Deut. 13:5), which means the binding and attach-

---

101. See below, selection 23, in which R. Zevi Elimelekh Shapira of Dinov poses a more specific question: how can *devekut* be achieved through mitzvot, which are merely physical acts?
102. Gloss to *Shulḥan Arukh*, Oraḥ Ḥayyim 6:1.
103. From the conclusion to *asher yatzar*, the blessing recited after attending to one's physical needs.

ment of the material in [man's] form to its Creator—how is that possible?[104]

Thus there must surely be an intermediary stage by means of which the binding and attachment of corporeal man unto God, who is utterly spiritual, becomes a possibility.

A clue may be found in a statement by Maimonides, Who wrote: "The truth of the matter is that man's mind is not equipped to perceive the reality of God's existence, as it is said: *Canst thou find out the deepness of God?* (Job 11:7). This is what Moses asked for when he said: *Show me, I pray Thee, Thy glory* (Exod. 33:18); Moses requested and obtained knowledge of His actual existence."[105] God said to him: The understanding that you seek is not within the realm of human ability, save as a gift of divine grace. I shall give it to you, so that you will perceive what no man has known before you or shall know after you.

Moses our teacher is the intermediary between Israel and the Holy One. Thus: *And they believed in the Lord and in His servant Moses* (Exod. 14:31). How can one cleave to God, for after all, faith in God and knowledge of God are expressions of *devekut*? Scripture answers: *they believed . . . in His servant Moses*; by believing in and becoming attached to Moses, who had attained knowledge of God and *devekut* with God as a gift of grace, they were able to know and believe in Him. . . . Thus, through Moses they were able to attach their minds and hearts to God.[106]

---

104. While God Himself works wondrously and in miraculous ways, He will not command man to do things that are impossible to perform in a natural, humanly feasible manner. For that would mean asking man to rely on the supernatural, a miracle, and not on his own capacity and will in order to lead his normal religious existence. See Nahmanides to Deut. 20:1 and *Minḥat Ḥinnukh*, mitzvah 425, end.

105. Maimonides, Hilkhot Yesodei ha-Torah 1:9–10. R. Yaakov Yosef is paraphrasing Maimonides but is true to his meaning. Our translation omits some minor references to other authorities.

106. Two conflicting understandings of *devekut* are resolved here, one that sees it as open to all, and the other reserving it for the spiritual elite. Each view has distinguished precedents in medieval exegetical authority. Nahmanides, commenting on "to love the Lord your God and to cleave to Him" (Deut. 11:22), holds that *devekut* is a mitzvah binding upon everyone. R. Abraham ibn Ezra (ad loc.) views it as a promise held out to the privileged among the faithful (see supercommentary *Avi-Ezer* ad loc., and cf. Ibn Ezra to Deut. 13:5). R. Yaakov Yosef synthesizes the two positions: *devekut* was meant as a precept for everyone but can be fulfilled only through the intermediation of Moses. R. Elimelekh of Lizhensk, in his *Noam Elimelekh*, offers a view close to Ibn Ezra's; when he speaks of *devekut*, he refers only to the zaddik, not to the ordinary man. Cf. R. Shatz, "Le-Mahuto shel ha-Tzaddik ba-Ḥasidut," p. 368.

20. BRIBING THE BODY
Source: R. Yaakov Yosef of Polennoye, Toledot Yaakov Yosef to Mishpatim, p. 69c

In order to achieve proper *devekut* with God it is necessary to indulge matter, for otherwise the "heaviness" of matter will prevent form[107] from attaining *devekut* by means of happiness with God. . . .

I have heard a solution based on this principle to a difficulty raised by the Tosafot to Talmud Betzah.[108] The Talmud teaches that the Holy One says to Israel, "Borrow on My account [to buy wine so as] to recite the Kiddush sanctifying the Sabbath day; and have faith in Me, and I shall pay you back." Whereupon the Tosafot raise the question that this conflicts with what is said by the Sages, "Better make your Sabbath like a weekday than rely upon other people."[109]

I heard from the Maggid, Rabbi Mendel,[110] that *levu alai* has two meanings, "borrow for Me [i.e., on My account]," and "be attached to Me,"[111] and one depends upon the other:[112] in order to bind and attach oneself to God, it is necessary to make the body and the material happy, so that they do not impede the soul's happiness and *devekut* in Him. And that is how we must understand the answer to our question: *levu alai*, if you borrow money so that you can attach yourself to Me, then I shall pay you back; but if you borrow only for your own pleasure, then it is better to make *your* Sabbath into a weekday, and not rely upon others. . . .

---

107. "Matter" and "form" are R. Yaakov Yosef's designations for matter and spirit. The dialectical tension between the two is a theme that runs through all his works and assumes many forms, e.g., the zaddik is the Man of Form, the common man is the Man of Matter.

108. Betzah 15b, s.v. *levu*.

109. Pesahim 112a, 113a; Shabbat 118a. The statement is not a dispensation to desecrate the Sabbath because of economic need, but a preference for doing without some of the festive accouterments that distinguish the Sabbath from the profane days in order not to have to beg or borrow from others. The question raised by the Tosafot is that this contradicts the dictum which has God urging the Jew to borrow money for Kiddush wine.

110. R. Menahem Mendel of Bar, an itinerant preacher (*maggid*), was an important member of the earliest hasidic circle. For his influence on the Besht, see J. G. Weiss, "Reshit Tzemiḥ ̇atah shel ha-Derekh ha-Ḥasidit," pp. 66–68.

111. The Hebrew root *l-v-h* has both meanings: for the first, see Deut. 28:12; for the second, Gen. 29:34.

112. The loan binds borrower and lender together. R. Menahem Mendel interprets the relationship homiletically.

If you should ask what bodily needs like eating and drinking have to do with *devekut* and attachment to God and with the soul, which is altogether spiritual and in no need of eating and drinking, . . . the answer is that matter and body cannot experience the joy of *devekut* with the Lord except in the corporeal acts of eating and drinking. When this is lacking, the body is saddened and prevents the soul from attaching itself to Him, which can take place only through joy. Hence: "Borrow on My account" to keep matter happy, so that both matter and spirit will be happy.

This is similar to the parable of the prince who was exiled by his father and fell in with people of low station. After many years, a letter from the king finally arrived for him. He wanted to celebrate [and to invite the others to share his happiness, but he knew that they would not understand the joy that reading the letter gave him. So] he ordered drinks for all the people of low station, to enable them to be happy with the material, while he was happy with the spiritual.

Afterword

The letter from the king symbolizes a secret message of imminent redemption by God, the Father-King. The parable teaches that one must collaborate with the body by indulging its form of happiness (bodily pleasure) in order to set the soul free to pursue the spiritual delights of *devekut*. The psychological rationale, that an unsatisfied body will frustrate one's spiritual aspirations, leads to an assessment of the body-soul relationship that is decidedly anti-ascetic. The interpretation of the parable as a pacification of the physical, permitting unfettered activity of the spirit in *devekut*, is more in accord with the theory of R. Nahman of Kossov, who advocated a simultaneous but unconnected pursuit of *devekut* in the midst of mundane activity. The Besht apparently moved from R. Nahman's way to that of R. Menahem Mendel (see introduction to this chapter). Nevertheless, there is a discrepancy between R. Menahem Mendel's exegesis and this parable. According to the parable, the material pleasures are a form of appeasement that allows the soul to be free for *devekut*; the corporeal lacks inherent worth. The exegesis sees a far more intimate connection: the physical indulgence enhances the contemplative activity. Weiss maintains that the far-reaching theory in the exegesis more accurately represents R. Menahem Mendel's thinking, and was advocated by the Besht too.[113] Other versions of the same parable attributed to the Besht in *Toledot Yaakov Yosef* (Shelah, p. 138c; Ki Tavo, p. 191a) support this interpretation.

21. DEVEKUT AND WORK
Source: R. Yaakov Yosef of Polennoye, Ben Porat Yosef, preface, p. 8c

An aspect of the excellence of the early Sages was that while they were engaged in mundane work with their physical limbs, their minds and souls were simultaneously attached to God and His Torah. . . . This explains the talmudic saying that "the early generations made the study of Torah their main concern,"[114] i.e., even while occupied with work, their minds were fastened on the Torah and in *devekut* with God.

This also explains the saying in Avot: "It is an excellent thing to combine the study of Torah with some worldly occupation."[115] Not only should your mind be free from worldly concerns while you are engaged in Torah and prayer, but even when you are occupied with worldly matters, your mind and soul should be involved in Torah and *devekut*.[116]

This is suggested in the verse *The secret things belong unto the Lord our God; but the things that are revealed belong unto us and to our children* (Deut. 29:28); when we are occupied with material concerns, such as providing sustenance for ourselves and our children, the activity

---

113. Weiss, "Reshit Tzemiḥatah shel ha-Derekh ha-Ḥasidit," p. 66-68.
114. Berakhot 35b. *Keva*, in this context, is usually and correctly translated as "main concern." R. Yaakov Yosef uses another shade of meaning: "fixed" or "attached to a certain place."
115. Avot 2:2.
116. A similar interpretation of this mishnah is given by R. Levi Yitzhak of Berditchev (*Bet ha-Levi* on Avot 2:2) and, later, by the Komarno Rebbe, R. Yitzhak Isaac Yehiel Safrin (*Notzer Ḥesed* on Avot 2:2). This calls in question Scholem's contention that it was R. Elimelekh of Lizhensk who turned *devekut* into a value that may be realized even during social activities, but only at the price of binding *devekut* to the institutions of zaddikism (see Scholem's "Devekut, or Communion with God"). As seen from these sources, *devekut* is a social value independent of zaddikism.
R. Hayyim of Volozhin also recommends the practice of "double consciousness," but substitutes Torah study for *devekut*; those who are unable to devote enough time to study should devote their thinking to Torah while occupied with mundane activities. He uses the same mishnah in Avot as a source (see my *Torah Lishmah*, pp. 72–73 and p. 130 n. 85), but admits that "it is a difficult task and not everyone can do it" (ibid.) R. Yaakov Yosef seems to reserve feats of this kind to "the early generations," which were presumably superior to our own.

should be limited to what is revealed, namely, the overt physical limbs; our *secret things*, however—the mind and soul—must remain even then attached to the Lord our God, as mentioned.

22. AN IMMORTAL PLEASURE
Source: R. Menahem Mendel of Vitebsk, Peri ha-Aretz to Ki Tissa

Devekut requires that there be no impediment between man and God; only then is *devekut* possible. As in the parable of the Besht, it is impossible to join silver coins together with glue unless some of the coin is scraped away where the attaching takes place. Only then will they hold well and become as one. If, however, there is rust or some other intervening substance, the pieces cannot be joined together. This indicates the meaning of *If thou seek her as silver, then shalt thou understand the fear of the Lord and find the knowledge of God* (Prov. 2:4). Such must be the *devekut* to God. You must scrape away part of your self to make sure that there is no rust or other substance capable of creating an obstructive partition. Only then can *devekut* take effect. However, there is no connection when you hold on to something other than the divine. As is known, attachment to the corporeal causes pleasure so strong that the mind is unable to think about anything else; one's thought are focused only upon that one thing. This holds true for every form of pleasure, such as the love of money, which takes up all man's thoughts.

The general rule is that [studying] Torah and [performing] mitzvot will all be useless, heaven forbid, if they are done without *devekut*, as mentioned. Man's potential degree of *devekut* may be surmised from his capacity for *devekut* in corporeal matters. People differ from each other in this respect. All depends upon what the individual experiences in this particular *devekut*, i.e., physical pleasure: to that degree is he obligated in the service of Lord and in *devekut* with Him.[117] For all

---

117. R. Menahem Mendel links man's capacity for spiritual *devekut* with his capacity for physical *devekut*, defined as corporeal or mundane pleasure. The more passion and pleasure one is capable of experiencing in everyday life, the more one can and must strive for spiritual *devekut* with God. Immediately before this passage, R. Menahem Mendel alludes to Genesis Rabbah 80:7, which comments on the scriptural description of Hamor, who raped Dinah, the daughter of Jacob (Gen. 34). Hamor's soul "cleaved" (the Hebrew uses the root of *devekut*) to Dinah; he "loved" her; his soul "longed" for her; he "had delight" in her. The Midrash shows how the same words are used to describe the love of the Holy One for Israel. R. Menahem Mendel reverses it and suggests that Hamor's illicit passion is the paradigm for proper *devekut* with God.

there is to man is intellect, [appropriate] attributes, and *devekut*. All of man's above-mentioned perceptions[118] must therefore be directed toward the Eternal Creator, in order to assure the immortality [of his soul] after he dies and it separates from the body. If man succeeds in using all these perceptions in *devekut*, God will give him much pleasure. However, if he does not so train his perceptions and pleasures while he is still alive, but allows them to dwell upon ephemeral and transient physical things, when he sheds his material self, and his body perishes and is lost, what blessing will he leave after him? How will he begin the life of delight, using his personal capacities [for spiritual *devekut* and pleasure] if he does not learn the way of the living and eternal God while he is still alive?[119]

23. DEVEKUT AND MITZVAH
Source: R. Zvi Elimelekh of Dinov, Benei Yisaskhar, Tishrei 5:3

Immortality and ultimate happiness are achieved only through the service of God that comes about specifically by means of physical acts. It is an established rule that the whole Torah and all its mitzvot require actual performance, as opposed to the opinion of the philosophers, whose speculations led them to question how immortality and ultimate bliss can possibly be achieved through physical acts performed in this corrupt world.[120] This view was angrily disputed and ridiculed by the great rabbi, the author of *Gur Aryeh*.[121] He asserts that

---

118. That is, intellect, personal traits, and the capacity for *devekut*. The language is unclear, probably because of a corrupt text.
119. This brief passage, translated from a corrupted text, yields three important insights: *devekut* requires total concentration and the deliberate removal of all distractions; the capacity to enjoy this-worldly pleasures is a form of *devekut* which indicates the magnitude of one's capacity to achieve spiritual *devekut*; spiritual *devekut*, unlike the corporeal kind, survives the body and is man's means of immortality and eternal pleasure in God.
120. The problem treated here is the conflict between the high spiritual demands of *devekut* and the apparently this-worldly quality of the Torah's commandments. The solution, in this rather polemical passage, is to see the physical act as a mere garb for the essence of the mitzvah, which is the divine will. The problem is but another facet of the more general challenge of the potentially antinomian character of *devekut*: if what really counts is spiritual communion, why must it be achieved through mitzvot? While the question is acute for hasidic thinkers because of their special emphasis on *devekut*, it was discussed in a general way by the medieval philosophers.
121. Rabbi Judah Loewe (the Maharal of Prague; ca. 1525–1609). *Gur Aryeh* is a commentary on the Pentateuch: The reference is to *Tiferet Yisrael*, chap. 5.

we should ignore the physical nature of the mitzvot and only pay heed to the One who commands the mitzvah, and whose will is infused (*davuk*) in the mitzvah. When man, in performing the mitzvah, becomes attached (*davuk*) to the will of the Command Giver, his soul is in *devekut* with the Life of life. . . .

Now [actional] mitzvot, such as tzitzit, tefillin, and mezuzah, seem like additions to the Torah.[122] The reason given for tzitzit, for example, *That ye may look upon it, and remember all the commandments of the Lord* (Num. 15:39), seems to indicate that there is no independent need for this mitzvah, and it is merely an act that reminds us of the Torah's other mitzvot. This may provide a pretext for someone to assert that since he has a good memory, he has no need for such signs, or he will make a different reminder for himself. Similarly for tefillin and mezuzah: *That you may remember the day when you came forth out of the land of Egypt all the days of your life* (Deut. 16:3).[123] Here again one may find excuses, heaven forbid, to desist from actually observing these mitzvot, since it is not their performance per se that is required, but their function as reminders to observe the rest of the Torah, and hence they themselves are superfluous. Far be it from us to say so! Rather, we are duty-bound to fulfill His commandments in actual practice exactly as God commanded us. These acts are in fact the assurance of our ultimate bliss and the immortality of our souls.

Now, these thinkers [the philosophers] invented rationales for some of the commandments, as when they sought to explain the sacrifices. God, so they reasoned, commanded the sacrificial offerings so that people would no long make offerings to demons, as in the pagan worship practiced in Egypt. As proof for this explanation they cite the verse *And they shall no longer sacrifice their sacrifices unto the satyrs, after whom they go astray* (Lev. 17:7).[124] One might conclude that any intelligent person who does not follow such foolishness should be exempt from the obligation of sacrifices. Far be it from us to say so!

---

122. These three commandments—the fringes on four-cornered garments, the phylacteries on arm and forehead, and the scriptural passages on the doorposts—seem to be but reminders to perform the Torah's other commandments and thus, in themselves, superfluous.

123. The passage quoted does not pertain to tefillin and mezuzah, but to the observance of Passover and the Passover sacrifice. However, a similar reason is given for tefillin in Exod. 13:16: "And it shall be for a sign upon your hand . . . for by strength of hand the Lord brought us forth out of Egypt."

124. The view so vehemently criticized here is that of Maimonides in *Guide of the Perplexed* 3:46. Cf. the criticism of Maimonides in Abarbanel's introduction to Leviticus.

The true purpose of the commandments is *devekut* unto the Life of Life. There is absolutely no way or possibility for the human mind to fathom the essence of the divine Intellect. . . . We are required to perform the mitzvot as they were given, in actual practice. We must look, however, not to the corporeal nature of the commandment but to the will of the blessed Commandment Giver which is infused (*davuk*) in the commandment. . . .

When man becomes attached to the Higher Will by performing a mitzvah, his soul attains *devekut* with life forevermore.

24. A PARADOX
Source: R. Zevi Elimelekh of Dinov, Agra de-Kallah to Lev. 19:2, II, 40c

Ye shall be holy, for I the Lord your God am holy (Lev. 19:2).

We must understand the reason offered in this verse, namely, *for I the Lord your God am holy.* How is it possible to compare the holiness of a material creature to His blessed holiness?

I believe that the answer is as follows: The Creator commanded us not to follow the desires of our hearts even when we are engaged in necessary mundane activities, such as eating and drinking and marital relations. At such times, we must intend only to do His will—to proceed, using the strength derived from the eating, to the service of God and to extricate the sparks of holiness, and so forth; and also in marital relations, to fulfill the commandment to perpetuate the species, but divest ourselves of any pleasure from the physical act.

Now, if the Creator had commanded us to be completely separated from, and not at all engage in, materiality and corporeality, and had He created us in such a fashion that we could exist without involvement in materiality and corporeality, then it would be very simple for us to do so. However, as things are now, it is necessary for us to be connected to the corporeal; nevertheless, we were commanded to be separate from it,[125] i.e., not to satisfy our desires while engaged in physical activities except for a higher purpose. This is very difficult for a corporeal being to understand. It is also difficult to understand why the Lord fashioned the human race in this manner.

Thus it is written *Ye shall be holy,* so that you will be separated from materiality (for holiness, as we know, means separation from the corporeal and material); as the Rabbis said, "Sanctify yourself [by refrain-

---

125. The Rabbis interpret "Ye shall be holy" as "Ye shall be separate," i.e., transcend your material nature (Sifra to Lev. 19:2).

ing from indulging] in all that is permitted to you."¹²⁶ Even when you are involved in what is permitted, you must be holy and separate, and not connected to corporeality.

If you should ask how it is possible to maintain two opposites, and why the Lord made man this way, Scripture offers the reason: *for I, the Lord your God, am holy*. We are commanded to *walk in His ways* (Deut. 28:9). And the Creator is concealed and separated from all human thought and has no connection to creatures. Nevertheless, if, heaven forbid, His providence and His grace (*shefa*) and His life-force were withdrawn from them for but an instant, they would be annihilated. No created being can move except by means of His overflowing grace (*shefa*) and life-force. In order to teach this perfect faith, we were commanded to walk in His ways, and to engage in corporeality both by connection and separation.¹²⁷

Understand this subject, and you will give delight to your soul, for these words are profoundly wise. Thus Scripture says, *for I the Lord* (am separate from all created beings;¹²⁸ and nevertheless I am) *your God*, who relates to you and is your Cause.¹²⁹

25. JOSEPH'S ACHIEVEMENT
Source: R. Yehudah Aryeh Leib of Gur, Sefat Emet to Vayigash, I, 246 (in the name of his grandfather, R. Yitzhak Meir Rothenberg of Gur [1799–1866], author of Ḥiddushei ha-Rim)

And Joseph made ready his chariots, and went up to meet Israel his father, to Goshen; and he presented himself unto him, and fell on his neck, and wept on his neck a good while (Gen. 46:29). Rashi comments: Joseph wept on the neck of Jacob, but Jacob did not weep on the neck of Joseph or kiss him, because, our Rabbis said, Jacob was occupied in reciting the Shema.

In that case, why wasn't Joseph too reciting the Shema?¹³⁰ I believe that Joseph, who [retained his spiritual eminence and moral integrity

---

126. Sifre on Deut, Re'eh 14:21; Yevamot 20a. See also Nahmanides to this verse.
127. That is, man's paradoxical relation to the material world reflects, by virtue of *imitatio Dei*, God's paradoxical relation to the universe as such—absolute and related, transcendent and immanent.
128. The Tetragrammaton implies transcendence, absoluteness.
129. The reference to *"your* God" implies relatedness.
130. The obligatory recitation of the Shema is limited to the first three hours of the day. If it was a time when Jacob had to recite the Shema, wasn't Joseph under the same obligation?

while he] was in the house of his Egyptian master, represents the class of those who achieve *devekut* with the Lord even when occupied in mundane matters, and do not feel the least bit separated from Him. However, Jacob was beyond nature, and therefore was in *devekut* with the Lord and could not kiss at that time.[131] (And the discerning will understand.)[132]

26. THE ZADDIK'S DEVEKUT AND HIS PASTORAL DUTIES
Source: *R. Elimelekh of Lizhensk, Noam Elimelekh to Shelah, s.v. be-derekh aher alu zeh*

Introduction

R. Elimelekh emphasizes that the zaddik's social mission, i.e., his use of his privileges and metaphysical powers to help the common people satisfy their mundane needs, comes into conflict with his spiritual function of uninterrupted *devekut*. When his thoughts are totally absorbed in divinity, he cannot worry about his people and call down heavenly grace (*shefa*) upon them. Since the zaddik must not relinquish his communal obligations, he experiences a temporary lapse of *devekut*—a descent. However, inasmuch as it is for a good purpose, because God wants the zaddik to act on behalf of the people's material needs, his descent from *devekut* is a great mitzvah. Elsewhere, R. Elimelekh states that while the zaddik makes a sacrifice by descending for the sake of his followers, he is then able to cleave spiritually with them, which is also a form of *devekut*, i.e., with his people.

*

The zaddik who ascends ever higher, from rung to rung, is always in great *devekut* with the Creator. When he is in such *devekut*, his mind is distracted from people and thus he is unable to act on behalf of people's needs, for he is in no way part of this world. The zaddik, there-

---

131. Accordingly, and remarkably, Joseph was capable of superior spiritual potency; he was able to achieve *devekut* even while engaged in profane activity, i.e., his emotional release in meeting and kissing his father. Jacob, however, was "beyond nature"; since his *devekut* was all-absorbing and incompatible with mundane activity, he could only recite the Shema (= *devekut*) but not simultaneously greet his son with a kiss.
132. See the critical comments of R. Yitzhak Ze'ev Soloveichik of Brisk (1886–1959), quoted in the *Bet ha-Levi* Haggadah.

fore, must occasionally let go of his *devekut* for the sake of people's wants, so that he can do something on their behalf, whether by praying for their physical or economic needs or by other evocations of divine *shefa*, which is the zaddik's responsibility.

By occasionally letting go of his *devekut*, the zaddik performs a great mitzvah, for [his doing so] is the will of the Creator.[133]

27. THE ZADDIK EATS
Source: R. Elimelekh of Lizhensk, Noam Elimelekh to Korah, end

The zaddik, while praying, is, of course, in a state of *devekut* and sanctity, in pure, clear, and pellucid thought. When he eats, since eating is physical, it is as if a sword were hanging above his head lest he become grossly material and be cut off from holiness, heaven forbid, so while eating he strengthens himself and strives to sanctify himself ever more, in order to bind himself to God with great attachment and *devekut*. Thus, while eating, the zaddik sanctifies himself even more than during prayer.

However, this is not the case with other people. They are better able to sanctify themselves while praying than while eating.

ADDITIONAL NOTE

*1. The identification of *talmud torah lishmah* ("the study of Torah for its own sake") with *devekut* is a recurring theme in the writings of the Besht's disciples. While the Besht defined the association of *lishmah* and *devekut* as derived from the light of the Ein-Sof inherent in the letters of Torah, his disciples simplified the connection. They held that *devekut* is the basis and purpose of Torah study and, in effect, the definition of *torah lishmah* (e.g., see *Toledot Yaakov Yosef* to Shelah, sec. 4, pp. 499 ff.). Similarly, the Maggid R. Dov Baer: since God "has confined himself to the four cubits of Halakhah" (Berakhot 8a), the learner's thought becomes accessible to Him who is present at this very spot (*Or ha-Emet, Torah Lishmah*; p. 217 [n. 80]).
Elsewhere R. Yaakov Yosef quotes the Besht as saying that the requirement for divine inspiration during Torah study and prayer makes it advisable to study less when one occasionally senses a reduction of spirituality, for a respite will revitalize the spirit and make it possible to experience more truly spiritual devotion. He interprets Mishnah Avot 4:12, "R. Meir said: Decrease your occupation and busy yourself with Torah," as: "Decrease your occupation" does not refer to toil for worldly goods, but to occupation in Torah. The meaning that emerges is to temporarily lessen one's cognitive study of Torah in order to assure contemplative vigor during subsequent study (*Toledot* to Hukkat, sec. 3, p. 541a).

---

133. See *Noah Elimelekh* to Naso, p. 70a. Cf. G. Nigal, "Mishnat ha-Ḥasidut be-Kitvei R. Elimelekh mi-Lizhensk u-Veit Midrasho," pp. 94–95.

R. Hayyim of Volozhin, who rejects the hasidic identification of *lishmah* with *devekut*, and sees *devekut* as a hindrance to the intellectual perception of Torah (see *Nefesh ha-Hayyim* 4:2–3, and cf. my *Torah Lishmah*, pp. 230–232), holds that Torah study in itself constitutes a form of *devekut* to God (*Nefesh ha-Hayyim* 4:10; cf. *Torah Lishmah*, pp. 114–115). See below, chap. 7.

6

Worship, Service of God

INTRODUCTION

Of the many aspects of religious life, none is so intimate as the service of God as manifested in the act of prayer; yet nothing in man's private spiritual life is so enmeshed in the public realm. Many have lived without devoting themselves to contemplation of the deeper religious mysteries, but every observant Jew daily brings himself to God in prayer. Hence it is not surprising that prayer, more than any other area of Jewish existence, exhibits the interplay of theoretical probing and practical implications. The specific contributions of hasidic thought on prayer are rooted in its mystical, kabbalistic orientation and its stress on mental purity and emotional intensity. But we cannot understand the background to the selections presented in this chapter without noting the halakhic and social debates that framed the early history of Hasidism.

The question of focus or attention (*kavvanah*) is central to the "service of the heart" that is prayer. Proper intention is a halakhic requisite of prayer. By the period we are discussing, the minimal standard had been lowered, in recognition of human frailty,[1] but the God-seeking individual was naturally unwilling to settle for an inferior act of worship. Hasidic masters were aware that prayer was threatened by the crisis of the individual frustrated in his desire to summon the

---

1. See N. Lamm, *Halakhot va-Halikhot*, chap. 6, on the stipulation of implicit intention.

proper *kavvanah* (see selection 13). How to channel one's thoughts during prayer also raises the general problem of *maḥashavot zarot* ("alien [i.e., unwelcome] thoughts"), further addressed elsewhere in this volume (see chap. 11, "Elevation of Character"). The desire for sustained attention also inspired specific hasidic practices, on which more below.

But what is the content of the *kavvanah* that is to be attained? The halakhic backbone of prayer is petition. For many religious persons, however, petition seems fatally tinged with selfish desire and with the presumption that man can somehow wheedle God into conforming to his wishes.[2] While some hasidic teachers deal with the philosophical problem—how man can change God's will (see selections 9–10)—much attention was devoted to elaborating a kabbalistic theory that "elevated" the idea of petition. According to this view, the Shekhinah suffers cosmic exile, in sympathy with man's own suffering. The purpose of prayer is not to realize the petitioner's goals, but to redeem the Shekhinah. One prays, then, not for his own sake, but for the sake of God, as it were. This redefinition of the element of petition is shared by mitnaggedic kabbalists like R. Hayyim Volozhiner.

Kabbalistic theory occasionally influences both the general mood and the specific thoughts that accompany prayer. Thus R. Dov Baer, son of R. Shneur Zalman, the founder of Habad Hasidism, painstakingly mapped the terrain of contemplative and ecstatic prayer. Contemplation (*hitbonenut*) involves meditation on God's presence in the world and the detailed structure of the sefirot and their interrelationships, while genuine ecstasy (*hitpa'alut*) grows out of this rigorous meditation.[3] An approach of this kind restricts the emotional spontaneity we customarily associate with the hasidic world, and was far from being universally adopted. A striking contrast is evident in the selections from R. Nahman of Bratslav, for whom prayer is a virtual conversation between man and his Maker.

Another kabbalistic notion with broad implications for the halakhic and social standing of Hasidism is represented by the special *kavvanot* associated with R. Isaac Luria, the Holy Ari. These mystical "intentions" attached to the text of the liturgy shifted the emphasis from the manifest content of the prayer to the kabbalistic secrets

---

2. For a defense of petitionary prayer, sustained by the thought of R. Joseph Soloveitchik, see S. Carmy "Destiny, Freedom and the Logic of Petition."

3. R. Dov Baer's writings are not represented here. For an outline of his approach, see L. Jacobs, *Hasidic Prayer*, pp. 84–92, 98–103.

encoded therein.[4] As the *kavvanot* were introduced into a modified version of the Sephardic prayerbook, adopting them required the Eastern European Jew to relinquish the Ashkenazic text of his fathers, and this change of custom added a halakhic difficulty to the innovation. In fact, the new text was used privately by several renowned non-hasidic rabbis, including R. Moshe Sofer (the Hatam Sofer) of Pressburg (following his teacher, R. Nathan Adler), who objected, nonetheless, to its acceptance by laymen.

Hasidic thinkers were impelled to endorse the popular employment of the Lurianic text. To justify the deviation from the inherited communal practice, they argued that the tradition of each group of Jews was authoritatively ordained as the unique channel to God for that group; the Lurianic version, however, remains supreme and was never rejected by the elite.[5] But what right have simple Jews to use *kavvanot* that they do not understand? To this R. Elimelekh of Lizhensk answered that the average man need not dwell upon the mysteries of the text, and indeed it would be presumptuous of him to do so; his *kavvanot* are taken care of, so to speak, through his faith in the zaddik.[6]

It may be instructive to compare this characteristic approach with that of R. Hayyim of Volozhin. R. Hayyim insists that prayer should concentrate on the simple meaning of the words, using the authoritative text, and eschewing any other thoughts. What of the esoteric reasons hidden in the recesses of the text? Since we cannot penetrate the full meaning intended by the Men of the Great Assembly, who fixed the text, we must remain faithful to their conception.[7] Note that the function of talmudic authority in R. Hayyim's framework is similar to that of the zaddik in R. Elimelekh's scheme, namely, to enable the common man to pray simply, without worrying about the deeper *kavvanot*.

The propensity of Hasidism to encourage the recitation of esoteric formulas also came to the fore in the controversy about *le-shem yihud*. This phrase serves as a preface to the performance of a mitzvah, expressing the desire to unite *Kudsha Berikh Hu*, the sefirah of Tiferet

---

4. For more on Lurianic practice and early Hasidism, see R. Shatz-Uffenheimer, *Hasidism as Mysticism*, chap. 10; and J. G. Weiss, "The Kavvanoth of Prayer in Early Hasidism."

5. See Jacobs, *Hasidic Prayer*, p. 168 n. 3.

6. Epistle appended to *Noam Elimelekh*. Cf. what his disciple, R. Kalonymus Kalman Epstein, states in his name, *Ma'or va-Shemesh*, end of *Nitzavim*, cited by Jacobs, *Hasidic Prayer*, pp. 80–81.

7. *Nefesh ha-Hayyim* II, p. 13.

(symbolically identified as masculine), with the Shekhinah (the sefi-rah of Malkhut, regarded as feminine). In a famous responsum, the eminent talmudist R. Ezekiel Landau of Prague criticizes the popular-ization of this practice.[8] He does not see the need for elaborate for-mulations of *kavvanah* in general, and is particularly concerned that a worshiper preoccupied with striving to articulate secret intentions risks falling into erroneous ones instead.

Distinct from the mystical affiliations of hasidim at prayer that divided them from other Jews, the emotional intensity fostered by the movement also tended to confirm their social apartness. In addition to the cultivation of melody as an element in worship, hasidic prayer was marked by dramatic gestures. While physical demonstrativeness in prayer has a respectable talmudic pedigree, hasidic behavior often called forth the satire of their opponents, and sometimes internal crit-icism as well.[9] A parable attributed to the Besht will make the point. A drowning man gesticulates wildly because he is trying to save him-self; similarly, an individual for whom prayer is a matter of life and death will make violent gestures while praying. Neither action should arouse scorn in the spectator.[10]

The scheduling of prayer presented a more serious halakhic and social cause of dissension. Because of the emphasis on proper inten-tion, hasidim habitually recited the set prayers after the time man-dated by Halakhah had elapsed, for such intention cannot be sum-moned up instantly; it requires deliberate and often time-consuming effort. Their elaborate preparations for prayer included resort to tobacco in order to bring about the right frame of mind, seemingly immoderate attention to physical purity, immersion in the mikveh, and so forth. Beyond the apparent halakhic transgression, laxity with respect to the set times for prayer unavoidably led hasidim to worship separately from their non-hasidic brethren. Especially in a period when the specter of the Sabbatean heresy had not been banished, the establishment of separate *minyanim* could not fail to reinforce suspi-cions. Thus, for example, when R. Yaakov Yosef turned to Hasidism, his final rupture with his community is said to have resulted from his instituting his own prayer services.[11]

---

8. *Noda bi-Yehudah,* Yoreh De'ah 93. For more on the issue, including hasidic counter-arguments, see Jacobs, *Hasidic Prayer,* chap. 12.

9. See n. 69 below. See also selections 20 and 24, and Jacobs, *Hasidic Prayer,* pp. 62 ff.

10. *Keter Shem Tov,* pp. 24a–b, cited by Jacobs, *Hasidic Prayer,* p. 59.

11. *Shivḥei ha-Besht,* no. 48; see D. Ben-Amos and J. R. Mintz, *In Praise of the Baal Shem Tov,* pp. 62–63.

Once they began to pray, hasidim were also known for the length of their worship. This was a natural consequence of the emphasis on whole-hearted intention and emotional involvement, though there were noteworthy exceptions, such as R. Menahem Mendel of Kotzk, who completed his prayers rapidly precisely because he upheld the highest standard of concentration. For their adversaries, the very duration of their devotions was a mark against the hasidim, for it seemed to reverse the hierarchy which placed the study of Torah above prayer. Hasidic thinkers, in fact, often argued for the merit of prayer as a central institution of religious existence.[12]

One last sociological note is struck by the late Jacob Katz. The hasidic approach to the institutions of prayer liberates the spiritual life, in effect, from the tyranny of the clock, be it halakhic or economic: "The rational use of time, that is, its division and fullest exploitation for practical purposes and for the realization of religious values, was basically impaired by making a virtue out of waiting hours until the opportune moment arrived for communion with God."[13] Whether one approves of this mode of structuring time or not, it ought to be recognized that much in the hasidic outlook is fundamentally out of harmony with what we call modernity, characterized by the Weberian concept of rationality.

Hasidism's response to this aspect of the challenge of modernity is at one with its responses to other aspects of the challenge: withdrawal. By withdrawing from the professions, and from any occupation that requires higher education, or, in some instances, even secondary education, hasidim avoid the threat of confrontation with modern modes of knowledge. By restricting their economic activities to a limited range of entrepreneurial enterprises, especially small businesses, they can in large measure control their own schedules. And, indeed, in hasidic areas, most retail businesses open at 10:00 A.M. or later, enabling their owners and workers to attend to their prayer obligations.

A Story

Once the Baal Shem Tov and his disciples were on a journey. In a forest along the way, they chanced upon an abandoned synagogue

---

12. See selections 7–8 and notes thereto.
13. J. Katz, *Tradition and Crisis*, p. 244.

and decided to pray the Minhah service there. The disciples opened the door and invited their master to be the first to enter.

Just as he was about to step into the shul, the holy Baal Shem Tov stopped and would not cross the threshold. The hasidim were perplexed but reluctant to question their master. But after a while, when the sun began to set and it would soon be too late for Minhah, they summoned up the courage to ask why he would not enter the shul.

The Baal Shem Tov replied, "I can't go in because it is so crowded; there is no room for us." The hasidim were astounded, because the shul was empty. Taking note of their confusion, the Besht explained: "A prayer, when uttered sincerely and wholeheartedly, always sprouts wings and soars upward to the Throne of Glory of the Creator Himself. But I feel that the people who once prayed here had no *kavannah*. Their prayers had no wings and collapsed and fell upon one another, so that the shul is now densely packed with dead, wingless prayers—and there is no room for us."

"And You Shall Serve the Lord Your God"

1. PURE MOTIVES
Source: *Geulat Yisrael,* quoted in *Sefer Baal Shem Tov to Bereshit, no. 17*

The essence of worshiping God is to serve Him truthfully, as is stated in the preface to *Tikkunei ha-Zohar. . . .*

The general rule that emerges from this is that we must constantly ponder and probe our every act, even our good deeds and the mitzvot we perform, making sure that they contain no admixture of ulterior motive, God forbid, or self-interest.

Our service should be only for the sake of His holy, glorious, and revered Name. All our deeds should have one purpose only: to serve God in truth and wholeheartedly.

2. THE PLEASURE PRINCIPLE
Source: *R. Levi Yitzhak of Berdichev, Kedushat Levi to Vayehi, s.v. ve'zot asher dibber*

On the verse *at your right hand stands a queen in gold of Ophir*[14] (Ps. 45:10), our Rabbis commented: "Because Israel loves the Torah as

---

14. The literal meaning of *shegal* is "queen" (see Rosh Hashanah 4a and Koren edition of the Bible), but the Talmud also understands it as "sodomy." R. Levi Yitzhak, as will

much as the nations of the world love sexual intercourse, you [Israel] have merited gold of Ophir as a reward."[15]

This presents a difficulty. Why was this gentile lust in particular compared to Israel's love for Torah? Do not the nations cherish any other lusts?

The answer is as follows: When you contemplate an act of lust, whether sexual or other, reflect that it comes from God, "and everything that God created in His world He created for His glory."[16] God is the end and purpose of this covetous thought, and the cause of the thought's occurring in your mind. Now a thing's purpose and cause is always more important than the thing itself. Therefore, reason to yourself, "Why should I desire something insignificant and transient? Isn't it better for me to serve the Creator and to love God, Who is the purpose of everything? If I desire something and satisfy the desire, I only satisfy that one lust at that one moment. But when I serve God with equal enthusiasm, I achieve all pleasures, for He is the totality of pleasure!" By this method of elevating lustful thoughts, you can elevate your evil urge from the depths to the greatest heights.

However, even though this method is a good one, it is not the ultimate in divine service. The reason is that one who employs this method is like one who serves himself, because he derives pleasure from his service of God.[17]

The ideal object of divine service is to give satisfaction to the Creator, so that He has the same type of pleasure that a father does when he plays with his precocious son, as it is written: *My son, if your heart is wise, my heart*[18] *shall rejoice, too* (Prov. 23:16). *May the Lord rejoice in His works* (Ps. 104:31) refers to the same thing.

Now, [most] worldly lusts give pleasure to man, and man is the recipient of the pleasure. But the sexual appetite is just the opposite.

---

become evident in the selection, understands it as "sexual intercourse" (see Deut. 28:30, where the written text [*ketiv*] is *yishgalenah* but the lection [*keri*] is *yishkavenah*). For our purposes the two are similar, but see Rashi ad loc. for the difference between them.

15. Rosh Hashanah 4a.

16. Avot 6:11, Yoma 38b.

17. With other hasidic thinkers, R. Levi Yitzhak did not deny the validity of deriving pleasure from religious observance, but considered it to be spiritual hedonism, inferior to the selfless form of worship expressed as giving pleasure to, rather than receiving pleasure from, God.

18. "My heart," according to the allegorization here, means God's heart. "My son" is God's son, man.

Man gives and woman receives, but man derives pleasure from giving even though he gives to someone else. This is the meaning of the previously cited passage in the Talmud, "Because the Torah is as beloved by Israel as sexual intercourse is by the nations of the world." Even as the giver in intercourse derives pleasure from the act of giving, so Israel loves Torah [study] and divine worship, for the essence of divine service is *bestowing* joy and pleasure, in the form of *shefa* [an overflowing of divine grace], upon the Creator.

This explains the meaning of the statement in the Talmud: "R. Hisda said to his daughters, 'Take a pearl in one hand.'"[19] It means that God, Who is called Great in Mercy,[20] tells the upper worlds, which are called daughters of the Holy One, to assist man in his worship of God, in accordance with the principle "He who comes to be purified is assisted [by divine aid]."[21]

Now in the first method [in which man intends to receive personal spiritual pleasure], man obtains aid easily. But the second method [in which man only desires to bestow pleasure upon God] is much more difficult, and is attained only by great effort. These two methods correspond to the functions of two parts of the female anatomy: the breasts, which give, and the womb, which receives. This explains the meaning of God's saying to the upper worlds, "Show the pearl," i.e., in the beginning be like breasts, which give, by bestowing an abundance of grace (*shefa*) to man from which he benefits. This is the first method. But the second method is when man is stimulated and willing to exert great effort in order to attain the objective: then man is to bestow satisfaction upon the Creator and the entire celestial realm. When ready for this higher form of worship, he is allowed to proceed to the womb, i.e., to give spiritual pleasure.[22]

---

19. Shabbat 140b. R. Hisda advises his daughters to allow their husbands to fondle their breasts ("take a pearl in one hand") in erotic foreplay, but to delay as long as possible the moment the husband's other hand reaches for their private parts, so as to enhance the pleasure.

20. There is an interesting allegory here based on a similarity in sound between the key words in the talmudic text. R. Hisda represents the *Rav Ḥesed* (lit., "God Who is abounding in kindness"; see Exod. 34:6, Num. 14:18), i.e., God Himself. He tells his daughters to "take a pearl in one hand," a euphemism for the breasts lovingly offered by a woman to her husband. R. Levi Yitzhak understands this as God telling the upper worlds (the "daughters" of God) to assist in the human worship of the Creator, the two erogenous zones symbolizing receiving (the womb) and giving (the breasts).

21. Shabbat 104a.

22. Thus, when it comes to worship or prayer, man's petition should not be self-centered, to meet his own needs (thus receiving pleasure) but *tzorekh gavo'ah*, for the sake of heaven: a theocentric petition for God's needs or pleasure, as it were.

3. DAILY PROGRESS
Source: R. Elimelekh of Lizhensk, Noam Elimelekh to Hukkat, s.v. o yomar de-hinneh, and Noam Elimelekh to Yitro, s.v. o yomar de-hineh

The holy people of Israel cannot possibly remain forever on the same [spiritual] level. Every day they ascend from level to level in the service of God because each of them possesses [within him] a portion of God above. This portion arouses each of them to the service of the Lord. Every day this portion grows stronger within him, for the service he performs today has a strengthening effect, arousing him the next day to even greater service; and so for every day thereafter. There is no end or limit to the service of God. Similarly, when one's service is defective, heaven forbid, one regresses from his level and needs reinforcement anew.

That is the meaning of *Ye shall be holy, for I the Lord your God am holy* (Lev. 19:2): i.e., because I, the Holy One, dwell within you and arouse you always [to new heights].[23] This makes it virtually impossible for you to be stationary; rather, you must move on in My service from level to level.[24]

Move steadily forward in the service of God so that each day you reach a [spiritual] height beyond that of the day before.

For instance, even if you spend the day studying Torah for its own sake *(lishmah)* and in *devekut*, with fear and with love, the next day examine your conduct; perhaps yesterday's Torah study was inadequate, and you did not do your duty. [This will awaken in you] a need to study today with greater holiness, purity, and abstinence, trembling with awe. And so [shall it be] every day.

---

23. R. Elimelekh interprets the biblical verse not as "ye shall be holy," but as "ye shall become holier," i.e., always progressing in holiness. Cf. Midrash Tanhuma, Lev. 4 (according to the version in Yalkut Shimoni ad loc., sec. 604), where the verse is interpreted as: "You shall be holy with many kinds of holiness, just as He is holy with all kinds of holiness," which may perhaps refer to the constant striving for a higher level of holiness. A similar exposition can be found in *Or ha-Ḥayyim*, by the saintly R. Ḥayyim ibn Attar, a contemporary of the Besht who was held in great esteem by the hasidic masters. Cf. *Sefat Emet* to this verse, homilies of years 5641 and 5634.

24. The terms *omedim* ("stationary") and *holekhim* ("moving") apparently refer to Zech. 3:7, "Thus said the Lord of hosts: If thou wilt walk in My ways . . . then I will give you access *(mehalekhim)* among these that stand by *(omedim)*." Angels are defined as *omedim*, i.e., nonmoving beings, because they can never achieve a higher level of holiness. Man, however, is a *mehalekh*, a mover, for he is capable of moving ever higher on the ladder of holiness, and the level of his prayer, or service of the Lord, is always changing.

4. TWO WAYS TO PURE PRAYER
Source: R. Yaakov Yosef of Polennoye, Toledot Yaakov Yosef to Vayishlah, s.v.
od yesh lomar

There are two methods in the great principle of serving the Lord. One
is to cleanse your thoughts first and then perform the mitzvah,
whether of deeds or words, so that it will be pure and lucid, without
any ulterior motive.

That is the mystery of [the verse] *And Isaac went out to meditate in
the field at the eventide* (Gen. 24:63). *Eventide* refers to alien and evil
thoughts, of which Isaac would carefully rid himself before he began
to pray.[25] By so doing he made sure that his prayer would be as clear
as the very heavens, as bright as day.

But there is another way, deeper than the first. . . . I heard from my
master [the Besht] that we should begin studying Torah, praying, or
performing a mitzvah in association with the evil urge, and not for
their own sake.[26] In this way, we prevent the *yetzer ha-ra* from attacking us, so that we will be able to complete [our session of studying
Torah, praying, or doing mitzvot] for its own sake.[27]

The conclusion is to first try to deceive the evil urge by cooperating
with it, and then, showing ourselves to be mighty as lions, to perform
the Lord's service for its own sake.

Admittedly there is a danger involved [in this approach]. You may
be captivated by the *yetzer ha-ra* while associated with it, and then
there is no telling who will emerge victorious. Perhaps you will no
longer be able to separate from it afterwards.

Nevertheless, remember that if you are careful you may succeed,
and pray to God to help you in the struggle against the evil urge. This
way may well turn out to be better than the first one mentioned
above.

---

25. Two puns on *lifnot erev*, "at the eventide": *lifnot* is interpreted as *lefannot*, "to
remove, to empty"; *erev* as "alien thoughts," either because "evening" and darkness
becloud the mind, or because *arov* means to "mix" or "pollute."
26. That is, do not seek to achieve the highest standard of spiritual and mental purity at the outset, but begin in a less-than-desirable frame of mind.
27. By appearing to conspire with the *yetzer ha-ra* one can neutralize it. The Besht real-
istically discouraged too high a standard at the outset, preferring that purity of
thought be reserved for the end of the process. He stressed the word "always" (*le-
'olam*) in the well-known talmudic dictum that "a man should *always* study Torah not
for its own sake (*she-lo lishmah*), for as a result of this he will come to study Torah for
its own sake (*lishmah*)." The great mitnaggedic theoretician, R. Hayyim of Volozhin,
said the same thing. See my *Torah Lishmah*, pp. 180–181.

5. THREE PRINCIPLES IN SERVING GOD
Source: R. Yaakov Yosef of Polennoye, Ben Porat Yosef to Vayera, s.v. u-neva'er pasuk[28]

Serving God through Torah study and prayer consists of attaching yourself to the letters [of the Hebrew alphabet], which are called *nefesh* ("soul"), as stated in the Zohar and in the Tikkunim, [which say] that the [Hebrew] letters are termed *nefesh*.[29] By drawing vitality from Above into the letters, man is able to elevate them to their roots, and thereby can elevate his own soul, by way of his attachment to the letter. That is the true purpose of learning Torah [or praying] for its own sake (*lishmah*). . . .

It may [also] be the meaning of the verse *Escape for your life (al naf-shekha)* (Gen. 19:17), namely, by attaching yourself to the letters which are called *nefesh* ("life, soul") . . . [and through them] to God, the Life of all living, you may well save your soul from all misfortune; for you are, after all, attached to life itself. . . .

This is one principle in serving God.

A second [principle is]: *Look not behind you* (ibid.). . . . View yourself as if you were standing before God all alone, with no one standing beside you or behind you.[30] . . .

A third [principle]: *Do not stay all in the plain* (ibid.). . . . Do not stay on the same [spiritual] level, but always keep perfecting yourself and moving on from rung to rung. . . . For [one who does not progress] is said to be standing on a *plain* [plateau]. Rather, you must *escape to the*

---

28. This message is excerpted from a homily on Genesis 19:17, in which the angels, warning Lot about the imminent destruction of Sodom, tell him: "Escape for thy life; look not behind thee, neither stay in all the plain; escape to the mountain, lest thou be swept away." In keeping with the homiletic style of the time, and as is characteristic of most hasidic exegesis, R. Yaakov Yosef's interpretation has little or nothing to do with the historical context to which the plain meaning of the verse refers. Instead, the intent of the verse is universalized and spiritualized by ingenious if often far-fetched plays on words.

29. The idea or technique of attachment (*devekut*) to the letters is a meditative practice introduced by the Besht's disciples as a substitute for the complicated, deeply mystical *kavvanot* of the Ari. See J. G. Weiss, "The Kavanot of Prayer in Early Hasidism," and Jacobs, *Hasidic Prayer*, pp. 74–78. Regarding letters as *nefesh*, see my "The Letter of the Besht" to R. Gershon of Kutov, especially p. 117, and below, no. 121, and Additional Note 9.

30. The second principle emphasizes the feeling of solitude in the presence of God. Man is more likely to strive for elevation when he sees himself as alone, with no one behind him or below him.

mountain (ibid.), that is, move steadily onward to greater heights of perfection, like a mountain climber. . . .

In material things, look backward [to those who are behind you], but in matters of the spirit, direct your gaze forward, to the level of the one who is above you.

6. SELF-ANNIHILATION AND SELF-AFFIRMATION
Source: R. Levi Yitzhak of Berdichev, Kedushat Levi to Lekh Lekha, s.v. u-Malki Zedek

In general there are two types of servants of the Creator. One worships the Creator by means of self-sacrifice, and the other worships Him through the commandments and good deeds. The difference between them is that the former's service is in the category of nothing (*ayin*).[31] He who serves God through the mitzvot is in the category of something (*yesh*), i.e., the existent or substantive, because the commandments themselves are in the category of *yesh*.[32] Therefore, he who worships through self-sacrifice, and [is in the class of] *ayin*, cannot draw God's abundant grace (*shefa*) down upon himself.

While worship through mitzvot and good deeds is in the category of *yesh*, it contains an element of *ayin*. Whoever draws upon the divine *shefa* through the commandments attaches himself to both *ayin* and *yesh*. This is so because through his intention to create pleasure for God, he places himself in the category of nothing. But performing commandments and good deeds involves him in the reality and in substance, the something (*yesh*) through which he brings down divine abundance upon himself from God.[33] Thus man sometimes sustains himself through his good deeds.

---

31. Self-sacrifice (*mesirat nefesh*) normally means willingness to die for a higher cause. In Hasidism, however, it implies not only physical but metaphysical self-surrender: willingness for one's identity, spiritual as well as corporeal, to be obliterated in the face of God's holy omnipresence. Self-annihilation of this kind is the mark of mystical devotion.

32. The second type of worshiper is normative rather than mystical. His divine service proceeds not through contemplation to self-annihilation, but through religious and ethical acts to self-affirmation. His goal is *yesh*, the opposite of *ayin*, and his medium is performance (rather than contemplation), which is something definable and limited, hence substantial.

33. The normative worshiper has a mystical dimension, in that the God whose law he observes is the Ayin or Ein-Sof of the Kabbalah, so that his religious life partakes of both *ayin* and *yesh*. The point is important, because R. Levi Yitzhak is here wrestling with an important problem for hasidic thought in his generation. On the

Prayer

7. THE COMMANDMENT TO PRAY
Source: Letter of R. Shneur Zalman of Liady to R. Alexander Sender of Shklov, Iggerot Baal ha-Tanya, ed. Heilman, p. 33 f.

Those who say that the commandment to pray is only rabbinic [in origin] have never seen the light. For while the text of the prayers and the requirement that they be recited thrice daily may be rabbinic,[34] the essential concept and content [of the mitzvah to pray] are the foundation of the whole Torah: to know the Lord; to acknowledge His greatness and glory with perfect and serene knowledge and an understanding heart; to contemplate them to such an extent that the intellective soul is inspired to love the Name of the Lord, to cleave to Him and His Torah, and to crave His mitzvot. All this can be achieved nowadays only by reciting the Pesukei de-Zimra[35] and the blessings before and after the Shema,[36] with full and audible articulation that arouses the concentration of the heart. Would that it were so, and more!

For R. Simon bar Yohai and his colleagues,[37] however, it was sufficient merely to recite the Shema in order to attain all the above. They were able to achieve it in the blinking of an eye because of their humil-

---

one hand, the mystical approach, which emphasizes man's self-obliteration through ontological absorption into the divine, is clearly a superior form of devotion, in the same way that the Ein-Sof, the great divine Nothing, is infinitely superior to the sefirot, which, because finite, are considered *yesh*. On the other hand, Halakhah forms the mainstream of Judaism, and the normative cannot be overlooked. See Additional Note *1.

34. On the question of whether the obligation to pray is of rabbinic origin or biblical (and therefore of a higher order), Maimonides holds that the principle of daily prayer is biblical, based on the Sifre's interpretation that "to serve Him with all your heart" (Deut. 11:13) implies prayer, but that the exact mode and wording, etc., of the prayer are only rabbinically mandated. See Maimonides' *Sefer ha-Mitzvot*, Positive Commandment No. 5, and Nahmanides' gloss; also his Hilkhot Tefillah 1:1 and *Kesef Mishneh* ad loc. Cf. R. Shneur Zalman's *Kuntras Aharon*, s.v. *hinneh lo tovah*. See also B. Naor, "Two Types of Prayer," which compares several hasidic approaches to prayer with that of Rabbi J. B. Soloveitchik.

35. The psalms recited before the benedictions preceding the morning Shema.

36. The Shema consists of Deut. 6:4—9, 11:13—21; and Num. 15:37—41.

37. The Talmud (Shabbat 11a) decides that while everyone else must interrupt Torah study in order to recite the Shema and the Amidah at the right time, R. Simon bar Yohai and his colleagues were exempted because they were constantly engaged in scholarship to the exclusion of any other occupation. On the relative merits of study and prayer, see my "Study and Prayer," and also the next selection.

ity and loyalty to the Covenant. But nowadays, whoever is close to the Lord and has even once imbibed the taste of prayer, knows and perceives that without prayer one cannot begin to serve the Lord in truth, [and can do so] only by rote.[38]

8. PRAYER AND TORAH
Source: R. Nahman of Bratslav, Likkutei Moharan, II, 25, s.v. gam

It is also good to transform Torah into prayer; when you study [Torah] or hear a Torah discourse from a true zaddik, make it into a prayer.[39] Beseech and plead with God that you will merit the fulfillment of everything that was said in the discourse, for [at present you perceive yourself as] very far from it.

If you are wise and love truth, God will lead you in the way of truth, which will enable you to understand by analogy how to conduct yourself in this respect, so that your words will be gracious and your pleas properly presented, pacifying God so that He will draw you nearer to His service in truth.

The subject of this conversation [i.e., the prayer][40] rises to very great heights, for especially when you transform Torah into prayer you cause an exceedingly high degree of delight up above.[41]

---

38. Paraphrasing Isa. 29:13.
39. R. Nahman here raises the issue of the merits of prayer vis-à-vis Torah study. The talmudic view is that Torah takes precedence over prayer, as pointed out in the preceding selection, and rebukes those who prolong their prayers unduly for "putting aside eternal life [Torah study] to engage in temporal existence [prayer]" (Shabbat 10a). The early hasidic masters stressed the supremacy of prayer over every other mitzvah, including Torah study. While they sensed this to be an innovation, they viewed it as a necessary and justified departure. R. Hayyim of Volozhin, the leading mitnagged, held a diametrically opposite view. See Additional Note *2.
40. R. Nahman often refers to prayer as a *sihah* ("conversation") between man and God; see below, selections 15 and 16.
41. R. Nahman's view is more radical than R. Shneur Zalman's. He recommends that Torah itself should be transformed into prayer. Accordingly, not only is prayer superior to Torah study, but the value of Torah study is measured in terms of the prayer developing from it. R. Nahman's view may be understood as an attempt to reconcile an even more extreme hasidic approach with the traditional view, and in this respect is similar to the view expounded by R. Kalonymus Kalman Epstein of Cracow, a contemporary of R. Nahman's, in his *Ma'or va-Shemesh* to Vayehi (Gen. 49:22). After stating that hasidim since the Besht's time have seen prayer as the exclusive means by which man can refine his character, R. Epstein continues: "However, in order to attain to pure prayer, it is necessary to engage . . . in studying Torah and in performing good deeds so as to learn how to pray with true fear and great love." See too his commentary to Gen. 28:16–17. Cf. Jacobs, *Hasidic Prayer*, pp. 18–20.

9. DOES PRAYER CHANGE GOD'S WILL? (1)
Source: R. Menahem Mendel of Vitebsk, Peri ha-Aretz, Mikhtavim, pp. 57 f.

I heard from the holy mouth of our master and rabbi [R. Dov Baer], the Maggid [of Mezeritch], when I was with him in the land of Volhynia, a commentary on the verse *He will fulfill the desire of those who fear Him, and He will hear their cry and will save them* (Ps. 145:19).

If you serve God in utter truth, you should have no desire or lust for anything except to do His will. How, then, do you come to pray and seek divine mercy for yourself, or even for others—attempting to change and reverse God's will, so to speak? If it is because of your own quality of compassion that you cannot endure [your fellow man's anguish] and cannot refrain from praying for him, why, as believers and the sons of believers, we ought to know that the quality of mercy implanted in the heart of man is but the outcome of a long process originating with God, evolving from world to world until it descends to the material world![42]

Take the totality of mercifulness to be found in the material world, including all living species, human and nonhuman. If it were possible to conceive and imagine that the totality of this trait in the whole world were concentrated in one person, it still would not measure up to an infinitesimal fraction of God's mercy. And if [despite all this compassion] the divine thought and will decided [to be harsh], who would dare to encroach upon the Lord's mystery? Isn't a servant of the Lord ashamed to pray for something [or someone], even when his compassionate yearnings are great?

But this can be explained as follows: God longs for the prayers of the righteous (*zaddikim*), and therefore contracts and conceals His mercy, while creating a desire [for His mercy] within the righteous. This results in their self-arousal, bringing about an awakening-from-below to pray and plead for His compassion, much as a son playfully ingratiates himself with his father. It is God's pleasure and delight; there is no need to elaborate.

---

42. In other words, even if a religious man's prayer issues not from a desire to change the divine decree, but simply as an expression of irrepressible sympathy with the person for whom he prays, that very sympathy or compassion is of divine origin (a concept underscored in Hasidism because of its doctrine of immanentism); hence, it is in apparent opposition to the divine decree which caused the grievous situation against which the prayer is directed.

This explains the brazenness of the righteous in attempting to alter God's will, when Scripture says explicitly: *I the Lord change not* (Mal. 3:6).

For in truth this does not constitute a change [in the divine will], inasmuch as it was His will all along. Compare a father who wishes to give something precious to his son whom he loves dearly for his great wisdom. But the father restrains and toughens himself, concealing his own wishes, and giving his son the impression that he will in no way give it to him. The father only wants his son to entreat him urgently, to the point that he is unable to refrain from giving, because of the abundant pleasure he derives from his son's pleading with him.[43] The comparison is obvious. There was no change of will [in either case], only a reinstatement of the original desire.[44]

This, then, is the meaning of "God will make[45] the desire of those who fear Him," thus providing Himself with an opportunity to *hear their cry and come to their rescue* (Ps. 145:20) because God yearns for their prayer.[46]

---

43. The father in the parable should not be misunderstood as engaging in a cruel manipulation of his son. The pleasure of which the Maggid speaks is that of enhanced love between father and son. The withholding and subsequent submission by the father increases the dramatic tension in the filial relationship, and the result is a stronger and more loving bond between father and son. Analogously, God wants man to pray so that he will not be merely a passive recipient of divine largesse, but an active partner in a love relationship.

44. For a different approach to this problem, see the next selection.

45. The word *ya'aseh* in the biblical quotation at the beginning of the discourse, usually translated "He will fulfill," is rendered literally as "He will make," i.e., God will instill or awaken in those who fear Him a desire to pray in order to fulfill His own yearning for the righteous to pray to Him. Without God's self-contraction and intervention, the zaddik would never pray, since he feels no personal needs and desires; to pray for others because of a feeling of mercy may seem improper to the righteous man because it is like doubting God's all-compassionate nature. Hence, the need to "make him a desire"—artificially, as it were—to pray.

46. This interpretation is quoted in *Maggid Devarav le-Yaakov*, no. 161. Elsewhere in the same work the Maggid expresses a similar thought in a different manner: "When one prays, God forbid that he should direct all his desire toward the corporeal thing for which he asks, for there is no more selfish motive than this. He should rather have the following in mind: Our Rabbis say that the cow wishes to suckle more than the calf wishes to suck (Pesahim 112a. Cf. Yevamot 113a, Lev. R. 34:8). This means that a giver has a greater desire to give than the beneficiary has to receive. So it is with God: His pleasure in benefiting His creatures is greater than that of the creatures whom He benefits" (*Maggid Devarav le'Yaakov*, p. 221, no. 129; cf. Jacobs, *Hasidic Prayer*, pp. 29–30).

Actually, the Talmud says as much explicitly: "Why were our patriarchs [and matriarchs] barren? . . . because God longs for the prayers
of the righteous.[47]

Now, the righteous man truly wants his service of the Lord and his
devekut to transcend time, namely, to be directed beyond the sefirot,
where there is no alien intrusion whatsoever and no lack of anything,[48] as is well known.

Praying for anything that is under [the influence of] time and its
needs is tantamount to a descent from the high level of *devekut*, but
he cannot possibly avoid doing so, since it is God, so to speak, Who
created this desire within him in order to produce in him the awakening-from-below, for God desires the prayers of the righteous, as
mentioned above.

10. DOES PRAYER CHANGE GOD'S WILL? (2)
*Source: R. Zevi Elimelekh of Dinov, Benei Yisaskhar, Ma'amarei ha-
Shabbatot 8:8*

The early thinkers asked how prayer can be efficacious. Does not it
imply, heaven forbid, a change in God's will? Before the prayer, He
willed things one way, and afterwards His will is altered.[49]

---

47. Yevamot 64a. R. Menahem Mendel adds an interpretive comment to the Talmud's
question: God showed Adam every generation and its scholars (Sanhedrin 38b),
including Isaac and Jacob and the children of Rachel by Jacob. Since this indicates that
God never intended the fathers of the nation to be barren, it confirms the conclusion
that their childlessness was merely a temporary obstruction by His divine will to
induce them to pray.

48. The truly righteous person (zaddik) does not want to pray for anything physical,
but directs his worship to God in His capacity as Ein-Sof, beyond the ten sefirot. In
the world of Ein-Sof there is no differentiation, no relationship, and hence no perception of want or need. Such alien intrusion characterizes the world of the sefirot in
which God turns outward to relate to man.

49. God's impassibility is one of the classical problems of medieval Jewish philosophy.
God does not change His mind, for as the Bible states: "The Glory of Israel will not
lie or repent; for He is not a man that He should repent" (1 Sam. 15:19), or (as in Mal.
3:6), "I the Lord change not," cited in the preceding selection. However, a deterioration in man's moral condition seemingly evokes a corresponding change toward man
in God. See, e.g., 1 Sam. 15:11, "I repent that I have set up Saul as a king" (cf. Hertz,
Pentateuch and Haftorahs, p. 998 n. 29), or "And it repented the Lord that He had made
man on the earth" (Gen. 6:6). The same is also true when man changes from evil to
good, as in the case of Nineveh: "And God saw [the people of Nineveh] . . . that they
turned from their evil way; and God repented of the evil which He said He would do
unto them, and He did it not" (Jonah 3:10). It is this apparent inconsistency that concerns R. Zvi Elimelekh. See Additional Note *3.

Disciples of the Besht, in attempting to solve this problem, wrote that by means of prayer, man becomes [spiritually] attached to a higher plane and is transformed into a different person. As a result, the harsh verdict that hung over him is no longer applicable. When man prays to God, Who brings everything into existence, he becomes attached to a much higher plane and is transformed into a new being. Thus God's will is really not changed, for there was never a harsh decree against the being now in existence.

In my own humble opinion, there is another way to solve this difficulty, based upon a tradition I [have learned] from [well-known] authors.

Our Sages said: [at Creation] God stipulated with the Red Sea that it would divide its waters for the Children of Israel.[50] The same is true in other such instances, as the Rabbis stated in the Midrash[51] and also in the Zohar.[52] They said this for the same reason, namely, how can there be a change of will in [God, Who is utterly] One and without admixture.   Why should the Craftsman destroy His handiwork, changing the laws of nature that He instituted in accordance with His will at Creation? It must be said, therefore, that at the time of Creation, the Holy One stipulated with everything He created that their order of functioning might change at certain times and in certain ways, if such-and-such a thing occurred.[53] Now, man has free will. Hence, if the Egyptians had let the Israelites go immediately [when God ordered them to] and had not pursued them, the sea would not have split. But because the Egyptians hardened their hearts and pursued the Israelites, who in turn cried out to God, the sea was split.[54]

---

50. Genesis Rabbah 5:4.

51. Ibid. Cf. Exodus Rabbah 21:6; Mekhilta de-Rashbi and Midrash ha-Gadol to Exodus 14:27.

52. Zohar II, 49a, 170a.

53. There is a long history to the theory that miracles are not sudden occurrences but part of the order of Creation. See Maimonides, *Guide* 2:29 (and briefly in the eighth chapter of his introduction to Avot and in his commentary to Avot 5:5); Maharal, *Gevurot ha-Shem*, second preface (and briefly in chap. 42); *Tosafot Yom Tov* to Avot 5:5; and R. Bahya b. Asher to Exod. 14:27. All base this idea on the midrash cited here by R. Zvi Elimelekh. Rabbenu Bahya (citing Pirkei de-R. Eliezer) concludes: All miracles, signs, and wonders that have occurred since Creation were incorporated in the natural scheme of things to take place at a given time. To the onlooker (who sees something he is unaccustomed to) it seems supernatural, but in reality there is no reversal of God's will in these events, since it is not anything He wills now and did not want before. It was His original will that the predetermined change in nature would come into focus in its time through the righteous in the given generation.

54. See Exod. 14:8–17.

This, however, was the outcome of God's primordial will that such-and-such would happen if certain things occurred at a given time.

The same holds for prayer. There is no change in the divine will. It is all part of God's original plan that when a certain individual prays at a given time in a certain way, such-and-such will happen.

11. PRAYER OUT OF LOVE AND OUT OF AFFLICTION

Source: R. Yaakov Yosef of Polennoye, Toledot Yaakov Yosef to Shelah, s.v. ve-li nireh lefaresh

Maimonides writes in Hilkhot Lulav:[55] The joy one feels while performing the mitzvot, and for the love of God Who commanded them, is a great service. One who abstains from such rejoicing deserves to be punished, as it is written: [*And all these curses shall come upon thee . . .*] *because thou didst not serve the Lord thy God with joyfulness and with gladness of heart, while having an abundance of everything* (Deut. 28:45–47). In a similar vein wrote the Ari of blessed memory: [The joy of serving God should be] greater than any other joy in the world,[56] and [this verse] comes to teach us that Torah and prayer require a state of joyousness.[57]

To be sure, it occasionally happens that we are pained and depressed by suffering, or that something else grieves us, so that it is impossible to pray with joy. Nevertheless, prayer in pain and tears is acceptable and, moreover, becomes a wrapper to [envelop] all prayers . . . as the Zohar[58] interprets [the verse]: *A prayer of the afflicted when he is faint* (Ps. 102:1)—the prayer of the afflicted envelops all other prayers.[59]

---

55. End of chap. 8.

56. The Ari interprets the words *me-rov kol* as "greater than all other [joys]," rather than the usual "while having an abundance of everything."

57. R. Isaac Luria, *Sha'ar ha-Mitzvot*, beginning. Serving God with joyfulness (*simḥah*) is a basic tenet of Hasidism. It applies to every religious activity, including the study of Torah and the performance of mitzvot, as well as prayer. The zenith of joy, however, should find its expression during prayer. Here the servant of God who truly loves Him demonstrates his joy and happiness through ecstasy. The term often used in hasidic literature to describe the ecstatic state in prayer is *hitlahavut* (from *lahav*, "flame")—burning enthusiasm. See Additional Note *4.

58. Zohar III, 195a. cf. Zohar I, 23b.

59. The Hebrew reads *tefillah le-'ani ki ya'atof*. The root of the last word is *a-t-f*, which admits of three meanings. The first, especially in the verb's reflexive form, is "to be faint"; hence the standard translation, "A prayer of the afflicted [or poor] when he fainteth." The second is "to cover" or "to wrap up," as in Ps. 65:14. A third but much

If you are afflicted by trouble, suffering, poverty, and pain, bear in mind that what happened is merely a reminder to pray for similar wants in the Shekhinah, because the righteous are the deputies of the Matrona (another name for the Shekhinah, or Divine Presence). Your prayers will bring about a *tikkun* up above, and this will automatically result in a similar improvement down below.[60]

Hence there are two types of prayer. The first is based on love [of God alone, not on some felt personal need]. The second comes from a heart broken by poverty and affliction. Each type [is important] in its own time, and the second is equally acceptable in spite of being recited with pain and sadness.[61] There is, however, a major difference

---

rarer use of the verb is "to turn aside," as in Job 23:9. R. Yaakov Yosef generally adopts the second meaning in his homilies. There is a fourth possibility which some scholars have used in translating the cognate Aramaic *ittufa* in the Zohar passage (III, 195a) cited by R. Yaakov Yosef. The Zohar says that the poor man's prayer is superior to all others, even those of Moses and David, because the poor man offers his prayer from a broken heart, and it is that which God cherishes most. The fourth meaning is "delay, lateness"; see Rashi to Gen. 30:42. Hence, when the Zohar says that the poor man's prayer causes *ittufa* for other prayers, some (e.g., I. Tishby, *Mishnat ha-Zohar* II, p. 338) translate as "it turns aside" (i.e., overwhelms, weakens) other prayers. Others (e.g., Simon and Sperling in the Soncino translation of the Zohar V, pp. 277–278) understand it as "delay": the poor man's prayer takes precedence, making all others wait while it rises up before God. R. Yaakov Yosef seems to borrow the last definition as secondary. His primary translation is "covering up" or enveloping, and that in a double sense: certain prayers are "late" or delayed, a sign of their deficiency and inefficacy, and thus may be described as covered up in the sense that they are not worthy of standing exposed before God, especially in comparison to the excellence of the poor man's prayer; and covered up in the sense of being enfolded, i.e., the poor man's prayer envelops the other, weaker prayers in order to strengthen and elevate them at the right time. According to R. Yaakov Yosef, the Zohar passage thus reads: [the poor man's] prayer created a covering (*ittufa*) for all the world's prayers, which do not ascend until his prayer ascends. The Holy One says: let all the prayers cover themselves, while this prayer rises up before Me.

60. Mishnah Sanhedrin 6:5 teaches the principle of divine sympathy for human suffering: "When man is in pain, the Shekhinah says, as it were, 'My head is ill at ease, my arm is ill at ease.'" Hasidism teaches that man ought to pray for the *tikkun*, or restoration, of the Shekhinah's integrity or "health," and thus deflect his concerns onto God. When the prayer is answered, and the Shekhinah is "healed," man too will be cured of his suffering. See Additional Note *5.

61. This seems to contradict the earlier assertion that the second type has more power than the first and may even serve as a "cover" for it. The present statement should be understood as an adumbration of preferences, namely, that every effort should be made to pray with joy, out of love, even when one's heart is broken. However, if one is unable to overcome his affliction and depression, and prays in such a state of mind, it may be advantageous, as stated in the Zohar.

between these two kinds of prayer, and it can be most instructive for the service of the Creator. . . .

The general principle in serving the Lord by studying Torah and praying is to do so out of love. This is the root of everything. . . . Those who serve from love succeed in binding and attaching all of their 248 limbs, making them all as one. This is lucidly stated in a passage of Maimonides: When a man fulfills even one mitzvah out of love, it is accounted to him as if he had fulfilled all 613 mitzvot.[62] For the 248 positive commandments are parallel to the 248 organs in man's body, and the 365 negative commandments are parallel to his 365 sinews.[63] Therefore when a man performs even one mitzvah out of love [with the participation of] all his organs and sinews, the totality of 613 mitzvot becomes incorporated in his performance of the one mitzvah; for *ahavah* ("love") is the numerical equivalent of *eḥad* ("unity").[64] But when he performs a mitzvah not as an act of love, but as a *commandment of man learned by rote* (Isa. 29:13), sadly and sluggishly, it accounts for only one organ. As a result, he must fulfill all 613 mitzvot for each of his 248 organs and 365 sinews.[65]

There are two types of men. The common people perform the mitzvot as if learned by rote, in a state of laziness. It is as if they were asleep, which is a partial death.[66] The Rabbis said of them that the wicked are considered dead even while alive.[67] Then there are the zaddikim, who perform [their duties] out of love, eagerly, as if fully alert, as it is written, *but my heart is awake* (Song of Songs 5:2), unlike those who are in a state of *I am asleep* (ibid.). Thus the righteous are said to be alive (*ḥai*),[68] meaning full of zeal. Moreover, because of his love of God [the zaddik] cleaves to Him Who is called the living God, as it is

---

62. Maimonides' Commentary on Mishnah, end of Makkot. According to the Talmud, the human body has 248 organs and 365 sinews. The parallelism with the Torah's 248 positive and 365 negative commandments was often stressed in homiletic-kabbalistic and, of course, hasidic writings. R. Yaakov Yosef here reads this analogy into Maimonides' statement.
63. See Makkot 23b, end, and Rashi, who asserts that the 365 negative mitzvot are also parallel to the days of the solar year.
64. Both words have the same numerical value, 13.
65. One mitzvah performed with passion is the equivalent of all 613 performed without fervor and devotion. Hasidism emphasized the experiential dimension of religious life, as is here emphasized by the numerical equivalencies between the human body and the sum of the commandments. See below, nn. 69, 84.
66. Berakhot 57b: Sleep is one-sixtieth of death.
67. Ibid. 18b.
68. Ibid. 18a.

written, *To love the Lord your God, to walk in all His ways, and to cleave unto Him* (Deut. 11:22) . . . in other words, by walking in all God's ways one may achieve a state of loving Him and subsequently cleaving to Him, and then, *You that did cleave unto the Lord your God, are all alive this day* (ibid. 4:4).

This explains the meaning of *He that regarded the prayer of the wakeful (ar'ar)* (Ps. 102:18); the word refers to those who are wakeful when praying.[69] From them God accepts even a solitary prayer because they serve Him lovingly, and love is all-embracing [activating the 248 organs and 365 sinews] even when its practitioner is merely an individual on his own. True, God does not reject the prayers of the common people either, although they come forth in a laggardly manner, in a state of *I am asleep*, but only if the prayer is communal—only then *hath He not despised their prayer.*[70]

Now we may understand [the verse] *A prayer of the afflicted when he is faint and poureth out his complaint before God* (Ps. 102:1). The meaning is as follows: Occasionally a zaddik is compelled to pray [not out of love and joy but] out of affliction and pressure, because poverty and suffering have befallen him. This is truly prayer of the afflicted (*tefillat ha-ar'ar*), and the reason for it is a need to envelop the covered [i.e., embarrassed or imperfect] prayers which are inert and laggardly. The zaddik [finding himself in the same situation as everyone else] will then pray from the depths of his heart for the Shekhinah and the God of Israel to be unified,[71] thus repairing the deficiency. The zaddik's prayer then becomes the wrapper for all the covered [imperfect] prayers of those who habitually pray out of pain and by rote—those who would otherwise have to engage in communal prayer to be accepted.[72] Therefore it is said, *and [he] poureth out his complaint before God*, meaning alone, for in this instance even solitary prayer is accepted willingly.

What we also learn from this is that the [zaddik's] "lazy" prayer occurs only when it is necessary to repair other lagging prayers that need to be enveloped. . . .

---

69. The word *ar'ar* is usually translated as "the destitute," following Rashi and Ibn Ezra. *Metzudat David*, however, explains it in a way close to R. Yaakov Yosef's.
70. This explains why the verse begins with a reference to solitary prayer, using the singular *tefillat ha-ar'ar*, and ends with the plural, *tefillatam*. See Additional Note *6.
71. The kabbalistic ideal of all divine service is to unite the Shekhinah and the Holy One, i.e., to effect the integration and reunification of the sefirot.
72. The zaddik helps along the prayers of the common people even if they are recited privately and not communally.

This type of prayer, the prayer of the afflicted, has a graduated series of aspects, as I have learned from books and teachers.

The lowest grade is of the person who prays for himself, [asking] that his own wants be filled. . . .

Above that is the one who intends to repair a lack in the Shekhinah up above, which automatically results in his own improvement here below through the *tikkun* of his roots above. For the uppermost and the nethermost are all one single, indivisible unity.[73] In any event, he must not entertain any selfish motive in repairing either the above or the below. . . .

There is, however, another, still greater level: that even for the *tikkun* up above he does not insist that his entreaty be fulfilled. . . .

The best counsel for the wise man is to do his duty and pray as the occasion demands and then leave it to the Master of all to do as He pleases. This aspect [of prayer] is the most outstanding, for it involves serving God without expectation of reward.[74]

12. JOYFUL PRAYER
Source: R. Menahem Mendel of Vitebsk, Peri Etz to Emor

When you perform a mitzvah for the sake of heaven, i.e., *lishmah*, to fulfill the wishes of God, Who spoke and His will was done,[75] you arouse all the worlds, from the lowly, compound[76] world of Asiyah, through the countless worlds of Yetzirah, Beriah, and Atzilut,[77] up to

---

73. See above, n. 60.

74. Avot 1:3. Cf. *Degel Mahaneh Ephrayim* to Haftarat Ki Tetzei, p. 253. The conclusion is rather interesting in that, after reviewing a series of graduated spiritual exercises, R. Yaakov Yosef advises that it is best to be spontaneous and pray simply in response to circumstances, relying upon God to do as He wishes with the prayer. R. Hayyim of Volozhin similarly concludes that, with all the sophisticated distinctions between levels of spiritual complexity in prayer, it is best to pray with simple intent and leave it all to God. See his *Nefesh ha-Hayyim* 2:13.

75. Performing a mitzvah or studying Torah *lishmah* means that it is done sincerely and without any ulterior motive. The normal translation, "for its own sake," is not necessarily accurate, as the term is open to several definitions (see below, chap. 7). Here the major hasidic interpretation is offered parenthetically: an act performed purely for the sake of God, to fulfill His will.

76. A philosophical term denoting the inferior quality of mundane existence: compound as opposed to simple, which is spiritually superior because it is one, and therefore less prone to deterioration and conflict.

77. The four worlds, in Lurianic Kabbalah, mediate between the Ein-Sof and the mundane realm. R. Menahem Mendel identifies Asiyah as the scene of human, profane activity.

the Supernal Will.[78] For God, in His simple will,[79] chose to create the worlds for the sake of Israel, who are called "the beginning,"[80] because they accepted the Torah and the yoke of His kingdom, and as a result the descent of the worlds took place, bringing about the fulfillment of the practical mitzvot.[81]

When you perform one of God's commandments with all your strength and emotions, even including joyous inspiration in fulfilling a mitzvah, you arouse all the worlds with this joy, adding strength to the heavenly family, so to speak, and elevating all the worlds, including yourself, up to the Supernal Will. From there you return, bringing down grace (shefa) from world to world, all the way to this lowliest and nethermost of worlds.

The Rabbis said: "One must not rise to pray in sadness . . . only in the joy of performing a mitzvah."[82] Man's loftiest quality is the spirit of joyfulness. If joy is derived from doing a mitzvah, it [produces] a yihud ("unification") that is superior to everything.

Prayer, as is well known, is called the Soul of David, which is the Shekhinah. That is why prayer is associated with nefesh, as in I poured my soul (nefesh) before God (1 Sam. 1:15).

The saying of the Sages that "the Shekhinah down below serves a purpose up above"[83] obviously means the following: Since His Kingdom is sovereign everywhere, even in the outermost parts of the worlds, if you petition or pray for something that you need, your only intention should be to fulfill the Shekhinah's wants [not your own], inasmuch as it is simply unfitting for something to be missing from the King's palace.[84] Prayer of this kind is a mitzvah: it is the prayer of

---

78. A synonym for Keter, the highest realm in the sefirotic system of emanations, hence the source of the other sefirot.

79. See above, n. 75.

80. Midrash Tanhuma (ed. Buber), Gen. 3. Cf. Rashi to Gen. 1:1.

81. The positive mitzvot that entail action. The point is that the purpose of creation is the performance of mitzvot. Doing them lishmah and joyously activates the creative order of the cosmos, raising it, as it were, to the highest point and, when it returns, bringing new vitality and the abundance of divine grace (shefa) to our worldly sphere.

82. Berakhot 31a.

83. See Megillah 29a.

84. For a fuller treatment of the rabbinic and kabbalistic theme of the Shekhinah's sympathy for suffering man, and the hasidic emphasis on projecting one's own needs on the Shekhinah and praying for it, see the preceding selection. The text of the present selection indicates that the prayer should be based upon the premise that any defect in the divine realm is unthinkable, and hence the suffering of the Shekhinah must be alleviated.

the pious. However, if your purpose in praying is to satisfy your own lusts and wants, your prayer will not ascend up above; on the contrary, it will descend deep below into the impure shells (kelipot), God forbid, and will be declared impure.

The general rule is this: When a man performs even one mitzvah with the proper motivation (lishmah) and sanctifies himself below, he arouses all worlds up to the most high. And then he is hallowed up above, by means of [his bringing down the divine outpouring via] the descent of all the worlds awakened by his joyfulness in serving God.[85]

That is the meaning of *I will run the course of Thy commandments, for Thou dost enlarge my heart* (Ps. 119:32): the pathway produced by the joy of performing a mitzvah turns into a paved highway where travel is fast, since there is no obstacle or resistance. A mitzvah performed for the sake of God "Who spoke and His will was done" is, in fact, His will, thus dispersing all the forces of evil, the kelipot, for they have no place in the realm [of the divine Will].

13. A PRAYER TO PRAY
Source: R. Levi Yitzhak of Berdichev, Kedushat Levi to Va'ethanan

The Talmud concludes that the words "God, open Thou my lips" [recited at the beginning of the Amidah][86] are not considered an interruption between [the benediction of] Redemption (Geulah) and the Amidah even during the Shaharit service,[87] for inasmuch as the Rabbis decreed that it is to be recited, it is regarded as an extension of the Amidah. But then the [Talmud's] statement should have been, "The Rabbis decreed it as prayer."[88] One must conclude that this phrase was

---

85. Cf. Maimonides' Commentary to the Mishnah, end of Makkot: man achieves perfection by performing even one of the 613 mitzvot with true love and devotion to God.

86. The Amidah, also known as the Eighteen Benedictions (Shemoneh Esreh), is recited while standing and is regarded as the prayer par excellence.

87. The Talmud (Berakhot 4b, 9b) teaches that one must proceed to the Amidah, without interruption, immediately after the Geulah benediction, which is the conclusion of the reading of the Shema. The brief sentence mentioned is permitted, and is not considered an interruption, because it is regarded as a prayer, i.e., part of the Amidah.

88. Why, R. Levi Yitzhak asks, the unnecessarily cumbersome way of justifying the prefatory petition, i.e., because the Rabbis decreed its recitation we regard it as part of the text of the Amidah? Why not simply state that because the Rabbis enacted it, it is not considered an interruption? After all, the Talmud teaches that the Amidah

not included in the original enactment [of the liturgical text] by the Men of the Great Assembly, and when its recitation was decreed later, it was regarded as an extension of the Amidah [rather than as part of the original enactment].

Thus, "God, open Thou my lips" should be understood as a prayer for the ability to pray. The tannaim and their predecessors had no need to pray for this, for surely their prayers were pure. Only later, when "hearts diminished,"[89] did they feel compelled to add a prayer that our prayers [i.e., the prayers we are about to recite] should be pure.

Hence there are two aspects to prayer: the prayer itself, and a prayer for the ability to pray [properly].

14. PRAYER IN THE VERNACULAR
Source: R. Nahman of Bratslav, Likkutei Moharan, Tinyana, no. 25

Solitude is a superior virtue, greater than all others. At regular intervals, seclude yourself for an hour or more in a room or a field to converse openly with your Creator, [whether] offering arguments or apologies, in words that are grateful, pacifying, and conciliatory, beseeching and imploring Him to bring you close to Him in order to serve Him sincerely.

This prayer and conversation should be in the vernacular, Yiddish, since you may find it difficult to express yourself fully in the Holy Tongue (Hebrew). Furthermore, since we do not customarily speak Hebrew, your words would not come from the heart. But Yiddish, our spoken language and the one in which we converse, more readily engages the emotions, for the heart is more attracted to Yiddish. In Yiddish we are able to talk freely and open our hearts and tell God everything, whether remorse and repentance for the past, or supplications for the privilege of coming closer to Him freely from now on, or the like, each of us according to his own level. Try carefully to make this a habit, and set aside a special time for this purpose every day. [Then] you will be happy the rest of the day.

---

itself was composed by the Men of the Great Assembly, whose decrees and enactments are considered rabbinic. One must conclude that the Rabbis who added this supplementary phrase were not the same as those who composed the Amidah, and that the latter (i.e, the Men of the Great Assembly) did not know of this phrase or consider it necessary.

89. When spirituality had so declined that it was difficult to sustain purity of intention in prayer.

Such conduct is an exceedingly great virtue. It is a highly advisable way to come close to God. It is a comprehensive plan, for it includes everything. [It provides an opportunity for every one of us] to converse with God and to entreat Him if we feel deficient in our divine service, or if we feel completely remote from His service. Even if you occasionally fumble for words and can barely open your mouth to talk to Him, that in itself is [still] very good, because at least you have prepared yourself and are standing before Him, desiring and yearning to speak even if you cannot. Moreover, the very fact that you are unable to do so should become a subject of your discussion and prayer. This in itself should lead you to cry and plead before God that you are so far removed from Him that you cannot even talk to Him, and then to seek favor by appealing to His compassion and mercy to enable you to open your mouth so that you can speak freely before Him.

Know that many great and famous zaddikim relate that they reached their [high] state only by virtue of this practice. The wise will understand from this how important such practice is and how it rises to the very highest levels. It is something that everyone, great or small, can benefit from, for everyone is able to do this and reach great heights through it. Happy is the one who takes hold of it![90]

15. IN SOLITUDE
Source: R. Nahman of Bratslav, Likkutei Moharan, I:52

We merit reabsorption into our [spiritual] roots—once again becoming part of the Unity of God, whose existence is necessary[91]—only by means of self-annihilation. It is impossible to attain self-nullification without solitude. Only in solitary talk with our Creator can we abolish all our lust and evil traits to the point that we completely negate our material existence and are reabsorbed in our roots.

The best time for such solitude is at night, when the world is free of worldly occupations. Daytime, the time of worldly pursuits, is distracting and confusing, preventing us from becoming attached and reunited with God. Even if you are not personally occupied [with the material and corporeal], it is hard to achieve self-nullification when

---

90. See Additional Note *7.
91. Necessary existence, as opposed to contingent existence, is a medieval philosophical concept applied to God, whose existence is absolute and without cause, and whose nonexistence is unthinkable. All else is contingent existence. But see the end of this selection.

the rest of the world is busy pursuing this-worldly vanities.

The solitude should take place in a secluded area, outside the city limits, where there are no people milling about. A place where there is [usually] traffic during the day, with people pursuing their worldly affairs, is not conducive to solitude and reabsorption in God, even if there is no one around at the moment. Therefore, both nighttime and a lonely road or place are needed.[92]

During these solitary sessions, empty your head and mind of all worldly interests, negating everything until you truly attain self-annihilation. In your loneliness at night in a secluded area, begin by reciting prayers and conversing frequently [with God] until you have succeeded in abolishing one or another lust or bad habit. Then continue your solitude until another of your passions and evil traits is voided. And continue in the same way for a longer time, until you have rid yourself of all of them . . . until there is nothing left of you . . .[93]

And only then, when you have attained true self-annihilation, does your soul rejoin its roots, namely, Him Whose existence is necessary. Then all the world is included with your soul [as it is reabsorbed in its divine] root, whose existence is necessary, for everything depends upon Him. Thus is the whole transformed into necessary existence.[94]

---

92. This discourse revolves around Mishnah Avot 3:5, "He who keeps awake at night and goes on a road alone while turning his heart to vanity, such a one forfeits his soul." The author deduces that to secure the eternal life of one's soul by rejoining its root and source, one should do the things mentioned in the Mishnah, namely, be awake at night and go on a road alone, but instead of turning one's heart to vanity, one should utilize the solitude of night and the lonely road for the kind of meditation that leads to spiritual self-annihilation. (There is a clever homiletical pun here on the words *battalah* ["vanity"] and *bittul* ["negation" or "self-annihilation"].)

93. The *bittul*, or self-nullification, of R. Nahman would seem, from this passage, to be more ethical than essential or ontological, as is the case with R. Shneur Zalman and the Habad school. The self whose annihilation R. Nahman advocates is not the adept's identity, but the totality of his evil qualities (e.g., avarice, lust, etc.). However, a parenthetical passage indicates an ontological *bittul*. After the adept has annihilated all his desires and evil traits, something may still remain of him, in that he has not completely annihilated his pride and presumption, and considers himself a "something" (or "somebody"). "He must resort to ever greater effort in solitude until nothing remains of him . . . and then he has truly achieved annihilation." Nevertheless, R. Nahman's emphasis is clearly ethical-moral.

94. It is heresy, R. Nahman says in an earlier passage, to ascribe necessary existence to anything but God. What about the error of certain heretics who consider the world's existence necessary rather than contingent? He answers that when the adept succeeds, through solitary prayer, in being reabsorbed in his root, i.e., his place in the

16. PRAYING ALOUD
Source: R. Shneur Zalman of Liady, Tanya, Iggeret ha-Kodesh 22

I come as one who remembers and recalls former things[95] in general, and in particular to those who willingly conduct their services of prayer with raised voices.[96]

Let them strengthen themselves with all might and power against anyone from within or without who seeks to impede them. For it is the *will of those who fear Him* (Ps. 145:19),[97] transcending the wisdom and understanding God gave them in order to know and do all that God commanded with intelligence and knowledge.

There should be but a simple will and a spirit of voluntary offering in everyone whose heart prompts him to engage in perfect service and cause gratification to the Creator. . . .

Preparing for Prayer

17. FIRST WORDS
Source: Besht, Keter Shem Tov, p. 20b; Likkutim Yekarim, p. 12

Guard your mouth and tongue from any kind of talk [before praying]. Our Rabbis even prohibited permissible statements (i.e., statements that would be legitimate in other circumstances) before praying, such as greeting another person,[98] because this too may be detrimental to prayer.

As is well known, the world was created through thought, speech, and deed. The beginning of everything is thought; speech is a branch of thought, and deed is a branch of speech.

Godhead, he is united with and thus becomes an integral part of the necessary existent. By means of Jews who undergo this spiritual transition, the existence of the whole world is transformed from contingent to necessary. R. Nahman's thesis is not philosophically cogent, but when we recall that he is concerned more with ethics than with theories of existence (see the preceding note), his words become more meaningful. He is using metaphysical terminology to underscore a spiritual and ethical teaching.

95. See Keritot 8a.
96. See Additional Note *8.
97. The end of the verse is significant in this context: "He will hear their cry and save them."
98. Berakhot 14a.

So it is with man. When he rises from sleep he becomes a new creature, as it is written: *They are new every morning* (Lam. 3:23). If he starts his day with [profane] talk, even the permissible kind, and surely [if he begins] with improper speech, even if he prays and studies Torah afterwards, it will be considered merely a continuation and ramification of his first words. For just as speech is a branch of thought, and subordinate to it, so words derive from and follow the first words.[99] Something similar is written in the Zohar[100] and in the writings of R. Isaac Luria concerning the duty to honor an older brother.[101] Because the eldest brother, the firstborn, takes the principal share, the other brothers are regarded as branches of the first [and are secondary to him].[102] The same is true here.[103]

Therefore, carefully hallow and purify your first words [each day], and similarly cleanse your first thought, so that it is attached to holiness, thus ensuring [the sanctity and purity] of all your subsequent words.

18. THE ODOR OF PRAYER
Source: R. Elimelekh of Lizhensk, Noam Elimelekh to Beha'alotekha, s.v. va-yishma Mosheh

The angels appointed to bring the prayers of Israel before the Holy One distinguish between proper, lucid prayers and those disqualified by unseemly thoughts, for a thought of this kind will not be a *sweet aroma to God* (Lev. 1:9 ff.).[104] This is so even according to those who

---

99. The first words a man speaks each morning determine the quality of his words and deeds the rest of the day. Therefore, one should begin the day with prayer.
100. Zohar III, 83a.
101. See Ketubbot 103a, "Honor your father and your mother" (Exod. 20:12): the *vav* of *ve-et imekha* ("and your mother") serves to include the older brother; Maimonides, Hilkhot Mamrim 6:15; *Shulḥan Arukh*, Yoreh De'ah 240:22.
102. This reasoning would limit the duty to honor the older brother to the firstborn. However, Maimonides and the *Shulḥan Arukh* understood the reference to mean any older brother; see n. 101.
103. Just as the younger siblings are subordinate to the firstborn, so the first words a person speaks in the morning are his "firstborn," and everything else he says during the day is conditioned by them.
104. The idea that prayers should be fragrant is derived from the fact that prayer was enacted as a substitute for the Temple sacrifices (Berakhot 26b), which provided "a sweet aroma to God" (Lev. 1:9 ff.; cf. Menaḥot 110a). Halakhah requires that the act of prayer resemble the sacrificial service for which it substitutes (*Tur* and *Shulḥan*

hold that angels do not discern human thoughts. How then can they tell [which prayer is pure and which impure]? By their divinely granted talent for "smelling" prayers to determine their quality.

A man who carefully avoids everything evil throughout the day, such as flattery, lies, buffoonery, anger, haughtiness, hatred, rivalry, and other things that have a damaging effect, and instead occupies himself in Torah, acts of kindness, and the performance of mitzvot—when a man of this sort comes to pray, all his good deeds infuse a pleasant aroma into his prayer, just as spices produce a good smell in cooked food. The opposite [kind of behavior] will, God forbid, cause a foul odor in one's prayer.

19. SERVICE AND CHARACTER
Source: R. Elimelekh of Lizhensk, No'am Elimelekh, Lekh Lekha, s.v. va-yomer ha-Shem

Now the Lord said unto Abram: Get thee out of thy country, and from thy kindred, and from thy father's house, unto the land that I will show thee (Gen. 12:1).

We must serve the Creator on three levels, each higher than the next. To begin with, we must break the power of desire which is part of [our] natural constitution, such as the desire to eat and drink, by making sure that our eating and drinking take place in sanctity and purity. Thereby we break the power of other gods, for by *gematria* (arithmetical substitution), the word *elohim* ("gods") is identical with *ha-teva* ("nature"), both equaling eighty-six.[105] Second, we must break our own lowly qualities, which have been part of our character from the day we left our mother's womb. Some of us are inferior to others with regard to certain character traits, such as anger.[106] After we break

---

Arukh, Orah Hayyim 98:4). On fragrance resulting from good deeds and attributes, see Genesis Rabbah 61:4 on "And Abraham took another wife and her name was Keturah"; says R. Judah, this was Hagar (his former concubine), but she is called *keturah* (from *ketoret*, "perfume") because her conduct and good deeds spread a fragrant aroma, as does incense. The basic idea is that prayer cannot be isolated from its human context. A man's ethical conduct invariably affects his prayer in ways that are immediately evident.
105. Man's natural lustfulness is equated with idolatry. By destroying the other gods (whether literally idols or, symbolically, his material nature), man succeeds to the service of the living God. This level of service is called *yir'ah*, "fear" (of God).
106. R. Elimelekh differentiates universal appetitive attributes, the result of man's corporeality (e.g., hunger and thirst), and individual character deficiencies (e.g., anger).

the power of these low and despicable qualities, we move on to the category of *ahavah*, love of the Creator.

Finally, we must arrive at the third level, *tiferet* ("beauty").[107] We have already explained above, in the portion of Noah, that all man's deeds must be beautiful and glorious; thus the tanna stated that the right path a man must choose is "All that brings glory (*tiferet*) to him who adopts it and also brings him honor (*tiferet*) from men."[108]

All this is suggested by our verse. *Get thee out of thy country*[109] symbolizes the first level, that of the physical and earthly desires which are part of the material nature that we must transcend.

And from thy kindred[110] hints at the second level: the inferior qualities which are man's at birth.

And from thy father's house implies the third level. Most of man's odious boasting consists of arrogance and pride because of his father or grandfather's greatness.[111] We must abandon this lowly quality for a different type of Tiferet [i.e., going from self-glorification to glorification of God] which is good in the eyes of both God and man, as mentioned above.

Unto the land that I will show thee, the conclusion of the verse, refers to a high land.[112]

---

107. There is a play on words here. *Tiferet* is honorific, denoting beauty or glory in the service of God. Its reflexive form, *hitpa'arut*, denoting pejorative self-glorification, is abominable. Note that the three desirable traits, fear, love, and beauty, are counterparts, respectively to the three sefirot of Yirah (the equivalent of the better-known Gevurah), Hesed, and Tiferet. R. Elimelekh is saying that man must overcome his natural appetites and attain fear (of the Living God); neutralize his character limitations and attain love for God; and transform his egocentricity or self-glorification (*hitpa'arut*) to the glorification of God, serving Him with beauty (*tiferet*).

108. Avot 2:1. This is the whole passage, which is not cited in its entirety by R. Elimelekh.

109. *Eretz*, the Hebrew word for "country," also means "earth" and thus suggests corporeality or earthliness.

110. Literally, "that from where [or whom] you were born," suggesting the traits peculiar to specific individuals.

111. The hasidic penchant for boasting because of a distinguished pedigree was apparently already sufficiently widespread to warrant castigation.

112. By elevating the three basic characteristics we arrive at a higher level where the lowly, crass qualities are transformed into means of divine service.

Contemplative Prayer

20. THE ECSTATIC AND THE EROTIC
A. Source: Besht, Keter Shem Tov, p. 4a, no. 16

From the Besht: *From my flesh I shall see God* (Job 19:26).[113] Just as you cannot sire [a child] in physical copulation unless your organ is "alive" and [you are filled with] desire and joy, so it is with spiritual coupling, that is, with regard to the words of Torah and prayer: when it is done with a live organ, in joy and pleasure, then you can be fecund.

B. Source: R. Pinhas of Koretz, Likkutim Yekarim, 18

Prayer is [an act of] coupling with the Shekhinah,[114] and just as there is shaking at the beginning of copulation, so must you shake at the beginning of prayer. Afterwards you can continue standing without any motion, and remain attached to the Shekhinah in great *devekut*.

21. SIMPLICITY
Source: R. Pinhas of Koretz, Imrei Pinhas, no. 187

It is told in the name of the rabbi[115] that he was very concerned lest we strain ourselves to attain *kavvanah* (mental concentration during prayer) in order to reach the upper strata.[116] [He taught] that instead we should serve [the Creator] in simplicity. If we are worthy of attaining [communion with the highest strata], it will come to us of itself.

---

113. The plain meaning of the verse is, "When I leave my flesh and my skin is destroyed, i.e., when I die, I shall see God." Hasidism, following the Kabbalah, interpreted it to imply a correspondence between the upper mystical spheres and the human body, so that one can contemplate the heavenly spheres by studying man and his experience as a microcosm. Note, in this and the following selection, the "Freudian" interpretation of the traditional Jewish penchant for swaying during prayer, emphasized to the point of exaggeration by the hasidim. The quite explicit sexual analogy is all the more remarkable for its lack of self-consciousness, indicating that the sexual metaphors used in theological discussions by hasidic thinkers are often purely symbolic.
114. See Zohar II, 10b.
115. Rabbi Pinhas of Koretz.
116. The highest levels that prayer could reach.

[R. Pinhas,] may his lamp shine,[117] told about someone who prayed to attain the divine spirit (*ruah ha-kodesh*). His prayers were fulfilled halfway. He received spirit (*ruah*) but it was not holy.[118]

The meaning of the verse *And Jacob went on his way, and the angels of God met him* (Gen. 32:2) is also told in the rabbi's name: [Jacob went his own way, but] he did not go after them. Understand [this]![119]

22. RENEWAL AND FRESHNESS
Source: R. Yaakov Yosef of Polennoye, Toledot Yaakov Yosef to Ekev, no. 3, s.v. u-khedei lehavin

Regarding prayer, I have learned from my teachers and read in [various] books that every day we must pray with a different *kavvanah*.

Now it is obvious that we cannot each day think the same thought that we did yesterday or the day before.[120] This should be reflected in prayer. It should contain new thoughts every day in accordance with our perceptions. To achieve this we need breadth of mind and great concentration so that our mouth, heart, and thought will be fully coordinated, as is well known.[121]

---

117. Since this honorific was used when the words or deeds of a living person were recorded, this must have been written during the lifetime of R. Pinhas.

118. There is a pun here. *Ruah ha-kodesh* is the designation of the holy spirit; *ruah* alone means "wind." He was granted the first half of his prayer detached from the second half: all wind, no holiness.

119. R. Pinhas' prescription for prayer and his preference for simplicity portends a tendency among hasidic thinkers to deviate from the intricate kabbalistic meditations that formed the basis of the Lurianic conception of prayer. Hasidism generally opted for *kavvanah* rather than *kavvanot*—simple intention over elaborate meditations— even though the early generations of hasidim (e.g., the Maggid; see *Sefer Derekh Hasidim*, pp. 173–174) were still devoted to *kavvanot*. Thus, when one says, "Blessed art Thou, O Lord," one should not meditate the Lurianic *kavvanot*, but should think simply: "God, you are blessed." R. Pinhas protested the overintellectualization of prayer, and held that in order for it to be meaningful one should pray simply but devoutly.

120. Our thinking is not static. We think a thought one day, and go on to another the day following. Similarly, as the text of the prayers is fixed, every day's prayer must be infused with a fresh intention (*kavvanah*) and not merely repeat the thoughts that occurred during the same prayer in the past. R. Yaakov Yosef here attempts to integrate the halakhic requirement for a fixed and immutable text with hasidic spontaneity.

121. Apparently referring to the well-known definition of *kavvanah* as contemplation. The Besht's famous letter to his brother-in-law, R. Gershon of Kutov, which was to

This does not occur, however, when you pray by rote,[122] the same way you did yesterday and the day before, your tongue forming words and your head bowing at Modim[123] out of habit, but without heart. As the Tosafot wrote[124] in the name of the Jerusalem Talmud:[125] "We should be grateful to the head, for when we reach Modim [in the Amidah] it bows by itself."[126]

23. REDEEMING IMPROPER PRAYERS
Source: *Leshon Ḥasidim, Tefillah, no. 51 in the name of R. Yaakov Yosef of Polennoye*[127]

Thou wilt direct their heart, Thou wilt cause Thy ear to attend (Ps. 10:17).

This means that when they pray with proper intention of the heart,[128] You will *cause thy ear to attend* and fulfill their wishes. Similarly: *Thou hath given him his heart's desire, and the request of his lips Thou hast not withholden, selah* (ibid. 21:3). This means that a mere *request of the lips* without *kavvanah* may not impede the fulfillment of the duty to pray, but your *heart's desire* will not be granted unless you

---

have been delivered by R. Yaakov Yosef (but never was), says: "In every single letter [of prayer and Torah study] there are worlds and souls and divinity, and [these] ascend and bind up with each other and unite with each other. Afterwards, the letters bind up and unite with each other and a word is formed, and they unite in a true unity with divinity. Include your soul with them in every single step of the above. [Then] all the worlds unite as one and rise up, and there is [thus] great joy and pleasure without limit" (see my "The Letter of the Besht to R. Gershon of Kutov"; also, below, chap. 17). According to the Besht, the Hebrew letters and words uttered in prayer or while studying Torah are earthly counterparts of God's creative power. In praying, one should aim to assist in the unification of these creative forces through concentrated contemplation on the letters and words. See Additional Note *9.

122. The word translated as "by rote" is *keviut*. It refers to a statement in the Mishnah (Berakhot 4:4), cited by R. Yaakov Yosef in the introduction to this chapter, which reads: "One who treats his prayer as a perfunctory obligation (*keva*) is not [really] praying for mercy." To ensure that prayer is not perfunctory and mechanical, it is necessary to continually renew one's *kavvanah*. See Additional Note *10.

123. A benediction in the Amidah which requires bending of the head and body at its beginning and end.

124. Rosh Hashanah 16b, s.v. *ve-iyyun tefillah*.

125. Berakhot 2:4, end.

126. R. Yaakov Yosef interprets the text from the Jerusalem Talmud as sarcastic or sardonic self-deprecation. Cf. below, selection 26 and notes.

127. See the elaborate discourse recorded in R. Yaakov Yosef's *Ketonet Passim* to Metzora, pp. 23 ff.

128. That is, with *kavvanah*. The root of *kavvanah*, k-v-n, means "to direct," and is the same as the root of *takhin*, the word in the verse cited here.

have prayed with proper intention at least once.[129] This one prayer will elevate all the delayed prayers which are then enveloped in it. This is indicated in [the verse] *A prayer of the afflicted when he is faint* (ibid. 102:1), which the Zohar interprets as enveloping,[130] namely, that all prayers are enwrapped into the prayer of the afflicted [thus reaching their destination along with it]. The same holds true in regard to *kavvanah*.[131]

That is what is meant by *Thou hast not withholden, selah*: although no benefit is derived at present [from a prayer which is a mere utterance of the lips], it may ultimately be beneficial, as attested by the word *selah*, which means "forever."[132]

The same may be said in regard to Maimonides' ruling that [the absence of] *kavvanah* is a hindrance to prayer.[133] He means to say that *kavvanah* hinders or defers the prayer's elevation and acceptance (to the point that its requests are fulfilled) until one prays at least once with intention.

Prayer with proper *kavvanah* is a biblical commandment; prayer without it is only a rabbinic duty. This reconciles the opinions of Maimonides and Nahmanides.[134]

---

129. A prayer without *kavvanah* may fulfill the halakhic obligation to pray, but it is inadequate to move God to do as one wishes. However, as the passage will now say, "improper" prayers accumulate until one "proper" prayer elevates them.

130. See above, n. 59 and the text there. The root *a-t-f* means both "faint" and "envelop" or "wrap."

131. The one prayer recited with *kavvanah* redeems or elevates all previous inadequate prayers.

132. See Eruvin 54a. An intentionless (*kavvanah*-less) prayer is not necessarily lost forever (*selah*), because a suitable prayer anytime in the future may bring about its elevation.

133. Hilkhot Tefillah 4:15: "Any prayer that is without *kavvanah* is no prayer at all." Cf. ibid. 10:1. For Maimonides' definition of *kavvanah* in prayer, see *Guide of the Perplexed* 3:51.

134. Maimonides and Nahmanides are usually seen as disagreeing on the nature of the obligation to pray. Maimonides (*Sefer ha-Mitzvot*, Positive Commandment 5, and Hilkhot Tefillah, beginning; see *Kesef Mishneh* ad loc.) holds that the duty to pray is of biblical origin, while Nahmanides (in his critique of the *Sefer ha-Mitzvot*, ad loc.) maintains that it is only rabbinic. R. Yaakov Yosef suggests that there is no conflict, for Maimonides agrees that intentionless prayer is only rabbinic, while Nahmanides may admit that prayer with proper *kavvanah* (according to the selection, the "envelope" or "wrapper" for defective prayers) is a biblical commandment. See Naor, "Two Types of Prayer," on hasidic harmonizations of the Maimonides-Nahmanides dispute (esp. p. 32, n. 15).

24. DECORUM
Source: R. Shneur Zalman of Liady, Tanya, Iggeret ha-Kodesh, chap. 24[135]

My beloved brethren, you who are beloved friends of your Maker and
odious to your evil urge:[136] I beg you, do not act wickedly! Do not
make yourselves wicked before God in the one hour[137] He has chosen
of the whole day [for His people] to gather and stand before Him to
come into the minor sanctuary,[138] to attend to His glorious Shekhinah,
Who dwells with them in the midst of their impurity (Lev. 16:16).[139] This is
a time when it pleases Him to reveal Himself and be available to those
who seek and beseech Him and hope for Him.

If you talk about your needs,[140] you show that you do not care to
contemplate and to see the manifestation of His majestic glory. Hence
you become an impure chariot to the supernal fool,[141] of whom it is
said: *The fool does not desire understanding* (Prov. 18:2), as mentioned in
the Zohar[142] and by the Ari. This is so because you do not wish to contemplate and to see the precious splendor of the greatness of the King
of all kings, the Holy One, Who reveals Himself during that hour up
above—and also below, to those who desire to behold His glory and
greatness, which envelops and vests itself in the words of the prayer,
as arranged for everyone, and which is revealed to each of us in accordance with our intellect and the root of our soul, as it is written, *Man*

135. Some use has been made in this passage of the English translation and footnotes
of Rabbi Jacob Immanuel Schochet in the Kehot 1972 English edition of *Tanya*, vol. 4.
136. A play on the words *yotzeram* ("their Creator") and *yitzram* ("their *yetzer ha-ra*
[evil urge]") occasionally employed in the Talmud and midrashim. See Berakhot 61a,
Ruth Rabbah 3:1.
137. A paraphrase of a popular talmudic phrase (see Eduyot 5:6, Niddah 13a). The idea
is to keep the hour appointed for prayer free from profane distractions; one who does
otherwise is wicked.
138. Designation of the synagogue and the house of Torah study; Megillah 29a.
139. Cf. Yoma 56b—57a.
140. Meaning, if you indulge in conversation about personal matters instead of focusing on your prayers.
141. The supernal fool is the principal source of evil and impurity, according to the
Zohar and the Ari.
142. See Zohar I, 179a.

is praised [yehullal] according to his intellect (Prov. 12:8); the *ketiv*[143] being *yehallel* ("he praises").[144]

The Kingdom of Heaven is similar to a kingdom on earth.[145] A king customarily conceals his majesty in the innermost chambers, with many guards at the doors, so that people have to wait for years to see his might and glory. When the [king] wishes to be revealed to everyone, he proclaims throughout his kingdom that they should all assemble and stand before him, in order to be shown his majestic glory and the precious splendor of his greatness. Now, if anyone were to stand before him without bothering to look at him, and instead focused on his own needs—how inferior, foolish, and stupid he would be; *he is like the dumb beasts*[146] in everyone's eyes. Moreover, it dishonors the king to demonstrate before him that one regards the pleasure and delight of beholding his glory and splendor as less valuable than preoccupation with one's own needs. [The person who acted this way] would forfeit his life to the king by publicly insulting and dishonoring him. Of him it is said, *And the fool offers up the insult* (Prov. 3:35), which implies that even a fool should not offer up insult by making his contempt [for the king] apparent to everyone.

Our Sages therefore ordained that when praying we should be "as if standing before the King."[147] At the least, we should give this impression to anyone who observes our actions and words with physical eyes, even if our mind is as blank as a fool's. All the prayers were enacted for this purpose, if one reflects on the matter properly.[148] Those who fail to act this way forfeit their very lives. Of such a person does the Zohar say that "he directs insult against the Supernal

---

143. The written text of the Torah, as opposed to the way it is read aloud. See, for instance, Sanhedrin 4a. Ordinarily, this refers to a situation in which there is a discrepancy between the traditional spelling and the traditional reading. In this case, however, the deviant reading, based on the way the consonantal text could be vocalized, is produced for homiletical purposes.

144. Thus reading: "man praises—-or prays—-according to his intellect." The content of one's prayer reflects one's intellect and, correspondingly, the degree of revelation elicited by the prayer.

145. See Berakhot 58a, where the reverse analogy is used. Cf., however, Zohar I, 197a.

146. Paraphrasing Ps. 49:13, in accordance with Rashi's interpretation of the word *nidmu*.

147. Berakhot 33a.

148. Since the prayers were enacted, at least in part, to provide an opportunity for everyone, even the fool incapable of grasping their precise meaning, to publicly demonstrate that God is the King of the universe, one should stand before God appropriately.

Order, and shows that he is separate from and has no part in the God of Israel,"[149] heaven forfend!

Therefore I come on behalf of our Sages to enact a decree that will apply equally to everyone: No idle words may be spoken from the moment the prayer leader begins to recite the service until the end of the last Kaddish at Shaharit, Minhah, and Arvit.[150] Anyone who deliberately disobeys shall sit on the ground [in disgrace] until he begs three men to release him from the supernal excommunication—"As he repents, so he will be healed."[151]

25. IN THE PRESENCE OF GOD
Source: R. Zadok ha-Kohen of Lublin, Zidkat ha-Zaddik, no. 208

Man's contest with his *yetzer ha-ra* lies mainly in [his struggle with] his fantasies and the thoughts of his heart and mind.[152] Regarding this the *Tikkunei Zohar* says: "One who is victorious in battle is given the king's daughter," meaning prayer.[153] For prayer is the recognition of the Presence of God, as if one were standing before the king, as the Talmud states.[154] It is the heart and mind of man that stand before Him, for God looks into the heart (1 Sam. 16:7). If, heaven forbid, you are overtaken by alien thoughts or extraneous mental images, you are not, in that instant, standing before God.[155] Therefore, one who conquers his *yetzer ha-ra* and prevents it from emerging as imagination and extraneous thought is awarded the king's daughter, namely, God's Presence at the time of prayer.

---

149. Zohar II, 131b.

150. The morning, afternoon, and evening services, respectively.

151. Paraphrasing Isa. 6:10. He who profanes the prayers as indicated must consider himself under a divine ban until he is released by a court of three.

152. R. Zadok's pejorative use of "fantasies" or "imagination" (*dimyonot*), to which he largely devotes nos. 203–209 of this work, is probably influenced by Maimonides, who used the term in contrast to "intellect" (*sekhel*). The *dimyonot*, representing subjectivity, are detrimental to the acquisition of truth. Cf. Maimonides, *Guide for the Perplexed* 1:73, 3:15, inter alia. On the hasidic concern with alien thoughts, see below, chap. 11.

153. End of tikkun 13 and beginning of tikkun 21. These passages speak of the princess as the prize for slaying the primordial serpent responsible for the death of Adam and all his descendants. In this selection, the serpent symbolizes man's evil inclination, but the princess, here identified as the gift of prayer, is susceptible of other interpretations as well. See R. Zadok's *Mahshevot Harutz*, p. 46a.

154. Eruvin 64a. See above, selection 24.

155. Standing before God is defined as the concentration of heart and mind on God. The intrusion of a strange thought marks their absence.

This is what is meant by the requirement of "connecting redemption to prayer,"[156] for redemption from Egypt implies liberation from the realm of the imagination.[157]

The Rabbis said: Who may be considered a son of the world-to-come? One who connects redemption to prayer.[158] The Talmud further states that one who recites *Tehillah le-David* (Ps. 145) thrice daily is *assured* that he will be a son of the world-to-come.[159] [Why the different language?] In *Tehillah le-David*, one praises God for providing sustenance to all living, in alphabetical order, which is the order of all creation, since everything is arranged by God.[160] This is called the category of *emunah* ("faith"); such a one is included in the Congregation of Israel, thus granting him assurance that he will be a son of the world-to-come. However, one who is liberated from imagination achieves the level of *emet* ("truth"). In connecting redemption to prayer, he merits the recognition of the Presence by means of prayer, unifying truth and faith [and unifying] the Holy One and His Shekhinah.[161] Such a person becomes a son of the world-to-come now,

---

156. Berakhot 4b, in the name of R. Yohanan. Geulah, the benediction for the redemption from Egypt recited after the Shema, must be followed immediately and without interruption by the Amidah.

157. See the end of the next selection (excerpted from the same work).

158. The talmudic text states that one who connects redemption to prayer is a son of the world-to-come, i.e., he is one who *now* enjoys the spiritual bliss of eternity.

159. Ibid., in the name of Ravina. Note the added "is assured that he will be," etc., in contrast to the preceding quotation.

160. Psalm 145 is an acrostic of the Hebrew alphabet. R. Zadok sees this as a worshipful recognition of the orderliness of Nature, which is God's creation. He now categorizes this as faith, in that the acknowledgment of the orderliness of creation is an intellectual affirmation that may lead to, but is not at present, a spiritual-psychological awareness of the Divine Presence. This is contrasted with the connection of redemption to prayer, which R. Zadok previously defined as the kind of prayer that issues from one who has liberated himself from the realm of profane imagination and extraneous thoughts, and hence is standing before God. In this condition, profoundly aware of the Divine Presence here and now, the worshiper is in a state higher than faith, namely, truth: he is actively aware of the Presence as a psychological and spiritual fact rather than an abstract belief. Therefore, he is immediately "a son of the world-to-come," whereas the other worshiper, meritorious though he may be, is merely assured that he *will be* a son of the world-to-come. The words are commensurate with the level of religious devotion; he who *believes* in God is *assured* that he will be entitled to eternal bliss; he who *experiences* the Presence is *now* a son of the world-to-come.

161. The aim of all devotional activity, according to the Kabbalah, is the unification of the two aspects of divinity called Holy One and Shekhinah, representing, respectively, the nine upper sefirot and Malkhut.

and with complete awareness, not merely as a matter of confidence. For *emunah* is defined as confidence: faith in the Eternal One (i.e., confidence that God is indeed eternal). But *emet* denotes that which is immediately obvious, thus eliminating the need for confidence. One who is privileged to achieve this state is a son of the world-to-come in fact—palpably and manifestly—so that the term *muvtah* ("is assured") is no longer relevant.

26. DIFFICULTY CONCENTRATING
Source: R. Zadok ha-Kohen of Lublin, Zidkat ha-Zaddik, no. 209

Fantasies[162] especially threaten to overcome us during prayer. This is the "lack of devotion in prayer" [of which the Rabbis said] that we cannot escape from them every day.[163] Tosafot and R. Nissim [Ran][164] cite the Jerusalem Talmud, "R. Hiyya said: I have never in my life had devotion [in prayer],"[165] and take it literally.

However, it is implausible to say this of such great men,[166] especially R. Hiyya, about whom it was related that when he prayed "Thou causeth the wind to blow and the rain to fall," a wind began blowing and rain started falling.[167]

The phrase "I never had devotion" may be interpreted to mean "I never felt a need for it." The halakhah requiring concentration was meant for those who are liable to be distracted by fantasies and [stray] thoughts;[168] those whose tongue says one thing while their heart is

---

162. Or "imaginings." See n. 152 above.
163. Bava Batra 164b. *Iyyun tefillah* is interpreted by R. Tam (Tosafot ad loc. and Rosh Hashanah 16b) as "lack of devotion," citing as proof the J.T. text (see next note), which R. Tam took literally. Most commentators, including Rashi, R. Gershom (Bava Batra, ad loc.), and R. Hananel (Rosh Hashanah, ad loc.), as well as Tosafot citing another opinion, explain it as meaning: calculating the effect of prayer, i.e., expecting the granting of one's wishes as a claim upon God, hence a form of thaumaturgy.
164. On Rosh Hashanah 16b.
165. Berakhot 2:4. *Kavnit*, referring to *kavvanah*, means, in this context, concentration of thought on what is being recited, or devotion to the task at hand.
166. The Jerusalem Talmud quotes others besides R. Hiyya who made similar assertions regarding their devotional (*kavvanah*) practices. The commentators, sensing the difficulty, gave the statements a variety of different interpretations. For R. Yaakov Yosef's view, see selection 22 above.
167. Bava Metzia 85b.
168. Note that *kavvanah* is related to *kivvun*, "direction." The Aramaic *kavnit* also means "I directed." One whose head is filled with idle, stray thoughts needs *kavvanah* to direct them to God; since R. Hiyya usually concentrated, this was not the case.

elsewhere. R. Hiyya, however, never experienced any other thought except the Presence of God before him, and whenever he spoke he was conscious of addressing the King of kings. [In consequence, he had no need for concentrated devotion at any specific time.] "One day I attempted *kavvanah*"[169] refers to a time when he was particularly troubled by his thoughts—perhaps it was the day when the prophet Elijah caused him and his sons anxiety during their prayers.[170] At that time he tried hard to direct and settle his thoughts properly, but to no avail because the distraction came from heaven.

The same is true of the other amoraim.[171] They felt a lack of devotion only when afflicted by anxiety of heavenly origin. Generally, however, they had no special need for *kavvanah*. Their heartfelt outcries to God during prayer were to them a natural state of mind, characteristic of those untroubled by fantasies. But for all others [who do not possess this unusual trait], lack of devotion in prayer is an almost inescapable daily occurrence, as stated above.

For this reason it was ordained that before [the actual Amidah] we recite the words: *O God, open Thou my lips, and my mouth shall declare Thy praise* (Ps. 51:17). The divine name used in this verse, *Adonay*, denotes the presence of His Shekhinah in the hearts of the children of Israel. We entreat the Shekhinah—coming from the heart—to open our mouths [in prayer], so that our mouths will not speak by themselves [mechanically]. For the Holy One is indeed the heart of Israel, as it is written, *God is the rock of my heart and my portion for ever* (Ps. 73:26),[172] referring to the divine name mentioned, as is well known.

The prayer [Amidah] concludes with *Let the words of my mouth and the meditation of my heart be acceptable before Thee, O God, my Rock and my Redeemer* (Ps. 19:15).[173] This is a plea to accept the meditation of the heart just completed, even if it happened to be adulterated with fantasies and alien thoughts, since "You are my Rock," meaning "the Rock of my heart," as mentioned above, and thus You are the source of all my thoughts. *My Redeemer* refers to the redemption (*geulah*), as

---

169. In the continuation of the Jerusalem Talmud's account of R. Hiyya: "one day I attempted *kavvanah*, and I thought to myself," etc.
170. See Bava Metzia 85b, end. Elijah prevented R. Hiyya from forcing a premature resurrection of the dead with the *mehayeh ha-metim* blessing of his Amidah prayer.
171. The others, mentioned in Jerusalem Talmud, loc. cit., who admitted to having different thoughts while praying.
172. In accordance with the exposition of the verse in Song of Songs Rabbah 5:2.
173. Cf. Berakhot 4b.

explained in the preceding chapter;[174] it symbolizes the redemption of the truth from the fantasies in which it is entangled.

ADDITIONAL NOTES

*1   R. Levi Yitzhak may be grappling here with the conflict between the mystical quietism of his teacher, the Great Maggid, and the normative rabbinic Judaism which his opponents, the mitnaggedim, accused the hasidim of abandoning, a charge that he and other hasidic leaders denied. In this selection he finds a way out of what appears to be an unavoidable conflict by asserting that the normative devotional life is simultaneously *yesh* and *ayin*, both self-affirming and self-annihilating. His interpretation of Hasidism reconciles mystical quietism with the normative affirmation of man's existential reality, seemingly tipping the scales in favor of the halakhic way. Later in the passage he attributes both ways to Abraham: outside the land of Israel, he served God through self-sacrifice (i.e., contemplation and annihilation), whereas "in the Land of Israel he didn't need this, because he was able to serve Him by means of commandments." The purely mystical way may be spiritually superior, involving a direct perception of divinity ("actually with one's eyes"), yet Abraham is assured that the normative way ("through a glass") will bring him great reward, evoking the divine grace (*shefa*).

*2   See my article "Study and Prayer," and *Torah Lishmah*, pp. 121–132. While R. Shneur Zalman reveals a certain ambivalence on the subject, R. Hayyim unequivocally reasserts the supremacy of Torah study.

*3   Most biblical exegetes, however, do not ascribe any change to God as a result of changes in man in either direction. When man improves, he avoids calamity, since the punishments mentioned in the Torah or predicted by the prophets are all conditional on persistence in sin (Radak et al. to Jonah, ad loc.; for more detail, see Malbim, ad loc.). In the reverse case, man has only himself to blame. By exercising his free will improperly, he spoils the natural order of creation, bringing about a change detrimental to his own well-being (Malbim to Gen. 6:6); cf. R. Zvi Elimelekh's use of the volition argument as a solution to the problem. See also Albo, *Sefer ha-Ikkarim* IV:18, for a view similar to the one cited here in the name of the Besht.

*4   In *Torat ha-Maggid*, ed. I. Klepholtz (Tel Aviv, 1969), vol. 1, pp. 3–9 (cited and translated by Jacobs, *Hasidic Prayer*, pp. 97–98), a disciple of the Maggid, R. Hayyim Haikel of Amdur, describes some rules of *hitlahavut* in prayer based on the teachings of his master: "A man should allow his intellect to prevail when he recites the words of the prayers so as to shatter the barrier which separates [him from God] until he cleaves to Him. For every letter [of the alphabet used for sacred purposes, and not necessarily for prayers, as Jacobs understood; see above, selection 5 and n. 29] is a great world extending upwards *ad infinitum*, and with every letter he utters with his mouth he bestirs those worlds up above. Consequently, he should recite the words [of his prayers] with great enthusiasm (*hitlahavut*), with great joy, and with great attachment (*devekut*). . . . At times one is like unto a drunkard in the joy he has of the Torah because a great love burns in his heart. At times one is able to recite his prayers at

---

174. *Zidkat ha-Zaddik* 208, translated in the preceding selection.

great speed because the love of God burns so powerfully in his heart and the words emerge from his mouth automatically."

*5   The idea that even in time of need one should pray not for oneself but for the sake of the Shekhinah is a recurring theme in Lurianic Kabbalah, and deeply influenced hasidic thinking. According to the Besht, while petitionary prayer is answered automatically, often in a way not discernible to the petitioner, the *kavvanah* of one's prayer should not be concentrated on oneself, "for if one has the intention of seeing his prayers answered [in a personal way], he introduces something corporeal into his prayers, whereas the proper thing is for them to be purely spiritual, for the sake of the Shekhinah and not for the sake of worldly things" (*Keter Shem Tov*, p. 9a). The Maggid states that all worship should be for the sake of the Shekhinah, "and there should be nothing of self in it," not even a feeling of "personal delight from the act or worship" (cf. Jacobs, *Hasidic Prayer*, p. 98).

Here is how the Besht interpreted the verse *for this* (*zot*) *let every pious man* (*ḥasid*) *pray* (Ps. 32:6): "this" (*zot*), the feminine indicative, represents the Shekhinah; it is formed from the letters *zayin/alef/tav*, which together hint at the seven lower sefirot. In contrast to the upper three, which characterize divine intellect, they represent divine character or personality, and culminate in the tenth sefirah, Malkhut, which is identical with the Shekhinah. The *zayin* in *zot*, with its numerical value of seven, represents the seven lower sefirot, while the *alef* and *tav*, the first and last letters of the Hebrew alphabet, denote the zenith and nadir of the sefirotic realm. When the *alef* and *tav* are united with the seven sefirot, the Shekhinah becomes whole. Thus *zot* represents the Shekhinah in its relationship with all the sefirot and the whole of creation, and it is for *zot* that every *ḥasid* prays.

*6   In referring to the proper way of praying as the prayers of the *awake*, R. Yaakov Yosef is apparently alluding to the liveliness of hasidic prayer, as distinguished from non-hasidic, or mitnaggedic, forms of prayer, which the hasidim deemed tepid and laggardly. Hasidism encourages forceful movements and even gestures and melodies during the Amidah, often quoting the talmudic statement that R. Akiva would cut short his public prayers, but when praying alone would bow and prostrate himself so much that he began in one corner and finished in another (Berakhot 31a; and see, e.g., the letter of R. Shmelke of Nikolsburg, a disciple of the Maggid of Mezeritch, cited by M. L. Wilensky, *Ḥasidim u-Mitnaggedim*, vol. 1, pp. 84–88). R. Shneur Zalman of Liady, in a letter to R. Alexander of Shklov, discussing the proper posture during prayer, writes: "They [the mitnaggedim] demand that we pray as they do, i.e., only hurriedly and without any bodily movements or raising of the voice, just like those angels on high that have reached a state beyond which there is no higher, as it is said, *When they stood, they let down their wings* (Ezek. 1:24). But this . . . does not apply to the other ranks [of angels], as it is said [in the benedictions before the reading of the morning Shema], 'And the ophanim and the holy beasts with a noise of great rushing.' Even of the seraphim it is written, *A noise of tumult like the noise of a host* (Ezek., loc. cit.)." (See Hillmann, *Iggerot Baal ha-Tanya*, pp. 33–34. Cf. Jacobs, *Hasidic Prayer*, pp. 54–58.) R. Yaakov Yosef's juxtaposition of the two kinds of postures during prayer should be seen in light of this difference between hasidim and mitnaggedim.

*7   The tone of this passage seems to bear out the contention of Joseph G. Weiss (*Meḥkarim be-Ḥasidut Bratslav*, pp. 91–93) that the approach of the Maggid and the Habad school of R. Shneur Zalman differed radically from that of R. Nahman of

Bratslav. Weiss holds that the Maggid and Habad saw prayer as an opportunity for contemplation and ecstasy, whereas Bratslav saw it as an opportunity for a personal conversation between man and his Maker. He identifies Habad as the school of mystical religion and Bratslav as the school of faith-religion. For the mystical school, the climax of prayer is attained when man abandons his own needs and prays for the needs of the Shekhinah. Not only does he surrender his personality, but he strips his prayer of all materiality. For Bratslav, the existential situation and personal relations predominate. This distinction may be affirmed by comparing the present selection (14), as well as selection 8, another discussion of prayer and Torah study from the same part of *Likkutei Moharan*, with selection 24, a chapter from the *Tanya* dealing with decorum during prayer. (Cf. Jacobs *Hasidic Prayer*, pp. 93 ff.) However, Weiss is wrong in ascribing the concept of *bittul ha-yesh*—the self-annihilation and self-abandonment that occur at the highpoint of *devekut* and total immersion in prayer—entirely to the mystical school, attributing to the faith school of Bratslav the view that prayer is merely a means of self-improvement. In the next selection from *Likkutei Moharan*, it is obvious that R. Nahman too sees the ultimate goal of his kind of prayer—in solitude—as the achievement of total *bittul ha-yesh*, to the extent that one's soul "joins its roots" and becomes "absorbed by Him, blessed be He" (see especially n. 93).

Additionally, Weiss maintains that R. Nahman of Bratslav did not practice, or write, any mystical prayers. In this, Weiss is followed by Arthur Green (*Rabbi Nahman of Bratslav*, pp. 54–60), who maintains that in the fascinating *etzot* literature of the Bratslav movement, we find only very rare mentions of R. Nahman endeavoring to follow the early hasidic masters in mystical prayer and the importance of *devekut*, which all but disappeared later on. However, this claim does not stand up under further investigation. See Z. Gries, "Quntres Hanhagot Ne'elam le-R. Nahman mi-Bratslav," p. 767, n. 17, who maintains that whereas it is true that none of R. Nahman's prayers are *technically* mystical (i.e., include the *yihudim*), many of them can be described as mystical in the sense that they seek an unmediated *unio mystica*. For other features of R. Nahman's teaching on solitude, see the sources cited by M. Hallamish, *Mavo la-Kabbalah*, pp. 51–52.

*8   On raising the voice during prayer, see Nahmanides (Exod. 13:16): "This is the meaning of the Rabbis' comment on *Let them cry mightily unto God* (Jonah 3:8): from here you learn that prayer needs [a raised] voice: 'arrogance conquers shyness.'" (The source of this rabbinic comment is *Pesikta de-Rav Kahana, Shuva* [Parma version]; see *Pesikta* [Buber ed.], p. 161a, n. 89. The printed edition, as well as Jerusalem Talmud Ta'anit 2:1, and Yalkut to Jonah, ad loc., leave only the last comment: "arrogance.") According to Nahmanides, the statement calling for prayer to be out loud is not to be taken literally. What it really means, he says, is that people should designate a place in which to assemble for communal prayer, thereby declaring publicly to the world: "It is true that God created us and we are His creatures." However, Rabbi Aaron ha-Kohen of Lunel (*Orhot Hayyim*, Tefillah 72) quotes the same passsage and accepts its literal meaning. Similarly, *Sefer Hasidim* 820 says that benedictions should be recited out loud, citing Ps. 103:1 as the source. As for prayer (*tefillah*), the Talmud states explicitly that raising one's voice is forbidden (Berakhot 31a). The codifiers accepted this as law (halakhah) with some exceptions. See *Shulhan Arukh, Orah Hayyim* 101:2, also *Shulhan Arukh ha-Rav*, ibid. See also S. Carmy, "Destiny, Freedom and the Logic of Petition," pp. 29–32 and 36 n. 26.

*9   Other early hasidic sources elaborate on this theory of the Besht's. Thus, in his homily on *A light shalt thou make to the ark* (*tevah*) (Gen. 6:16), explaining that the word *tevah* was a substitution for its homonym, "word," he said: "This means that the word should be illuminated. For in every word there are worlds, souls, and divinity" (*Zavaat ha-Rivash* p. 8; *Sefer Besht*, vol. 1, pp. 118 ff.; *Degel Maḥaneh Ephraim* to Noah. Cf. Jacobs, *Hasidic Prayer*, pp. 75–77).

The contemplative innovations required every day, according to the author, seem to indicate that one should concentrate each day on a different word, each of which contains "worlds, souls, and divinity," and thus assist, by one's *kavvanah*, in unifying them. "Mouth, heart, and thought" are equivalent to "worlds, souls, and divinity." To achieve unity in the latter, full coordination of the former is needed.

*10   Earlier R. Yaakov Yosef cites Talmud Berakhot 21a, "If one can add something new to his prayer," but takes it out of context. In the Talmud, the requirement of novelty only concerns repeating the prayer after having already fulfilled the statutory obligation (see text and Tosafot ad loc.). He transposes the idea of novelty in *tefillat nedavah* ("voluntary prayer") to the fixed, ordained prayers.

7

Torah Study

INTRODUCTION

For over two hundred years, Hasidism has been described, by popular mind and polemical pen, as a movement antagonistic to the primacy of Torah study in the religious hierarchy of Judaism. Yet it was one of the most eminent of nineteenth-century hasidic leaders, R. Menahem Mendel of Lubavitch, who publicly declared that the major contribution of Hasidism was the elevation of the concept of Torah study *lishmah* ("for its own sake").[1] It may be helpful to sort out the disputes underlying these contrasting assessments.

Much of what appears to be a depreciation of Torah study in Hasidism is actually the consequence of hasidic cultivation of other religious activities. Thus, the hasidic emphasis on man's emotional life expanded the place of prayer both qualitatively and quantitatively. The preference for prayer seems to fly in the face of the talmudic dictum that classifies prayer as "temporal life" (*ḥayyei sha'ah*), as opposed to Torah study, which constitutes "eternal life" (*ḥayyei olam*); time allotted to prayer may encroach upon the imperative of perpetual study. In addition, hasidic masters frequently rank practical mitzvah performance over the intellectual analysis of the performance. This may also derive from the need to offer ordinary people the prestige

---

1. See my *Torah Lishmah*, p. 226, n. 66.

and motive for intense religious service. Lastly, the idea that man can serve God through his "secular" pursuits may be viewed as an alternative to the traditional highway of Talmud Torah.[2]

What is more remarkable about the hasidic way, however, is the nature of its Torah study. Here Torah remains the primary focus of the religious activity, even as it takes on a character that is somewhat alien in the eyes of the critics of Hasidism. We may distinguish three kinds of *lishmah* with respect to the study of Torah: the functional (to know what to do); the devotional (for the love of God); the cognitive (to know the Torah).[3] Mitnagdism, as exemplified by R. Hayyim of Volozhin, subscribes to the cognitive approach; Hasidism, while not monolithic, tends to emphasize the devotional.

The hasidic orientation toward the devotional manifests itself at several levels. Several of the selections in this chapter assert that the purpose of Torah study is *devekut*, and promote it as such. This thesis inevitably affects the nature of the study: it places Talmud Torah in the service of a higher religious ideal; it also encourages the kind of preparation for learning and concentration during study that will foster the proper devotional consciousness. The other side of this accent on intentions is a seeming indifference (as perceived by critics) toward intellectual thoroughness and knowledge of Torah. Thus R. Hayyim of Volozhin, the premier exponent of the cognitive approach, stresses that study should aim at thorough knowledge of the entire halakhic corpus, and that preoccupation with devotional experience necessarily interferes with one's full intellectual involvement.

Hasidic Torah study is also associated with an expanded curriculum, one that, in keeping with its devotional orientation, prominently features Kabbalah. In doing so, hasidic learning differs from those approaches that relegate Kabbalah to a secondary role, with halakhic study front and center, and from those who would reserve kabbalistic inquiry to the elite, to those who have already thoroughly mastered the halakhic foundation of Torah. The Besht, by contrast, shared kabbalistic insights with his community. To be sure, he carefully translated the mystical concepts from the metaphysical abstractions accessible only to the cognoscenti into a psychological frame of reference pertinent to the life of the less-sophisticated Jew. At any rate, hasidic literature makes free and familiar use of Kabbalah, thus exposing itself to the charge of downplaying Halakhah.

---

2. See chapter 9 (Worship through Corporeality), and also my *Torah Umadda*, chapter 10.
3. This typology is elaborated in *Torah Lishmah*, chap. 5.

How far the experiential thrust of Hasidism molds its conception of Torah study can be illustrated by a defense of hasidic Talmud study:

> When they study Talmud they garb themselves in awe and trembling and apprehension and great reverence before God, so that their Torah glows on their faces. And when they mention the name of the tanna or other transmitter of a tradition, they imagine that tanna standing alive before them, or the root of his light emanating from the Supreme Chariot. . . . Thus there falls upon them a fear and great reverence of God, without end or limit; and the love of Torah and its light burns in them ceaselessly. When they emerge from their study, miracles and wonders are done for them as in earlier generations, so that they heal the diseased.[4]

What is emphasized here is the *devekut* of the hasidic master as an outgrowth of his knowledge. But what is equally striking is the nature of the knowledge so highly esteemed. It is less a matter of the content of the talmudic discussion than the breakthrough to a personal relationship with the titans of the tradition.[5]

Within Hasidism there is also room for heavy emphasis on Torah study. Among the early masters it is most notable in R. Shneur Zalman, who is also the only one to produce a major halakhic work. The *Tanya* identifies knowledge of Halakhah, in all its prosaic details and intellectual rigor, with knowledge of God. It should be recognized that R. Shneur Zalman's doctrine differs from the mitnaggedic version of the cognitive view, as represented by R. Hayyim of Volozhin. This dispute is rooted in their respective views of divine immanence and transcendence, and is treated in the first chapter of this book.

The importance which Hasidism attached to the experiential element in the study of Torah is reflected in the attention devoted to the problem of learning *shelo lishmah* ("with deficient intention"). On the one hand, the spiritual orientation of the movement mandated that the student make every effort to attain the level of learning *lishmah*, and not to be satisfied with "mere" intellectual competence. On the other hand, the hasidic writers were too realistic to ignore the dangers of overconscientious attention to one's spiritual state, leading to

---

4. *Iggeret ha-Kodesh* (appended to R. Elimelekh of Lizhensk's *Noam Elimelekh*). Cf. selection 19 below, from R. Nahman.
5. The last section of Rabbi Joseph B. Soloveitchik's *U-Vikkashtem mi-Sham* can be viewed as a synthesis of the classical Lithuanian exaltation of cognitive achievement with the existential hasidic appreciation of the personal dimension of authentic religious knowledge.

either despair (and the abandonment of study) or smugness. Both of these concerns find expression in the texts below. Fear of exploiting mastery of Torah *shelo lishmah*—to build a grand reputation—may partially explain the unwillingness of most early hasidic leaders to publish works containing novel halakhic investigations.

The present volume concentrates on the early generations of hasidic thought. But our picture of Torah study as an ingredient of hasidic thought would be incomplete without remarking on a late-nineteenth-century development among the disciples of R. Menahem Mendel Morgenstern of Kotzk. The Kotzker is generally identified with a streak of radical individualism and a ruthless stripping away of false motivations. At the same time, his extant statements put enormous emphasis on the conventional study of Torah.[6] And in spite of his own aversion to publication, his two closest disciples, his son-in-law, R. Abraham Borenstein (the author of *Avnei Nezer* and *Eglei Tal*) and R. Yizhak Meir of Ger (the author of *Ḥiddushei ha-Rim*) were prolific halakhic writers whose oeuvre is comparable to that of their most celebrated non-hasidic contemporaries.

The historical dialectic implicit in this development has been taken up in the general introduction to this volume. For our purposes in this chapter it will suffice to quote the treatment of *lishmah* in the preface to *Eglei Tal*:

> I have heard some people who deviate from the path of reason with respect to the study of our Holy Torah. They say that whoever studies and produces new insights and rejoices and delights in his learning—that this is considered to be less a study *lishmah* than is simple study that yields no delight, and is pursued exclusively to fulfill the commandment: for when the student delights in his learning, there is mingled in his learning personal pleasure as well. But truly this is a striking error. On the contrary, it is of the essence of the commandment of Torah study to be joyful and delight in his study, for then the words of Torah are absorbed in his blood. And since he takes pleasure in the words of Torah, he becomes attached (*davuk*) to the Torah. . . .
>
> I concede that he who studies not for the sake of the commandment to study, but solely because he enjoys his study, this is what is called *shelo lishmah*, like someone who eats matzah not for the sake of the commandment but for the pleasure of eating. . . . But he who studies for the sake of

---

6. See Y. Levinger, "Torato shel ha-Rebbe mi-Qotzk le-Or ha-Amarot ha-Meyuḥasot lo al yedei Nikhdo R. Shmuel mi-Sokhochov," *Tarbits* 55 (5755), pp. 109-135, see pp. 113-115. See A. Brill, *Intellectual Mysticism of R. Zadok ha-Kohen of Lublin* (forthcoming).

the commandment and [at the same time] delights in his learning—this is study *lishmah*, and it is all holy, for the delight too is a mitzvah.

By the time of the *Eglei Tal*, Hasidism has passed the century mark. By then, one might suggest, much of the conflict between Hasidism and its opponents, with respect to Talmud Torah, had been overcome.[7] Rigor and fervor, intellect and devotion, harmoniously flow together toward the sea of Torah that is their common destination.[8]

The Purpose of Study

1. TORAH STUDY AS A TABERNACLE
Source: R. Shneur Zalman of Liady, Tanya, Likkutei Amarim, chap. 34

It is well known that the Patriarchs themselves constituted the Chariot (*Merkavah*),[9] for throughout their lives they never, not even for a moment, abstained from binding their mind and soul to the Lord of the universe, with total self-surrender to His blessed unity.[10] So for all the prophets after them, each according to the level of his soul and

---

7. See the contemporary Satmar scholar David Yoel Weiss, *Megadim Ḥadashim* to Berakhot (Jerusalem, 5749), pp. 130 ff., on whether the benediction on the study of Torah can be view as a *birkat hana'ah* (a benediction recited before enjoyment). He cites several hasidic texts on both sides of the question, with the Besht insisting, in contrast to others, that it is indeed a *birkat hana'ah*, for "the ordinances of God . . . give joy to the heart" (Ps. 19:9).
8. See R. Abraham Isaac Hakohen Kook, *Eder ha-Yekar* (Jerusalem, 5727), p. 26. R. Kook remarks that later Hasidism "became very concerned . . . to elevate the value of halakhic inquiry and to expand it, albeit entirely in the spirit of Hasidism and its primary stamp, that the feeling of inner sanctity be a spontaneously ascending flame."
9. "The Patriarchs are truly the Chariot" (Genesis Rabbah 47:6). The Chariot in Ezekiel's vision (Ezek. 1) was understood as a means for each individual to accommodate the Divine Presence and carry out God's purpose in the world. Thus the Patriarchs, as the world's spiritual elite, exemplified this process of self-nullification before God and their total surrender of self and their absorption into His unity, so that they themselves in effect became "chariots." Our midrashic saying regarding the Patriarchs is explained by R. Shneur Zalman in chap. 23: When the organs of the human body perform a commandment of the Torah, such that the divine soul's faculty of action is immanent in it at the time, they become a vehicle (*merkavah*, i.e., "chariot") for the Supreme Will.
10. Cf. *Likkutei Amarim*, chap. 23. One's transformation into a *merkavah* for the divine will requires total self-surrender and self-annihilation in the presence of the One.

his perception. However, the rank of Moses our teacher surpassed them all, for concerning him it was said, "The Shekhinah speaks out of Moses' throat."[11]

At Mount Sinai the Israelites experienced something similar [to this union], but they could not endure it, as the Rabbis said: "At each [divine] utterance their souls took flight,"[12] . . . which is an indication of the annihilation of their existence, as mentioned. Therefore God commanded at once that there be made for Him a Sanctuary, containing the Holy of Holies, so that there might dwell therein His Shekhinah, which is the revelation of His blessed unity. . . .

However, since the Temple was destroyed, God has no other sanctuary or habitation for His blessed unity save the "four cubits of the Halakhah,"[13] which is His will and wisdom as embodied in the laws which have been set out for us. Therefore, after reflecting deeply on the subject of this self-nullification, according to his capacity, as discussed above, one should reflect deeply [as follows]: My mind and the root of my soul are too limited to constitute a chariot (merkavah) and an abode for His blessed unity in perfect truth, since my mind cannot at all conceive and apprehend Him in any manner or degree of perception in the world, not even an iota of the perception of the patriarchs and the prophets. This being the case, I shall make for Him a tabernacle and habitation by engaging in the study of Torah, as my time permits, at appointed times by day and by night in accordance with the law which was given to each individual as specified in the laws of the study of Torah.[14]

2. THE GREAT VOICE OF SINAI
Source: R. Zevi Elimelekh of Dinov, Benei Yisaskhar, Sivan, ma'amar 5, Ma'alat ha-Torah 7

The verse *These words the Lord spoke unto all your assembly on the mountain . . . with a great voice, and it went on no more* (Deut. 5:19) is trans-

---

11. Zohar III, 232a. Cf. Zohar III, 7a; also *Tikkunei Zohar*, tikkun 38, end.
12. Shabbat 88b.
13. Berakhot 8a.
14. *Shulḥan Arukh*, Yoreh De'ah 246:1 and Rema to ibid., in light of Menahot 99b and see *Shulḥan Arukh ha-Rav*, Hil. Talmud Torah 3:1–6.

lated in the Targum as "and it went on without end."[15] The meaning of this is that man ought to reflect upon that "great divine voice" with a sense of wholeness and with love for the Torah. This promotes enough understanding of the laws, even at the simple level. This will make it possible for "new Torah" also, to issue from him.[16]

However, one who makes no effort to gain understanding of the Torah and its laws in depth will achieve neither perception of the mysteries of the Torah nor inspiration of the Holy Spirit (ruaḥ ha-kodesh). For man cannot be cleansed from his earthliness except through profound understanding of Halakhah in accordance with the truth of Torah.

This is the "voice of the Sinaitic words," because of which and in which are given the most recondite and unfathomable secrets.[17]

3. THE SINAITIC EXPERIENCE OF TORAH STUDY
Source: R. Shneur Zalman of Liady, Torah Or to Yitro

The most important aspect of the receiving of the Torah is that which is written in the Ten Commandments: *And God spoke all of these words,* leimor *(saying)* (Exod. 20:1).[18]

At first blush the word *leimor* is incomprehensible. It is not comparable to any other *leimor* in the entire Bible, which is ordinarily interpreted as "saying" to another.[19] Here it is impossible to explain it in

---

15. Onkelos ad loc. Rashi, citing the Targum, explains the seeming contradiction between the literal meaning of *ve-lo yasaf,* which is "and it went on no more," and the Targum's interpretation, which is just the opposite. It has to do with the manner of divine speech as opposed to that of man. The latter must stop from time to time in order to catch his breath, while God's voice goes on ceaselessly. R. Zevi Elimelekh, however, gives new meaning to the Targum interpretation, namely, that God's great voice at Sinai caused a chain reaction in the development of Torah that continues to reverberate forever, especially in the esoteric sense (*razin de-oraita,* "mysteries of the Torah").

16. The reference here is to new insights of an esoteric nature into Torah (*razei Torah*).

17. See Deut. 4:12.

18. For R. Elimelech's homily on this verse, see below, selection 12.

19. Thus, when God instructs Moses in any law or message *leimor,* it is a charge to Moses "to say," i.e., to convey that law or message to another—-usually the Children of Israel.

this manner, for all Israel heard when God spoke to them face-to-face, those then present and those not present.[20]

The correct interpretation of *leimor* in this verse is: to utter and speak all of the words of the Torah that were already stated to Moses in the entire Bible; for Mishnah, halakhot, and aggadot[21]—all of it was related to Moses at Sinai. Thus, although the Talmud cites the names of individual tannaim and amoraim as articulating a specific halakhah—as, for example, the House of Shammai states thus and the House of Hillel states thus—its meaning is that this word of God is the Law spoken to Moses at Sinai which emerged from the mouth of that tanna or amora. . . .

Israel was granted this power that the Law emerging from their mouth is actually the word of God spoken to Moses at Sinai, given at the time of the receiving of the Torah by Moses. . . . Hence *leimor* means: to say that which was already uttered. This is a case of *bittul*, of annihilation of self to Him, for the utterances did not become separate in relation to man, but issued forth from man's mouth as though they were his own speech. Thus the verse *My lips will repeat Thy utterances* (Ps. 119:172) means: "The Torah is Your (God's) utterance, and my tongue repeats it as one who repeats after the speaker what he has said."

The Ten Commandments are the Torah in its totality. For in receiving the Ten Commandments from the Almighty, Israel received the Torah in its entirety, achieving the state of self-nullification to the word of God emerging from their mouth. They were as one who repeats after the speaker; such was the relation of the revelation of infinite light below to that of above, i.e., one of an actual self-nullification.

When the intelligent person contemplates this during his study of Torah, awe and fear will engulf him as he takes to heart that this is actually the word of God spoken to Moses at Sinai.

This is what our Sages stated regarding the verse *Make them known to your children and your children's children* (Deut. 4:9), and in the next

---

20. The Rabbis, in Shavuot 39a, taught that all Jewish souls, including those of generations not yet born, were present at Sinai to accept the covenant. They derived this from the verses *Neither with you alone do I make this covenant . . . but with him that standeth here with us this day before the Lord our God, and also with him that is not here with us this day* (Deut. 29:13—14).

21. I.e., the entire repository of Jewish law and lore.

verse, *The day you stood before the Lord your God in Horeb* (i.e., Sinai) (Deut. 4:10). "Just as then in awe and fear, so likewise now," etc.[22]

At first glance it is difficult to understand the comparison of Sinai to the situation of "likewise now." For in their encampment about Mount Sinai, the entire nation *saw the sounds* (Exod. 20:15), and *God spoke to them face-to-face* (Deut. 5:4), which is not the case when an individual studies Torah by himself. But the matter should be understood as written above, that every individual's study of Torah, at all times, is actually the word of God spoken to Moses at Sinai. Thus, he who studies Torah will experience fear and awe as though he had received the Torah this day from Mount Sinai.

4. THE STUDY OF HALAKHIC CODES
Source: R. Nahman of Bratslav, Likkutei Etzot, Talmud Torah, no. 62

Every Jew is under a great obligation to study daily a portion of the halakhic codes. This should never be skipped, not even during an emergency, such as when one is busy or traveling. The least one should do in such an event is to learn a single paragraph in the *Shulḥan Arukh*, where he can, i.e., not necessarily at the place he is up to in his regular study of the *Shulḥan Arukh*. This way, not a single day in one's entire life will pass without the study of *Shulḥan Arukh*. On other days, when there are no emergencies, one should study in an orderly sequence all four parts of the *Shulḥan Arukh* until he has completed them. Afterwards, he should start again from the beginning and repeat the same orderly cycle.

This is the proper way for all of one's lifetime. It provides a great *tikkun* ("reparation"), purifying and repairing all the impairments one has caused by his sins. For the study of the codes (*poskim*) enables one to distinguish properly the good from the evil, which is the essence of all *tikkunim*.[23]

---

22. Berakhot 22a. Whenever Israel's descendents transmit the teachings of Torah, they should undergo the same profound emotions of awe and fear that they experienced at the time of the Sinaitic revelation.

23. The author's emphasis on the study of the practical codes, such as the *Shulḥan Arukh*, is in line with earlier hasidic masters who held that studying the Talmud text in all its intricate dialectics makes one susceptible to conceit and bragging. E.g., see G. Nigal's introduction to *Noam Elimelekh*, pp. 112—144. However, in n. 798 ad loc., Nigal cites the Maggid of Mezeritch as having praised intellectual creativity in talmudic dialectics as "purifying the mind for serving God." Cf. my *Torah Lishmah*, chap. 4, concerning R. Shneur Zalman, who gave preference to the performance of mitzvot

5. STUDYING TALMUD AND THE SPIRIT OF ERETZ ISRAEL
Source: R. Aharon of Zhitomir, Pitgamin Kaddishin, sub 5 Darkei Limmud

One who studies Gemara may be compared to one who dwells in the Land of Israel;[24] he will merit the lights of Eretz Israel, i.e., the spirit of the Holy Land.[25] For Mar the son of Rav Ashi was in Babylonia and situated between two mountains, when he arranged the final order of the Babylonian Talmud. He uttered an oath and four clouds arrived and surrounded him, then he uttered another oath that brought to them air from the Land of Israel; and then he arranged the Talmud.[26]

The Importance of Study

6. "WHO NEEDS A TORAH?"
Source: R. Levi Yitzhak of Berdichev, Kedushat Levi, Likkutim, end, s.v. ita be-Midrash

The talmudic saying that the patriarchs possessed the knowledge of the Torah in order to fulfill its commandments before the Torah was given[27] needs understanding. It may be explained as follows:

It is known that just as there are 248 limbs and 365 sinews in the corporeal human body,[28] so, too, there are 248 spiritual limbs and 365 spiritual sinews of the soul.[29] And just as there can be no vitality in the corporeal limbs without food and drink, so too there is no vitality in

---

over the study of Torah, unlike R. Hayyim of Volozhin, who held the opposite view. It is likely that this is the reason Hasidim were advised to study the codified decisions of Halakhah and Shulhan Arukh, knowledge mandatory for the proper fulfillment of the mitzvot. See also my "Study and Prayer: Their Relative Value in Hasidism and Mitnagdism," in S. K. Mirsky Memorial Volume (New York, 1970), pp. 37—52.

24. R. Aaron's assumption that the study of Talmud may serve as a substitute for dwelling in Eretz Israel is a novel approach for which it is difficult to find support in the sources. However, R. Yair Hayyim Bakhrakh expresses a similar thought regarding the study of Kabbalah; see his She'elot u-Teshuvot Havot Yair 210.

25. That is, the inspiration of the Holy Land.

26. I do not know the source of this legend. The point is that the study of Talmud is equivalent to being immersed in the sanctity of the Holy Land.

27. Mishnah Kiddushin, end. Cf. Yoma 28b.

28. Makkot 23b. As to 365 sinews, see Zohar I, 170b.

29. The source for this is unknown to me. See, too, Noam Elimelekh to Balak 84c, s.v. bameh devarim amurim, which implies: "When a zaddik studies for its own sake, he causes the creation of 248 spiritual limbs."

the spiritual limbs other than the fulfillment of the Torah commandments. Now, the Torah, God, and Israel are all one unity.[30] Thus the
souls of Israelites are derived from the identical source as the Torah,
and therefore the life-force of the souls depends upon the fulfillment
of the Torah and its commandments.

This, however, may lead one to wonder: Why did Israel need the
giving of the Torah and the study thereof in order to know how to fulfill God's mitzvot? Would they not have fulfilled the Torah automatically? Inasmuch as the Torah is the principal life-force of the soul, the
very substance of the soul ought to be attracted to Torah and mitzvot.
And just as there is no need to teach the corporeal limbs to eat and
drink and to fulfill other physical needs of the body, because on it
depends the body's basic vitality to which it is devoted by nature, likewise there should be no necessity to educate the soul in Torah and
mitzvot, which constitute the root of its vitality.

The explanation of this is, however, simple. Truly speaking, if not
for the fact that the soul is enclosed in a corporeal body, there would
indeed be no need for it. But the soul is garbed in a body, and this corporeal enclosure obscures and covers the soul; therefore the need for
the giving and the studying of the Torah.[31]

Therefore the patriarchs, who attained a state where they are
divested of corporeality, so that the bodies did not cover the souls, had
indeed possessed the power to know and fulfill the Torah on their
own. This was achieved before the Torah was actually revealed, since,
as said, the soul without the interference of the corporeal body is naturally drawn to Torah and mitzvot.[32]

7. ELEVATING THE SPARKS THROUGH STUDY
Source: R. Shneur Zalman of Liady, Tanya, Iggeret ha-Kodesh, chap. 26

The enlightened will understand something yet more wonderful, that
is, what happens in heaven above by the deliberation and elucidation
of a halakhic decision from the Gemara, through the early and later
codifiers, which prior to this deliberation was in a state of concealment. By means of this deliberation one elevates this ruling from the
kelipot that were obscuring and concealing it in such a way that it was

---

30. See Zohar I, 24a; II, 60a; III, 73a, and see Y. Tishby, "Qudsha Berikh Hu," Oraita ve-
Yisrael Kula Had Hu—"Meqor ha-Imrah be-Ferush 'Idra Rabba' le-Ramhal," Kiryat
Sefer 50 (5735), 480-492, and ibid., 668, 674.
31. See Additional Note *1.
32. See Additional Note *2.

not known at all or that its reason was not well understood.[33]

For the reason of the halakhah is the secret of the sefirah of the Supreme Hokhmah, the sparks of which fell into the *kelipot* at the Breaking of the Vessels. These sparks are there in a state of exile because the *kelipot* dominate them and hide the wisdom of the Torah from the higher and lower spheres. . . .

Now, the celestial beings do not have the power to select and cleanse that which is in the *kelipat nogah*[34] because of the Breaking of the Vessels. Only the terrestrial beings can do that, for they are vested in a material body, the "hide of the serpent," which is of the *kelipat nogah*. They sap its strength by breaking the passions and suppressing the *sitra ahara*,[35] so that all the agents of evil are dispersed.[36]

That is why the celestial beings come to hear novellae of Torah from the terrestrial beings,[37] when they uncover and reveal the secrets of wisdom which until then were suppressed in exile. Every Israelite is able to reveal secrets of wisdom, i.e., to reveal and to discover a new insight, whether in Halakhah or in Aggadah, in the revealed or in the mystic parts of the Torah, according to the level of his soul's root.[38] One is indeed obligated to do so in order to perfect his soul by elevating all the sparks that fell to it as its lot, as is known.[39] [And every word of Torah, especially one of Halakhah, is a spark of the Shekhinah, i.e., the word of God, as it is stated in the Gemara: "The word of God,

33. Earlier in the same chapter the author cites R. Isaac Luria's famous teaching that "the principal service of man and the basic purpose of his occupation with Torah and the commandments, is to disencumber the sparks." These sparks, as the author proceeds to inform us, issued from the primal catastrophe and fell into the "shells" (*kelipot*) from which man must liberate them. The sparks that come from the vessel or sefirah of Wisdom are the teachings of Torah.

34. See *Tikkunei Zohar*, introduction, 10b; *Etz Hayyim* 49:4. Cf. Pirkei de-R. Eliezer, chap. 20. This "shell of Venus" denotes the realm where good and evil "serve in confusion," and man's function is to purify the good from its contamination by evil. See the next selection, no. 2.

35. "The Other Side," i.e., the demonic forces.

36. Paraphrase of Ps. 92:10. With the purification of the good, the *kelipah* disappears of itself.

37. See Zohar III, 173a. Cf. Hagigah 14b.

38. See *Sefer Hasidim*, sec. 530, and comment of R. Hayyim Yosef David Azulai (Hida) in *Berit Olam*, ad loc. The efficacy of man's mystical achievements by virtue of his intellectual creativity in Torah is relative to his own talents and native spiritual proclivities.

39. Zohar I, 4b. Cf. *Shulhan Arukh ha-Rav*, by the author, Laws of Talmud Torah 1:4, end.

i.e., the Halakhah . . ."[40].][41] . . . Pertaining to this it is said in the Gemara: "Whoever occupies himself with Torah, God says of him, 'I account him as if he had redeemed Me and My children from among the nations of the world.'"[42]

8. STUDY TO REMOVE THE SHELLS
Source: R. Yaakov Yosef of Polennoye, Toledot Yaakov Yosef to Beha'alotekha, s.v. ve'agav neva'er

The purpose of studying the Oral Law, i.e., the laws of the forbidden and the permissible, of defilement and purity, of the ritually fit and the ritually disqualified, is as follows:

There are divine spheres of Loving-kindness (*Hasadim*) and Judgment (*Gevurot*). From Lovingkindness comes an expansion of the good and the holy of the right side, while Judgment causes the amplification of the evil urge from the left side.[43] The sin of the serpent engendered a state of confusion between the good and the evil,[44] thus creating a need to study the Six Orders of the Oral Law dealing with the categories of the three polarities mentioned above in order to separate the *kelipot* from the good, that is, the forbidden from the permissible, the impure from the pure, and the ritually unfit from the ritually fit.

When this separation of the defiled and the forbidden from the Shekhinah is accomplished, "the Bride" (*h-k-l-h*) is adorned with the letters *h-l-k-h* (Halakhah) of the right side, i.e., the presence of His blessed Name.[45] This is the meaning of the issuance of the *Bat Kol* ("Heavenly Voice") declaring that the Halakhah is in accordance with

---

40. Shabbat 138b.
41. The brackets are added in the source.
42. Berakhot 8a. Cf. Zohar III, 281a.
43. The right side of the sefirotic structure controls lovingkindness, mercy, and compassion in the world. The left side yields nonbeneficient power, might, and strictness in judgment.
44. The sin of the biblical serpent in tempting Eve to eat of the forbidden fruit of the tree of knowledge of good and evil (Gen. 3:1—6) caused good and evil to interpenetrate. Man must endeavor to restore the primal position of the good by separating it out of the enveloping shell (*kelipah*).
45. "The Bride" (Heb. *ha-kallah*) is a symbol of the Shekhinah, God's loving presence, and thus properly belonging to the "right" side, that of lovingkindness. The same Hebrew letters, by transposition, form the word *halakhah*. Thus halakhic analysis, which distinguishes between the three sets of polarities, is that which restores the pristine quality of the sparks and "adorns" the Bride as Shekhinah. See below, selection 18, and see my *Torah Lishmah*, p. 217, for further discussion.

the decision of Bet Hillel.[46] It was to announce the inclusion of Lovingkindness and Judgment in one unity. . . .

For it is the purpose of Torah study to remove the *kelipot* which are in the way of incorporating Lovingkindness and Judgment into one unity.[47]

9. STUDYING TORAH VERSUS STUDYING THE "WORDS OF TORAH"
Source: R. Zadok ha-Kohen of Lublin, Zidkat ha-Zaddik 59

The term "Torah" implies teaching, guiding,[48] for the Torah indeed serves man as teacher and guide. This does not necessarily refer to the educative value of its statutes and laws, for even if one studies the order of Kodashim,[49] he is considered engaged in Torah. But the guiding strength of Torah is its light, as our Rabbis said in the Midrash on Lamentations: "The Torah's luminary power will cause their return to the good."[50]

The light of Torah which saves and protects has its effect only on those who use it in the right way,[51] that is, they engage in its study for its own sake,[52] for then it is an elixir of life,[53] inasmuch as life and light

---

46. Eruvin 13b.

47. Bet Hillel, who usually took a more lenient attitude in Halakhah, is said to be symbolized by Lovingkindness, while Bet Shammai, whose decisions were usually stricter, is represented by Judgment. Although the *Bat Kol* decided in favor of Bet Hillel, it did not intend to utterly reject the opinion of Bet Shammai, for it also announced the "the opinions of both these and these are the words of the living God" (Eruvin 13b). So, both Lovingkindness and Judgment are necessary for the divine wholeness. Thus the true purpose of the heavenly message was to assert the unity of Lovingkindness and Judgment.

48. See Maharal of Prague, *Gur Arye* to Gen. 1:1, citing R. David Kimhi.

49. The fifth order of Mishnah and Talmud dealing mainly with sacrificial laws which are irrelevant today from a practical point of view.

50. Lamentations Rabbah, proem 3 (*petiḥa*). See Jerusalem Talmud Hagigah 1:7. In a parenthetic remark R. Zadok interprets the midrashic saying that the Torah's light restores man to the good, as having a dual effect. It protects a person from committing a sin, and it saves the sinner from the sin when it has been committed, in accordance with a statement in Sotah 21a and Rashi *ad loc*.

51. R. Zadok alludes here to a talmudic interpretation of the verse in Prov. 3:16: "Length of days is in her right hand; in her left hand are riches and honor." The reference here, according to Shabbat 63a, is to those who use the Torah to the right (*maiminim*), that is, those who study it the right way, and those who use Torah to the left (*masme'ilim*), those who use it in the wrong way. The right way is to study Torah for its own sake (*lishmah*); the wrong way is to study for personal advancement or other personal motives (*shelo lishmah*). See Rashi there, s.v. *le-masme'ilim* and Prov. *ad loc*.

are one and the same, as it says: *For with Thee is the fountain of life; in Thy light do we see light* (Ps. 36:10). But the one who studies Torah for personal motives (*shelo lishmah*) will not perceive its light, and consequently it does not become a guide to him, and it will not restore him to the good; moreover, the term "Torah" does not even apply to it, although it may be termed Torah language, which according to the Yerushalmi (at the end of Berkahot) is in itself a good thing.

This is why we say in the benediction, "to be occupied with words of Torah," [54] and not "to study Torah," for who can be confident that he is esteemed enough and distinguished enough[55] to be truly occupied with his study of Torah in the true way? Therefore we say "words of Torah," for in any event we do engage in Torah discourse, "mutterings of Torah," which are more fully articulated elsewhere,[56] and this is a mitzvah in itself. Thus the intended meaning of the benediction is this: "Blessed art Thou . . . who hast sanctified us with Thy commandments and commanded us" to engage in things that bring holiness into the heart, as is the purpose of all commandments. This may be deduced from the rabbinic interpretation of the command, *and thou shalt talk of them* [words of Torah] (Deut. 6:7), where it refers to the negative, that is, not to engage in idle talk.[57] This may cause one to wonder: why not say it is intended as stated, for the positive, since it is indeed a mitzvah in itself to utter words of Torah? Now, however, it may be said that the intention of the rabbinic command is indeed the positive, that is, one should engage in Torah talk even of the kind that is nothing more than an alternative to idle talk, i.e., the sort that cannot be defined as true Torah.

And therefore the benediction is followed by another one with the plea: "O Lord our God, we beseech Thee to make the words of Thy Torah pleasant in our mouth . . . so that we . . . may . . . study the

---

52. See previous note.

53. In accordance with the Talmudic saying in Taanit 7a: If one merits, Torah study becomes to him an elixir of life; if not, it turns on him as a deadly poison.

54. In the morning prayer.

55. R. Zadok uses here terms mentioned in Moed Katan 28a, which, according to Rashi *ad loc.* and *Arukh* (cited on the margin of the Talmud there), seems to have the meaning given here.

56. Even if we do not fully understand them now.

57. Yoma 19b.

Torah for its own sake."[58] Here the petition is to achieve Torah study
for its own sake by virtue of finding pleasantness and sweetness in the
words of Torah in our mouth. Thus the desire for Torah increases so
that the mere study of its words will lead to the achievement of the
higher level, the study of Torah itself, as our Sages said:[59] from studying for ulterior motives one attains to study for its own sake.

10. THE TORAH AND THE HEART
Source: R. Zadok ha-Kohen of Lublin, Zidkat ha-Zaddik, no. 225

Words of Torah which pass through the heart, that is, that the heart
feels and is affected by them, are defined as a "tree of life"[60] and an
"elixir of life."[61] For the heart is the source of vitality, as is written:
Above all thou guardest, keep thy heart, for out of it is the issue of life (Prov.
4:23). When one's enthusiasm is aroused by the words of Torah, the
very zest of his vitality is aroused, and engenders vitality in man.

This occurs when one's fear of sin comes before his wisdom
(Torah).[62] For fear of heaven is in the heart, as our Sages said on the
verse *to acquire wisdom when there is no heart* (Prov. 17:16).[63] Fear is the
female, and the Torah of truth is the male designed to instill peace and
joy in the heart, as it is said: *The precepts of the Lord are right, rejoicing
the heart* (Ps. 19:9). After the fear which engenders a broken heart and
sadness, the words of Torah are absorbed and sustained in the heart.

For the heart is the locality where the blood boils and through the
power of desire and yearning for the sweetness of the words of Torah
the element of fire is strengthened, as the Rabbis said: "The Torah
boils in him."[64] And it is well known that boiling causes absorption
with such strength that what is absorbed never escapes from it, a
quality absent in absorption by cool or cold elements, such as words
of Torah which do not pass through the heart. One may be perfectly
capable to conceive wisdom in his brain and to perceive matters of

---

58. In some texts the word *lishmah* (for its own sake) is omitted from this blessing
(see *Ozar ha-Tefillot*, pp. 116-117), an omission seemingly approved by R. Zadok. It
is, however, of no consequence at all for him, since in his view the expression
"study of Torah," used here instead of "study of the words of Torah" in the first
blessing, is itself an indication that the reference is to *Torah lishmah*.
59. Pesahim 50b.
60. Based on *She* [the Torah] *is a tree of life to them that lay hold upon her* (Prov. 3:18).
61. Yoma 72b.
62. See Avot 3:9.
63. Yoma, loc. cit.
64. Ta'anit 4a.

divinity and Torah while his heart remains totally unaffected by it all. For he is like one who studies external wisdom, which has no relation to him.[65] It is all the result of lacking the necessary prerequisite, that is, the fear of sin, which causes one to reflect on his shortcomings and to feel a need for the words of Torah capable of perfecting him; thus his wisdom will not endure. This is akin to what is said in the Gemara Sanhedrin regarding Doeg, that he forgot all his Torah learning because "God [Raḥmana] desires the heart,"[66] namely, that one's Torah should leave a sensible imprint on his heart. This is the principle: When one's heart is actively inspired in his study of Torah, then it has vitality and is absorbed internally.

Defining Study for Its Own Sake

11. THE INTELLECTUAL ASPECT OF TORAH LISHMAH
Source: R. Shneur Zalman of Liady, Tanya, Likkutei Amarim, chap. 5

When any intellect conceives and comprehends a concept with its intellectual faculties, the intellect grasps the concept and encompasses it. This concept is [in turn] grasped, enveloped, and enclothed within the intellect which conceived and comprehended it. The mind, for its part, is also clothed in the concept at the time it comprehends and grasps it with the intellect.[67] For example, when a person understands and comprehends, fully and clearly, any halakhah in the Mishnah or the Gemara, his intellect takes it in and encompasses it and, at the same time, is clothed in it.

Now, the particular halakhah is the wisdom and will of God, for it was His will that when, for example, Reuben pleads in one way and Simeon in another, the verdict shall be such and such. This is the case

---

65. Heb. ḥokhmah ḥitsonit, lit. "external wisdom," ordinarily refers to studies external to Torah. R. Zadok interprets these as studies that have no essential connection to the Jew.

66. Sanhedrin 106b. The talmudic text actually reads: "The Holy One, blessed be He, desires the heart." However, in Rashi ad loc., s.v. revuta, the term for this phrase is raḥmana instead of ha-kadosh barukh hu. The phrase is also raḥmana in the Zohar (e.g., Zohar III, 281b, Raya Mehemna). The term raḥmana in talmudic and midrashic literature denotes either God (as in Ta'anit 9b) or the Torah (as in Bava Mezia 3b). The author uses raḥmana here seemingly in referring to its other meaning, viz., the Torah; i.e., the Torah desires the heart.

67. A point demonstrated by the fact that when the mind is preoccupied with one thought it cannot, at the same time, engage in another.

even if such a litigation has never occurred and will never present itself for judgment in connection with such disputes and claims, since it is the will of wisdom of the Holy One blessed be He that in the event of one person pleading this way and the other litigant pleading that way, the verdict shall be such and such.

Therefore, when a person knows and comprehends with his intellect such a verdict, in accordance with the case as it is set out in the Mishnah, Gemara, or Codes, he has thereby comprehended, grasped, and encompassed with his intellect the will and wisdom of God whom no thought can grasp,[68] nor can His will and wisdom be grasped except when they are clothed in the laws that have been set out for us. His intellect is likewise clothed in God's divine will and wisdom.

This is a wonderful union, like which there is none other, and which has no parallel anywhere in the material world, whereby complete oneness and unity, from every side and angle, can be attained.

Hence the special rank, infinitely great and wonderful, of the commandment of knowing the Torah and comprehending it, over all the commandments involving action, even those relating to speech, and even the commandment to study the Torah, which is fulfilled through speech. For concerning all the commandments involving speech or action, God clothes the soul and envelops it from head to foot with divine light. With knowledge of Torah, however, besides the fact that through it the intellect is clothed in divine wisdom, this divine wisdom is also contained in it, to the extent that his intellect comprehends, perceives, and encompasses, as much as it is able to, of the knowledge of the Torah, each man according to his intellect and the strength of his knowledge and comprehension in *Pardes*.[69]

---

68. Introduction to *Tikkunei Zohar* 17a: "No thought can apprehend Thee." The author hints here that the preference for Torah study over the fulfillment of the mitzvot is based on the Torah's intellectual nature. Cf. *Torah Lishmah*, chap. 4, esp. pp. 147-149.

69. Lit. "orchard," but in Kabbalah and hasidic literature, based on Talmud Hagigah 14b, taken as an acrostic of the four Hebrew words denoting the four levels of scriptural interpretation: *peshat* (simple meaning), *remez* (intimation), *derash* (homiletical exposition), and *sod* (esoteric meaning). For a more elaborate discussion, including Maimonides' definition of *Pardes*, see my *Torah Lishmah*, pp. 174-176, and Albert van der Heide, "PARDES: Methodological Reflections on the Theory of the Four Senses," *Journal of Jewish Studies* 34 (1983), pp. 147-159, and also my *Torah u-Madda* (Northvale: Jason Aronson, 1990), pp. 80—81.
This intellectual definition of Torah for its own sake (*torah lishmah*) by R. Shneur Zalman is one of the three I have detected in his writings (see *Torah Lishmah*, chap. 6); cf. the other passages from R. Shneur Zalman cited in this chapter.

Since, in the case of Torah knowledge, the Torah is clothed in the soul and intellect of a person, and is absorbed in them, it is called the "bread" and "nourishment" of the soul. For just as physical bread nourishes the body as it is absorbed internally, where it is transformed into blood and flesh of his body, whereby he lives and exists, so too with knowledge of the Torah and its comprehension by the soul of the person who studies it well, with intellectual concentration, until the Torah is absorbed by his intellect and is united with it, and they become one. This becomes nourishment for the soul, and its inner life from the Giver of life, the blessed Ein-Sof, who is clothed in His wisdom and in His Torah that are absorbed in the soul.

This is the meaning of the verse *Yea, Thy Torah is within my innermost parts* (Ps. 40:9). It is also stated in *Etz Ḥayyim*, Gate 44, chap. 3, that the garments of the soul in the Garden of Eden (Paradise) are the commandments, while the Torah is the food for the souls which during life on earth had occupied themselves in the study of the Torah for its own sake. It is similarly written in the Zohar, regarding the meaning of "for its own sake," that it is study with the intent to attach one's soul to God through the comprehension of the Torah, each one according to his intellect,[70] as explained in *Peri Etz Ḥayyim*.[71]

12. LISHMAH AND SHELO LISHMAH
Source: R. Elimelekh of Lizhensk, Noam Elimelekh, Likkutei Shoshanah, 105a, s.v. ve-zehu yesh noḥalin

One's principal occupation in the holy Torah ought to be for its own sake (*lishmah*), for only through such study is one likely to attain knowledge of God, to recognize His greatness and His wonders, and to cleave unto the divine.

This is the meaning of *And God spoke all these words, saying, I am the Lord thy God* (Exod. 20:1—2), i.e., God told us all of these words, namely, the Torah in its totality, in order to say: *I am the Lord thy God*.[72] For it is the Torah which made it possible for Him to convey to us the perception of His divinity.

---

70. Zohar II, p. 21a ff. R. Shneur Zalman combines here the intellectual definition of *lishmah* prevalent in Mitnaggedic literature with the widely held hasidic interpretation where *lishmah* is associated with *devekut*. Rabbi N. Mindel, the translator of *Likkutei Amarim*, assumes (incorrectly, I believe that "we have here a departure from the conventional concept of *teshuvah* and *shelo lishmah*." Cf. *Torah Lishmah*, p. 228, n. 87.

71. See Additional Note *3.

72. The interpretation is based upon the apparently redundant *leimor* ("saying"). Cf. above, selection 3.

The Sages nevertheless relaxed somewhat the requirement of *lishmah* by saying that one should always engage in the study of Torah, even if not for its own sake, for this will eventually lead him to study for its own sake.[73] The fundamental root and principle of Torah study is still: for its own sake. The permission to engage in study with ulterior motives in mind is merely that man should not waste his time completely, Heaven forbid, and become bored.

This is the meaning of *Hear, my son, the instruction of thy father, and forsake not the teaching of thy mother* (Prov. 1:8). The first part of the verse refers to engaging in Torah for its own sake, and it intimates the proper approach to achieve this. That is, when studying the Torah one should sense in it the message or reprimand and chastisement demanding of him to study for its own sake and with *devekut*.[74] Through this kind of study one may be called a son to the Father—the Creator. The other part of the verse, *forsake not the teaching of your mother*, is addressed to study for selfish reasons, saying that in any case one must not totally neglect the Torah, Heaven forbid, and should study it even if not for its own sake.[75] This sort of study, however, is of the female type, for he is merely a receiver, not an emanator of spiritual bounty.[76]

---

73. Pesahim 50b.

74. On the meaning of *devekut*, see chapter 5. Elsewhere, R. Elimelekh points out that when one studies with *devekut* it makes no difference what and how much he learns. For every bit of such Torah engagement relates to an upper world of its own, and thus there are many ways of attaining *devekut* or ecstatic communion with God (*Noam Elimelekh* to Miketz, Nigal ed., p. 123). R. Elimelekh stresses repeatedly that the main purpose of *lishmah* is *devekut*. The one who studies for its own sake feels "as if he had just received the Torah anew at Sinai from the mouth of God. This [in turn develops in the learner] great love and a burning enthusiasm" leading to *devekut* with the Shekhinah (*Noam Elimelekh* to Zav, Nigal ed., p. 297).
The zaddik who studies *lishmah* has the power to "elevate" the Torah of those who study for merely personal reasons (*shelo lishmah*). The learner provides the body (*guf*) of Torah, as it were, and the zaddik causes it to be endowed with a soul (*neshamah*), namely *lishmah* (ibid.).

75. Cf. *Noam Elimelekh* to Bereshit, beginning.

76. Hence the difference in the scriptural text between "father" and "mother." Nigal, in his introduction to *Noam Elimelekh*, pp. 104-106, seemingly understands the last remark in our selection to mean that one who studies with an ulterior motive may merit honor and wealth but will not attain *devekut* (see Shabbat 63a). See Additional Note *4.

13. *SHOCKING ONESELF INTO STUDYING LISHMAH*
Source: R. Zadok ha-Kohen of Lublin, Zidkat ha-Zaddik, no. 167

In the study of Torah one is permitted to be anxious.[77] This means that one should fear that perhaps the Torah is for him a deadly poison, Heaven forbid.[78] The very fear will sweeten his study and thus transform his learning for selfish reasons into study for its own sake (*lishmah*).[79]

When one is afraid, it is his instinct (*mazal*) that senses some danger,[80] similar to a dream, which is also a form of vision that one's instinct (*mazal*) is seeing. Regarding the latter, the Rabbis said: "A bad dream is helped by its sadness,"[81] i.e., the mere fact that it causes one pain is sufficient to nullify its impact. Similarly, Torah becomes a dreadful poison to the one whose study has no merit, but if this thought agitates him, it suffices and the cause of his worry will automatically be alleviated.

A difficulty, however, arises: should not one be unafraid in [studying] the words of Torah? Does not Scripture say *The precepts of the Lord are right, rejoicing the heart* (Ps. 19:9) and *Wisdom is a stronghold to the wise* (Eccles. 7:19); and do not other biblical verses teach us that Torah bestows upon man strength and joy, the very opposite of fear?

It may be explained as follows: One rabbi said: "A man should always engage in the study of Torah, even if not for its own sake, for through its study for a selfish purpose he will attain a state of study

---

77. Berakhot 60a, in resolving two contradictory verses, *the sinners in Zion are afraid* (Isa. 33:14), implying that fear is sinful, and the other is *Happy is the man that feareth always* (Prov. 28:14). Rashi interprets this to mean fear of forgetting what one has learned. This is a commendable trait, for it causes one to study more diligently. R. Zadok, however, explains this fear as having to do more with the quality of Torah study than with its retention.

78. In accordance with "If one is deserving, [the Torah] becomes for him an elixir of life; if undeserving, a deadly poison" (Yoma 72b). Our author apparently connects this saying with another dictum in Shabbat 63a, regarding those who use the Torah the "left" way, which Rashi interprets to mean that they engage in it for personal motives (*shelo lishmah*).

79. See the preceding note. Regarding the author's association of "sweetness" in study with *lishmah*, see above, selection 9.

80. Megillah 3a. Normally, the term refers to destiny, one's stellar influence. Rashi interprets *mazal* in this case as each individual's guardian angel. Perhaps in a broader, more contemporary sense, one might understand the Talmud's use of *mazal* as intuition, or instinct.

81. Berakhot 55a; see Rashi ad loc.

for its own sake (*lishmah*)."[82] Now, he says "always," for in such a state, i.e., for a selfish purpose, one can go on studying continuously, which is not the case with study for its own sake. It is utterly impossible to do so constantly. For studying *lishmah* is synonymous with *devekut*, and such communion, like the conjugal duties of Torah scholars which are limited to once a week, "from Sabbath to Sabbath,"[83] or like strollers (*tayalin*), that is, those who make excursions into the esoteric *Pardes*, who can achieve this state of *lishmah* and *devekut* once a day, at the most, though regularly it is *shelo lishmah*.[84]

When the rabbis teach that from *shelo lishmah* he will reach *lishmah*, it means that the *shelo lishmah* itself, from its very nature and essence, will bring him to *lishmah*, i.e., the sobering fear. . . .

This is the meaning of *Happy is the man that feareth always* (Prov. 28:14), that is, he fears the form of Torah learning which is constant, i.e., study with ulterior motives. Such an individual will, on occasion, reach the level of *devekut*, where there is no reason at all to fear.

14. SELF-SCRUTINY IN STUDY
Source: R. Levi Yitzhak of Berdichev, *Pitgamin Kadishin, no. 13*

It has been said: A man should always study the Torah even if not for its own sake, for through the study for a selfish purpose he will attain the state of studying for its own sake.[85] This statement of the Gemara seems at first glance incomprehensible. If, in the final analysis, one must study for its own sake, why then is the term "always" used in

---

82. Pesahim 50b.
83. Ketubbot 62b. Hence, such a level of intention and devotion cannot be maintained in uninterrupted fashion. A similar analogy of *lishmah* with *devekut* and the subsequent comparison of such study with marital congress, based on the root of *devekut* in the Torah's command *ve-davak be-ishto* ("he shall cleave to his wife") (Gen. 2:24), was suggested by R. Yaakov Yosef; see elsewhere in this chapter.
84. Namely, mystics, those who engage in the study of Kabbalah. The author engages here in word-play. Mishnah Ketubbot 61b states that the marital duties of strollers (*tayalin*) is once every day. The Gemara (ibid. 62a) illustrates this by one who eats and drinks and sleeps in the shade of his orchard. *Pardes*, the Hebrew word for "orchard," is the talmudic term for mysticism (see Hagigah 14b). The study of mysticism is thus described by kabbalists as "strolling in the orchard" (*tiyul ba-pardes*). Hence the author's suggestion that strollers in Pardes may achieve *devekut* and *lishmah* once every day.
85. Pesahim 50b.

relation to self-serving study? The true meaning of this saying, however, is as follows:

The Torah teaches man wisdom and the knowledge of how to attain the wondrous level of perception that enables him to serve God in truth and for its own sake, and the Torah implants in him ideas as to how to reach this goal. The best advice is that whenever one studies the Torah and worships God, he should afterwards scrutinize his activities concerning these matters thoroughly and repeatedly and with great subtlety. In all likelihood he will discover that he has been deficient in studying *lishmah* and in serving God in complete truth in accordance with his own ability and prior achievements. This degree will encourage his efforts to attain genuine *lishmah*. In the future he will thereby gain fresh determination and vigor to achieve the privileged levels of *lishmah* and truthfulness.

One must not heed the misleading claim of his Evil Urge (*Yetzer ha-Ra*), which attempts to convince him that he has already attained full maturity in studying *lishmah* and truthfulness in his service of God. Only a fool will believe this. A wise man, however, will recognize in this the seductiveness of the Evil Urge, which attempts to cast him into the nethermost pit with his wicked counsels and smooth tongue. "He who seeks purification receives heavenly assistance."[86] God in His abundant compassion will grant him the attainment of the state of *lishmah* in utter truthfulness in the study of His holy Torah and in all other aspects of His service.

This is what is meant by "always," that is, one's study of Torah ought *always* to contain the aspect of *shelo lishmah*, in that he should perceive intellectually that all his previous study was merely *shelo lishmah*. As a result of [expressing] such self-serving he will indeed attain the inner spiritual fortitude necessary to attain the level of *lishmah* and utter truthfulness in his divine service.[87]

15. THE REWARD OF STUDY FOR ITS OWN SAKE

Source: R. Zevi Hirsch of Zhidachov, *Sur me-Ra va-Aseh Tov*, and see *Zevi Hirsh Eichenstein, Turn Aside from Evil and Do Good*, trans. Louis Jacobs, London, 1995, pp. 134-135.

The purpose of Torah study for its own sake is as described by R. Meir

---

86. Shabbat 104a. Cf. Zohar I, 54a; II, 79b—c; and III, 53b.
87. Cf. chapter 5 on *devekut*. That the feeling of insufficiency provides a challenge and a stepping-stone for loftier achievement is a popular theme in hasidic literature.

in tractate Avot: "Whoever occupies himself with Torah for its own
sake merits many things . . . and it prepares him to become just, pious,
upright, and faithful."[88]

Torah for its own sake (*Torah lishmah*), as defined in the preface of
the saintly R. Hayyim Vital to the teachings of R. Isaac Luria is: Torah
for the sake of Torah; this in reality means, for the sake of God, since
this is what Torah is all about, as indicated by its name: a guide, as in
moreh derekh[89] for ascending the mountain of the Lord, the Holy One,
God of Jacob.[90]

Now, dear reader, is there much benefit in pointing the way to the
lame or the blind to climb a mountain or to a stupid man who has no
more intelligence than an animal? So does the Zohar describe those
who lack wisdom, those who have never even tasted the wisdom of
the Torah, which is compared to honey and the droppings of the hon-
eycomb (Ps. 19:11); the Zohar calls them "those with clogged hearts
and sightless eyes."

This is the meaning of the tanna's saying, "Whoever is engaged in
studying Torah for its own sake," namely, who studies in order to perceive and understand the vitality inherent in Torah; it is this that prepares him to become just and pious, etc. That is, the Torah transforms
him into a vessel ready to receive these qualities of being just and
pious, etc. It points the way to the path on which to walk unhindered
by lameness and blindness, to be perfect, of full height without a
defect in any limb. That is, each of his limbs will correspond to its
equivalent in Torah,[91] and hence the talmudic rule: Any addition of a
limb is considered as if the limb is completely absent,[92] will not be
applicable to him.

---

88. Avot 6:1.
89. For the interrelationship between the words *torah* and *moreh derekh*, see S. J. Finn,
Ha-Otzar (Warsaw, 1921), vol. 2, p. 311. R. Zvi Hirsch defines the guiding nature of
Torah as pointing the way for the ascent to God. See selection 9, above.
90. R. Zvi Hirsch sees no distinction between the devotional definition of *lishmah*
meaning "for the sake of God," and its intellectual definition, "for the sake of Torah
itself." See my *Torah Lishmah*, pp. 190 ff. More likely, R. Zevi Hirsch synthesizes the
Besht's definition ("for the sake of God"; see *Torah Lishmah*, pp. 215-218 and notes ad
loc.) and the one adopted by R. Hayyim of Volozhin, "for the sake of the Torah itself"
(ibid., pp. 231ff.).
91. Makkot 23b. "Man has 248 limbs, parallel to the 248 positive commandments in
the Torah" (Zohar II, 170b). Cf. Midrash on Psalms 32:4 and see selection 6, above.
92. Hullin 58b. The original halakhic context is that of the kashrut of animals.

However, if a man does not reflect on the full measure of his stature—his two eyes, two ears, ten fingers, ten toes, and every joint of his 248 limbs—as to why and for what purpose each of these limbs was created, and which aspect of wisdom it teaches, he may find himself with an additional limb which is considered a deficit, and he thus becomes disqualified (*terefah*).[93] Then, of course, he is no longer prepared to be just, pious, and upright.

Lishmah and Devekut

16. DEVEKUT DURING TORAH STUDY
Source: Besht, Zava'at ha-Rivash, nos. 29–30, pp. 4b–5a[94]

When one studies, he should rest a bit every now and then, in order to attach himself to Him. Even though it is impossible to attach oneself to God during the time of study, nevertheless study one must, for the Torah "polishes" one's soul, and *it is a tree of life to them that lay hold of it* (Prov. 3:18). And if one did not study, he would be distracted from his *devekut*.[95] One should, however, recognize that just as one cannot maintain a state of *devekut* when he is asleep or when he senses a drop in his spiritual alertness, so too he may feel an even more severe interruption during his Torah studies. Nevertheless, one ought to reflect every so often on the state of his *devekut* to the blessed Creator.

When one talks,[96] he should not have any other thoughts except his *devekut* to God. True, at the time of study one's mind ought to be occupied with thoughts of learning; by virtue of this activity he becomes properly attached to Godliness. Thus one must occupy himself with Torah at every opportunity, since, as said, it is *a tree of life*.

---

93. Ibid. What R. Zevi Hirsch seems to be driving at is that in the absence of a religious purpose for the study of Torah, the ego intrudes and becomes, as it were, a superfluous organ in the corpus of one's Torah study. This, in keeping with the halakhic metaphor, is equivalent to a major defect and one is *terefah* (non-kosher).
94. Kehot ed. The same passage (with negligible changes) also appears in *Darkei Yesharim* (or *Hanhagot Yesharot*) (Lemberg, 1800), a small booklet consisting mainly of quotations from R. Menahem Mendel of Premyshlyany, p. 2a. See Jacob Shochet's footnotes to the Kehot ed. of *Zava'at ha-Rivash*, ad loc. Later editions of *Darkei Yesharim* tend to attribute its content to the Besht and the Maggid.
95. See Additional Note *5.
96. Sec. 30 of the Kehot ed., which adds in parentheses: "during study," implying that the "talks" in this passage refers to words during Torah discussion, as opposed to the formal study of the Torah text, and that here one's mind should be on *devekut*.

However, when one merely talks words,[97] relying on the *devekut* he already achieved, he ought to take great care to avoid occasional falling away from the attained *devekut*.

17. FOR THE SAKE OF LETTERS
Source: R. Yaakov Yosef of Polennoye, Toledot Yaakov Yosef to Aharei, end

I heard from my teacher the Besht in the name of Ramban [Nahmanides], who reportedly said to his son that he would sense immediately that his study of Torah is for its own sake (*lishmah*), if he is overcome with fear and love [of God]; then he will know assuredly that his Torah ascends before God and is acceptable to Him.

I heard from my teacher a reason for the tannaitic statement that "whosoever is occupied with the study of Torah for its own sake merits many things."[98] What exactly is meant by studying "for its own sake"? He explained as follows:

Everything in nature (*ma'aseh bereshit*), whether small or large, was created through the letters of the "231 gates," as is well known from the *Book of Creation*.[99] Because of his sins, however, man deposes the sacred souls—which are the holy letters—from their vital source to the realm of the *kelipot*, Heaven forbid, either into the mineral or other non-human domains, and so on.

---

97. The Kehot ed. adds the word *betelim* ("idle talk") here, thus implying that during Torah study maintaining a proper level of *devekut* simultaneously with his cognitive activity is not much of a problem. This sentence, therefore, would refer to ordinary idle talk, cautioning that one cannot rely on a previous "high" of *devekut* to carry him through the more prosaic periods of one's day. Cf. this passage in a different, slightly modified version, cited by Shochet in his footnotes. See also his remarks and bibliographic references to Kabbalah and hasidic works pertaining to these passages on p. 41a. For an analysis of the various versions, based on an examination of the manuscript material, see Z. Gries, *Safrut ha-Hanhagot*.
98. Avot 6:1
99. Lurianic Kabbalah teaches that the worlds came about through the divine power latent in the letters of the Hebrew alphabet. Specifically, there took place a "combination of letters" of the Ten Utterances (Avot 5:1), i.e., the nine separate references to "and God said" in the Genesis account of creation, plus the initial "in the beginning God created." This calls for the arrangement of the twenty-two letters of the Hebrew alphabet in two-lettered permutations which yields a total of 462 permutations (22 x 21). Of these, half are the exact reverse of the other half, e.g., AB, BA; CD, DC, etc. Hence, there are 231 two-letter combinations in direct order and the same number in reverse order. Cf. R. Shneur Zalman's *Shaar ha-Yihud veha-Emunah*, chap. 2, where the Lurianic doctrine of letter mysticism is described briefly. The Hebrew names of all created things are the very "letters of speech" that create and sustain them. These derive,

When man corrects his deeds and studies the Torah for its own sake, i.e., for the sake of that certain letter that he has debased, he repairs the damage. By engaging in study with awe and love, meditating on the elevation of the letter, which is a soul, from the realm of the *kelipot*, he may bring about its reascension and reattachment to its source.

Now, from the place of the *kelipot* up to the supernal heavenly realm where the letters are rooted, there are myriads of levels. Thus, in the process of ascension generated by his study, all levels lying in between, whose source in existence is derived from that letter, are elevated as well unto their highest roots.[100]

Hence the tanna states very well: "Whosoever is occupied with the Torah for its own sake merits many things." For indeed, "many things" are done with this letter, and all of them are repaired and elevated each to its root described as "beloved, a lover of the All-Present, a lover of mankind."[101]

18. STUDY IN PREPARATION FOR AND ACHIEVEMENT OF DEVEKUT
Source: R. Yaakov Yosef of Polennoye, Toledot Yaakov Yosef to Shelah 4

The sacred Torah is called "halakhah," as our Sages said: "God has in His world only the four cubits of Halakhah."[102] Two explanations may be given as to why the Torah is called "halakhah." One, because the word implies movement (*halikhot*), as it is said: *His goings are as ever* (Hab. 3:6).[103] The other interpretation is its literal transformation into

---

level by level, from the Ten Utterances recorded in the Torah, by means of substitutions and transpositions of letters through the "231 gates," until they reach and become invested in that particular created thing to give it life. These permutations of the creative power of the original Ten Utterances are necessary because individual items of creation are not capable of receiving their life-force directly from the Ten Utterances; the creative vitality of the latter is far greater than the absorptive capacity of the former and will overwhelm them. They can receive this life-force only when it "descends" and is progressively diminished, degree by degree, by means of the substitutions and transpositions of the letters, so that it is appropriate for that specific object. It is understood that such items in the created world are not homogeneous.

100. *Sefer Yezirah* 2:4–5.
101. See Additional Note *6.
102. Berakhot 8a.
103. Megillah 28b.

the word *ha-kallah* ("the bride").[104] . . . Both of these interpretations are true.

As to the first interpretation: Even though our Sages permitted the study of Torah for ulterior motives—as they said, "A man should always engage in the study of Torah, even if not for its own sake"— one should not take this to mean that he may remain, Heaven forbid, on that level. It is meant only as a point of departure for further achievement: One ought to "go" (*h-l-k*), move upward continually from rung to rung, until he reaches the level of studying for its own sake. As indeed they said in the conclusion of the preceding statement: "for through learning for a selfish purpose he will arrive at the state of studying for its own sake (*lishmah*)."[105] Thus they explicitly stated that the main purpose of study is for its own sake.

The second interpretation is based on the identical letter composition of *halakhah* and *ha-kallah*.[106] It is said: *from my flesh I shall see God* (Job. 19:26).[107] The bride dresses in many kinds of ornaments in order to arouse the lust for sexual union, and at the moment of intercourse she removes all her adornments and garments, and then the man *cleaves to his wife, and they become one flesh* (Gen. 2:24), without any clothing. So, too, is it with the ornaments of the Torah, namely, mind-sharpening study (*pilpul*), or learning Torah for any ulterior reason— even if only for the purpose of gaining a share in the world-to-come. This is not the principal objective, for these are all mere ornaments of the heavenly bride Torah designed to arouse the holy supernal coupling. And then, as it were, He sheds His garments and "bone cleaves to bone."[108]

Similarly, when a man attaches himself to the form of the letters of the Torah, which is the bride, merging his total self with the inner essence of the Torah letters; this is the true spiritual coupling, that is, shedding the garments of selfish motivation, benefit, or reward, and

---

104. See above, selection 8, n. 45.

105. Pesahim 50b.

106. Both words consists of the same four letters, *h-l-k-h*, but in *ha-kalah* the *kaf* is dotted with *dagesh forte*, giving it the sound of *k* instead of *kh*. The word-play on *halakhah/ha-kallah* is taken from Zohar, *Tikkunim, Zohar Ḥadash* to Song of Songs, and *Shulḥan Arukh* of the Ari, Kavvanot Talmud Torah 2. See my *Torah Lishmah*, p. 55, n. 217 and above, selection 8.

107. This verse implies, for R. Yaakov Yosef, that a passionate, ecstatic religious yearning for God is not dissimilar in some ways from sexual arousal—the corporeal passion of "my flesh." The erotic simile is now further expounded.

108. A conflated paraphrase of Gen. 2:23 and Ezek. 37:7.

concentrating only *lishmah*—on the love of Torah and cleaving to her (*devekut*) for her own sake.[109] This is the root and purpose of everything. As it is written: *And unto Him you shall cleave* (Deut. 13:5); this is the root of all the 613 commandments. The commentator to the Code of Maimonides (at the beginning of chapter 2 of *Hilkhot Yesodei ha-Torah*) similarly observed that all 613 commandments were given only in order to enable us to achieve these levels of love of God and *devekut* to Him.

This is the meaning of "Do not read 'movements' (*halikhot*) but 'laws' (*halakhot*)," referring to the bride (*ha-kallah*).[110] That is, one must not leave the bride in her adornments, but should proceed from this level to the highest level, which is coupling without garments and ornaments, namely, *devekut* of his inner self with the inner essence of the Torah.[111]

19. ATTACHING ONESELF TO THE AUTHOR WHEN STUDYING
Source: R. Nahman of Bratslav, Likkutei Etzot, Talmud Torah, no. 13

One ought to know at the onset of his study that at the moment when he settles down into learning, the zaddik in the Garden of Eden in whose Torah dicta he is then engaged is attentive to his voice. He should therefore attach himself to the tanna or the zaddik who innovated or revealed this Torah material which he is now studying. This develops into a state defined as "kissing," which is an aspect of spiritual cleaving between the souls of the student and the author, which causes great delight to the tanna or the zaddik. Through this, one will also merit to do penance (*teshuvah*), i.e., to rejuvenate his days which had passed in silence.

This is true only if one studies Torah for its own sake (*lishmah*), that is, in order to fulfill the commandment of studying the Torah, which is equal in importance to all other commandments[112] and through which he may merit to fulfill the precepts of the Torah.

---

109. R. Yaakov Yosef here alludes to the Besht's definition of study for its own sake, which he cites numerous times in his books, namely: for the sake of the letters themselves. See the selection immediately preceding this one.
110. See above, n. 104
111. Torah study for its own sake (*lishmah*) is thus understood by our author as a means for the attainment of true cleaving (*devekut*) to God; for this, the achievement of *devekut*, is man's essential purpose. See Additional Note *7.
112. Mishnah Peah 1:1.

However, if one studies not for its own sake but for selfish reasons, such as to be called a scholar, then even a carcass is better than he.[113] With this kind of study one can surely not become attached to the spirit of the tanna. On the contrary, since one cannot perceive the truth through such learning he becomes a foe and a disputer of the true zaddikim.

This is the "exile of the Shekhinah," i.e., the Oral Law (*Torah she-be-al Peh*) is exiled into the mouth of the scholars (*lamdanim*).[114]

ADDITIONAL NOTES

*1   R. Elimelekh of Lizhensk raises a similar question (*Noam Elimelekh* to Va-Yeshev, beginning, 19a). He answers that a purely spiritual, contemplative worship would overwhelm and annihilate man.

*2   R. Elimelekh explains the talmudic teaching regarding the patriarch's observance of the Torah commandments by referring to the exceptional state of *devekut* they achieved, for every mitzvah has its root in the upper worlds. Thus Abraham, whose contemplative powers were constantly concentrated in the upper worlds, discovered all the mitzvot on his own, without benefit of revelation. See *Noam Elimelekh* to Yitro, s.v. *va-yedaber*. Cf. ibid. to Devarim, s.v. *o yomar eleh*, where R. Elimelekh adds on the same theme that "every mitzvah has a world of its own."

*3   Elsewhere in *Likkutei Amarim* (chap. 39) R. Shneur Zalman defines *lishmah* as study "inspired by fear and love" of God. "For just as a person does nothing for his companion in carrying out the latter's will, unless he loves him or fears him, so one cannot truly act for God just to carry out His will without recalling and arousing any love or fear of Him in his mind and thought." As to *shelo lishmah* he writes: "When a person is engaged [in Torah] not indeed for its own sake but for some personal motive, with a view to his own glorification, as, for example, in order to become a scholar, and so forth, then that motive, which originates in the *kelipat nogah*, clothes itself in his Torah, and the Torah is temporarily in a state of exile in the *kelipah* until he repents. . . . On the other hand, if a person acts without any particular motivation, neither for its own sake nor for selfish reasons, then it is not contingent upon repentance; rather, as soon as he learns again the same subject for its own sake, then even that which he had learned without any particular intent conjoins itself with this study and ascends on high."

---

113. According to Leviticus Rabbah 1:15, where this is said of a scholar who has no wisdom (*da'at*). Thus, in the author's view Torah *lishmah* is synonymous with true Torah wisdom (or knowledge).

114. See the immediately preceeding selection, no. 18 and Additional Note 7, where the titles *lamdan* and *hakham* are distinguished. (Even more acerbically, those who study Torah in order to be honored are called "Jewish devils" by R. Yaakov Yosef and others (*shedim yehuda'in*). See G. Scholem, *Von der Mistischen Gestalt der Gottheit*, Zurich, 1962, p. 117, 287 n. 61. See G. Nigal in the introduction to his edition of *Noam Elimelekh*, Jerusalem, 1978, pp. 101-102, n. 697.) The reference in this passage to Torah being "in exile in the mouth of the *lamdan*" may refer to this pejorative evaluation.

*4   R. Elimelekh's view that study *shelo lishmah* serves a good purpose is shared by R. Yitzhak Isaac of Komarno. In his commentary on Avot 1:13 he remarks on Hillel's statement, "And he who does not study deserves to die; and he who makes a worldly use of the crown of Torah shall waste away (halaf)": "Some foolish hasidim refuse to study the Torah because of their fear that the study will be *shelo lishmah*. They fail to appreciate that it is impossible to begin with devekut; a degree of *shelo lishmah* is essential at first. Later, when one eventually attains to the state of *lishmah*, his previous Torah is transformed and elevated. Hence, "he who does not study," even *shelo lishmah*, "deserves to die." He thus interprets the last part of Hillel's saying in a novel way. *Halaf* does not mean to "waste away" or to be "extirpated," as interpreted by all commentators. Rather it means "transformed" (as in *hiluf* of money = exchange). That is, one who makes worldly use of Torah will eventually be transformed, as the Talmud teaches (Pesahim 50b): from *shelo lishmah* he will come to *lishmah*.

*5   Joseph G. Weiss, "Talmud Torah be-Reshit ha-Hasidut," Hadoar 45, no. 3 (August 6, 1975): 615—617, points to this quotation as evidence that the study of Torah was here to be preparatory to the attainment of *devekut*. Thus, study is not a value in itself, but polishes or prepares the soul for the higher function, that of *devekut*. However, this is not necessarily so. While Weiss may be correct regarding the thinking of R. Menahem Mendel, a contemporary of the Besht who belonged to his own circle of pneumatics which held the extreme view that *devekut* took preference over the study of Torah, this may not reflect the opinion of the Besht. The latter held the theory of (to use R. J. Werblowsky's felicitous locution) "double-consciousness"— that *devekut* could be experienced even during the time of study; he apparently applied to intellectual experience what he had learned from R. Nahman of Kosov about *devekut* being practiced even during one's social experience. The remainder of our passage confirms this as the Besht's view. R. Menahem Mendel kept up the classical distinction between Torah and *devekut*. In this he followed the kabbalists, except that he gave much greater emphasis and attention and time to *devekut* over Torah study. R. Menahem Mendel indeed requires a decreasing of the time devoted to the study of Torah, as seen from the following passage in *Darkei Yesharim* (loc. cit.): "Another important principle is not to study too much. In earlier generations, their intellect was strong, and so they studied with great supernal sanctity; they did not have to bother themselves with [a conscious appearance of] fear [*yir'ah*, piety]. Their fear was always present, and therefore they could study much. But we, whose intellects are weak, if we removes our thoughts from *devekut* in the Lord and study much, the fear of the Lord will, heaven forbid, be forgotten by us. . . . Therefore one must study less and [instead] meditate always on the greatness of the blessed Creator."

*6   In his preface to *Toledot Yaakov Yosef*, R. Yaakov Yosef mentions this definition of *lishmah* in the name of the Besht, without citing its original source. He writes: "I heard in the name of my teacher that *lishmah* means for the sake of the word or the letter itself; i.e., to attach it to its root" (preface, sec. 3). This theory is closely related to the Lurianic idea of elevating the sparks. There is, however, a clear distinction between the two. The Besht does not emphasize, as Luria does, the elaborate theosophic mechanisms guided by the intermediacy of study conducted with the proper contemplative concentration of the student, but rather on a general attachment to the Torah and its letters. To the Besht it is a means to the attainment of *devekut*. By striving to bring about the reattachment of the letters to their supernal source, one achieves his own high level of *devekut*. Cf. my *Torah Lishmah*, p. 215. See also J. G.

Weiss, "Talmud Torah le-Shitat R. Yisrael Besht," in *Tiferet Yisrael* (the Brodie Festschrift), pp. 154—156.

*7   Elsewhere R. Yaakov Yosef cites the Besht as saying that the basic goal of Torah study is to attach oneself to the inner spirituality of the light of the Ein-Sof immanent in the letters of the Torah (*Toledot Yaakov Yosef* to Vayetzei 10). The identi-fication of *halakhah* and *ha-kallah* underscores the same idea, namely, the paramount importance of *devekut*. The knowledge of Halakhah is secondary in rank to *devekut*, which is the ultimate purpose of Torah. Elsewhere our author makes a distinction between *hakham* and *lamdan*. "A *hakham* is one who studies for the sake of his Maker . . ." One who does not study this way, even if he is learned in the whole Talmud and its related literature, may be called a *lamdan* ("learner") but not a *hakham* ("wise man"). *Toledot Yaakov Yosef* to Shofetim 9, citing *Sefer ha-Kaneh*. Cf. *Torah Lishmah*, pp. 216—218 and notes ad loc.

8

The Zaddik

INTRODUCTION

General Observations

In Hasidism, community is exceedingly important. Hasidic values and hasidic life are lived in the context of other devout Jews who share the same aspirations and hold to the same principles. It is, by any definition, a religious community. The structure of the community is built around the relationship of the members to each other and the members to their leader. The ordinary member is called a *ḥasid* (plural: *ḥasidim*), meaning, generally, "pious one," but in Hasidism specifically one of the members of the devout community committed to the ways of Hasidism. And the role of the leader is of the utmost theoretical and practical significance in Hasidism.

In the early history of the movement, the leader was called a *zaddik* ("righteous one"), a term reserved for the charismatic leader of the hasidic community, with each different hasidic community—and there were hundreds—having its own zaddik. Nowadays, and probably for over a century, the term of choice for the hasidic leader is *rebbe*, the Yiddish for "rabbi." But the change in terminology does not seem to possess any conceptual significance. The literature of the movement used the appellation zaddik exclusively, and that is the term we shall employ here.

Traditionally, the term *hasid* denotes a man of higher spirituality and devotion than does the term *zaddik*. In talmudic and rabbinic literature, *zaddik* refers to the good, God-fearing person dedicated to the study of Torah, prayer, the performance of mitzvot, and the doing of good deeds. The term *hasid* was considered superior to *zaddik* and denoted a man of exceptional piety and saintliness. Hasidism reversed these definitions. Hence, the term zaddik was applied to the exceptional, saintly man who was held to possess charismatic gifts, whereas ordinary members of the movement were called hasidim. As a consequence, many talmudic and midrashic statements in praise of the zaddik were applied as well to the hasidic zaddik, further enhancing his leadership role of the devout community.[1]

Similarly, many of the laudatory descriptions glorifying the *talmid hakham*—the term for the scholar of Torah—and the privileges granted to him in Jewish life and under Jewish law were applied to the hasidic zaddik as well. For the zaddik, averred R. Nahman of Bratslav, must be both a scholar of Jewish law and a pious man of good deeds;[2] therefore, *talmid hakham* and *zaddik* are used interchangeably by R. Nahman as well as by others in much of the hasidic world.[3]

There is, however, a basic difference between the typical biographies of each of these.[4] Thus, the usual biography of the rabbinic scholar of recent centuries, unlike some of the talmudic sages, such as R. Akiva, of whom it is told that he was an ignoramus until the age of forty, speaks of a straight and unimpeded intellectual growth. He usually begins as a child prodigy, whose greatness becomes apparent at an early age and who astounds his teachers. He then outgrows his school and goes from yeshiva to yeshiva, while his career as a genius is obvious to everyone.

To the contrary, the hagiography of many great zaddikim contains the motif of surprise. There is always a turning point that is astounding. First we find a period of concealment, a "double life," so to speak,

---

1. See A. Wertheim, *Halakhot ve-Halikhot be-Hasidut* (Jerusalem, 1960), appendix 1, pp. 232–233 [English ed., *Law and Custom in Hasidism*, Hoboken, NJ: Ktav, 1992, pp. 353-355]; L. Jacobs, *Hasidic Prayer*, chap. 11, pp. 126 ff.

2. See below, selection 3.

3. E.g., see the fragment from *Toledot Yaakov Yosef*, below, selections 27 and 192; see also selection 35, n. 225.

4. J. G. Weiss, *Mehkarim be-Hasidut Bratslav*, Jerusalem: Mosad Bialik, 1974, pp. 5-6.

as in the legendary biographies of the Besht and other zaddikim. Then comes their "revelation," which is not seen as a revolutionary, stormy crisis, but rather as a short, condensed process.

The period of concealment is not primarily a matter of religious humility, but is rather a "cover" for mystical preparation before stepping out into public life. We find here a dialectic of spiritual self-confidence and humility. Note the life of the Besht: the first thirty-six years are a period of *hester* ("concealment"); after his revelation at this age his life changes from one extreme to another: he exchanges his loneliness and anonymity for charismatic leadership.

As said, this dramatic point does not usually occur in a single revelatory act, but rather in a short slice of life which proves fateful. Thus, the "conversion" of R. Yaakov Yosef of Polonnoye is rather typical. At the outset, he is a *talmid ḥakham*, of the usual cast, and also an opponent of Hasidism, who for one reason or another comes to the zaddik and is "turned on," leaving as a hasid who accepts the spiritual hegemony of the zaddik.

Hasidic zaddikism begins with the initiator of the movement, or even earlier. J. G. Weiss presents some proof that the Besht was not the first to function as a zaddik. The role and doctrine of the zaddik preceded the Besht, in the group which Weiss calls the "pre-hasidic circle of pneumatics," consisting to a large extent of preachers (*mokhiḥim* and *maggidim*), and some *ba'alei shem*, who developed a "zaddikology" of their own.[5] According to this early zaddikology, the charismatic activity of the zaddik took place only in the realm of the spirit, and even then it had one spiritual object, and that was the rectification of sin (a reflection of their own professional role as preachers). This is quite remote from the classical type of zaddik as developed later in Hasidism, who is concerned with changing Justice (Din) to Mercy (Raḥamim), with "Sweetening of Judgment" (*hamtakat ha-dinim*), with the flow of divine grace (*shefa*), and so forth.[6]

---

5. J. G. Weiss, "Reshit Tzemiḥatah shel ha-Derekh ha-Ḥasidit," *Zion* 17 (1951): 48-50. Some members of the circle were R. Yehudah Leib, the *mokhiaḥ* of Polonnoye, R. Menaḥem Mendel of Bar, R. Naḥman of Horodenko, R. Naḥman of Kosov, and the Besht. Cf. Weiss, "A Circle of Pneumatics in pre-Hasidism," *Journal of Jewish Studies* 8 (1956): 199-213, and now Abraham J. Heschel, *The Circle of the Baal Shem Tov: Studies in Hasidism*, Chicago: University of Chicago, 1985.
6. See below.

For the earlier group, the zaddik was charged with working for all of Israel; the differentiation, whereby he is concerned mainly with his own community of Hasidim, is a later development.[7]

The leadership role of the zaddik is critical to the vitality and success of the hasidic community. Hasidic theory purports to base its conception of the zaddik on the talmudic precept of *emunat hakhamim*, faith or belief in the sage. While this may indeed be the respectable origin of zaddikism, this later development went far beyond its ideational progenitor. Many theoreticians of hasidism (such as R. Nahman of Bratslav) elevated the zaddik to levels far beyond that of the classical *talmid hakham*, and hasidim began to take the zaddik's word as law even in mundane matters, to attribute to him infallibility, and to consider him the prime candidate as a potential Messiah.

Defining the Zaddik

The Besht defines the zaddik as one who conducts himself in a supernatural manner.[8] He reportedly stated that just as we find two people where one becomes the "garment" or "chair" for the other, so too one who conducts himself in a supernatural way has his needs performed for him by people who conduct themselves in a natural way.[9] The latter therefore become the "chair" for the former,[10] and when combined with each other they become one organism.

To the Besht's disciple, R. Yaakov Yosef, the zaddik is the soul of the Jewish nation while the rest of the people are its body. And just as an individual Israelite consists of matter (*homer*) and form (*tzurah*)—

---

7. Cf. Weiss, "Reshit Tzemihatah," pp. 70, 73. See below that some early masters of the Hasidic movement perceived the zaddik's concern as the "totality of Israel." This becomes clear from many passages of R. Yaakov Yosef, R. Elimelekh of Lizhensk, and R. Nahman of Bratslav below in this chapter.

8. Possibly referring to the charismatic leader. Thus is he quoted by his disciple in *Toledot Yaakov Yosef* to Mishpatim 2, s.v. *uva-zeh yuvan*.

9. These terms in Hasidic literature denote instruments; the one serves the purpose for another, presumably superior, to sit, and the garment is secondary to the body.

10. G. Scholem, in "Demuto ha-Historit shel R. Yisrael Baal Shem Tov," *Devarim Be-go*, Tel Aviv, 1976, p. 312, sees this as the source of later misuse and criticism of the doctrine of zaddikism. However, the Besht never made practical use of this theoretical dispensation to accept gifts from others, as did later zaddikim. The Besht left the world as poor as he entered it. He never exploited and abused his own charisma. As to the legal, mystical, and ethical reasons for such practices by the later masters, see below, selection 13.

his limbs and veins, flesh and blood comprising his material being and the soul in all its layers (*nefesh, ruaḥ,* and *neshamah*) providing the form—so too is it with the totality of Israel. Likewise, as it was the objective of the creation of individual man that he should transform his "matter" into "form" and solidify both into one unity, so too is it the purpose of the zaddik, whom R. Yaakov Yosef calls the "Man of Form" (*ish ha-tzurah*) to transform, on a national scale, the *ḥomer* into *tzurah*. The zaddik, however, is for him not a man of supernatural gifts, but one who is dedicated to the Torah and the serving of God in an exceptional way (see selection 8).

The other great disciple of the Besht, R. Dov Ber, the "Great" Maggid of Mezeritch, who functioned as a full-fledged zaddik with thousands of hasidim, gave the zaddik a thoroughly mystical conception. Weiss maintains that the Maggid attributed to the zaddik a "magical" function: change (*hishtanut*), for the Maggid, is brought about by the soul's near annihilation as it retreats to the sphere of Ayin ("Nothingness"), identified as Hokhmah ("Wisdom"), in which all contradictions vanish.[11] This is brought about by means of pure contemplation and is thus a "magical" feat: a *reductio ad infinitum* to the ontological phase of Hokhmah from which it reemerges in a new form. The Maggid assigns this contemplative feat to the zaddik.[12] (This definition of the zaddik and his function is in sharp contrast to those of R. Elimelekh of Lizhensk[13] and R. Nahman of Bratslav, as will be seen later.)

Although, as stated earlier, zaddikism is as old as the movement, it is generally agreed that it was R. Elimelekh, disciple of the Maggid,

---

11. J.G. Weiss, "The Great Maggid's Theory of Contemplative Magic," *Hebrew Union College Annual* 31 (1960): 137–147, now "Petitionary Prayer in Early Hasidism" in J. Weiss, *Studies in Eastern European Jewish Mysticism,* pp. 126–130.
12. Weiss calls this magic because, unlike prayer, results are guaranteed if the rules of mental concentration are followed. This is also the basis of *hamtakat ha-dinin* ("sweetening the judgment"), a crucial function of the zaddik in Hasidism, as it was already for the Besht (see below).
13. This is pointed out by Weiss in "The Great Maggid's Theory of Contemplative Magic." For a detailed analysis of the Maggid and R. Elimelekh, as well as of Weiss's thesis, see below selections 14 and 15 and notes thereto. Briefly stated, R. Elimelekh holds that the zaddik and the magician are two contradictory types, notwithstanding their superficial similarities. The difference is that the magician conceives his operations as working within strict causality founded on physical necessity, while the zaddik realizes the uncoercive character of his activities. Thus, the zaddik would marvel at the success of his efforts which are not critically dependent upon the proper carrying out of a technical procedure. The zaddik is essentially a man of prayer.

who gave the doctrine of the zaddik its fullest treatment in his *Noam Elimelekh*, published posthumously in 1788 by his son Eliezer, which is largely dedicated to the development and elucidation of hasidic zaddikology. The chapter that follows this introduction contains a variety of excerpts demonstrating the different aspects of zaddikism. A brief review of R. Elimelekh's basic points will now be attempted in order to get an overall insight into his definition of the zaddik and his contribution to the doctrine.

To begin with, the zaddik whom R. Elimelekh placed at the center of his universe and hasidic theory is not an egocentric personality; rather, his entire concern is to serve his flock. Neither is he completely a spiritual person. R. Elimelekh sought and achieved the synthesis between the leader of a real, living community and the solitary mystic. The zaddik in his doctrine realizes in his life both the *devekut* ideal of the mystic and the concern for his congregation.[14]

The zaddik is one who works within society. R. Elimelekh vigorously opposed seclusion for the purpose of mystic intensification. The zaddik, even while relating to people, does not experience any confusion of his higher thoughts, because he is bound in constant *devekut* with his Creator. It is characteristic of the teachings of R. Elimelekh that he considers both *devekut* and social action as vital. He defines the institutional zaddik: "This shall be the sign: if people follow him, then he is a zaddik." But how does the ordinary man know whom to choose as his zaddik? He must observe the zaddik's conduct and assure himself that the zaddik acts according to the Torah, that he not deviate in any way from the law, and that his heart is aflame with *yiḥudim* (mystical unification).[15]

In R. Elimelekh's typology of the zaddik, the tension between the two types—the zaddik who is segregated and the one who is socially involved—is resolved in favor of the latter; the social element eventually overpowers the mystical one.[16] R. Elimelekh holds that the world

---

14. See Gedalia Nigal, *Mishnat ha-Ḥasidut be-Kitvei R. Elimelekh mi-Lizensk u-Vet-Midrasho* (dissertation, Hebrew University, 1972), pp. 19–20. Cf. notes to the appropriate passages of *Noam Elimelekh* in Nigal's critical edition of the book, published by Mosad ha-Rav Kook (Jerusalem, 1978). See Additional Note *1.

15. See *Noam Elimelekh* to Bo, p. 37c, s.v. *o yomar* and Nigal, op. cit. pp. 65–66. Cf. Nigal's review of the *Maor va-Shemesh* by R. Elimelekh's disciple R. Kalonymos Kalman Epstein, "Mishnat ha-Ḥasidut be-*Sefer Maor ve-Shemesh*," in *Sinai* 75 (1974): 147, where identical views are expressed by the disciple in the name of his teacher.

16. See Rivkah Shatz, "Le-Mahuto shel ha-Zaddik be-Ḥasidut," *Molad* 18 (1960): 370.

needs both types. He greatly admires the mystical, spiritual zaddik, but his whole doctrine of relationships between zaddik and community refers only to the second, or social, kind. The two realms, the mystical-spiritual and the social, are in inverse relationship; one must be achieved at the expense of the other.[17]

One of R. Elimelekh's euphemisms for the zaddik is *kelalut yisrael,* "the totality of Israel." This is appropriate because, as the most important spiritual personality among his people, all the souls of the people are, as it were, concentrated in him, and also because the ambitions of a zaddik are all dedicated to satisfying the needs, spiritual or physical, of the totality of Israel. His disciple, R. Kalonymos Kalman Epstein, points out that the term *kol* is applied to the zaddik because, in Kabbalah, Yesod is called *kol,* and this is the sefirah of the zaddik (*zaddik Yesod Olam*).[18]

In every generation God chooses one Jew to be the head of the generation—the *zaddik ha-dor.* Although it is possible for one to become a zaddik through his own efforts in subduing his evil inclination and serving God with *devekut,* it is both extremely difficult and very rare.[19] Normally there are three ways in which a man can become a zaddik: his ancestors may have been zaddikim and he inherits his charismatic gifts from them; he may have been named after a zaddik; or he may have been a zaddik in a previous existence.[20] The semimagical aid of either parental endowment or the force of the special name or the metempsychosis is generally necessary.[21] Furthermore, the ability of the zaddik to give adequate spiritual advice to his followers depends on his knowledge of their previous existence. He alone knows for which purposes they have been sent down again into this world, and which matters they have to put aright because of their failures in their

---

17. Ibid., p. 371.

18. Nigal, op. cit., p. 77. Also in the introduction to his edition of *Noam Elimelekh* (Jerusalem, 1978), p. 50.

19. *Noam Elimelekh,* 69a, end. Cf. Nigal, introduction to his edition of *Noam Elimelekh,* p. 19-20. And see *Noam Elimelekh* to Emor, beginning.

20. *Noam Elimelekh* to Mishpatim, 44a, s.v. *ki tikneh,* and to Naso, beginning. The transmigration of the soul comes to correct another zaddik's deficiency during his lifetime (or his own shortcomings in a previous life),

21. See *Noam Elimelekh* to Ki Tissa, s.v. *zeh yitnu,* to Emor, beginning, and to Be-Midbar, s.v. *se'u et rosh.* Cf. L. Jacobs, "The Doctrine of the Zaddik in the Thought of Elimelekh of Lizensk," in *The Rabbi Louis Feinberg Memorial Lecture in Judaic Studies* (University of Cincinnati, February 1978).

earlier lives, so that he alone can guide them through their stormy path in this existence.[22]

R. Nahman of Bratslav took a diametrically opposite view as to the predetermination of the zaddik. While he places the zaddik high above the perceptional capabilities of the people who have not attained closeness to him (see selection 4), he was strongly opposed to the belief that the zaddik reaches his high state by virtue of having been endowed with a very lofty soul. The zaddik, he holds, became who he is mainly through his struggles with his Evil Urge, and thus any person can reach the highest levels. Furthermore, the zaddik has no monopoly in influencing man's heart to true faith in God and the fear of heaven, man's paramount achievements. One may receive such an awakening from any Jew to whom he turns for help in these matters. There is something of a zaddik in everyone (selection 6).[23]

In Habad, as defined by R. Shneur Zalman of Liady, the zaddik is one who has successfully eliminated all obstacles on the path of man which prevent him from reaching the higher sphere of spirituality and holiness. Thus, the zaddik is one who has already earned the title "Servant of God" (*eved Hashem*), in contrast to the one who is still effectively engaged in the struggle against the wicked side of his nature and is called *oved Elohim*, one who is in the process of serving God (see selection 2).

Zaddikim are not all on the same spiritual level. First there is the classical talmudic distinction between the complete zaddik (*zaddik gamur*) and the incomplete zaddik (*zaddik she-eino gamur*). Habad, however, defines these two kinds of zaddikim in a characteristic and novel way. The complete zaddik is synonymous with the zaddik who prospers (*zaddik ve-tov lo*), where prosperity does not allude to the material or social realm, but is taken in an ethical-psychological sense: a man in whom the evil has not been merely obliterated and abandoned, but transmuted into goodness. Hence he utterly despises all

---

22. *Noam Elimelekh* to Naso, beginning. Cf. Jacob, "Doctrine of the Zaddik." This does not necessarily burden R. Elimelekh with the Maggid's "magical" conception of the zaddik. The former's mystical aids may be the prerequisites to becoming a zaddik, but R. Elimelekh clearly is at variance with the Maggid as to the source of the zaddik's accomplishment and basic function (see above, n. 13).

23. R. Nahman also seems to be in complete disagreement with the Habad doctrine on this point. R. Shneur Zalman stresses the innate prenatal stratification of human beings. The complete zaddik (*zaddik gamur*) seems to be born to total triumph over evil, whereas the overwhelming majority of people are considered mediocre (*benonim*) or less (see selection 1). See Additional Note *2.

physical desires and natural appetites, and seeks gratification only in the service of God. The incomplete zaddik is synonymous with the zaddik who suffers (*zaddik ve-ra lo*), i.e., one in whom a fragment of evil still lingers on, thus preventing him from completely effacing it; hence his hatred for the Other Side (*sitra aḥara*) is not absolute (selection 1).

The categorization of zaddikim is also found frequently in R. Elimelekh, not as a hierarchy, as in the case of R. Shneur Zalman's conception, where one zaddik reaches a higher rung than the other, but rather as different kinds among peers. As R. Elimelekh explains, there are bound to be differences among the zaddikim, since the opportunities for serving God are as limitless as the Creator Himself. Even a zaddik who has reached the loftiest rungs on the ladder of saintliness can only see the "tops of the mountains."[24] Nevertheless, some zaddikim are more mature than others. Since humility is the hallmark of the true zaddik,[25] maturity may make a big difference. When the zaddik is still a novice in the path of holiness, his newly discovered delight in God's service and his heightened spiritual powers are so novel and deliciously exciting that he can easily fall into the trap of pride. Mature zaddikim, however, are never proud, knowing as they do from experience in self-mastery how remote they still are from their goal, and grieving as they do constantly over Israel's bitter fate.[26] In this respect, he points out a paradox: in the light of holiness, one who imagines that he is near to God is in reality remote from Him, while the true zaddik grieving over his remoteness from God, is very close to Him.[27] Thus the true zaddik always sees himself as far from achieving the status of a true zaddik.[28]

---

24. *Noam Elimelekh* to Noah, s.v. *veha-mayim*.
25. *Noam Elimelekh* to Noah, beginning, s.v. second *elleh*, and to Vayetze, beginning, s.v. *o yomar*.
26. *Noam Elimelekh* to Shemot, beginning. Cf. Jacobs, "Doctrine of the Zaddik."
27. *Noam Elimelekh* to Be-Ḥukkotai, 67a. For this reasons, remarks R. Elimelekh, all benedictions begin in the second person ("Blessed art Thou") but continue in the third person ("Who sanctified us with His commandments"). This thought is attributed to the Besht in *Toledot Yaakov Yosef*, p. 107b. Cf. Jacobs, "Doctrine of the Zaddik."
28. *Noam Elimelekh* to Noah, beginning, s.v. *elleh*. Elsewhere R. Elimelekh admits that some zaddikim are more advanced than others, depending on their endowments at birth. A zaddik who attains to saintliness through his own efforts is less advanced than one born in a state of sanctity (*Noam Elimelekh*, 44b, p. 234 of the Nigal ed., s.v. *im be-gappo*). See above, nn. 19–20. See Additional Note *3.

The world is always in need of the two types of zaddikim, according to R. Elimelekh. The contemplative type, who concentrates on the higher worlds and meditates on mystical unifications (*yihudim*), is the Menasheh type of zaddik. The other one, the Ephraim type, does not indulge overmuch in these exercises of spiritual ascent. Rather, his aim is to draw down the divine affluence (*shefa*) in order to satisfy the needs of the people of Israel for sustenance, blessing, and life.[29]

There are also differences among zaddikim in their way of worship. R. Elimelekh sees here three distinct types: (1) the zaddik around whom people gather in order to learn from his saintliness (Kehat type); (2) the zaddik who engages in mortification of the flesh (Merari type);[30] (3) the zaddik who is so humble that he sees himself as a stranger upon earth with no real title to existence (Gershom type). All these types must exist if the world is to be perfected.[31]

The true zaddik is like unto a seraph (fiery angel).[32] His burning enthusiasm for the divine is such that he would be in danger of expiring in his longing for God were it not that God saves him by cooling his ardor.[33] The zaddik nevertheless occasionally experiences times of spiritual dryness when he desperately needs the kind of recreation provided by good conversation. Yet the zaddik never detaches himself from God. Even his worldly talk is full of spiritual guidance and elevated counsel.[34]

Related to the above, the Besht reportedly held that the zaddik, in his zeal for the spiritual edification of his generation, uses idle talk as one of the means of influencing people. For there are some who cannot be elevated by his teaching and prayers, save by his casual conversation.[35]

The zaddik, in R. Elimelekh's scheme, must avoid at all costs exercising his sexual imagination. He should never gaze at women and, if his wife is beautiful, he should not be aware of it. When Adam "knew" his wife, Cain, the first murderer, was born (Gen. 4:1). R. Elimelekh interprets the word *yada* ("knew") literally. The true zaddik

---

29. *Noam Elimelekh* to Vayehi (below, selection 10). Cf. ibid. to Terumah, beginning.
30. On this type of ascetic zaddik, see Nigal, introduction to *Noam Elimelekh*.
31. *Noam Elimelekh* to Naso, beginning. Cf. Jacobs, "Doctrine of the Zaddik," pp. 70–72.
32. *Noam Elimelekh* to Beshallah, 39b-c s.v. *ve-atah*, in the name of the Maggid.
33. *Noam Elimelekh* to Vayishlah, 16c, s.v. *o yomar va-yehi*.
34. *Noam Elimelekh* to Tazria, 57b, (Nigal ed., p. 314), s.v. *o yomar*.
35. R. Moshe Hayyim Ephraim of Sudlikov, the Besht's grandson, in the name of his grandfather. See below, selection 12 and notes thereto.

does not *know* he is with his wife, because his mind is absorbed in meditation of the divine at the time of cohabitation.[36] Abraham first knew that his wife Sarah was beautiful when he came near to Egypt.[37] It was his proximity to the lewd Egyptians that brought him down from his state of complete attachment (*devekut*) to God.[38]

The Zaddik's Power and Its Source

The zaddik is granted extraordinary spiritual powers. The talmudic saying that God decrees and the zaddik nullifies the decree[39] came to mean, in hasidic thought, that the zaddik is endowed with supernatural powers. God grants him the power to bring down the flow of divine grace (*shefa*) from the highest sefirotic realms into this world, or to control its flow, by virtue of his prayers or, sometimes, even by merely exercising his will.[40]

The zaddik's greatest source of power is his prayer. Through his prayers, the sick are healed, the people of Israel are saved from persecution and oppression, they are able to earn their daily living, and they are blessed with worthy children. The zaddik's concern is for the physical and material as well as for the spiritual needs of his own community of Hasidism, and also of the totality of Israel. The means for providing all of this are his prayers.[41] In early Kabbalah, the talmudic

---

36. *Noam Elimelekh* to Bereshit, s.v. *veha-adam*. In a letter to R. Zekhariah Mandel, printed at the end of his book, he writes that the true zaddik would be incapable of having intimate relations with his wife were it not for the fact that God grants him special desire on Friday nights sufficient to enable him to perform the divine precept. Cf. Jacobs, "Doctrine of the Zaddik." See also Additional Note *13 below.

37. See Rashi on Gen. 12:11.

38. *Noam Elimelekh* to Lekh Lekha, 5d, s.v. *va-yehi ra'av*. Cf. ibid. to Vayishlah, s.v. *o yomar va-ye'avek*, that the act of coition can never be entirely pure and hence no benediction is recited over it, unlike the performance of other commandments or even eating, over which a benediction is recited. S. Dubnow, in his *Toledot ha-Hasidut*, pp. 470–471, writes that the mitnaggedim, in their writings, criticize the *Noam Elimelekh* for its alleged obsession with sex. Cf. Jacobs, "Doctrine of the Zaddik."

39. Mo'ed Katan 16b.

40. See below. As to the hasidic interpretation of the talmudic dictum, see, e.g., *Kedushat Levi* to Rosh ha-Shanah (Munkacz, 1939; reprint ed., New York, 1962), p. 94c, s.v. *bi-gemara*.

41. See L. Jacobs, *Hasidic Prayer*, chap. 11, pp. 127–130. Cf. Shatz, "Le-Mahuto shel ha-zaddik be-Hasidut," pp. 373–374. R. Yaakov Yosef, who sees the zaddik as the soul of his generation, maintains that the zaddik alone knows the "soul" of prayers (*Toledot Yaakov Yosef* to Yitro 6, p. 190b). Similarly, R. Nahman of Bratslav holds that the zaddik alone perceives the essence of prayer (see selection 19).

statement that children, life, and sustenance do not depend upon merit but upon *mazal* (lit. "the constellation[s]," and derivatively, "luck"),[42] was interpreted as coming from the word *nezilah*, i.e., in the "trickling down" of grace (*shefa*) from the higher worlds. And, Hasidism maintained, since this flow of divine grace is under the zaddik's control, or through his intermediacy,[43] it follows that the statement is a reference to the zaddik.[44]

The zaddik, according to the Maggid, is like the high priest on Yom Kippur, who could by his divine service cause the thread of crimson wool to turn white.[45] But whereas the high priest could bring about change (*hishtanut*) only on Yom Kippur, the zaddik can do so any time he wishes (see selection 14).[46]

Zaddikism makes no claims for prophecy or prophetic powers for the zaddik. In these generations, admittedly, there are neither prophets nor divine heavenly voices. Nevertheless, the zaddik is inspired by the Holy Spirit (*ruaḥ ha-kodesh*), which is for him a source of miraculous powers that enable him to perform supernatural acts in order to strengthen the faith of Jews.[47] This Holy Spirit is, according to R. Nahman of Bratslav, an aspect of prophecy. The true zaddik is one who has developed perfection in faith, which requires imaginative clarity; and what is prophecy if not a clearly developed sense of imagination (see selection 7; cf. selection 6)?[48]

How the zaddik possess such supernatural powers in our time of exile is explained by R. Elimelekh, who cites a parable of the Maggid. When the king is at home in his palace, he may leave it to stay for a while in a splendid mansion where full regal honors can be paid to him. But when the king is traveling he is prepared to enter the most humble dwelling in which hospitality is offered to him, provided it is

---

42. Mo'ed Katan 28a.
43. See below.
44. See Shatz, "Le-Mahuto shel ha-Zaddik be-Ḥasidut," loc. cit.; Jacobs, *Hasidic Prayer*, loc. cit.
45. Mishnah Yoma 6:8. White symbolizes the purification from sin and the changing of evil decrees.
46. Maggid, *Or ha-Emet*, 55c.
47. According to R. Elimelekh and his disciple, R. Kalonymos Kalman. See Jacobs, *Hasidic Prayer*, pp. 131-132, and "Doctrine of the Zaddik"; G. Nigal, "Mishnat ha-Ḥasidut be-*Sefer Maor va-Shemesh*," *Sinai* 75 (1974): 149.
48. See selection 7, and see selection 6, and n. 96 below, where R. Nahman advises the zaddik not to use his powers except to bring stray Jews back to their source.

clean. Thus, nowadays when the Shekhinah is in exile, God dwells in every pure soul free from sin.[49]

Another source of the zaddik's extraordinary spiritual strength is his great faith, which R. Nahman of Bratslav calls "the song of silence." The zaddik who has attained the "primal faith" transcends mere wisdom, identified as "speech." By means of this "silent song," of the zaddik, all the souls who fell into the heresy of the "empty space"—the primordial vacuum which resulted from God's self-constriction (tzimtzum) that enabled creation to take place—ascend and escape from it.

The zaddik is granted the power of "sweetening the judgment" (hamtakat ha-dinim), i.e., the complete sublimation of evil by turning Din (Judgment) into Hesed (Lovingkindness). This too is accomplished through prayer. The Besht was reportedly told by Ahijah ha-Shiloni (the biblical prophet whom the Besht considered his personal teacher and master) that the way to "sweeten the judgment in its source" is by prayer, meditating on the interaction of the appropriate sefirot. In Lurianic mysticism, the dinim are mentioned in the same breath with the kelipot; thus is it the "impure shells" (kelipot) that the zaddik must "sweeten," a conception continued by R. Elimelekh.[50]

The elevation of din to its source and its sweetening is considered a "change." This may be accomplished through a transmutation of the letters and words of Torah and prayer, i.e., the zaddik can, through his study of Torah, transform tzarah ("distress") to tzohar ("window," i.e., an opening for escape from tzarah).[51]

All of these powers of the zaddik to change heavenly decrees and sweeten judgments sharpen the problem raised by medieval Jewish

---

49. *Noah Elimelekh* to Vayeshev, 21a, (Nigal ed.), pp. 109–110. Cf. Nigal's introduction, p. 98. Citing the Maggid's parable, Nigal points out that whereas the Maggid seems to suggest that everyone may achieve *ruah ha-kodesh*, R. Elimelekh limits this to the zaddik.

50. For a review and analysis of the sources, see G. Nigal, "Mishnat ha-Hasidut be-Kitvei R. Elimelekh mi-Lizensk," pp. 103–104; see more in his introduction to his edition of *Noam Elimelekh*, pp. 40-56, pp. 40–42. R. Elimelekh claims biblical precedent for this mystical potency (Nigal, loc. cit.). The zaddik who did not nullify or sweeten the *dinim* has not fulfilled his mission, and must undergo a transmigration of his soul (*gilgul*) in order to complete it (Nigal, "Mishnat ha-Hasidut," p. 105). Cf. Nigal's introduction to *Noam Elimelekh*, pp. 42 ff.

51. *Toledot Yaakov Yosef* to Noah 3; *Noam Elimelekh* to Noah, s.v. first *be-inyan aher*. Cf. Nigal, introduction to *Noam Elimelekh*, p. 54, and his "Mishnat ha-Hasidut," p. 114, and his "Mishnat ha-Hasidut be-*Sefer Maor va-Shemesh*," p. 159.

philosophy: how can one bring about the change of God's will in the light of the teaching that God never changes? Hasidic teachers essayed a number of resolutions of this dilemma (see selection 18).[52]

The Social Function of the Zaddik

The zaddik is considered by the Maggid and R. Yaakov Yosef as the intermediary or the channel which transfers the divine grace (shefa) from the higher worlds to his contemporaries. For R. Yaakov Yosef, the shefa is a two-way process: the "men of form" (zaddikim) draw shefa to the "men of matter" (ordinary people), and the latter, in turn, supply the material needs of the former.[53]

For R. Elimelekh, the zaddik performs a double task; he brings men near to God, and he brings down the divine shefa from heaven to earth. Through his close attachment (devekut) to God, he can influence others to fear God. The zaddik's prayers for banei ("children"), hayyei ("life"), and mezonot ("sustenance")[54] help the congregation attain these blessings (see selection 28).[55] The drawing of shefa by the zaddik depends upon the restoration of harmony to the divine world. This requires an "initiative from below" in which the zaddik restores wholeness to the three "worlds" (sefirot) of Yir'ah (Fear), Ahavah (Love), and Tiferet (Beauty). The totality of spiritual and physical needs of the congregation supplied by the zaddik are drawn down to the congregation by virtue of the zaddik's divine service on the levels of love-fear-beauty.[56]

R. Elimelekh also designates the zaddik as the "channel" through which the shefa enters this world. The question as to why God needs an intermediary or channel was answered in two ways. One answer refers to certain difficulties connected with the flow of shefa. The sec-

---

52. See selection 18 and accompanying notes; Nigal, "Mishnat ha-Hasidut," pp. 112–114, and introduction to his edition of Noam Elimelekh, pp. 44–49. See too above, chapter 6, selections 9 and 10.

53. Toledot Yaakov Yosef to Ki Tissa 3 and elsewhere; see selections 24-27 and 36-37. The Maggid and R. Yaakov Yosef used the terms memutza (intermediary), tzinnor (channel), or merkavah (vehicle) to describe the zaddik's function of intermediacy in bringing down shefa. Cf. Nigal, introduction to Noam Elimelekh, pp. 24–27.

54. See Mo'ed Katan 28a.

55. See Noam Elimelekh to Toledot, s.v. va-yisa Yitzhak and compare to Vayeira, beginning, and to Bo.

56. Nigal, "Mishnat ha-Hasidut," pp. 88–89, based on various passages of Noam Elimelekh. Cf. Nigal's introduction, pp. 29–30.

ond is the social explanation of the zaddik's activity. The first goes back to the Maggid, who, discussing the "intermediary" aspect of the zaddik, speaks of the "power of the recipient." Ordinary man is not equipped to receive and absorb the fullness of the *shefa*, especially since it is essentially spiritual. It is the zaddik who must concentrate and focus it for the ordinary man. R. Elimelekh occasionally resorts to this answer. But he also offers a much different solution—not theosophical but practical. The zaddik must carry the *shefa* to man, spreading its beneficence far and wide. This is more hasidic and less purely "mystical."[57]

When *shefa* is not forthcoming, it is mostly the fault of the common man. It may be his sins or his lack of faith in the zaddik, which is tantamount to lack of trust in the Creator.[58] The arresting of *shefa* may also result from the inability or unwillingness of the zaddik to interrupt his higher *devekut*. (The two terms indeed seem contradictory: *devekut* usually implies a lonely and solitary life, socially detached, while *shefa* implies involvement with one's environment.) This possibility causes R. Levi Yitzhak of Berditchev to say that some zaddikim are so absorbed when they come before God in prayer or in *devekut*, that they forget all about worldly needs—including the need to bring down *shefa* for their people, a need which only the zaddik can accomplish adequately. Thus we have the paradox, R. Levi Yitzhak observes, that the lesser zaddik may be more instrumental and effective in providing *shefa* than a zaddik of a higher spiritual station. The former is still sufficiently remote from God to feel a need for worldly things and pray for them, while the latter is so close to God when he prays that he forgets all about his mission.[59]

As pointed out earlier, the relationship between the zaddik and his contemporaries is reciprocal. Weiss observed that in early Hasidism, common man prays for material blessing, and the man of the spirit benefits from this; just as the man of spirit prays for spiritual blessing

---

57. Nigal, "Mishnat ha-Hasidut," pp. 90–91; idem, introduction to *Noam Elimelekh*, pp. 30–32.
58. See the excerpt from R. Yitzhak Yehudah Yehiel of Komarno (selection 37) that *shefa* brought down by the zaddik for common men is preconditioned by their faith in and love of the zaddik. See also section 35, from *Toledot Yaakov Yosef*, that cleaving to the zaddik is like having *devekut* with God. Cf. Nigal, "Mishnat ha-Hasidut," pp. 92, 96–99; idem, introduction to his edition of *Noam Elimelekh*, pp. 37–38.
59. *Kedushat Levi* to Song of Songs, pp. 65b–c, s.v. *al tir'uni*.

and ordinary people benefit from that.[60] According to R. Elimelekh, the spiritual benefit of the people is indirect. The zaddik only inspires by his personal example, and the relationship between the zaddik and the one who seeks his help is such that the petitioner knows that the *shefa* comes from the Holy One; in fact, then, it is the individual man who presents his request directly to God and who receives the *shefa*. At the moment of encounter between the zaddik and the petitioner, all personal barriers fall and they are as one. The zaddik in his descent, and the common man in his ascent,[61] are unified. This is the true social mission of the zaddik.[62]

R. Kalonymos Kalman, R. Elimelekh's disciple, teaches that one who comes to the zaddik must be moved to complete repentance, to be inspired with love of Torah and prayer and faith. The zaddik too must derive benefit from those who come to him, for through them he is inspired to greater holiness from God, to new intellectual powers to create greater *ḥiddushim* (novellae) in Torah, and to new ideas and means of serving God in truth, each according to his own ability. Furthermore, it inspires the zaddik himself to *teshuvah* when he feels inadequate to the tasks thrust upon him, and considers himself a lesser person than imagined by his hasidim.[63]

What is it that draws certain hasidim specifically to one zaddik rather than another? This is explained by R. Elimelekh as well as by R. Kalonymos Kalman by the concept of propinquity of the "sparks" of the souls of the hasidim to the "root of the soul" of the zaddik. Those whose source is shared with or close to that of the zaddik find their way to him. This common spiritual source is a condition for the successful affiliation between the zaddik and his people. When he wishes to influence them, he must "bind their souls to his". This is more than a question of sympathetic identification but rather a mystical synthesis, one which merges, even if only for an instant, the leader and the follower into one personality. In this manner, the vital energies of *shefa* are transmitted from the zaddik to the one who cleaves to him. In the moment that the common man draws close to the zaddik, he himself becomes a zaddik. Hence, it is inadvisable for

---

60. J.G. Weiss, "Reshit Tzemiḥatah shel ha-Derekh ha-Ḥasidit," p. 78; now in A. Rubenstein, ed. *Perakim be-Torat ha-Ḥasidut*, pp. 122-181, 154. Cf. R. Shatz, "Le-Mahut shel ha-Zaddik be-Ḥasidut," pp. 373–374.

61. See below, "Descent of the Zaddik."

62. Shatz, "Le-Mahut shel ha-Zaddik," p. 375.

63. G. Nigal, "Mishnat ha-Ḥasidut be-*Sefer Maor va-Shemesh*," pp. 150–151.

the zaddik to develop any relationship with those coming from sparks and roots of a soul distant from himself.[64]

The condition of reciprocity between the zaddik and the common man makes it mandatory that they support him and satisfy his material needs.[65] As R. Elimelekh sees it, the zaddik's followers support him with their worldly goods in order that they become attached to him through his dependence on them.[66] R. Kalonymos Kalman explains the matter very simply: Thousands of hasidim come to the zaddik and cause him great expense. Therefore it is only fitting that they help cover the expense. When the zaddik reaches true heights and opens the flow of divine grace for all, the question is no longer relevant. His followers are returning to the zaddik what is actually his.[67]

The "Descent" of the Zaddik

R. Yaakov Yosef remarks that sometimes the common people will not obey the zaddik because of defects they discern in him. But little do they know that the zaddik's fault is for their benefit, since this creates a bond between them and the zaddik which helps him to elevate them (see selection 27).[68] R. Yaakov Yosef is hinting here at the hasidic doctrine of the zaddik's descent in order to enable the ascent of his followers (*yeridah le-tzorekh aliyah*), a doctrine elaborately elucidated by him elsewhere (see selection 40).

Weiss describes the evolutionary development of the doctrine. The pre-hasidic circle experienced a crisis in their profession and a feeling of failure, and therefore developed the new idea of the descent of the

---

64. Ibid., and Nigal, "Mishnat ha-Hasidut be-Kitvei R. Elimelekh," pp. 78—79. Cf. idem, introduction to *Noam Elimelekh*, pp. 21–24.

65. This constitutes one of the solutions to the problem which arose at the very beginning of Hasidism: Why cannot the zaddik, who releases *shefa* for others, take care of his own material needs? Why should he accept money and charity from those who come to him? See Nigal, "Mishnat ha-Hasidut be-Kitvei R. Elimelekh," p. 99, and introduction to *Noam Elimelekh*, pp. 38–39. This was a major cause of criticism of Hasidism; see Dubnov, *Toledot ha-Hasidut*, Tel Aviv: Devir, 1960, pp. 182–183.

66. *Noam Elimelekh* to Pekudei, beginning; to Korah, s.v. *va-yedabber* (Nigal ed., p. 422).

67. Nigal, "Mishnat ha-Hasidut be-*Sefer Maor va-Shemesh*," pp. 152–153, 158. Cf. his introduction to *Noam Elimelekh*, pp. 38–39, where he cites R. Elimelekh's division of zaddikim who take charity (*tzedakah*) from their followers into three categories. In his dissertation (see n. 15 above), Nigal cites another answer: that charity is given to the zaddik in order to serve as a key which unlocks the stream of *shefa*. See selection 13, where R. Zevi Elimelekh of Dinov treats this problem analytically and at some length.

68. *Toledot Yaakov Yosef* to Bo 11.

zaddik from his *devekut*.[69] In this circle, the major concern was the role of the religious leader in regard to sin. The moderates held that one must befriend the sinner. The radicals held that one must risk entering into the sinful situation itself. For both, this was a concept of "descent" in order to elevate the sinners.[70]

The nature of the descent is the limited lapse of consciousness in the course of *devekut* in which, willingly or not, the zaddik confronts an intruding sinful thought and thus identifies with all his people, reminding him that he too is part of the organism that includes the sinners, and he too is soiled by sin.[71]

There are two possible aspects to the descent. First, the zaddik may deliberately lower himself in order to rescue and elevate the sinner. Second, the causal situation is reversed: The transgressions of the sinners distract the zaddik from *devekut* via "strange thoughts" (*mahshavot zarot*), thus forcing his descent.[72]

The Besht held both ideas, i.e., that the fault which precipitates the descent can be both that of the zaddik and that of the people.[73] However, the problem of the descent of the zaddik was not the Besht's central concern. It is R. Yaakov Yosef who creatively developed the doctrine, using as his sources the ideas of the "pneumatic circle" which preceded the Besht instead of those of his teacher, the Besht.

The Maggid, however, has almost nothing to say on the descent of the zaddik. And yet his students, in developing their zaddikology, spoke a great deal about descent and developed it tremendously.[74] From one point of view, the descent is the result of a *natural failure of contemplation*—already noted by R. Menahem Mendel of Bar. Man's communion with God cannot continue uninterrupted, because of his physical and spiritual limitations. His soul, like the divine worlds, is in a constant dynamic tension of rise and fall, ebb and flow, for this is the nature of the world: reaching and not-reaching (*mati velo-mati*). Therefore, when the zaddik wishes to reach a higher level, he must

---

69. J. G. Weiss, "Reshit Tzemihatah shel ha-Derekh ha-Hasidit," 68, *Perakim*, p. 144.
70. Ibid., p. 69.
71. Ibid., p. 78.
72. Ibid., p. 82. In the first way, where the zaddik initiates the descent, it is also understood that this is the *cause* of the descent insofar as he causes people to fall deeper into sin as a result of his carelessness, allowing himself to be distracted from his *devekut*.
73. Ibid., p. 84.
74. Ibid., p. 88.

recede and rest and then advance to a yet higher level. This dynamism in man's soul enables him to stay alive, for the *full* implementation of the ideal *devekut* would mean the end of man's existence.[75]

The social aspect of this doctrine is developed, characteristically, by R. Elimelekh. The social mission of the zaddik requires his descent from his contemplation of divinity, which cuts him off from all mundane concerns. Only the cessation of his concentration, or at least its weakening, makes it possible for him to worry about his people and evoke the *shefa*. Furthermore, the descent is necessary also to allow the spiritual communion of the zaddik with his followers.[76] R. Elimelekh considers the social zaddik who descends for the sake of his people to be offering a personal sacrifice. He is maintaining the moral balance of the world, and it is for this purpose that he must mingle with the sinners.[77]

For R. Yaakov Yosef as well as for R. Elimelekh, the descent of the zaddik is an aspect of *averah li-shmah* (sin for a good purpose), of which the Talmud speaks;[78] it was considered crucial for the contact between the zaddik and the sinner. The hasidic thinkers rejected the extreme antinomian implications of this doctrine. Ordinarily they applied it to the situation where the zaddik is forced to concentrate on material matters instead of spiritual ones.[79] However, both R. Yaakov Yosef and R. Elimelekh allow for an occasional minor "equivalent" transgression by the zaddik, in order to form a binding connection with the sinner which will raise him from his fall. Thus, Moses became angry at those who were engaged in the war against the Midianites when he suspected them of pagan worship; anger is considered a sin equivalent to idol worship (see selection 40). Or, according to R. Elimelekh, if someone is a habitual liar, the zaddik resorts to an identical sin, e.g., denying that he is a zaddik (see selection 41).

---

75. See Rivkah Shatz, "Le-Mahuto shel ha-Zaddik be-Hasidut," *Molad* 18, p. 371-373; Nigal, "Mishnat ha-Hasidut be-Kitvei R. Elimelekh," p. 171, and introduction to *Noam Elimelekh*, pp. 95–97.

76. See *Noam Elimelekh* to Naso, 69a, s.v. *o yomar* (Nigal ed., pp. 375–378). Interestingly, the association of the ordinary people with the zaddik too is termed *devekut*. Cf. the passages of *Noam Elimelekh* translated in this chapter (selections 41, 42, and 43). See also Nigal, "Mishnat ha-Hasidut be-Kitvei R. Elimelekh," p. 94, and introduction to *Noam Elimelekh*, pp. 35–36.

77. See *Noam Elimelekh, loc. cit.* See Additional Note *4.

78. Nazir 23b, Horayot 10b.

79. See Nigal, "Mishnat ha-Hasidut be-Kitvei R. Elimelekh," p. 95.

In defining the descent of the zaddik as part of his social obligations, R. Elimelekh sees the closing of the circle. The sinner causes the zaddik to descend by bringing the latter to sinful thoughts or unintentional sinful acts. The descent of the zaddik redeems the sinner from his actual, intentional sin, but in the process a new sin is engendered—the very descent of the zaddik is considered sinful. The sin is atoned for by the sinner who does repentance. Hence it is not only the zaddik who provides *tikkun* ("repair") for the sinner, but the reverse as well: the sinner assists in the enhancement of holiness.[80]

Defining the Zaddik

1. THE COMPLETE ZADDIK AND THE INCOMPLETE ZADDIK
Source: R. Shneur Zalman of Liady, Tanya, Likkutei Amarim, chap. 10

When a man strengthens his divine soul and wages war against his animal soul[81] to the degree that he expels and eradicates its evil from the left ventricle[82] of the heart—as is written: *And thou shalt root out the evil from within you* (Deut. 21:21)—and yet the evil is not actually converted into goodness, such a man is called an "incomplete zaddik" or a "zaddik who suffers" (*zaddik ve-ra lo*).[83] That is to say, there still lingers in him a fragment of wickedness in that left ventricle except

---

80. See Shatz, "Le-Mahuto shel ha-Zaddik," p. 373.

81. In chap. 9 the author describes the "abodes" of both the divine and animal souls. Within every Jew the animal soul (*ha-nefesh ha-bahamit*) dwells in the left ventricle of the heart that is filled with blood. The divine soul (*ha-nefesh ha-elohit*) dwells in the brain and in the right ventricle of the heart "wherein there is no blood." The two souls "wage war against each other" over who shall control the body and all its limbs." The contemporary reader should not be put off by the outdated biology, but consider the ideas it represents.

82. In the earlier chapter he states that this abode of the animal soul is the source of "all lusts and arrogance and anger," and all evil.

83. R. Shneur Zalman's interpretation of *zaddik ve-tov lo* as a zaddik who has rid himself of evil and is therefore completely good (*tov lo*), and *zaddik ve-ra lo* as a zaddik who still possesses a measure of evil, enables him (in chap. 1) to harmonize this talmudic typology of two kinds of zaddikim with another one, namely the "complete zaddik" (*zaddik gamur*) and the "incomplete zaddik" (*zaddik she-eino gamur*). In the Talmud too these types are occasionally brought together, as, for example, in Berakhot 7a, but only as one being a reward for the other (e.g., *zaddik ve-tov lo* to reward *zaddik gamur*), while R. Shneur Zalman conceives each term as complementing the other to define the personality of the zaddik. (An interpretation similar to his may be implied in Kiddushin 40a).

that it is overwhelmed and nullified by the good because of the evil's minuteness. Hence, he imagines that he expelled it and it has completely disappeared. In truth, however, had all the evil departed entirely, it would have been converted into actual goodness.

The explanation of the matter is that a complete zaddik, in whom the evil has been converted to goodness, and who is therefore called a zaddik who prospers (*zaddik ve-tov lo*), has completely divested himself of the filthy garments of evil. This means, he utterly despises the pleasures of this world, finding no enjoyment in human pleasures of merely gratifying the physical appetites instead of seeking the service of God, inasmuch as these are derived from and originate in the *kelipah* ("impure shells") and *sitra ahara* ("other side").[84] For whatever is of the *sitra ahara* is hated by the perfectly righteous man with an absolute hatred by reason of his great love of God and His holiness, with profound affection and delight, as stated above.[85] For they are antithetical to each other, as it is written: *I hate them with utmost hatred; I count them mine enemies. Search me, O God, and know my heart* (Ps. 139:22–23). Hence, the degree of hatred toward the *sitra ahara* and the sense of the utter repulsiveness of evil is in accordance with one's love of God. For disgust is as much the opposite of real love as is hatred.

The incomplete zaddik is one who does not hate the *sitra ahara* with an absolute hatred; consequently he also does not absolutely abhor evil. And as long as the hatred and revulsion toward evil are not absolute, there must remain some vestige of love and delight in it, and the fouled garments have not been shed entirely and completely. Thus, the evil has not actually been converted into goodness, since it still has some hold in the soiled garments, except that it is nullified because of its minuteness and is therefore accounted for nothing. Hence, he is called a zaddik to whom evil remains subjugated and subservient.[86] Accordingly, his love of God is also not perfect, and thus he is called an incomplete zaddik.

2. THE ZADDIK AND THE OVED
Source: R. Shneur Zalman of Liady, Tanya, Likkutei Amarim, chap. 15

The difference between who *serves* God (*oved Elohim*) and one who is *righteous* (*zaddik*) is that *oved* is in the present tense, implying one who

---

84. These two expressions are kabbalistic terms for evil and the demonic.
85. In *Tanya*, chapter 9 (see n. 1).
86. *Zaddik ve-ra lo* is thus interpreted by the author as a zaddik of whom it can be said that the evil (*ra*) is subservient to him (*lo*).

is in the midst of serving God, namely, he is still effectively engaged in the struggle against his Evil Urge (*yetzer ha-ra*), seeking to overcome his wicked nature and to expel it from the "small city,"[87] that it should not invest itself in the organs of his body. Verily, it entails much effort and toil to wage constant war with it. This is the *benoni*–the "mediocre" servant of God.[88]

The zaddik, however, is designated "servant (*eved*) of God," which is a title already earned, just as the title "sage" (*ḥakham*) or "king" (*melekh*) is bestowed upon one who has already become a sage or a king. Thus, the zaddik is one who has already successfully accomplished the task of waging war against the evil within him, resulting in its total expulsion and disappearance. His heart has become void within him.[89]

3. THE ZADDIK AS SCHOLAR
Source: R. Nahman of Bratslav, Likkutei Moharan I, 31:9, p. 97b

The zaddik must be both a scholar in Torah and pious in good deeds. He must be a scholar because the rabbis said, "The ignoramus cannot be pious."[90] But to be a scholar alone certainly does not count for anything, because it is possible to be a scholar and completely wicked at the same time, as the Rabbis said: "If he uses the Torah the right way, it becomes a life-giving elixir for him, but if he does not use it the right way, it becomes a deadly poison for him."[91] Therefore, the zaddik must be both a scholar and a pious man.[92]

---

87. This refers to the verse "There was a little city with few men within it" (Eccles. 9:14—15), which according to the Talmud (Nedarim 32b) and many commentators is an allegory for the human body and its limbs. "And there came a great king against it and besieged it and built great bulwarks against it" (ibid.) refers to the *yetzer ha-ra*.
88. *Tanya*, chap. 1, defines the *benoni*, not as an individual of middling virtue, but as one who is perfect in his behavior, yet still suffering from inner conflict.
89. A paraphrase of Ps. 109:22, "And my heart is wounded (*ḥalal*) within me." In the Talmud, the verb *ḥalal* (which in Scripture is written with a *patah* under the first *lamed*) is read as a noun (with a *kamatz* under the *lamed*), which means a corpse or empty space. Thus David states that his Evil Urge (*yetzer ha-ra*) within him is dead, thus leaving an empty space in his heart (see Bava Batra 17a, Avodah Zarah 4b, end, and Rashi).
90. Avot 2:5. And, *a fortiori*, if one is not pious (*ḥasid*), he cannot be a righteous man (*zaddik*). There might well be a reference here to the institutionalized categories of hasid and zaddik.
91. Yoma 72b. The knowledge of Torah alone is no guarantee of righteous conduct. In the wrong hands, it can be destructive. Cf. Yevamot 109b, "One who says I have only Torah, he does not have even Torah."
92. R. Nahman's assertion that the zaddik must necessarily be a Torah scholar (*talmid*

Perceiving the Zaddik

4. THE RETINUE OF THE ZADDIK
Source: R. Nahman of Bratslav, Kitzur Likkutei Moharan I, 140

It is impossible to attain any conception of the zaddik himself, for he is completely beyond our intellectual grasp. However, it is possible to understand the exalted level of the zaddik through the people who are close to him,[93] and from whom the common people are not yet so distant.

5. THE MERIT OF THE ZADDIK
Source: R. Nahman of Bratslav, Likkutei Etzot, Zaddik, no. 85

The opposition which confronts the zaddikim really works to their advantage in that it acts to conceal them before they have matured sufficiently to be revealed to the world. The opponents of the zaddikim themselves would love to obliterate them entirely, God forbid. But God does not abandon them or deliver them into their hands.

R. Nahman was very upset with people who thought that the major merit of the zaddik and his perception was attained only because of the soul, i.e., because he has a very high soul. He said that that was not true, but rather it mostly depended upon the good deeds, the struggles, and the service of a person. He said explicitly that any person in the world can reach the highest levels if only he will direct himself thoroughly to what is truly the good way for him.[94]

ḥakham) justifies his hasidic predecessors' usage of this term *talmid ḥakham* as a synonym for a zaddik and their interpretation of talmudic and midrashic statements regarding Torah scholars as referring to the zaddikim (e.g., see R. Yaakov Yosef in selections 27 and 35).

93. The people close to the zaddik (*mekoravim*) and his disciples are called, in the parlance of the developer of the doctrine of zaddikism, R. Elimelekh of Lizhensk, a contemporary of the author, "small zaddikim" (*zaddikim ketanim*) or "beginner zaddikim (*zaddikim matḥilim*); see *Noam Elimelekh* to Shemot, beginning; to Shelah, 73d-74a, s.v. *o yomar va-yishlaḥ*. Cf. G. Nigal, introduction to his edition of *Noam Elimelekh* (Jerusalem, 1978), p. 21. This sheds light on R. Nahman's statement here.

94. R. Nahman here explicitly denies the popular hasidic notion that the zaddik is preordained because of naturally superior spiritual endowments. He affirms that moral effort, good conduct, toil, and spiritual struggle are the ingredients available to any human being who aspires to the level of the zaddik. In selection 6, R. Nahman goes a step further. Not only is the level of a zaddik *within the reach of everyone*, but

6. THE ZADDIK IN EVERYONE
Source: R. Nahman of Bratslav, Likkutei Etzot, Zaddik, sec. 42–43

The true zaddik is the focal point of all Jews. Therefore it is of prime importance to be connected to zaddikim and to speak with them regarding the fear of heaven, i.e., spiritual matters, and they will enlighten and arouse one's heart by virtue of the holiness concentrated in them.

One should, however, also speak also with his friends regarding the fear of heaven, in order to assimilate the good traits of these friends. For there is a positive aspect in every Jew, something valuable that only he and no one else possesses. This point of goodness in everyone is an aspect of the zaddik, enabling him to influence and illuminate the other's heart; and the other should receive willingly the inspiration coming from him. Hence, there is between them a relation of reciprocity, an aspect of "and they receive from one another."[95]

The general principle of the zaddik's authority is this: The zaddik has the power to act as he wills, as our Rabbis said: "Who rules over Me? The zaddik."[96] The zaddik, however, should use this ruling power vested in him for illuminating and arousing the hearts of Jews to the service of the blessed Name. Therefore, it is of fundamental importance that one should bind himself to true zaddikim and speak with them regarding matters of serving God. From them he may receive the strength, enlightenment, and inspiration to serve the blessed Name, so that he will return to God.

---

there is a bit of a zaddik in everyone. The accessibility of the status of zaddik is also implied in the homilies of R. Elimelekh, who in turn follows in the footsteps of his master, the Maggid. Both frequently speak of men generally while meaning the zaddik, implying that every man in Israel has the potential to become a zaddik. See Nigal's introduction to *Noam Elimelekh*, pp. 19–20.

95. Based on Isa. 6:3, "And one [of the Seraphim] called unto another and said: Holy, holy, holy is the Lord," which the Targum translates (and which is included in the daily morning liturgy) as "And they receive [sanction] the one from the other." Cf. selection 5 as to the power of an ordinary Jew according to R. Nahman's zaddikology. See also below, selection 31 and n. 203 thereto.

96. Shabbat 63a, Mo'ed Katan 16b. Cf. Zohar II, 15a; III, 15a. In all sources cited, the example given as to the zaddik's power is: "For I [God] decree, and he [the zaddik] nullifies that decree." R. Nahman here counsels the zaddik not to avail himself of these powers over the divine except to bring people closer to Him. For more on this subject see below, selections 14-24, esp. selection 20 as to R. Nahman's view on the zaddik's powers.

7. THE ZADDIK'S PROPHETIC VISION
Source: R. Nahman of Bratslav, Likkutei Etzot, Zaddik, no. 98

The genuine leader of every generation possesses a quality of prophet-ic spirit. Even now, after prophecy has ceased[97] and he cannot possibly have real prophetic vision, he is still necessarily the possessor of the holy spirit (*ruah ha-kodesh*), something of which the rest of the people are incapable. This holy spirit is an aspect of prophecy. The zaddik, the authentic leader, has a clearly developed faculty of imagination, from which is derived a perfected holy faith. For the roots of perfec-tion in faith are in accordance with the clarity of the imaginative fac-ulty.

8. THE "MAN OF FORM" AND HIS MISSION
Source: R. Yaakov Yosef of Polennoye, Toledot Yaakov Yosef, preface, sec. 4

Just as the stature (*komah*) of the individual man consists of 248 limbs and 365 sinews, which constitutes only the body of man but is not man himself—for it is the *nefesh* (lower soul), *ruah* (middle soul), and *neshamah* (upper soul) within him that are worthy of being called man—so too for the totality of the people of Israel as a nation. The Jewish nation too consists of a configuration (*komah*) embodying 248 limbs and 365 sinews, but it is the righteous (*zaddikim*) of a generation who provide the soul and the life-force for the totality of their gener-ation. The same is also true of the world in general. There are in it sev-enty nations, but it is Israel which is the soul and vitality of the entire world of nations....

For man was created of matter (*homer*) and form (*tzurah*), which are two opposites. The *homer* is inclined to follow obstinately the materi-al body, which are the *kelipot* impure (shells); the *tzurah*, however, desires and longs for things spiritual. The purpose of man's creation is for him to transform the matter into form and merge both into one unity; they should not remain separate entities.

And just as this is the purpose of individual man, so too it is with the totality of the Israelite nation. The common men of Israel are called *ammei ha-aretz* ("people of the land"), for their principal occupa-tion is with earthly matters. Therefore they represent the material

---

97. With the destruction of the Temple in Jerusalem. See Bava Batra 12a. Cf. Zohar II, 6b. See Additional Note *5.

part of the nation. Not so the zaddikim, who occupy themselves with Torah and the service of God; they are the form. And here too the main objective is to transform the *homer* into *tzurah*.[98]

9. TWO TYPES OF ZADDIKIM: THE ABRAHAM TYPE AND THE NOAH TYPE
Source: R. Levi Yitzhak of Berdichev, Kedushat Levi to Noah, s.v. ve-eleh tole-dot Noah

There are two types of zaddikim who serve the Creator. One zaddik serves the Creator with great enthusiasm, but he is concerned only with himself, making no effort to invite the wicked to serve the Creator with him. Another zaddik serves the Creator while encouraging others to join him. Our Father Abraham was the latter, for we know that he converted gentiles to Judaism.[99] It is further stated in the writing of R. Isaac Luria that it is precisely for the sin of not reproving the wicked of his day that Noah was punished. Noah's soul therefore transmigrated to Moses, who was charged with the task of correcting Noah's error, and he did so by constantly reproving the Children of Israel for their wrongdoings.[100]

Our rabbis referred to this differentiation between the two zad-dikim when they said, "One who is good to heaven, i.e., God, and good to mankind is the true zaddik."[101] He who worships God while simultaneously bringing the upright closer to God is referred to as a man who is good to heaven, because *he* worships the Creator, and as good to mankind because he also invites God's creatures to worship Him. But Noah was not this type of zaddik, because he did not call upon mankind to serve God with him, as we explained . . .

The reason that the Torah states, *Noah walked with God* (Gen. 6:9), is to emphasize that Noah "walked" *only* with God, but did not associate with other humans in an attempt to encourage them to worship the Creator. . . .

---

98. R. Yaakov Yosef frequently comes back to this theme of the zaddik as the "man of form," whose function it is to transform the material aspects of the totality of Israel. Cf. Gedalia Nigal, "Al Demut ha-Zaddik be-Hasidut," *Molad* 30, N.S. 7 (1975): 176–177, and introduction to *Noam Elimelekh*, pp. 25–27, 97.
99. Gen. 12:5, according to Genesis Rabbah 39:14; see too Sifrei Va'ethanan 32.
100. On the kabbalistic doctrine of metempsychosis, see Scholem, *Major Trends in Jewish Mysticism*, pp. 281–284.
101. A paraphrase of Kiddushin 40a.

The explanation of *but Noah found ḥen* (favor, charm, beauty) *in the eyes of the Lord* (Gen. 6:8) is as follows. The Torah should have stated, "And Noah had *ḥen* in the eyes of the Lord." Why is the term "found" used? According to our interpretation, the verse is well stated. It is well known that the generation of the flood was immoral while Noah was a complete zaddik.[102] Noah elevated *ḥen* to the realm of the sacred, while the generation of the flood saw *ḥen* only in the *kelipah*. But Noah did not reprove his neighbors. Thus, "And Noah found *ḥen* in the eyes of *the Lord*," Noah observed that *ḥen* exists in the world, but he "found" or discovered it only in the "eyes of the Lord," i.e., he elevated it from the profane world to the sacred, spiritual world; but his sin consisted of elevating the *ḥen* only with regard to his own spiritual welfare, while making no effort to enlighten the rest of his generation. . . .

Noah was a righteous man, yet he belittled himself in his own eyes. He had little faith in himself that he could influence the divine will. He thought that he differed little from the rest of his contemporaries and reasoned that if he would be saved, so would the rest of mankind. On this point Rashi remarks that "Noah was of those people 'little' in faith"[103] indeed, for Noah appeared little in his own eyes, thinking that he was not great enough a zaddik to influence the divine will.

10. THE EPHRAIM TYPE AND THE MANASSEH TYPE
Source: R. Elimelekh of Lizhensk, Noam Elimelekh to Vayehi, s.v. va-yikaḥ Yosef

And Joseph took them both, Ephraim in his right hand toward Israel's left hand, and Manasseh in his left hand toward Israel's right hand, and brought them near unto him. And Israel stretched out his right hand, and laid it upon Ephraim's head, who was the younger, and his left hand upon Manasseh's head, guiding his hand deliberately; for Manasseh was the firstborn (Gen. 48:13–14).

The primary intent of Scripture is to inform us that the firstborn was at the right of Israel, and the younger at his left. Is it not, then, redundant to tell us that they were, respectively, at the left and right of Joseph?

---

102. Gen. 6:1—4.
103. Rashi to Gen. 7:7.

I believe that Father Jacob's main purpose was to perpetuate His grace (*shefa*) and blessings for the people of Israel. Jacob sought to do this by means of these two zaddikim, Ephraim and Manasseh, as he said, *By thee shall Israel bless, saying, "God make these as Ephraim and Manasseh"* (Gen. 48:20)..

Why through these two zaddikim? Because the world is always in need of two types of zaddikim, one who will always contemplate the higher worlds and meditate on mystical unifications (*yiḥudim*), in order always to augment light in the higher spheres, and the other to think about the needs of this world, the people in need of sustenance and blessing and life, and other such necessities.

By means of these two kinds of zaddikim the world exists, and Jacob therefore sought to achieve this through his two grandsons. For Manasseh, as the firstborn, was by nature desirous of always rising spiritually from level to level and not thinking about mundane matters at all. But Ephraim was younger in his divine service as well. He did not indulge so much in these spiritual ascents. Rather, he always pondered how to draw down the divine grace (*shefa*) upon the people of Israel. Our Father Jacob considered this extremely important, for his main purpose was to draw down goodness upon Israel.

Now, Joseph's intention was just the opposite. He reasoned that Manasseh was more important because of his great concentration and his spiritual ascent, and that is why he placed Ephraim at his own right. For Joseph too wanted the people of Israel to receive blessings through these two zaddikim. But he felt that the power of his own right hand was sufficient for Ephraim to achieve blessings for the people of Israel. However, Joseph considered Manasseh as more important, for he served God through great spiritual attainments, and therefore he placed him to the right of his father Jacob.

But our Father Jacob disagreed. He took the opposite view, and since Ephraim was younger,[104] he crossed his hands in order to bless Ephraim with his right hand. For the primary function of Jacob was to do good to the generations after him, that they be prepared for every good effluence and mercy. This was symbolized by Ephraim.

This is what Jacob meant when he said, *I know it, my son, I know it* (ibid. 19). That is, "I know of the idea of my son Joseph, namely, that Manasseh has attained a higher level than Ephraim. *But his younger brother*, in his own way, *shall be greater than he, and his seed shall become*

---

104. Thus, presumably, in need of strengthening.

a multitude of nations—the world will on his account be full of His grace and His goodness. Therefore is he more beloved in my eyes." Hence, *And he set Ephraim before Manasseh* (ibid. 20).

This is the meaning of *The counsel of the Lord is with them that fear Him; and His covenant, to make them know it* (Ps. 25:14). *Them that fear Him* are the zaddikim who draw down blessings upon the world, and they must do so in secret and in hiding so that the accuser Satan will not denounce all of this goodness.[105] *His covenant* refers to the zaddik who conducts himself according to the covenant and the Torah. *To make them know it* means to do so openly, so that people will learn from him this proper way.[106]

11. GREATNESS AND SMALLNESS (IN ZADDIKISM)
Source: R. Elimelekh of Lizhensk, Noam Elimelekh to Shelah, 74a, s.v. o yomar va-yishlaḥ

It appears difficult to understand how it could enter one's mind to say that Jonah fled from before the blessed Lord Whose *glory fills the whole earth* (Isa. 6:3) and Whom *the heavens and the heavens of heavens cannot contain* (2 Chron. 6:18).

However, the answer is that Jonah's intent was to commit a transgression for the sake of heaven (*lishmah*),[107] for "great is a transgression

---

105. Satan seeks to indict the Ephraim-type zaddik, who must therefore perform his service of the Lord secretly. It is unclear from the text whether the author means that this zaddik stands accused of neglecting his own spiritual integrity in his communal preoccupations and must therefore perform his service on behalf of the people secretly; or that Satan seeks to nullify the goodness this zaddik brings down upon the world by attacking the zaddik in the area of his own spiritual elevation, and therefore this zaddik must conceal that aspect of his life devoted to attaining ever higher spiritual levels. The latter seems the more reasonable interpretation. Accordingly, the other type of zaddik has no reason to hide and must practice his purely spiritual service without any attempt at concealment in order to educate the people by his example. This may be a form of apology for the emerging hasidic zaddik—an Ephraim type—by hinting that despite his apparently full involvement in mundane matters he does have an active spiritual side to his personality that he deliberately conceals for the good of the people.

106. For more elaboration on the theme of the zaddik as the drawing force of divine grace (*shefa*), see below, selections 35–39.

107. The meaning of *lishmah* varies with the context.

for the sake of heaven,"[108] provided that it is accompanied by holy intentions. Thus, Jonah found it difficult to carry out his prophetic mission to the inhabitants of Nineveh lest, by repenting from their wickedness, they cause Israel to be accused, heaven forbid.[109] For the Talmud relates that the nations of the world, when admonished, are liable to repent at once.[110] Therefore, Jonah sought to become preoccupied and to distract himself with the details of his sea journey in order to interrupt his *devekut* and so by severing his connection with the Source of prophecy, avoid uttering this prophecy; for prophetic inspiration comes essentially through *devekut*.

However, there is also a zaddik of a much higher level who is always in a state of *devekut* and suffers no distractions, such that even if he should discuss mundane matters and appear to others to have interrupted his *devekut*, he does not in reality do so. Even when engaged in these lowly matters, he entertains the most sublime intentions. . . .

Lesser zaddikim are not permitted to accept mundane burdens, lest they interrupt their *devekut*. They . . . must keep themselves in a state of "smallness," in extreme meekness. The great zaddikim are not permitted to be in a state of perpetual "smallness," for at times they must rise up to a state of "greatness,"[111] as they are governed by the divine wisdom that is within them, that they might draw down blessing and great *shefa* upon the world.

12. THE ZADDIK'S IDLE TALK
Source: R. Moshe Hayyim Ephraim of Sudlikov, Degel Maḥaneh Ephraim to Metzora

I heard from my grandfather the Besht of blessed memory that there can be no uplifting of man, save through the leaders and the righteous of the generation. The zaddik can elevate man's character and his speech. There are two methods of this elevation.

---

108. Nazir 23b. The talmudic passage concerns Jael (Judg. 4:17—22, 5:6, 24—27) and suggests that at times the power of intention can transform an evil deed into a good one. The hasidic teachers often made use of this passage, but the mitnaggedim were wary of it because of the obvious risk of exploiting it for Sabbatean or antinomian purposes.
109. That is, Israel will suffer by comparison.
110. Rashi to Jonah 1:3.
111. "Greatness" in this context refers to the zaddik's spiritual self-confidence and intercessionary assertiveness.

1. There are those whom the zaddik elevates through his teachings of Torah and his prayers.

2. There are those whom he cannot raise except by means of casual conversation. This follows from the interpretation of our rabbis of the verse *and whose leaf does not wither* (Ps. 1:3): his casual conversation, i.e., a mere "leaf," has a purpose (does not "wither") even though it appears to be only idle speech. For indeed the zaddik elevates the person through these apparently idle words which he speaks with him.

Not everyone can prove himself worthy of this, as my grandfather said about the Mishnah: "She was seen talking to one."[112]

Enough said.

13. THE ZADDIK'S "MATERIALISM"
Source: R. Zevi Elimelekh of Dinov, Agra de-Pirka, sec. 7

Regarding the established custom that when a Jew comes to the zaddik to pray for him, he gives him money for it. . . .

Now, I found in the homilies of Rabbenu Nissim (Ran) stating—in connection with the admonishment of Ezekiel (13:19) to the false prophets who prophesy for breadcrumbs and similar gifts—that such a custom was no doubt also the practice of the true prophets.[113] For if this were not an accepted usage, it would be unthinkable that Jews could be led astray by false prophets. The mere fact of their requesting material reward would have opened their eyes to their deceitfulness, since true prophets did not ask for such reward. One must conclude from this that the real prophets acted likewise. Similar proof

---

112. Ketubbot 13a. The mishnah concerns a woman who was seen "talking" with a stranger. Upon inquiry she identified the man as one of halakhically valid lineage, and the Sages disagree as to her credibility. The word *medabberet* ("talking") of the Mishnah is interpreted in the Talmud as a euphemism for intimate relations. The Besht, giving the Mishnah a symbolic-mystical rather than halakhic meaning, interprets the word *eḥad* ("one" in "seen talking to one") to refer to the outstanding "one" (the zaddik) of the generation, and he gives *medabarret* a double meaning: idle speech and intimate connection. Hence the implication that the zaddik's idle talk has a penetrating, intimate effect on man, causing his elevation.
It should be noted that the author's grandfather (the Besht) was known for engaging in casual conversation, even with women and adulterers, as recounted in *Shivḥei ha-Besht* 118: "Once . . . a man came to see the Besht. The Besht was very fond of him and they talked together. That man was a well-known adulterer."
113. *Derashot ha-Ran*, second homily; Feldman ed. (Jerusalem, 1977), p. 21, in connection with Isaac's request to bring him tasty food (*mat'amim*) before blessing his firstborn (Gen. 27:4).

may be found in the case of King Saul. When he went to Samuel the prophet, he attempted to offer him a gift.[114] (True, Samuel did not accept it. But this is because he was an exception in this regard, as our Rabbis said: If one wishes not to derive pleasure from others for spiritual service, like Samuel the Rammati, he may do so.[115] However, this in itself proves our point, for seemingly only Samuel, not others, abstained from taking gifts.) Another case is that of the wife of Jeroboam when she went to the prophet Ahijah the Shilonite (1 Kings 14:2–4). From all this it becomes clear that genuine prophets also practiced this custom of accepting remuneration, which on the surface seems a strange thing.

The solution to this difficulty is as follows: During the solitude required for prayer and prophecy one ought to elevate his intellect and reduce his crude corporeality in order to receive the divine grace with a mind prepared for greatness. Now, the coarseness of matter has a tendency to overwhelm one. The roar of his lust leaves no room for intellectual preparedness which requires mental concentration. The advisable thing to do, then, is to feed his corporeal appetites something that appeases them so that his material self will not disturb him in his solitude and prayer. A similar explanation is given for the sacrifice of the he-goat on the Day of Atonement [which is sent to Azazel][116] . . . This is the content of the Ran's words.[117]

The saintly master R. Pinhas of Koretz of blessed memory offered a somewhat different solution to the problem. His explanation is this: When a man comes to pray to God for another person, it may be considered an impudence, heaven forbid. Others may think: Your friend does not pray for himself; hence you obviously are a conceited person, for you consider yourself more worthy than your friend to pray before the Creator. Therefore, one is advised to take some reward for it. This may serve as a rebuke to the "accuser," saying, I pray for him because he paid me to do so, and I am thus obliged to fulfill my mission.[118]

---

114. In 1 Sam. 9:7—8 Saul prepared a gift for Samuel when he went out for his first encounter with him. Scripture does not state, however, that he actually offered the gift to Samuel or that Samuel rejected it.

115. Berakhot 10b, and see Rashi ad loc.

116. See Nahmanides to Lev. 16:8, citing Pirkei de-R. Eliezer, chap. 46, that one of the he-goats is given to Samael (Satan) on the Day of Atonement as a kind of bribe not to interfere with the sacrifice.

117. R. Nissim does not say all this explicitly; it is largely R. Zevi Elimelekh's elaboration of a casual comment by R. Nissim.

118. See Additional Note *6.

14. THE EFFICACY OF THE ZADDIK'S PRAYER
Source: R. Dov Ber, the Maggid of Mezeritch, Or ha-Emet 55c

It is well known that the high priest on Yom Kippur could atone for the sins of Israel by his service of speech[119] and confession. Thereby, he would cause the thread of crimson wool to turn white.[120] Through his efforts, its color became white, because all hues can impart color, except for white, which is the original appearance of all. Therefore it changed into white, to show that everything had already been "sweetened in its source."[121] . . .

Now, the zaddik can bring about change (hishtannut) any time he wishes, whereas the high priest could do so only on Yom Kippur. And this is the difference between Israel and the nations of the world, that the nations of the world cannot perform change (hishtannut), but can only move things from place to place,[122] but Israel, because they are in devekut with God can return things to the Source of Sources from which all things are formed. And God, because of His love, transforms things at all times from evil to good, even without prayer being offered to Him, as with R. Hanina b. Dosa, who merely revealed his will.[123] This is the meaning of the verse *He does the will of them that fear*

---

119. That is, by the various readings, prayers, and recitations which formed part of the prescribed service of the high priest on Yom Kippur.
120. The sign of divine forgiveness. See Mishnah Yoma 6:8.
121. The whitening of the crimson thread at the door of the Sanctuary is interpreted as the symbol of the doctrine of *hamtakat ha-dinim be-shorasham,* "the sweetening of judgments in their source," i.e., the regression via contemplation of what is apparently evil and harsh to its roots in the sefirot, where it undergoes a metamorphosis to the good and the beneficent. The exact scheme will be discussed below. In the symbolism of the Yom Kippur service, white represents the neutral source, to which the red, symbolizing evil, is now returned, and in which it loses its malevolent character.
122. Change in substance is different from change in place. See Maimonides, *Guide* 2:4. The spiritual impact of the nations of the world is not nearly as radical as that wrought by the people of Israel.
123. Mishnah Berakhot 5:5. R. Hanina b. Dosa is reported, upon praying for the sick, to have said, "This one shall live, this one shall die." When asked how he was able to determine this, he answered that if his prayer went smoothly, he knew that the one he had prayed for had been "accepted" and would live, but if his prayer was not smooth, he knew that the patient was doomed. The Maggid takes this as indicating that R. Hanina b. Dosa's prayer was not supplicatory and intercessionary, in the usual sense. See Additional Note *7. Rather, instead of normative prayer, the *tefillah* of R. Hanina b. Dosa was simply an expression of his (own) will, by which he no doubt means the contemplative mystical technique of restoring things to the "source," shortly to be identified as Ayin or Hokhmah, and therefore more certain, more causal, and more coercive than supplicatory prayer. (The point is made by Weiss himself in the essay mentioned above. See Additional Note *8).

Him (Ps. 145:19). Thus too [the saying of the Sages], "There is no planetary influence, nothing is *mazzal* over Israel."[124] This means that Ayin ("Nothing") is the planet [or: source of emanation] for Israel.[125] Ayin is the name for the sphere of Hokhmah (Wisdom), as it is written, *But Hokhmah is found from Ayin* (Job 28:12).[126] From it were all things formed: "Thou hast formed all by means of Hokhmah"[127] and *mazzal* ("planet") implies flowing (or: emanation), as in *Water shall flow (yizzal) from his branches* (Num. 24:7).[128]

15. THE ZADDIK IS NOT A MAGICIAN
Source: *R. Elimelekh of Lizhensk, Noam Elimelekh, Vaeira, 35a, s.v. ki yedabber alekhem*

When Pharaoh shall speak unto you, saying, "Show for yourselves a wonder . . . " (Exod. 7:9)

The word *lakhem* ("for yourselves") seems to be inaccurate. It should have been written *li* ("for me"), for certainly Pharaoh wanted them to provide a sign for *him*. Furthermore, one may ask: After Moses and Aaron showed him the wonder of the rod turning into a serpent, and then his magicians did the same, why was it necessary that Pharaoh's heart be hardened, as it is written, *And Pharaoh's heart was hardened* (Exod. 7:13)? After he had seen the magicians too perform the miracle, his heart did not require further hardening.

But it appears to be quite simple. When a man is experienced in miracles, for God performs a miracle for him at any time, then it is

---

124. Shabbat 156a. Also, "Israel is not subject to astrological influence [*ein mazzal le-yisrael*]" (Nedarim 32a).
125. The letters *a-y-n* are repointed by the author to read, not *ein* ("there is no"), as in the talmudic saying quoted in the preceding sentence, but as *ayin* ("nothing"), which the Maggid identifies with the sefirah of Hokhmah (Wisdom), and hence that metaphysical zone which is the matrix of all emanations and in which all things are equal and in equilibrium. Hokhmah-Ayin is thus indicated as the source in which all "judgments" are "sweetened" and in which all changes, such as the nullification of evil decrees, as well as all other changes, are effected. By contemplation, the object to be changed is mystically transported back to this sphere where it is momentarily annihilated and re-created in its new form, and then emanated back to existence.
126. See Additional Note *8.
127. From the daily liturgy, where the plain meaning is, "Thou hast formed all *in* wisdom (*hokhmah*)."
128. The play on *mazzal-yizzal* thus concludes the reinterpretation of *ein mazzal le-yisrael* ("there is no planetary influence over Israel") to "Ayin ['nothing,' synonym for Hokhmah] is the source which emanates onto Israel."

always a source of novelty and wonder in his eyes. Even though God always performs miracles for him, nevertheless he is amazed at them and considers them a great novelty. However, one who performs something remarkable even once through sorcery or the like, then the second time it no longer appears novel at all, since he has himself done so once before.

This is what God said: *When Pharaoh shall speak unto you, saying, "Show for yourselves a wonder,"* i.e., perform the kind of wonder that will be marvelous and novel *for you* too. Then you will know that it is certainly the word of the Lord.

That is why it is written, *And Aaron cast down his rod before Pharaoh and before his servants* (Exod. 7:10). Whereas concerning the magicians it is written, *And they also . . . did in like manner* (Exod. 7:11), but it does not say, *before Pharaoh.* The reason is that the casting of the rod of Aaron was a great novelty for Pharaoh; he understood that this was the word of the Lord because he saw that even in the eyes of Moses and Aaron it was a novelty. But what was done by the magicians was no novelty, neither for them nor for Pharaoh, for he knew that they were doing this by means of their follies [i.e., magic].

Hence it is written, *And Pharaoh's heart was hardened.* It was necessary that his heart be hardened, because he understood that the act of the magicians was insubstantial.[129]

16. POWERS OF THE ZADDIK
Source: R. Elimelekh of Lizhensk, Noam Elimelekh to Va'ethanan, s.v. ha-yom ha-zeh

We read in the Talmud, "The Holy One decrees, and the zaddik annuls,"[130] as it is written, *Thou shalt also decree a thing and it shall be established unto thee* (Job 22:28). Now, how does this verse prove that the zaddik can annul judgments, i.e., harsh decrees which the Holy One ordains? The obvious meaning of the verse is that when the zaddik ordains, the Holy One fulfills the decree.[131] However, we may understand this passage according to what has been said earlier[132]:

---

129. See Additional Note *9.
130. See Mo'ed Katan 16b.
131. But not the bolder thesis that the zaddik has the power to annul a divine decree.
132. In the earlier part of this passage (not translated here), R. Elimelekh offers a rationale for the supernatural ability of the zaddik to contravene a divine decree. It is based upon a passage in Midrash Tanhuma (Mishpatim 4) that "If there is *din* (judgment or

When the zaddik ordains here below, there is no *din* ("judgment") up above, and thus the decrees vanish of themselves.

However, we must endeavor to understand: From where does the zaddik derive the ability to heal the sick through his prayers and to sustain him in continued life? After all, even the zaddik does not live forever; his life is only contingent.[133] How can a contingent being give life to a person? The blessed Lord, Who exists and lives forever and Whose life is absolute, can bestow life upon man who is merely a contingent being. But this cannot be done by man whose own life is contingent.

The answer is that the zaddik attaches (*medabbek*, from *devekut*) himself to God, and his life is thus connected to the eternal and absolute life of God. The life of the zaddik, too, thus becomes absolute and eternal because of this intimate attachment, like organs of the same body.[134]

In this manner does the zaddik have the power to bring life to the sick.

However, one might ask: If so, should not the zaddik live forever? That is impossible, because the zaddik is not always in *devekut*. Sometimes he is interrupted from his *devekut*, because that is the nature of the world; complete *devekut* can be approached but not fully maintained (lit., "reached and not reached"). The zaddik must always move up from level to level, and in his desire to rise to the very highest level he must sometimes regress and descend to a somewhat lower level, and then rise to the highest one. When the time comes for the zaddik to go the way of all the earth, to the "world of truth," and he is interrupted in his *devekut*, he then passes away, and is gathered unto his people.

Indeed, this is the will and desire of God, that all of us be in *devekut* with Him. That is what the commandments *I am the Lord thy God* and

---

justice) here below, then there is no *din* up above." This dictum uses the word *din* as a homonym; it means both justice, as in a legal decree, and (harsh) judgment or punishment. Hence, if humans act justly ("there is *din* here below"), God will refrain from punishing ("there will be no *din* up above"), and its converse. Hence, if the zaddik issues a decree (*din*), God refrains from punishing us (then, there is no *din* up above). The result: by exercising his own *din*, the zaddik "annuls" the *din* of the Almighty, for He, as it were, made His own use of *din* contingent upon man's *din*.

133. In the philosophical sense: as opposed to essential, absolute. In this selection R. Elimelekh is offering a religious and philosophical analysis of the zaddik's power to affect the operations of divine providence.

134. Lit. "like bone attached to bone," a reference to both Ezek. 37:7 and Job 19:20.

There shall be no other gods are all about.[135] *I am* is the positive precept, and *There shall not be* the negative precept, concerning Godliness, and both are matters of *devekut*.[136] Thus God Himself spoke to us, saying that we shall be in *devekut* with Him, with eternal life.[137]

17. THE ZADDIK AS SPIRITUAL SUPERMAN
Source: R. Elimelekh of Lizhensk, Noam Elimelekh, very first passage

It is written in the Mishnah, "The world stands on three things: on Torah, on divine worship [exemplified by the commandment to bring the first fruits], and on acts of kindness [symbolized by Israel, the community which is bound together by acts of goodness]."[138] It is also written in the Mishnah: "The world exists on three things: on law [corresponding to divine worship], on truth [corresponding to Torah], and on peace [corresponding to acts of kindness]."[139] It can be said that both Mishnah passages teach the same lesson.

These three elements may be explained in the following manner: There are three levels in the service of the exalted Creator. The first is Torah, to study for its own sake (*lishmah*). Because this level of motivation is so difficult to attain and can be reached solely by exerting great effort in the service of God, the Rabbis, in truth, permitted the study of Torah even not for its own sake, as it is written, "One should always study Torah even not for its own sake, because from this one proceeds to study Torah for its own sake."[140] Therefore, even if one has not attained the level of studying Torah for its own sake, one should not neglect its study because of this; for a man cannot easily attain the study of Torah for its own sake, except through great exertion in the service of the blessed Lord [using] all one's good qualities.[141]

---

135. Makkot 24a.
136. That is why these commandments were heard "from the mouth of the *Gevurah* (God)."
137. See Additional Note *10.
138. Avot 1:2. The material in brackets is based on Genesis Rabbah 1.
139. Avot 1:18.
140. Pesahim 50b. The terms *lishmah* and *shelo lishmah* may be variously interpreted. For a more elaborate analysis of the hasidic view, see my *Torah Lishmah*, pp. 215–220.
141. The study of Torah is thus considered by R. Elimelekh as the *lowest* of the three levels, surely an inversion of the traditional hierarchy of values. The reason for this is that since Torah study may be pursued "not for its own sake," i.e., without purity of intention, it is an exoteric activity; it does not challenge man to the kind of psychological motivation that corresponds to the sustained purity of contemplation. (Indeed, for Hasidism study *lishmah* meant primarily for the sake of *devekut*. See my *Torah Lishmah*, loc. cit.) Even the common man, incapable of maintaining unbroken contemplation, can undertake the study of Torah.

The second level is prayer, for this is the essence of "the service of the heart," as it is written: *"To serve Him with all your heart* (Deut. 11:13): this is prayer."[142] The heart is the seat of understanding and therefore, by means of prayer which issues from the heart, one may ascend to *devekut* with the Creator, to bind himself to Him. For *tefillah* ("prayer") is derived from the word which means "a knot,"[143] because one binds himself to the Creator with great *devekut* during prayer. This is suggested by the knot of the phylactery of the arm,[144] the function of which is to bind the thought of the heart with God.[145] Great effort is required in order to pray constantly to God that He should help the worshipper lest he be distracted by the Evil Urge from *devekut* with the Creator. The reason for this is that man, by his very nature, is prone to think constantly about his own matters and worldly affairs.[146]

This, too, is a meaning of the verse *The Lord saw that the wickedness of man was great on the earth, and that every imagination of the thoughts of his heart was only evil continually. And it repented the Lord that He had made man on the earth; and it grieved Him at his heart. . . . But Noah found grace in the eyes of the Lord* (Gen. 6:5–8).

As long as man is on earth and his wickedness is great, even he who wishes to serve God and do no evil, nevertheless, his thoughts pull him toward *only evil continually*. *It repented the Lord* means that He was

---

142. Ta'anit 2a.

143. See Rashi to Gen. 30:8.

144. *Tefillah* and *tefillin* are related etymologically.

145. The phylactery of the arm rests opposite the heart.

146. The second level is thus reserved for a category intermediate between the common man and the zaddik. (It is possible that R. Elimelekh considers this as a "lower zaddik" in his typology; in the next paragraph, elaborating this second level, he refers to Noah as a zaddik, in accord with the scriptural description of Noah as a *zaddik* ["righteous man"] [Gen. 6:9].) It demands of the worshipper that he resist the natural tendency to distraction, breaking the continuity of his concentration. While this is unquestionably a higher category than the first, it still requires divine assistance. Normal human initiative is insufficient; failure is common. But God, knowing well man's weakness, his faltering powers of concentration, and his wavering attentiveness, is compassionate and forgives man his lapses in *devekut* as he strays after worldly or even immoral thoughts. At best, those represented by this second type can not only resist the mental lapses and reject the demands made upon their attention by their very physicality; they can also transform the obstacle of corporeality and channel its energies and vitality into service of God through contemplation. Yet, despite this ability to raise the sparks and effect worship through corporeality, the *devekut* is not constant.

consoled because man had an excuse for his conduct before Him.[147] *For He created man*[148] means, as the Sages said, "If not for three verses, Israel's enemies (a euphemism for Israel) would have fallen. One of them is, *that I caused evil in their hearts*—that I gave them an Evil Urge."[149] *And it grieved Him at His heart* means that God was grieved because of the heart of man, in that He gave him such a heart of stone.[150] *But Noah found grace* means that Noah was a zaddik and that he transcended his nature, which was prone to separate him from *devekut* with the exalted Creator, and strengthened himself in order to attach himself to the Creator.[151] *Noah found grace* (*ḥen*); by transforming the order of the letters of his name, Noah (*N-H*) found grace (*H-N*) in the eyes of God.[152]

The third level is deeds of kindness. In the upper worlds *raḥamim* ("compassion") prevails, i.e., love and mercy, for God loves the zaddik in accordance with the holy deeds performed by him in the world He

---

147. *Va-yinnaḥem*, in the scriptural context, means that the Lord "regretted" or "repented." But the word is a homonym and may mean "He was consoled." It is this second meaning which our author adopts for his exposition.

148. *Ki*, in context, means *that* He created man. But the word may also read *for*, serving the author's homiletic purposes.

149. Berakhot 32a. This supports the idea that man's evil nature is his excuse and hence the reason for his survival. Thus, too, "God was *consoled, for* He created man."

150. R. Elimelekh explains *"his* heart" to mean the heart of *man*, rather than the heart of *God* (the literal meaning).

151. R. Elimelekh here ascribes to Noah, who typifies the second category of zaddik, the capacity for *it'hapekha* ("transformation") of the Evil Urge into the Good Urge. This concept of the sublimation and channeling of the erotic energies of man, was already known to the Sages of the Talmud (Berakhot 54a, Sukkah 52b). But most hasidic teachers, beginning with the Besht, developed it rather elaborately in connection with the doctrine of worship through corporeality. Thus, the Besht, in *Zavaat ha-Rivash* (n.p.); R. Yaakov Yosef of Polonnoye, *Ketonet Passim* 13d, 34b; *Toledot Yaakov Yosef* (Vayishlah), n. 3; and elsewhere. It is interesting that R. Elimelekh attributes worship through corporeality and transformation to this intermediate class. He seems here to reflect the ambivalence of his teacher, R. Dov Ber, the Maggid, as to whether the common man too can successfully undertake this spiritual activity (the view of the Besht), or whether ordinary people ought to be dissuaded from doing so because of the obvious dangers, and that only the zaddik should be encouraged to risk this spiritual venture (R. Shneur Zalman and other students of the Maggid). R. Elimelekh apparently wants to solve the problem by positing this intermediate class, superior to the ordinary man in that he can worship through corporeality, but inferior to the zaddik in that, nonetheless, the *devekut* of the latter is unbroken.

152. Thus Noah's very name suggests the *it'hapkha*, or the transformation of evil into good. The source for this transformation of letters is Zohar I, 58a.

made. But here, God's actions of love and mercy are called *ḥesed* ("kindness"), i.e., God acts kindly, and provides for the needs even of those who have not earned His love.[153] But the zaddik who has reached such a level that he can elevate all corporeal things, i.e., he can raise the holy sparks from the material things, such as food and drink which contain them, and whose thoughts when involved with such corporeal things are centered solely on elevating these holy sparks—a zaddik of this sort does not require this *ḥesed* or unearned "kindness," whereby his mundane needs are satisfied as an act of *ḥesed*. Rather, God provides him with all his needs in accordance with the standards of justice, by virtue of his good deeds.[154] This is the reason for the expression *gemilut ḥasadim* ("the bestowing of kindness"). *Gemilut* is derived from *He weaned (va-yigamal) his son Isaac* (Gen. 21:8).[155] The zaddik does not require the level of *ḥesed* ("kindness"). Rather, he has earned his reward because of God's love for him.

Thus the zaddik binds himself with eternal life in the exalted spheres above; even while in this world, he attains the bliss of the supernal world which derives from eternal life. This is the meaning of the talmudic benediction, "You shall see your world in your own lifetime."[156] Through the actions and movements which one undertakes in holiness, purity, *devekut*, joy, love, and awe, he will attain the bliss of the world-to-come, while yet in this world.[157]

One may also say that this is the meaning of the verse *But you who cleave to the Lord your God are yet all alive today* (Deut. 4:4). Through the *devekut* by which you cleave to the Creator, you will attain eternal life even *today*, in this world.

The verse *Moses commanded us the Torah, an inheritance of the congregation of Jacob* (Deut. 33:4) also refers to the three levels of divine ser-

---

153. See Berakhot 7a.
154. Cf. Berakhot 17b, "The world is sustained with charity, but they [the zaddikim; see Rashi ad loc., s.v. *ve-hem*] are sustained by force [of their merits]."
155. Kindness is related to weaning because of the root word *gamal*, which is common to weaning and *gemilut ḥesed*. The zaddik too receives the divine goodness in a limited fashion—limited to the corresponding good deeds performed by the zaddik.
156. Berakhot 17a. This is the literal meaning. R. Elimelekh's interpretation, not too far from the literal, is: "You shall attain eternal life ('your world') during your lifetime in this world."
157. By sustaining unbroken *devekut*, the zaddik, the highest of the three types, transfers *all* his corporeality into expressions of worship (unlike the second class, which experiences only limited success in this venture). Hence "this world" has been effectively sublimated into an unblemished spiritual existence, identical with that of the world-to-come.

vice. *Commanded us the Torah* means that He commanded *us* to study His Torah even if not for its own sake; *us* implies that *each person* should study according to his own level. The second level is *inheritance*—to elevate the holy sparks, which are called "inheritance of the fathers," as is known. God gave us the opportunity to elevate the holy sparks as a form of inheritance, for the sparks remain as an heirloom for us. That is what is meant by "and He keeps faith with those who sleep in the dust."[158] God "keeps faith" with the sparks, raising them from "the dust" to holiness.[159] The third level is "the congregation of Jacob." This refers to the complete *devekut* to which the zaddik attains and by which he emanates goodness to all of Israel. He is the *inheritance of the congregation of Jacob*, who takes shelter under the shadow of His wings to obtain His grace (*shefa*).[160]

18. THE ZADDIK'S METHOD OF EFFECTING CHANGE (THROUGH PRAYER)
Source: R. Elimelekh of Lizhensk, Noam Elimelekh to Emor, s.v. elleh mo'adei

We must understand how it is that when the zaddik prays, his prayers are answered. This seems to imply a change in God, but Heaven forbid that we ascribe change to the True One!

But here is the explanation. The zaddik prays for a certain person. He prays with all 248 limbs and 365 sinews of his body, without the interference of any alien thoughts, and binds to himself the person for whom he prays, and thus sanctifies him.

Thus his prayer is answered. Because, from where comes a lack or need in a person? Certainly it is the result of a punishment for some sin committed by one of the body's limbs. Now when the zaddik spiritually surrounds and covers that person in prayer, the limbs of that person become as one with the limbs of the zaddik, and the person is restored to wholeness. Since the sin has been atoned for by the process of *tikkun* ("restoration"), the punishment vanishes.

---

158. This is taken from the second benediction of the Amidah, the prayer of the Eighteen Benedictions.

159. The passage literally refers to resurrection. The author interprets the phrase as referring to the Lurianic doctrine of the raising of the sparks, which many hasidic thinkers associate with worship through corporeality. The symbol of the *kelipot*, or "shells," in which the sparks are incarcerated is the "dust," or corporeality.

160. For R. Elimelekh, the zaddik is the "inheritance of the congregation"; he personifies his hasidic community, or even all of Israel.

Thus we may also explain the verse *All my bones shall say, Lord, who is like Thee, who delivers the poor from him that is too strong for him, and the poor and the needy from him that robs him?* (Ps. 35:10).[161] When a person sins, that sin causes him to entertain alien thoughts, and thus his mind is defiled, heaven forbid. *All my bones*, etc., means that when I pray with pure and clean thought, and all my limbs cooperate with me in this divine service, thereby I *deliver the poor* who is poor in some respect because of a spiritual defect caused by one of his limbs, and he is saved, because I the zaddik pray for him and bind him to me, as I have said above. . . .

The Holy One is above time, and there is no change in Him. But Scripture says, *These are the times (seasons) of the Lord* (Lev. 23:4), implying that sometimes we can discern in the Creator time and change; i.e., if yesterday there was a certain evil decree, and today the decree was changed for the better. How can this be said of the true Creator? ...

The answer is, by means of the prayer of the zaddikim, who pray with all of their limbs, identifying with the one for whom they pray, with all of the body, whole and without any admixture of alien thoughts. ...

The worlds . . . are subject to time. The zaddikim who pray with *kavvanah* are the ones who sustain the worlds, and emanate goodness and vitality to all the worlds. Thus they are the cause of changing the attribute of Justice, i.e., harshness, to complete Love, because they determine all, by virtue of the vitality they emanate.[162]

19. ONLY THE ZADDIK PERCEIVES THE ESSENCE OF PRAYERS
Source: R. Nahman of Bratslav, Likkutei Etzot, Zaddik, no. 16

The true zaddikim elevate prayer through great ascensions until they reveal His Godliness and His blessed Kingdom to all who dwell on earth, even to those who are exceedingly remote from Him, such as the wicked and the idol worshippers. For this is basically what the greatness of God is all about: that those who are far removed from Him, even pagans, come to recognize that there is a God Who governs and rules.

---

161. It is unclear from the text whether R. Elimelekh intends the "from him that is too strong for him" to refer to the power of sin and alien thoughts or perhaps to the zaddik. In the latter case the prefix *mem* in *meḥazak* would meant not "from" but that the poor are delivered "by means of" the zaddik, who is spiritually more powerful.
162. See Additional Note *11.

Hence, one who has a illness or any other sorrow in his house ought to go to zaddikim that they petition for God's compassion upon him. This causes great satisfaction to Him, because God longs for the prayers of the righteous (*zaddikim*).[163] For only the zaddikim perceive the essence of prayer.[164]

20. THE SONG OF THE ZADDIK
Source: R. Nahman of Bratslav, Likkutei Moharan I, 64:5

Every branch of wisdom has its own singular song and melody, and that melody is reserved for that wisdom. . . . And from the song is derived its wisdom. . . . Even the wisdom of heresy has its own special song and melody. . . .

The greater the degree of wisdom, the more sublime its melody, and so on, from level to level . . . all the way up to the first point of Creation, which is the beginning of Atzilut, than which there is nothing higher.[165] Nothing surpasses that wisdom save the light of the Ein Sof which surrounds the Great Void (*he-halal ha-panui*) and which contains all of creation and wisdom.[166] But the wisdom that is bathed in the light of the Ein Sof is imponderable and ineffable, for the Ein Sof is God Himself, and His wisdom is beyond all comprehension.

Nothing exists in those realms other than faith—the faith in Him and that His infinite Light surrounds and envelops all the worlds. Faith too has its unique song and melody. Thus, just as idol worshippers sing their songs in their houses of worship, so does their misguided faith in their idols have its own song. So, in reverse, is it with the holy; every article of faith has its own song. And the song that applies to the faith in the light of the Ein Sof which encompasses all the worlds, the faith that is higher than all forms of wisdom and articles of faith, is likewise higher than all songs and melodies in the world. And all the songs and melodies of all the forms of wisdom derive from that supernal song and melody. . . .

---

163. Yevamot 64a, Hulin 60b. Cf. Zohar I, 137b, 167b. For more on this, see chap. 6 (Worship), selection 9.
164. See Additional Note *12.
165. Atzilut is the first and thus holiest of the four spiritual worlds in which God, as the Ein Sof, reveals Himself.
166. The Great Void, according to Lurianic Kabbalah, is a gigantic vacuum formed by the Ein Sof's primordial self-constriction, and in it the Creation took place.

It is only the singular zaddik of the generation who merits the melody of that supernal faith, for he is in the category of Moses and the category of silence...which is beyond the category of speech.[167] ...

By means of the song of the zaddik, all the souls which fell into the heresy of the Void escape and ascend from it,[168] for the zaddik's song is in the category of the prime faith (rosh emunah), i.e., the highest form of faith. By means of this melody and this faith are all heresies nullified and encompassed in this song from which all other songs are derived.[169]

21. THE ZADDIK AS A MIRACLE WORKER
Source: R. Nahman of Bratslav, Likkutei Moharan I, 49:7, p. 124b

The zaddik, whose heart is open to wisdom . . . can renew the work of Creation, and perform miracles and wonders in the world. For it is

---

167. The zaddik, and especially the most eminent zaddik of the generation (zaddik ha-dor), is, for R. Nahman, one who has transcended mere wisdom and attained faith. If wisdom is identified with speech (as in the Greek logos), then faith is that silence which surpasses speech. The zaddik, as preeminently a man of faith, is thus identified with Moses, who reached the highest rung, that of faith, symbolized by silence. (It is Moses who is referred to in the Torah as "slow of speech and slow of tongue" [Exod. 4:10]; see Likkutei Moharan I, 64:3.) Paradoxically, only after relinquishing "speech" and even "song" and embracing the "silence" of faith does the zaddik find the "song" of faith, by means of which he redeems the souls of the heretics.
168. See previous note. Because the Ein Sof is "absent" from this Void, it is the province of evil and, especially, of heresy (epikorsut), which R. Nahman calls "unwise wisdoms" (Likkutei Moharan I, 64:2), and which are spurious wisdom. The arguments of the heretics ("those who engage in philosophy") are insubstantial (both on account of their inherent fallaciousness and because they issue from the Void); hence, there is really no "answer" to them. An "answer," for R. Nahman, implies a legitimate question, so that question and answer are in genuine dialogue, such that "both these and these are the words of the living God." Unlike ordinary men, the zaddik of the generation may study the words of the heretics not primarily to refute them, but to rescue and elevate the souls of the heretics who have fallen into the Void. As the one symbolized by Moses, and hence by silence, the zaddik is qualified to approach the eternally mute Void in order to deliver the hapless souls entrapped within it by means of his "song" (see the preceding note). The silence-song and duality of faith is apparently the response to the ambiguous nature of the Void from which God is absent and in which He is, in a deeper sense, present.
169. The wordless melody of the zaddik is thus infinitely more than his aesthetic self-expression. It is a song of faith—-that which surpasses mere intellection and is the source of all wisdom—-and has redemptive powers. The victims of heresy or faith-lessness are caught up in the zaddik's song and pulled by it out of their incarceration in the Void.

said, "and in His goodness He renews every day, constantly, the work of Creation";[170] and "goodness" refers to the zaddik who is called "good," as it is written, *Say ye of the righteous (zaddik) that it shall be good for him* (Isa. 3:10).[171]

22. THE ZADDIK'S SELF-CONFIDENCE
Source: R. Nahman of Bratslav, Likkutei Moharan I, 61:5

There are those zaddikim who suffer controversy against them because they do not have faith in themselves. They do not believe in their own original novellae in Torah (*ḥiddushei torah*)[172] and do not believe that the Almighty derives great delight from their novellae. Because they do not have faith in their own novellae, they are neglectful of them. That is why they are beset by controversy.[173] As a result of this controversy they repent, and their own novellae become important to them, and they resume their creative thinking, and of this a book is made.[174]

Thereby is a book composed up above as well, as it is written, *Then they that fear the Lord spoke one with another, and the Lord hearkened and heard, and a book of remembrances was written before Him* (Mal. 3:16).[175]

---

170. Prayerbook, morning service.

171. See Yoma 38b. The interpretation of the passage from the prayerbook is that God, by means of the zaddik who is called "goodness," renews Creation. The zaddik, as the essence of goodness, therefore has the capacity to renew Creation and, possessing this power over the natural order, can perform miracles. Elsewhere, however, R. Nahman suggests that the zaddik ought not utilize his powers over creation and nature, which is the realm of the divine, but rather use these powers to change the will of people who have fallen astray from the service of God. See above, selection 6 and note 96.

172. Original and creative interpretations of Torah.

173. The text is somewhat confusing as to cause and effect. The meaning of the passage is that the zaddik's lack of self-confidence is the cause, and the controversy against him is the effect. He lacks confidence in himself, which leads to his neglect of his creativity in composing novellae, and this inadequate fulfillment of his spiritual office results in the disputes against him.

174. Earlier in this chapter, R. Nahman maintains that all genuine controversies result in the composing of a book, of the responsa genre, for controversy is a result of question and answer, stimulus and response. All such controversy-books are important for the world. They clarify in a way that ordinary didactic writing does not.

175. The "controversy-book" of which R. Nahman speaks is not merely a literary creation but a spiritual one as well. He finds reference to this in the verse cited.

23. THE ZADDIK AND SECULAR LEARNING
Source: R. Nahman of Bratslav, Likkutei Moharan I, 49:7, s.v. ve-zehu perush le-shemesh

The spiritual attainment of the zaddik comes about only through the people of Israel. . . . And when Jews, heaven forbid, indulge in the secular wisdom of the nations, then the zaddik falls from his level of perception, and his vision is covered and obscured. But when Jews leave the wisdom of the nations, then the zaddik is *as a bridegroom coming out of his chamber* (Ps. 19:6),[176] i.e., the zaddik emerges from his concealment which he had experienced heretofore. Then *he rejoiceth as a strong man to run his course* (ibid.), for the zaddik is like a hero in doing and obeying the word of God;[177] indeed, it requires strength to run this course, which one must traverse at the time that Israel is in a state of rebuke, and upon which course one can now run with great speed.[178]

The Social Functions of the Zaddik

24. THE ZADDIK AND THE COMMON MAN
Source: R. Yaakov Yosef of Polennoye, Toledot Yaakov Yosef to Ki Tissa, sec. 3

And now I would like to add my explanation of the reason why the Israelites were commanded to donate, as part of the census, *half* a shekel (Exod. 30:13).

---

176. The verse itself refers to the sun in the great "nature psalm." However, in this homily R. Nahman equates the sun with the zaddik, referring to Kiddushin 72b. "Chamber" (*huppah*) implies concealment and obscurity; the zaddik's spiritual vitality is contained and restrained.

177. See Ps. 103:20, "ye mighty in strength that fulfill His word."

178. The zaddik is one who "runs the course" of doing God's bidding. He does so even when confronted with the handicap of Israel's estrangement from God because it engages in profane studies (and, since the zaddik derives his powers from Israel, he is weakened in his activity). But when Israel abandons its preoccupation with secular studies, the zaddik can "run the course" much more speedily. At the end of this chapter in *Likkutei Moharan*, the editor adds an interesting explanation that he heard from R. Nahman: When one repents over some past misdeed, he indeed succeeds in undoing his sin. However, while the consequences of the sin are cancelled, the time spent in this period of estrangement cannot normally be recaptured by repentance alone. Therefore one must "run the course" as speedily as possible, i.e., accelerate one's spiritual improvement, to make up for lost time. R. Nahman is quoted as saying to his hasidim, in Yiddish, "You must hurry very much in order still to be able to catch something."

The purpose of man's creation as a composite of matter and form, which are two opposites, is that he make the matter submit to the form.[179] And as it is with an individual person, so is it with regard to the whole world, or a country or a city. The zaddikim are the form, and the masses of the people are the matter, the bodily. The purpose of this division is that the zaddik should bring the masses to repentance, as Abraham did, as it is said, *And the souls they had gotten in Haran* (Gen. 12:5).[180] Thus is matter made subservient to form.

Now in one individual person, the soul or form must not boast of its superiority to the body by saying that it is a holy soul and hewn from a holy quarry, from under the Throne of Glory,[181] whereas the body derives from dust and the fetid drop, as the tanna teaches in Avot: "Consider three things and you will be spared from sin; know whether you came . . . from a fetid drop."[182] Despite this spiritual superiority of the soul, it descends into this world in order to perfect, through the organs of the body, all the commandments necessary for the restoration of its wholeness; whereas before this, it had to eat the "bread of embarrassment."[183] Certainly the body must not boast of its superiority to the soul, that is, because it supports the soul, for when the soul departs from the body the latter becomes malodorous as it decomposes. Thus they need each other, like man and woman, each of which alone is only half a body.

So, collectively, the scholars and the zaddikim must not say that they do not need the masses of the people, for the latter are the supporters of the Torah,[184] and also because of many of the practical commandments which are fulfilled by them. Certainly, the masses of the people should not say that they do not need the scholars, or act arrogantly toward them because they support them, for that is not so. On the contrary, it is as the Rabbis say, that God says, "The entire world is supplied with food because of the merit of my son Hanina, and my

---

179. "Matter" and "form" are, for R. Yaakov Yosef, equivalent to the physical and the spiritual, but with broader and more symbolic connotations. See the excerpt from *Toledot Yaakov Yosef* in selection 8 above.

180. The verse is interpreted by the Midrash to refer to the pagans whom Abraham and Sarah converted to the monotheistic faith. See Genesis Rabbah 39:14.

181. The Throne of Glory is considered the realm beneath the sefirot but above the Intellects from which *neshamah*, the highest aspect of the soul, derives.

182. Avot 3:1.

183. The "embarrassment" is that of eating what one has not earned, so to speak.

184. That is, by maintaining scholars and schools of Torah.

son Hanina himself suffices with a kav of carobs from Friday to Friday."[185]

If so, everyone must feel that he is only *one half* as is the half-shekel. If the matter and form come together, whether in the collectivity or in the individual, man becomes one and complete.

25. THE ZADDIK'S LADDER
Source: R. Yaakov Yosef of Polennoye, Toledot Yaakov Yosef to Vayetzei, sec. 3, s.v. ve-li nireh

The world in general is called one *partzuf* ("countenance").[186] The common men are its legs and the zaddikim its eyes, as they are called *the eyes of the assembly* (Lev. 4:13).[187] . . . Thus it is said that the world in general is called a "ladder," as it is written, *And he dreamed, and behold, a ladder set up on the earth, and the top of it reached to heaven* (Gen. 28:12). The common men are *set upon on the earth* inasmuch as they are called the legs of the world, and the scholars (*talmidei hakhamim*, i.e., zaddikim), as its head or eyes, are those who *reach to heaven*. And since all of them combined constitute a completed configuration and a single entity (*partzuf*), therefore the "angels of God," namely the zaddikim who have not betrayed the mission assigned to them by their Creator, *ascend on it* (Gen. 28:12). That is to say, a generation whose deeds are proper stimulates its heads (leaders) to ascend even higher. So was it at Mount Sinai, where we are told, *And Israel encamped there before the mount* (Exod. 19:2), meaning that they rested in penance,[188] and then *Moses ascended unto God* (Exod. 19:3). The converse is equally true: when the generation's deeds are improper, the zaddikim descend, Heaven forbid, as our Sages said of Samuel the Small, that he merited that the Shekhinah should rest on him but his generation was not fit for this.[189] For in that case, the ladder which represents the totality of

---

185. Berakhot 47b, Ta'anit 24b; Zohar III, 216.

186. *Partzuf*, or "countenance," is a term used in Lurianic Kabbalah to denote one aspect of the deity. The *partzuf* is considered a whole entity in its own right, merging its constituent parts into one unity. R. Yaakov Yosef uses the term not in its general sense but to show how the zaddikim and the masses relate to each as parts of one whole organism.

187. Cf. Num. 15:24 and Rashi to Ta'anit 24a, s.v. *me-einei*: "the eyes of the assembly" refers to "the elders who illuminate the eyes of the people." Cf. G. Nigal, "Al Demut ha-Zaddik he-Hasid," *Molad* 30 (1975): 177. See also below, selection 36.

188. Mekhilta to Exod. 19:2.

189. Sotah 48b.

the world's common people serves as a means of descent for the zaddik. For just as when a man's legs are lowered into a pit, the head too is lowered and when his legs are planted on a mountain his head is raised even higher, so it was with the effect of the spiritual state of the masses upon the zaddikim.

26. RECIPROCAL FUNCTIONING OF THE ZADDIK
Source: R. Yaakov Yosef of Polennoye, Toledot Yaakov Yosef to Yitro, sec. 6, s.v. u-meshani

He who leads the community for the sake of heaven i.e., unselfishly, should strive to keep the people on the straight path in all matters, both mundane and spiritual, not merely in rhetoric and in practice, such as chastising and reprimanding them, but also in his thought. He must bind himself to God mentally together with his contemporaries, to elevate and cause them to cleave to Him. But this is on condition that they too attach themselves to the heads of the generation, i.e., the zaddikim, for only then can the latter take them by the hand and elevate them.[190]

27. LOOKING UP TO THE ZADDIK
Source: R. Yaakov Yosef of Polennoye, Toledot Yaakov Yosef to Bo, sec. 11, p. 157b, s.v. uva-zeh yuvan

And it came to pass, when Moses held up his hand, that Israel prevailed over Amalek (Exod. 17:11). "Were, then, the hands of Moses making war? But what the verse refers to is this: As long as the Israelites were looking upwards, they were victorious."[191] This means that they constantly contemplated ways to ascend higher, and as a result the learned men, the zaddikim of the generation, became important in their eyes,

---

190. This and similar statements of R. Yaakov Yosef were seen by the mitnaggedim as a request that the hasid "relegate his thoughts to the zaddik" in prayer, which in their view was a grave sin on the order of idol worship. The most pronounced criticism on this point came from R. David of Makov in his Shever Poshe'im, p. 58, cited by M. Wilensky, Hasidim u-Mitnaggedim (Jerusalem, 1970), pp. 149–150. He refers to Nahmanides' comment on the verse "Thou shalt have no other gods before Me" (Exod. 20:3) to the effect that the ancient pagans had a similar practice: "When the people of a country saw an individual like Nebuchadnezzar [who] had great power and his star was very much in ascendance, they thought that by taking on his worship upon themselves and directing their thoughts toward him, their star would also ascend with his." See below, selection 39, n. 245, for R. Nahman's view on this.
191. Rosh ha-Shanah 29a.

for they longed to reach the zaddik's level.[192] And since within the Israelite nation itself the head (= the zaddik) did not bow downward, therefore in the totality of nations too, Israel—which is called the "head" of the nations—prevailed and subsequently ruled.[193] However, when within the Israelite nation itself the heads of the people, namely, the scholars (talmidei ḥakhamim) were not held in esteem,[194] so too in the totality of nations was Israel defeated. . . .

And so it is always whenever Jews look upwards, meaning that they heed the Torah and ethical teachings of those who are above them, they are strengthened and cured, as Maimonides wrote: "Just as there are illnesses of the body so too there are sicknesses of the soul. . . and the scholars (talmidei hakhamim) are the healers of the soul, providing they are obeyed, but when they are not obeyed the common people fester away."[195]

True, they have a complaint. They do not heed the scholar (talmid ḥakham, zaddik), they say, because they have found in him some fault. The truth, however, is that even conceding they are right, the scholar's fault is for their benefit, so that they have some common ground with him in order that he raise them,[196] as in the parable of the minister of the crown who changed his clothing.[197]

28. THE EXALTED AND THE HUMBLE
Source: R. Nahman of Bratslav, Kitzur Likkutei Moharan II, 7:7

The sage and the zaddik[198] who merits these makkifim[199] must teach

---

192. A zaddik is one who is both pious and a scholar (see above, selection 3). Thus talmid ḥakham and zaddik are here used interchangeably.
193. See above selection 8, where R. Yaakov Yosef states that Israel is "the soul and vitality" of all the nations.
194. See n. 192.
195. Mishneh Torah, Hilkhot De'ot 2:1.
196. R. Yaakov Yosef is hinting briefly at the doctrine of the descent of the zaddik, which he elaborates elsewhere. See below, selection 40.
197. The author is referring here to a parable which he uses frequently. A minister disguises himself as a common citizen in order to "reach" the prince, who has sinned, so that he may inspire him to return to the king. Cf. the excerpt from Toledot Yaakov Yosef below, selection 40 and n. 248.
198. See Likkutei Moharan II, 7:6, where the sage-zaddik is more elaborately described as "the sage of the generation who is the Rebbe of the generation."
199. In Likkutei Moharan II, 7:6, the author uses the term makkifim for supernal entities which "surround" the zaddik and which he bequeaths to his disciples by teaching them. These makkifim are longevity and immortality, in which the greatest spiritual delight is in knowing that we do not know.

both the more exalted and the more humble. That is, he must show those who are of high station that they know nothing about God and, contrariwise, those of humble station who grovel in their sins on the very ground in utter degradation, that the Lord is still with them and close to them, thus encouraging them never in any way to despair, Heaven forbid.

29. A ZADDIK'S STRANGE CONDUCT
Source: R. Nahman of Bratslav, Likkutei Etzot, Zaddik, no. 57

One ought to know that the zaddikim who are true leaders vary in their approaches regarding the guidance of worldly men who desire to be close to them. At times, the zaddik makes himself very much available to the world. At other times he conceals himself and hides from them so that they are unable to come near him. He may also provoke questions about his objectionable and astonishing behavior, to the point that their mind becomes twisted and confused because of his strange conduct with them. All this, however, is for the benefit of those who seek his closeness.[200] Therefore, do not allow your thoughts about this to frighten you, for it is all for your benefit.

30. THE ZADDIK'S INFLUENCE
Source: R. Nahman of Bratslav, Likkutei Etzot, Zaddik, no. 108

The true leader of the generation ought to be a great zaddik indeed, which means that he must be saintly and ascetic, completely separated from sexual lust with great holiness.[201] Only then is he fit to be a leader of Israel. After achieving such a state, he is capable by mere contemplative observation, reflecting on each Jew, to bring sparkle and light into everyone's mind and intellect, distributing greatness to each in accordance with his capacity and the quality of his mind. This, in turn, bestows on everyone the worthiness to create the original *hiddushim* (novellae) on the Torah befitting him. Also, each one of the Jews is brought along into a state of holiness and abstinence from lust,

---

200. The author hints here at the doctrine of the descent of the zaddik in a similar manner as does R. Yaakov Yosef elsewhere; see above, selection 27. Cf. the introduction to this chapter, "Descent of the Zaddik." It is also a fairly obvious reference to his own "strange conduct" which both attracted and repelled many of his potential acolytes, and which he here interprets as being for their good.
201. See Additional Note *13.

by virtue of the leader who is a great saint. They are also privileged through this—namely, the influence of the zaddik's reflection upon them—to achieve modesty and repentance and a true sense of humility which is an aspect of eternal life in the world-to-come.[202]

When the Jews, however, do not have such a leader, heaven forbid, then the whole world is in a state of confusion, and everyone who has a desire to appropriate the title of zaddik takes it, as is the case now, because of our many sins.

31. THE ZADDIK'S COMPASSION (AND PASSION)
Source: R. Nahman of Bratslav, Likkutei Etzot, Zaddik, no. 96

The true zaddik is very merciful toward his fellow Jews, inasmuch as his compassion for Jews is of the genuine kind, i.e., to inculcate in them the sacred knowledge so that they know that the Lord is God, thus diverting them from sin. For Jews, this is the principal pity, greater than all other kinds of compassion; because Jews, as a holy nation, are incapable of carrying upon them the load of sin for even one day. For the zaddik knows the degrees of Israel's holiness and their devekut and their spirituality, how utterly removed they are from iniquity, so much so that sin does not befit a Jew at all.[203] Therefore, the zaddik always stands up for them self-sacrificingly, to divert them from sin, and he entreats the blessed Name to forgive them all their guilt. He also knows how to regulate his compassion. He will not extend mercifulness of the kind that may hurt one, Heaven forbid, and he will not have mercy on one whom it is forbidden to pity.

The zaddik also strives to perpetuate his wisdom for generations to come. This constitutes the principal perfection of the zaddik after his departure. For even if he is privileged after his death to ascend very high, to the ultimate heights, his achievement is not really complete by being on high alone. His true perfection is achieved only when, after his departure, he continues to illuminate down below as well, through a son or a disciple who received his sacred wisdom, and pro-

---

202. Here there is no reciprocity mentioned. It is a one-way affair. The zaddik is the giver, and his generation the takers. For a differing view, see introduction, "The Zaddik and His Generation."
203. See Additional Note *14. Cf. below, selection 40 and n. 253. In that selection, R. Yaakov Yosef limits the inability to sin or to persist in sin to the zaddik only. R. Nahman's view is in line with his contention that there is a bit of the zaddik in everyone (see above, selection 6).

ceeds to spread that light in the world from generation to generation—eternally.[204]

32. MEASURED ENTHUSIASM
Source: R. Nahman of Bratslav, Likkutei Etzot, Zaddik, no. 100

The zaddikim who are the true leaders of the generation cast out from the hearts of Jews all melancholy and sadness, thereby enabling them to develop a burning enthusiasm (hitlahavut) for God.[205] At times, however, one generates an excessive burning for God, beyond the proper measure. This too is not good, for it is an aspect of tempestuousness which is called "destruction." Zaddikim are also watchful to subdue the stormy spirit so that they are not consumed by excessive ecstasy. It is thus the role of the zaddik to assure that the heart of every Jew be enthusiastic as it should be, with measured temperament.[206]

33. TRUE ZADDIKIM AND "JEWISH DEVILS"
Source: R. Nahman of Bratslav, Likkutei Moharan I, 12:1

The controversies we observe, in which scholars (lomdim) oppose the zaddikim and speak of them with scorn, arrogance, and contempt—all this expresses a great divine purpose.[207] For there are two kinds of religious leaders: Jacob and Laban. Jacob is the zaddik who formulates new interpretations (hiddushim) in Torah,[208] and who studies Torah for its own sake (lishmah).[209] His reward is stored away and hidden for the

---

204. R. Nahman seems preoccupied with the perpetuation of his teachings, if not by offspring, then through disciples. He ascribes this passionate desire to every zaddik.
205. Atzvut ("sadness") is a major topic in R. Nahman's discourses (sihot) with his hasidim. He considered this the biggest deficiency in the development of the hasid, inasmuch as Hasidism demands serving God joyfully and with enthusiasm.
206. The need for emotional balance even in hitlahavut during service and prayer may be based on Maimonides, Hilkhot De'ot 1–2, as are several other tenets of Hasidism. See chaps. 5 (Devekut), 6, (Worship), and 10 (Repentance).
207. The author is obviously referring to the erudite mitnaggedim.
208. The author intends talmudists who are creative and whose studies result in new interpretations and concepts, generally in Talmud, by means of the traditional method of dialectic. His praise of hiddushim may also be inspired by his awareness that Hasidism itself was an innovation—and opposed because of it.
209. The term lishmah admits of many definitions but may be loosely translated as "for its own sake." See chap. 5 (Devekut) on this theme. The early hasidic leaders criticized the rabbinic establishment of their day, charging that their study of Torah was not lishmah.

future, as the Sages said, "Tomorrow they will receive their reward."[210]
. . . Laban refers to the scholar (talmid ḥakham, lit., "disciple of the
wise") who is a "Jewish devil,"[211] who studies only in order to boast
and to controvert others. Of a scholar of this sort do the Sages say that
"a carcass is better than he."[212]

It is well known that one is called a scholar only if he studies the
Oral Law. One who studies only Scripture is not called a scholar; for
this he must be conversant with the Talmud and the Codes. Now,
when one studies without knowledge (daat), he is called Laban, on
account of the deviousness which enters into him.[213] He then despises
and persecutes the zaddikim, both the Higher Zaddik and the Lower
Zaddik. For the Shekhinah dwells between two zaddikim, as it is written in the Zohar on the verse *the righteous (zaddikim) shall inherit the
land* (Ps. 37:29), that it refers to *two* zaddikim.[214] These two zaddikim
are the Higher Zaddik, who initiates new interpretations in the Oral
Torah, and the Lower Zaddik who studies these novellae.[215] Now, the
Oral Torah is known as the Shekhinah, as it is written: Malkhut is represented by the mouth (peh), and is called the Oral Torah (torah she-
be'al peh).[216] Now, when the Shekhinah, which is called the Oral
Torah,[217] enters into a scholar who is a "Jewish devil," this is known as

---

210. Eruvin 22a.
211. A term of opprobrium applied by the Zohar (III, 253) to students of Torah who
abuse the Torah and distort its ends in their studies. The term was used often by R.
Yaakov Yosef of Polennoye in his polemical writings.
212. Leviticus Rabbah 1:15. The full statement reads: "A scholar who has no knowledge (daat), a carcass is better than he."
213. Laban is notorious in Jewish tradition for his dishonesty and treachery. One who
possesses learning without daat ("knowledge"), i.e., one who misuses his intelligence,
is identified by R. Nahman as Laban.
214. Zohar I, 153b and 245b.
215. See Additional Note *15.
216. *Tikkunei Zohar,* second introduction. Malkhut, the last and lowest of the sefirot,
represents the culmination of the divine will to be revealed. It is thus symbolized by
the mouth (in the diagramming of the sefirot according to the pattern of Adam
Kadmon, the primordial man), which is the culmination of the process which begins
with the initial thought and culminates in speech. Here it is also identified with the
Oral Torah—Mishnah and Talmud and its literature—which in Hebrew is literally
"Torah of the mouth."
217. Shekhinah is identified, throughout the Kabbalah, with the sefirah of Malkhut,
and hence is also known as the Oral Torah.

the exile of the Shekhinah.[218] Then it uses its "mouth" to speak ill of the zaddik, etc.

When a man studies, in sanctity and purity, some law or halakhic decision taught by a tanna or other righteous man (*zaddik*), this comes in the category of "kissing,"[219] and "kissing" means the cleaving together (*hitdabkut*) of spirit with spirit. Now this halakhic decision is the "speech" of the tanna, and speech is the vitality of a man; for the verse *and the man became a living soul (nefesh ḥayah)* (Gen. 2:7), Onkelos translates, "a speaking spirit." This "speaking spirit," i.e., the *living soul*, derives from the Oral Torah, as it is written, *Let the earth bring forth nefesh ḥayah (the living creature)* (Gen. 1:20).[220]

Hence, when the tanna formulates his new interpretation, and utters it, this utterance itself is in the category of Oral Torah, for that is its origin, as it is written, *Let the earth bring forth nefesh ḥayah*. When we now learn this new interpretation, and introduce this teaching and this new interpretation into our mouth, we are in effect linking ourselves (*middabbekim*) to the spirit of the zaddik, i.e., the originator of the teaching, with the "speaking spirit," i.e., with the speech of the one who is now studying this interpretation. This is the cleaving of "spirit unto spirit," which is called "kissing." Thus, when we study a law which the tannaim taught, the spirit of the tanna thereby cleaves to the spirit of the student, and it is as if the student and the tanna kissed.

But when a scholar who is a "Jewish devil" studies Talmud or a halakhic decision, of him Scripture says, *the kisses of an enemy are importunate* (Prov. 27:6). For the tanna cannot bear the spirit of such a scholar who is a "Jewish devil," for who can bear to kiss a carcass, much more so one than whom a carcass is better?!

And even with regard to zaddikim who have gone to the other world, when we study their teachings of Torah, we thereby cause our spirits to cleave to theirs, as the Sages taught, "Their lips move in the grave,"[221] this being accomplished by the category of "kissing."

---

218. This is a concept often dealt with in the Kabbalah. See Zohar II, 14b, 216b; III, 75b. For talmudic use of the term, see Megillah 29a. R. Nahman here uses the concept to attack mitnaggedic scholars who defame the "true zaddikim."
219. See Zohar III, 220a.
220. R. Nahman here identifies the Oral Torah as the "earth" or "ground" from which issues speech-vitality.
221. Yevamot 97a, "When a tradition is recited, in this world, in the name of scholars [who have died], their lips move in the grave."

34. A NEGATIVE EFFECT OF THE ZADDIK
Source: R. Yitzhak Yehudah Yehiel of Komarno, Hekhal ha-Berakhah to Shelah, p. 103a

It is known from our master the divine Baal Shem Tov that when a zaddik commits a small sin he causes a plain man to commit a grave sin.[222] Thus it happened once the Besht saw one of the common people desecrate the Sabbath and he began to groan exceedingly over it. He was wondering in what way he himself violated the Sabbath to cause another Jew to desecrate the Sabbath so openly. And it was revealed to him from heaven that he made profane use of a scholar (*talmid ḥakham*) whose designation is "Sabbath."[223] And for a man of the Besht's caliber this was considered desecration of the Sabbath.[224]

The Zaddik as Provider of *Shefa* and *Devekut*

35. ATTACHING ONESELF TO THE ZADDIK
Source: R. Yaakov Yosef of Polennoye, Tzafnat Pa'ane'aḥ, p. 128

The purpose of all is, *and to Him shalt thou cleave* (Deut. 10:20). However, the Sages interpreted this by saying: "Is it, then, possible to cleave unto Him, about whom it is said that *the Lord thy God is a devouring fire* (Deut. 4:24)? The verse means, then, cleave to Torah scholars (*talmidei ḥakhamim*)."[225]

---

222. See *Toledot Yaakov Yosef* to Ki Tetze, sec. 3, "I heard from my master [the Besht] that any little sin committed by the head of the generation (*zaddik ha-dor*) may cause the common man of his generation to commit a major transgression."
223. Zohar III, 29b, "A scholar (*talmid ḥakham*) is like the Sabbath day." To abuse a scholar, such as sending him on a worldly errand, etc., is thus akin to desecrating the Sabbath.
224. The author relates other instances to prove his point.
225. Ketubbot 111b. The quotation is not entirely accurate. Actually, the verse the Talmud comments upon is in Deut. 4:4 ("But ye who cleave unto the Lord your God are alive every one of you this day") and specifies that this cleaving is to be accomplished by marrying one's daughter to a Torah scholar (*talmid ḥakham*), engaging in business on his behalf, and benefiting him from one's own resources. The author apparently refers here not to the talmudic comment on this verse but to the comment by Sifre to an identical verse (Deut. 11:22), "And to cleave unto Him." Here the Sifre asks the same question as the Talmud (loc. cit.) and replies: "It means necessarily to cleave to the scholars and their disciples, and He will credit you as if you ascended to heaven [i.e., as if you cleave to Him]" (Sifre, Ekev 13). Talmudic and midrashic references to Torah scholars (*talmidei ḥakhamim*) are often interpreted in hasidic literature, and especially by R. Yaakov Yosef, as referring to zaddikim. See above, selection 3, that the zaddik must also be a Torah scholar and see Additional Note *16.

We must seek to understand why the Sages explained the verse in a manner other than its plain meaning. For Scripture states *and to Him shalt thou cleave,* literally to cleave to God. Yet they interpreted that to mean that we must cleave to the scholars.

However, this is not really a difficulty. For in man there exists a dwelling place for God, as it is written, *And I shall dwell among them* (Exod. 25:8).[226] It is the righteous man (*zaddik*) who is called "the temple of the Lord" and "the sanctuary of the Lord" in which the Lord dwells, as is well known from the writings of our earlier Sages. Now, when a man attaches himself to the scholar (*talmid ḥakham*), in whom the Shekhinah dwells, he is *ipso facto* attached to Him in actuality.

Thus we may understand the verse *And they believed in the Lord and in His servant Moses* (Exod. 14:31). They believed in God by their faith and *devekut* in Him. But, as the Talmud asked, how is it possible to cleave to Him in *devekut*? Therefore Scripture explains: *and in His servant Moses.* For whoever believes in and cleaves to the "shepherd of Israel,"[227] is *ipso facto* in *devekut* with Him, as the Sages commented.

This will explain why the Sages interpreted the verse *Thou shalt fear the Lord thy God* (Deut. 10:20) to mean: "including the Torah scholars."[228] For the scholar is called "sanctuary" and "fear." And that we must fear the sanctuary is explicit in the Torah; thus, *and ye shall reverence* (fear) *My sanctuary* (Lev. 19:30). Thus too is it written, concerning Amalek, *and he feared not God* (Deut. 25:18).[229] Understand this.

In this manner we may understand the verse *and I will hide My face from them* (Deut. 31:17). The *talmidei ḥakhamim* are known as the "face of God," and it is they whom God will hide from Israel, i.e., their punishment will be that I will deny them physicians of the soul because they humiliate the Torah scholars.[230] Consequently, *and many evils and troubles shall come upon them, so that they will say on that day, are not these evils come upon me because my God is not within me* (Deut. 31:17)—the latter phrase referring to the Torah scholars, for the Jews failed to

226. The verse should have read, "Let them make Me a sanctuary and I shall dwell *in it*," namely, the Sanctuary. Instead, the verse reads *"among them,"* implying the indwelling of divinity in man or, in the specific interpretation of our author, the zaddik who symbolized the sanctuary.
227. That is, Moses, who is here taken as the archetype of the *talmid ḥakham*—zaddik.
228. Pesahim 22b.
229. Is this an implied criticism of the mitnaggedim?
230. The Torah scholars (*talmidei ḥakhamim*) are "the physicians of the soul." See n. 195 above.

cleave to them, and thus they did not cleave to Him. That is why *all these evils are upon us*, etc.[231]

36. THE ZADDIK AS A VEHICLE FOR SHEFA
Source: R. Yaakov Yosef of Polennoye, *Toledot Yaakov Yosef* to Aharei, sec. 6

I heard from my teacher the Besht concerning the mishnah that says: "He with whom the spirit of mankind is pleased (*noḥaḥ*), with him the spirit of the Omnipresent (God) also is pleased."[232] As I have mentioned elsewhere, man is called a microcosm (*olam katan*). All of Israel is included in this maxim;[233] one is considered the head, and another the foot. So those who are called the heads of the generation are "the eyes of the assembly."[234] When the head of the generation makes himself a vehicle (*merkavah*) for the bestowal of the Divine Spirit (Shekhinah), then from him the Divine Spirit issues forth to the rest of the generation. Thus it is said the "the spirit of the Omnipresent is pleased" (*noḥaḥ*) in the sense of "bestowed on him." The spirit of God reposes[235] on the whole world by means of the zaddik. Such too is the meaning of "the spirit of mankind is pleased with him."[236]

The converse is also true: When the spirit does not repose on the world, he should not blame his generation. The fault is his, the zaddik's.[237] This, then, is the meaning of the latter part of the mishnah: "He in whom the spirit of his fellow men finds no delight, in him the spirit of the Omnipresent takes no delight." Here again it does not

---

231. See Additional Note *17.
232. Avot 3:13.
233. R. Yaakov Yosef refers to the Jewish people, rather than to an individual, as a microcosm, as the term is normally used. See next selection. The use of the analogy to depict certain individuals or classes as eyes, head, feet, etc., is more appropriate to the macroanthropos than to the microcosm concept. But the result, the purpose of the author's homily, is the same, see Additional Note *18.
234. Cf. above, n. 187.
235. The word *noḥaḥ* ("is pleased") means, in R. Yaakov Yosef's interpretations, "reposes on, bestows upon," and not, as the commentators on the Mishnah read it in context, as meaning "delight, pleasure," as in *rei'aḥ niḥo'aḥ* (Lev. 1:9 et passim).
236. This is how R. Yaakov Yosef understands the above-quoted mishnah according to his interpretation of the word *noḥaḥ*, giving at the same time a different twist to the word *heimennu*. In the new context, it is meant as an explanation of the first part of the sentence: When [God's] spirit [i.e., His *shefa*, or grace] is bestowed on mankind, it is through him [the zaddik] or because of him (*mimmennu*). Cf. the next selection and n. 241.
237. Ibid.

refer really to delight but to the bestowal of *shefa*. Namely, if mankind is deprived of the *shefa* because the spirit of the Omnipresent does not rest on the zaddik, it is the zaddik's fault; he, and not the generation, is the cause of it.

Though this is not the precise language of the Besht it is, in any event, his implication; and *the words of a wise man's mouth are gracious* (Eccles. 10:12).

37. FOR THE LOVE OF THE ZADDIK
Source: R. Yitzhak Yehudah Yehiel of Komarno, Notzer Hesed to Avot 3:13

Man is a microcosm ("small world"). One is a head; another one, a foot.[238] The heads of the generation are called *the eyes of the assembly* (Lev. 4:13).[239] When the head of the generation finds himself in wonderful *devekut* and great illumination, and he becomes a vehicle (*merkavah*) for the Shekhinah—i.e., he has reached a state when his study of Torah, prayer, and the performance of the commandments are fulfilled with divine illumination and marvelous *devekut*, which in turn, brings down upon him divine grace, light, and vitality—then these same qualities expand to include the people of his generation who are attached to him. They too become part of his chariot (*merkavah*) and his intellectual concentration on divinity (*mohin*). The same may apply to those who, although not attached to him, at least are not his adversaries.

This is the meaning of the statement in the Mishnah, "He with whom the spirit of the Omnipresent (God) is pleased."[240] The words *nohah heimennu* should be understood not as "is pleased with," but "are pleased because of him." Hence the Mishnah tells us: When the people's spirit is pleased and inspired, it is surely from him–the *talmid hakham*, the zaddik. It is from his light that all people are illuminated.[241] For he is the channel through which divine grace and good will

---

238. See n. 233 above.
239. See above, selection 25 and n. 187; also selection 36, where R. Yaakov Yosef quotes the Besht on this, adding, "and all of Israel is included in this maxim." R. Yitzhak Yehudah Yehiel proceeds to interpret the mishnah in Avot 3:10 in a similar vein. However, while the basic idea is the same, the details and the conclusions are not.
240. Avot 3:13.
241. R. Yitzhak Yehudah Yehiel seems also to suggest a different interpretation of the word *kol* at the beginning of the tannaitic statement, meaning "all" rather than "anyone." In Hasidism generally, the term *kol*, which is the kabbalistic term for the sefirah of Yesod (Foundation), is used to refer to the zaddik, who is referred to as *Yesod*

descend upon all the world and extend to all people of his generation. And the tanna proceeds to explain why this is so because the spirit of God, the divine light which emanates to all of his generation, is brought on by him and through him.

As a general rule, however, the spirit and illuminating power of the zaddik affect and inspire only those of his generation who are favorably disposed toward him. They have no complaint against him, and his deeds are sweet to them. Which brings us back to the original meaning of the tanna's statement: Anyone, namely any zaddik of whom it is the case that the people are pleased with him, and hence become attached to him lovingly, with heart and soul, the spirit of God too is pleased with him, causing divine grace and light to rest on all those who cleave to him. But those people who are displeased with him, thus showing no inclination to bind themselves to him with heart and soul, may have no benefit from the divine spirit emanating through him, for it has no effect on those who are displeased with the zaddik and thus unwilling to bind themselves to him.

38. THE ZADDIK AS INTERMEDIARY
Source: R. Elimelekh of Lizhensk, Noam Elimelekh to Bo, s.v. bo el par'oh

The blessed and exalted Creator takes great pleasure in doing good and bestowing *shefa* (grace) upon all the world and upon all creatures.

However, because the Creator's *shefa* is so great, it is impossible to receive it except through an intermediary. This intermediary is the zaddik, who receives the *shefa* from above and in turn bestows it even upon those who are not worthy or qualified to receive it directly. Thus, when the zaddik bestows *shefa*, he is like one who does a favor (*hesed*) to the whole world, for he receives this grace from above and distributes it to all below. But the source of this grace is the blessed Creator.

This is the meaning of the verse *Alone He works great marvels* (Ps. 136:4): the Holy One does marvels by Himself for His people Israel. *For His mercy endures forever* (ibid.). This means that God's grace *le'olam*

(*zaddik yesod olam*). This is so because the zaddik binds the souls of all Israelites to their roots. He thus incorporates within himself "the whole assembly of Israel." (See *Toledot Yaakov Yosef* to Vayak'hel, sec. 1.) Hence the term *kol* may at times refer simultaneously to the zaddik and to all of Israel, which may be the case here according to the author's interpretation of the Mishnah.

("to the world")[242] is brought about by the zaddik's favor [rather than *His mercy*).[243] . . .

Now, when the zaddik, who bestows *shefa*, first wishes to receive this divine grace from above, he must conduct himself with great humility. Afterwards, while bestowing grace on the world, he spreads out expansively in order to bestow grace on the world. He is like a man who walks expansively through all his rooms and attics and bringing into them all he owns in order to fill them with all that is good.[244]

AFTERWORD

There is thus a two-step process in the zaddik's role in transferring the *shefa*. The first was learned by R. Elimelekh from his teacher the Maggid (see *Maggid Devarav le-Yaakov*, no. 83, ed. Schatz-Uffenheimer, pp. 144-146) and it is essentially a theosophical point with moral consequences: the *shefa* issuing from the Infinite is incapable to being absorbed by finite and mortal creatures. Hence it must undergo the process of *tzimtzum*, or contraction. The locating and tapping of the resources in this severely contracting *shefa* is reserved for the zaddik. In response to the divine mystical *tzimtzum*, the zaddik must experience ethical and psychological retreat and self-constriction, i.e., humility.

The second step, here introduced by R. Elimelekh, adds the social dimension to the zaddik's *shefa* function. He must now "expand," in the sense of communicating with his community and involving himself in their affairs in order to bring the *shefa* to them. Note that the theory of the intermediacy of the zaddik is discussed in only one direction, i.e., from God to man, and not from man to God. By this I mean that there is no discussion of the role of the zaddik in bringing the Jew's prayer to God; apparently, every Jew can do that by himself. Rather, the major function of the zaddik is to increase the *shefa*, and thus act as an advocate and helper of the people by expanding the volume of divine goodness toward Israel.

---

242. The author here plays on the word *le'olam*, which in biblical Hebrew means "(endures) forever," but in later Hebrew takes on a spatial rather than temporal significance. Hence, "to the world."

243. *Ḥesed* is used both in the original sense of "mercy" or "love," and in the derivative sense of a "favor," as in *gemilat ḥesed*.

244. The expansiveness referred to in this passage should not be confused with arrogance or conceit. It implies, rather, a beneficient outgoingness, as opposed to the withdrawal and retreat into one's self by the man of humility and meekness.

39. INTELLECTUAL SUBMISSION TO THE ZADDIK
Source: R. Nahman of Bratslav, Likkutei Moharan I, 123

The root and the foundation on which everything depends is that one bind himself to the zaddik of the generation and accept his words on any subject without departing from his words, heaven forbid, right or left; to cast off from himself all his prior learning, and to remove his mind from it as if he has no thoughts except what he receives from the true zaddik and rebbe. As long as there remains with him some of his own thinking, he has not attained perfection and he is not bound to the zaddik.[245]

The Descent of the Zaddik

40. IDENTIFYING WITH THE ZADDIK
Source: R. Yaakov Yosef of Polennoye, Toledot Yaakov Yosef to Aharei, sec. 5

The commandment *that he* (Aaron) *come not at all times into the holy place . . . Herewith shall Aaron come into the holy place* (Lev. 16:2–3) may be explained by means of the composite verse that results when the following two phrases are combined: *When the leader sins* (Lev. 4:22) *for the guilt of the people* (Lev. 4:3). . . .

In my humble opinion this fits my explanation of the talmudic ruling, "Anyone who is not obligated in the performance of a commandment cannot, by his performance, relieve others of their obligation."[246] This is in accordance with the Yerushalmi: "Samuel the prophet wore

---

245. Here the author is stretching the doctrine of *mesirat ha-maḥashavot la-zaddik* ("relegating one's thoughts to the zaddik") to the extreme. As mentioned earlier (see above, n. 190), this idea first developed and advanced by R. Yaakov Yosef caused a tremendous uproar among opponents of Hasidism, who saw in it a form of idolatry. The present selection from R. Nahman represents an even more radical version of this innovation.

246. Rosh Hashanah 29a. This ruling is classically understood to refer to positive commandments. Hence the permission of having only one Jew perform a mitzvah and by his act relieving other Jews (who are in attendance and wish to associate themselves with his mitzvah performance) from actually performing it would apply only when the performer is himself obligated to do it. In this instance, the mitzvah is accredited to the others just as if they had actually done it themselves. (The ruling is based on the concept that "all Israelites are responsible for each other"; see Rashi ad loc.) The author gives this ruling an additional interpretation involving sin. Only he who bears guilt himself can help others to be raised out of their guilt. The basis for

the cloak of Israel and said, 'I sinned.'"[247] as mentioned in the parable of the minister of state who changed his garment.[248]

This may be explained as follows: The guilt of the people who commit a deliberate sin causes the heads of the generation to sin unintentionally, so that they may have some connection with the people in their state or level of sin in order to be able to raise them from their level. This is similar to what I wrote on the verse *And Moses was angry* (Num. 31:14): "Perhaps you relapsed to worship the idol Peor."[249] . . . We know that he who is angry, it is as if he worshipped idols.[250]

Such an approach gives the zaddik an opening to which to connect his repentance so as to repair all those low spiritual levels, both his own and the people's. And so does the Talmud teach: "When an individual repents, he himself is forgiven, and the whole world is forgiven too."[251] This is effective when he has linked himself with them on their level.[252]

This thesis also explains the words of King David, peace be on him, *And you will forgive my sin, for it is numerous* (Ps. 25:11) and, in chapter 65 (v. 4), *Sins have overwhelmed me, our sins You will forgive*. Now this

this interpretation is that the word *ḥayyav* ("*kol ha-meḥuyyav be-davar*") used in this ruling has two meanings: (a) obligated (as in the performance of a commandment), and (b) guilty (as of sin).

247. J.T. Ta'anit 2:7.
248. A parable often used by R. Yaakov Yosef. A minister of state disguises himself as a lay person in order to "reach" the prince who has sinned so that he may inspire him to return to the king. The zaddik acts likewise. Cf. above, selection 27 and note 197.
249. See Shabbat 64a.
250. Zohar III, 179a. The author explains the sin of Moses, who lost his temper and is considered, hyperbolically, tantamount to idol worship. It is precisely because of this equivalency that Moses was able to relate to the people's sin of the worship of Baal Peor while engaged in the war in Midian, and thus raise them out of it
251. Yoma 86b.
252. As understood classically, this talmudic passage is meant to exalt the merits of *teshuvah* (repentance), in that not only is the penitent individual forgiven but God in His mercy forgives others because of the merits of his repentance. R. Yaakov Yosef sees in this dictum proof for his thesis that the repentance of the zaddik helps bring forgiveness for all people. This, of course, is the reason why he, the zaddik, sinned in the first place, so as to be able to identify with them on their level, and thereafter to elevate them along with him. Elsewhere (*Toledot Yaakov Yosef* to Vayak'hel, sec. 1) the author writes that the zaddik must himself be aroused to *teshuvah* first and then it becomes easy for him to persuade all of his generation to *teshuvah*, since the zaddik is the foundation (*yesod*) of his generation. But he must take care to persuade them softly, leading them gently—holding their hand, so to speak. However, if he acts offensively to them, then "there is no cure for his wound."

poses a difficulty. Quite the contrary, if the sins are numerous, heaven forbid, is this a reason to be forgiven? Also, why is *overwhelmed me* in the singular, and afterward *our sin* in the plural?

But according to the above this is understood. The sin that happened to him was not appropriate for him by his own nature; the reason that he sinned was in order to attain some relationship with the masses because, as I explained the mentioned talmudic ruling, only the "guilty" can absolve others.[253] Thus the words of David can be understood: *You will forgive my sin*, which came about *because it is numerous*, i.e., for there are many people at this level and I have to elevate them.[254] This also explains the second verse mentioned: Sins have overwhelmed me, so that *our sins you will forgive*.[255]

Accordingly, we may explain the talmudic passage, that really David was not capable of committing that act, i.e., the sin with Bathsheba. The only reason he committed the sin was to teach the people of Israel how to do *teshuvah*.[256] . . . According to our interpretation, this works out well. For David immediately realized that the sin occurred to him for the sake of others—to elevate them through identifying with his repentance.[257]

Now, one might, heaven forbid, fall into the error of thinking that he should sin intentionally so that he may identify with the lower lev-

---

253. Note the expression "happened to him" (*she-nizdamen lo*), which connotes even less than an unintentional sin. This seems to imply, as does the whole doctrine espoused by R. Yaakov Yosef, that the zaddik himself is not capable of sin at all. The only reason he "chances upon" sin is in order to help raise the people out of their sin. Cf. above, selection 31 and note 203, where R. Nahman of Bratslav expresses a similar view about Jews generally, and see Avodah Zarah 4b.

254. The simple meaning of the verses is that the *sins* are numerous. R. Yaakov Yosef, however, explains that the *people* who sin are numerous, i.e., the masses and their intentional transgressions are the cause of the unintentional sin of the zaddik. Hence the word *ki*, with the second half of the verse explaining the first.

255. Thus the grammatical problem is solved. I sinned (singular) so that the masses' sins (plural) be forgiven along with my repentance and subsequent forgiveness.

256. Avodah Zarah 4b.

257. R. Yaakov Yosef thus goes a step further than the Talmud. David sinned not just in order to teach the people *how* to repent, but that through his repentance the people were *actually brought to a state of* penitence; they were raised from their low level of sin to spiritual heights along with him (the zaddik), and thereby they too were forgiven.

els in order to raise them, as the heretics have erred.[258] It is for this reason that the verse says, *That he come not at all times into the holy place.* It means so say that, *To everything there is a season* (time) (Eccles. 3:1), and there are fourteen good "times" and fourteen bad "times,"[259] for God so created the good and the bad to counterbalance each other.[260] Thus it is written, *that he come not*, intentionally, *at all times*, including also bad times, i.e., to commit a sin willingly, heaven forbid, so that through it he will identify with those low levels to elevate them "to the holy." For this is complete heresy.[261]

41. THE ZADDIK'S "EQUIVALENT SINNING"
Source: R. Elimelekh of Lizhensk, Noam Elimelekh to Vaeira, s.v. re'eh netatikha

And the Lord said unto Moses, "See, I have set thee in God's stead to Pharaoh" (Exod. 7:1). One ought to understand what the words *see* (*re'eh*) and *God's stead* mean.

The zaddik wants to elevate a base man and separate him from his folly and lowliness. But he cannot break down this foolishness except with something that is somewhat similar to it. This means that the zaddik must descend a bit from his spiritual level and place himself in a situation somewhat similar to that of the base man.

Now, Pharaoh asserted that he was a god, as Rashi explains in his comment on the verse *Lo, he goeth out unto the water* (Exod. 7:15).[262]

---

258. The reference here is to the Sabbateans and Frankists, who affirmed the doctrine of the holy sin (see G. Scholem, "Redemption Through Sin" in *The Messianic Idea in Judaism*). The followers of Shabbetai Zevi maintained that he intentionally lowered himself to the depths of the *kelipah* by converting to Islam in order to retrieve the "sparks." R. Yaakov Yosef is warning against carrying his doctrine to this radical extreme. He is not advocating that the zaddik sin intentionally in order to elevate the masses. He is simply explaining the phenomenon that the unintentional sin of the zaddik may serve this lofty purpose of universal dimensions.
259. In Eccles. 3:2–8 there are altogether twenty-eight repetitions of the word *et* ("time"), referring to a variety of actions, situations, and feelings during a man's lifetime. Fourteen of these are positive times, and fourteen negative.
260. See Eccles. 7:14.
261. R. Yaakov Yosef proceeds accordingly to quote the Mishnah: "If one says, 'I will sin and I will repent,' . . . he is not given the opportunity to repent" (Yoma 8:9). It refers, he indicates, to the one who says, "I will sin intentionally so to help the lower levels of man repent alongside with him." See also above selection 27 and nn. 196–197.
262. Rashi ad loc., s.v. *hinneh*: "He [Pharaoh] goes to the Nile to attend to his physical needs before daybreak (then no one can see him) because he pretends to be a god, having no such needs."

Therefore, the Lord said to Moses: *See, I have set thee in God's stead* (lit., I have set you as a god) *to Pharaoh*. You must perform before Pharaoh signs and miracles, acts of a divine nature. Through this performance you will break down his foolishness that makes him regard himself as a god, because he will think that *you* are a god.

"Therefore, *see (re'eh)*, i.e., pay careful attention to this so that you will not become arrogant, heaven forbid."[263] This in essence is the meaning of the talmudic maxim, "An intentional transgression is better than a commandment done not for its own sake."[264] The zaddik must descend from his level to break down the base man's folly, thus purposely transgressing. For example, if someone is a habitual liar, the zaddik must neutralize him with something similar. Certainly this does not mean that the zaddik should lie, heaven forbid. Rather, we find that our Sages permitted a scholar to conceal his knowledge of a tractate.[265] Or, similarly, the zaddik denies that he is a zaddik, although this is a lie because he really is. He purposely transgresses in order to break the liar's strength.

According to the Gemara, "Truth said, 'Let man not be created, because he is compounded of falsehood'; righteousness (*zedek*) said, 'Let him be created.'"[266] That is the meaning of *I have preached righteousness (zedek) in the great congregation* (Ps. 40:10). Where there is a great congregation, it is impossible that there should not be one liar amongst them. The zaddik raises him—the liar—from his foolishness and falsehood by descending into a state similar to his, as was described before. Thus the zaddik becomes a "preacher of righteousness (*zedek*), which, [i.e., *zedek*], propitiously said, "Let him be created."

42. THE ZADDIK'S SELF-SACRIFICE
Source: R. Elimelekh of Lizhensk, Noam Elimelekh to Shemini, s.v. va-yissa Aharon

The zaddik is constantly in a state of *devekut*, and is attached to the higher worlds. However, because he always yearns for the welfare of

---

263. That is to say, "do not forget that you are merely a mortal playing the role of God." The author indicates here the potential danger of the zaddik's descent to sin, even unintentionally. For even Moses, renowned for his inimitable modesty, had to be warned not to become proud when appearing as a "god" before Pharaoh.
264. Nazir 23b.
265. Bava Metzia 23b. This is done out of modesty; see Rashi ad loc., s.v. *be-masekhet*.
266. Actually this is not found in the Talmud but in Genesis Rabbah 8:5.

Israel, that the blessed Lord may favor them with all kinds of *shefa* and blessing, he descends somewhat from his high spiritual station and from his *devekut*. Nevertheless, he does good by descending somewhat from his *devekut*, for when people notice how great is his longing and his desire for their welfare, he implants within their hearts the fear and the love of God, so that they are all moved to serve God. . . .

In order to bring blessing upon the people, the zaddik must come down from his level. For the level of the zaddik is one of constant self-examination, in which he is concerned lest he committed even some minor infraction or entertained some sinful thoughts. . . . He thinks at all times thoughts of repentance. . . . The zaddik, by virtue of his *devekut*, establishes peace amongst the heavenly hosts. Still, because of his longing to bestow *shefa* upon his people, he is willing to descend somewhat from his exalted spiritual level.[267]

43. THE ZADDIK AND HIS "HOUSEHOLD"
Source: R. Elimelekh of Lizhensk, Noam Elimelekh to Shemot, s.v. o yomar al pi

An alternative interpretation may be given to the verse *And these are the names of the sons of Israel who came into Egypt with Jacob* (Exod. 1:1).

The spirituality of a man and his soul are referred to as "names."[268] A name, such as Reuben or Simeon, refers to a man's soul and not [only] to his body.

The proof of this matter is that a sleeping person can be awakened far more easily by calling his name than by arousing him bodily without calling his name. This is because when one sleeps, the soul rises and departs from the body; that is why it is more difficult to wake him by physically shaking him than by calling his name.[269]

The verse *And these are the names of the sons of Israel* may thus be explained as follows: The Torah wonders, how is it that these holy zaddikim, who are called "Israel,"[270] the highest level of holiness, *came*

---

267. For a fuller conception of this form of descent and self-sacrifice of the zaddik, see the introduction to this chapter, "Descent of the Zaddik."

268. See Zohar I, 83a; III, 121b. Cf. I. Tishby, *Mishnat ha-Zohar*, vol. 2, pp. 134–138. See also *Toledot Yaakov Yosef* to Shemot 2.

269. Calling one's name is tantamount to summoning his soul to return, since his name represents his soul, which is not the case when he is touched physically.

270. "Israel" connotes a higher spiritual level than "Jacob"; see. e.g., Gen. 32:28 and cf. Nahmanides to Gen. 46:2.

into Egypt, i.e., descended to the level of Egypt?[271] The answer to that is that they came *with Jacob*, i.e., they lowered themselves for the sake of the common people who are called "Jacob."[272] For the zaddik must descend from his high spiritual station so that he may become attached to the common people and thereby elevate them to holiness. Indeed, if such were not the case, the zaddik would have no connection with the people.

The verse proceeds to explain how the zaddik goes about raising the common people to holiness. Every man came to Egypt *with his household* (Exodus, loc. cit.). The zaddik is called "man," and his inwardness is called "his household." When the zaddik stimulates his inner spiritual resources, he arouses likewise the inner resources of the common people, and thus they rise together to greater levels of holiness.

This is the meaning of *I will give great thanks to the Lord with my mouth and praise Him among the multitude* (Ps. 109:30). That is because thought determines everything. It supersedes speech, because one can encompass in his thought much more than he can express orally. Nevertheless, King David, of blessed memory, said, *I will give great thanks unto the Lord with my mouth*, which means, "Although it is impossible to express all my thoughts, still *I will give great thanks to God with my mouth*, which is of a lower spiritual sphere. Why so? Because I seek to *praise Him among the multitudes*—to extol His name among the many, i.e., the ordinary people.

For when a zaddik descends to a lower spiritual level, it enables him to lift up the common people to a higher station of spirituality and holiness.

ADDITIONAL NOTES

*1   Elsewhere I have pointed out my disagreement with Scholem in his article in *Molad*, p. 217, cited above n. 10 who holds that R. Elimelekh turned *devekut* into a social value only by linking it to the institutions of zaddikism, a connection completely foreign to early Hasidism. See my *Torah Lishmah*, p. 130f, n. 85, where I dis-

---

271. "Egypt" is the symbol of evil, corruption, and spiritual contamination.
272. Such an interpretation of this verse was already advanced by Nahmanides to Gen. 46:2. Nahmanides suggests that the reason God called him Jacob at that time, just as he was about to embark on his descent to Egypt, after He had told him, "Thy name shall be called no more Jacob, but Israel" (Gen. 32:28), is that Egypt represents descent from spiritual heights to slavery. Nahmanides then proceeds to expound the first verse in Exodus, dealt with here, in a similar manner.

prove this thesis with quotations from R. Levi Yitzhak of Berdichev and R. Yitzhak Isaac Yehiel Safrin, the Komarno Rebbe.

*2   I believe that Weiss (*Mehkarim be-Hasidut Bratslav,* pp. 93–95) is in error in drawing a firm distinction between the two schools in Hasidism regarding the zaddik: the mystic, represented by the Maggid and Habad, and the faith school, represented by R. Nahman of Bratslav. For the Maggid and Habad, Weiss, maintains, the zaddik is merely an exceptional personality. Bratslav, however, was very extravagant in emphasizing the role of the zaddik: the zaddik is a phenomenal occurrence, a singular personality in the world who is its hidden leader, the paradoxical zaddik-Messiah in whose hand all is given over. There is, at the least, an apparent misunderstanding on his part of the Bratslav view, in light of what has been demonstrated here on the basis of the source material.

*3   Jacobs, in his "Doctrine of the Zaddik," translates the relevant passage as "born in a state of sanctity because his father had holy thoughts at the moment of his conception." This appears to be a misinterpretation of the worlds *kadosh me-rehem* used by R. Elimelekh. Jacobs's conclusion that in R. Elimelekh's scheme the "self-made" zaddik is less advanced than the preordained zaddik needs some modification. While it is true that the latter may rise faster, he may also fall more forcefully because he takes himself for granted, thus falling prey to conceit. The self-achieved zaddik (*ha-zaddik me-atzmo*), having struggled so hard to attain his high level, is exceedingly careful not to dissipate his hard-earned status. See *Noam Elimelekh* to Naso, beginning. Cf. Nigal, introduction to *Noam Elimelekh,* p. 20–21.

*4   See Shatz, "Le-Mahuto shel ha-Zaddik," p. 371. Shatz points out that there is an echo here of the Sabbatean paradox (see also the passage from *Toledot,* selection 40, end), but with a distinct sense of moderation. The zaddik does not descend into the *kelipot* in order to destroy them; he goes down to the man himself who is caught up in the act of sin in order to save him (Shatz, loc. cit.). R. Yaakov Yosef (*Toledot Yaakov Yosef,* loc. cit.) refers to the Sabbateans as "complete heretics," for they allowed the intentional descent of the zaddik for the sake of "ascent," where he speaks of unintentional sin; or, if intentional sin is needed in order to form a union with the sinner for the purpose of his elevation, it must be a minor sin such as anger or the cessation of *devekut* (see introduction, "Descent of the Zaddik," last two paragraphs).

*5   Cf. Responsa *Divrei Hayyim* by R. Hayyim Halberstam of Sanz (a hasidic master and a younger contemporary of R. Nahman), pt. II, Yoreh De'ah 105: "I do not know why you doubt that *ruah ha-kodesh* exists even now for the one who deserves it, even though prophecy was abolished. . . . Even now, after the destruction of the Holy Temple, a spirit of prophecy rests on those that are worthy, namely, a holy spirit of wisdom; for prophecy is one thing and a holy spirit of wisdom (*ruah ha-kodesh de-hokhmah*) is something else. This [holy spirit of wisdom] was never abolished, and only a heretic will deny this." After proceeding to prove this view from the Talmud (loc. cit., that prophecy was "taken away" from the prophets, but not from the wise) and Maimonides (in his *Guide,* without stating the exact location) and Nahmanides, he concludes: "Even in our own time, the genuinely wise who do not indulge in the material have *ruah ha-kodesh.*"

    The author, however, speaks of "imaginative powers" for the zaddik, a quality that Maimonides ascribes to prophecy itself. See *Guide* 2:36. See more on this subject in the introduction to the chapter, "The Zaddik's Power," and nn. 48–49.

*6   For more on the subject of the zaddik accepting (and even requesting) material gifts for his spiritual services, see *Iggeret ha-Kodesh* of R. Elimelekh, published at the end of *Noam Elimelekh*, Nigal ed., p. 601. Cf. Nigal's introduction to *Noam Elimelekh*, pp. 38–39, and his review of the hasidic ideas of R. Kalonymos Kalman Epstein, R. Elimelekh's disciple, in "Mishnat ha-Hasidut be-*Sefer Maor va-Shemesh*," pp. 152–153, 158.

*7   The words *she-gilah retzono bi-levad* in the text can be read: "who merely revealed *His* will," implying that the prayer was simply a technique for disclosing the divine decree (so J. G. Weiss, *Hebrew Union College Annual*, 1960, p. 142). However, this would treat R. Hanina b. Dosa's prayer as a form of divination, which is entirely irrelevant to the point of the passage.

*8   A homiletic interpretation of the verse which is ordinarily translated, in context, as, "But wisdom, where shall it be found?" What is remarkable about this interpretation is that kabbalists have usually seen in this verse the identification of Keter ("Crown"), the highest sphere of the ten sefirot and the one immediately preceding Hokhmah, as Ayin ("Hokhmah is found from Ayin"). For the Maggid, however, Hokhmah is identified as Ayin, not derived from it. See Weiss, "Great Maggid's Theory," p. 139. For the Maggid to be able to identify Hokhmah as Ayin and the source of all else, it is necessary to accept the opinion of those kabbalists who considered Keter too remote and numinous to be included in the ten sefirot, and thus regarded Hokhmah as the first of the sefirot, adding Da'at as the third, immediately following Binah. (This is the schema of R. Shneur Zalman, who obviously got it from his teacher, the Maggid, and which is expressed in the acrostic "Habad.")

*9   J. G. Weiss, in his "Petitionary Prayer in Early Hasidism," contrasts the Maggid (in the preceding excerpts), for whom the contemplative act is thaumaturgically assured provided the technique is strictly followed, and for whom the element of causality thus converts the act into one of magic, with R. Elimelekh's approach, regarding the efficacy of the zaddik's prayer. The latter transformed the art of the zaddik (in his *hamtakat dinim* or *hishtannut*) "into a religious act," i.e., a genuine act of prayer, in which God can either accept or reject man's or the zaddik's supplication and thus was not theurgical.

Weiss cites part of the passage translated here as evidence of R. Elimelekh's attitude; and what is implicit here, is made explicit in the work of his students, especially in *Maor va-Shemesh*. In this passage R. Elimelekh does not even mention the zaddik, but it is fairly obvious that in discussing Moses and Aaron as opposed to the Egyptian magicians, he is alluding to the true zaddik as opposed to the sorcerer. Of course, it should not be expected that R. Elimelekh would quote the Maggid, his master, in order to disagree with him directly, even assuming Weiss is right in his analysis of the Maggid. However, see next Additional Note, on selection 16, regarding Weiss's interpretation of R. Elimelekh.

*10   This passage does not fully support the thesis of J. G. Weiss (see previous Additional Note) that whereas the Maggid's view of the zaddik's powers was "magical," R. Elimelekh's was "religious," and not a matter of theurgical causation. It is true that in many passages R. Elimelekh does indeed incline to a more "religious" view, but sometimes, as the current selection demonstrates, there do indeed appear theurgical elements.

*11   R. Elimelekh thus seems to offer two answers to the philosophic problem raised by Hasidism's ascription to the zaddik of the power of *hamtakat ha-dinim*

("sweetening of judgment"), the changing of divine decrees from harmful to beneficial. The first one is that by prayerful attachment to the sinner, the zaddik in effect
transforms the identity of the sinner to that of a zaddik, and thus the reality has been
changed, not the divine decree. This is not far removed from the traditional solution
to the problem of prayer as such, i.e., by praying, one changes oneself and hence the
original divine judgment no longer applies to him.

The second answer suggested by R. Elimelekh is far more radical. The zaddik is above
time and simultaneously subject to time. God, Who is above time and thus beyond
change, acts in the world, which is under time, through the zaddikim. The latter can,
as it were, exercise their spiritual powers so as to effect changes in the world, the *hamtakat ha-dinim*, by virtue of their spiritual superiority to the time-conditioned reality
of the world. "Change," as medieval Jewish philosophy insists, cannot be attributed
to God. According to R. Elimelekh, it is the zaddik to whom change applies.

Elsewhere R. Elimelekh suggests other solutions to the problem of prayer effecting
changes of God's will. To mention some: In one he explains that the soul of the zaddik soars so high during prayer that it reaches those worlds where there had never
been any decree of suffering and death because there only mercy reigns (*Noam
Elimelekh* to Vayetzei, s.v., *ve-yaakov*; in Nigal's edition, pp. 79 ff.).

According to another of his solutions, in a harsh decree of heaven only the letters of
the decree are created without forming any words, and the zaddik, by his prayers,
succeeds in combining those letters in a different order so as to form words of blessing rather than curse. But these Hebrew letters are the letters in which the Torah is
written, and the Torah is given in love. Consequently, only great love, of a kind
beyond the grasp of the ordinary man, can succeed in putting the letters together in
their right order so as to change the decree for good. The zaddik has that great love
for God and for all men, gentile as well as Jew. *Noam Elimelekh* to Vayetzei, s.v. *va-yisa*
(Nigal ed., pp. 74–75); cf. Jacobs, *Hasidic Prayer*, pp. 129–131.

*12   In a similar vein, R. Yaakov Yosef states that the Zaddik alone knows the soul
of the prayers. See *Toledot Yaakov Yosef* to Yitro, cited by Jacobs, *Hasidic Prayer*, pp.
131–132.

*13   A similar view regarding the zaddik's total separation from sexual lust is to be
found frequently in the writings of R. Elimelekh; e.g., see *Noam Elimelekh* to Bereshit,
s.v. *ve-ha-adam*, and in his letter to R. Zekhariah Mendel printed at the end of the
standard edition, pp. 112a, b (in Nigal's ed., pp. 603–604). Cf. L. Jacobs, *The Doctrine
of the Zaddik in the Thought of Elimelekh of Lizhensk*, and nn. 34–39 ad loc. See also the
introduction to this chapter, "Defining the Zaddik," and nn. 36–38.

*14   An identical view is expressed more elaborately by a non-hasidic luminary, a
contemporary of R. Nahman. R. Aryeh Leib ha-Kohen, the famous author of *Ketzot
ha-Hoshen* writes in his preference to *Shev Shemaateta*, s.v. *ha-neshamah*, that essentially a Jew is incapable of sinning and, if he did, to persist in it.

*15   R. Zev Wolf of Zhitomir, *Or ha-Meir* to Noah, s.v. *et kashti*, proposes a different theory about the two zaddikim of the Zohar. The Lower Zaddik (*zaddik tahton*) is
the one who brings delight to the Shekhinah by his scholarship of Torah and performance of mitzvot. The Higher Zaddik (*zaddik elyon*) is the one who can discover and
reveal Godliness even in the realm of the corporeal where such Godliness resides in
deep concealment. The Shekhinah receives more delight from the latter zaddik than
from the former.

*16   See A. Wertheim, *Halakhot ve-Halikhot ba-Ḥasidut*, pp. 161–164 (English ed., *Law and Custom in Hasidism*, pp. 241–246); T. Yslander, *Studien zum Beschtschen Hasidismus*, pp. 324–326; S. H. Dresner, *The Zaddik*, p. 130. Cf. Jacobs, *Hasidic Prayer*, p. 132–133.

*17   In his *Toledot Yaakov Yosef* to Yitro 6, the author expresses the same ideas in a much longer and more elaborate discussion, part of which was translated by Jacobs, *Hasidic Prayer*, pp. 131–132.

*18   See *Keter Shem Tov* (Kehot ed.), sec. 125. The part beginning "All of Israel . . ." appears in *Toledot Yaakov Yosef* in parentheses. It is, however, part of the regular text in *Keter Shem Tov*.

9

Worship Through Corporeality

INTRODUCTION

Worship through corporeality, or *avodah be-gashmiyut*, is one of the most important contributions of Hasidism to Jewish religious thought. The concept, which involves the service of God both in and through the profane world, follows from the monistic conception of *devekut* taught by the Besht. Most of the relevant concepts have been discussed in the introduction to chapter 4, to which the reader is cordially referred.

Worship through corporeality brought into the domain of religious significance the entire range of human activity, even beyond the considerable aspects of human life already covered by the mitzvot and the Halakhah—the forbidden and permitted and required. *Divrei reshut*—all that is neutral halakhically, that upon which Halakhah makes no explicit judgment but which occupies most of one's waking day—was now seen as a challenge and an opportunity to achieve *devekut* and thus to serve the Creator.

Eating is as good an example of *avodah be-gashmiyut* as any. As an intimate physical activity, the ingestion of food, no less than its evacuation, embarrassed the ancients. The Greeks solved the problem by means of aesthetics; they imposed etiquette on ingestion, thus validating it as an acceptable public exercise. Jewish tradition added a sacred dimension: the appropriate blessings before and after eating, attention to the dietary laws, etc. The response of Hasidism was *avo-*

dah be-gashmiyut: sanctifying the very act of eating itself, beyond the rules of "proper behavior" (*derekh eretz*) and Halakhah.

This idea of worship through corporeality addressed another problem as well. Hasidism had set for its adherents an enormously difficult challenge, that of uninterrupted *devekut*. How could such a high state of rapture or even fundamental God-consciousness be maintained when a myriad of prosaic and mundane details demanded attention in the course of each day? When these very mundane activities themselves became the vehicle for *devekut*, that problem disappeared. The physical or social involvements were exalted and the *devekut* was continued, albeit in a new form. Whether eating and drinking, plying one's trade or dealing in business, one must intend to release the "sparks" that vitalize all that exists and reveal the immanence of the Creator in His creation.

Worship through corporeality is thus an alternative form of prayer, study of Torah, or performing any of the other mitzvot, in the practice of *devekut*. The two universal states—the major state of "greatness" and the minor one of "smallness"—apply to *devekut* as well. The major state, that of heightened inspiration and directness, is *devekut* in the course of performing the mitzvot. This is referred to as *avodah be-ruḥaniyut*, worship through spirituality. This is the higher goal, even though it is easier to achieve than *avodah be-gashmiyut*. The lesser, minor form of *devekut*, is available to every Jew, not only the zaddik, but it is more difficult than that *devekut* which applies to doing the mitzvot, such as study or prayer, because the Evil Urge is stronger and more dominant in the material realm.

This worship through corporeality implies not the sacralization of the material world itself but (contra Buber; see the introduction to chap. 4) "binding oneself" to the divine immanence, the spiritual element, within the natural order. It is thus not Nature, but the spirituality that inheres in it, that is the focus of *avodah be-gashmiyut* which, as stated, is clearly inferior to *avodah be-ruḥaniyut*, the state of "greatness," and of which the former is derivative.[1]

---

1. See Rivkah Shatz, "Le-Mahuto shel ha-Zaddik ba-Ḥasidut," p. 368. For a contemporary application of this essential hasidic concept, see my *Torah Umadda*, chap. 10.

1. SPARKS EVERYWHERE
Source: Besht, Zava'at ha-Rivash, no. 109

"The Torah spared the money of Israelites."[2]

Why is that so? Because it is an important principle that whatever man eats or wears, or any vessel that he uses, he benefits from the vitality present in that object.[3] For without that spiritual life-force, it would be devoid of existence. Moreover, in each of these substances there are holy sparks that relate to the root of his soul.[4] I heard that this is the reason why one man likes a certain thing while another hates it, but instead loves something else.

Hence, when one uses that vessel or eats that food, even if he does so only to satisfy his physical needs, he thereby repairs the fallen sparks. For the strength that he acquired from that garment or meal or whatever, he now uses to serve God, thus causing their repair (*tikkun*).

Therefore, it occasionally happens that after one has completed the repair of all the sparks present in the object which relates to the root of his soul, God takes that vessel away from him and He gives it to someone else, so that the other should repair the remaining sparks of that vessel, for they relate to the other's soul.[5]

---

2. Rosh ha-Shanah 27a, Menahot 76b, 86b, 88b. This means that the Torah, in legislating the commandments, took into consideration the economic welfare of the people and avoided waste of their resources.

3. The "vitality," or ontological source of any object, is spiritual in nature: the indwelling presence of God.

4. The idea that a spark of divinity inheres in every object and is responsible for its very existence is a Lurianic teaching. These are the sparks that scattered after the Breaking of the Vessels and were ensconced in the *kelipot*, and which beg to be "redeemed" or "elevated" or "repaired" by man in the course of performing a mitzvah or engaging in the proper (kabbalistic) meditations. The climax of the accumulated repairs (*tikkunim*) will usher in the messianic age. In Hasidism these "sparks" became the symbol of divine immanence or spiritual "vitality" which ensured the continuing existence of the object in which they dwelt. What the Baal Shem Tov now adds is the idea that these sparks are not all identical and interchangeable, but that some relate to or come from the vicinity of one soul (or Root of the Soul) while others relate to other soul-roots.

5. We now have the answer to the question posed at the beginning of this passage. If the Torah was so concerned not to squander our resources, surely we must be equally careful. And the reason now is obvious: every object, regardless of its pecuniary value, is sustained by divine sparks which must be redeemed. If we waste the object, we have wasted the opportunity to perform the *tikkun*.

2. THE BODY SAVES THE SOUL
Source: R. Yaakov Yosef of Polennoye, Toledot Yaakov Yosef to Tazri'a, sec. 2

I heard from my teacher [the Besht] an explanation of the verse, *And the living creatures ran and returned* (Ezek. 1:14).[6]

It is fitting that the soul, having been hewn from a holy source, ought always yearn to return to its origin. However, lest its existence be annihilated [as a result of its reabsorption in its spiritual source], it was ensconced in matter so that it might also engage in material acts, such as eating, drinking, business, and the like, so that it not be constantly aflame in serving God. This in keeping with the mystery of *tikkun* and the maintenance of body and soul.

3. MATTER AND SPIRIT
Source: R. Yaakov Yosef of Polennoye, Toledot Yaakov Yosef to Mishpatim, sec. 12

In order to achieve proper *devekut* with God, it is necessary to indulge matter, for otherwise the lugubriousness of matter will impede form from attaining *devekut* by means of happiness in Him.[7] . . .

In accordance with this principle, I heard a solution to a difficulty raised by the Tosafot to the Talmud, tractate Betzah.[8] The Talmud teaches that the Holy One says to Israel, "Borrow on My account [to buy wine] so as to recite the Kiddush, sanctifying the Sabbath day; and have faith in Me and I shall pay you back." Whereupon the Tosafot raise the question that this conflicts with what is said by the

---

6. The "living creatures" which, in Ezekiel's famous vision of the divine chariot, ran to and fro (*ratzo va-shov*), has generally been interpreted by kabbalists as the principle of alternation from the exquisite bliss of being in God's company to the crest-fallen state of alienation and estrangement. The Besht here applies the metaphor to his conception of ambivalence toward corporeality. The spiritual realms are obviously superior to the physical world, yet the soul must be connected to the body lest an exaggerated and ascetic spiritualism defeat the function of *tikkun*. The soul thus runs "to and fro" between its supernal origin and its material abode.

7. "Matter" and "form" are the terms used by the author for matter and spirit. The dialectical tension between the two is a theme that runs through all his works and assumes many forms, e.g., the zaddik is the "Man of Form," the common man is the "Man of Matter."

8. Betzah 15b, s.v. *levu*.

Sages, "Better make your Sabbath like a weekday than resort to the help of others."[9]

I heard from the Maggid, Rabbi Mendel,[10] that *levu alai* has two meanings; one, "borrow for Me" (i.e., on My account), and two, "be attached to Me,"[11] and that one depends upon the other.[12] That is, in order to bind and attach oneself to God, it is necessary to make the body and the material substance happy, so that they not impede the happiness of the soul and its *devekut* in Him.

In this manner, the answer to our question may be understood. *Levu alai*, if you will borrow money so that you can attach yourself to Me, then I shall pay you back. However, if you borrow only for your own pleasure, then better make *your* Sabbath into a weekday, and do not rely upon others.

If you will ask: What do bodily needs, such as eating and drinking, have to do with *devekut* and attachment of the soul to Him, when the soul is altogether spiritual and not in need of eating and drinking? . . . The answer is that matter and body experience no joy in *devekut* with the Lord, except in the corporeal acts of eating and drinking. When this is lacking, the body is in sadness, and this prevents the soul from attaching itself to Him, which can take place only in joy. Hence, "Borrow on My account" to keep matter happy, so that both matter and spirit will be satisfied.

This is similar to the parable of the prince who was exiled by his father and fell in with people of low station. After many years a letter from the king finally arrived for him. He wanted to celebrate [and invite the others to share his happiness, but he knew that they would not understand the joy that came from reading the letter. Therefore]

---

9. Pesahim 112a, Shabbat 118a. The statement is not a dispensation to desecrate the Sabbath because of economic need, but a preference for doing without some of the festive accoutrements of the Sabbath that distinguish it from the profane days, in order not to have to beg or borrow from others. The question raised by the Tosafot is that this contradicts the previous dictum, which has God urging the Jew to borrow money for kiddush wine.

10. R. Menahem Mendel of Bar, an itinerant preacher (*maggid*), was an important member of the earliest hasidic circle which included the Besht. For his influence on the Besht, see J. G. Weiss, "Reshit Tzemihatah shel ha-Derekh ha-Hasidit," pp. 66-68.

11. The same Hebrew root, *l-v-h*, has both meanings. For the first, see Deut. 28:12; for the second, Gen. 29:34.

12. Cf. the Latin *obligatio*. As a result of the loan, the borrower and the lender are bound together. R. Menahem Mendel, of course, interprets the relationship homiletically.

he ordered drinks for all the people of low station, so that they might rejoice with the material whilst he rejoiced with the spiritual.[13]

4. TWO KINDS OF SELF-INDULGENCE
Source: R. Shneur Zalman of Liady, Tanya, Likkutei Amarim, chap. 7

The existence and vitality of any mundane thought, word, or deed—which are neutral, in that they are not in any way forbidden and are unrelated even remotely to any of the 365 negative commandments, whether of biblical or of rabbinic provenance, but they are not directed "for the sake of heaven" in that their purpose is not necessarily to serve God with the body, even if only to sustain it in life—are no better than the thought, word, or deed of the animal soul itself.[14] . . .

---

13. The "letter from the king" symbolizes the secret message of imminent redemption by God, the Father-King. The analogy is that one must collaborate with the body by indulging its form of happiness, namely, bodily pleasure, and meanwhile the soul is free to pursue its spiritual delights of *devekut*. The psychological rationale, that an unsatisfied body will frustrate one's spiritual aspirations, thus leads to an assessment of the body-soul relationship that is decidedly anti-ascetic. The interpretation of the parable as a pacification of the physical, permitting unfettered activity of the spirit in *devekut*, is more in accord with the theory of R. Nahman of Kossov, who advocated a simultaneous but unconnected pursuit of *devekut* in the midst of mundane activity. The Besht apparently moved from the way of R. Nahman to that of R. Menahem Mendel (see introduction to chapter 5). Nevertheless, there seems to be a discrepancy between R. Menahem Mendel's exegesis and the parable. According to the parable, the material pleasures are apparently a form of appeasement, allowing the soul to be free for *devekut*; the corporeal lacks inherent worth. According to the exegesis, there is a far more intimate connection: the physical indulgence enhances the contemplative activity. Weiss (*Zion* 17 [1951]: 66–68) maintains that the former, more far-reaching theory more accurately represents R. Menahem Mendel's thinking, and was advocated by the Besht too. Other versions of the same parable, attributed to the Besht, in *Toledot Yaakov Yosef* (to Shelah, n. 12, and to Ki Tavo, n. 4), support this interpretation.
14. Earlier, in chaps. 1–2, the author describes the well-known theory of the Ari (as cited by his disciple R. Hayyim Vital in *Etz Ḥayyim*, gate 50, chap. 2) according to which every Jew, whether righteous or wicked, has two souls; one originates in the *kelipah* and the *sitra aḥara*, and is clothed in the blood which gives life to the body; the other soul is the portion of God above, and is the source of man's intellect and wisdom. The former is called the animal soul; the latter, the intellective soul. The animal soul is the source of all of man's pernicious characteristics deriving from the four evil elements which are contained in it. They are anger and conceit, which are derived from the element of fire, the nature of which is to move upwards. The appetite for pleasure emanates from the element of water, for water is the source of all kinds of enjoyment. Frivolity and scoffing, boasting and idle talk issue from the element of air, and sloth and melancholy from the element of earth.

Kelipat nogah is an intermediate category between the three completely unclean *kelipot* and the holy[15] . . . , and at times it is absorbed
and elevated to the level of holiness, as when the good that is intermingled in it is extracted from the evil and prevails and ascends until
it is absorbed in holiness. Such is the case, for example, of one who
eats fat beef and drinks spiced wine in order to have the mental leisure
to serve God and His Torah, as Rava said, "Wine and fragrance make
man's mind more receptive,"[16] or in order to fulfill the mitzvah of the
enjoyment of the Sabbath and the festivals.[17] In such a case, the vitality in the meat and wine originating in the *kelipat nogah* is distilled and
ascends to God like a burnt offering and sacrifice. Such is the case, too,
when one utters a humorous remark in order to sharpen his wit and
gladden his heart in God and His Torah and His service, which should
be practiced joyfully, as Rava was wont to do with his pupils, prefac-
ing his discourse with some witty remarks to relax the students.[18]

However, one who gluttonously consumes meat and wine in order
to satiate his bodily desires and animal soul . . . in such case the energy acquired through the consumption of meat and wine is degraded
and absorbed temporarily in the utter evil of the three unclean *kelipot*.
Hence, his body temporarily becomes a garment and vehicle for
them—until he repents and returns to the service of God and His
Torah.

For inasmuch as the meat and the wine were kosher, they have the
power to revert and ascend with him when he returns to the service
of God. This is implied in the terms "permissible" (*heter*) and "permitted" (*mutar*), which mean becoming untied and no longer bound by

---

15. The Kabbalah posits four *kelipot* ("shells" or "husks") which are the symbol of evil.
Three are uncontestably so, but the fourth, called *nogah* (Venus or "glow," the time
which mediates between daylight and darkness), is the intermediate stage between
the truly evil *kelipot* and the holy and good. Because of its position between good and
evil—and because, indeed, it represents the mixture of both and is thus a metaphor for
"real life" in this mundane scene—*kelipat nogah* is a source for sustaining evil and,
equally, the realm in which the good can be "extracted" or "separated" from the evil
and the "sparks" thus redeemed and elevated. For more elaboration on this theme, see
below, selection 7.
16. Yoma 76a.
17. See Maimonides, Hilkhot Shabbat 30:7; see below, selection 7, for a comparison of
this position with that of R. Zevi Elimelekh of Dinov.
18. Pesahim 117a. This is a Beshtian idea. See *Keter Shem Tov* (Kehot ed.), no. 37; *Keter
Shem Tov (ha-Shalem)*, 9b.

the power of the "extraneous forces" ([*ha-koḥot*] *ha-ḥitzonim*)[19] which prevent him from returning and ascending to God.

5. BEAUTY IS OF GOD
Source: R. Elimelekh of Lizhensk, Noam Elimelekh to Beshallah, s.v. va-yikaḥ Mosheh (38b)

Our father Jacob served God with his particular attribute, which is Tiferet (Beauty).[20] Hence, whatever he said, heard, did, or ate, he derived from it a lesson for the glorification (*hitpa'er*) of the Creator.[21] For instance, when he ate something delicious, he considered that the food was created, and who then instilled the good taste in it if not the Creator? And if the food has such a delicious taste, then surely the goodness of the taste reflects the Creator Himself, without limit. So did Jacob view material things.[22]

6. THE ZADDIK AND THE COMMON MAN
Source: R. Elimelekh of Lizhensk, Noam Elimelekh to Korah, end

The zaddik, during the course of his prayer, is of course in a state of *devekut* and sanctity, in pure, clear, and pellucid thoughts. When he eats, because eating is physical, a fright seizes his head[23] lest he become grossly material and be cut off from sanctity, heaven forbid. He therefore strengthens himself and strives increasingly to sanctify himself while eating, in order to bind himself to God with great attachment and *devekut*. Thus, while eating, the zaddik sanctifies himself even more than during prayer.

---

19. The Hebrew term *mutar* literally means "released"; (*ha-koḥot*) *ha-ḥitzonim* is a kabbalistic term synonymous to *kelipot*.
20. Each of the patriarchs, according to the Kabbalah, represented one of the first three of the seven lower sefirot, in accordance with his human qualities and the nature of his service of God. Hence, Abraham stands for Hesed (Loving-Kindness), Isaac for Gevurah (Strength or Justice), and Jacob for Tiferet (Beauty).
21. Cf. *Sefer Besht* to Bereshit, no. 36.
22. See below, n. 38.
23. *Mora* ("fear") is a play on *morah* ("a razor shall not come upon his head").

However, that is not the case with other people. They are able to sanctify themselves more during prayer than during eating.[24]

7. THE SABBATH AND THE WEEKDAY MEALS
Source: R. Zevi Elimelekh of Dinov, Benei Yisaskhar, Maamarei ha-Shabbatot 10:5

It is well known that all things and all living creatures which the Torah forbids us to eat derive their vitality from the three unclean *kelipot*.[25] These were altogether prohibited by the Torah because the three unclean *kelipot* can never achieve *tikkun* and are destined for total annihilation when the Messiah will come. These are symbolized by the three shells (*kelipot*) of a nut which are totally unfit for eating and are therefore discarded.

But all those things and living creatures which are kosher and are permitted to us by the Torah, derive their soul and vitality from the fourth *kelipah*, that of *nogah*, which occupies the border between holiness and profanity, and thus possesses aspects of both good and evil.

Now, when a man eats of these kosher foods with the proper intention, for the sake of heaven, and he utilizes the strength acquired from this meal to study the Torah and to serve God, he elevates thereby the *kelipat nogah* to high levels of holiness, and all the forces of iniquity will be scattered.[26] That is, the three unclean *kelipot* disappear into the "abyss of the great deep," for after the *kelipat nogah* is absorbed into holiness, the other *kelipot* lose their vital base.

By contrast, when a man eats merely to satisfy his gluttony and to gratify his body, even if the food is kosher and permitted to us by the Torah, he inclines the *kelipat nogah* to the three unclean *kelipot*. Indeed, the holy Zohar refers to the *kelipat nogah* as a "scale" because, like a balance, it can be tipped in either direction. This is the mystery of the

---

24. Here the practice of worship through corporeality is restricted to the zaddik. Elsewhere, however, R. Elimelech permits it to the common man; see his *Tzettl Katan*, no. 15, and cf. Nigal, introduction to *Noam Elimelekh* (Jerusalem, 1978), pp. 76-77. See also Rivkah Shatz-Uffenheimer, "Le-Mahuto shel ha-Zaddik ba-Hasidut," *Molad* 18 (1960): 368-369. For a detailed review and analysis of the Hasidic practice of worship through corporeality, see her *Hasidism As Mysticism*, pp. 28-30, 52-57.
25. See above, selection 4, for further treatment of the theme of the *kelipot*, especially *kelipat nogah*, in this context.
26. Paraphrase of Ps. 92:10.

fourth shell of the nut; it can be eaten with the fruit, but never by itself.[27] Understand this.

Now this holds true only for weekdays. However, on the Sabbath, since the Torah declares it a mitzvah to delight the body with food and drink in honor of the Sabbath, one can, by means of the corporeal pleasures, elevate the vitality of *kelipat nogah* to the realms of holiness.[28]

8. A PARADOX
Source: R. Zevi Elimelekh of Dinov, Agra de-Kallah to Lev. 19:2, 40c

Ye shall be holy, for I the Lord your God am holy (Lev. 19:2).

It is necessary to understand the reason offered in this verse, namely, *for I the Lord your God am holy.* How is it possible to compare the holiness of a corporeal creature to His blessed holiness?

I believe that the answer is as follows: The Creator commanded us not to follow the desires of our hearts even when we are engaged in necessary mundane activities, such as eating and drinking and marital relations. At such times we must intend only to do His will—to use the strength acquired from the eating for the service of God, and to extricate the sparks of holiness, and the like; and also, in sexual intercourse, to fulfill the commandment to perpetuate the species, and remove from ourselves any pleasure from that sensual act.

Now, if the Creator had commanded us to be completely separated from, and not at all to engage in, the material and the corporeal, and had He created us in such a fashion that we could exist without involvement in them, then it would be very simple for us to do so. However, as things are now, it is necessary for us to be connected to the corporeal, and nevertheless we were commanded to be separate

---

27. Just as the three outer shells of a nut are always discarded, so the three major *kelipot* will vanish when the Messiah comes and the good and holy will prevail. *Kelipat nogah*, however, the "fourth shell," is analogous to the fourth, or innermost, shell of a nut. It is often eaten together with the fruit itself, but never stripped off and eaten separately. So this fourth *kelipah*: if it is associated with and used for holiness, it is holy and contributes to the strength and vitality of the holy, but if it is separated from the holy, then it too must perish because it reverts to evil.

28. R. Zevi Elimelech apparently disagrees with R. Shneur Zalman on this point. The latter (see selection 4 above) implies that even on the Sabbath one ought to consciously intend his indulgence in food and drink for the sake of heaven. For R. Zevi Elimelech, the fact that the Torah commanded such indulgence automatically qualifies it as "for the sake of heaven," and no conscious effort is required.

from it,[29] i.e., not to satisfy our desires whilst we are engaged in physical activities except for a higher purpose. This is apparently very difficult for a material being to comprehend. It is also difficult to understand why the Lord so fashioned the human race.

Thus it is written, *you shall be holy*, that you shall be separated from sensuality (for holiness, as we know, means separation from the corporeal and the material); as the Rabbis said, "Sanctify yourself by refraining from indulging in what is permitted to you."[30] Even when you are involved in what is permitted to you, you must be holy and separate, and not be connected to corporeality. If you will ask how it is possible to maintain two opposites, and also why the Lord made man so, Scripture offers the reason: *for I the Lord your God am holy*. Now, we are commanded to *walk in His ways* (Deut. 28:9). And the Creator is concealed and separated from all thought and has no connection to creatures. Nevertheless, if, heaven forbid, His providence and His grace and His life-force were withdrawn from them for but an instant, they would be annihilated. No created being can move except by means of His grace and His life-force.

In order to teach this perfect faith, we were also commanded to walk in His ways, blessed be His Name, and to relate to corporeality both by connection and separation.[31]

Understand this subject and you will give delight to your soul, for these words are profound in wisdom.

This is what Scripture meant when it said, *for holy am I the Lord*, separate from all created beings;[32] and nevertheless *your God*, who is connected to you and is your Cause.[33]

9. CORPOREALITY ITSELF AS WORSHIP
Source: R. Zevi Hirsch of Zhidachov, *Sur me-Ra va-Aseh Tov, Ketav Yosher Divrei Emet, 116a*

One can perform unification of action[34] in all mundane activities, such as business dealings, eating, drinking, and sexual intercourse, in a

---

29. The Rabbis interpret "you shall be holy" as "you shall be separate," i.e., transcend your material nature (Sifra to Lev. 19:2).
30. Yevamot 20a.
31. That is, man's paradoxical relation to the material world reflects, by virtue of *imitatio dei*, God's paradoxical relation to the universe as such—absolute and related, transcendent and immanent.
32. The Tetragrammaton implies transcendence, absoluteness.
33. *Elohekhem* ("your God") implies relatedness.
34. See below.

more exalted manner than the one described in *Duties of the Hearts,*[35] in the chapters called "Unification of Deeds" and "Service of God." Based on the verse *He that sacrificeth unto the gods, save unto the Lord only, shall be utterly destroyed* (Exod. 22:19), the author sees eating, drinking, and sleeping as a means to strengthen one's body for the service of the Creator; likewise, the purpose of business dealings is to provide sustenance for himself and for his family.

Now, my brother, while it is indeed the sign of a good heart when one's every action is for the sake of God and he does everything with heaven in mind, nevertheless, this is not what we call "the perfect service" in the tradition we have received. So did I hear in the name of the Maggid (R. Dov Ber of Mezerich), with regard to the talmudic saying, "What is a perfect service? One after which no other service follows."[36] The Maggid said: "When one's eating is intended only to strengthen his body for Torah study and worship, how can one call this a perfect service? While eating, he neither prays nor learns; hence this is merely an act of service for the sake of and which leads to the true service which follows." However, if the eating is done in accordance with the meditation of R. Isaac Luria—to extract and elevate the holy sparks in the food . . . and especially if one has been privileged by the Almighty to perceive and visualize with his mind the roots of His blessed Names, as explained in the Lurianic writings regarding the proper meditation by scholars for eating—then he can create *yihudim* ("unifications")[37] as much with his eating as he can with his prayer.[38] Happy is he and happy is his lot!

Similarly, each of his business matters can become a service in its own right, provided that he deals honestly. This is equally true of all mundane matters, whether plowing or sowing or reaping—any work of the field.

---

35. One of the most popular philosophical and devotional works, by the eleventh-century Spanish Rabbi Bahya ibn Pakuda.

36. Yoma 24a.

37. A synonym for the act of elevating the sparks and reuniting them with their supernal source.

38. This is characteristic of the significant "advance" of hasidic thinking over the normative approach, represented by R. Bahya, and codified in the standard code of Jewish law, the *Shulhan Arukh* (Orah Hayyim 231:1), that the proper intention during physical activity is to derive the strength or means or wherewithal to worship God in the accepted manner, i.e., prayer or study or mitzvot. This latter keeps the mundane activity at one remove from actual "service." Our author, however, here articulates the Hasidic concept of *avodah be-gashmiyut* as the corporeal or mundane act in and of itself constituting "service" if the right intentions accompany it.

10. UPLIFTING THE WORLD
Source: R. Levi Yitzhak of Berdichev, Kedushat Levi to Vayiggash, s.v. ve-od nir'eh

It is written in the *Shulḥan Arukh*, Oraḥ Ḥayyim 231:1, that a man's intention while eating, drinking and performing all of his other physical and material needs, should be to gather strength in order to serve the Creator, and thus fulfill the verse *In all thy ways acknowledge Him* (Prov. 3:6).

There is a profound analysis of these matters in the writings of the Ari [= R. Isaac Luria]. Probably both the *Shulḥan Arukh* and the Ari intended the same idea, namely, that God created in His world four levels of beings: minerals, plants, animals, and humans. Because of his lovingkindness (*ḥesed*), He desires that all these things be elevated to a higher rung.[39] That is, that the mineral should be elevated to the category of plant,[40] and as the animal eats the plant it elevates the plant to the animal level and, moreover, helps raise the mineral to the animal level. Afterwards, when man eats the meat of an animal, all the lower levels are raised to that of humans. . . .

This explains why the benedictions on food use the present tense: "Blessed art Thou . . . who creates (*borei*) the fruit of the tree or the earth, etc.," rather than the past, "He created." For when a man eats and enjoys food, all the elements comprising that food are elevated from the categories of mineral, plant, and animal to that of the human. Hence, by the act of eating, new creations take place as lower beings are raised to the level of man. Thus the term *borei* ("He creates"), in the present tense, is used correctly.[41]

---

39. Accepting the ancient division of the world as divided into four hierarchic levels, R. Levi Yitzhak maintains that God, in His goodness, desires that each level be raised to a higher rung. Note that the author here makes the assumption that the *Shulḥan Arukh* and Luria agree. This assumption is not necessarily warranted; see above, n. 37. R. Levi Yitzhak probably finds it more prudent to avoid positing a controversy between them and having to choose one side over the other. Moreover, note too that he comes down on the side of the more radical interpretation of *avodah be-gashmiyut*, but does not spell out the necessity for conscious awareness and meditation in such worship through corporeality.
40. By virtue of the minerals serving as nutrients for the plants.
41. Hence, by means of *avodah be-gashmiyut*, man exercises a creative function, in imitation of the divine Creator. As to his halakhic excursus, the assumption of the author that *borei* implies a present and ongoing process is in dispute in the Talmud and among the codifiers. See Berakhot 52b and *Magen Avraham* to Oraḥ Ḥayyim 167:8; also Rashi to Berakhot 52b, s.v. *borei*.

11. SPIRITUAL FOOD
Source: R. Hayyim Halberstam, Divrei Ḥayyim on Yom Kippur, s.v. ba-pasuk ha-ḥodesh, pp. 8a-b

It is told[42] in the name of the Ari [= R. Isaac Luria] that on Yom Kippur we are nourished from Above with the "food of angels," and that this is "nourishment of the Torah"—actual spiritual food. Now in truth, a man is capable of living several days without food and . . . nourishment, depending upon his individual strength and intake prior to the fast. If one ate a great deal, it is natural that this food will sustain him longer. So is it clearly explained in the verse, *Arise and eat, because the journey is too great for thee . . . and he went on the strength of that meal forty days and forty nights* (1 Kings 19:7—8). Thus, that with which man sustains himself while *not* eating is not in the class of "spiritual nourishment"; it is just that the material food eaten earlier still animates him.

Hence, with regard to Yom Kippur, one would think that in actuality one is not nourished by spiritual food but owes his existence to the material food which he had eaten earlier. Therefore the holy Torah enlightened us by making it a mitzvah to eat on the eve of Yom Kippur. Thus, this meal constitutes the fulfillment of a commandment and, consequently, the sustenance on Yom Kippur derived from this obligatory meal . . . is considered spiritual nourishment.[43]

---

42. This passage offers an explanation of the Talmud's dictum that one who eats and drinks on the ninth day of Tishri (Yom Kippur eve) is considered as if he fasted on Yom Kippur (Berakhot 8b), i.e., that eating on that day is a mitzvah. The Talmud derives this from Lev. 23:32.

43. R. Hayyim proceeds to clarify why all other "obligatory meals" are not considered pure spiritual nourishment. In all other mitzvah meals, one experiences bodily pleasure at the moment of eating, while the obligatory meal of Yom Kippur eve nourishes on the Day of Atonement, when there is no longer any bodily pleasure to be gained from it; only the spiritual, "angelic" nourishment derived from the mitzvah remains. This meal on Yom Kippur eve is an example of *avodah be-gashmiyut*.

10

Repentance

INTRODUCTION

Repentance (*teshuvah*) is a central foundation of Judaism. In addition to the specific commandment to repent of one's sins, the imperative to repent takes pride of place in the penitential season leading up to Yom Kippur, and the desire for repentance appears frequently in the daily liturgy. Thus one can hardly regard the emphasis on repentance as a distinctively hasidic contribution. Yet certain themes characterize hasidic writings on repentance. Let us note some of those that appear in the selections below.

At the theoretical level, hasidic thought on repentance bears the imprint of other hasidic doctrines. To begin with, it often reflects kabbalistic concepts of repentance. Thus, human repentance is connected to the processes of cosmic renewal. The return to God is equivalent to the elevating of the sparks through the sefirotic structure, and the different qualities of repentance are rooted in different sefirotic origins. From this perspective, it is also possible to speak of return to God as a spiritual movement independent of antecedent sin.

Other hasidic themes have a more direct psychological cash value. A great threat to the process of repentance is pessimism about the efficacy of repentance, and despair about the vitiated state of the sinner. These problems, which any religious psychology must deal with, evoke specific hasidic ideas. Thus the idea of "descent for the purpose of ascent" reconciles man to past failure by integrating it into the higher state to be inaugurated through repentance. Hence a special emphasis on the rabbinic idea that ideal repentance lifts one to a higher level than that attained by the righteous individual who has never stumbled. Hence also the integration of repentance on the part of the individual with the process of elevation on the part of the Jewish community as a whole.

Kabbalistic language permits the hasidic writer to discuss the question of initiative. At one level, free repentance requires man to take the first step toward God. At the same time, however, placing the entire onus upon man can well lead to discouragement over man's limited powers. Again rabbinic sources in kabbalistic garb adumbrate a process in which God initiates the human response of repentance and augments the modest beginning made by man.

At the practical level, Hasidism encouraged its followers to treat repentance as an all-pervasive aspect of religion, rather than being merely the effort to obtain pardon for specific sins. Thus an ongoing imperative to repentance transforms it into a way of life, permeating all religious life. This is in keeping with the general tendency of Hasidism to maximize the place of religious *feelings* in Judaism. The same appreciation of spontaneous feelings may also lead hasidic writers to respect the possibility of sudden, instantaneous repentance more than parallel mitnaggedic thinkers do.

Hasidic authors also took it upon themselves to suggest to their followers the proper emphasis to be placed on different aspects of repentance. Halakhah demands regret for the past, confession, and resolution for the future. The individual may experience difficulty in determining the order of these essential ingredients. The threat of being overwhelmed by these requirements may bring the prospective *ba'al teshuvah* to despair, which is to be avoided at all costs. The attempt to regulate these factors can be found, for example, in R. Zadok's emphasis on one's determination for the future as taking precedence over the need to reconcile the errors of the past.[1]

The same educational purposes leads several of our authors to define the appropriate place of ascetic practices in the context of repentance. Ascetic behavior has an atoning function, beyond the specific forms of abstinence integral to the Halakhah (such as fasting on Yom Kippur). In this connection, it becomes important to distinguish between the essence of repentance as a turning toward God and the

---

1. See selection 4 below, and Additional Note *1.

austerities that are worthwhile, if at all, as a means toward reconciliation with Him.

The Lurianic asceticism is prevalent in many Hasidic texts, including those of R. Nahman of Bratslav and R. Elimelekh of Lizhensk. R. Shneur Zalman's writings reveal the ambivalence he undoubtedly experienced between the ascetic bent of Lurianism, whose influence was still quite powerful in the early decades of the Hasidic movement, and the anti-ascetic reaction that Hasidism engendered and that emerges both from the Halakhah (see, inter alia, *Responsa Noda bi-Yehudah*, Oraḥ Ḥayyim 35) and a long tradition in medieval Jewish thought. R. Shneur Zalman attempts to reconcile the two tendencies.

1. REPENTANCE AND ASCETIC PRACTICES
Source: R. Shneur Zalman of Liady, Iggeret ha-Teshuvah, chaps. 1-3

The commandment of repentance, as required by the Torah, is simply the abandonment of sin.[2] The sinner must resolve with his whole heart never again to revert to folly and rebel against His rule, and never again to violate the King's command, God forbid, neither a positive nor a negative commandment.

This is the basic meaning of the term *teshuvah* ("repentance"): to return[3] to God with all one's heart and soul, to serve Him and keep all His commandments. *Let the wicked abandon his way, and the sinful his thoughts, and return to God* (Isa. 55:7). Such statements abound: *Return unto the Lord your God and hearken to His voice . . . with all your heart* (Deut. 30:2), and *Return, O Israel, unto the Lord your God* (Hos. 14:2), and *Bring us back, Lord, unto You* (Lam. 5:22).

This is not at all the common conception that repentance is identical with fasting.[4] Even where the completion [of the process] of atonement requires suffering, as in the case of sins punished by excision (*karet*) or execution, this means that God brings the sufferings on the sinner.[5] For when the repentance is acceptable to Him, as man

---

2. Sanhedrin 25b; *Shulḥan Arukh*, Ḥoshen Mishpat 34. Contrition over errors of the past and, as R. Shneur Zalman will point out, ascetic practices are inadequate for repentance. At bottom, *teshuvah* requires a change in way of life: abandoning one's sinful ways.
3. *Shav* is the Hebrew root of both "repentance" and "returning."
4. Note the equation of the two in many editions of the High Holiday Mahzor, in the prayer Unetanneh Tokef.
5. I.e., the afflictions mentioned are not self-imposed but are brought on by God as part of the divine process of atonement and forgiveness.

returns to God with all his heart and soul out of love, then following the initiative-from-below, i.e., human initiative . . . there is an awakening-from-Above, i.e., divine response, arousing the love and kindness of God, to scour his sin through affliction in the world. *For whom the Lord loves He chastises* (Prov. 3:12).[6]

Therefore Maimonides and *Sefer Mitzvot Gadol* make no mention of fasting in [connection with] the mitzvah of repentance, even for sins involving the punishment of excision or capital sins. They cite only confession and the plea for forgiveness: *They shall confess their sins* (Num. 5:7).

But what of the verse *Return to Me with all your hearts, with fasting and weeping* (Joel 2:12)?[7] This was to nullify the heavenly decree that had already been issued, to expunge the sin of [that] generation through the affliction of locusts. That is the justification for all fasts undertaken because of any trouble threatening the community, as in the Book of Esther.[8]

There are descriptions in the Musar literature, particularly the *Rokeah* and *Sefer Hasidim*, of numerous fasts and mortifications for excision and capital sins. The same is true of sins punished by death by divine agency (*mitah bi-yedei shamayim*), like wasteful emissions of semen, as the Torah recounts of Er and Onan (Gen. 38:7—10). These fasts and mortifications are intended to avoid the punishment of suffering at the hand of Heaven, God forbid, and also to urge on and expedite the end of the process of atonement of the sinner's soul. . . .

However, all this refers to atonement and forgiveness of the sin; [even without these ascetic practices,] he is pardoned completely for having violated the command of the King once he has fully repented. No charge or semblance of accusation is made against him on the day of judgment to punish him for his sin, God forbid, in the world-to-come. He is completely exonerated from the judgment to come.[9]

---

6. Thus, the afflictions attendant upon sin and repentance are the "scouring" of sin by a merciful God and have nothing to do with the penitent sinner voluntarily undergoing fasting, mortification of the flesh, or other such ascetic practices.

7. Does this not indicate that man must fast and undergo mortification as part of his penitence?

8. Thus, fasting and mortification are appropriate in order to avoid far greater suffering decreed by heaven as punishment for one's sins, such as the locust plague in the case of Joel, or genocide in the case of Esther. Such fasting may be classified as an adjunct of prayer rather than repentance.

9. Formally, repentance without fasting or any other form of mortification is adequate to atone for the sin.

Nonetheless, that he may be acceptable before God, as beloved of Him as before the sin, that his Creator may derive delight from his service—in past times he would bring a burnt offering (Lev. 1:3). This offering was brought even for violating an ordinary positive commandment that involves no excision (*karet*) or execution. . . . It is a "gift" [that the penitent offers to God] after he has done penance and the punishment has been commuted.[10]

[An illustration:] If one displeases his king and appeases him through an intercessor, and the king does forgive him, still he will send some token gift to the king that the king might agree that he appear again before his sovereign. . . .

Today we have no offerings to call forth God's pleasure, so fasting replaces the offering. The Talmud says, "May my loss of fat and blood be regarded as though I had offered before You. . ."[11] Therefore there are many cases of talmudic sages who, to expiate some minor transgression, underwent a great many fasts. . . .

With this precedent, R. Isaac Luria taught his disciples, according to kabbalistic principles, the number of fasts for many transgressions, though they entail no excision or death by divine agency. . . .

In general, the mystery of the fast is remarkably effective for the revelation of the Supreme Will, similar to the offering, of which it is said, *an aroma pleasing to God* (Lev. 1:13). In Isaiah we find, *Do you call this a fast and a day desirable to God?* (Isa. 58:5). Obviously, an acceptable fast is a "desirable day." . . .

However, all this applies to the strong and healthy, whose physical vigor would not be sapped at all by repeated fasts, as in past generations. But whoever would be adversely affected by many fasts, and might suffer illness or pain, God forbid, as in contemporary generations, is forbidden to engage in many fasts. This ban concerns even fasts for sins of excision or execution, and certainly the positive and negative commandments that do not involve excision. Instead, the criterion for fasting is one's personal estimate of what he is sure he can tolerate.

For even in those early talmudic generations, only the robust who could mortify themselves fasted so frequently. But whoever cannot fast and [nevertheless] does so, is called a sinner.[12] This applies even to

---

10. Zevaḥim 7b.

11. Berakhot 17a. My fasting, and the consequent "loss of fat and blood," is in place of an animal sacrifice.

12. Ta'anit 11a; *Shulḥan Arukh*, Oraḥ Ḥayyim 571.

one who fasts for specifically known sins, as Rashi explains there. . . .[13]

It goes without saying that a student of Torah who fasts is a sinner and is doubly punished, for the weakness resulting from his fast prevents him from studying Torah properly.

What, then, is his alternative? *Your sin redeem with charity* (Dan. 4:24). The codifiers of Torah law specified for each fast-day of repentance approximately eighteen [coins].[14] The wealthy should add to this, each according to his means. . . .

Nonetheless, every man of spirit who desires to be close to God, to repair his soul, to return it to God with the finest and most preferred repentance, should be stringent with himself. He should complete, at least once during his life span, the number of fasts for every grave sin incurring death, if only death by divine agency. . . .

Briefly, then, he may redeem his fasts with charity if he cannot mortify himself, as noted. Though this might amount to a considerable sum, he need not beware the injunction, "Do not distribute more than one-fifth."[15] For these circumstances are not "distribution" to charity, since he does this to release himself from fasting and affliction. This is no less necessary than medicine for his body or his other needs.

The number of fasts enumerated in the above-mentioned penances is exceedingly great. Therefore, all who revere the word of God are now accustomed to being unstintingly generous with charity, for the prevalent lack of hardihood prevents them from mortifying themselves overmuch.[16]

2. REPENTANCE AND INTEGRITY
Source: R. Zevi Elimelekh of Dinov, Benei Yisaskhar, Tishri 4:6 no. 21

It is known that many people are mistaken about the mitzvah of repentance. Some hold that repentance is [accomplished] through many fasts and mortifications. Others maintain that [it is accomplished] through the recitation of great numbers of psalms and prayers for atonement. All these people are greatly mistaken, for these acts are simply incidental and mere details.

13. See Rashi and Tosafot to Ta'anit 11a, s.v. *ve-khi*.
14. *Shulḥan Arukh*, Oraḥ Ḥayyim 334:26.
15. Ketubbot 50a. R. Shneur Zalman advises the penitent not to be concerned about giving to charity in excess of the maximum permitted amount of 20 percent.
16. See, for example, *Responsa Noda bi-Yehudah*, Oraḥ Ḥayyim 35, and compare R. Shneur Zalman's *Iggeret ha-Teshuvah*.

The essence of repentance, however, is total contrition with a heart filled with remorse, whereby one regrets from the depths of one's heart every aspect of sin, transgression, and crime which he committed and [through which] he betrayed and angered his Creator. One admits and confesses to his Creator every detail. He abandons the sins in which he is engaged, and sincerely resolves never to return to that folly in any manner, even at peril to his life.

But this must be done honestly and sincerely, from the depths of the heart, for since man knows that the law of repentance is such, it is possible that he will recite the formula to God without genuinely meaning to regret the past and without honest resolve regarding the future. This [lack of integrity] occurs to man because the light of the soul becomes murky as a result of the denseness of his material element. [Therefore] the soul does not function properly in the body. This is like a candle which cannot give off light because its wick is full of dirt. One must shake the wick and pound the dirt off it until the flame can adhere to the wick and become one with it. The purpose of mortification is, similarly, to break down the material element of the body in order that the soul may function properly. Thus can repentance be performed sincerely, i.e., the essence of repentance as described above.[17] But the mortifications [as such] are not the essence of repentance. Consider this carefully.

Now, there are various distinctions [concerning mortification]. During a time of [divine] will and mercy, when His right hand is extended to receive penitents, the penitent receives divine assistance and, immediately upon deciding to repent, as he commences with confession and beseeching of his Creator, God turns to him mercifully from His abode and infuses the light of the soul into the body. The bodily limbs are thus aroused, and the repentance will be sincere and from the depths of the heart. There will be no need to afflict the body with various mortifications.

However, when, God forbid, the attribute of Judgment prevails, man has little divine assistance, and the accusations against him [for his moral failings] are overpowering, so that [even] when man desires to repent, he is prevented from doing so by the material element, because of his many sins and transgressions. Thus, [at such times,]

---

17. Thus, the mortification of the flesh is only a preparation for *teshuvah*.

one must afflict his body in order to purge it of its filth;[18] and who knows if he can bear it?

3. ALTERNATIVES TO ASCETICISM
Source: R. Zevi Elimelekh of Dinov, Benei Yisaskhar, Tishri 4:11, no. 36

Our master the Ari, [R. Isaac Luria] of blessed memory, wrote that repentance ("Te-She-u-V-aH") is an acrostic for ta'anit ("fasting"), sak ("sackcloth"), va-efer ("and ashes"), bekhi ("weeping"), hesped ("wailing"). This teacher wrote that in this weak generation (especially in our exile, which gets worse every day), it is impossible for everyone to observe [all these five elements]. One must at least take care to observe five other matters which sustain repentance: Torah [study], Shabbat, vidduy ("confession"), bushah ("shame"), hakhna'ah ("submissiveness").

We have already written, concerning fasts and afflictions, that one should not become depressed and think that because he cannot observe everything his repentance will not be accepted. For immediately upon performing repentance properly,[19] [even without these additional forms of renunciation], it is effective.

4. THE MINIMUM FOR REPENTANCE
Source: R. Zadok ha-Kohen of Lublin, Zidkat ha-Zaddik, no. 12

There are two elements in repentance, one relating to the future and one to the past. That is why two things are necessary: purification, for the future;[20] and atonement, to make amends for the past and wipe away the sin. This [latter] is effected by means of a sacrifice or its equivalents: prayer or fasting or charity.

---

18. This passage should be compared to the previous excerpt from Iggeret ha-Teshuvah. There R. Shneur Zalman addresses the advisability of mortification and fasting as such, while Benei Yisaskhar focuses on the question of the penitent's sincerity.
19. I.e., following the second acrostic set.
20. The text adds, in parentheses, that the purification must take place "in the waters of knowledge," referring to Isaiah's metaphor of the world being filled with the knowledge of the Lord "as the waters cover the sea" (Isa. 11:9). This immersion in Torah (identical with the "knowledge of the Lord") saves one from sin and helps one to return to the right way. Thus, as indicated in Leviticus Rabbah 25 and elsewhere, teshuvah requires that if one normally studies one page of Talmud, he should now study two.

The law is that atonement[21] is not a prerequisite for repentance.[22] Thus, even if one intended repentance [only] in his heart, he is considered completely righteous.[23] However, this is true only insofar as [partaking of] the *terumah* (the offering to the priests) is concerned, which is brought from totally profane stuff; [in this sense, one can become] a righteous person. However, for *kodashim* (partaking of the meat of a sacrifice), in order to sanctify oneself and become holy, one must also cure [the ills of] the past.

AFTERWORD

R. Zadok here plays on a halakhic theme found in Berakhot 2a. The Mishnah teaches that the earliest time to recite the Shema in the evening is when the priests begin to eat their *terumah*, the priestly gift that Israelites put aside from their grain, wine, and oil. The Talmud identifies this as nightfall, when the stars have come out. Why does the Mishnah not state this directly? The Gemara's answer is that the Mishnah wishes to teach us an additional lesson in passing: that priests who have been ritually defiled may eat of the *terumah* as soon as the stars appear, and need not wait until they have offered up the requisite sacrifice the next day. All that is required is that they immerse in the mikveh (ritual pool) during the day and wait for the appearance of the stars, even without the atonement provided by a sacrifice. So much for eating of the *terumah*.

However, the same priest, who had immersed himself in the mikveh and passed nightfall, but had not yet brought his sacrifice as atonement for his impurity, may *not* partake of the sacred meat of a sacrifice, whether his own or any other. R. Zadok establishes, on the basis of this text, that there are two levels of achievement in

---

21. By means of sacrifice or its equivalents, which restores the former status of the sinner.

22. In the sense that the absence of sacrifice or its equivalents does not rule out successful *teshuvah*.

23. The mere thought of *teshuvah* redefines a man as righteous even without any of the various forms of atonement, such as sacrifice, prayer, fasting, or charity. The source for this is the Talmud, Kiddushin 49b, which rules that if a man betrothed a woman "on condition that I am a complete zaddik," the marriage is valid even if he was known to be thoroughly wicked, for it is possible that at that moment he entertained a thought of *teshuvah*; hence the thought alone is effective repentance. See too *Minhat Hinnukh* 364, and my "Teshuvah: Mahshavah u-Maaseh," in *Bet Yitzhak*, 26 (1989).

the *teshuvah* process: honest resolve for improved future conduct and reparation for the past. The former, which he calls "purification," is akin to the purification (or *mikveh*, "immersion") of the defiled priest (after night has come); at that point he may partake of the *terumah* (which, while it may not be eaten or even touched in a state of impurity, is not "sacred"); by analogy, the penitent is accepted as a righteous person.

However, the higher level is that of the achievement of sanctity, equivalent to the priest who, in addition to immersion and nightfall, also brought his (sacred) sacrifice. Atonement (symbolized by sacrifices or its equivalents: prayer, fasting, charity) is prerequisite to the higher level of sanctity. R. Zadok adds that the recitation of the Shema—which is the "acceptance of the yoke of the Kingdom of Heaven," i.e., the acceptance of the Jewish faith—is contingent upon the time for eating the *terumah*, not the sacrifice; or, to put it in more familiar terms, upon that level of repentance in which one resolves to abstain from evil in the future. It does not require the more stringent atonement for sins of the past. Sacrifice, prayer, fasting, almsgiving—all these are beyond the minimum of *teshuvah*, which is the simple mental act of inner resolve to change. The essence of repentance is future-oriented. Confronting and dealing with the past is a higher stage.

5. REPENTANCE AND TZEDAKAH
Source: R. Shneur Zalman of Liady, Iggeret ha-Kodesh, chap. 10

The essence of repentance is in the heart, for through remorse from the depths of the heart one arouses the depths of the Supreme Light. But in order to elicit [this light] so that it radiates in the upper and lower worlds, it is essential that there be a tangible "awakening from below," in the form of an active deed, such as charity and kindness, that is without limit and measure.

For insofar as man bestows *rav ḥesed*[24] upon the poor and destitute who have nothing of their own, without setting a limit and measure to his giving and distributions, God likewise emanates His light and benevolence in the form of *ḥesed ila'ah* ("supreme kindness"), referred to as *rav ḥesed* (Exod. 34:6), which radiates infinitely within the upper and lower worlds, without limit and measure. For in relation to Him,

---

24. R. Shneur Zalman adds here: "i.e., *ḥas-dalet*." This refers to the division of the word *ḥesed* into *ḥas* ("having compassion") and *dalet* (the last letter of *ḥesed*), "those that have nothing"; the word *dal* or *dalet* means "poor, destitute."

all are in a state of destitution,[25] for they possess nothing of their own and are as naught before Him. All the blemishes that man caused above, in the upper and lower worlds, through his iniquities, are rectified thereby.

This may explain the verse, *To do charity and justice is more acceptable to the Lord than sacrifice* (Prov. 21:3): sacrifices are restricted by measure, quantity, and limit, while charity has no limits. One may give away all he owns without restraint in order to atone for his transgressions.

As for the ruling of the Rabbis that "a [liberal] donor should not squander more than a fifth,"[26] this applies only to one who has not sinned, or who has already repaired his sins by means of self-mortification and fasts, as required for the rectification of all blemishes [caused] Above. But for one who stills needs to remedy his soul, surely the healing of the soul is not inferior to the healing of the body, where money does not count, as it is written: *Everything one has he will give for his life* (Job. 2:4).

6. REPENTANCE AS ELEVATION OF THE SPARKS
Source: Besht, Keter Shem Tov, pt. 1, no. 53

A great principle: Everything in the world contains holy sparks and nothing is devoid of them. In all of one's deeds, even the sins he commits, there are sparks from the Breaking of the Vessels.[27] What are these sparks?[28] They are repentance, and [therefore] when one repents a sin, he elevates the sparks contained there to the upper world.[29]

---

25. See the preceding note. According to the Kabbalah, the upper and lower words, both the sefirot and this mundane arena, are devoid of any potency, even of existence itself, without the animating power of the Ein-Sof. This is especially true for R. Shneur Zalman, the author of this passage.

26. Ketubbot 50a. This is one of the enactments (*takkanot*) of the Sanhedrin at Usha, that one should not give to charity more than one-fifth of his wealth, so that he should not himself be reduced to rely on charity. See Rashi, ad loc.

27. This is the Lurianic conception of cosmic cataclysm when the light of the Ein-Sof overflowed from the created sefirot (the "vessels"). These sparks exist in and sustain all objects and acts, and await redemption by man by means of his study of Torah and performance of the mitzvot, and also such mundane acts as eating when done with the proper intention. *Ben Porat Yosef* to Miketz 74a; *Ketonet Passim* to Beha'alotekha 35b; see Glossary.

28. That is, how can the divine sparks be said to inhere in a sinful deed?

29. The Besht's answer is that sin can be repealed by means of repentance, and the potential for *teshuvah* is the holy spark that is immanent in sin itself. Note how this effectively side-steps the antinomian conclusion of the Sabbateans. See G. Scholem, "Redemption Through Sin," pp. 94–95.

7. THE INNER REPENTANCE
Source: R. Yaakov Yosef of Polennoye, *Toledot Yaakov Yosef* to Behar, sec. 11

Man, constituted of good and evil, never stays on one level, but constantly rises and falls. Because of the incitement to sin by the ubiquitous Evil Urge, he sometimes sinks into the depths of concupiscence in this material world and falls from his high station. If he then wishes to return on the high road to the Lord—whose service, Torah, fear, and love are a flame in his heart—but cannot, because of his sins which have led him into darkness over the years and form an iron curtain between him and our Father in Heaven; then the following advice is proffered to him. The [fundamentally] righteous person (= *zaddik*) can act in one of two ways in order to regain his former high level.

First, as Maimonides suggests, he can follow the "middle path."[30] One who has erred by going to one extreme must bend toward the opposite extreme, in order finally to arrive at the middle path.[31] We learn this from medical science.[32] So it is with regard to the ways of the Lord. If one has fallen from his high station by going to one extreme, he must repent by going to the other extreme. This is known as the "higher repentance," whereby one unifies Father and Mother.[33]

But there is another, deeper way for the zaddik to make his own; this is not meant for everyone, as is the first method mentioned above. It is more difficult, and is intended only for those initiated into the mysteries of the Lord.[34]

---

30. Maimonides' ethical philosophy (largely following Aristotle, but with clear differences to accommodate it to authoritative Jewish teaching) calls for man to follow the mean, or middle path, between the two antipodes in each band of character. For instance, generosity is the mean between profligacy and niggardliness, and courage is the mean between foolhardiness and cowardice. See Maimonides' *Eight Chapters*, chap. 4; idem, Hilkhot De'ot 1:4.

31. On the basis of his theory, Maimonides recommends to one who has overreached to one extreme to strive for its opposite, so that ultimately he will emerge on the middle path and succeed in attaining moderation. See Hilkhot De'ot 2:2.

32. It is Maimonides (ibid.) who applies a medical principle—medication urging the body in the opposite direction of its malfunction in order to reestablish its balance—to repentance, or therapy of the soul.

33. Symbols of the sefirot of Hokhmah ("Wisdom") and Binah ("Understanding") respectively; see Glossary.

34. The second method is esoteric and should not be offered as a popular spiritual technique. The Lurianic idea of the sparks scattered throughout creation, even evil, was referred to by the Besht in the preceding selection. Only the zaddik, adept in Kabbalah, can be trusted to free the sparks, in the manner here suggested, without being further ensnared by sin. R. Yaakov Yosef is cautious in recommending such potentially dangerous mediations, lest people lapse once again into Sabbateanism and its antinomian embracing of sin in order to liberate the divine sparks.

. . . He must be wise enough to know that, whatever the level to which he has descended, there too resides the glory of the blessed Shekhinah, in accordance with the mystery of *His kingdom ruleth over all* (Ps. 103:19).[35] Hence the reason for his descent to this level was to connect to himself those levels of sparks of the Shekhinah that exist there, so that he might rise with them as part of the mystery of his repentance. Although this is a "lower repentance," nevertheless it leads him more deeply into the sanctuary.[36]

8. THE SUPERIORITY OF THE PENITENT OVER THE RIGHTEOUS
Source: R. Dov Ber of Mezeritch, Maggid Devarav le-Yaakov 194 (Shatz-Uffenheimer ed.), p. 312

The Rabbis said: "He who performs repentance out of love, his pre-meditated sins are transformed into merits."[37] One can perhaps say that this is hinted at in the verse, *Who is a god like Thee that pardons iniquity and passes by the transgression of the remnant of His heritage?* (Mic. 7:18). He who repents out of love is a *nosei avon*,[38] i.e., he elevates and bears and raises [the sin] upward so that it turns into merits, thus evoking the higher love which is Hesed.[39] It is known that the sefirah of Tiferet inclines toward Hesed,[40] and when one repents out of love and elevates the iniquity to merit,[41] he greatly stirs up the prevalence of Hesed and powerful love and great beauty for Tiferet-Israel.[42] This

---

35. One of the verses often evoked to support hasidic immanentism. The reference is, apparently, to the preposition *ba* in *ba-kol*, lit. "His kingdom ruleth *in* all."
36. This phrase alludes to the extended homily from which this passage is taken. The characteristically kabbalistic-hasidic technique of *teshuvah* is "lower" but also "deeper" or "more inward."
37. Yoma 86b. Through repentance out of love instead of fear, one's worst sins, the premeditated ones, not only are accounted as nondeliberate transgressions, but they are considered as if they were meritorious deeds.
38. A play on words. The Hebrew word *nosei* can means "pardons," as the ordinary sense of this passage indicates, but the same root also means "elevates" and "bears."
39. The fourth of the sefirot, that of divine grace (*shefa*), associated with divine love; see Glossary.
40. Tiferet ("Majesty" or "Beauty") is the sixth of the sefirot which dialectically reconciles Hesed ("Love") and Gevurah ("Power"). Tiferet, R. Dov Ber asserts, is closer to Hesed than Gevurah.
41. For by raising the sin to the sefirotic levels indicated, it loses its evil character and becomes converted to its opposite: merit.
42. By this composite term R. Dov Ber indicates supernal as opposed to mundane Beauty. Israel, or Jacob, is the third of the three patriarchs, who each symbolized, respectively, one element of the triad, Hesed-Gevurah-Tiferet.

is what is meant by *And it is his glory [tiferet] to pass over a transgression* (Prov. 19:11);[43] hence all his sins are forgiven.[44]

This is occasioned by the penitent more than by one who was righteous all along, for the latter causes constant delight up Above, whereas the penitent causes a much greater delight, for [his action] comes after despair, and it is like one who has found something very precious that he had lost.[45] This is especially so since the penitent must make ever greater efforts in the service of the Creator.

9. THE INITIATION OF REPENTANCE
Source: R. Yaakov Yosef of Polennoye, Ketonet Passim to Kedoshim[46]

There are two kinds of repentance. In one, the initiative for repentance comes from man, who then receives assistance from Above. In the other, man makes no step [in the direction of repentance] until he is prodded by Heaven. This, our Rabbis tell us, is an ongoing dispute between God and the Congregation of Israel. God says, *"Return unto Me* (first), and then *I will return unto you"* (Mal. 3:7). The congregation

---

43. Scripture describes the gracious character of the wise man—it is his glory or beauty to overlook a transgression or insult—and the author here applies it to God. Hence, it is His quality of Tiferet which causes him to forgive sins.

44. The line of reasoning includes one element mentioned in the original text preceding this translation portion: the talmudic assertion that the face of Jacob-Israel is engraved on the Throne of Glory; hence, the verse "Israel, by whom I [God] will be glorified" (Isa. 49:3), the last word being a verb-form of *tiferet*. When an Israelite repents of a sin, and does so out of love, he stirs the sefirah of Tiferet, which in turn arouses Ḥesed, the result of which is the transformation of sin to merit and the pardon of past iniquities.

45. This is a characteristic hasidic element, though rooted in the talmudic teaching that "penitents stand where the perfectly righteous cannot" (Berakhot 34b); see also Maimonides, *Eight Chapters*, chap. 6. The transformation or sublimation of evil to good, of sin to merit, creates "greater pleasure" in heaven than the consistent goodness of the righteous man who never had to overcome moral failure and despair, and who affords heaven merely "constant pleasure" which, according to the Besht, can hardly be called pleasure at all. The superiority of the penitent over the righteous man who never failed is not merely a preference for the adventuresome and creative spirit over the routinely righteous, but also touches upon a kabbalistic note, the "elevation of the sparks" (see above, pp. 332–334 and below, pp. 379 f). This is implied in R. Dov Ber's reference to finding that which one lost, i.e., the divine sparks were "lost" in sin, and by means of repentance out of love the penitent redeems and elevates them back to their Source. (See Shatz-Uffenheimer's notes to this passage.)

46. The same passage appears in the R. Yaakov Yosef's *Ben Porat Yosef*, homily for Shabbat Teshuvah, year 5521 (= 1760).

of Israel replies: "We have no strength to begin; therefore, *Thou turn us unto Thee and we shall return*" (Lam. 5:21)—God should take the first step.[47]

The difference [between the two approaches] is this: When a human is the initiator, it may be compared to when the female is the first to emit seed, in which case she gives birth to a male child, the symbol of compassion. When the process starts from Above, such as because of troubles visited upon people [by Heaven], it is like when the male is the first to emit seed, in which case the offspring is female.[48]

I have heard something similar from my master [the Besht] on the verse, *Fire shall be kept burning upon the altar continually* (Lev. 6:6), on which the Rabbis commented: Although fire, for the burning of the sacrifices on the altar, comes down from Heaven, it is a mitzvah to bring earthly fire.[49] The fire from Above (the Besht said) was meant to be only a reaction to the effort of humans, who should first stir up the flames below.

This may also be the intention of the introductory statement in the *Shulḥan Arukh*: One must strengthen himself as a lion and rise [early] in the morning to serve his Creator; that he shall awake the

---

47. Lamentations Rabbah 5:22.

48. According to R. Ammi in Berakhot 60a (in an obvious reference to Lev. 12:2), the sex of a child is determined by which of the parents came to climax first. If the mother, the child will be a boy; if the father, a girl. In the Zohar, "male" and "female" are taken as symbolic of the masculine/feminine polarity in the sefirot, a polarity further developed in Lurianic Kabbalah. In the latter, from which Hasidism borrows heavily, we find the terms "female waters," the waters of earth and the abyss, representing the passive elements in divinity, and "male waters" of heaven, the active elements. As with the other instance of male/female imagery, the symbolism seeks to express the yearning for unification and the overcoming of the fragmentation and dissonance within the sefirot. For a successful conjunction of both elements, it is necessary that the "female waters" be elevated first, in preparation for the "male waters," rather than coercion by the latter of the former. If the "female waters" are thus the initiators, then the meeting of the two is felicitous, and vice-versa. This now fits in with the talmudic dictum, as the hasidic teachers identify "female waters" with mankind, and "male waters" with God. If the female is aroused first, i.e., if the process of reconciliation begins with human initiative, from down "below," then the result will be a "male child," symbol of compassion and felicity. If, however, we wait upon the "male waters," or divine initiative, then the result is a "female child," symbol of *din* ("judgment"). The lesson is clear; a person must not sit idly by, waiting until God coerces him to turn to Him by visiting various afflictions upon him. Rather, he must turn to God out of love, and by his own initiative.

49. Yoma 21b.

dawn."[50] The reference here is to repentance. One should repent in his youth, when all is well with him, and not wait until he is awakened from Above through troubles and distress. And thus the consequent remark: "But the dawn does not awaken me."[51] I do not wait, said David, for an awakening from Heaven to do repentance, but I begin on my own. When assistance from Above ("dawn") follows, that is called a "male child," and is a token of divine compassion.[52]

Nevertheless, if man cannot arouse himself [to do repentance], he must at least endeavor to experience it when a sign for awakening comes from Above.[53]

10. TWO KINDS OF REPENTANCE
Source: R. Gedaliah of Linitz, Teshuot Ḥen, Shemini, s.v. uve-ofen aḥer, ed. Jerusalem, p. 83b

The Zohar teaches that there are two aspects to repentance, a higher and a lower repentance.[54] This may be explained as follows: The fear of Heaven comes in two forms, yir'at ha-onesh ("fear of punishment") and yir'at ha-romemut ("reverential fear"). The former is called the lower yir'ah, the latter, the higher yir'ah.

The kind of repentance which results from the fear of punishment is basically inferior and is designated the Lower Repentance. It is, however, a stepping stone to the Higher Repentance, which is the outcome of reverential fear, [that which overwhelms man when he contemplates] the very greatness of God.

There is also another level of penitence which may be called Repentance of Repentance, or Binah of Binah.[55] This means that when a man achieves the Higher Repentance, his heart begins to ache with

---

50. Oraḥ Ḥayyim 1:1.
51. Based on Ps. 57:9, "I will awaken the dawn." The implication is: "but the dawn will not awaken me." That is, David says that he will initiate the arousal or the turn to God, and not wait for God to arouse him to His service. This concluding remark ("but the dawn will not awaken me") is not found in the Shulḥan Arukh, but is recorded in the Tur (Oraḥ Ḥayyim 1:1), the source of the Shulḥan Arukh's citation.
52. As in n. 48 above.
53. Thus, even though he will not have achieved the optimum, at least he will have succeeded in doing some form of teshuvah.
54. Zohar (Raya Mehemna) III, 122a—123b.
55. Binah ("Understanding") is the third of the ten sefirot, and is identified by Raya Mehemna (Zohar III, 122a) as equivalent to, or the mystical source of, teshuvah.

regret for not having achieved such a state of returning to Him out of awareness of His mighty greatness earlier.[56]

11. REPENTANCE OUT OF LOVE
Source: R. Shneur Zalman of Liady, Tanya, Likkutei Amarim, chap. 7

"Repentance out of love," the Rabbis say, [carried the privilege that] "one's premeditated sins are transformed into merits."[57]

This refers to repentance that comes from the depths of the heart, with great love and fervor, and from a soul passionately desiring to cleave to God, and thirsting for Him like parched desert soil. For, inasmuch as the sinner's soul has been in a barren wilderness and in the shadow of death, which is the *sitra ahara* ("Other Side"),[58] and infinitely removed from the light of God's countenance, his soul develops a thirst for Him even more than do the souls of the righteous (*zaddikim*). As the Rabbis said: "In the place where penitents (*ba'alei teshuvah*) stand, not even the perfectly righteous (*zaddikim gemurim*) can stand."[59] It is in reference to repentance out of such great love that they say that the penitent's willful sins become like virtues, since these—his sins—brought him the attainment of this great love.[60]

However, in the case of repentance not motivated by such love, even though it too is a proper way of penitence and God will pardon

---

56. This thought is close to that of the author of *Benei Yisaskhar* (see above, selection 19). See also n. 106 below.
57. Yoma 86b.
58. The kabbalistic term for evil. There are ten sefirot in the world of *tum'ah* ("impurity") just as there are ten sefirot in the world of *kedushah* ("holiness"). The latter are called *sitra de-yamina* ("the right side") or *sitra da* ("this side"). The former are designated *sitra di-semala* ("the left side") or *sitra ahara* ("the other side").
59. Berakhot 34b. R. Shneur Zalman gives the talmudic comment on *ba'alei teshuvah* a novel interpretation. It does not necessarily refer to a higher reward but to a loftier sense of spiritual elevation and achievement. For Maimonides, for instance, this passage does refer to greater reward, because of the greater effort needed to overcome a heretofore triumphant *yetzer ha-ra*. See Hilkhot Teshuvah 7:4, and cf. his *Eight Chapters*, chap. 6.
60. The perfect zaddik, who never sinned, can never experience the thirst of the soul to return to a pristine state as much as the *ba'al teshuvah*. Consequently the zaddik's *teshuvah*, in the sense of returning, cannot produce such great love and joy. However, R. Shneur Zalman elsewhere presents a broader concept of *teshuvah* which is independent of sin, i.e., the yearning of the soul to return to its divine Source. Such *teshuvah* does not allow a distinction between the penitent and the completely righteous person. See R. Shneur Zalman's *Likkutei Torah*, beginning of Ha'azinu.

him, his iniquities are not transformed into merits. His sins will not be released from the *kelipah* (contaminating shells) until the End of Days, when death will vanish forever.

12. THE MANY GATEWAYS TO REPENTENCE
Source: R. Gedaliah of Linitz, Teshuot Ḥen, Shofetim, s.v. veha-nir'ah, ed. Jerusalem, p. 1031-b

The fifty gates of wisdom[61] are simultaneously fifty gates of repentance, for there are fifty ways to return to the Holy One and come nearer to Him. Six of these are elucidated in the name of the Ari, of blessed memory. We shall mention two of them briefly. They are as follows:

The first is contentment [with a minimum of worldly pleasures]. One contemplates his own exceeding inferiority relative to the King of kings, the Holy One, and he becomes satisfied with a frugal existence which would have been impossible without such meditation. He is happy to live like that in order not to be distracted by worldly matters so as to devote more time to the service of God and to return to Him closely.

The second gateway [of repentance] is that of pride. To be sure, here again the solid base is humility. What is meant, however, is the kind of pride ascribed to [King] Jehoshaphat: *And his heart was lifted up in the ways of the Lord* (2 Chron. 17:6). When man contemplates his lowliness in comparison to God, he begins to understand that a lifetime of serving Him will not be sufficient to repay Him for even one of His favors.[62]

And so it is with all of the fifty gates, each of them dealing with a specific way of returning to God. The fiftieth (i.e., the highest) gate is all-pervasive, in the sense that all the others contain an element of its main feature, which is: digging a tunnel beneath the Throne of His Glory.

Our sins alienate us from our Father in Heaven. This "obstructive partition" is the cause of our forgetting to return to Him. But God "digs a tunnel" beneath His Throne [while] concealing its existence

---

61. Rosh Hashanah 26b. Traditionally, there are fifty levels, or "gates," of wisdom.
62. The "pride" element is man's endeavor to respond to God's goodness with service, even though he knows it must forever remain inadequate. "His heart you lifted up," in the verse cited, is a biblical idiom for pride.

from the "accusers."[63] This opening serves as a reminder to transgressors to repent for their sins, for "there is no forgetting before the Throne of Glory."[64]

This "tunnel" is also the cause for the repentance thoughts that are a daily occurrence to everyone. The wise man whose *eyes are in his head* (Eccles. 2:14) will take advantage of it and keep a watchful eye on his affairs, ensuring thereby his return to God in perfect repentance. The fool, however, *repeats his folly* (Prov. 26:11) and diverts his attention to empty talk or to drinking wine.

I heard a similar thought from the Rabbi-Preacher,[65] in the name of the Besht, concerning the matter of the *bat kol* ("heavenly voice") that goes forth every day from Mount Horeb (Sinai).[66]

This explains the Exodus from Egypt. The Israelites in Egypt were so utterly sunk in impurity that it became virtually impossible for them to return to God, for they had all but fallen into the fiftieth gate

---

63. In the talmudic metaphor, a person's sins become "accusing angels" against him. The idea of God digging a clandestine tunnel so that a sinner might do *teshuvah* and return to Him without interference from the angels is mentioned in both the Babylonian and the Jerusalem Talmudim and in midrashim in connection with Manasseh, the wicked king of Judea. See Sanhedrin 103a; J.T. Sanhedrin 10:2 (51b), Midrash Ruth 5:6, and elsewhere. (See also *Yefeh Enayim* to Sanhedrin, ad loc., for bibliographical references and for correct reading and interpretation of the Babylonian text.) The text in the Jerusalem Talmud reads as follows: "The angels sealed the windows [of heaven] so that the prayers of Manasseh would not ascend to God. The angels said: 'Master of the world, here is a man who worshipped pagan gods and set up an idol in the Temple; how can You accept his *teshuvah*?' God replied: 'If I do not accept his *teshuvah* I would be closing the door for all *ba'alei teshuvah*.' What did God do? He dug an opening beneath the Throne of His Glory and He accepted his [Manasseh's] supplication." R. Gedaliah's assumption that this heavenly "tunnel" was intended for all *ba'alei teshuvah* seems to be implied in the words of God: "If I do not accept Manasseh's *teshuvah* I would be closing the door . . ." The idea behind the imagery is that God seeks out the sinner and offers him the opportunity of *teshuvah*, even when his own resources are exhausted. One should never, therefore, despair of returning to God.
64. From the Rosh ha-Shanah Musaf service.
65. The popular title for R. Aryeh Judah Leib of Polonnoye, a disciple of the Besht.
66. See *Toledot Yaakov Yosef* to Beha'alotekha 1: "The Rabbis said: 'Every day a *bat kol* goes forth from Mount Horeb, proclaiming, "Woe to mankind for contempt of the Torah"' (Avot 6:2). On this the Besht asked: 'What is the purpose of the *bat kol* if it cannot be heard? And if it is heard, why has it no effect?' He explained that the *bat kol* expressed the *teshuvah* in thoughts that frequently occur to people." These *teshuvah* thoughts, causing man to question himself and suggesting a reorientation of his life, are not random events, but are messages or summonses by God.

of *tum'ah*.[67] Then God revealed His Divine Glory to them by digging a "tunnel" to them from beneath His Throne of Glory. This raised them above the realm of the natural and ignited in their hearts a burning flame to return to Him truthfully.

This similarly explains the many repetitions in Torah concerning the Exodus from Egypt. It was intended to teach us not to follow the advice of the Evil Urge, which "tells those who ate garlic (and exude a bad smell) to eat garlic again,"[68] for that is incurably wrong. The Exodus disproves such an argument: God acted wondrously with His people, granting them strength to return to Him, after they were sunk in the Egyptian furnace of iron, by providing for them a "tunnel" to Him.

13. THE ROLE OF THE ZADDIK IN REPENTANCE
Source: R. Elimelekh of Lizhensk, Noam Elimelekh to Metzora, 59b s.v. ve-od

A most important principle [in serving God] is *To walk humbly with thy God* (Mic. 6:8). All man's ways should be modest. Whatever one does publicly and with fanfare, even worshipping God, may easily become self-serving and lead to arrogance. But the [good deeds] that one performs privately will not become self-serving, for no one sees him.

This principle of acting modestly applies only to one who [is pious but] wants to improve his service of God. The *ba'al teshuvah*, however, who wishes to repent transgressions committed publicly, such as slander and other such sins, must of necessity do repentance in a like manner, namely, in public. This accords with [the halakhic rule], "As the absorption [occurred], so must the discharge be,"[69] namely, forbidden food is disgorged the same way it was absorbed. It follows, therefore, that for transgressions one committed secretly he should repent

---

67. The lowest level of impurity, hence ultimate defilement.
68. An allusion to the talmudic comment, "One who ate garlic and exudes a bad smell, should he eat garlic again to exude an even worse smell?" (Berakhot 51a). Having been given an opportunity by means of the divine messages to return, man should not ignore it and return to his wonted "smelly" ways. The Exodus is the paradigm of the availability of *teshuvah* for those on the very lowest moral and spiritual levels, and hence should emancipate us from the inertia of evil.
69. Pesahim 74a. The rule concerns the absorption of forbidden foodstuffs by a vessel. The vessel can be repaired by causing it to exude the material in the same manner it initially absorbed it, whether by fire, hot water, lukewarm water, etc. R. Elimelekh now uses this principle as a metaphor for repentance.

privately, while for the open, public sins he must repent openly and publicly.[70]

This, however, poses a problem. When one repents in public, he may [perhaps] do so for self-serving reasons (as mentioned above) and thereby waste any benefit from [his repentance], God forbid.

The solution to this problem is to visit the perfect zaddikim. This will save him from selfish involvement, for the Evil Urge is powerless in the presence of zaddikim. Moreover, one cannot possibly be affected by selfishness while in the company of zaddikim, for when one observes the abundance of their [unselfishly good] deeds, it causes him to tremble and think: How can I be proud of my humble doings, in comparison to the [great] practices of the zaddikim?[71]

14. REPENTANCE AS THE LIBERATION OF THE SHEKHINAH
Source: R. Elimelekh of Lizhensk, Noam Elimelekh to Vayehi 29a, s.v. o yomar

Everyone possesses within him a part of God above. Even when one commits a transgression, may it never happen, were it not for the part of God in him, he would be left with no strength to make any physical movement or shake a limb. This divine component is compelled to enwrap itself in garments upon garments in order to withstand the great suffering [that is the result] of the sin. This is the mystery of the exile of the Shekhinah.[72]

---

70. Maimonides and Raavad deal with the problem of public vs. private repentance (Hilkhot Teshuvah 2:5, based on Yoma 86b). According to Maimonides, for ritual sins the repentance should be private; for ethical sins, however, it should be public. Maimonides makes no distinction between publicly and privately committed transgressions, as R. Elimelekh does here. Raavad, however, maintains that all publicly committed sins, ritual or ethical, must be confessed and repented publicly. (But according to the interpretation of R. Joseph Caro, in his Kesef Mishnah, Maimonides does not dispute this view.)
71. See chapter 8 for the highly developed theory of the role of the zaddik in the writings of R. Elimelekh of Lizhensk.
72. In the Talmud, the exile of the Shekhinah has a national connotation. "Says R. Simeon bar Yohai: 'Come and see how beloved [the nation of] Israel is of God, for whenever they were exiled, the Shekhinah went along with them." R. Elimelekh, however, spiritualizes and personalizes this concept and applies it to every individual, inasmuch as everyone has a part of God within him. The "exile" of God Who dwells in man is caused by sin, and repentance is therefore an act of liberation of the Shekhinah.

Later on, when the sinner repents and weeps over his transgressions, he is [thereby] bewailing the exile of the Shekhinah. This, in turn, tears away the "garments" which the divine part within him was compelled to don, [and it is then that the divine within him] is revealed in its perfected form—when the sin is repaired.

15. MIXED EMOTIONS OF REPENTANCE
Source: R. Zadok ha-Kohen of Lublin, Zidkat ha-Zaddik, no. 129

As soon as one intends to do repentance, he is in the category of one who attempts self-purification, and [heavenly] justice demands that he be assisted [from Above].[73] When this heavenly support is granted, the spirit of purification expands of itself, eliciting an even greater intervention from Above in his support [to match his newly acquired purity]. The new, enhanced assistance again engenders a more vigorous longing for purity, and so the process keeps on repeating itself until an opening the size of a needlepoint expands to the size of the open doors of the Temple vestibule.[74]

[A question thus arises:] How is it that occasionally one wishes to do repentance but does not accomplish it, as the Rabbis say: "Transgressing Jews are full of remorse"?[75] An explanation for this may be found in Midrash ha-Ne'elam, Zohar Hadash, end of section Bereshit. It says: "When one is ready to do repentance, his Evil Urge[76] begins a great accusatory campaign (kitrug) against him. The time of the kitrug is, thus, [usually] on Rosh Hashanah, which is called When

---

73. See Yoma 38b: "He who comes to cleanse himself [from sin] will be assisted [from Heaven]."
74. This is a slight variation of the midrashic statement which has God saying to the Jews: "My children, open unto Me a door of repentance as the point of a needle and I will open before you doorways in which coaches and wagons can enter" (Song of Songs Rabbah 5:3); the latter part of this midrash is popularly quoted in the didactic religious literature in the form referred to by R. Shneur Zalman, namely, "and I will open before you a door the size of the entrance to the Temple vestibule." This is probably a conflation of Song Rabba with Eruvin 53a. R. Zadok here provides an original analysis of the mechanism of such a sanguine approach to repentance.
75. Eruvin 19a, Hagigah 27a. These sources, however, read: "are full of mitzvot."
76. "Evil Urge" and "Satan" are interchangeable terms; thus, "Satan, the Evil Urge, and the Angel of Death are one and the same" (Bava Batra 16a).

He may be found" (Isa. 55:6)[77] and *An acceptable time* (Ps. 69:14).[78] Satan's *kitrug* uses a variety of accusations in order to demonstrate that [this repenting sinner] does not deserve divine assistance, [thus interrupting the upward spiral of repentance]. The penitent must, therefore, seek heavenly compassion when he is ready for self-purification, in order to obtain divine support.

A good plan for counteracting [Satan's schemes] is [to maintain] joyousness and to trust that God, in His abundance of mercy and goodness, will surely accept him [and enable him] to do perfect repentance before Him. Within,[79] he should also experience a feeling of great wretchedness for his transgression. This is similar [to the shofar sounds] *tekiah, shevarim, teruah, tekiah* performed on Rosh Hashanah. As is generally known, [the sound of] *tekiah* denotes rejoicing, while *shevarim* and *teruah* signify the opposite. These are called "groaning and trembling sounds."[80] This causes Satan to be confused.[81]

It is written in the *Song of David when Nathan the prophet came to him* (Ps. 51:1), *O God, be gracious to me according to Thy mercy; in accordance with Thy abundant compassion, blot out my sins* (ibid. 2). [Note that] it begins with an expression of joy and song (*a song of David*),[82] confident that God will answer him; and as with all other entreating psalms, it ends on a note of deliverance and consolation. This parallels the order of sounds on [Rosh Hashanah]. Those of groaning and trembling [*shevarim, teruah*] are preceded by the straight sound [*tekiah*], symbolizing joy and song, and are also followed by *tekiah*, to end on a note of salvation and consolation.

---

77. See Rosh Hashanah 18a.
78. See Berakhot 8a and Rashi, ad loc. The Ten Days of Penitence, beginning with Rosh Hashanah, are most propitious for the reconciliation between God and man; and it is such a time, therefore, that the demonic and destructive forces within man most actively try to frustrate him.
79. Meaning either within the sense of joy and trust or within himself.
80. Rosh Hashanah 16b. Thus, just as the shofar sounds embrace both joy and lamentation, so man who begins repentance (especially in the Rosh Hashanah season) must experience both contrasting emotions. In both cases, joy both precedes and follows the lamentations.
81. This is a novel paraphrase of Rosh Hashanah 16b, according to which we sound the *tekiah* and *teruah* twice during the service, whilst "sitting" and whilst "standing," in order "to confuse Satan." R. Zadok attributes the "confusion of Satan" not to the repetition of the sounding of the shofar, but to the paradoxical emotions caused by sounding both *tekiah*, symbolizing joy, and *shevarim-teruah*, which express lamentation.
82. For the happy connotations of *mizmor* ("song"), see Berakhot 7b.

The same is true with repentance. With the attainment of perfect repentance there comes—in one hour; indeed, one moment—light and revelation, which are the joy that follows.[83] Similarly, it is written, for example, *I melt away my bed with my tears* (Ps. 6:7) and, soon after, *For God heard the voice of my weeping* (ibid. 9). A similar [joyous] state also occurs always before [repentance], as indicated in [the words of the prophet] *Before they call, I will answer* (Isa. 65:24). Surely when God answers, the impression is felt in all the worlds. Thus man's heart senses even before his "calling" [to God in repentance] a bit of joy and trust.

When man trains his heart to act thus, even if the joy does not come of itself because of God's answering him, he may nonetheless attain such joy by his own [emotional efforts]; for they leave their mark in heaven, and this is the way it really becomes. This is implied, as is well known, in the verse, *The Lord is thy shade upon thy right hand* (Ps. 121:5).[84]

16. THE LEAP OF THE PENITENT
Source: R. Levi Yitzhak of Berdichev, Kedushat Levi (Likkutim) 110b

It should be understood that repentance does not meanly only repentance for sins committed. When our Sages said that one should spend all his life in *teshuvah*,[85] they surely did not address themselves to repentance for sins. What they meant was that one should always feel heartbroken and empty for being so far from God.

By concentrating his thoughts and meditating deeply and steadily on God's greatness, a person will recognize his own unworthiness, his lack of any significance whatsoever. He will realize that he has not even begun to serve Him in a manner commensurate with His mag-

---

83. Hence, like the shofar, the anguish and inner ferment of the repentance experience must deliberately be preceded by joy and confidence, and they produce, as a consequence, similar feelings of consolation and deliverance afterwards.
84. An interpretation of this verse that is widely quoted in hasidic circles and that is attributed to the Besht (though it is older than him too) has it that this establishes a relationship between God and man. Just as the shadow follows the activity of the hand, so God reacts to man's gestures. Hence, if man wills himself into a joyous frame of mind, as a prelude to repentance, such a state of gladness and serenity will be granted him by God. The efficacy of spiritual "role-playing" is an oft-repeated theme in hasidic literature.
85. Shabbat 153a.

nitude. [This will instill in him] a feeling a humility and personal dissatisfaction resulting in an awakening to worship God with sublime fear, our of self-nullification, until he reaches the [spiritual] heights needed for standing before God.

This is what the Rabbis were referring to in their comment, "In the place where the penitent (ba'alei teshuvah) stand, not even the perfectly righteous can stand."[86] Those who worship God from the aspect of repentance, namely, out of sublime fear [for Him] and self-nullification, are in a higher state of serving God than even the perfectly righteous. For the latter, even though they are perfectly righteous—worshipping God by studying the Torah, observing the mitzvot, and performing good deeds—still may not have achieved the state of inner, profound heart-brokenness that comes with the contemplation of God's greatness, which is the real mark of a ba'al teshuvah.[87]

The Rabbis' comment, however, should also be understood to refer to a repentant sinner, one who committed many transgressions, incurred guilt, and deserves God's punishment [but wishes now to return to Him].[88]

This, however, poses a problem. How can one who violated the laws of God repeatedly; who became estranged from and has forgotten the divine ways and the lofty paths through which one ascends to the presence of God; whose heart became utterly coarse and dull[89]—how can such a soiled and abominable person return to God? How can he, moreover, ascend to spiritual stations higher than those of the perfectly righteous who never ceased worshipping god?

The answer[90] is: The repentant sinner, precisely because of his depraved state, his surrender to passions and ugly deeds, and his complete estrangement from the true eternal life, was at the brink of spir-

---

86. Berakhot 34b.
87. Cf. above, n. 60.
88. In the first part of this selection, R. Levi Yitzhak offered a novel interpretation of the classical talmudic text elevating the ba'al teshuvah above the completely righteous person. The teshuvah (lit. "return") refers not to every sin but to man's existential estrangement from his Creator, a gap that can be bridged only by annihilating one's ego and thus narrowing the distance, albeit imperfectly, between himself and God. He now offers another interpretation of the same text, accepting the term ba'al teshuvah in its usual sense of one who repents from specific transgressions that he committed.
89. R. Levi Yitzhak refers here to Yoma 39a, "Sin dulls the mind of man; read not venitmetem bam ['you will be defiled by them'] (Lev. 11:43) but nitamtem bam [you will become dull-hearted by them']."
90. R. Levi Yitzhak here includes a long parable, here omitted.

itual extinction and despair. His decision to return is the result of a silent, bitter outcry from the depths of his soul to God. His repentance comes from self-sacrifice and self-annulment. This is why he is privileged to ascend to the upper stations of spirituality even more than the completely righteous. The latter, although they serve God thoroughly and with perfection, ascend the spiritual heights only gradually, each in proportion to [the quality of] his service. The *ba'al teshuvah*, however, whose achievement comes from an abandonment of his very selfhood and utter reliance on the essence of the Holy One, reaches the upper echelons of spiritual sublimity [all at once], inasmuch as the "awakening from below" brings about immediately an "awakening from Above."[91]

17. THE SINNER HELPS THE RIGHTEOUS
Source: R. Elimelekh of Lizhensk, Noam Elimelekh, Metzora

An interpretation of the talmudic comment: "In the place where the penitents stand, not even the perfectly righteous can stand."[92]

One who is engaged in the service of God must examine himself very carefully so as not to fall prey to any ulterior motive or feeling of haughtiness from serving Him. For if, God forbid, he has any such ulterior motive in his study of Torah or in his prayer, his service does not ascend to heaven.

However, when a wicked person repents his grave sins, such as, God forbid, robbery, sexual immorality, and other such, [his repentance is accepted] because there is nothing that stands in the way of *teshuvah*.[93] And when [the sinner] accomplishes a complete repen-

---

91. According to this second interpretation of the talmudic dictum asserting the superiority of the repentant sinner, the spirituality of the righteous person is relative to his own incremental activities, whether of prayer or study or mitzvot or acts of social kindness. His rise is therefore gradual and centered on himself. The repentant sinner, however, has despaired of such evolutionary improvement. He feels worthless and nonexistent, hence incapable of spiritual growth by tapping his own inner resources. Instead, out of his despair, he simply offers a wordless cry and throws himself upon God's mercy. His repentance, therefore, is focused on his Creator upon whom he can rely and who can save him. His "leap of faith" is accepted, and a corresponding "leap" of divine forgiveness brings him to an even higher spiritual station than the saintly person whose ascent to God is not motivated by sin. See Additional Note *1.
92. Berakhot 34b.
93. See J.T. Pe'ah 1:1 and Sanhedrin 10:1, "Nothing stands in the way of *ba'alei teshuvah*."

tance, honestly and faultlessly, he elevates [alongside his own sins] those prayers of the zaddik[94] which were not perfect because of some selfish motive in them.[95]

Therefore, even the perfectly righteous (zaddikim) cannot stand where the ba'alei teshuvah stand, because the ba'al teshuvah attains a higher state of spiritual elevation than the former; it is he who elevates the [imperfect] Torah and prayer of the righteous (zaddik).

18. WHEN REPENTANCE IS FELT TO BE INADEQUATE
Source: R. Zadok ha-Kohen of Lublin, Zidkat ha-Zaddik 134

Sometimes it may seem to a man that he has already repented and that his sins were forgiven; yet later, he is stirred up again and is aggrieved over his transgressions. He feels that both of these [apparently contradictory] thoughts are not imaginary. Indeed, both are true.

The law states: Transgressions which one confesses this Yom Kippur he confesses again the following Yom Kippur.[96] This [presumably] includes sins of which the Halakhah says one is forgiven at once the moment he does repentance.[97] [This may be understood in light of the following:]

There is no limit to the spiritual level of one's repentance, just as there is no limit to the heights man can reach [in every other spiritual endeavor]. One's repentance is commensurate with the degree of his attainment and perception. All human qualities are relative [to one's spiritual state]; man is not a static being.

---

94. As often happens in reading the writings of R. Elimelekh of Lizhensk (as well as R. Yaakov Yosef of Polennoye), it is difficult to discern when the author refers to a "righteous person" in the ordinary, traditional sense, and when he intends the zaddik in the new role being set for him by these hasidic theoreticians.

95. The spiritual exercise of repentance does not occur in a vacuum, but as a social or even cosmic act which affects others as well. A successful spiritual act pulls along others as well, elevating others toward God. Hence, when the sinner repents of his sins, he brings along with him the zaddikim who, while they technically committed no sins, performed their good deeds in a less than perfect manner.

96. Yoma 86b. This is the opinion of R. Eliezer b. Yaakov. The alternate opinion holds that one should not reconfess if he has not returned to the sin since last Yom Kippur. Maimonides (Hilkhot Teshuvah 2:8) and the Shulḥan Arukh (Oraḥ Ḥayyim 607:4) accept the former view. For differing opinions regarding the halakhah in this controversy, see Meiri to Yoma, loc. cit., Klein ed., pp. 217–218.

97. See Yoma 86a, Maimonides, Hilkhot Teshuvah 1:4.

This was the complaint of Moses: *I can no longer come and go* (Deut. 31:2).[98] So is it written: *In death one becomes free* (Ps. 88:6).[99] Thus too the talmudic idiom for death is, "his soul has rested." In this world, however, one never stays still, even though one does not feel it.

He whose roots are good—and there is a tradition that one who is [essentially] good will not turn bad[100]—keeps moving up higher and higher in goodness. The same is true in the opposite direction. As our Sages said: The older that scholars grow, the more clear-minded they become; the older that ignoramuses grow, the more confused they become.[101]

Therefore, when one reaches a higher level [it occurs to him] that [in his present state] he has not even begun to do repentance. Thus, as he climbs from height to height, his sin always appears before him. (That is, when he is in a lesser state, he has atoned for his sin relative to that state. This holds for all spiritual levels and worlds. When this happens, the sin vanishes, without leaving a trace. Nevertheless, when he attains a more exalted state, the sin reappears in all its strength. There is profound wisdom in this.)[102]

As the individual progresses in spiritual attainments, the impure thoughts of his youth stand revealed. Surely one who entered Pardes[103] and reached great heights, probably repents for the impurities and sins of his youth.[104]

This may be the meaning of the Rabbis' saying: "Whoever is greater, his *yetzer* is greater too."[105] For sin is man's greatest defect, and so is his *yetzer*.[106]

---

98. Thus Moses' impending death is signaled by his inability to move. Life implies movement.

99. Meaning: he is not expected any longer to move to greater spiritual heights. This is based on the rabbinic interpretation of Shabbat 30a.

100. See Berakhot 29a.

101. Kinnim 3:6.

102. This passage appears in parentheses in the text.

103. The term for esoteric wisdom. See Hagigah 14b.

104. Referring mainly to wasteful discharge of semen, called *ḥatat ne'urim* ("youthful sins").

105. Sukkah 52a. The *yetzer* is man's instinctual, usually lustful drive.

106. The last paragraph apparently refers to what was said earlier, that the more one grows spiritually, the more he feels the impact of past sins and consequently a greater need for repentance. Thus the saying that the *yetzer* grows commensurately with one's progress in spiritual greatness was not meant in a substantive sense but in the *ba'al teshuvah's* perception of it, i.e., the same defect of sin or *yetzer* is more disturbing to one of greater spiritual excellence. See Additional Note *2.

19. PERPETUAL REPENTANCE
Source: R. Zevi Elimelekh of Dinov, Benei Yisaskhar, Tishri, gedolah teshuvah, 5:19

The saintly author of the *Duties of the Hearts* wrote: "The pious men
of the olden days repented all their lives, even for a single transgression." Let me explain his words briefly.

It is known that according to the laws of the Torah pertaining to
[fines for] "degradation" in personal injuries, its evaluation is always
relative to the offender and the offended.[107] If the offender is a lowly
person, the one offended feels more slighted. Similarly, a great man
suffers more humiliation from an insult than does an ordinary individual. It follows from this that where the offender is a very lowly
person and the one slighted is a very great one, the payment assessed
should be very high because the humiliation is great. The situation
may be similar in other instances, such as an outburst of anger against
someone.[108] The process of conciliation would similarly depend upon
the relative status of the personalities involved.

Now, the greatness of God and His exaltedness are infinite, and
man is a tiny creature, insignificant in knowledge. Even were he to
live a million years, man could not adequately placate the anger of the
Creator of all things. But sin blinds the eyes of man, rendering him
unable to contemplate and be sensitive to God's greatness.

When one repents, his eyes are enlightened, and he is able to judge
and appreciate more clearly Whom he affronted. He can now, with his
improved reasoning powers, better understand God's greatness and
exaltedness. [With his new perceptions,] it becomes clear to him that
yesterday's repentance was not enough. He did not have then the
knowledge of God's greatness that he has today. Now that he is
enlightened, he needs to repent anew. The new repentance, in turn,
again stimulates the process of enlightenment [as to the greatness of
God and the insignificance of man], causing a need for new repentance. But even if man lived a thousand years, he can never attain
fully the knowledge of His greatness; hence, he must always be in a
state of repentance, even over one sin.[109]

---

107. Bava Kamma 83b, according to the view codified in Hoshen Mishpat 420:24.
108. The reference here may be to an outburst of anger against someone who admon-
ishes him for a sin he supposedly committed; see Maimonides, Hilkhot De'ot 6:7–8.
109. Similar ideas may be found in the citations from R. Nahman of Bratslav and R.
Zadok ha-Kohen in this chapter. See especially Additional Note *2.

20. NONE IS EXCLUDED FROM REPENTANCE
Source: R. Gedaliah of Linitz, Teshuot Ḥen, Ha'azinu, s.v. ke-nesher, ed. Jerusalem, p. 112a

Even if one had committed many transgressions, he must not allow the Evil Urge to seduce him into thinking that God will never forgive him. Heaven forbid! This empty prattle is merely [the Evil Urge's] way of pushing one away from God.[110] For there is nothing that stands in the way of repentance, as it is written in early devotional books: "Thou turnest man to *daka* ('contrition') [and sayest: *Return, ye children of men* (Ps. 90:3).]" The acrostic of *daka* is: *dam* ("blood"), *kefirah* ("heresy"), and *ishah* ("woman"). [The verse thus implies that] even if one committed the gravest of sins, which are adultery (*ishah*), murder (*dam*), and idolatry (*kefirah*),[111] he may still find atonement through repentance.

Moreover, the argument of the *yetzer* has no basis on account of the [constant] reminder [to repent] coming from God. As mentioned earlier, a heavenly voice (*bat kol*) goes forth daily, proclaiming, *Return, O backsliding children* (Jer. 3:14).[112] If it were true that such sinners are denied repentance, it would make no sense to call upon them to repent.

21. FAITH IN THE EFFICACY OF REPENTANCE
Source: R. Zevi Elimelekh of Dinov, Benei Yisaskhar, Tishri, s.v. gedolah teshuvah, 14

Return, O Israel, unto the Lord thy God (Hos. 14:2). The verse may be understood in accordance with the assertions of both the early and

---

110. See Ezekiel 33:10, "You speak, saying: Our transgressions and our sins are upon us, and we fester away in them; how then can we live?" Rashi (ad loc.) comments: "You show no desire to repent because you think that repentance will no longer help you."

111. These three sins are the only ones for which one must sacrifice his life (see Pesahim 25a–b).

112. See above, selection 12, in the name of the Besht. There, however, the reference is made to Avot 6:2, according to which the *bat kol* warns against contempt for Torah. The only mention of a *bat kol* calling to repentance is in Hagigah 15a in the case of Aher (= Elisha ben Abuyah, a scholar who became a heretic and cooperated with the Roman government in its actions against Torah study), where it seems to be directed solely at him, and is not said to be a daily occurrence. R. Gedaliah has apparently, perhaps unwittingly, conflated both sources.

the later halakhic codifiers that one of the stipulations for the effectiveness of repentance is having faith in it.[113] The sinner must believe that repentance brings atonement even if he has committed countless transgressions and prayed many times to God for forgiveness and each time returned to his rebelliousness. Nevertheless, the good and forgiving God will accept his repentance.

Let me explain this to you according to reason.

A human being, if he possesses good personality traits, such as compassion and forgiveness, will readily pardon all who vex him. Nevertheless, he will lose his patience with the repeater who persists in provoking him day after day, and he will refuse to forgive him anymore. Now, there are many levels of such forbearance. One who is more compassionate will be more patient. But finally every human being reaches his limit, for mortals are by nature finite beings and therefore their characters are limited.

However, this cannot occur in the relation of God toward man. The reason for this is that, unlike man, God's existence is eternal and boundless; His attributes, too, are limitless. And inasmuch as He is merciful, compassionate, good, and forgiving, all of these attributes too have no limit or end.

The sinner, therefore, must not be overcome by a feeling of resignation: How can I lift my face to return to Him when so many times before I have expressed contrition over my sinful ways, prayed for forgiveness, promised God that I would not sin again, only to return to my wonted ways again and again? How will God ever accept my repentance again? One should never say this. [One must always keep in mind that] His graciousness and forgiveness are infinite, just as He Himself has no limit.

This, then, is what the prophet meant by saying: *Return, O Israel, to the Lord thy God.* He is eternal and boundless [and therefore unlimited in His attributes of goodness], and He will therefore assuredly accept your repentance at all times. Even if you erred often, He Who is good and forgiving will pardon your sins and forgive you.[114]

---

113. See Maimonides, Hilkhot Shegagot 3:10; Rema, *Shulḥan Arukh,* Oraḥ Ḥayyim 607:6. The atonement of Yom Kippur is effective only for those who believe in it. Yom Kippur does not expiate the sins of the skeptic who says, "Of what use is this day?"
114. The exegesis, though not completely clear, is as follows: *Return* is made possible by *to the Lord your God.* Just as the latter is infinite, so His attributes of compassion and forgiveness are boundless, and hence there are unlimited opportunities for Israel to "return."

22. REPENTANCE FOR REPENTANCE
Source: R. Nahman of Bratslav, Likkutei Etzot, Teshuvah 7:6

Even when one is sure that he has repented in a perfect way, he should repent again:[115] repentance for his original repentance, because initially his repentance was relative to his perceptions at that time. After repentance, however, one's knowledge and perception of God surely deepen and, in comparison with his present understanding, the previous one was, as it were, gross and corporeal. Therefore he has to repent for his original repentance, which was tantamount to a corporeal conception of His exalted divinity.[116] Happy is the one who is privileged to repent in such a way.

. . . One must repent ceaselessly, inasmuch that even at the moment when one says, "I sinned, I transgressed, I committed crimes," it is unlikely that there is no ulterior motive involved in his saying so. He must therefore repent to atone for his original repentance declaration.[117]

23. SIN'S REDEEMING VIRTUE
Source: R. Zadok ha-Kohen of Lublin, Kedushat Shabbat 5, p. 13b

After the terrible sin [of Adam and Eve partaking from the Tree of Knowledge] had brought darkness upon all future generations by causing God's decree of death upon man, Adam nevertheless merited the great light of the Sabbath.[118] For this is the way of Creation of the world: First darkness and then light, for thus, [by experiencing darkness first], does one appreciate the superiority of light. Thus too Adam

---

115. Based on Yoma 86b. See above, n. 96.

116. R. Nahman does not, of course, refer to an actual belief in the corporeality of God. This did not constitute a problem for Hasidism or, indeed, for Judaism, since the Middle Ages. What he means is that as one grows religiously, each spiritual repentance, *relative to the one following it*, appears coarse and unrefined—corporeal, as it were, compared to the subsequent and more exalted and refined spiritual experience.

117. Thus, every new stage in the process of spiritual growth invalidates the preceding stage. See Additional Note *2.

118. The Bible teaches that Adam and Eve were created on the sixth day of Creation. According to the aggadic-midrashic tradition, the whole episode of their sin and their expulsion from Paradise occurred on the same day before nightfall, on the eve of the Sabbath. Darkness—the first he had ever experienced—terrorized Adam, and when dawn broke on the morning of the Sabbath, he gratefully uttered the psalm for the Sabbath, later included in the Psalms of David as psalm 92.

merited the "vestments of light"[119] only after the sin, when he saw that he was naked.

AFTERWORD

"And the eyes of [Adam and Eve] were opened [after eating the forbidden fruit] and they knew that they were naked, and they sewed fig-leaves together and made themselves girdles" (Gen. 3:7). Their sense of shame after committing the sin led them to cover up with clothing. But, according to the Midrash as interpreted by R. Zadok, their repentance earned for them a different set of "garments"—light. Adam and Eve therefore achieved, by means of repentance (an idea introduced by the Aggadah), a spiritual level superior to that which characterized them in their previous state of innocence. Darkness has led to light, and the darkness serves only to emphasize, by contrast, the desirability of the light. The idea is rather startling. Sin begets a reaction (repentance) which leaves man in a more exalted state than he was originally. Sin, paradoxically, is the stimulus for man's spiritual growth. Later in the same discourse R. Zadok cites for support the famous rabbinic dictum that "in the place where the *ba'alei teshuvah* ['penitent'] stand, even the zaddik ['righteous'] cannot stand" (Berakhot 34b). This passage now appears as more than encouragement to the wayward transgressor, but teaches a profound and somewhat disquieting truth—as R. Zadok says a few lines later—that when the merely "good" is involved in a struggle with evil and emerges victorious, it becomes "very good." Evil, hence, has a redeeming virtue.

---

119. After the curse which followed the sin, and immediately before the expulsion, we read that, "And the Lord God made for Adam and his wife garments of skin and clothed them" (Gen. 3:21). The Hebrew for "skin," *or*, is written with an *ayin* as the first letter. If an *alef* is substituted for the *ayin*, then with barely any change in pronunciation the word means "light." According to the Midrash (Genesis Rabbah 20), the Torah scroll written by R. Meir (the great tanna, who was himself a scribe) was found to contain this variant reading, *or* with a *alef*, hence "garments of light."

ADDITIONAL NOTES

*1   This thesis of R. Levi Yitzhak should be contrasted to the conception of *teshu-
vah* by R. Hayyim of Volozhin, the leading ideologist of the mitnaggedim, opponents
of Hasidism. R. Hayyim maintains that true repentance can take place only as a result
of the study of the Torah. The latter is never accomplished in "leaps," but is, rather,
like a well which slowly builds up strength; similarly, repentance, tied to the cognitive process of study of Torah, must be gradual rather than spontaneous and impul-
sive. See R. Hayyim's *Nefesh ha-Ḥayyim* 3:21.

*2   R. Zadok's concept should be compared to that of R. Nahman of Bratslav (see
below, selection 24). According to the latter, spiritual growth by means of repentance
entails doing repentance for one's previous repentance, i.e., the more exalted one's
spiritual attainment is, the more picayune and even gross does his previous religious
experience appear; so much so, that it requires penitence. For R. Zadok, however, it is
not the prior repentance experience that now appears niggardly and primitive; rather
the sin that occasioned it—and for which the previous repentance was adequate at
that time—now appears much more serious (because the penitent now considers it
from the vantage of his more refined spiritual character) and hence requires repentance all over again. For R. Zadok, the distress and tension of spiritual growth is the
result of old sins which produce a new guilt feeling. For R. Nahman, it is the quality
of each previous religious (or repentance) experience that proves embarrassing as one
ascends the spiritual ladder.

Another interpretation of the endless repentance process, different from these
two, is offered in *Benei Yisaskhar* (see the next selection), which concentrates neither
on guilt nor on the inadequacy of the repentance experience, but on the greater capacity for religious knowledge of God which, in turn, creates greater sensitivity to the
"insult" to God entailed in the initial sin. This seems to cover the middle ground
between R. Nahman and R. Zadok.

11

Elevation of Character

The biblical teaching that man was created in the divine image runs through the entire history of Jewish religious thought to our very own day. It is the foundation of Judaism's anthropology, the bedrock on which must be constructed any validly Jewish conception of man and mankind.

This doctrine, known as *tzelem Elohim*, allows for a number of interpretations. During the enormously fertile period of Jewish thought that we call the Golden Age of Spanish Jewry, it was interpreted as the rational nature of man, the capacity for creativity, human freedom, and so on. Later, under the influence of the Kabbalah, Jewish thinkers saw in it the teaching of man's vast spiritual potencies: like God, his Creator, man the creature has it within his power to exercise a decisive influence over all the worlds, spiritual and physical, for good or for evil. The common denominator of these various expositions of the biblical doctrine is that the *imago dei* is a proprium of the human species: man possesses by nature some affinity with the divine, and this affinity grants him a core of unimpeachable value. Because the artist somehow inheres in his art, because the creation bespeaks its Creator, man has infinite value as a reflection of the Infinite Who called him into being.

Hasidism put its own stamp on the concept, a stamp that pulled together ideas already known but now presented in a new configura-

371

tion. Quoting the verse *From my flesh I behold God* (Job 19:26), the school of the Great Maggid, especially Habad, derived the teaching that just as God revealed Himself through the ten sefirot, so man's soul reveals itself in ten different attributes, which are likewise referred to as the ten sefirot of man's divine soul. The image of man is a true reflection of the divine life. Thus, Hasidism opened up for investigation a whole new psychology based upon the sefirot. The interrelationship between God and man is to be explored on the basis of the sefirotic structure that both share. Moreover, this provided not only for diagnosis, but also for the therapy of spirit and human character.

Accordingly, for instance, if man committed a sexual sin, whether in deed or in thought, this was considered a defect in the sefirah of Ahavah, i.e., in the world of love, which is the fourth of the ten sefirot, or worlds, of his soul. Now this corresponds to the fourth of the ten divine sefirot, Hesed ("Love," "Lovingkindness"). Hence the therapy consists of "repairing" the human failing by restoring the human love to its root, the divine sefirah of Hesed. This restoration and repair is a profound mental process, a directed contemplation with mind and heart, during prayer or study and even, at times, during profane activities.

Since all human character traits can be described in terms of the ten sefirot of man's divine soul—especially the fourth (love, equivalent to Hesed), the fifth (fear, equivalent to Gevurah), and the sixth (glory or beauty, equivalent to Tiferet), these following upon the first three, which are intellectual in nature—it follows that man must seek self-perfection by restoring his human sefirot to their roots in the ten divine sefirot.

This process is known as *ha-ala'at ha-middot*, the "elevation of the attributes" to their source in the ten sefirot. The excerpts presented in this chapter deal with these elevations.[1] One very special case of *ha-ala'at ha-middot* is that of alien thoughts (*maḥshavot zarot*), stray thoughts that enter man's consciousness, especially during times of religious devotion, distracting him from his concentration and sullying his mind with extraneous, vulgar concerns. These strange or alien thoughts are usually (but not always) erotic in nature.

This posed a special problem for Hasidism, with its extravagant emphasis on thought over action and inwardness over externality (the

---

1. See the introductions to chapters 9 and 6 for further discussion of this subject.

Besht taught that "a man is where his mind is"), but it is significant for all of Judaism, which identifies holiness with purity of thought. In contrast to ancient (and perhaps contemporary) paganism, Judaism does not abide the commingling of the spheres of spirituality and sexuality. Where the Canaanite pagans had prostitutes, both male and female, among the cultic personnel of their temples, and orgies as part of the worship service, Judaism defined *kedushah* ("holiness") as *perishah* ("separation," e.g. from the sensual). Without condemning the sexual as *eo ipso* sinful, without considering marriage a concession to man's base nature, and without developing a monastic order for the spiritual elite, Judaism nevertheless drew a strong line and set firm boundaries so as not to allow the libido to infringe upon the spirit. Hence the halakhah requiring a "separation" (generally a belt) between the heart and the private parts (where the style of clothing was such that there were no separate garments for the upper and lower portions of the body), and hence too the separation of the sexes at prayer services.

Alien thoughts can indeed wreak havoc with efforts to concentrate upon prayer or any of the mitzvot. The promptings of the evil urge (*yetzer ha-ra*) clutter the terrain of consciousness with unworthy distractions, and set up the idols of lust and concupiscence in the most sacred precincts of man's heart.

What makes matters worse is a special perversity of human nature, worthy of serious study by psychologists: the more one seeks consciously to banish a thought, the more persistently does that very thought intrude upon one's thinking and cling to it like a barnacle. The reader can perform his own little experiment. At exactly nine o'clock this evening, sit down, close your eyes, and determine that even for one single minute you will not think about alligators . . .

How then is one to deal with alien thoughts, especially those that are most taboo during prayer or meditation or Torah study? As mentioned, the problem is aggravated in the case of Hasidism because it placed such a high premium on *taharat ha-mahshavah* ("purity of thought"). Understandably, therefore, *mahshavot zarot* becomes a major issue for hasidic teachers instructing their followers in spiritual discipline and moral self-perfection.

In the hasidic view, an alien thought may be engendered not only by sin but also by the metaphysical nature of the world as a result of the Breaking of the Vessels. According to most hasidic writers, the Lurianic doctrines of the Breaking of the Vessels and the Raising of the

Sparks[2] explain the source of the alien thoughts and also provide the means for elevating them. When the light of the Ein-Sof entered the "vessels" (i.e., the sefirot), the seven lower ones broke, and the sparks of the overspill of the divine light descended from one world to the next until they finally embedded themselves in the "shells" (*kelipot*)—the "other side" (*sitra aḥara*, the repository of evil). Man's task is to redeem the incarcerated sparks by consecrating his mundane existence, thus raising them back to their divine origin. Although these ideas, as mentioned, are often held to be of Lurianic origin, Joseph G. Weiss maintains that they represent a purely Beshtian theory that can well get along without the Lurianic doctrine.[3]

Alien thoughts were regarded as messengers of the evil urge, shock troops of the *sitra aḥara*, omens of evil itself.[4] Does one undertake a frontal attack, pouring one's mental energies into the campaign to destroy the enemy, banishing alien thoughts and so enabling prayer to triumph? Or, perhaps, is there a more subtle and effective approach, whereby one steals the enemy's weapons and emerges from the contest all the stronger?

This, in turn, is based upon yet other considerations, some highly theoretical, some more practical. The theoretical question: Are the *mahshavot zarot* truly evil, or, like evil itself, are they only disguises for the holy, so that when the mask is ripped off, the power of holiness emerges? Indeed, are these intruders really couriers from the realms of holiness, challenging the worshiper to reach new heights? Are they, in the language of Lurianic Kabbalah, sparks of holiness, the residue of the primordial Breaking of the Vessels, come to the righteous to beg for their release from the husk of evil, pleading to be liberated and restored to the upper regions, those of the ten sefirot? And more practically, even if they are, is everyone qualified to undertake so spiritually sophisticated a maneuver, or should projects of this kind be restricted to the elite, while *hoi polloi* attack the problem frontally?

The selections in this chapter deal with just such problems. Consistent with its general view of evil, Hasidism tended to see *mahshavot zarot* as disguises, as holy sparks begging for release, and therefore putting man under the obligation to elevate them and restore them to their upper roots. Note the statement by the Maggid

---

2. See L. Jacobs, *Hasidic Prayer*, pp. 106 ff.
3. Weiss, "Reshit Tzemiḥatah shel ha-Derekh ha-Ḥasidit," p. 101.
4. See the introduction to chapter 6 in conjunction with these lines.

that alien thoughts are both *tam* and *mar*, pure and bitter. And note too the problem dealt with either directly or indirectly by a number of the thinkers represented in this chapter, on the question of whether elevating alien thoughts is recommended only for the zaddik or for the common man as well. Thus, the discussions by R. Shneur Zalman on the difference between suppression and transformation, and when and by whom each strategy is to be used.

1. THE ELEVATION OF BROKEN THOUGHTS

Source: *R. Dov Baer of Mezeritch, Maggid Devarav le-Yaakov, no. 26, pp. 43–44*

If a king has a son in a filthy place, he will go there out of love for his son, in order to remove him from it. So too, at times, a thought originating in the worlds above will come to someone. If he is wise, and can discern the locus of the thought, whether love, fear, or glory,[5] he is able to elevate it even if the thought is this-worldly in the sense of physical desire. He must realize that the thought needs to be repaired at this specific time. Whether it comes from the world of love or fear or glory, which degenerated because of the Breaking of the Vessels, now is its time to be elevated.

That is the very reason why this thought descended from the upper worlds and came to him: in order to be raised from its state of brokenness. This is accomplished when man cleaves unto God through this quality (or sefirah), whether it be love, fear, glory, or any other of the seven lowest sefirot.[6] Therefore a man should always contemplate the sefirah from which the thought was engendered—love, fear, or glory—in order to be able to elevate it.

The same holds for eating and drinking. When love is engendered in someone in the course of eating and drinking (i.e., love for the food he is eating), he should take this pleasure and elevate it to the Creator.[7]

---

5. Synonyms for the sefirot of Hesed, Gevurah, and Tiferet. Note that only the wise can effect this elevation.

6. See my "Matter and Spirit" (Gesher 5741) for a more elaboration description of the process of elevation by means of meditations and *devekut* as developed by R. Shelomoh Lutzker, a disciple of the Maggid.

7. Here we find the transition from the elevation of alien thoughts to more generalized elevations of all human activities, even the purely physical, the concept of *avodah be-gashmiyut* discussed in chapter 9. The wise person will be able to justify his ordinary eating and drinking to the level of authentic service of the Lord by dint of the process of elevation.

The Creator emanates into everything, *for the whole earth is full of His glory* (Isa. 6:3). He must elevate the essence of the thing (e.g., the alien thought, eating or some other physical sensation, pride or some other emotion), each in accordance with its quality of the seven lower sefirot, thus causing the inner essence to cleave unto the Creator.

2. BITTER, YET PURE
Source: R. Dov Ber of Mezeritch, Maggid Devarav le-Yaakov, 55, pp. 80–81

And she sat in the entrance of Enaim. . . . When Judah saw her he thought her to be a harlot, for she had covered her face (Gen. 38:14).[8]

The name Tamar is composed of the words *tam* ("innocent, pure") and *mar* ("bitter"). The alien thought is bitter (*mar*), but in truth it is pure (*tam*).[9] Thus it is written: *I saw slaves on horses* (Eccl. 10:7). *Horses* refers to words of prayer.[10] When an alien thought rides upon them, and a man sees this, he is astounded that a mere slave is riding on the king's horse.[11] But when he bears in mind that they are holy words, and it is only their configuration that is wrong, he can contemplate the letters by bringing them to the world of permutation, and from these words other configurations can be made—words of Torah

---

8. This is a homily on the story of Judah and Tamar (Gen. 38). Tamar was widowed, successively, by two of Judah's sons, and he was reluctant to have his youngest son marry her or to marry her himself, as was called for by the system of levirate marriage in force in pre-Sinaitic days. In order to obtain what was rightfully hers, Tamar disguised herself as a harlot, seduced Judah, and became pregnant by him. On discovering that she was with child, Judah adjudged her guilty of adultery (as was the pre-Sinaitic law with regard to a widow waiting to be married by her brother-in-law) and condemned her to death. When Tamar revealed that she had pretended to be a harlot and he was the father of her child, he conceded his error. The child ultimately became an ancestor of King David.

9. The sparks of God's immanence pervade all existence, even the realm of evil, and extend to the mental spheres. The alien thought that distracts man from pure, unadulterated worship and contemplation, ruining his unbroken *devekut*, is itself sustained by a divine spark and thus is inwardly pure and innocent.

10. In kabbalistic and hasidic writings, mundane terms are sometimes used as metaphors for the idea of one state of being supporting another, superior one. Thus *kissei* ("chair, throne"), *merkavah* ("chariot"), or, here, the horse. That which is borne by this medium is of a higher nature and may be said to inhere in the medium. In the present case the words of prayer are the "horse" upon which the Divine Presence "rides" or "rests"; i.e., its inner essence.

11. Words of prayer should support the king, i.e., the Holy One, but He is dismounted when an intruding alien thought gains control of the horse.

instead of nonsense.[12] This is what is meant by *she sat in the entrance of Enaim*: the one through whom all look toward the Holy One.[13] *When Judah saw her, he thought her to be a harlot [zonah]*, i.e., *zo na'eh* ("this one is comely"), for it is an organ of the Shekhinah.[14] But then the question is: If it is indeed an organ of the Shekhinah, why is it dressed in such nonsensical words? The answer is, *for she had covered her face.*[15]

3. MATTER AND FORM
Source: R. Yaakov Yosef of Polennoye, Toledot Yaakov Yosef to Yitro, sec. 1

As is well known, man is composed of matter and form, i.e., a body and a soul. The soul is constantly aflame with longing to be attached to her Maker, but the material body is an obstacle to this attachment (*devekut*). That is why the soul also desires material things, such as eating and sexual intercourse. These too serve a higher spiritual purpose: raising the holy sparks, and so on. Only at certain times does form [soul] manage to gain the upper hand over matter [body] to

---

12. This is an instance of what J. G. Weiss calls "the atomization of *devekut*." The contemplation takes place by concentrating, not upon the obvious concept relayed by the plain sense of the word, but upon its constituent letters, its "atoms," which are interchangeable according to set rules. The idea behind this exercise is that the world consists of a discrete number of neutral elements which, depending upon man's moral-spiritual character and contemplative powers, can be organized into a configuration for good or for evil—for words of Torah or for nonsense, in the Maggid's language. Hence the alien thought is not intrinsically evil; its constituent elements are capable of bearing divinity itself and thus are pure. But man, by submitting to their allure, allows these selfsame letters to adopt the configuration of the alien thoughts, allowing the "slave" to displace the "king" riding on the "horse." And that is "bitter." By elevating his alien thoughts to the world of permutation, the divine sphere where the configurations of the same elements can be transformed from evil to good, man restores the thoughts to their roots, creating Torah out of nonsense and purity out of bitterness.
13. Enaim is the name of the place where Tamar seduced Judah, but for the purposes of the homily the Maggid adopts the word's common meaning, "eyes." The phrase "entrance of the eyes" refers to the Shekhinah, another name for Malkhut, the nethermost of the ten sefirot, which, as closest to man, is the necessary channel through which he may reach out or look up to the Holy One, or the upper sefirot.
14. The Hebrew word for "harlot" is broken down into its two phonetic components, yielding "this is comely"; i.e., although the alien thought is a "harlot," it is intrinsically pure, pleasant, and fitting, a part of the Shekhinah itself.
15. The holy, pure element of the divine spark immanent in all creation disguises itself by covering itself with "words of nonsense" or the "harlot's clothing." Divine immanence is a fact, but it is in disguise, and man must bend every effort to reveal the godliness within nature and within himself and his activities and words.

achieve *devekut* with God.[16] This is the mystery of *And the living creatures ran and returned* (Ezek. 1:14).[17] This is called smallness (*katnut*) and greatness (*gadlut*).[18]

4. ELEVATING THE SPARKS IN THE MUNDANE
Source: R. Yaakov Yosef of Polennoye, Toledot Yaakov Yosef to Mishpatim sec. 5, mitzvat keniyat eved kena'ani, s.v. ve-hinneh

A great principle in serving God is this: in everything you do for the sake of heaven, see to it that what you do will immediately be a service of the Lord.[19] When eating, do not say that you are eating for the sake of heaven in the sense that the food will give you strength to serve the Lord. Although this too is a good intention, the ultimate perfection is for the act itself, in and of itself, to be an act for the sake of heaven, i.e., to elevate the sparks.

---

16. When the soul is in eclipse, it indulges in material needs and pleasures, but these can be made to serve a fundamentally spiritual purpose: the redemption of the material world based on the Lurianic notion of the elevation (or clarification) of the sparks.
17. The oft-cited source for the kabbalistic idea of alternation. The mystical experience—and the normative religious experience as well—consists of alternating periods of joy and sadness, closeness to God and infinite remoteness. In Hasidism, these are usually referred to as "greatness" and "smallness." When the soul openly engages in *devekut*—when man is consciously engaged in worship—it is in the state of greatness. The soul's indirect connection with God, by means of indulging in corporeal matters and elevating them, is an instance of smallness. See chap. 12B.
18. Note that the text does not stress any need for special contemplation while performing the body's material and physical functions, as R. Yaakov Yosef mentions elsewhere. The higher purpose is achieved in the ongoing natural alternation between *katnut* and *gadlut* of the one who strives to be a true servant of God.
19. The element of consecration or spiritual meaningfulness should not be at one remove, so that a profane act is performed now to enable you to perform a sacred act later, but it should be direct: the profane act must be done in way that makes it an act of divine service. This is an important principle of Hasidism. A variation on the theme is enunciated in *Zava'at ha-Rivash*: by eating to sustain one's body, one repairs the sparks *because* he will afterwards have the strength to serve God. This does not, however, detract from the main point: the Lurianic notion of raising the sparks lends immediate significance to every mundane act and endows it with the possibility of sanctity. Cf. R. Yaakov Yosef's comments elsewhere in the same work (Bo, no. 8): "There is a great principle: *In all thy ways acknowledge Him* (Prov. 3:6). This is explained by Maimonides (Hilkhot De'ot 3:3) to mean that one should contemplate even in all one's mundane activities [that one dedicates them] for the sake of heaven. . . . It seems to me that there is a deeper meaning to this. Just as the intention in spiritual matters, such as Torah, prayer, and the performing of the mitzvot, relates to the purifying [and repairing] of the sparks . . . so too does it in corporeal matters, such as eating, drinking, and every kind of mundane work."

The mystery of the Sabbath meals is known to all initiates into the divine mysteries.[20] All of man's activities ought to be [carried out] in the same manner. *That the wise man may hear and increase his learning* (Prov. 1:5).

5. THE LIBERATION OF THE PRINCE
Source: R. Yaakov Yosef of Polennoye, Ben Porat Yosef to Miketz, pp. 74a–b

Here is how the Ari [= R. Isaac Luria] explains, in his *Kavvanot*, the matter of sifting out the holy sparks that were scattered among the *kelipot* during the Breaking of the Vessels:

Man is given the task of selecting and elevating the sparks from the mineral world to the world of plants, and then to the animal and human worlds, so that each holy spark may be extracted from the *kelipot*. . . . And that is the purpose of every Jew in his service of God by means of studying Torah, observing mitzvot, and contemplating while eating.[21] . . .

As is well known, every one of the sparks in minerals and plants, etc., constitutes a complete structure (*komah shelemah*)[22] of 248 limbs and 365 sinews. While the spark is inside the mineral or plant, etc., it is like a prisoner in a dungeon, unable to extend his hands and legs or to speak, but lying in a cramped position, head bent over stomach and knees.

Someone who is able to concentrate his thought well enough to elevate the holy spark from plant to animal to human, brings it forth

---

20. The kabbalistic interpretation views the Sabbath meals, the "meals of faith," as sacred acts on which the sustenance of the rest of the week depends. They represent the joyous fulfillment of divine unification; they are comprehensive and all-inclusive, and observing them is tantamount to observing the whole Torah (Zohar II, 88a–89a). The underlying idea, for R. Yaakov Yosef, is that they are an end and not a means to some other end in the service of the Lord. See chap. 9 above, selection 8, n. 33, for more on the difference between the hasidic interpretation of the talmudic requirement that all acts be for the sake of heaven and the standard rabbinic view enunciated by R. Bahya and codified in the *Shulḥan Arukh*.
21. See above, chap. 9, selection 8 and selection 9.
22. In Kabbalah and hasidic literature, every element of the material world is held to be a complete configuration of the divine sefirot in miniature. For examples, see selections 11, 22, 23 from R. Yaakov Yosef in chap. 6.

unto freedom. There is no greater redemption of captives,[23] as I heard from my teacher [the Besht]. . . . For surely there is no greater reward than when the prince, imprisoned in a dungeon, is released from captivity by a man who manages with much effort to bring him forth from slavery unto freedom.

6. SUPPRESSING EVIL
Source: R. Shneur Zalman of Liady, Tanya, Likkutei Amarim, chap. 27

This is the quality of the intermediates (*benonim*) and their service: to subdue the evil impulses and thoughts that ascend from the heart to the brain, and to turn one's mind away from evil completely and reject it with both hands.[24] . . . Whenever one rejects it from his mind, the *sitra ahara*[25] below is suppressed[26] and the arousal from below evokes the arousal from above.[27] Thus is suppressed the *sitra ahara*

---

23. Ransoming captives is the highest form of charity; see Bava Batra 8a–b and Maimonides, Hilkhot Matnot Aniyim 8:10. According to the Besht, elevating the sparks is like ransoming a prince from captivity, and is the highest form of redemption.
24. In R. Shneur Zalman's system, the *benoni* is a person of intermediate quality. This does not imply spiritual and moral mediocrity, for the *benoni* has attained full righteousness insofar as one can do so by his own efforts. He is, in fact, a completely saintly person by virtue of having struggled with evil and overcome it, but he retains the propensity for evil. The *benoni* knows evil (which, in R. Shneur Zalman's mystical anatomy, issues from the left ventricle of the heart), and this evil, in the form of one's animal soul, is in constant struggle with one's divine soul. In the *benoni* the divine soul is the victor, but the animal soul has not been extirpated. It is only in the person of the zaddik (fully righteous person) that evil is entirely banished. This state is a charismatic gift, issuing from divine grace, and is unattainable by human initiative alone. The attitude here recommended in dealing with evil and alien thoughts is addressed to the *benoni*. The *Tanya*, the work from which this passage is taken, is an exoteric work, directed to the wide public of R. Shneur Zalman's followers. His other, more esoteric works are intended for the spiritual elite and the initiates among his hasidim. Note the rejection and negation of evil thought (and "suppression" of evil drives) recommended in *Tanya*, chaps. 27 and 28, and the movement toward elevation and transformation in selection 7, from the more esoteric *Likkutei Torah*.
25. Lit. "the other side.," the counterpart of the spheres of divine holiness. This is the kabbalistic term for evil and the demonic. The text here speaks of a *sitra ahara* in this world and another one in the upper worlds.
26. *Itkafia* ("suppression"), the voiding or rejection of evil and evil thoughts, rather than the channeling of their powers to spiritually and morally constructive ends. Suppression is a lower form of approaching evil than transformation, in which the potencies of evil are not dismissed but salvaged and used for the good. See below n. 30 and in greater detail the introduction to chap. 15.
27. The first term refers to human initiative, the second to divine initiative.

above, which soars like an eagle, thereby fulfilling *Though you raise yourself like the eagle . . . I will bring you down from thence, saith the Lord* (Obad. 1:4). Similarly, the Zohar elaborates on His great satisfaction when the *sitra aḥara* is suppressed, for then the glory of the Holy One rises above everything, even more so than because of any other praise, and this ascent is greater than any other, etc.[28] Therefore do not lose heart and feel deeply grieved even if you are engaged in the conflict with evil all your life, because it may be the reason for which you were created—always to suppress the *sitra aḥara* . . . always striving to turn your mind away from evil thoughts and temptations in order to suppress the *sitra aḥara*, [but] never able to annihilate it completely, for only zaddikim can do that.[29]

There are two kinds of satisfaction that God above derives: one, when the zaddikim completely annihilate the *sitra aḥara* by its transformation[30] from bitter to sweet and from dark to light. And second, when the *sitra aḥara* is suppressed while rising up like an eagle, in all its power and strength. For the Lord will bring it down, in response to the arousal from below by the *benonim*.

7. TRANSFORMING EVIL
Source: R. Shneur Zalman of Liady, Likkutei Torah to Exodus, p. 3a

The function of the Tabernacle is the settling of the Shekhinah in Israel. Thus it is written, *And let them make Me a sanctuary that I may dwell among them* (Exod. 25:8);[31] and also, *The Temple of the Lord are themselves* (Jer. 7:4).[32] This conforms to what the Rabbis said: "The Holy One desired an abode in the lower world."[33]

---

28. Zohar II, 128b.
29. See n. 24 above.
30. *It'hapkha*, lit. "turning upside down," the alternative to *itkafia*, "suppression." It may be helpful to think of the transformation of evil as akin to the Freudian notion of sublimation. R. Shneur Zalman recommends the methods of suppression to the *benonim* and by implication to lesser individuals, reserving transformation for the zaddikim or spiritually elite.
31. *Be'tokham* ("among them") is interpreted by the Sages as "in them," implying the presence of the Shekhinah within man. See *Tzedah la-Derekh* to Exodus, ad loc., citing the early Rabbis (*kadmonim*) as the source.
32. *Hemah* ("are these") is similarly interpreted: "they," i.e., humans, are the dwelling place (symbolized as the tabernacle, sanctuary, or temple) of the Lord. See Alshekh to Jeremiah, ad loc.
33. Midrash Tanḥuma to Naso 16.

Now this must be understood: Why did God seek to dwell in this world? After all, even without this we already know that He is present here, as it is written: *Do I not fill heaven and earth?* (Jer. 23:24).[34]

The matter may be explained as follows: "Abode" means that His blessed divinity will be revealed, and hence this abode must specifically be in the lower worlds. For "lower world" is not meant spatially, inasmuch as the category of space does not apply to Him. . . . [The terms] "upper worlds" and "lower worlds" refer to degree and level. This lowly world is the nethermost and lowliest; i.e., it is the culmination and end of all the levels of the progressive devolution of the worlds. Therefore, the perception of divinity in this world is concealed and greatly contracted—*darkness shall cover the earth* (Isa. 60:2). The Holy One desired especially to be in it as an abode, in the revelation of His divinity, specifically to illuminate the darkness. This illumination and revelation take place by means of Torah study and doing mitzvot, as we know from the statement of the Rabbis: "Better one hour of repentance and good deeds in this world than all the life of the world-to-come,"[35] for thereby one makes possible a greater revelation of divinity than in the life of the world-to-come.

The actualization of this abode and revelation takes place by means of the suppression of the *sitra ahara*, which is identical to the *yetzer hara*,[36] as the Zohar says: when the *sitra ahara,* is suppressed, the glory of the Holy One rises up above everything, etc. In the beginning, one must attempt to suppress the *sitra ahara*, but afterwards one must attain the level of transforming darkness to light. The suppression takes place with all five senses: that of sight—by closing one's eyes so as not to see evil,[37] and similarly with regard to hearing, etc. And the same with speech, action, thought, and all other dispositions of the body and mind.[38]

---

34. Since we already know that God is immanent throughout creation, what sense can we make of His desire to dwell in the lower world within man?
35. Avot 4:17.
36. The demonic in man expresses itself in his inclination to rebel against God and do that which is evil.
37. That is, not to see what is immoral or forbidden to behold.
38. Yevamot 20a.

8. THE ELEVATION OF BEAUTY
Source: R. Levi Yitzhak of Berdichev, Kedushat Levi to Vayetzei, s.v. va-yishak

And Jacob kissed Rachel (Gen. 29:11). And Rachel was of beautiful form and fair to look upon (Gen. 29:17). And Jacob loved Rachel (Gen. 29:18).

It seems quite amazing that Jacob, the elect of the patriarchs, about whom the Torah itself states, And Jacob was a perfect [i.e., whole-hearted, pious] man (Gen. 25:27), and one who observed all the Torah's commandments even before they were revealed at Sinai, as he himself said, "With Laban I have sojourned, but the 613 commandments I observed"[39]—it is amazing that he should have paid attention to physical beauty. It is especially amazing because the zaddik, by nature, is exactly the opposite, as it is written: Grace is deceitful and beauty is vain, but a woman that feareth the Lord, she shall be praised (Prov. 31:30).

I heard from my holy teacher, the holy illuminato, the Maggid Dov Ber, that the explanation is as follows: Our father Jacob, as is well known, worshiped God by means of the attribute of beauty.[40] He elevated every spark of beauty, even if it was encased in gross corporeality, and returned it to its source.... That is why we are told that Jacob kissed Rachel, who was beautiful, and that he loved her; for Jacob saw that Rachel possessed the spark of beauty, and by elevating it to its supernal root, he served the Lord.[41]

9. ELEVATION AND THE HALAKHAH
Source: R. Levi Yitzhak of Berdichev, Kedushat Levi to Pekudei, s.v. meha-Besht

[Here is how] the Besht interpreted the idea of the raising of the sparks:[42]

When we see the element of corporeality in something or, heaven forbid, of evil, then we are to serve the Lord with it by virtue of the

---

39. Rashi to Gen. 32:5.
40. Beauty in this case refers to the sefirah of Tiferet. The patriarchs are said to symbolize sefirot; e.g., Abraham is Hesed, Isaac, Gevurah, and Jacob, Tiferet (sometimes called Rahamim [mercy]).
41. See chap. 5, selection 4, where R. Shneur Zalman interprets these verses as a parable for devekut. R. Levi Yitzhak reads them as referring to the elevation of the sparks, but he probably regards devekut as necessary before the elevation can be achieved.
42. According to the Lurianic doctrine, after the primordial Breaking of the Vessels, when the sefirot could not contain the light of the Ein-Sof, sparks fell into the shells (kelipot). It is the purpose of religious life and observance to elevate or restore these divine sparks to their origin by means of the proper contemplation.

love or fear or other such quality that it possesses. In this manner we elevate it. For instance, we contrast a good love to the evil love, for it was only for the purpose of loving God that love was emanated by the Creator into this world. This is what the raising of the sparks means. So it is with regard to fear and other traits. If we see an evil fear anywhere,[43] heaven forbid, we must elevate it to the realm of holiness. Other traits must be elevated in the same manner.

The dismantling of the Tabernacle means that the traits symbolized by the various parts of the Tabernacle are not connected to the performance of commandments.[44] When the Children of Israel in the desert chanced upon a place where there was an unworthy love, they stimulated this love to become the love of God, Who is the source of all love. So too for the attributes of fear and beauty.

Afterwards, when they had already elevated the traits of love and fear, they erected the Tabernacle. That is to say, they connected these attributes to the commandments of the Creator. For when a man possesses love of God or fear of God, but refrains from performing the mitzvot that apply to these attributes, the love or fear cannot endure. But when he does perform the mitzvot that apply to a specific attribute, the attribute itself will continue to exist. Therefore they erected the Tabernacle after they elevated the sparks, connecting the attributes to the commandments symbolized by the erection of the Tabernacle, in order to ensure their permanent existence in sanctity.[45]

---

43. Evil fear, like evil love, refers to prohibited fear, such as the fear of man rather than God, or social embarrassment which inhibits the fulfillment of religious obligations.

44. The Tabernacle was the portable sanctuary which accompanied the Israelites in the wilderness. R. Levi Yitzhak sees its parts as symbols of the various *middot* (attributes, traits, or qualities), usually exemplified by fear, love, and beauty (or glory), all of which are alternative names for the sefirot of Hesed, Gevurah, and Tiferet. That these qualities are identified as parts of the Tabernacle, the abode of the Divine Presence, indicates the possibility of elevating mundane dispositions to the level of the sacred. R. Levi Yitzhak now adds a new and important note for the hasidic notion of *ha-ala'at ha-middot* ("elevation of the attributes"). The fact that the Tabernacle can be dismantled and reerected implies the ephemeral effect of elevation brought about by contemplation. What is built up by the contemplative uplifting is soon taken apart. In order to make the elevation permanent, it must be associated with a mitzvah, i.e., the normative. The spiritual achievements of contemplation must be normativized if they are to survive. The act of erecting the Tabernacle, in response to the specific divine command to do so, symbolizes the rooting of the act of elevation in a normative context, i.e, the Halakhah.

45. A play on words: *kimah* ("erection") and *kiyyum* ("existence" or "endurance").

However, only Moses was able to erect the Tabernacle, thus connecting the Tabernacle to the Torah.[46] . . .

If, heaven forbid, the love and fear are not directed toward the Creator, then it is as if they were not at rest. But when they are directed toward the Creator, they are considered at rest, because they are fulfilling the purpose for which they were emanated from the Creator. But there is another step: when the attributes are constantly connected to the mitzvot, they can release *shefa* from above.[47]

The state of being constantly connected . . . occurred only in the Temple in Jerusalem. There, the vessels were connected to each other and to the commandments. But the level at which the attributes were at rest, i.e., when they fulfilled their function in the worship of the Creator, this obtained in the Tabernacle also, as suggested by the fact that the Tabernacle had no roof. This indicates that there was rest but no permanent connection or relatedness.

---

46. "Torah" and "commandments" are used here interchangeably to signify the halakhic or normative moment.

47. R. Levi Yitzhak here develops the two steps in the spiritualization of character traits. The first, elevation, consists of achieving a state of rest, in the sense of fulfillment. The second step, linking the contemplative with the normative, takes the traits or attributes beyond mere rest or fulfillment to a more creative and aggressive posture, that of influencing the higher worlds and releasing *shefa* (divine abundance) for the world. In the next paragraph the two levels are symbolized by the (portable) Tabernacle in the desert (= elevation) and the (fixed) Temple in Jerusalem (= normative obligation).

12A

Joy and Dejection

INTRODUCTION

Hasidism was born into a world of lingering doom and dejection. Jewish society showed all the signs of collective clinical depression—and for good reason. The Sabbatean and Frankist heresies had left it reeling, with a bitter after-taste of frustration from the failures of the pseudo-Messiahs. Anti-Semitic persecutions and pogroms were commonplace. Economic conditions were devasting. And, in many areas, there was felt a growing distance between the learned classes and the ignorant common folk; the rabbinic leadership seemed to be out of touch with the rest of the community.

Thus, swaddled in sorrow and nursed in frustration, the infant movement had to overcome depression, its greatest emotional threat. Hence, the hasidic emphasis on *simḥah*, joy. Only by actively pursuing a happy frame of mind can one overcome the menace of melancholy and its consequent damaging effect on one's religious life, one's "service of the Lord."

Joy and the display of joy thus come to be universally regarded as a hallmark of Hasidism. Hasidim seem to be involved in a perpetual round of singing, dancing, fellowship, and drinking. To admirers of the movement, these emotions and actions inject a welcome vitality into what they regard as the gray solemnity of religious life. To detractors of Hasidism, from the earliest period on, they betray a lack of seriousness. The reality, as reflected by the texts in this chapter, is more com-

plex. It is necessary to consider the meaning of joy for Hasidism and
its connection to other aspects of the spiritual life. In addition, we
shall note the historical question: how much of hasidic teaching in
this area is innovation, how much a continuation of earlier themes in
Kabbalah and homiletical literature?

The most general positive thrust behind the hasidic emphasis on
joy is the fundamental hasidic preoccupation with the nearness of
God. Because the world is God's creation, because He has befriended
man, the appropriate feeling for man, the grateful and happy beneficiary, is joy (see particularly selections 1 and 2).

Much of the discussion, however, goes beyond the proclamation of
joy to grapple with religious factors that qualify, or even threaten to
diminish it. Sadness (atzvut) is often associated with sorrow over one's
sins, including guilt for relatively minor transgressions (see selection
3). Depression, which ostensibly spurs one to repentance, can also
undermine the confidence required for self-mastery (see selection 4).
Sadness mimics the most important religious feelings—the "broken
heart" so dear to God (see selection 6), humility, punctiliousness,
remorse—but it is not identical with these authentic religious states,
and one should therefore avoid it. And the wrong kind of joy is no
virtue; one must beware of confusing the joy connected to fulfillment
of the mitzvot with mere frivolousness and other such unworthy
manifestations of joy. The hasidic teachers, in effect, take into
account the criticisms of their adversaries.

It should be noted that for many of the hasidic masters, depression
is a recurrent temptation.[1] The lure of melancholy may well be rooted in certain features of the spiritual endeavor. The high goals that one
sets for the community and for oneself cannot be met by mere flesh
and blood. Moreover, man's quest for God is, *by its very nature*, asymp-
totic: the goal is always elusive, hence there is a built-in grief. Lastly,
as the mystics have taught, the principle of alternation (*ratzo va-shov*)
characterizes the mystical experience, and corresponds to oscillations
of mood. The ever-loooming threat of depression obviously plays a
role in the tremendous hasidic emphasis on joy and the proscription
of sadness.

What was new in hasidic doctrines of joy? Ezriel Schochet has
adduced many similar ideas about the value of joy and its superiority
over ascetic practices beyond the customary, in the earlier literature.[2]

---

1. This is stressed, for example, by Elie Wiesel in his *Souls on Fire* and *Four Hasidic
Masters and Their Struggle Against Melancholy*.
2. See his "Al ha-Simḥah be-Ḥasidut."

Yet we may locate areas where early Hasidism sounded its own note.

For one thing, Hasidism taught that joy, in its physical manifestations, should not be isolated from its spiritual dimensions. This idea is powerfully expressed in R. Yaakov Yosef's important parable about the king's son who celebrates when he receives a letter from his father (= the spiritual) by entertaining his companions (= the body) with drink. The reader will find this in chap. 9, selection 3.

Hasidism also democratized the idea of serving God in joy rather than self-mortification. The *Shelah*, a sixteenth-century work that strongly influenced the writers in this chapter, speaks of great men who imbibe, "not to fill their bellies . . . but to seek wisdom, for when the bodily powers are fortified, so are those of the soul."[3] However, he warns against including the masses in such activity, lest they drink to excess. The hasidic teachers were apparently more open in disseminating these ideas and the practices associated with them.

1. IMMANENCE AND JOY
Source: Besht, Zava'at ha-Rivash, no. 45 (ed. Kehot, p. 15)

Weeping is very bad, for one must serve [God] in joy. However, if one weeps out of joy, then it is very good.[4]

2. CONTINUOUS JOY
Source: Besht, Zava'at ha-Rivash, no. 137 (ed. Kehot, p. 25b)

One should always be in a state of joy. He should reflect and behave in perfect faith that the Shekhinah is within and watches over him; that he beholds the Creator, and the Creator beholds him; the Creator can do anything He wishes—destroying all the worlds in a moment or creating them in a moment; that in Him are rooted all the boons and rigors[5] of the universe, for His vitality and grace (*shefa*) pervade everything, and I [therefore] trust and fear nobody but Him.[6]

---

3. Cited by Schochet, ibid., pp. 37–38.
4. Cf. Oraḥ Ḥayyim 288:2 (Rema's gloss and *Turei Zahav*) concerning the permissibility of weeping on the Sabbath as an expression of *devekut*. See also Z. Gries, *Sifrut ha-Hanhagot*, p. 218.
5. Lit. *dinim* ("judgments"), in the sense of punishment.
6. Note how hasidic immanentism leads directly to the emphasis on joy. It is the ubiquitousness of the Divine Presence, the "beholding" of each other by God and man, that ignites in man the spark of happiness. This thesis is further developed by R. Shneur Zalman; see the next selection.

3. IMMANENCE AND THE HEART'S JOY
Source: R. Shneur Zalman of Liady, Tanya, Likkutei Amarim, chap. 33

The true joy of the soul can be further heightened, especially when one recognizes, at times, that he must purify and illuminate his soul by the joy of the heart.[7] Let him reflect deeply and meditate with his intelligence and understand the true divine unity which fills all the upper and lower worlds, and whose glory even fills this very world; how all that exists is actually as nothing in His presence; how He is alone in the upper and lower worlds just as He was before the six days of creation; how God above even occupied this very space in which this world—heaven and earth and all their hosts—was created before its Creation, and how too [after Creation] He does so, alone, without any change whatsoever.

When one reflects very deeply on this, his heart will rejoice and his soul will be glad with joy and singing, with all his heart and soul and might, in this superb faith, for this is the very [experience of the] nearness of God. The entire purpose of man, the purpose of his creation and the creation of all the upper and lower worlds, is to make a dwelling place for Him here below. . . .

How great is the joy of the ordinary and lowly man who is befriended by a human king who lodges and lives with him in (his modest) house! How infinitely more so for the nearness and indwelling of the King of kings, the Holy One. . . . We ought to rejoice over our heritage, bequeathed to us by our ancestors, i.e., the true unity of God, such that even here on this earth there is none other than Him. This is, indeed, His dwelling place in the lower worlds.

4. HALAKHIC STRINGENCIES AND RELIGIOUS EXPERIENCE
Source: Besht, Zava'at ha-Rivash (ed. Kehot), 7b, 8a, nos. 44, 46

(44) Sometimes the Evil Urge misleads man and tells him that he has committed a major transgression even though it was nothing but a

---

7. In the preceding chapter, the famous chapter 32 of the *Tanya* (see below, chapter 13, selection 8), the author develops his thesis that by abnegating the physical self and aspiring to spiritual felicity, one can achieve true love of his fellows. This spiritual felicity, or "joy of the soul," sometimes requires the assistance of the "joy of the heart," a state of emotional bliss arrived at through intellectual contemplation. This meditation on divine immanence, in its characteristic *Tanya* or Habad form, as a source of joy, is in the Beshtian tradition; see above, selection 1.

mere stringency (*ḥumra*)[8] or not even a transgression at all. Its intention is to make a person sad and, through sadness, disrupt his divine service.

Man must be alert to this deception. He should say to his Evil Urge: "I care not about this stringency, for your intention is to interrupt me from His service and you are speaking a lie. Even if it is a bit of a sin, my Creator will be better pleased if I am not preoccupied with this stringency, for you want to cause me gloom while serving Him. On the contrary, I will serve Him in joy. For this is a great principle: My intention in serving Him is not for my benefit, but rather to please God.[9] Therefore, even if I do not concern myself with this stringency you are talking about, the Creator will not be exacting with me. The reason I do not pay attention [to this stringency] is that I should not interrupt my divine service; how can I interrupt my service of God for even one moment?"

(46) One should not be overly punctilious in all that he does [i.e., in his performance of the mitzvot], for it is the design of the Evil Urge to instill in man fear that he may not have discharged his obligation through this act, thus leading man to sadness, and sadness is a great obstacle to divine service. Even if one is ensnared by sin, God forbid, he should not be overly despondent, for that would deter him from his divine service. Rather, he should be sorrowful about the sin, then return to rejoice in God, because he fully regrets [his action] and plans never in any way to repeat his foolishness.

Even if a man knows with certainty that he did not discharge his [mitzvah] obligations because of various impediments, he should not become fretful. [Rather,] he should reflect that the Creator, who plumbs man's heart and conscience, knows that he wishes to do the best but simply cannot. Thus, one should endeavor to rejoice in the Creator.

---

8. An extra measure of punctiliousness in the performance of a mitzvah, beyond what is required in a formal halakhic sense. The Besht's critique of excessive stringencies is that the guilt they engender over the failure to abide by them detracts from the emotional stability necessary for the proper religious experience. By attributing such anxiety to the Evil Urge, he effectively designates the *ḥumra* tendency as destructive of the genuine spiritual enterprise. Such an attitude, of course, did not endear early Hasidism to its contemporary critics, for whom such strictures were indications of greater piety. Later Hasidism, it should be pointed out, did not continue this Beshtian critique of the *ḥumra*.

9. Note the emphasis on intention as opposed to action. This is characteristically hasidic.

It is written: *It is a time to act for the Lord; they have made void Thy Torah* (Ps. 119:126).[10] Sometimes, if there is a mitzvah [the performance of] which entails a trace of sin, he should not listen to the Evil Urge which seeks to deter him from performing the mitzvah. Let him say to the Evil Urge: "I have no intention in performing this mitzvah other than to afford pleasure to my Creator." In this way the Evil Urge will disappear, with the help of God. Nevertheless, one ought to weigh in his mind whether or not he ought to be performing this mitzvah.[11]

5. SPIRITUAL DEPRESSION
Source: R. Shneur Zalman of Liady, Tanya, Likkutei Amarim, chap. 26

It should be stated as a great principle: When one seeks to triumph in a physical contest, as in the case of two individuals wrestling, each trying to throw the other, if one is lazy and sluggish he will easily be defeated and felled though he is stronger than the other, so exactly is it in the contest with one's Evil Urge (*yetzer*): It is impossible to conquer it in indolence and weariness, which come from sadness and a heart as dull as stone, but only with diligence which derives from joy and from a heart that is open and carefree, with no trace of worry and anxiety at all.

The verse *In all sadness there would be profit* (Prov. 14:23) seems to indicate that sadness yields some benefit and virtue.[12] On the con-

---

10. The extant copies of *Zava'at ha-Rivash* indicate this verse as a proof-text for the preceding sentence. However, the editor of the Kehot edition suggests, correctly in my view, that it forms the beginning of a new idea: that when a single act comprises a major mitzvah and a trace of *averah* ("sin"), one should overlook the sinful element and do the act for the sake of the mitzvah. The most prominent use of this verse in rabbinic literature is as warrant to commit the Oral Law to writing and publication; one must sometimes "make void Thy Torah" [violate the prohibition of publication of the Oral Law] in order "to act for the Lord" [save the Oral Law from oblivion]. The theme is now universalized, as the author applies it to any situation of a mitzvah which entails a trace of *averah*. He ascribes to the prompting of the Evil Urge the excessive caution (in the spirit of *ḥumra*) which would prefer to abandon the opportunity for mitzvah lest its performance entail some trivial infraction.

11. Because the anti-*ḥumra* tendency may have obvious anti-halakhic consequences, the author cautions against taking that inclination to an extreme and counsels the use of common sense. He is for softening what he regards as excessive halakhic rigor when it contradicts authentic religious experience; he is not against Halakhah as such.

12. Note that Rashi, Ibn Ezra, and other standard commentaries do not translate the word *etzev* in this verse as "sadness."

trary, however, the wording implies that gloominess in itself has no merit, except that it can lead to some benefit, namely, the true joy in the Lord God. [This joy] often comes in the wake of genuine anxiety over one's sins, with bitterness of soul and a broken heart, which can break the spirit of impurity and of the *sitra aḥara*, i.e. Satan, and the iron wall that separates man from our Father in Heaven. . . .

This is the simple reason why R. Isaac Luria ordained that Psalm 51 be recited after the midnight prayer (*Tikkun Ḥatzot*) before one studies—in order that one might study (Torah) with the true joy in God which follows remorse.[13] For that joy has a superiority like that of a light emerging after, and from, the very darkness. . . .

I offer this advice on how to purge one's heart of all anxiety and of every trace of worry about mundane matters, even about "children, health, and sustenance." Everyone knows the dictum of the Rabbis that "just as one must recite a blessing for the good [so must one recite a blessing for misfortune]."[14] The Gemara explains that one should accept bad news with the same joy with which he would greet manifest and obvious good news, "for this too is for the good,"[15] except that it is not apparent and evident to human eyes, for it derives from the "hidden world" which is higher than the "revealed world." The latter emanates from the letters *vav* and *heh* of the Tetragrammaton, whereas the "hidden world" issues from the letters *yod* and *heh*. Hence the verse *Happy is the man whom Thou, O God*[16] *chasteneth* (Ps. 94:12).

The Rabbis, therefore, commented that the verse *But they that love Him shall be like the sun going forth in its might* (Judg. 5:31) refers to those who rejoice in their afflictions.[17] For this is the joy which comes from desiring God's nearness more than anything in this mundane life, as it is written: *Because Thy lovingkindness is better than life* (Ps. 63:4). The nearness of God is infinitely more powerful and sublime in the "hidden world," for *the concealment of His strength is there* (Hab. 3:4) and *the Most High abides in secrecy* (Ps. 91:1). Therefore [one who rejoices in his afflictions] merits to see the "sun going forth in its might," i.e., in the

---

13. The midnight prayers, a Lurianic innovation, emphasize mourning over the destruction of the Temple. For our context, note particularly v. 14 of the psalm.

14. Mishnah Berakhot 9:5.

15. Berakhot 60b.

16. Written as *YH* (*yod-heh*). Thus the "misfortunes" mentioned in the verse are blessings in disguise, originating in the "hidden" worlds.

17. Yoma 23a.

world-to-come, when the sun will emerge from its sheath in which it is enclosed in this world.[18] This means that then the "hidden world" will be revealed and will shine in a great and mighty revelation to those who had taken refuge in Him in this world and had taken shelter under His shadow, i.e., the shadow of divine wisdom (ḥokhmah), rather than from revealed light and goodness.

As for the sadness in regard to spiritual matters,[19] one must devise ways to rid oneself of it, and most certainly so at the time of divine worship, when one must serve God with joy and a glad heart.[20] But even if one is a man of business and worldly affairs, and finds himself gripped by anxiety or melancholy about spiritual matters during the time of his business affairs, he should know that it is clearly a plot of the Evil Urge in order to ensnare him afterwards in lust, heaven forbid, as is known. Were it not so, why would genuine sadness, derived from love or fear of God, come to him in the middle of his business affairs?

Hence, whether the melancholy seizes him during divine service— Torah study or prayer—or it befalls him at some other time, he should persuade himself that now is not the time for genuine sadness, not even for worry over serious transgressions, God forbid. For this one needs set times and the right occasion to reflect with a calm mind on the greatness of God, against whom he has sinned, so that thereby one's heart may truly be rent with sincere contrition. It is explained elsewhere when this time should be and, further, that as soon as his heart has been broken during these specific times, he should completely remove the anxiety from his heart and believe with a perfect faith that the Lord has dismissed his sin and is abundantly forgiving. This is the true joy in God which comes after anxiety, as mentioned above.[21]

---

18. Cf. Nedarim 8b.

19, The anxiety that comes about as a result of moral and religious introspection and self-criticism.

20. See Deut. 28:47.

21. Thus R. Shneur Zalman does not invalidate moral anxiety, which plays such a large role in Jewish pietistic literature, and religion generally, but instead limits it to specific times and occasions (see the next selection). Anxiety which is deemed acceptable only if it comes on schedule, and even then must be endured quickly and transcended, no longer poses a major threat to the hasidic emphasis on joy as a religious desideratum.

6. SADNESS AND BITTERNESS IN WORSHIP
Source: R. Shneur Zalman of Liady, Tanya, Likkutei Amarim, chap. 31

One should not be troubled if, by prolonging deep concentration on the above matters[22] for an hour or two, in order to acquire a humble spirit and a contrite heart, he lapses into deep despondency. Sadness stems from *kelipat nogah*[23] and not from that of holiness, regarding which it is written, *Strength and gladness are in His place* (1 Chron. 16:27) and "The Shekhinah rests on one only in moments of joyfulness, including that of halakhic discourse."[24] If the sadness arises from concern with spiritual matters, it derives from the element of goodness that is within *nogah*.[25] (Therefore R. Isaac Luria, of blessed memory, wrote that even worry about sins is appropriate only during the confession, and not during prayer and Torah study, which should be conducted with the joy that derives exclusively from holiness.)

Nevertheless, the way to subdue the *sitra ahara* ("Other Side") is on the latter's own ground,[26] as the Rabbis said: "From the forest itself is taken the axe wherewith to fell it,"[27] and "He met his equal."[28] With regard to this is it written: *In all sadness there is benefit* (Prov. 14:23), the profit being the joy that follows sadness, as will be seen below.

In truth, however, a broken heart—or the bitterness of the soul because of its distance from the light of the divine countenance and its being clothed in the *sitra ahara*—is not called *atzvut* ("sadness") in Hebrew. *Atzvut* implies that the heart is dull as stone and devoid of vitality. But in the case of the bitter, broken heart, the contrary is true: There is vitality in the heart expressed as agitation and bitterness, except that this vitality stems from the attribute of the holy *gevurot*

---

22. Referring to the thesis developed in *Tanya*, chap. 30, on the need to engage in unending struggle against one's animal nature and the dire consequences of failure.
23. The "translucent shell," the kabbalistic symbol of the realm in which good and evil are intermingled.
24. Shabbat 30b. Cf. Zohar I, 180b.
25. Thus, anxiety over one's moral inadequacy is a virtue, but of a lower order. It derives from the realm of *nogah* and is a "natural" form of the good, rather than issuing from pellucid sanctity.
26. The Kabbalah's term for evil. The author is recommending turning the weapons of the enemy (despondency) against him; sadness itself prepares the way for joy. See *Tanya*, chaps. 26 and 33 (above chapter 7, selection 7 and above, selection 5).
27. Sanhedrin 39b.
28. Shabbat 121b.

(severity), whereas joy comes from the attribute of *ḥasadim* ("kindness"), for the heart is comprised of both of them.[29]

It is sometimes necessary to arouse the attitude of the holy *gevurot*. . . . The most propitious time, specifically appropriate for most people, is when one is in any case troubled by mundane worries or dejected, without apparent cause. Then is the right time to transform the sadness by becoming one of those "masters of self-examination" mentioned earlier . . . thus ridding oneself of the dejection occasioned by mundane affairs.

Following this he will arrive at true joy, as he reflects in his heart . . . and says to himself: "Truly and without doubt I am far removed from God, and I am abominable and despicable . . . yet all this is myself alone; that is, the body with its animating soul. But there is within me truly a portion of God—as there exists even in the most worthless of men—namely, the divine soul with a spark of veritable godliness, enclosed in it and vitalizing it, except that it is, so to speak, in a state of exile. Therefore, on the contrary, the farther away I am from God and the more contemptible and loathsome I am, the deeper in exile is my divine soul and the more greatly is it to be pitied. Therefore I shall make it my whole aim and desire to extricate it from this exile, in order to restore it *to her father's house as in her youth* (Lev. 22:13), before it was clothed in my body, when it was yet absorbed in His blessed light and completely united with Him. Now it will again be thus absorbed and united with Him, if I make it my whole purpose with regard to the Torah and the mitzvot . . . especially the commandment of prayer, to cry unto God in the Shekhinah's distress of exile in my despicable body, to liberate it from its prison, so that it may attach itself to Him, blessed be He."

This is the essence of "repentance and good deeds,"[30] the latter being the good deeds which one performs in order to restore the "portion of God" to the Source of good of all the worlds. Thus will the service of God throughout his life be in great joy—the joy of the soul in

---

29. R. Shneur Zalman here makes an important distinction between melancholia (*atzvut*, "sadness, depression") and anxiety ("the broken heart and embittered spirit"). The former is a state of passivity, the latter one of agitation. The former, in the mystical framework, derives at best from *kelippat nogah*, that realm where natural good and evil commingle, whereas the latter issues from the exclusively sacred realms in which severity (*gevurot*) and kindness (*ḥasadim*) are the two sides of the same sefirotic structure. In this scheme, anxiety and joy are two sides of the same coin, which cannot be said of melancholy or depression (*atzvut*).
30. See, e.g., Avot 4:11.

its release from his despised body and "returning to her father's house as in her youth,"[31] while he is engaged in Torah and worship.[32]

7. A BROKEN HEART AND SORROW
Source: R. Nahman of Bratslav, Likkutei Etzot, Hitbodedut, no. 23

A "broken heart" and sadness (atzvut) are not the same at all. Sadness is expressed in anger and irritability, whereas broken-heartedness is like a son cleansing himself before his father,[33] [or] a child crying and complaining that he has been set far from his father. The latter type is dearly beloved by God. It would be best for man to experience such a "broken heart" all day long. But, because most people would easily be led from a broken heart to sadness, which is exceedingly injurious, as I have explained many times, one ought to set aside some period during the day to pray with a "broken heart," restricting his broken-heartedness to that period alone, while the rest of the day is spent in joy.[34]

8. POSITIVE JOY AND NEGATIVE JOY
Source: R. Yaakov Yosef of Polennoye, Toledot Yaakov Yosef to Toledot, sec. 3, middle

The Talmud states: "It is written, And I praised joy (Eccles. 8:15), and it is also written, and as to joy, what does it achieve? (ibid. 2:2). The contradiction is only apparent. The answer is: the former deals with the joy of a mitzvah; it is this to which I praised joy applies. The verse and

---

31. Paraphrasing Lev. 22:13, as above.
32. The liberation of the divine spark from the body does not refer to death but to the spiritual elation of Torah study, prayer, and the performance of mitzvot. Paradoxically, the more one contemplates one's own abjectness, the more is one moved to assert his God-like nature, and in this triumph over his corporeal self lies the secret of man's felicity and happiness.
33. The expression of an intimate and loving relationship of a son who, in confessing his wrongdoings, is primarily disturbed by the absence of a direct and immediate encounter with his father. This purifying desire for reconciliation is R. Nahman's interpretation of the "broken heart."
34. This excerpt should be compared with that from R. Shneur Zalman (the previous selection). Both distinguish between atzvut ("sadness") and lev nishbar ("broken heart"), but each offers a different interpretation of the contrast. Both, however, adopt the same strategy of limiting even the preferred form of emotional and spiritual distress to specific times, thus devoting the rest of one's time to simḥah ("joy").

as to joy, what does it achieve? applies to joy which is not related to a mitzvah."[35] ...

It is known that the reward of a mitzvah is another mitzvah, and the reward of a transgression is another transgression.[36] Thus it is written: *And I praised joy (et ha-simḥah),*[37] which signifies only the joy of a mitzvah which is the mitzvah itself. The reward of the mitzvah draws forth an additional mitzvah; whereas *as to joy, what does it achieve?* does not activate [an additional force] for good. Joy in a mitzvah, however, creates further joy, for it is derived from the aspect of the soul which is called "Abraham." The difference between the two is as follows: *Abraham gave birth (holid et) to Isaac* [Heb. *yitzḥak*, lit. "he will laugh"] (Gen. 25:19) to add further laughter and joy, whereas sorrow follows the joy that is unrelated to a mitzvah, as is stated in the Zohar.[38] But the joy of a mitzvah generates further joy.

9. JOY LEADS TO CLAIRVOYANCE
Source: R. Nahman of Bratslav, Likkutei Etzot, Simḥah, nos. 2–3

One must perform the mitzvot with such great joy that one does not even want any heavenly reward for it. He wishes only that God should prepare another mitzvah for him, for he derives pleasure from the mitzvah itself. Through this one may know what has been decreed for the world, whether the decree has been confirmed or not, and upon whom the evil has been decreed, heaven forfend.[39] One thus knows how to pray for the world, for after the judgment has been decreed, *zaddikim* must clothe their prayers in the form of stories. One merits all this by performing the mitzvah in great joy derived from the mitzvah itself. This [in turn] may be merited by praying fervently and with great awe and love.

---

35. Shabbat 30b.
36. See Avot 4:2.
37. The Hebrew word *et* (which has no meaning in translation) appears in the verse. The verse being comprehensible without the inclusion of this apparently superfluous word, the author expounds a reason for the inclusion of *et*: it signifies further joy, for such is the nature of spiritual joy, i.e., the *simhah* of mitzvah, as opposed to the ordinary forms of joy.
38. *Midrash ha-Ne'elam* to Toledot, p. 135a.
39. By desiring only that joy which comes from the sacred act in itself, and waiving all rights even to spiritual rewards, one achieves that distance or independence from the worlds through which alone he can see them as they truly are. This distancing seems to be reflected in R. Nahman's next remarks on the value of storytelling where direct petition is no longer possible.

10. HUMILITY AND SADNESS
Source: R. Elimelekh of Lizhensk, Noam Elimelekh to Bemidbar, s.v. o yomar va-yedaber

The Torah teaches man how to conduct himself. Thus, the Torah was given at Sinai in order that man should learn always to be humble and self-deprecating, even as God scorned the high mountains and chose Mount Sinai, which was the lowest mountain of all. This is the meaning of *in the desert of Sinai* (Num. 1:1).[40]

Nevertheless, man must strive to avoid despondency, for self-abasement can cause him to fall into melancholy, which is a great impediment to the service of the Creator. Therefore, the Torah cautioned man always to be in a state of joy, for the divine spirit does not repose upon a depressed person.[41] This is the meaning of *in the tent of meeting (moed)* (ibid.): One should place himself in the tent of the *moed*, which is synonymous with joy, for *moed* means "a holiday."[42]

On the first (day) of the second month (ḥodesh) (ibid.) [may be interpreted to mean]: If one would say, "How can I rejoice after having sinned so much?" the Torah says: "Nevertheless, let him repent joyfully and say courageously, 'It is as if I had been born today, and I shall never again return to [such] foolishness.'" This is called "renewal," for he is like a newborn creature.[43]

---

40. "Desert" connotes barrenness and humility, even as Sinai is the symbol of lowliness.
41. Shabbat 30b.
42. *Moed* literally means "appointed time." The tent of meeting in the desert was called the *ohel moed* because the encounters with God there were held at set times. A festival is called a *moed* because it occurs at a designated time. Hence the play on words, yielding "the place of joy."
43. "Month" is *ḥodesh* in Hebrew. *Ḥodesh* comes from the root *ḥ-d-sh*, meaning "new," for a new month is marked by a new moon. Hence the play on words so typical of hasidic homilies: rebirth, the dominant existential dimension of repentance, rids one of the dejection that comes from the awareness of accumulated sins. The fundamental problem dealt with by R. Elimelekh, similar to that which concerned R. Shneur Zalman (see above, selections 5 and 6), is the conflict between Judaism's demand for humility and one's consequent mood of self-deprecation as a morally inadequate creature, and Hasidism's high emphasis on happiness as a prerequisite to proper religious experience, especially that of ecstasy.

11. JOY AND FREEDOM
Source: R. Nahman of Bratslav, Likkutei Etzot, Simhah, nos. 7, 10, 26, 27

(7) Joy is in the category of "illuminated faces" and "truth and faith." Its opposite, sadness, is in the category of idolatry and the "faces of darkness and death." One merits joy primarily through upholding the covenant,[44] and through closeness to the true zaddikim, who are the joy of all Israel. Thereby one binds himself up with God and deserves to behold the pleasantness of the Lord and to bask in the luminous countenance of the King.

(10) One must keep very far from sadness, for the shells[45] have the aspect of sadness and are "judgment intensified" [i.e., the essence of punishment]. When sadness prevails, the Shekhinah, which is the joy of Israel, is in exile. The negation of the shells and the ascent of holiness take place primarily through joy.

(26) Sadness and melancholy are like dust which fall upon the heart of a Jew which is thus unable to burst into flame and be inspired [with the love] of God. With their holy spirit, the true leaders of the generation blow away the dust, i.e., melancholy, from the heart of the Jew. Thus they inspire the hearts of Israel toward God.

(27) Because of melancholy and sadness, the mind and intellect are "in exile," and it is difficult for one to reflect on returning to God; thus one remains far from God. The reason that the world (i.e., mankind), is so far from God is that people do not reflect properly on the purpose of the cosmos. However, through joy, the mind is stable and one can think properly; for joy is the realm of freedom. Therefore, when one brings joy to his mind, he liberates it from exile, and he can direct it wherever he wishes and thus reflect properly on his purpose in all his worldly enterprises, and thus return to God.[46]

12. DANCE, SONG, AND HUMOR
Source: R. Nahman of Bratslav, Likkutei Etzot, Simhah, nos. 12, 14, 15, 29

(12) Dances of mitzvah—as when one drinks wine on the Sabbath or holidays or at a wedding or at other feasts of mitzvah, and does so

---

44. A euphemism for stringency in abiding by the sexual scruples of Judaism and atoning for one's past moral lapses.
45. *Kelipot*, the kabbalistic symbol for evil.
46. By removing extraneous emotional burdens, joy makes possible one's spiritual-intellectual cogitation on his ultimate purpose in the world, and this leads him to God. Religious experience does not flourish in depression.

moderately and for the sake of heaven, to rejoice in Israel and in God Who chose us from among all the people, and thereby arouses such joy that it penetrates down to his feet, i.e., that he dances out of joy—expel all the outward [shells] which cling to the feet.[47] They sweeten and nullify evil decrees, and one becomes worthy of all of the blessings. The enthusiasm of such dances is an *offering of sweet savor to the Lord* (Num. 28:8). However, he who dances with the passion of his Evil Urge, this is a *strange fire* (Lev. 10:1), heaven forbid, and the wine which he drinks is but profane wine of intoxication to which cling the outer shells, heaven forfend.[48] Thus, dances of holiness sweeten evil decrees, as does the *pidyon*.[49]

(14) Listening to a musical melody on instruments played by a pious musician for the sake of heaven can be very helpful in attaining joy, and also subdue and clarify the imagination.[50] Through this, one merits awareness and concentration of his thoughts on the world-to-come and to perceive the clues which God provides for him every day on how to draw closer to Him. By means of such song and joy, one can even attain prophecy and the holy spirit.

(15) Through song and joy, one can "pour out his words like water in the presence of the Lord."[51] Therefore, by being happy throughout the whole day, one should be able to pray in solitude properly.[52]

(29) One should make strenuous efforts to attain joy in any way possible, searching within himself for those good qualities which lead to joy. . . . At the very least, one ought to be happy at the privilege of

---

47. By expressing religious joy with one's legs, one thereby rids himself of all sinful or immoral acts which involve these limbs. ("Shells" are the euphemism for evil.)

48. The "strange fire" on the altar that caused the death of the two older sons of Aaron is interpreted by R. Nahman as that passion which issues from impure motives rather than the desire to serve the Lord.

49. "Redemption" money given to the zaddik in return for his intercessionary prayers and which "redeem" the hasid from any harmful heavenly decrees which may have been issued against him.

50. The pejorative use of "imagination" in Jewish literature goes back to Maimonides, for whom it symbolized emotion or affect and deterrence to reason. For R. Nahman, an anti-rationalist, it represented unbridled passion. Such "imagination" could be "subdued" or "clarified" (i.e., its sinful aspects separated from its potential as a means of divine service) by true joy for the sake of heaven.

51. Paraphrase of Lam. 2:19.

52. A cheerful frame of mind enables one to pray with greater ease, especially the special "prayer in solitude" recommended by R. Nahman. See on this chapter 6, selection 15.

being born a Jew and not a pagan. This is surely a wonderful, unlimited, and unadulterated joy, for it is an act of God Himself.[53] One should accustom oneself to proclaim joyfully, by word and in full heart, "Blessed is our God Who created us for His glory and separated us from those who stray, i.e., pagans."[54] Thus one can be in a state of joy throughout all his life no matter what befalls him.

Sometimes one must become jovial through frivolity and humor. Because of the many tribulations which man suffers—physically, psychologically, and financially—he usually cannot be happy without silliness, by playing the fool in order to be cheerful. The very vitality of body and soul depend upon this. In the upper worlds, too, a great "unity" is created through man's jocular state of mind, namely, feeling joyous.

---

53. Being born Jewish is a fact determined by God, in which he had no choice. Hence the joy in one's Jewishness is uncorrupted by pride in one's individual achievement.
54. This benediction is recited as is part of the morning prayers.

12B

Smallness and Greatness

The terms *katnut* and *gadlut*, "smallness" and "greatness," play a significant role in the Hasidic conception of the service of God.

Indeed, the two were universalized and became adjectives for the two basic states of all beings, from the divine sefirot to the most trivial of material objects.

The Besht borrowed this language from Lurianic Kabbalah, where this terminology had specific but complex and esoteric meaning, and converted it into relevant human application. The translation of the term *katnut* (also *katnut ha-mohin* and, alternatively, *mohin de-katnut*), "smallness of mind," is used with a certain reluctance, because while the term includes the intellectual component it is not at all confined to the cognitive realm and does not refer exclusively to the brain. *Mohin*, literally "brains," which come in the small and great forms, should be understood, rather, as consciousness or awareness—the combination of the rational, emotional, and volitional aspects of man's consciousness.

"Smallness" is the "minor state" (as Gershom Scholem prefers to translate it, rather freely), that of imperfection, sadness, estrangement, mechanical performance out of habit or compulsion.

403

"Greatness" (and also *gadlut ha-moḥin* and *moḥin de-gadlut*), or the "major state," is one of freedom, joy, love, fulfillment. Service of God in smallness is performed by rote, and the worshipper is burdened by his inability to leap upward, to take wing, to break out in rapture and insight, his very defeat exacerbating his depression. Greatness represents his breakthrough, his triumph over his emotional-intellectual-spiritual limitations, and the expression of his latent powers.

The relationship of *gadlut* and *katnut* to *devekut* and the "descent" from *devekut* is problematical. Scholem seems to equate *gadlut* and *devekut*, even while granting that a "modest" form of *devekut* can be achieved through smallness.[55] In addition to being contradicted by a report of a Beshtian saying in *Zava'at ha-Rivash* (see below, selection 1), one can hardly ascribe any, even modest, experience in "smallness" to *devekut* if, indeed, the two are basically antonyms. Furthermore, note selection 2 below, in which the Besht speaks of "great *devekut*," even during periods of smallness. For the Besht, it would seem, *devekut* is not necessarily a purely emotional experience. Indeed, it is possible to achieve it through cognitive meditation alone (below, selection 7), even though *devekut* is usually attained out of a state of *gadlut*.

The selections that follow make plain that the two states were not clearly formulated or defined by the early hasidic masters. The lack of a firm delineation of the concept is reflected in the variety of interpretations offered. In the most general way, one can refer to them as the state of inspiration and its converse.

Hasidism's originality lies not in positing two forms of divine service, nor even in broadening their scope to other areas of existence, but in stressing the value of persisting even during the cold, blasé, alienated periods of smallness. Despite the Sabbatean doctrine of the necessary descent of the Messiah, and the condemnation any similar theory would have incurred as a result of the debacle of Sabbateanism, the Baal Shem Tov finds value in the service of the Lord during smallness per se, as well as in exploiting smallness as a point of departure to attain the more exalted subsequent greatness. Thus, for the Besht, in a state of *katnut* one can still serve God by telling stories, engaging in idle talk, jesting, and laughing.

The point is made in a charming homily by one of the greatest of the Polish zaddikim of the nineteenth century, R. Yitzhak Meir of Gur, renowned as the author of *Ḥiddushei ha-Rim* and leader of the largest

---

55. Scholem, *The Messianic Idea in Judaism,* pp. 218–222.

of the hasidic dynasties. He cites the passage in the Talmud (Shabbat 88a) which says that at the revelation of the Torah at Sinai, God raised the mountain over the heads of the assembled people of Israel and said to them, "If you accept the Torah, good and well; if not, here shall be your burial place!" Tosafot (ad loc.) asks the most obvious question: How can the Sages of the Talmud assert that Israel was coerced into accepting the Torah when Scripture states explicitly that the response of the Israelites was, "We shall do and we shall obey" (Exod. 24:7; the latter verb is taken by the Sages to denote understanding, thus proclaiming the priority of submission to rational consent), thus implying their readiness to accept the Torah on faith?

The answer he offers is that indeed both are true; paradoxically, the Children of Israel were both coerced into their historic mission and they accepted it voluntarily. Essentially, their attitude was that given by Scripture: a warm and happy response of readiness to assume the burden of servitude to God. But the Sages insisted upon a note of reluctance as well, in order to teach successive generations that one must serve the Lord not only in *gadlut*, implied by the "we shall do and we shall obey" verse, but also in the darker moments of life when the human spirit is subdued and weary and vulnerable, the state of *katnut* when one must force himself obstinately and relentlessly to do God's will even while his own spirit is unresponsive. The Almighty must be served not only in the presence of the theophany of revelation at Sinai, but even during the grim periods when the mountain seems about to crash over our very heads.

Indeed, persistence in serving God during the alienation of *katnut*, the stubborn commitment to religious performance even in the absence of any redeeming religious experience, is a sign of spiritual authenticity and heroism. Yet one must always aspire to worshiping and serving God in greatness.

1. DEFINING KATNUT AND GADLUT
Source: Besht, Zava'at ha-Rivash, no. 129

In order to understand what is *katnut* ("smallness") and what is *gadlut* ("greatness"), consider this example: If one studies Torah without understanding, he is in a state of smallness, for his intellect is not whole. If, however, he studies with understanding and enthusiasm, then he is in a state of greatness, for he is attached to higher levels [of divine service]. The same holds true for prayer. In every mitzvah that one performs, there is *katnut* and *gadlut*.[56]

2. DEVEKUT IN "SMALLNESS"
Source: Besht, Zava'at ha-Rivash, no. 67

There are times when a person is incapable of worship except in a state of smallness, i.e., he does not enter the upper worlds at all but thinks that [since] *the whole earth is full of His glory* (Isa. 6:3), that His presence is close to him. At that moment he is like a child whose intellect is underdeveloped. Nevertheless, even though one worships in smallness, he can do so with great *devekut*.[57]

3. DEVEKUT IN "SMALLNESS" (continued)
Source: Besht, Zava'at ha-Rivash, no. 137

One ought to consider that the whole world is full of His glory; that His Shekhinah is always nearby; that He is completely spiritual (lit. "thinner than the thinnest," i.e., not corporeal or tangible); that He is the master of all that exists in the world; that He can do anything which I desire; and therefore it is not proper for me to trust in anyone but Him. [When] one thinks [thus], he beholds the Shekhinah in the same manner that he perceives physical things. This is the service of God in smallness.[58] . . .

At times his mind can discern that there exists above him a multitude of rounded heavens, and he stands at one point on this small

---

56. See also R. Zevi Elimelekh Shapiro of Dinov, *Agra de-Pirka* 137: "When one studies, prays, or performs a mitzvah without an inner desire and a sense of connectedness, it is called *katnut*, for he is like a child (*katan*) whose brain is small and who, if he does the right thing, does so fortuitously, like a blind man who finds a window by instinct (or happenstance), i.e., without reflection. However, when one performs the commandment with longing, seriousness, and purposeful intention, it is called *gadlut*."

57. See ibid., 69.

58. The Kehot edition has this passage in two paragraphs, the first ending with "anyone but Him," and the second beginning, "One ought to think that just as He beholds . . ." The first paragraph is thus irrelevant to the theme of *katnut* and *gadlut*. However, I have here followed most other editions in which the material is conflated, and have provided the translation in English. Accordingly, smallness reflects a state of awareness of God's immanence and closeness as well as personal trust in Him, but lacks that special spiritual energy and drive that characterize *gadlut*.

earth; that all the world is as nothing compared to the Creator; that He is infinite and performed the *tzimtzum*, making room within Himself and creating in that space all the worlds. Yet, though he understands all this intellectually, he cannot ascend to higher worlds.[59] This is the meaning of *The Lord hath appeared from afar to me* (Jer. 31:3)—that he can perceive Him [only] from afar.

4. SMALLNESS AS A PREPARATION FOR GREATNESS
Source: R. Mosheh Hayyim Ephraim of Sudlikov, Degel Maḥaneh Ephraim to Vayetzei, beginning

This is the secret of smallness and greatness: It is well known what is said in the name of my master and grandfather [the Besht], may the memory of the righteous be a blessing: *And the living creatures ran and returned (as the appearance of a flash of lightning)* (Ezek. 1:14).[60] It is impossible to remain at the same level perpetually. Rather, one must either go up or go down. The descent is for the purpose of ascent, provided one realizes that he is in a state of smallness and prays to the Lord [that he rise to greatness].[61] Thus, *From thence ye will seek the Lord thy God and thou shalt find Him* (Deut. 4:29); *from thence* implies: from wherever you happen to be.[62]

5. SMALLNESS AS THE EXPERIENCE OF GOD'S ABSENCE
Source: R. Yaakov Yosef of Polennoye, Ketonet Passim, Shemini, p. 11a

Where has thy beloved gone, O thou fairest among women? (Song of Songs 6:1). This can be understood by reference to *and the living creatures ran*

---

59. Thus smallness is identified with passive contemplation, and greatness with an active, inspired, exuberant reflection.

60. In Ezekiel's vision of the divine chariot, the celestial creatures (*ḥayyot*) run to and fro. The Besht takes this as applying to a constant change of state between smallness and greatness. Ḥayyot is read by him as ḥiyyut ("life-force"), which keeps on oscillating.

61. Hasidism's emphasis on ecstasy and a high level of inspiration created for it the dilemma of how to assess and account for all those periods of spiritual stagnation and psychological dullness, and especially how to cope with the despair they might engender that a spiritual "high" (i.e., greatness) will never be attained. Hence the Besht assumes that one's spiritual life is never stable, there are always ups and downs, and ought to look upon his period of smallness not as a permanent incarceration but as preparation for a new ascent to greatness. See Toledot Yaakov Yosef to Vaeira, sec. 1, for the same Beshtian idea in a somewhat different form.

62. Even in a state of smallness.

and returned (Ezek. 1:14).[63] God, the Life of Life,[64] is called *thy beloved*, Who had gone up above, so that the congregation of Israel, called *the fairest among women*, is left in a state of smallness.[65] When the service of the Lord is done without love or awe, but by compulsion and as if it were a great inconvenience, and without pleasure—those are the days of smallness, as I heard from my teacher [the Besht].

6. LEVITY LEADS TO GREATNESS
Source: Besht, *Keter Shem Tov*, p. 2

The reason for saying something humorous before study[66] is that *the living creatures ran and returned* (Ezek. 1:14);[67] man [too participates] in the mystery of smallness and greatness. Through joy and jest one emerges from smallness to greatness to study and cleave to God. Thus it is said about two jesters that they banished a man's trouble through a joke;[68] thus did they draw him close and elevate him. Likewise, it is written, *And [Abraham] took his two young men with him and Isaac his son* (Gen. 22:3); through laughter for the sake of heaven, one can elevate the years of youth with him.[69]

7. GREATNESS AND SMALLNESS IN THE RATIONAL AND DEVOTIONAL REALMS
Source: R. Dov Ber of Mezeritch, *Maggid Devarav le-Yaakov*, no. 205

---

63. R. Yaakov Yosef is applying the Beshtian theme of smallness and greatness, as he heard it expounded on the verse in Ezekiel and the verse in Song of Songs.

64. Hinted at in Ezekiel's "living creatures."

65. The experience of God's absence, what might be called *hester panim*, "the hiding of His face," leaves one in that mood of estrangement and abandonment called smallness.

66. See Shabbat 30b.

67. See the previous selection and the Besht's interpretation of this verse as it relates to smallness and greatness.

68. Ta'anit 22a.

69. The name Isaac (Yitzhak) derives from *tzehok* ("laughter"); see Gen. 17:17, 19. "Two young men" (*shenei ne'arav*) is, by means of a characteristic hasidic play on words, transmuted to *shenei* or *shenot ne'urav* ("the years of his youth"). Thus the surprising and altogether welcome conclusion that levity—laughter, humor, jesting—can, if done in the right spirit ("for the sake of heaven"), not only help one to ascend to a state of greatness, but somehow retroactively elevate all his past, "the years of his youth," endowing a lackluster past with a newfound inspiration.

The Talmud states that he who wants to live should kill himself.[70] It also states that the words of Torah exist only for one who kills himself for them,[71] as it is written, *The is the law (torah) when a man dieth in a tent* (Num. 19:14).[72] It is important to understand: What is the pertinence of death here?

The matter can be understood by an analogy to a teacher instructing his pupil. When the pupil does not understand what his master is teaching him, then he relates to his master's words "back to back," for he finds no satisfaction in these words, as they do not penetrate his heart. The teacher, too, is as if his face were turned away, for he understands well that his words are not being grasped by his listener. Afterwards, however, when the student applies all his heart and mind to his teacher's words, and he understands them very well, joy and love and fraternity are created between them, and they relate "face to face."

But one must try to understand whence it comes about that in the beginning he did not know what his master said, and later he did grasp the content and intention of the teaching. The answer is that at first he did not approach it with intellectual depth, but learned superficially, with little understanding. Later, however, he grasped the contents of the subject by diverting his attention from everything else, and concentrating on it with great intellectual profundity, to the limit of his wisdom and theoretical ability—so much so, that were a person to call him, he would not answer, almost not seeing even what is before his very eyes, so completely distracted is he [from all else by virtue of his focus] on this subject. And so he arrives at the ultimate true meaning of the teachings.

Now, this extreme diverting of attention [from all else] is almost a form of death[73]—or sleep, which is considered one sixtieth of death[74]—

---

70. Tamid 32a: "Alexander the Great asked the [Judean] elders of the Negev, 'What shall a man do in order to live?' and they replied, 'Let him kill himself.'" Rashi comments: "make himself lowly," i.e., humility is the way to greater attainment in life. The Maggid, in this passage, interprets the answer in an epistemological rather than moral sense.

71. Shabbat 83b. Mastery over Torah cannot be attained without the sacrifice of one's own needs and comforts.

72. Ibid. The proof-text connects the word for "law," *torah*, to dying. Hence: One can attain Torah only by being ready to die for it as he devotes his time to the "tent of Torah."

73. In ordinary English too, one involved in intense concentration on an object is referred to as "dead to the world."

74. See Berakhot 57b.

for all one's life-force rises upwards and he thereby receives new
moḥin.[75] This is the secret of the verse *They* [the Lord's mercies] *are new
every morning* (Lam. 3:23). This too is the secret of the chilling of the
thighs before birth; for he is then on the lowest level, as if he does not
exist and understand anything, for his mind has ascended all the way
up, so that his mind gave birth and he now understands the truth of
the [master's] words.[76] Thus . . . in the beginning, the teachings
appeared very constricted, for he did not understand them in breadth;
he was only on the level of Abba ("Father").[77] Afterwards, by his
intense and elevated distraction [by virtue of his focused attention on]
the content of the words [of the teaching], they appear to him in all
their breadth, he understands them thoroughly, and he relates to them
"face to face."

The same holds true for words of prayer.[78] When one begins to
pray, he is still in a state of smallness of mind, and he cannot pray
with *devekut*. He is then on the level of Abba. However, when he then
diverts his attention from anything and everything else, and is mindful of Him before whom he stands, and of the substance and permutations and Names and lights in the words [of prayer],[79] and he attaches himself to them in most wondrous *devekut*, then he relates to these
words "face to face," and they are seen in all their breadth . . . and

---

75. See Introduction above, for a definition of *moḥin*, which we here, with reluctance,
translate as "mind."
76. R. Dov Baer is making use of a sexual analogy, as indeed the earlier terms, "face to
face" and "back to back," are well-known kabbalistic terms based on erotic imagery.
Just as one's other organs are drained of heat and vitality at the act of sexual climax
(the words "before birth" in the text actually refer to the act of siring, hence orgasm),
so epistemologically the act of learning, at its climax of perception, is accompanied by
total distraction from all else.
77. Synonym for the second of the ten sefirot, Hokhmah ("Wisdom"), which represents cognitive potential. It is only in the next sphere, Binah ("Understanding"), also
called Mother, that the full realization of intellectual potential is attained and implemented. The author's use of the terms Father and Mother is a continuation of the
erotic metaphor.
78. The Maggid now applies his theory of learning to prayer. Just as total, deliberate
obliviousness to all extraneous sensation (= "death") is a prerequisite to intense attention in cognitive apprehension, so do the same schematics apply to the devotional
meta-rational realm.
79. The mystical elements in prayer that the kabbalist can invoke, via his spiritual
techniques, in order to achieve *devekut*.

what was narrow before is now greatly expanded, and he feels separated from his physical existence.

8. HOLDING ON TO GOD DURING GREATNESS
Source: R. Elimelekh of Lizhensk, Noam Elimelekh to Emor, s.v. be-inyan

When one is involved in Torah study or prayer or in any holy deed, he is in a state of greatness of the mind.[80] Such is the way of the righteous (zaddikim): Before they pray, they meditate and direct their minds to reflect on Him to whom they pray. This holiness elevates the mind during this period. However, after the conclusion of the prayer or the holy deed, the zaddik falls to a state of smallness of mind because he is involved with temporal vanities.[81] But this is not the purpose of wholesome service, for one must constantly be in holiness and purity, without even a brief interruption. Therefore one must so bind himself to God during the period of his greatness of thought that his thought should be connected to God even when he leaves it [for his daily chores].[82]

9. YOUTHFULNESS AND MATURITY
Source: R. Levi Yitzhak of Berdichev, Kedushat Levi to Yitro, s.v. o yevo'ar anokhi

The Sages taught that the Lord appeared to Israel at Sinai as an old man, while at the Exodus he appeared to them as a young lad.[83] This alludes to the two forms of the service of the Creator. In the first, a person serves the Creator simply because "He is the Great Ruler." He does not consider the goodness and lovingkindness that the Lord bestows upon him, because such favors and pleasures are as nothing compared to the great delight of [the very act of] the service of the

---

80. Mohin, which we have translated as "mind," literally means "brain." However, as indicated in the introduction to this chapter, mohin should be understood, rather, as intentionality.

81. Cf. Sefer Baal Shem Tov to Noah, Amud ha-Tefillah, sec. 167.

82. R. Elimelekh's prescription for surviving the periods of smallness is to reach the highest level of devekut during greatness and have the afterglow sustain him in his low periods. Note that R. Elimelekh's concept of the two states is less complex than the other definitions mentioned earlier. Greatness, for R. Elimelekh, is, it appears, the very act of being involved in sacred activity, with no mention of the emotional involvement, and smallness is simply the involvement in one's daily, prosaic routines.

83. Pesikta Rabbati 21:5.

Creator. Such a person knows that he worships the great and power-ful King, whose servants number in the millions, and whose "glorious chariots" are infinite in number. This is called greatness of mind, wherein one serves the Creator with the greatness of his intellect.[84]

There is another kind of worship in which one serves the Creator because the Creator grants him much kindness and goodness. This person worships the Creator with smallness of mind.[85]

At the Exodus, the Israelites beheld God's miracle and wonders: the punishment of the Egyptians by the ten plagues, the splitting of the Red Sea, and the spoils of Egypt. They then worshipped the Lord with smallness of mind. This is what the Rabbis meant when they said, "At the Red Sea, God appeared to Israel as a young lad," for a youth has a limited mind; and they served Him then out of smallness of mind. During the giving of the Torah at Sinai, "the pollution of the Israelites departed,"[86] so that no earthly pleasures held any importance for them compared with the service of the Creator. All of their service of the Creator was performed solely "because He is the Great Ruler." This is greatness of mind. This is what the Rabbis meant when they said, "At Sinai, the Lord appeared to Israel as an old man"; as one who possess-es a great mind.[87] . . .

Whoever serves the Lord with greatness of mind suffers no fear or trepidation from any external events. Even though it may appear that he is beset by tribulations, inwardly he does not consider it tribula-tion, for he is firmly confident that no harm will befall him. But he who worships God with smallness of mind is gripped even inwardly with great fear from everyday troublesome events. . . . Because of this, the forces of impurity encompass him and he falls under their control.

---

84. On the terms here translated as "mind" and "intellect," see above, n. 80.

85. In another passage (Yitro, s.v. *o yomar*) R. Levi Yitzhak explains that one who wor-ships God with greatness of mind is what Maimonides calls *oved lishmah*, worshipping God "for His own sake." Here the motivation is solely love for God, and not for reward or any other ulterior motive. One who serves the Lord either out of fear of punish-ment or for a reward worships *shelo lishmah*, or, in R. Levi Yitzhak's terms, in small-ness of mind. This definition of smallness and greatness differs from that of the Besht, who refers to the concepts as capacities for inspiration.

86. Shabbat 146a.

87. R. Levi Yitzhak is substituting Israel for God as the subject of the Midrash. The Midrash states that God appeared as a lad at the Red Sea and an old man at Sinai. R. Levi Yitzhak says that Israel was young at the Red Sea and old at Sinai, and that this determined Israel's perception of Him.

13

Peace

INTRODUCTION

The world of the commandments is commonly divided into those governing man's relation to God (*bein adam la-Makom*) and those regulating man's relationship to his fellows (*bein adam le-ḥavero*). Although the talmudic corpus, and particularly those tractates that form the core of organized study, emphasized Jewish civil law, the singularity of religion is generally located in the ritual laws rather than the interpersonal ethical imperatives. Yet Hasidism, like other Jewish movements of spiritual renewal, attempted to mold the realm of social relations according to its own distinctive orientation.

The hasidic contribution, as reflected in our selections, addresses the standards of ethical behavior, the metaphysical underpinnings of interpersonal relations, particularly among Jews, and the connections between relations among people and other aspects of the religious quest.

The command to love all Jews (*ahavat Yisrael*) and to judge them meritoriously is limited halakhically to those who are not wicked. Yet the inclusive "democratic" tendency of much hasidic thought and early hasidic practice is to reach out to the sinner, to justify the failing Jew. This can be illustrated by the following tradition: We are told that the Besht sought to elevate the spirit of the false messiah Shabbetai Zevi, who had defected to Islam almost a century earlier. The Besht abandoned his exertions only when it proved threatening to his spiritual destiny.[1] In addition to such stories about extraordinary efforts to save straying brethren, there are also tales of hasidic masters mobilized in defense of the Jewish people, interceding with God and standing up to Gentile persecutors. Here the name of R. Levi Yitzhak of Berdichev is prominent. He, and others, celebrated the importance of the Jewish people in God's plan for history, and attributed their failings to the tribulations of exile and persecution.

In the light of this, we may better understand the urgings, in the hasidic literature, to adopt supererogatory precepts in judging one's fellow Jew, be it his observance of the commandments or his actions toward others.

For the writers we are considering, the love of one's fellow man is rooted in characteristic doctrines about man. Thus, for instance, R. Menahem Mendel of Lubavitch, the third of the seven generations of Habad leaders, discusses the negative formulation by Hillel of the commandment to love one's fellow man and elucidates its psychological basis (see the last selection in the chapter). Among other insights, the organic nature of Jewish existence is especially significant: all Jews are bound up with one another like limbs of one body; what affects one cannot but affect all others. This interrelationship is also tied to man's creaturely situation: all humans share this fundamental identity from which derives the commitment to others. Because it is the relation with God that is primary, it is important that love for men become more than the pleasure of companionship; it must be subordinated to the divine perspective.

The themes we have noted adumbrate the idea of the "Pintelle Yid," the inextinguishable kernel of Jewish identity to be found even in the alienated and the sinner. The outcome of this principle is a reluctance to write off various segments of the Jewish people. This notion developed a bit later in the history of hasidic thought, during the late nineteenth century, when diluted commitment became more widespread; hence it is not represented in our selections.[2] Yet the basic continuity of this idea with earlier hasidic thought should be obvious.

Hasidic literature is also aware of the need for peace and mutual esteem as a means to one's individual spiritual growth. If the individual's own outlook is limited, meeting with others promises the essen-

1. *In Praise of the Baal Shem Tov*, trans. D. Ben-Amos and J. Mintz, Bloomington: Indiana University Press, pp. 86-87. If this story does not reflect the Besht's own activities, it surely expresses the views of the hasidic editors of *Shivhei ha-Besht*.
2. See M. Piekarz, *Hasidut Polin* (Jerusalem, 1990), chap. 5.

tial expansion and completion of one's religious knowledge. Strife
among people cripples the individual spiritually by isolating him existentially.[3]

Peace, at the metaphysical level, is a sublime concept, reconciling
apparent opposites in the name of the divine perspective. From this
messianic perspective, not only are opposites tolerated; they no longer
exist: peace is a simple reality, rather than the goal of strenuous
effort.[4]

It is a melancholy feature of hasidic history that prosaic, earth-
bound peace often eluded the hasidic world. In the very beginning, it
was bitterly opposed by the communal establishment, the *kahal*, and
by the rabbinic leadership. The early hasidic masters were often persecuted by the less moderate mitnaggedim—and some answered in
kind. Internally, personal controversy frequently pitted one master
against the other, and the picture was a painful one, whether the strife
was rooted in different paths in the service of God or conflicts revolv-
ing around money and turf. It is particularly poignant that R.
Nahman of Bratslav, who speaks so eloquently about the blessing of
peace and the curse of strife, feuded bitterly with almost every one of
his peers whose life touched his.

The ideal of peace, indeed, is a heavenly conciliation; on earth it
remains a struggle.

Love of Fellow Man and Peacefulness

1. THE LOVE OF MAN
Source: R. Elimelekh of Lizhensk, Noam Elimelekh, Hanhagot ha-Adam, no. 8

One must be on guard not to hate any Jew, except for the wicked, and
even then only if one knows clearly that it is impossible to find any
merit in them.[5] However, if it is at all possible to judge them merito-

---

3. For the idea that truth can best be attained through the strategy of peace, i.e., the
recognition of a spectrum of complementary outlooks that are to be reconciled with
one another, see my "Peace and Truth: Strategies for their Reconciliation—A
Meditation," in *Reverence, Righteousness and Raḥamanut: Essays in Memory of Rabbi Dr.
Leo Jung*, ed. Jacob J. Schachter, Northvale: Jason Aaronson, 1992, pp. 193–199.
4. See A. Ravitzky, "Paradigms of Peace in Jewish Thought," in his *Al Da'at ha-Makom*,
Jerusalem: Keter, 1991, p. 17 and n. 25.
5. This view seems to diverge from that of Maimonides in his comment on the
Mishnah, "Judge all men in the scale of merit" (Avot 1:6). According to Maimonides

riously, one is duty-bound to love [them] as oneself, to fulfill the commandment, *Thou shalt love thy neighbor as thyself* (Lev. 19:18).

2. THE PROPER ATTITUDE
Source: R. Elimelekh of Lizhensk, Tefillah Kodem ha-Tefillah

Save us from jealousies between one man and another. May no jealousy enter our hearts, and may others not be jealous of us.[6] On the contrary, grant that we learn to see each other's virtues rather than faults. May we talk with each other in a forthright and acceptable manner before Thee. May we feel no hatred for one another, heaven forbid.

3. PEACE AMONG OPPOSITES
Source: R. Nahman of Bratslav, Likkutei Etzot, Shalom, no. 10

The essence of peace is to unite two opposites. Therefore do not be alarmed when you meet someone whose opinions are diametrically opposed to yours, causing you to believe that it is absolutely impossible to live with him in peace. Similarly, when you see two people of extremely contrasting natures, do not say that it is impossible to make peace between them. On the contrary, the very essence of peace is to strive for harmony between opposites, just as God makes peace in His heavens between the contrasting elements of fire and water.[7] One merits peace by committing oneself to Sanctification of the Name, and thus also merits prayer with the right intention.[8]

---

and Rabbenu Yonah in his commentary, ad loc., one whose wickedness is firmly established does not deserve to be judged meritoriously. On the contrary, any possible merit in such an individual should be viewed with suspicion, for it may be a cover-up for a scheming act of evil. It is possible, however, that R. Elimelekh would concede that one ought to beware of such an individual without hating him. See my "Loving and Hating Jews as Halakhic Categories" in *Tradition* 24/2 (*Festschrift in Honor of Walter S. Wurzburger*), 98-122.

6. This prayer against having, or being the object of, jealousy is also included in a supplement to the text of the concluding prayer of the Amidah: "O my God, guard my tongue from evil . . ." See *Otzar ha-Tefillot* I, 374.

7. See Ḥagigah 12a, where, according to one interpretation, the word *shammayim* ("heaven") is a combination of *esh* ("fire") and *mayim* ("water"). See Additional Note *1.

8. See Additional Note *2.

4. IDENTIFYING WITH THE OTHER
*Source: R. Menahem Mendel of Vitebsk, Peri ha-Aretz u-Peri ha-Etz,
Shofetim*

An explanation of the talmudic story of the proselyte who came
before Hillel to be converted on condition that he teach him the whole
Torah while standing on one leg, and Hillel taught him "What is hateful to thee, do not do unto others."[9]

The proselyte who came to be converted sought, in all sincerity, to
base himself on "one leg," i.e., on one powerful and unshakable article
of faith.[10] . . . In his answer, Hillel laid down the general principle that
it is utterly impossible even to begin to serve God unless one deeply
believes that even the barest minimum of faith in Him comes from
Him. For it is God who grants [to the faithful] a knowledgeable heart,
seeing eyes, and listening ears, as it is written: *Hear, ye deaf, and look,
ye blind* (Isa. 42:18) and *And I will give them a heart of flesh* (Ezek.
11:19).[11]

Even though the Rabbis taught that "everything is determined by
Heaven except the fear of Heaven,"[12] this referred only to the awakening-from-below which is a prerequisite for the awakening-from-
Above.[13] For the heavenly blessing is not bestowed upon a void,[14] as is
indicated in the statement of [the prophet] Elisha: [*Tell me,*] *what has*

---

9. Shabbat 31a.
10. R. Menahem Mendel here makes reference to his interpretation elsewhere of the
term "one leg" as a powerful article of faith. The proselyte was not frivolously seeing
to learn all of Judaism during the time he could stand on one leg, but was genuinely
searching for the single most important principle of faith. Interestingly, the Hebrew
word for leg is *regel*, and the Latin *regula* means a rule or precept. Was the Roman
pagan's request, and Hillel's answer, intended for the Hebrew or the Latin term—or
both...?
11. Like all else, faith in God derives from God.
12. Berakhot 33b. How, then, can faith be ascribed to God?
13. Meaning; man has to arouse himself first toward the need to receive the divine
shefa or grace before he can become its beneficiary.
14. God's abundant goodness will not take hold unless a "vessel" has been prepared in
advance for its reception. See Tosefta Berakhot 6:13: "Blessing will not take hold
except when man has exerted himself." Thus man must actively prepare himself for
the divine gift. Man must initiate the dialogue with God in which he receives from
Him the capacity of faith.

thou in the house? (2 Kings 4:2).[15] Similarly, [with regard to man's faith in God,] without the Holy One's help [in providing for such faith] man could never achieve it.[16] In the words of our Rabbis: "God says, 'You open unto Me an opening [of faith and repentance] like the point of a needle, and I will open before you doors [wide enough] for wagons and carts to enter."[17] With the awakening-from-below, the windows of heaven are opened [and emanate toward him] a stream of love [of such force] that many waters cannot quench it, each one receiving according to his own measure, for not all are alike.[18]

One may ask: Is there any favoritism in this?[19] [The answer is:] These are mysterious matters, incomprehensible to you; "what have you to do with the secret ways of the Merciful One?"[20] Who knows the spirit of man, whether it goes upward, with the ease of an eagle; and the spirit of the beast—and man—whether it goes downward into the depths of the *kelipot*, may God save us from them.[21] Perhaps your sins [caused your fellow man to be distant from God] and your transgressions prevented [God's] goodness from reaching him, since "all Israelites are responsible for one another"[22] because they are all in their root composed of one soul.[23] . . .

---

15. In order to prepare the miracle of the cruse of oil expanding so as to provide the widow with the wherewithal to survive, Elisha tells her to borrow many vessels, all of which are filled with oil from the overflow of the small container. The rabbis learned from this that God's blessings to man do not occur in a vacuum, but must have a base, or "vessel," on which to rest. Miracles are not the same as magic. See, too, Zohar II, 153b on *And thou shalt make a table* (Exod. 25:23).

16. See Kiddushin 30b.

17. Song of Songs Rabbah 5:3.

18. The divine grace is sensed by everyone according to his specific spiritual rank. Therefore every individual's perception is unique.

19. Does this not violate the principles of equality before God and freedom of the will?

20. Berakhot 10a.

21. Paraphrase of Eccles. 3:21. R. Menahem Mendel's response is that the matter is a mystery, beyond human comprehension. Different people are endowed with different spiritual capacities, yet this does not violate the principle of divine justice.

22. Shavu'ot 39a.

23. R. Menahem Mendel is deriving an immensely important application from the foregoing. The absence of uniform religious capacity by all individuals, in the face of the undifferentiated gift of faith bestowed upon human beings by their Creator, does not automatically predestine one to eternal bliss and the other to perdition. We are judged not *for* but *by* our faith and religious capacities. The concept of human interrelatedness, as in the talmudic dictum concerning the co-responsibility of all Israelites or the kabbalistic idea that all souls are branches of one comprehensive human soul,

The basic principle of all this is that man is powerless to perform any mitzvah or good deed and to cling to the ways of God on his own; only God [can help him to do this], He Who illuminates man with the lights of fear and love [of God]. Should He say, "I have no desire of you," then nothing in the world will help man to sanctify himself. For man cannot impose himself on the Almighty. One's righteousness does not avail him. How then can one bring upon himself divine holiness and *devekut*? Only by virtue of His compassion and lovingkindness for all His creations, as it is written: *Unto Thee belongeth mercy; for Thou renderest to everyone according to his deeds* (Ps. 62:13).[24] . . .

The more one feels and understands this truth, that his [spiritual] achievements are not his own—for he can do nothing because of the gross corporeality of his body and thought—but that it is the spirit of God that speaks through him, that it is His word that is upon his tongue, and that his love [for God] is but a firebrand plucked from the divine fire; the greater will be his ecstasy, in boundless measure, so that neither parchment nor ink will suffice to describe the might and magnitude of his heart which truly loves, and his words will ascend like flames heavenward.[25]

By means of this love one becomes automatically attached to all human beings, to all people in the world like himself. Inasmuch as such love is not a personal achievement, which is utterly impossible, but a heavenly blessing which God was willing to grant to him, if He had given this same gift to someone else, that other would have been just as enthusiastic in his devotion to His blessed name. In what way, therefore, is he any better than his fellow man? . . .

When reaching such a state of perception, one feels that he *is* that other person, even if that other be an ordinary glutton, and thus he

---

implies that my fellow man's diminished faith may somehow be the effect of my transgressions, even though I begin with a greater spiritual potential. Credit or blame are therefore both irrelevant and reprehensible; all comparisons between different individuals as to their moral-spiritual standings are invidious. R. Menahem Mendel makes this explicit in part of the passage that we have not translated here.

24. In the paragraph that follows, which is untranslated here, R. Menahem Mendel relates the idea to the hasidic concept of divine immanence. Since the divine permeates all, indeed *is* all, then my love and devotion are not my own but His, and I have no right to feel proud of my service of the Lord.

25. The very knowledge that one's religious experience is not really one's own, but a divine capacity implanted in him by an act of divine grace, intensifies that experience. The removal of the egotistical element serves not to diminish but to enhance the quality of authentic religious experience.

comes to love every Jew, even the wicked ones. For he truly understands and knows how close he is to them, that he is [intimately]
related to them, that they are as one man, that he is in no way superior, for whatever [spiritual qualities] he possesses are but a gift from
heaven. Consequently, when such a person ascends to greater heights
in the love of God, he raises everyone, even in the thousands, along
with him, and he and they are one soul. . . .

However, one who imagines that his achievements in the study
and observance of Torah are the result of his own power and initiative,
is considered as one who hates Jews, indeed, as if he had no God . . .
for he effectively denies that it is the power of God that enabled him
to do this. . . .

The general rule in this matter is thus as follows: One who serves
the Lord in the manner indicated above, loves everyone and elevates
all those who are related to his category. Conversely, one who hates
anybody, even the wicked, indicates thereby that he views himself as
a righteous person whose righteousness is self-promoting arrogance.
[Such a person] is *deceitful above all things* (Jer. 17:9).

This, then, is what Hillel, in his humility, meant when he taught
the proselyte the whole Torah "on one leg": that the commandment
Thou shalt love thy neighbor as thyself (Lev. 19:18) is the basic principle
of faith.[26] The verse *Do not I hate them, O Lord, that hate Thee?* (Ps.
139:21) refers only to willful heretics who hate God, but not to those
who commit transgressions to satisfy their lust and appetite. Who
knows if you too will someday be in their position!

---

26. The reader is expected to pull together all the elements in this passage and conclude the homily coherently. Hillel's response—that "Thou shalt love thy neighbor as
thyself" (whether in its biblical positive form or in Hillel's Aramaic negative formulation) is the "one leg" the proselyte sought—is much more than the mere imperative to
behave lovingly to others in a social context. This love implies a fundamental, metaphysical identity of all human beings regardless of the differences in their moral or
spiritual attainments, because it derives from the fundamental article of faith that all
derives from God, that whatever excellence we possess is not of our own doing but is
ours merely by the grace of God. Because all issues from God, no one human being is
entitled to feel superior to any other, no matter how low the other has fallen. It is in
this *faith* that all derives from God that our common humanity is grounded and thereby is our love reinforced. This faith is the "one leg" that Hillel asserted is implied in the
commandment of neighborly love and which he taught to the proselyte as the foundation of all Judaism.

5. THE LIMBS OF ONE BODY
Source: R. Shneur Zalman of Liady, Iggeret ha-Kodesh, chap. 22

It is written: *All the men of Israel . . . knit together as one man* (Judg. 20:11).[27] Just as one man is composed of many limbs, and when they become separated it affects the heart[28]—for "out of it are the issues of life"[29]—so, since we are all truly as one man, the service [of God] will be established in the heart.[30] Therefore it is said: *To serve Him with one consent* (Zeph. 3:9); only so.

Therefore, my beloved and dear ones: I beg of you to strive with all your heart and soul to implant in each one's heart the love for your fellow man, and not ever to consider a wicked thought about another, as it is written: *And let none of you devise evil in your hearts against his neighbor* (Zech. 8:17). If such a thought should ever arise, let him banish it from your heart, even as smoke is driven away,[31] for this is truly like an idolatrous thought. [As the Rabbis taught:] Slanderous talk is as grave [a sin] as idolatry, adultery, and the shedding of blood all taken together.[32] If this is so with speech[, then it is surely so with thought]. For the advantage of proper thought over [proper] speech, whether for good or for better,[33] is already known to the wise of heart.[34]

---

27. Cf. Hagigah 26a. In Mekhilta de-R. Shimon b. Yohai to Exod. 19:6, ed. Epstein-Melamed (Jerusalem, 1955), p. 139: "As one body and one soul." On the halakhic aspects of this theme and this passage, see my *Halakhot ve-Halikhot* (Jerusalem, 1990), pp. 160–167.
28. See ibid., end of Mekhilta de-R. Yishmael, ed. Horovitz-Rabin, repr. Jerusalem, 1970, Yitro 2, p. 209; Tanhuma, ed. Buber, Nitzavim 5; Leviticus Rabbah 4:6.
29. Paraphrase of Prov. 4:23.
30. That is, the heart is that sensitive organ which reflects the integrity of the whole body and the harmonious cooperation of all its limbs (cf. *Kuzari* 2:35 ff.). All Israel is as one body, and all its individuals are limbs, and hence the traditional phrase "serving the Lord in the heart" (as in Deut. 11:13) implies that the service of the Lord is contingent upon the feelings of unity and love in Israel. R. Shneur Zalman adds here: "and from the affirmative you may infer the negative." See Sifre Deut. 46.
31. See Ps. 68:3.
32. Yerushalmi Peah 1:1; Midrash Tehillim 112:2. Cf. Arakhin 15b and Maimonides, Hilkhot De'ot 7:3.
33. R. Shneur Zalman apparently means "for good or for evil," but uses a euphemism for the latter based upon the idea that evil can be transformed or sublimated into the good, or something "better."
34. See *Tanya* 16 and *Torah Or* to Yitro, 71a, where R. Shneur Zalman asserts the superiority of thought over speech and action in the realm of the spirit. Cf. Maimonides, *Guide* 3:8.

May the good Lord, *Who blesses His people with peace* (Ps. 29:11), set among you life and peace forever.

6. LOVE AND HUMILITY
Source: R. Zevi Hirsch of Zhidachov, *Sur me-Ra va-Aseh Tov 3, s.v. kodem, 64a*

R. Akiva said, concerning the commandment to love one's neighbor: "This is a great principle in the Torah."[35] R. Isaac Luria (The Ari) said,[36] and I quote him in brief, "Know that all Israel constitutes the mystery of one organism containing the souls of every individual Jew; every Jew is therefore a single limb of this organism, which explains why each Jew is responsible for all others."[37] . . . I similarly heard it said in the name of the Besht that if one notices in another person some defect or impurity, let him imagine that he is looking into a mirror, and the [marred] face he sees is his own, not his friend's.[38] The Besht's thought is identical with that of the Ari: by means of the wise insight into the unity of the Eternal God, one perceives that all souls are aspects of one organism.[39] It is only a mindless fool who, looking into the mirror, thinks that it is someone else who stands in front of him.

Therefore, my beloved brother, know that this is a great principle of the Torah about which all of its details revolve. For the purpose of all knowledge is to know one's own lowliness, that there is no one in the world less worthy than oneself. One is bound to reach such a conclusion if he wisely contemplates the chain of cause and effect stretching back to the Ein-Sof, Who is the Prime Cause of all. This is the purpose of the *kavvanot* of all the mitzvot. This knowledge is the princi-

---

35. Sifra, Kedoshim 4:11; Yerushalmi Nedarim 9:4; Genesis Rabbah 24:1.
36. *Likkutei Torah* to Kedoshim.
37. Shavuot 39a.
38. Hence, the imperfection that I discern in others is really my own.
39. That is, the unity of the Creator is reflected in the essential spiritual unity of all humankind. The theme was especially powerful in the Kabbalah, which generally tended to a monistic view. Maimonides similarly asserts the unity of the world as flowing from the unity of the Creator; see *Guide for the Perplexed* 1:72. An exactly opposite position is that taken by Saadia Gaon, according to some historians of Jewish philosophy, who deduces from the unique unity of God that all else is composite. See my *Faith and Doubt* (New York: Ktav, 1971), chap. 2, esp. p. 66, n. 1; and, more elaborately, in my "The Unity of God and the Unity of the World: Saadia and Maimonides," in *Torah and Wisdom: Studies in Jewish Philosophy, Kabbalah, and Halacha, Essays in Honor of Arthur Hyman*, New York, 1992, pp. 113-120.

ple;[40] and this knowledge is the source and root of love, as indicated [in the verse] *Only you have I known of all the families of the earth* (Amos 3:2).[41]

When man is in a state of perfect knowledge, then the unity of God is perfect.[42] But when there is, God forbid, jealousy and hatred between man and his fellow man, when he does not regard the other with a benevolent eye but considers himself more knowledgeable, wiser, and better than his fellow man, of him is it said in the *Tikkunei Zohar, tikkun* 1, "He who separates himself from his fellow man, it is as if he caused a division in Thee." He is, God forbid, like one who "cuts the plants"[43] of the unity of the blessed Creator.

Even if one loves his fellow man, but considers himself superior to him, even as, for example, the head is superior to the leg, he remains imperfect, for the advantage of the head over the leg is that the head is the dwelling-place of knowledge; but [the head] knows that if the leg is lost it, [the head,] too will feel pain, and its thinking processes will be impaired. How then is it superior? The leg, then, is really on par with the head, since it causes the head to maintain its intellectual

---

40. By "knowledge" he intends humility: the awareness of one's own lowliness when compared with the Ein-Sof, an awareness inculcated by the performance of the mitzvot and reinforced by the mystical meditations or *kavvanot*. The "principle" referred to is the "great principle" of neighborly love asserted by R. Akiva, as cited at the beginning of this passage. R. Zevi Hirsch is now relating, if not identifying, the two: love of fellow man, which, as he mentioned, issues from the organic metaphysical unity of mankind, is in effect when individuals are profoundly aware of their own inadequacy, and hence are deterred from arrogance or malice toward their fellow humans.

41. The word "know" is used by Amos in the sense of "love," i.e., "You only have I loved," etc., hence proving that "knowledge" goes together with the "principle" of love. On the interpretation of "know" as "love" in this verse, see Rashi, ad loc.

42. R. Zevi Hirsch now reads the equation in the other direction. Having asserted that the unity of God leads to the unity of mankind, he now maintains that when men are as one—in a state of love, abetted by the "knowledge" of their own nihility in the face of the Ein-Sof—they contribute to the *yiḥud*, or unity, of God. Hasidism, following the Kabbalah, requires of people to enhance the "unification of God's Name." Conversely, when they are divisive because they do not act lovingly one to another, they incur disunity and fragmentation in God's Name.

43. The Kabbalistic euphemism for impugning the unity of God. The phrase is talmudic in origin, and is a synonym for "heresy." See Hagigah 14b–15a, and R. Hananel and Rashi ad loc.

perfection. How, then, can the head boast of superiority, seeing that they are [both part of] one body?[44]

Know, therefore, my brothers and friends, that the "external forces"[45] are concentrated precisely on this area, creating dissension among friends, among great and small, and among the righteous and those who serve the Lord. All this—while the Gentiles live in peace and serenity. The *sitra aḥara*[46] helps them to live peacefully with each other; in this generation they have achieved a unity that has never before existed.[47] Whereas, among scholars and servants of the Lord, the *sitra aḥara* can boast of sowing dissension.

Anyone whom God has favored with wisdom and understanding must strive [to implant] in every Jewish soul love, brotherhood, peacefulness, and friendship in order to perfect this attribute and to assure the utmost love for one's fellows and for all Israel.

7. ONE SOURCE LEADS TO ONE HUMANITY
Source: R. Levi Yitzhak of Berdichev, Kedushat Levi, *comments on aggadot*

It is known that all commandments of the Torah are divided into two categories. Some are mitzvot for Jews relating to their Father in Heaven. Others are mitzvot [which regulate the behavior] between man and his fellow man, and are included in the general commandment, *Thou shalt love thy neighbor as thyself* (Lev. 19:18), on which R. Akiva commented: "This is a great principle in the Torah."[48]

---

44. Love, in the sense of affection or pity alone, is inadequate. If, as R. Zevi Hirsch asserts, love issues from an awareness of the organic unity of all souls, and from the consciousness of the impotence of each solitary individual, then true love must be an expression of equality, in the sense that all pride and superciliousness must be banished.

45. The satanic powers.

46. A euphemism for Satan or demonic forces. R. Zevi Hirsch attributes the peace among non-Jews to Satan because it reveals by contrast the disunity that prevails among Jews, who worship the One God.

47. A bit of hyperbole which reflects the very human tendency to imagine that the grass grows greener on the other side. On the tendency to extol the ethics of Gentiles as a means to reprove Jews, see M. Saperstein, "Jews and Christians: Some Positive Images," *Harvard Theological Review* 79 (1986): 236–246. In any event, R. Zevi Hirsch, who died in 1831, lived through the Napoleonic wars, hardly an example of Gentile love and peace. Or could this passage have been written in the period just after 1815, when the Congress of Vienna ended the war and the Holy Alliance was signed in Europe? Or might he reflect the dissemination of the ideals of the French Revolution?

48. Sifra, Kedoshim 4:11; Yerushalmi Nedarim 9:4, Genesis Rabba 24:1.

However, it should be explained that the duties of man to his fellow man are included in the principle of the unity of God; this is so because the first two of the Ten Commandments, *I am the Lord thy God* and *Thou shalt have no other gods* (Exod. 20:2–3), were heard [directly] from the mouth of the Almighty[49] and these encompass the whole Torah.[50]

Let me explain to you now how these [duties of man to his fellow man] are included in the principle of the unity of the Creator. The whole community of Israel believes that we were created by one God. Also, all Jews together are called *Kenesset Yisrael* ("Congregation of Israel"), which is another name for the Shekhinah.[51] Since we all come from the same quarry, it follows that the pain of one person be felt by the other, just as one feels pain in his whole body when one limb hurts him. Similarly, when one Jew is happy, his fellow Jews should rejoice too, for, as said, we were created by one God, and all our souls come from the same source. This includes all the mitzvot between man and man. Hence, all these commandments between man and man are contained in the principle of the unity of the Creator.

This may be implied in the demand made by the proselyte to Hillel: "Convert me on condition that you teach me the whole Torah while standing on one leg,"[52] namely, that the explanation and reason of all mitzvot, including the social-ethical precepts, be based on the single principle of God's unity. Then I will be ready to convert and worship the one and only God. When I understand this, I will know that all laws, including those that guide society, are without reason, and yet even ordinary civil laws must be followed knowing that One God cre-

---

49. Makkot 24a.
50. See Maimonides, Hilkhot Yesodei ha-Torah 1:6 and *Guide* 2:33; also *Ḥinnukh* 26. These sources, however, do not indicate any connection between the comprehensive importance of these two commandments with the fact that they were heard by all directly from God. R. Levi Yitzhak seems to suggest that these commandments were deliberately singled out to be addressed to all the Children of Israel directly, instead of through the intermediacy of Moses, because the principle of the unity of God they proclaim provides the foundation for all the 613 commandments.
51. In the Kabbalah, *Kenesset Yisrael* is used to designate both the divine representation of the collectivity of Israel and the Divine Presence (Shekhinah), which is identical with Malkhut ("Kingdom"), the lowest of the ten sefirot. Hence the immediately implied correlation between the oneness of God and the feeling of unity within Israel.
52. Shabbat 31a.

ated us.[53] Hillel told him: "What is hateful to you, do not do unto others; this is the whole Torah, and the rest is commentary."[54] That is to say, the reason for the commandments between man and his fellow man—"what is hateful to thee," etc.—is that One God created us, and we all derive from one Source.[55] Hence the commandments between man and his fellow man, wherein we share both the pain and the joy of our fellow Jews, have as their reason the Oneness of the Creator.

Thus, the social laws of the Gentiles, though they do not understand their true nature,[56] and even the laws of states and civil laws [must be followed] in order to serve the One God and to understand that He is One and unique.

Therefore must all nations merge into one people, and we shall see realized the verses *that God will turn the people to the people of God* (Zeph. 3:9) and *that many nations shall say to the house of Jacob: Come, ye, and let us go in the light of God* (Zeph. 3:9 and Isa. 2:3–5).[57]

8. LOVE AND HATE
Source: R. Shneur Zalman of Liady, Tanya, Likkutei Amarim, chap. 32[58]

The suggestion mentioned above—viewing one's body with scorn and contempt, and finding happiness only in the joy of the soul—is a direct and easy way to fulfill *Thou shalt love thy neighbor as thyself* (Lev. 19:18) toward every Jew both great and small.

---

53. This passage in the Hebrew text is quite obscure. The passage may be read as I have translated it—that the reasoning behind individual commandments of the Torah's social-ethical legislation is irrelevant, because all that counts is that it issues from the One Creator—or that the proselyte is here contrasting the Torah's legislation to secular law: the latter is senseless, and only the former is valuable because it is based upon divine unity. Either way, the main point is that ultimately both the social and ritual laws of the Torah are based upon the Oneness of God from whence they issue.

54. Shabbat 31a.

55. Apparently, R. Levi Yitzhak's interpretation is that the first part of Hillel's response—"what is hateful," etc.—which implies the social-ethical commandments, is based upon "the whole Torah," i.e., is of one piece with the entire Torah, including the ritual laws.

56. The reference is to Ps. 147:20, as interpreted in Hagigah 13a.

57. This universalistic conclusion follows logically from the premises of the homily. The last part of the text conflates phrases from Zeph. 3:9 and Isa. 2:3–5.

58. Thirty-two, the number of this chapter, is the numerical equivalent of the Hebrew word *lev* ("heart") and is regarded by Hasidim of the Habad school as appropriate to the content of this chapter, which speaks of love even, paradoxically, when it comes together with hatred.

Since his body is despicable and repugnant to him, and the greatness of his soul and spirit are of inestimable excellence, inasmuch as their root and source are in the living God, all Jews are called real brothers because they are all of a kind and have one Father, by virtue of the root of their souls in the one God; only in their bodies are they separated. Hence there can be no true love and brotherhood among those who assign primary value to their bodies while regarding their souls as of secondary importance; [the love of the latter cannot last,] since it is dependent upon a [transitory] thing.[59]

This is what Hillel the Elder meant when he said in regard to this commandment: "This is the whole of the Torah; the rest is but commentary."[60] For the basic foundation of the entire Torah is to elevate and exalt the soul high above the body, reaching into the Source and Root of all the worlds, and also to draw down the blessed light of the Ein-Sof upon the Congregation of Israel, namely, into the fountainhead of the souls of all Israel, to become "one with One."[61] This is impossible if there is, God forbid, disunity among the souls, for the Holy One does not dwell in an imperfect place,[62] as we pray: "Bless us, our Father, all of us together, with the light of Thy countenance"[63]....

As for the talmudic statement that if one sees his neighbor sinning it is a mitzvah to hate him and also to tell his teacher to hate him,[64] this applies only to one who is his comrade in [studying] Torah and [the observance of] mitzvot—after having fulfilled the commandment, *Thou shalt repeatedly rebuke thy friend (amitekha)* (Lev. 19:17), referring to him who is "with you in Torah and mitzvot,"[65] and who

---

59. See Avot 5:16. Physical existence is ephemeral; hence if that is what brings people together, their relationship must be transient.
60. Shabbat 31a.
61. See Zohar II, 135a. "Congregation of Israel" is the collectivity of the Jewish people. It is also the kabbalistic name for the Shekhinah, the Divine Presence, identified as Malkhut ("Kingdom"), the lowest of the ten sefirot. Hence, at this point the unity of God meets the unity among Jews, enhanced by love and kindness.
62. Zohar, Genesis 216b.
63. The nineteenth and final blessing of the Amidah prayer.
64. Pesahim 113b.
65. R. Shneur Zalman applies here a talmudic word-play used elsewhere on the term *amitekha* to read *im she'itekha*, "one who is with you" or "like you" in Torah and mitzvah observance. See, e.g., Bava Metzia 48a, in regard to the injunction against cheating (see Rashi, s.v. *nakhri*) and Shavuot 30a concerning the commandment "You shalt judge your friend *(amitekha)* with righteousness" (Lev. 19:15). The Talmud does not

nevertheless has not repented of his sin, as stated in [R. Eliezer Azkari's] *Sefer Haredim*.[66]

But as for one who is not a comrade and is not on intimate terms with him, Hillel said: "Be of the disciples of Aaron, loving peace and pursuing peace, loving people [lit., creatures] and drawing them near to the Torah."[67] This means that even those who are removed from God's Torah and from His service, and are therefore classified simply as "creatures" (*beriyot*), one must attract them with strong cords of love, so that one might succeed in drawing them close to Torah and the service of the Lord. If one fails, he has still not forfeited the merit of the commandment of neighborly love.[68]

Moreover, even with regard to those who are close to him and who did not repent of their sins after he has rebuked them, such that he is enjoined to hate them, there still remains the duty also to love them. Both [approaches] are right: [they deserve] hatred because of the evil in them, and love for the aspect of hidden good in them, which is the divine spark in them that animates their divine soul. He should also arouse compassion in his heart for the divine soul [of his wayward friend], for it is held captive in the evil clutches of the *sitra ahara*[69] that triumphs over it in wicked people. For compassion destroys hatred and awakens love.

Love of Man and Love of God

9. CARING FOR OTHERS AND CARING FOR GOD
Source: R. Elimelekh of Lizhensk, Noam Elimelekh to Ki Tissa, 52b

There are people who ignore the commandment *Thou shalt love thy neighbor as thyself* (Lev. 19:18) and pay no attention to their friends' pain and troubles. They are only concerned with their own welfare. There are other people who share their fellow man's pain and troubles

---

record a similar interpretation of the commandment to rebuke, as does R. Shneur Zalman. However, see the Malbim's commentary (ad loc.) for a similar analysis, and cf. Malbim to Lev. 5:21, for a more detailed analysis of the talmudic usage of the term.
66. Chap. 4, sec. 29. Cf. the *Be'er Yehudah* commentary to *Sefer Haredim* (Jerusalem, 1966), pp. 60–61, for further analysis of the implications of this view. On the halakhic aspects of this theme, see my *Halakhot ve-Halikhot*, pp. 168–175.
67. Avot 1:12.
68. See Additional Note *3.
69. Euphemism for Satan and the forces of evil.

because they are soft-hearted and compassionate. This [latter] quality is a good one, but it is not true and fundamental.[70]

The true way [of loving others] is to feel distressed when Jews are in trouble because the holy Shekhinah is in pain since, [as it is written], *In all their affliction He feels afflicted* (Isa. 63:9).[71] One's purpose should be to draw down divine grace to channel abundance upon Israel in order to elevate the Shekhinah.[72]

10. LOVE OF GOD AND LOVE OF ISRAEL
Source: R. Yitzhak Yehudah Yehiel of Komarno, Ozar ha-Hayyim to Kedoshim, 170b.

It is a positive commandment to love every Jew as one loves oneself. Our rabbis said: "What is hateful to you, do not do unto others,"[73] as it is written: *Thou shalt love thy neighbor [reiakha] as thyself; I am the Lord* (Lev. 19:18).[74] Said R. Akiva: "This is a great principle in the Torah."[75] This mitzvah is indeed a general principle encompassing the whole Torah from beginning to end, for one who loves God loves Jews, has compassion for them, shares in their anguish, and does nothing to hurt or frighten another.[76]

Surely one must love the Jewish people as a whole, feel pain for their misfortune and for the exile of Israel and the Shekhinah,[77] and

---

70. Since it is subjective and sentimental, it does not attain its full and true stature as a Jewish spiritual precept.

71. See Ta'anit 16a, where this verse is the basis for the custom of placing ashes atop the ark on a fast-day.

72. The concept of praying for the alleviation of the pain of the Shekhinah, by ascribing one's own distress to the Shekhinah, was well known in Lurianic and hasidic circles (see chapter 6, selection 11). The author here applies it to the social realm as well, and offers it as the underpinning of human relationships. My feelings of commiseration should be directed not at my neighbor; such emotions are welcome, but they are unstable, and have no roots in a more comprehensive world-view. Rather, I must appreciate that the Creator, in His aspect of Shekhinah, sympathizes with suffering man and takes upon Himself man's tribulations and anguish. Hence, my motivation to alleviate the pain of my neighbor is my desire to restore the Shekhinah to health, as it were, and liberate it from its exile in suffering.

73. Shabbat 31a (Hillel's reply to the proselyte); see excerpts from *Kedushat Levi* and others in this chapter.

74. See Additional Note *4.

75. Sifre, Kedoshim 4:11. For other sources, see n. 48 above. Cf. *Hinnukh*, loc. cit.

76. See Additional Note *5.

77. Megillah 29a: "R. Shimon bar Yohai says: Come and see how beloved Israel is of God, for wherever they went into exile, the Shekhinah went along with them."

pray for [divine] mercy for them, both the people of Israel and every individual Israelite. He will not seek honor at the expense of another's degradation by comparing his own deeds with the deeds of the other so that he appears worthy and the other unworthy, for one who seeks honor by degrading another loses his share in the world-to-come.[78] Rather, one should love his fellow man as the pupil of his eye, love peace and pursue peace, love people and bring them near to Torah, and rejoice in the happiness of others. . . .

For God is the heart of Israel.[79] The holy Shekhinah adorns itself with the [good] deeds of Israel and repairs their souls. . . .

Reiakha (in Leviticus 19:18, usually translated as "thy neighbor" but here understood as "thy friend,") refers to God.[80] The expression "*to* thy friend" is meant to include all who join and cleave to "thy Friend," implying that one should love those who love God and serve Him, namely, the whole of Israel as well as individual Israelites who cling to Him.[81] But when it comes to the wicked who is far from God, one must hate the wickedness utterly.[82]

This commandment, therefore, includes the love of God and the love of Israel, His sanctified people. For indeed, one who loves God truly must also love Israel as the pupil of his eyes and is grieved by their troubles.

11. THREE LOVES
Source: R. Zadok ha-Kohen of Lublin, Zidkat ha-Zaddik, no. 196

There are three loves: the love of Torah, the love of the Holy One, and the love of Israel. They are all one, as we know from the Zohar;[83] one

---

78. Yerushalmi Hagigah 2:1, Genesis Rabbah 1:5.

79. Song of Songs Rabbah 5:2.

80. According to Rashi on Shabbat 31a, s.v. *d'alakh*, God is referred to as "thy friend" in Prov. 27:10, "thy friend and the friend of thy father (*reiakha ve'reia avikha*) do not forsake."

81. The Hebrew in Lev. 19:18 has a rather strange construction. In place of the expected *et* (*ve-ahavta et reiakha*), we find the preposition *le-reiakha*, which normally means "to thy friend." (This was already noted by Nahmanides, ad loc.) Our author interprets this homiletically to include the retinue of "thy friend."

82. The author recommends that one hate wickedness (*ha-ra*) rather than the wicked (*ha-rasha*). This is reminiscent of the explicit distinction by R. Shneur Zalman in *Tanya*, chap. 32, translated earlier in this chapter (see selection 8), and Beruriah's statement in Berakhot 10a.

83. That is, God, Torah, and Israel constitute a unity. See Additional Note *6.

without the others is inadequate. The love of God is the source of all. For love of Israel alone, without love of God, [might be construed as simply] the love of fellowship and companionship. This was the nature of the generation that built the Tower of Babel (Gen. 11:1–9); they too loved companionship.[84] (I have heard that it is because of this that Boaz legislated the practice of greeting one's fellow man with the Name of the Lord.[85] Boaz liked fellowship very much and feared that his love was for fellow humans only, without loving God. Therefore his opening remarks in company and his greetings were always in the name of God in order to demonstrate that he desired human companionship only so that he might thereby enhance the glory of heaven.)[86]

The love of Torah without love of God is but love of wisdom. This was [characteristic of] the generation of the Flood [in the days of Noah] (Gen. 6—8), about whom it is written in the Zohar that they were worthy of receiving the Torah because they loved learning so much.[87] (This is the reason that the *sons of God*, i.e., angels, came to the *daughters of men* [Gen. 6:2], for it is known that the female symbolizes desire and the male fulfillment. The angels possess wisdom and perception, but they do not have the Evil Urge and lust, as stated in the *Midrash ha-Ne'elam*.[88] Desire for the words of Torah too requires having an Evil Urge. Man has desire but lacks perception. Then the two are united[89]—but this is not the proper place to discuss this.) But without love of God, the love of wisdom leads to immorality.[90]

The Children of Israel, descendants of *Abraham who loved Me* (Isa. 41:8), have implanted in them from their very conception and birth the love of God. This love of God is the source of the other loves and corresponds to the sefirah of Keter ("Crown"), which is beyond man's perception. Hokhmah ("Wisdom") and Binah ("Understanding") rep-

---

84. Nahmanides on Gen. 11:2, citing Radak to 11:4.

85. Thus Boaz's greeting to the reapers, "The Lord be with you," and their response, "The Lord bless thee" (Ruth 2:4). See Berakhot 54a.

86. This passage appears in parentheses in the source. This holds as well for the other two parenthetical remarks in this excerpt. They were added by R. Zadok in later years.

87. Zohar III, 216.

88. Zohar I, 138a. The statement is also found in Genesis Rabbah 48:11.

89. That is, the marriage of the angels with the "daughters of men" symbolizes the combination of desire for knowledge with the knowledge itself. The latter without the former is inadequate for the true comprehension of Torah.

90. That is, the intellectual quest, without a religious foundation, leads to immorality. The generation of the Flood was guilty of immoral acts.

resent the love of Torah and the love of Israel, for Binah is associated with the heart, and the heart is the locus of the love of human beings, as it is written, *As in water face answereth to face, so the heart of man to man* (Prov. 27:19).[91] (Every sefirah is a complete structure. The above are the first three within the sefirah of Hesed ["Love"]; the lower seven ones represent the expansion of their potencies.)[92]

Now these [i.e., the loves that correspond to the three highest sefirot] are the powers of *nefesh, ruah,* and *neshamah*.[93] The connection between one Israelite and another is the aspect of *nefesh*. One's connection to Torah is the aspect of *ruah*. And the connection to God is the aspect of *neshamah,* which comes from under the Divine Throne.

It is for this reason that [the Sages ordained that in our daily prayers] we say: "My God, the *neshamah* which Thou hast placed within me is pure." For no corruption prevails [in the region of the Divine Throne, focus of the *neshamah*], because it is a part of God,[94] and the love of God is never shaken. There did the Sages say that God says, "Would that they forsook Me but observed My Torah."[95] For He cannot, as it were, be forsaken by the Children of Israel, as in the verse *Surely with a mighty hand and with an outstretched arm and with fury*

---

91. The author here structures the three loves according to the three highest sefirot. The love of God is equivalent to Keter, the transcendent source of all the other sefirot. The love of Torah is identified, obviously, with Hokhmah (Wisdom). Binah ("Understanding") is declared by the author as the sefirotic equivalent of love of man (or Israel) because in the kabbalistic structure of the sefirot as a macro-anthropos, Binah is identified with the heart, and the heart is the seat of emotions, hence love of fellow man. On his proof-text from Proverbs, see Rashi *ad loc.,* and see Tosafot Pesahim 113b, s.v. *she-ra'ah.*

92. This parenthetic remark qualifies the previous assertion. Every one of the ten sefirot is a "complete structure," hence it is itself composed of ten sefirot. The three highest sefirot, which represent the three loves, are all within the sefirah of Hesed ("Love"), and the lower seven sefirot within Hesed are the spelling out of the implications of the three loves symbolized by the first three sefirot.

93. In Kabbalah and Hasidism, the "soul" comprises several parts or layers. The three most basic of the five elements are, in ascending order, *nefesh,* the quality of biological vitality; *ruah,* the power of speech and intellect; and *neshamah,* the most spiritual and partly transcendent aspect of the soul that links man, ultimately, to God. See chap. 2 above.

94. As the most transcendent of the three souls, or levels of the soul, *neshamah* partakes of divine immutability, hence it is always pure. For the same reason the love of God, which our author identifies as equivalent to or emanating from *neshamah,* is unimpeachable.

95. *Petihta* to Lamentations Rabbah, beginning.

poured out will I be king over you (Ezek. 20:33).[96] Even if one increases his sins in order to provoke [God], he does not sever the root of the love of God, which corresponds to the sefirah of Keter, which is the concealed source of thought. "Even though one sins, he remains a Jew."[97]

12. THE OTHER MAN'S FAULTS
Source: R. Yaakov Yosef of Polennoye, Toledot Yaakov Yosef, end,[98] sec. 13

I heard from the venerable rabbinic scholar, R. Nahman, an interpretation of the words of [the Besht] that one should intend in every word that he utters submissiveness, separateness, and sweetness.[99] [The interpretation is that] one should leave the quality of Strength (Gevurah), in that he should not find fault with people but treat them with compassion and discover good in everyone.[100] Even when he notices something ugly in his friend, he should feel that it is for his good so that he might detect in himself some aspect of [that ugly

---

96. Hence, "Would that they forsook Me" is not to be taken literally but rhetorically, since it is impossible for the bond between God and Israel to be severed.

97. Sanhedrin 44a.

98. This passage appears at the end of the *Toledot Yaakov Yosef* in an appendix of teachings and interpretations that R. Jacob Joseph of Polennoye heard from "my teacher," the Besht. It is also quoted, with some minor variations, in the Lubavitch version of *Keter Shem Tov* (Brooklyn: Kehot, 1972), pt. II, no. 302, 39a-b.

99. The text here is obscure. The *Toledot Yaakov Yosef* version contains a puzzling abbreviation at this point which apparently eluded the editor of the Kehot edition. The editor of *Sefer Baal Shem Tov* (Spero Foundation, 1948), I, p. 83, n. 99, however, maintains that this indicates that several lines of the original text are missing, and that this lacuna contained R. Nahman's interpretation of the first two items in the Besht's dictum, "submissiveness" and "separateness." The extant text resumes after the beginning of the exegesis of "sweetness." The editor (generally assumed to be Shimon Mendel Vadnick from Govartchov, also called Shimon Mendel Govartchov, but more probably R. Nathan Nata Donner; see Yitzhak Alfasi's note in *Kiryat Sefer* 49, no. 4 [Elul 5734]: 659) speculates that the flow of ideas is as follows: in every word one utters, one must intend "sweetness," referring to the kabbalistic-hasidic notion of *hamtakat ha-dinim* ("the sweetening of Judgment"), or the neutralization of the harsh judgments that issue from the fifth of the ten sefirot, Gevurah ("Strength").

100. Donner (*Sefer Baal Shem Tov*, p. 84, n. 100) here cites a statement by R. Aryeh Leib, the Preacher of Polennoye and one of the Besht's earliest disciples, that the Messiah will be the most excellent and effective *melamed zekhut* (i.e., one who defends or discovers the good in others) of Israel, including the wicked. "A small *zaddik* ('righteous person')," he said, "loves small evildoers. A great *zaddik* loves [even] great evildoers. But Messiah will love and discover the good even in the completely wicked. Hence, those who discover the good in all [God's] creatures are in the category of Messiah."

quality], even if only in this thoughts, and thus he will repent of it.[101] This is all for his own benefit, for were he alone (without this friend whose ugly qualities displease him) he might think that he is pious; now he knows differently.[102]

I believe that this is the meaning of *It is not good that the man should be alone, I will make a help-mate [ezer] for him [ke-negdo]* (Gen. 2:18).[103] [The verse should be understood as follows:] "It is not good that man be alone"—for this reason, that "I will make a help" for him from his "opposite" (*ke-negdo*), by detecting that he too possesses some of that quality that displeases him in the others.

13. AS MAN LOVES, SO DOES GOD
Source: R. Yitzhak Yehudah Yehiel of Komarno, Ozar ha-Hayyim to Kedoshim, 172.

Thou shalt love thy neighbor as thyself, I am the Lord (Lev. 19:18). [The verse may be interpreted as follows:] If you will behave toward your fellow man with love and harmony, then *as thyself I am the Lord*, I your Lord will be like you.[104] This accords with the inner meaning of the verse *The Lord is thy shade* (Ps. 121:5), as interpreted by the Besht.[105] If

---

101. A similar thought may be found in the glosses of R. Jacob Emden to Sotah 3a: a jealous husband who suspects his wife of adultery may be projecting, in some measure, his own shortcomings.

102. That is, by internalizing and projecting upon himself the criticism of his fellow man, he grows in character. He must, therefore, be grateful to the friend whose character or deed he finds repugnant.

103. The Hebrew term *ke-negdo* may mean either "at his side," i.e., "fit to associate with him," or "as over against man" (see the Soncino Pentateuch, ed. Hertz). The rabbis saw *ke-negdo* as a contradiction of *ezer*. Thus, according to talmudic interpretation, *ke-negdo* indicates that on occasion she may turn out to be, instead of a helpmate (*ezer*), an opponent—"against him." See Rashi on Gen. 2:18. R. Yaakov Yosef's homiletic interpretation has the verse referring, not to one's wife but to any fellow human being. If he finds himself "opposed" to some displeasing characteristic or trait in his friend, he will use it to "help" himself in the sense of ferreting out of himself some trace of that same unattractive quality. Thus his friend's defect is for the good of his own character growth, and it is better than being "alone" and not encountering this friend who bears the imperfection. This interpretation accords with the Besht's dictum that one should view his fellow man as a mirror. See above, selection 6.

104. By dividing the verse differently from its plain sense, moving *ka-mokha* forward, thus, "Thou shalt love thy neighbor; as thyself I am the Lord," the author derives the idea that God loves man in the same measure as man loves his neighbor.

105. The plain meaning of the verse is that the Lord protects man, as his shade from the burning sun. The Beshtian interpretation is that the Lord is like a shadow: whatever man does, He does; i.e., God acts to man as man acts to his fellow man. The iden-

a man conducts himself toward his comrades and fellow men with love and good character, so will his "shade," i.e., so will God conduct Himself with him. This, then, [is the meaning of the verse:] *Thou shalt love thy neighbor; as thyself I am the Lord*, dealing with you in love and goodness.

14. WHOLENESS
Source: R. Yaakov Yosef of Polennoye, Toledot Yaakov Yosef to Ki Tissa, sec. 3

The reason for the mitzvah to give half a shekel[106] is offered by R. Solomon Alkabez,[107] cited by the Alsheikh,[108] as follows:

It was intended to teach the children of Israel the importance of unity, that no one should ever think that he ought to be separate from his fellow man. Rather, he should view himself as being merely half [a person], and only after joining all other Jews does he become complete. Therefore, everyone gives half [a shekel]. . . .

The commentaries wrote, [concerning] Haman's statement [to King Ahasuerus] that *there is a certain people scattered and dispersed among the peoples* (Esther 3:8),[109] that the Jews are a people divided and therefore easily conquered. Therefore did Esther cry out [through Mordecai], *God, gather together all the Jews* (Esther 4:16), meaning: [in order to repair the divisiveness] gather them together, in unity.

That is why the Torah commanded [that everyone] give half a shekel each year as *ransom for the soul* (Exod. 30:12). For this sin [of divisiveness] was not yet corrected, not until Elijah [the prophet] will come, who *shall turn the heart of the fathers to the children, and the heart of the children to their fathers* (Mal. 3:24). The [second] Temple was

---

tical interpretation is offered by the great mitnagdic leader, R. Hayyim of Volozhin, and, prior to both of them, is quoted on behalf of anonymous sources by R. Ephraim Shelomoh of Lunshitz (d. 1619). See my *Torah Lishmah* (Heb. ed. only), p. 47, n. 68.

106. Exod. 30:11–16. Proclamations reminding the populace to prepare the half-shekel offering were made on the first day of the month of Adar, and collections were made on the fifteenth of that month. Purim occurs on the fourteenth of Adar (and, for walled cities such as Jerusalem, on the fifteenth).

107. In his commentary *Manot ha-Levi* on the Book of Esther. Alkabez, one of the great Safed kabbalists of the sixteenth century, is the author of the famous hymn *Lekha Dodi*.

108. R. Moshe Alsheikh, in his commentary *ad loc.*

109. *Meforad*, usually translated as "dispersed," more accurately means "divided" or "separated."

destroyed in punishment for baseless hatred,[110] until God will send Elijah the prophet to repair this [sin].[111]

Hence the need to inspire the people on the first day of the month of Adar, before the reading of Esther, [by giving half a shekel each,] to inspire and arouse themselves to correct this sin, just as Esther sought to repair it when she sensed that the time was appropriate for it.[112]

15. DIVISIVENESS CAUSES ESTRANGEMENT FROM GOD
Source: R. Nahman of Bratslav, Likkutei Etzot, Shalom, no. 4

The world can be attracted to the service of God, to worship Him in unity, in accordance with the peace that prevails in a generation. When people are at peace with each other they talk with each other, and they ponder with each other: what is the purpose of this world and all its vanities? Thus they come to explain to each other the truth, that in the end nothing remains of man except what he prepared for himself for the world of eternity, for life after death. For man is accompanied at his death neither by silver nor by gold [nor by precious stones, but only by Torah and good deeds].[113] Thereby will every man cast away the false idols of his money,[114] and bestir himself to turn to God, His Torah, and His service, and to the embracing of the truth.

But if there is no peace, or worse, if there is controversy, God forbid, people do not get together and do not talk about the purpose [of life]; and even when they occasionally do so, the words do not penetrate into the heart because of the constant striving and quarrels and hatred and jealousy. For quarrelsomeness and the desire to triumph do not tolerate the truth. . . .

---

110. Yoma 9b.

111. Elijah, in Jewish tradition, is the harbinger of the Messiah, who will rebuild the Temple.

112. R. Yaakov Yosef thus relates the commandment of the half-shekel with the festival of Purim, on which the Scroll of Esther is read. Each warns against divisiveness and teaches unity and harmony. Similarly, Alkabetz, in his *Manot ha-Levi*, explains the mitzvah on Purim to "send gifts to one another": "its purpose is to emphasize love and caring for each other on the day when our enemies sought to destroy us for the lack of unity among ourselves." Cf. *Bayit Hadash* to *Tur*, Orah Hayyim 695, and Hatam Sofer to *Shulhan Arukh*, Orah Hayyim 685.

113. Avot. 6:9.

114. Paraphrasing Isa. 2:20.

The conclusion is, that the estrangement of most people from God comes from divisiveness.

16. NO TIME FOR QUARRELS
Source: R. Nahman of Bratslav, Likkutei Etzot, Maḥloket u-Merivah, no. 36

The whole world is full of quarrels: among the nations, in every city, in every home, among neighbors, between a man and his wife, and his family and his servants and his children, and so on. No one pays attention to the [bitter] end, that every day man dies. For the day that has passed will never return, and each day he draws closer to death. How does he find time to waste on quarrels?

Therefore, anyone of even minimum intelligence should take this to heart and learn patience and not waste his days in quarrels, large or small. One should restrain his emotions and his anger and live in peace with everyone.

17. THE NEGATIVE FORMULATION OF THE COMMANDMENT TO LOVE
Source: R. Menahem Mendel of Lubavitch, Derekh Mitzvotekha, 29a

The statement of Hillel, "What is hateful to you, do not do to your neighbor"[115] requires explanation. Why did Hillel formulate [the commandment "Love thy neighbor as thyself"] negatively, instead of the positive way it appears in Scripture (Lev. 19:18)—and as Onkelos translates it?

The answer is that Hillel's words are a deeper explanation of the mitzvah to love one's neighbor. The principle that a person does not see his own faults does not mean that he is totally unaware of his faults. On the contrary, a person can see and understand the depths of his inferiority better than anyone else, for another person can view him only with his eyes (i.e., from without) whereas he sees into his own heart. What it means, rather, is that his failing does not occupy his attention to any great extent, and it is as if it did not exist at all, because of the great love with which he loves himself. "Love covers all transgressions" (Prov. 10:12). This self-love covers all the faults of which he is aware, thus not permitting his knowledge to exercise him emotionally. That is why his knowledge of his own faults does not

---

115. Shabbat 31a.

occupy a place of prominence in his mind—he is insensitive to his own faults because they are overwhelmed and suppressed by his great (self-) love, which "covers all transgressions" and encloses him.

When another person sees and understands his fault, this angers him greatly, even though he knows that it is true . . . because the friend acknowledges this weakness as substantial and worthy of note, whereas what he himself recognizes in himself is covered up by his (self-)love. His ire is directed at his friend for exposing his fault, ignoring the love which covered it up thus making it virtually invisible, and now it appears real and significant.

That is what is meant by "what is hateful to you"—this exposure which is hateful to you, do not do to your friend. Do not "see" his faults and transgressions, whether social in nature or between man and God, and thus turn them into hard realities. Instead, let your love [for him] be so great that it "covers all transgressions" and does not permit them to emerge from [abstract] knowledge to attention-getting reality. He must be as one who is possessed of great and wondrous longing for his friend, which issues from the very depths of his soul, such that any evil he may have done to him despite the love he bore him means nothing to him and is nullified in the presence of the great love that he has for him.

ADDITIONAL NOTES

*1   Abarbanel, ed. Jerusalem, in the opening remarks to his commentary on Genesis, presents some proof from talmudic statements that angels too are called *shammayim*, for they are constituted of the two opposites, fire and water. See *Otzar ha-Tefillot* I, 189, for a similar interpretation of the verse "He who makes peace in His heavens," which concludes both the Amidah and the Kaddish. R. Nahman's point is that peace is not the absence but the overcoming of conflict and opposition, and is thus a dynamic rather than a passive concept, patterned after the divine imposition of peace in God's multifaceted empyrean realm.

*2   For a view according to which peace on high requires not coexistence but a change in the nature of one of the opposites, see R. Jonathan Eyebeschutz, *Ya'arot Devash*, translated by Marc Saperstein in *Jewish Preaching, 1200–1800*, (New Haven: Yale University Press, 1989), p. 340.

*3   This view is stated repeatedly in various parts of this chapter. While it is characteristic of the world-view of Hasidism, it is not unique to hasidic teachers. Thus, R. Meir ha-Levi Abulafia (Spain, 12th cent.) asserts that the commandment of neighborly love includes the wicked, even one who has committed a capital crime. Proof for this view is the Talmud's teaching that this commandment includes the injunction to choose "a dignified death" for the capital offender (Sanhedrin 52b). Similarly, R. Samuel Edeles (Maharsha; Poland, 1555—1631) maintains that *Thou shall not hate thy brother in thy heart* (Lev. 19:17) applies to transgressors as well; see my article on

"Loving and Hating Jews . . . " referred to above, n. 35. Hence, while this open attitude toward the evildoer has precedents in Jewish thought and literature—the above two references are but a sampling—it was Hasidism that highlighted this attitude of tolerance and compassion as part of the whole movement, especially in its earliest phases.

*4   The Talmud (Shabbat, loc. cit.) does not explicitly associate Hillel's statement with the commandment in Leviticus, but the commentators and some medieval halakhists (Rishonim) did. See, inter alia, *Ḥinnukh* 243; see also *Ha-Torah ve-ha-Mitzvah* (Malbim) to Lev. 19:18.

*5   The relationship between the two loves is presaged in Mishnah Avot 6:1, which teaches that one who studies Torah for its own sake "loves God, loves people."

*6   Actually, as Y. Tishby has pointed out in *Kiryat Sefer* 50:30 (Sivan 5735 = 1975): 480–492, there is no such passage in the Zohar. The nearest the Zohar comes to such an idea is in III, 73a, where the three elements are declared similar because they all share in the dual character of possessing both revealed and concealed aspects. This is not quite the same as asserting a mystical identity of God-Torah-Israel. The apocryphal Zohar passage is quoted first in hasidic circles by the Besht's grandson, R. Mosheh Ḥayyim Ephraim, and in mitnaggedic circles by R. Ḥayyim of Volozhin. Tishby has traced the source of the statement to R. Moses Ḥayyim Luzzatto. The imprecise ascription by our author does not, however, affect the logic of his discourse.

14

Pride and Humility

Hasidic authors display a keen awareness of the paradoxes and pitfalls of self-deception engendered by the tension between pride and humility. Thus the individual who strives mightily to attain humility may discover that the exhibition of humble behavior and attitudes of meekness coincides with the vice of pride in one's very accomplishment of humility. By the same token, a stress on humility can often lead to acquiescence in spiritual mediocrity.

In connection with this danger, one special socio-historical factor must be mentioned. In the eighteenth-century period during which Hasidism emerged, East European Jewry was in social, psychological, and spiritual disarray. As mentioned above in the introduction to chapter 12, the Sabbatean and Frankist heresies, the oppression of the Jews, the unrelieved poverty, and the distance between the scholarly elite and other sectors of the Jewish community cast a pall of depression over all Jewry. In addition to the usual moral concern with pride, it was important to emphasize the reverse—not allowing the sense of worthlessness to undermine one's spiritual gestalt, thereby leading to further alienation from the sources of spiritual vitality. Hence, the occasional reminder that a modicum of self-esteem was necessary for the proper service of God (see selections 10, 11).

Otherwise, Hasidism cultivates the same virtues as conventional Jewish teaching, halakhic or aggadic. However, here, as elsewhere, one

441

can nonetheless detect a special intellectual, spiritual, and historical emphasis.

In halakhic and ethical literature, the prohibition of arrogance or pride (*ga'avah*) and the corresponding virtue of humility (*anavah*) take two forms. In the context of man's relation to God, pride occurs when man bestows credit upon himself for his own attainments and status.[1] As an interpersonal quality, humility enjoins respect for one's fellow human being.

Both of these dimensions are stressed in the hasidic writings represented in this chapter. The selections from *Zava'at ha-Rivash* display the idea of nothingness that is so prominent in the works of the Maggid of Mezerich. Humility, from this point of view, is part of the spiritual quest whose goal is the annihilation of the self before God.[2]

At the same time, the interpersonal aspect of humility is not neglected. We find specific moral counsel—to refrain from responding to those who denigrate one's religious practices (selection 4), in addition to the development of respect for others as a moral principle (selection 7). Another insight is that of R. Nahman, who emphasizes the humility that is appropriate in comparing one's achievement to one's potential, or ego-ideal (selection 12).

1. EQUANIMITY
Source: Besht, Zava'at ha-Rivash, ed. Kehot, p. 2 a–b, nos. 2, 10

It is written: *I have set the Lord always before me* (Ps. 16:8). *Shiviti* ("I have set") is related to the word *hishtavut* ("sameness").[3] Whatever happens to a man, it should all be the same to him—whether people praise him or insult him; and so for all other matters. Thus, with regard to food, it should make no difference whether one eats delicacies or other things, since the Evil Urge has been removed from him completely. No matter what happens, one should say: This comes from God; if He deems it proper to do so [then that is sufficient for

---

1. Semag, for example, subsumes the prohibition of *ga'avah* under the rubric of idolatry.

2. See R. Shatz-Uffenheimer, *Hasidism As Mysticism: Quietistic Elements in Eighteenth Century Hasidic Thought*, Princeton University Press, 1993, pp. 72-73.

3. Both derive from the root *sh-v-h*. The noun form of the reflexive is *hishtavut*, and the reflexive verb generally means "to become equal" or "to become alike." The Beshtian use of *hishtavut* (which is explained in the sentences immediately following in the text) is truly reflexive, i.e., "it is all the same to me that X says such-and-such about me." Homiletically, the Besht places the comma immediately after the first word, *shiviti*. Thus—it is all the same to me, because the Lord is always before me.

me]. Man's intentions should be solely for the sake of heaven. As far as he himself is concerned, however, there should be no difference to him.[4] This is a very high degree [to attain] . . .

The great principle of *hishtavut* is that everything should be the same to you, whether people think you are an ignoramus or whether they think you know the entire Torah. What causes this [feeling] is the constant *devekut* with the Creator.[5] Because of your occupation with *devekut*, you have no time to think about such personal matters, for you are constantly busy in attaching yourself to God above. In anything which man does, he should think of the pleasure he is causing for the Creator, and not that he is doing it in any way to fill his own needs. Even if it happens that he attains pleasure from his divine service, it should not be for his own need.[6]

2. SHARED CREATURELINESS
Source: Besht, Zava'at ha-Rivash, no. 12

One should never think that he is greater than his neighbor because he serves God with greater *devekut*,[7] for man is like all other creatures that were created for the purpose of serving God. God has given his neighbor a mind just as He has given one to him. And in what way is he more important than a worm? A worm also serves God with its entire "mind" and power. Man too is but an insect, a worm, as it is written: "And I am a worm and not a man" (Ps. 22:7). Had God not given man a mind, he would have been able to serve Him just as the worm [serves Him], and therefore a man is not even more significant

---

4. That is, in dealing with others, one must do what is right, helpful, and satisfying to the other, one's intention thus being "for the sake of heaven." With regard to one's own self, however, one should cultivate this studied indifference.
5. This Beshtian indifference is thus far different from stoicism. The latter is rationalistic, fatalistic, and materialistic, while *hishtavut* is profoundly theistic and spiritual. The source of *hishtavut* is *devekut*; paradoxically, the rhapsodic experience of communion (see chap. 5) yields a character that is stoic in its outward manifestations: calm, serene, indifferent to compliments and slights alike. This is so, as we read in the next sentence, because one's "thoughts" are so actively engaged in the contemplation and experience of the Divine Presence that one has no time to concern himself with himself. Humility is thus a by-product of *devekut*.
6. As long as the sense of gratification ("pleasure") is not the goal of his divine service, its experience is acceptable. We may detect here an attempt to avoid the kind of asceticism which invalidated even the sense of spiritual pleasure in the religious enterprise.
7. See Additional Note *1.

in God's eyes than a worm, certainly not more significant than other human beings. One ought to think that he, the worm, and other small creatures are considered as fellows in the world, for they are all creatures and have no power other than what the Creator has granted them.[8] This ought to be constantly on man's mind.

3. MAN AS NONEXISTING
Source: Besht, Zava'at ha-Rivash, p. 6b, no. 53

One ought to consider himself as if he were not [in existence], as the Talmud (Sotah 21b) states on the verse *but wisdom will come from nothing* (Job 28:12).[9] The intention here is that one ought to think as if he does not exist in this world. Of what use is it, therefore, that he be deemed important in the sight of other people?[10]

4. AVOIDING RELIGIOUS STRIFE
Source: Besht, Zava'at ha-Rivash, no. 49

Another great principle: When a man is vilified by people because of his divine service in prayer or other matters, he should not respond to them, even with kind words.[11] Thus he will avoid controversy and boastfulness, which cause one to forget the Creator.[12] Our Rabbis said: "Silence leads to humility."[13]

5. SELF-NEGATION
Source: R. Pinhas of Koretz, Midrash Pinḥas, p. 27b, no. 38

Great miracles can be performed for a man who truly considers himself as nothing (*ayin*). For our Father Abraham, when he went to do battle with kings (Gen. 14), did not rely upon miracles. Rather, he went with sword and buckler, for he was on the level of *ayin*, and the

---

8. See Additional Note *2.
9. Literally, "but wisdom, *where* shall it be found?" *Me'ayin* means both "where" and "from nothing."
10. For further discussion of the hasidic concept of *ayin* ("nonexistence"), see below, selections 5 and 11.
11. This passage obviously reflects the indignities visited upon the nascent hasidic movement, especially the abuse heaped upon hasidim for the startling innovations in their manner of prayer.
12. The Besht is aware of the tendency of participants in religious polemics to substitute their egos for their ideals, and thus counsels silence as the best response.
13. See *Reshit Ḥokhmah*, Gate of Humility, chap. 3.

Holy One performed miracles for him and took rocks[14] which He cast upon them, and so he conquered them.[15] Therefore it is stated of Nahum Ish Gam-zu that he took of the dust of Father Abraham (Ta'anit 21a), i.e., the quality of *ayin* which is symbolized by dust, for dust represents the most inferior level [of humility].[16] Therefore was that miracle performed for him.

A man who is on the level of *ayin* is worthy of having the Shekhinah rest upon him. For of the Holy One we know that *the whole world is full of His glory* (Isa. 6:3); therefore, when man is as naught, God can dwell within him. But when man considers himself to be "something," God is not within him.[17]

6. SIGNS OF HUMILITY
Source: R. Pinhas of Koretz, Midrash Pinhas, p. 105, no. 26

The Torah cherishes humility. Therefore, in ancient times people studied on the ground.[18] And therefore, too, we eat dairy foods on Shavuot,[19] for this is a sign of smallness (*katnut*).[20]

---

14. Hardened soil; see Ta'anit 21a.
15. The reasoning is: Had Abraham relied upon miracles, that would have implied that he thought himself worthy, and thus no miracles would have occurred. However, Abraham considered himself as naught and thus resorted to natural means of warfare, and precisely for this reason was he aided by miraculous divine intercession.
16. The Talmud (Sotah 17a) praises Abraham for his humility in declaring, in his plea to God to spare Sodom, "for I am dust and ashes" (Gen. 18:37). Dust is thus the symbol of Abraham's self-effacement or, for R. Pinhas, ego-annihilation, the negation of self.
17. R. Pinhas of Koretz (whose sayings are recorded in this work by a student writing mostly in Hebrew but partly in Yiddish) here uses an almost crude spatial metaphor: When a man is humble to the point of denying or negating his self, then God's immanence dwells in him. However, if he considers himself "something" (*epes* in Yiddish), i.e., a being of worth and value, then he blocks, as it were, the divine immanence from entering him. It should be pointed out that similar disquisitions on the ethical import of the *ayin* concept may be found, albeit with a more mystical orientation, in the works of R. Dov Ber, the Maggid of Mezeritch, with whom R. Pinhas often disagreed. See, e.g., *Maggid Devarav le-Yaakov*, no. 120, et passim.
18. In talmudic days it was customary for students to sit on the earth rather than on benches or chairs (see Avot de-R. Natan, chap. 6, and Megillah 21a). Hence the relationship of Torah to humility. (See the preceding selection, where dust is used as a symbol of worthlessness.)
19. The festival commemorating the giving of the Torah, where custom dictates that we eat a dairy meal (Rema's gloss to Orah Hayyim 494:3). See also A. I. Sperling, *Ta'amei ha-Minhagim*, pp. 281–282 (secs. 621–625).
20. Dairy is lighter than, and hence inferior to, meat, and thus characterized as *katnut*, the state of "smallness" (on this term, see above, chapter 12). Here again Torah is related to humility.

7. HUMILITY BEFORE GOD AND MAN
Source: R. Yaakov Yosef of Polennoye, Toledot Yaakov Yosef to Koraḥ, no. 2, s.v. ve-nir'ah

"Be very, very low of spirit before every man."[21] The meaning of "before every man" is: God is called *Adam Elyon* ("Supernal Man").[22] He includes within Himself all the categories of man and the righteous ones who raise their eyes to Him. God stands in the presence of every man. Every person, therefore, in standing "before every man," stands before the Holy One, who is the Supernal Man, and must therefore be "very, very lowly in spirit."[23]

8. SPURIOUS HUMILITY
Source: R. Yaakov Yosef of Polennoye, Ben Porat Yosef to Vayeira, p. 35d

I have written elsewhere that Maimonides contradicts himself. First he writes that one should take the middle way even in the matter of pride.[24] Later he writes: "Be very, very lowly of spirit."[25] I explained this by a parable that I heard: A certain king asked the physicians what he should do in order to live forever. The physicians gave him this medicine: that he should keep far away from pride and adopt the

---

21. R. Yaakov Yosef here conflates two texts, "Be very, very lowly of spirit" (Avot 4:4) and "Be lowly of spirit before all men" (Avot 4:11). The first mishnah emphasizes the need to go to extremes in attaining humility ("very, very"; see Maimonides, *Mishneh Torah*, Hil. De'ot 2:3). The second adds "before *kol adam* [every man]," and it is this upon which R. Yaakov Yosef focuses in this passage.

22. The Kabbalah often uses the simile of the human body to symbolize the structure and interrelationships of the sefirot. This mystical anthropos is referred to as Supernal or Primordial Man (*Adam Elyon* or *Di-le'ela* and *Adam Kadmon*; see Gershom Scholem, *Major Trends*, p. 215). This symbolism allows R. Yaakov Yosef to interpret "before every man *(adam)*" in the passage from Avot as referring to the *Adam Elyon*, Supernal Man, or God.

23. The equation of "man" = [supernal] Man, i.e., God, thus leads to a profoundly spiritual explanation of the need for humility: When you stand in the presence of another human being, you stand before God, Who indwells in him, or, more accurately, before a creature so significant that he symbolizes his Creator's divine life, and hence you must be humble and meek in his presence.

24. Hilkhot De'ot 1:4.

25. Ibid. 2:3. Thus, with regard to humility one must abandon the path of moderation and go to the extreme.

quality of humility and lowliness. If the king knew he was humble, then he would feel that he was the epitome of pride.[26]

What is implied here is that there are two categories of humility. The first is true humility. The second is a spurious humility, which is the essence of pride, as explained in the above parable of the king. The difference between these two types of humility is as follows: It is known that the holy rabbi R. Yosef Ya'avetz wrote: "The source of all sins is pride, as explained in the Talmud, 'He who is haughty is as if he denied the existence of God, as it is written, *And your heart will be lifted up* [i.e., grow haughty], *and you will forget the Lord your God* (Deut. 8:14). Conversely, lowliness and humility are the root of the entire Torah'" (Sotah 4b). If one knows that he lacks humility and lowliness, and that he wallows in the trappings of pride, the root of all sins, then he knows that he must repent in order to repair the sin. However, if he considers himself humble and the paradigm of perfection, why should he repent? And if one despairs of repentance, then he is ripe for punishment.

9. THE NEED FOR PRIDE IN THE MORAL LIFE
Source: R. Yaakov Yosef of Polennoye, Ketonet Passim, Tzav, p. 5a

I heard a parable about a prince or king who prepared a feast for his servants who were getting ready to do their work for him, whether plowing or reaping in the fields. Both old and young came to the party. Said the adults: "What are these children doing here?" They were answered: "They too are considered men." Later, when it came to work and the young ones did not do the king's work, the older servants asked: "Why do they not perform the king's service?" They were answered: "They are but children." Whereupon they wondered: "What is going on? When it comes to eating and drinking, they are considered adults, yet when it comes to work, they are children."

Now the words of a wise man's mouth are gracious! (Eccl. 10:12). "Are you so important and honored that you can attain holiness and piety, something that is merited by only one or two persons in a genera-

---

26. The parable is not quite clear, but appears to mean this: The physicians prescribed humility. But when the king sought to possess this humility it eluded him, for when he knows he is humble he loses that humility by becoming proud of it. Hence, he must go to the extreme, that of "lowliness of the spirit," in which state he is not even aware of his own humility. Thus Maimonides, as a matter of principle, requires humility, the mean. But since this quality is paradoxically self-defeating, he prescribes the extreme of lowliness as a way of ensuring that true humility, not the spurious kind, will prevail.

tion?" Thus man neglects to climb the ladder of perfection in Torah and mitzvot, in saintliness and proper conduct, until ultimately he despairs of any [spiritual] achievement. Such humility causes him to leave the ranks of Torah. . . .

But in truth, this is not so, for as it is written: *Speak unto all the congregation of Israel and say unto them: You shall be holy* (Lev. 19:2)—*all* the congregation are capable of becoming holy and saintly. . . .

One ought to be a "man" and not a "child,"[27] the opposite of lowliness and smallness, and exploit pride, which is [otherwise] the source of the Evil Urge in all sins, so that he may go to the opposite of lowliness and smallness [in spiritual matters]. So it is written, *Know this day . . . that the Lord is God in heaven above and upon the earth beneath* (Deut. 4:39). With regard to wealth and honor, which is "earthly," one should be lowly and humble, "beneath" other people. But when it comes to spiritual matters, that which is "heavenly," one should be proud and "above" others. . . . This is the opposite of the Evil Urge, which seduces man, telling him, concerning wealth and honor, "Who is more worthy of it than you?" and concerning divine service, that it is the business [only] of very pious and holy people.[28]

10. HUMILITY, PRIDE, AND THE EVIL URGE
Source: R. Yaakov Yosef of Polennoye, Toledot Yaakov Yosef to Hukat sec. 1, s.v. u-vazeh yuvan

. . . Israel should adopt Moses' attribute, humility (Num. 12:3), and Aaron's attributes, glory and pride (Exod. 28:2), and use [both sets of] these attributes.[29] These are great principles and good laws for the entire [life of] Torah to assist one against the Evil Urge. If the Evil Urge

---

27. Referring to the parable of the adult and minor servants of the king.
28. R. Yaakov Yosef often stresses the dialectic of pride and humility in religious life. The next selection illustrates the same theme. There may be two reasons for this emphasis. The first is a psychological insight: man's ego cannot be squelched or wished away; it must be directed, not banished. The second may arise out of sociological need. The political, economic, and religious conditions of European Jewry in the mid-eighteenth century made Jews feel "lowly" enough and hardly justified categorical preaching against arrogance. Hence, while the aversion to haughtiness as a universal component of morality necessitated preaching against pride, R. Yaakov Yosef found it important to encourage self-awareness and confidence lest excessive humility destroy the will to continue the spiritual life of Judaism—or, in his own words, "to climb the ladder of perfection in Torah."
29. See previous note.

debases man [by convincing him] that he is unfit to become holy, then he should hold up against it the attribute of pride, namely, pride that [he has a] soul that makes him worthy of becoming holy. But if the Evil Urge glorifies man and tells him that he is already holy and pure, then man should denigrate himself based on the lowliness of his corporeality.

11. HUMILITY IN TORAH STUDY
Source: R. Moshe Hayyim Ephraim of Sudlikov, Degel Maḥaneh Ephraim to Vayikra, p. 149a–b

The Torah is compared to water,[30] and water is the symbol of Hesed.[31] Just as water trickles from a high place down to a low place, so the holy Torah will only be found in one who considers himself lowly.[32] It cannot exist in one who is proud and "high" in his own eyes, for then the Torah seems to be farther and higher than he is, for it is known of Torah that *its measure . . . is longer than the earth and broader than the sea* (Job 11:9). Only one who diminishes himself can perceive and see the truth of the Torah, for then the Torah contracts and compresses itself for him so that he can understand the depth of its secrets. . . .

I heard the following in the name of R. Yaakov Yosef of Polennoye: "The world says that the scholars (i.e., mitnaggedim) study but the hasidim do not."[33] The truth is that the scholars, the more they learn, the more they become great in their own eyes, and so it seems to them that they have learned so much that it is enough. The hasidim, however, the more they learn, the more they become insignificant in their own eyes. Their entire purpose is to teach themselves to be small and lowly in their own estimation.

---

30. Sifra, Ekev 12; M. Tanhuma, Vayakhel 8 and Tavo 3
31. In kabbalistic imagery, water is one of the symbols of the fourth sefirah, Hesed, or love.
32. *Derekh Eretz Zuta* 8. Cf. Sotah 21b. For a different utilization of this idea, see *Tanya,* chap. 4.
33. Lit. "the scholars study—yes; the hasidim study—no" (the text uses the Yiddish words for "yes" and "no"). R. Moshe Hayyim Ephraim proceeds to interpret this popular maxim quite literally, with special emphasis on "yes" and "no": The mitnaggedim study Torah, and as a result of their pride in their intellectual attainments, they think they are "yes," i.e., significant and "somebodies," whereas the hasidim study and derive from their studies the awareness that they are "no," i.e., unworthy, nonexistent. See the excerpts from *Midrash Pinḥas* on humility as the awareness of oneself as *ayin* (nonexistent) earlier in this chapter (selections 5 and 6).

12. HUMILITY IN RELATION TO ONESELF
Source: R. Nahman of Bratslav, Likkutei Etzot, Ga'avah ve-Anavah, no. 12

One merits Torah solely through humility. One must break down his pride through four categories of humility. He must make himself small in the presence of his superiors; in the presence of his equals; in the presence of his inferiors; and sometimes, when he is himself the smallest of the small, he must make himself small in relation to his own intrinsic levels: he must imagine that he is below his own level.[34]

13. ATTRACTIVENESS
Source: R. Nahman of Bratslav, Likkutei Etzot, Ga'avah va-Anavah, 165b, no. 17

The more man makes himself small, the greater his power to attract [and the greater his power] to draw the divine Shekhinah to the lower worlds, so that He might dwell among us—which has been His will since the day He created the world: to attract people closer to divine service and to bring down the effluences of goodness and blessing upon Israel. Thereby, too, he merits to be attracted and drawn near to the true zaddik.

14. HUMILITY AND LIFE
Source: R. Nahman of Bratslav, Likkutei Etzot, Ga'avah va-Anavah, 166a, no. 30

The meekness and humility of our Teacher Moses is implanted in every Jew, indeed in his every limb.[35] But this humility and meekness are concealed and are in the category of "death." Therefore, one does not feel this humility within himself, and remains distant from humility and lowliness. However, by drawing close to the true zaddik and seeing him, and certainly when one is privileged to hear Torah from his mouth, one attains a sense of shame and repentance. He thereby deserves that this humility and lowliness should be "alive"

---

34. An engaging idea: humility in relation to oneself, the sobering awareness that one has failed even to live up to his own petty standards.
35. The capacity for genuine humility is innate in man and not imposed upon his nature from without.

within him.[36] He then merits true humility, which is in the category of the eternal life of the world-to-come.[37]

15. MAN'S SELF-CONFIDENCE
Source: R. Nahman of Bratslav, Emet va-Zeddek, Emunah, no. 150

The vessels of divine grace[38] are, in the main, completed by means of words of prayer. This takes place through perfect faith, which is the essence of the capacity to receive goodness. Just as one must have perfect faith in God—that He is the Creator of all, that He governs and rules over and watches over all, and can change nature at His will, and can endow the world with goodness—so must one have faith in oneself, believing in perfect faith that God hears and listens and pays attention to every word of every Jew, even the worst of the worst. For He "hears the prayer of every mouth."[39] It is within the power of every Jew to make his petition efficacious in mercy before Him, if he prays to Him sincerely, as it is written, *The Lord is nigh unto all them that call upon Him, to all that call upon Him in truth* (Ps. 145:18). When man lacks the faith that he has the power to elicit the divine grace by means of his prayer, then he indeed lacks the vessel to receive the grace; his heart does not have within it the place or vessel to receive the grace. This is so because, according to his own thinking, he lacks the capacity to receive and elicit the the divine grace, since he does not believe in himself and does not believe that his prayer is efficacious. Therefore the essential formation by prayer of the vessel with which to elicit the the divine grace and to make one's petition efficacious is by means of the perfection of faith in all its aspects, whereby he believes that God is omnipotent, that He rules and governs and leads according to His will, and also that He is gracious and merciful, and hears the prayer of every mouth.

This is the meaning of what the Sages said: "A man should always offer his praise of God first, and only afterwards ask for what he

---

36. This potential humility is "death," i.e., man himself is unconscious of his moral potencies. It takes the "true zaddik" (see above, chapter 8, selections 6 and 31 for a discussion of what R. Nahman means by this term) to transform the potential ("death") to a "living" psychic reality.

37. "Life" is now taken to be more than a convenient metaphor for the realization of character potential; the attainment of true humility is the culmination of eternal life itself.

38. Man's capacity to receive the divine grace (*shefa*).

39. From the Amidah in the daily service.

needs."[40] By offering our praise of God, our faith is strengthened to perfection in all its aspects, as mentioned above; and thereby, too, our faith is strengthened within ourselves that He will have mercy upon us and hear our prayers and endow us with all that is good, even as He heard the prayers of our ancestors.

That is why we conclude [the middle section of the Amidah, which concerns the] asking for the fulfillment of our needs, with the blessing [of God as] "He Who hears our prayers," for that is the main thing: To believe in perfect faith that God hears the prayer of every mouth, and that the vessel to receive the divine grace is thereby perfected.

ADDITIONAL NOTES

*1   Because of the hasidic emphasis on *devekut* as the principal expression of religious activity in Judaism, rivaling the primacy heretofore accorded to the intellectual exercise of studying Torah, the Besht found it necessary to warn his followers against allowing the practice of *devekut* to lead them into a feeling of superiority over others. Interestingly, R. Yitzhak of Volozhin, the leader of the mitnaggedic world following the death of R. Hayyim of Volozhin, found it necessary to caution his students against the superciliousness that comes from the intellectual mastery of Torah (*Nefesh ha-Hayyim*, preface, pp. 6–7, and throughout the *Ruah ha-Hayyim*); see my *Torah Lishmah*, pp. 118–120. Each was motivated by the same moral force, but applied it in a different environment.

*2   This Beshtian teaching of the equality that issues from shared creatureliness is a somewhat more radical restatement of the talmudic passage (Berakhot 17a) which reports a "gem in the mouths of the scholars of Yavneh," that "I am a creature, and my friend [the peasant or nonscholar] is a creature. I work in the city, and he works in the country. I rise early to do my work, and he rises early to do his work. Just as he does not attempt to encroach on my occupation, so I do not attempt to encroach upon his.... As we were taught, '[it makes no difference whether one has achieved much or little], as long as he directs his heart toward Heaven.'"

---

40. Berakhot 31a, slightly modified. The Amidah begins with three blessings of praise, and these are followed by the middle section of thirteen blessings of petitionary prayer ("asking for our needs").

15

Evil and Suffering

The need to understand evil and suffering stands at the center of every religious outlook, the focus of theological thinking and ethical values.

Mostly, the problem is formulated as a conflict between God's omnipotence and His goodness. On the one hand, there is the presence of evil; on the other, if God is good and does not tolerate evil, why doesn't He do something about it? If He is unable to do so, He cannot be omnipotent; if He is ready to accommodate evil even though He could abolish it, He is no longer the absolutely Good. Denying either God's goodness or His omnipotence is not acceptable in a monotheistic religious system, and hence the need for theodicy, i.e., the effort to "justify" God in the presence of evil in the world.

The problem for Hasidism is formulated in a somewhat different fashion. The presumed conflict is not between God's omnipotence and His absolute goodness, but between His immanence and His goodness. This slight variation is not only the result of the hasidic preoccupation with immanence (as pointed out in the introduction to chapter 1) but, even more, its unconscious preparation, as it were, for a response that is existentially viable and morally and psychologically constructive, rather than one which is intellectually satisfying.

Classical Kabbalah's outlook was dualistic. Evil was considered to have an independent existence; it was real and present. The kabbalists saw life as a struggle between the constructive, creative forces of good and the destructive, malicious forces of evil. Hasidism, however, quite naturally tended to a monistic conception, in which the reality of evil was denied as an autonomous ontological entity. In other words, there exists only the good, and provision had to be made for the presence of pain, suffering, and malice by asserting the negative character of evil, either as illusory or as a necessary means for a higher good. Once the centrality of immanence is granted, as just mentioned, such a conclusion becomes almost inevitable.

The illusory nature of evil is a direct consequence of the all-pervasive presence of God. The Besht (quoted in *Toledot Yaakov Yosef* to Ḥayyei Sarah) taught, "When one notices some aspect of ugliness in another's conduct, he should know that there too does God dwell, for there is no place that is empty of Him." If God is present in everything, it is impossible for evil to be a reality.

Joseph G. Weiss shows how the dualism of the Kabbalah, especially the Lurianic Kabbalah, was maintained in form only, while hasidic thinkers, especially the Maggid and R. Shneur Zalman, reinterpreted the content in a monistic fashion.[1] For them, the *kelipot*, which for the kabbalists were the essence of real evil, were metaphors for a subjective experience unrelated to an objective reality.

This negation of evil was developed by the Besht's student, the Maggid of Mezeritch, who put the stamp of his sophistication on the standard hasidic conception of evil. In his view, evil is not merely the metaphysical antonym or antagonist of the holy. As Yoram Jacobson points out, Hasidism did not conceive of evil as an autonomous demonic being challenging Divinity, but as the end product of Divinity distorted, misused, abused.[2] This distortion is caused by man, who, as part of his illusory superiority, claims autonomous existence for himself in the face of the Ein-Sof. In the words of the Maggid, man fails to reflect the *ayin* ("Nothing") of the Ein-Sof and substitutes for it his *yesh* ("something," substance, the opposite of Nothing). The divine creation of the world is classically described in Judaism as *yesh* out of *ayin* (something out of nothing), i.e., *creatio ex nihilo*. For Hasidism, this meant creation by the Ein-Sof. Man's function, according to the Maggid, is to restore the *ayin*—to reverse the process, not by physical destruction, of course, but by spiritual efforts which

1. J.G. Weiss, *Meḥqarim be-Ḥasidut Bratslav*, pp. 87–95.
2. Y. Jacobson, *Toratah shel ha-Ḥasidut*, chap. 12.

include meditation but, above all, the annihilation (lit. the making into *nihil*, or nothingness) of man's bloated ego. It is when man resists this spiritual task, and insists upon seeing himself as a *yesh*, a "somebody," that evil is introduced into the world.

Evil is thus not an independent substance or being; it is real only insofar as it is a part of the human psyche. Hasidism is monistic in its conception of evil and, in the developing tradition of the Besht and the Maggid and his students, refuses to adopt a dualistic notion of evil and good as two separate forces arraigned against each other, the conception that dominated the thinking of the Kabbalah. Metaphysically it is monistic, for it denies separate reality to evil; but existentially and psychologically it is dualistic, seeing man as torn by the conflict between his evil and good urges or, to use the Habad terminology, his divine and animal souls. As long as man considers himself a *yesh*, evil will be real for him. In the "real" world, as viewed by the Ein-Sof, evil is not real at all. Man is challenged to sublimate the darker forces of his personality, to exploit the powers of the animal soul—which, as we shall see, exceed those of the divine soul because of its more supernal origin—and use them to attain a level of sanctity undreamed of, to return his soul to a spiritual locus that far transcends its original source. Thus evil is more a challenge than an obstacle.

A correction must here be made to the thesis of Joseph G. Weiss. In the article cited above, Weiss maintains that the monistic view is restricted to the Maggid and Habad (the hasidic school founded by R. Shneur Zalman), but was not accepted by R. Nahman, who reverted to the dualistic approach of the Kabbalah. I find this assertion unacceptable, and offer selection 4 in this chapter as proof. Here, R. Nahman clearly espouses a monistic view of evil and good. He holds that evil is fundamentally an illusion, and that in eschatological times its nonreality will be fully revealed. Clearly, R. Nahman stands in the mainstream hasidic tradition on the question of evil.

This does not mean that the monistic approach was uncontested, only that Weiss's structuring of a mystical-hasidic monistic view as against R. Nahman's nonmystical dualism is highly questionable. In subsequent generations of Hasidism, however, one does begin to notice a return to a dualistic conception. We have included two selections (nos. 6 and 7) to demonstrate two such exceptions to the earlier consensus advocating the nonreality of evil and the monistic view of good and evil.

In addition to the fundamental question of the reality or nonreality of evil, several other themes deserve attention. One offers a psycho-

spiritual "solution" to the existential problem. Since the problem arises, as stated, because of a conflict between God's immanence and His
benevolence, the Besht proposes that the very awareness of His inherence in pain and suffering itself alleviates such anguish; the contemplation that everything, even suffering, comes from Him, makes the
suffering bearable. The reader's attention is drawn to selection 9, and
to the reference to the "dudelle" of R. Levi Yitzhak of Berditchev, a
song (or ditty) which reflects the Besht's approach.

Another theme that runs through the hasidic treatment of suffering comes to it from the Lurianic Kabbalah, and, in turn, had talmudic and even biblical roots, namely, reciprocal sympathy between God
and man. Man suffers, but he must not lower himself to such self-con-
cern that he begs God to cure his ills. Instead, he must realize that God
suffers along with him; the Shekhinah takes upon Herself the pain of
suffering man. But in that case, we must extend full sympathy for the
Shekhinah in its suffering. This is far more than a "technique," a kind
of spiritual trickery. What it implies is that man must move off the
dead center of self-interest and be concerned with others—beginning
with the Other—and only then will he experience psychic and spiritual succor. (One is reminded of Maimonides' view of evil in his *Guide
of the Perplexed*; the formulation is totally different, but in essence the
approaches are compatible.)

Another way that Hasidism expressed its view of evil as illusory is
in its doctrine that evil serves as a lower level of the good. Evil is
indeed illusory, but what is the nature of the illusion, and what is its
underlying reality? The answer Hasidism proposes is that the good
comes in many forms, some more self-evident and "revealed," while
others are deeply embedded within experience, even suffering. It is the
lower form of the good that we commonly refer to as evil. An interesting formulation of this approach, cast in the classical hasidic mold
of greatness and smallness, will be found in selection 21.

There is yet another subtheme which, in the course of time, came
to characterize the Beshtian attitude toward evil and suffering, and
that is the idea of evil as a *kissei* (a "chair," in the sense of a vehicle or
stepping-stone, i.e., a means to a higher end) for the good. This is a
theme found throughout the writings of the Besht's students: evil is
the *kissei* for the good, for it inspires the zaddik to greater efforts in
his service of the Lord, and in extracting the sparks of holiness from
the evil and transforming the destructive qualities of the soul to constructive ones, such as fleshly love to love of God, and so on.

Having said this, it is best now to study the hasidic conception of evil against the backdrop of the hasidic view of the dialectical nature of human existence. Man, in Hasidism, partakes of a "psycho-cosmic" drama: his soul is hewn from the holiest quarry, part of the divine Existence itself; in its source, the soul is perfect, unblemished, and at peace. But it was hurled downwards to a mundane existence, assuming the form of flesh and blood, in order to rise again and ultimately return to its divine Source and its primordial roots.

The question then is: for what purpose? Why is this trip necessary?

The answer of Hasidism[3] was: to reveal the Ein-Sof, for all else was brought into being only in order to vanish, revealing the eternal Ein-Sof as the only reality. Hasidism used several expressions to describe man's cosmic experience in his dialectical destiny: "descent for the purpose of ascent," "first darkness, then light," "light in need of darkness," "revelation in need of concealment," and so on.

Habad went a step further. For R. Shneur Zalman of Liady, the descent was not only for the purpose of an ascent to the same empyrean level, but more: an ascent to a yet higher rung in the realms of holiness. The adventure of the soul thus culminates not in restoration, but in advance. And the reason for this leap into the highest regions is: the soul's encounter with evil.

In the material world to which the soul was exiled, the spark comes into contact with its *kelipah*, the divine soul with the animal soul. Man himself is the scene of this struggle of the titans, and it is he who must determine who shall emerge victorious. His goal must be not merely to suppress the evil within him but, like Jacob wrestling with the angel, to bend the strength and power of the adversary for his own holy purposes. The first but easier goal is *itkafia*, the suppression of evil; the ultimate desideratum is *it'hapkha*, the conversion or transformation of darkness to light, of the bitter to the sweet, of evil to good, of impure to pure. *Itkafia* operates on the assumption that evil is a reality to be conquered, even if theoretically one knows that it is, ultimately, a mere illusion. *It'hapkha* is based on the existential as well as the intellectual awareness that evil is an illusion, an illusion brimming with vast undirected and chaotic powers that need to be harnessed, oriented, and sublimated. This act of sublimation—and the Freudian term is particularly apt, for Hasidism anticipated by about a century some of the most trenchant discoveries that we tend to associate with

---

3. This is based on Jacobson's excellent summation.

depth psychology—allows the recoil of the soul to surpass its original level in the higher spiritual realms and to leap over it to new and higher reaches. And all this thanks to the power of evil.

This schema entails a remarkable insight: that somehow evil has a higher spiritual origin than the good, for it has the potential to catapult man's soul to a destination far more exalted than what would be available to him without the presence of evil. This is part of a universal principle which might be best summed up colloquially as "the higher they are, the harder they fall." Spiritually, the more elevated a thing's origin, the more destructive its potential in the mundane stage of existence; and conversely, the more destructive an idea or element in this world, the more supernal its origin in the spiritual realms. Or, to put it psychologically, lust is more powerful and effective than conscience, and therefore must be treated with more respect. R. Shneur Zalman points to the talmudic principle that one who repents, a *ba'al teshuvah*, is greater than a saint.[4] The encounter with evil leaves the penitent sinner with the power of the evil that he harnessed in his return to the ways of holiness, and his reach is therefore greater than that of the saint, who has never known sin. Moreover, R. Shneur Zalman maintains, *teshuvah* in its original sense means "one who returns," i.e., the soul which seeks to return to its heavenly source regardless of whether or not it sinned.

In order to prevent a possible misreading of these words, I have included a number of excerpts to show that the hasidic view of evil and suffering is not totally "new," based as it largely is on a transvaluation of earlier kabbalistic thinking, but represents as well a normal development of standard talmudic views and insights into the subject. Selections 10 to 15 largely deal with traditional material, especially the concept of *yissurin shel ahavah* ("affliction out of love"), and similar notions.

No discussion of the hasidic attitude to pain, suffering, and evil, no matter how brief, can be complete without at least passing reference to that watershed in Jewish history which exposed more evil in the world and the hearts of men than anyone had ever thought possible. The Holocaust was a revelation of evil, an apocalypse from which Jews are still tottering and which will continue to plague our consciences, destabilize our thinking, and jeopardize both faith and skepticism for decades and centuries to come. If there is one group that suffered more casualties than any other in that kingdom of the night,

---

4. Berakhot 34b.

as Elie Wiesel has termed it, it is the hasidic community with its hundreds of thousands of members and its varied and colorful "courts."

Have the various hasidic approaches to evil and suffering been vitiated by the unparalleled destruction of the Holocaust? Apparently, the Holocaust delivered a fateful blow to all negative interpretations of evil. The faith to see in it a means to a higher good is probably more than human.

Nevertheless, it is instructive to learn how one zaddik, who served his hasidim in the Warsaw Ghetto during the darkest of the dark days, from 1940 to 1943, and who himself was martyred in Poland in 1943, taught hasidic doctrine and dealt with the problems of evil in his public discourses in the ghetto before its destruction following the uprising.[5] The zaddik was the Piaseczner Rebbe, Rabbi Kalonymos Kalmish Shapiro, a descendant of R. Kalonymos Kalman Epstein, author of the *Ma'or va-Shemesh*, who had thousands of hasidim in Poland. The talks on the weekly Torah portions that he gave in the Warsaw Ghetto have been collected in *Esh Kodesh*. The themes he discussed in these talks sound like a catalogue of the hasidic thinking on evil in the first generations of the movement as adumbrated above. Following are just four themes which the reader will recognize, albeit in somewhat modified form:

1. Whatever emanates from God must be just.
2. Suffering is a form of *ḥesed nistar* ("hidden love"), and by means of prayer and study it can be transformed into *ḥesed nigleh* ("open love").
3. Suffering leads to an appreciation of nonsuffering.
4. Suffering should be accepted joyously, for the Shekhinah suffers with the Jew in his calamity, and it is incumbent upon the Jew to pray and repent so that the Shekhinah will be relieved of its pain.

Clearly, it was not only in the movement's remarkable regrowth in the postwar world, but even in the depths of unparalleled suffering, that Hasidism revealed its capacity to deal with the most troubling of questions for those of its adherents who did not lose their faith.

---

5. Most of this material is drawn from P. Schindler, *Responses of Hassidic Leaders and Hassidim During the Holocaust in Europe*.

Evil: Reality or Illusion?

1. EVIL AS A DISGUISE OF THE GOOD
Source: Besht, as cited in Pitgamin Kaddishin, Jerusalem: Lewin-Epstein, n. d., 3a.

The following is a true explanation of why evil often happens to man, when we know that God is good and bestows good upon all His creations, and that evil does not issue from Him; it is also an explanation of the correct meaning of the scriptural verse, *Out of the mouth of the Most High proceedeth not evil and good* (Lam. 3:38),[6] which seems incomprehensible; and also an explanation of the words of our Rabbis, who said that from God, Who gives and bestows all things, only goodness issues, and it is only because of man, the recipient, that evil comes about,[7] for this too seems incomprehensible.

The explanation in depth is this: God bestows two different categories of good upon man. At times, something patently good happens to a man; its goodness is manifest to everyone. At other times, the good comes concealed; it seems to be bad for him, but after a while it becomes obvious that, on the contrary, it is a great good.

Now, in truth, no evil issues to Israel, heaven forbid, from God, Who is good and bestows good. On the contrary, all His deeds are acts of great kindness, salvation, and solace. If man merits it, then the goodness comes to him revealed. But at times, because of his impure deeds—each person on his own level[8]—man does not merit it, and then, when God's goodness descends from above to man below, accusing angels appear who denounce him and prevent the goodness from reaching him.[9] Then the heavenly judgment is that the goodness, for

---

6. See the excerpt from *Kedushat Levi* in selection 20; and see n. 89. In the present selection, the Besht is not satisfied with the declarative interpretation, for if so the verse should have read, "Out of the mouth . . . not evil"; why add, "and good"? This question is answered at the end of the passage.

7. I have been unable to locate the exact source of this statement. But see R. Jacob of Lissa, *Ta'alumot Ḥokhmah* on Eccl. 7:29. See too Maimonides, *Guide of the Perplexed* 3:12.

8. The criterion of impure deeds is relative to a man's moral and spiritual stature. An untoward act by a great man will be held against him, while the same deed by an ordinary person will be ignored.

9. Spiritual worthiness and unworthiness are personified as defending and accusing angels in the metaphor of a trial before the Heavenly Court. "R. Eliezer b. Jacob said, he who does one good deed has gotten himself one advocate; and he who commits one transgression has gotten himself one accuser" (Avot 4:13). What the Besht is saying is that a man's misdeeds are often so serious that he will see that the good God wishes to bestow upon him as harsh and evil.

the present, will reach him in different permutations,[10] enclothed in evil, heaven forbid.

If man can withstand the test of goodness in concealment by reinforcing himself with perfect and steadfast faith that "all that the Merciful One does is for the good,"[11] and believing with certainty that what has happened to him is really a great good which has not yet been revealed to him as a good, then by virtue of the very faith whereby he believes and trusts in God, the permutations are reversed, and the original permutations of goodness emerge, as they were before his denunciation by the accusing angels; then God's beneficence will be manifest and apparent to all. Moreover, by virtue of this faith and trust, the goodness will increase and be constantly magnified in greater measure. From the evil itself a goodness will be formed even greater than that which God decreed for him at first. But if he fails this test, and does not put his faith and trust in God, then because of his lack of faith in God, the second set of permutations remain as they appeared below in the guise of evil following the accusations. That is the judgment of heaven. Think about it.

Therefore, when something of this sort happens to a man, heaven forbid, i.e., some evil event, let him repent and make confession and trust that no evil issues from God, only goodness and kindness and compassion, and that certainly this untoward event is really good. It is merely waiting upon him, until he strengthens his faith well, and then by virtue of his great faith and trust the judgment is sweetened,[12] transforming the attribute of Judgment into Mercy. He will then merit having the permutations transposed truly for the good, and great and intense goodness, salvation, and solace will then be revealed

---

10. The kabbalistic technique of *tzerufim*, or letter-combinations, often called *Hokhmat ha-tzeruf* ("the science of permutations"), is based upon the mystical powers of the letters of the Hebrew alphabet by which God created and sustains the world. Since each Hebrew letter has a numerical value, a word or series of words can be transformed by arithmetical and structural permutations. The Besht uses this concept to explain how, because of denunciations by the accusing angels, the good that God intends for man sometimes appears as good-in-disguise rather than as a manifest benefaction. The divine decree is unquestionably good, but by permutations of its letters it now seems to be evil; it is essentially good, but is concealed, or in disguise. Man, by the spiritual effort of repentance—or, as we shall see, by faith in the innate goodness of what appears to be other than good—can reverse the permutations and bring about the original and manifest, or revealed, goodness.

11. Berakhot 60b.

12. *Hamtakat ha-din*, the "sweetening" or transformation of divine judgment or harshness into love and compassion. See above, chap. 8, on the zaddik's role in this.

to him, speedily and but a short time thereafter. . . . This is the way of faith: to believe that "all that the Merciful One does is for the good."

There is, however, an alternative path for the man who is *surpassing in rank and exceeding in power* (Gen. 49:3): the way of faith expressed in the adage "This too is for the good"[13]—in other words, to believe in God Who is good and bestows good, so that the evil itself is created by Him for great good; i.e., from the evil will come about a good greater and more powerful than the initial good that existed before the accusations. This was the way of Nahum of Gamzu.[14] When a man believes in this way, he merits that the evil itself becomes a source of goodness for him, and the goodness is increased to greater measure and effect, surpassing by far the original goodness. That is the difference between the path of "all that the Merciful One does is for the good" and the path of "this too is for the good."[15]

That is why, when the incident of the treasure chest befell Nahum of Gamzu—whereby all the money and jewels it contained were stolen and replaced by earth, and he presented this as tribute to the emperor of Rome—his faith and trust in God were so powerful that he cried out, "This too is for the good," and indeed it did turn out to be a great good, even more than if he had given the gold to the king. That is what is meant by the statement that everything depends on the recipient, as mentioned above.

And that is what is meant by "out of the mouth of the Most High," etc.; i.e., since God is good and does good, *there proceedeth not evil and good* (Lam. 3:38); even this category of the good in the guise of evil

---

13. Ta'anit 21a; see next note.
14. Nahum of Gamzu was renowned for his pious acceptance of whatever happened (his motto, "This too is for the good," came from the elements *gam* ["too"] and *zu* ["this"] in the name of his town, added to *le-tovah*, "for good"). Because of his piety and his propensity for miracles, he was selected to deliver tribute to the emperor of Rome on behalf of the Jews of Palestine. At an inn where he spent the night, robbers took the valuables from his treasure chest and filled it with earth. Nahum, unperturbed, said, "This too is for the good." The emperor was incensed when he saw the earth in the chest and wanted to kill him. Nahum's responded, "This too is for the good." Whereupon the prophet Elijah appeared in the guise of a Roman official and suggested that the earth in the chest had magical powers. When the emperor tried it in a battle against a heretofore invincible province, the earth turned into swords and arrows. In consequence they refilled Nahum's chest with gems and pearls, and sent him home in honor.
15. See Additional Note *1.

which later is revealed as good by dint of man's faith, even this does not issue from God. Only goodness and kindness, and great compassion, uncombined with any evil emerges from God, and it is only because of the accusing angels that the appearance of the good as evil comes about, as mentioned above. Because God is good and bestows good, then even from the very vestments of evil in which the good is disguised does there emerge a surpassingly great goodness when man returns in repentance, as described above.

2. A LOWER LEVEL OF THE GOOD
Source: Besht, Zava'at ha-Rivash, p. 16b

And God saw all that He had made, and, behold, it was very good (Gen. 1:31).

It may be asked why the Torah says, about the Creation of the world, *Behold, it was very good* (Gen. 1:31), and in other passages, *It is good* (Gen. 1:4, 10, 13, 18, 21, 25), yet in Deuteronomy it says, *See, I have set before thee this day life and good, and death and evil* (Deut. 30:15). Where did evil come from?

This evil should not be understood as actual evil; for evil is also good, only it is on a lower level than absolute good.

The Zohar hints at this concerning *mi-le'el* and *mi-le'ra*.[16] When one does good, evil itself is transformed into good. However, when one sins, actual evil occurs.[17] For example, the broom used to sweep the house was made with the purpose of cleaning the house. It has a partial measure of good, but on the lowest level. Nevertheless, it is good. But when it is used to strike a child who misbehaves, the broom becomes completely evil, and it is used to hit the child.

---

16. See Additional Note *2
17. The language is unclear. The passage apparently denies the existence of evil, yet speaks of it coming about one way or another. There are two ways of reading the passage. In one, God did not create evil as such, only the potential for evil. This solves the problem of the existence of evil, a dilemma for any theology which identifies God too closely with Nature. The other denies the absolute reality of evil, maintaining that it is purely situational; its existence or nonexistence depends on what we do in specific circumstances. Either way, the main point is that evil can be transformed into good, and the ethical imperative to do so is far more important for Hasidism than the metaphysical problem per se.

3. FROM EVIL TO GOOD
Source: R. Levi Yitzhak of Berdichev, Kedushat Levi to Vayeishev

An alternative explanation of the verse *and Jacob dwelt in the land of his father's sojournings, in the land of Canaan* (Gen. 37:1): The principle is that we should contemplate our ways and deeds, making sure that they are all for the sake of heaven; for "whatsoever the Holy One created in His world, He created but for His glory";[18] and this includes mundane objects. Thus, your eating and drinking should be for the express purpose of strengthening the body, the better to be able to serve the Creator.[19] Likewise, when engaged in the conjugal act, your thoughts should be directed to fulfilling the commandment of marital relations (*onah*; Exod. 21:10). Similarly, all of your material, mundane actions should be intended primarily for the glory of heaven, elevating the holy sparks to their Source. For every material object contains love, fear, and beauty;[20] when you desire to eat, drink, or engage in some other mundane activity, and you intend it for the love of God, you elevate the material desire to a spiritual one, releasing the holy sparks in these corporeal objects.

This is the mystery of *netilat yadayim* (the ritual washing of the hands before breaking bread). The word *netilah* ("washing") implies raising, as is seen in the verse *and he bore them and carried them (va-yenattelem)* (Isa. 63:9). In washing (*netilat*) the hands, one raises and elevates them, e.g., the three hands, namely, the great hand, the high hand, and the strong hand, which refer to the three attributes mentioned above.[21] With the correct intentions, one raises them and returns them to their Source.

This is also the secret of the blessing "Who bringest forth the bread from the earth." Bread signifies holiness, for the mystery of bread (*lehem*) consists of its thrice manifesting the Name of God.[22] "The earth" symbolizes the mundane and material. "Bringest forth bread" implies that the sparks of holiness are lifted up from "the earth" of the material.[23] When you conduct yourself in the aforementioned manner,

---

18. Avot 6:10.
19. See above, chap. 9.
20. The three sefirot of Hesed, Gevurah, and Tiferet.
21. Great hand, high hand, and strong hand all describe the hand of God (see Exod. 14:31, 14:8, and 13:9, respectively). See Additional Note *3.
22. The Tetragrammaton is numerically equal to 26, and the gematria of *lehem* ("bread") is 78.
23. See Additional Notes *3 and *4.

you demonstrate your mighty love of God. There is no greater way than this, for it enables you to serve your Creator wherever you go and whatever you do, even in the most material aspects of the physical world.

This is also the mystery of the verse *Oh, that you were really my brother, who had sucked the breasts of my mother, that I might find you in the street and kiss you* (Song of Songs 8:1). We find that there are two types of love: hidden and revealed. Hidden love is that between husband and wife, practiced in the confines of one's own dwelling. Revealed love is that of brother and sister, who often kiss each other openly, for there is no shame in doing so. The verse, then, describes a yearning for the revealed love of brother and sister. That is, even when "I find the sparks of Your holiness in that which is gross and material (the 'externals,' or that which is 'outside,' equivalent to conjugal love), I wish to *kiss* them," i.e., raise them to their holy Source without becoming entrapped in thoughts of material lust, for this is the secret of *kissing*. This is the mighty love described in the verse *for love is as mighty as death* (Song of Songs 8:6).

You must also calmly and joyfully accept all that God metes out to you. As our Rabbis taught, loving God *with all thy might* (*me'odekha*) (Deut. 6:5) means that whatever measure (*middah*) He metes out (*moded*) to thee, thank Him (*modeh*) greatly (*me'od*) and say that "whatever the All-Merciful does is for the good."[24] You should firmly believe that there is great good even in something that seems to be evil, for evil cannot derive from the divine. This was the manner of Nahum Ish Gamzu, who, because of his great faith in God, accepted everything that happened as a manifestation of the goodness of the divine will (*gam-zu,* "this too" is for the good).[25] In this way he sweetened the judgments (i.e., transformed the harsh decree into mercy) and changed the evil into the good.

This attitude is reflected in the verse *who brought you water out of flint rock* (Deut. 8:15), which embodies the mystery of the raising of the holy sparks to their divine Source. Water symbolizes God's goodness and mercy, while the rock symbolizes His power and might, and hence, Judgment. Your pure, firm thoughts can change God's attribute of Judgment into the attribute of Mercy, when you believe that all that God does is for the good, and thus express your great and mighty love of God.

24. Berakhot 54a.
25. Ta'anit 21a.

This was the type of faith and trust that characterized Jacob. On the verse *And Jacob dwelt in the land of his father's sojournings* (Gen. 37:1), Rashi explains that Jacob wished to dwell in peace, i.e., Jacob always sought to accept, calmly and with equanimity, that all was for the good, even *in the land of his father's sojournings* (*megurei*), i.e., even when surrounded by fear (*magor*) and trepidation, the characteristic attribute of his father Isaac.[26] Jacob's righteousness and faith in God furnished him with a sense of calm and equanimity, accepting all that befell him.

4. EVIL AND THE ULTIMATE GOOD
Source: R. Nahman of Bratslav, Likkutei Moharan I: 65, 3

On the verse *On that day shall the Lord be One and His Name One* (Zech. 14:9), the Rabbis commented: "Is not He One now too?" R. Aha b. Hanina said, "The world-to-come is not like this world. In this world, one pronounces the blessing 'Who is good and bestows good' upon hearing good tidings, and the blessing 'the true Judge,' upon hearing evil tidings, whereas in the world-to-come there will be only one blessing: 'Who is good and does good.'"[27]

The word *one* implies the ultimate purpose, which is altogether good.[28] For even if, heaven forbid, all the pain and suffering and evil in the world befall a man, he will recognize, if he thinks about their purpose, that they are not evils at all but great goods. All suffering comes from God with the specific intent to do good for man, whether to remind him to turn in repentance or to grind away his sins. Thus, suffering is a great good, for by sending it God intends to do good.

If you consider the purpose, i.e., God's intent, in all the evils and suffering that afflict you, you will experience no suffering at all. On the contrary, you will be filled with joy. . . .

---

26. Isaac's attribute was *gevurah* (fear). Jacob's faith in God and sense of equanimity were so great that he was able to maintain them even in the face of his father's attribute, i.e., fear. Rabbi Levi Yitzhak reads *megurei* ("sojournings") as *magor* ("fear"). Thus, Jacob dwelt or accepted everything calmly, even in the face of *gevurah*.

27. Pesahim 50a. At present there are two blessings, one for good tidings and the other for bad, but at the end of days there will be only *one* blessing, for good tidings; hence, "the Lord will be *One*." R. Nahman says that there will be no objective change, but our powers of perception will be altered, and we will escape the duality of good and evil that we accept in our mundane lives; our new insight at the end of days will lead us to the monistic view: everything is good; pain, suffering, and evil are all illusory.

28. By "ultimate purpose" (*takhlit*), R. Nahman means God's goal in creation, which is to do good to His creatures.

Indeed, there is no evil in the world, only complete goodness. The suffering that comes from all the afflictions that beset us results from the lack of knowledge that makes us unable to consider the ultimate purpose, which is all good, and hence we feel the pain and the hurt. But when we have knowledge and consider the ultimate purpose, we feel no pain or suffering, as mentioned above.[29]

Thereby you will understand something hidden and secret that is stamped into the soul of man: when he endures great pain, heaven forbid, such as the amputation of an organ, he closes and shuts his eyes tight. We all know that when you want to look at something far away, you close your eyes, squinting and constricting your vision in order to see the distant object you wish to behold. . . . Similarly, when considering the ultimate purpose which is altogether good, altogether *one*, you must shut your eyes and direct your attention to that goal. . . . That is, shut your eyes to this world, closing them very tight so as not to see all the world's desires and vanities. Then you will be able to see and perceive the light of this wholly good purpose. Then all the above-mentioned sufferings will be abolished of themselves.

5. FAITH, WISDOM, AND EVIL
Source: R. Shneur Zalman of Liady, Iggeret ha-Kodesh, chap. 11

The creation of being *yesh me-ayin* (*ex nihilo*, "from nothing") occurs constantly and at every moment; all creatures come into being from His blessed wisdom, which animates everything. When a man wisely and profoundly contemplates and concentrates his attention upon his coming into existence *yesh me-ayin*—truly every moment—how can he possibly think about his troubles, or about afflictions related to family, health, and making a living,[30] or any other worldly suffering? For the *Ayin*, His blessed Hokhmah,[31] is the source of life, welfare, and delight. It is the Eden which transcends the world-to-come[32] except

---

29. See Additional Note *5.
30. Or, "children, life, and sustenance," man's basic needs, mentioned in Mo'ed Katan 28a and see Zohar I, 181a. This trilogy is often mentioned in hasidic literature. See above, chap. 6.
31. In the Habad system, the highest of the sefirot, Hokhmah ("Wisdom"), is closest to the Ein-Sof—the Nothing (*Ayin*). Because of its position, Hokhmah is the source of all existence, and also the least understood. Hence, God's goodness is misunderstood as evil or suffering when, in fact, it is not that at all.
32. The antecedent of "It" is the divine Nothing—the *Ayin* or Ein-Sof. Eden is identified with Hokhmah, and the world-to-come with Binah. See earlier in *Iggeret Kodesh*, chap. 5.

that, because it cannot be perceived, one imagines that things are bad or that one is suffering afflictions. In fact, however, no evil descends from above and everything is good, though this is not always understood because of its immense and abundant goodness.

The essence of the faith for which man was created is to believe that "there is no place void of Him"[33] and *in the light of the king's countenance there is life* (Prov. 16:15), and therefore, *strength and gladness are in His place* (1 Chron. 16:27), because He is exclusively good all the time. Therefore, first of all, man ought to be happy and joyous at all times, and truly live by his faith in the Lord, Who animates him and is good to him at every moment. He who is grieved and laments acts as if he is experiencing something bad and is suffering and lacks some element of goodness; he is like a heretic, heaven forbid. That is why the kabbalists strongly rejected the trait of sadness.

He who has faith, however, is not indisposed by afflictions. With respect to worldly things, "yes" and "no" are all the same to him, truly equal.[34] He to whom they are not the same reveals that he is one of the *erev rav*[35] who act only for themselves, removing himself from divine influence in order to live the life of a heathen; such is his self-love, and that is why he desires the life of the flesh, family, and material well-being—for that is what he considers his good. It would have been better for him had he not been created. For the purpose of man's creation in this world is to be tested by these trials, to ascertain what is in his heart:[36] whether he will turn his heart toward other gods, the passions of the body that evolve from the *sitra aḥara,*[37] and desire them, or whether his desire and wish is to live the life of truth as it issues from the living God.

We must believe that man really lives in the life of truth, and that all his needs, and everything related to him, truly evolve in all their details not from the *sitra aḥara,* but *from the Lord by whom the steps of man are established* (Ps. 37:23), and therefore that everything is absolutely good, except that it is not apprehended.

---

33. *Tikkunei Zohar* 57. Cf. Exodus Rabbah 2:5.
34. The hasidic concept of *hishtavut,* or indifference. If everything comes from God, then everything is good, and it makes no difference whether it *seems* pleasant or unpleasant. See above, chap. 14, selection 1.
35. The "mixed multitude" that accompanied the Israelites out of Egypt (Exod. 12:38); i.e., one not of the truly faithful, the "believers, descendants of believers." Cf. Zohar I, 25a.
36. See Deut. 8:2, 2 Chron. 32:31.
37. The "other side," or demonic forces.

If we really believe this, everything becomes good—even in appearance. For by such a faith, when one believes that the very substance of what seems to be evil is in fact of the Supreme Good . . . through this faith, the imagined evil is truly absorbed and sublimated in the concealed Supreme Good.

6. DEATH AND EVIL
Source: R. Zevi Elimelekh of Dinov, Benei Yisaskhar, Nisan 4, Tiyyul ba-Pardes, derush 5

Pay careful attention and listen to the words of the wise and their hidden implications.[38] God made man upright,[39] and he was wholly good. God then commanded him not to eat from *the tree of the knowledge of good and evil* (Gen. 2:17), lest evil enter into him, causing a commingling within him of good and evil. Because he transgressed God's command, accepting the counsel of Samael, who came mounted upon the serpent,[40] as is well known, his substance became coarse, and evil entered into him. That is why death occurs, so that his matter, the body, can decompose, death being a malady and scourge for all the world. But by means of death, suffering, and punishment, each according to his just deserts, evil is separated from man, and only the good remains.[41]

7. THE ROOTS OF EVIL AND GOOD
Source: R. Zadok ha-Kohen, Peri Zaddik, pt. I, Kedushat Shabbat 7, pp. 22a–b

Esau and Jacob are the roots of all the good and evil in the world. In the realm of action, darkness comes first, but in that of thought it is reversed.[42] Thus Israel (i.e., Jacob) was the first to be conceived, for as

---

38. Paraphrase of Prov. 22:17 and 1:6.
39. Paraphrase of Eccl. 7:29.
40. *Pirkei de-R. Eliezer* 13. Samael is the legendary archdemon. See too Zohar I, 35b.
41. The writers of the preceding selections held to the standard monistic conception, which denies the reality of evil. In this and the following selection, two later hasidic thinkers seem to be returning to a pre-hasidic, kabbalistic notion of evil as real.
42. Empirically, darkness precedes light, so evil precedes good, and Esau is born before Jacob (Gen. 25:25—26). However, in conception (both intellectually and in the sense of impregnation), the good precedes the evil. Hence, Jacob comes before Esau.

we read in Genesis Rabbah,[43] Jacob is the firstborn of creation. By himself he brought all creation into complete *tikkun*, and that is why the Rabbis said: "Jacob our father did not die."[44] Adam, the primordial man, could not fully effect *tikkun* in order to nullify the divine decree that man must die, not even after he repented for his sin. Such *tikkun* can occur only when evil is totally separated from good, which Adam could not accomplish during his lifetime because of the enormity of his sin; or his repentance was inadequate. . . .

But our father Jacob, who was privileged to become the father of the Israelite nation . . . repaired the sin of Adam all by himself. . . . He separated all the evil from himself and transmitted it to Esau, the evil part that came with him [Jacob] on account of the commingling of good and bad that occurred through the eating from the Tree of Knowledge,[45] and because of which there is in every human being a mixture of good and bad. . . . Every righteous person has a wicked person as a counterpart because of the commingling of good and evil, one opposite the other.[46] When the righteous attains merit, he absorbs all the good even from his evil counterpart . . . and the wicked absorbs all the evil, and then they are separated from each other.

Suffering as a Disguise of the Good

8. TZIMTZUM *AND SUFFERING*
Source: R. Yaakov Yosef of Polennoye, Toledot Yaakov Yosef to Ekev, sec. 2[47]

My teacher the Besht asked, concerning the verse *Thou shalt love the Lord thy God with all thy heart and all thy soul and all thy might* (Deut. 6:5): Of what benefit is it to Him if mere mosquitoes like us love Him—the great and awesome King? Is it not like nothing at all?!

---

43. Actually, in Tanhuma, Shemini 3, based on "And thou shalt say unto Pharaoh: Thus saith the Lord: Israel is My son, My firstborn" (Exod. 4:22). Cf. Shabbat 89b, where the same source designates the people of Israel rather than Israel (Jacob) the man.
44. Ta'anit 5b.
45. According to the Kabbalah, the primordial sin of the Tree of Knowledge of Good and Evil caused good and evil to be admixed in Adam and Eve and all their descendants. Man's function is to separate the good from the evil and restore it to its pristine state before the adulteration. Note that evil is not treated as illusory (see above, n. 42).
46. See Eccl. 7:14 and Hagigah 15a—the principle of the symmetry of good and evil in the world.
47. The translation follows the text of *Toledot Yaakov Yosef* with borrowings from the somewhat more elaborate variant in *Sefer Baal Shem Tov*.

I heard from him a wonderful answer to this question. The Creation of the world took place by means of divine Judgment, which is the same as the *tzimtzum*.[48] In every one of the succeeding worlds there occurred a *tzimtzum,* whereby He contracted His light of the Ein-Sof to the point where His light could be received and His greatness perceived by each one according to his capacity. Withal, the original light of the Ein-Sof before the *tzimtzum,* and the sefirot or vessels which resulted therefrom and which contain the light of the Ein-Sof after the contractions, are a unity—that of the Ein-Sof. In His omnipotence, He is able to *seem* subject to limitation and contraction; but He comprises everything, one unity.

Man's afflictions and suffering constitute the body for the soul, the spiritual life which illuminates man; and this is His divinity, the light of the Ein-Sof that gives life to all.[49] When man accepts his suffering in love and joy, a *yihud* ("unification") is performed, whereby he attaches, combines, and unifies the vessel—the body, the result of *tzimtzum* and Din, signified by the divine Name Elohim—with the soul, which is identical with joy and spiritual vitality. Thereby, the Din is nullified (and is transformed into Rahamim).[50]

Thus, the counsel that is given is *Thou shalt love the Lord thy God.* The term Elohim ("God") represents Din; [we are to] accept it in joy and bind it to the former Name, the Lord, the Tetragrammaton, which is the soul.[51]

---

48. The contractions of the light of the Ein-Sof, by means of which the Infinite became finite and hence able to create and to reveal Himself to the creatures He created. Because this process, elaborated upon by Luria and the Lurianic kabbalists, entailed curbing the light of the Ein-Sof, it is considered a function of divine Judgment (Din) rather than Mercy (Rahamim). See introduction to chap. 1.

49. This is the key to the entire passage. The well-known body-soul relationship is applied to suffering. Just as the body is merely a vessel for the soul, so human misery is the body, or external framework, that contains the essence—divinity, in all its glory and joy.

50. In the normal relation of body and soul, man can, through the appropriate spiritual exercises, achieve a mystical awareness of the ultimate Oneness of everything, the oneness of the Ein-Sof, and hence the nullity of the body and corporeal existence. Similarly, pain and misery are considered corporeal attributes (not because they are organic in nature, but in the sense of a mystical ratio: suffering is to joy what body is to soul), and when man intuits the underlying unity of the creation, he is aware of the nullity of the body, or suffering.

51. Having already stated that the existential "body" of suffering and Din is symbolized by the name Elohim, R. Yaakov Yosef now informs us that the soul, or joy, is represented by the Tetragrammaton; the four-letter proper Name of God (usually trans-

9. GOD'S PRESENCE IN SUFFERING
Source: Besht, quoted in Toledot Yaakov Yosef, Vayak'hel, sec. 3, s.v. levaer, end

Understand that God Himself is present in all the suffering we endure, whether physical or spiritual, and that the pain is a kind of garb for God's presence. When we know this, the garb is removed, and the pain and all the evil decrees are removed.[52]

Suffering in Love

10. HEAVENLY LOVE IN A GARMENT OF AFFLICTION
Source: R. Shneur Zalman of Liady, Tanya, Iggeret ha-Kodesh, chap. 22a

For whom the Lord loves He chastises (Prov. 3:12). This is analogous to a compassionate, wise, and righteous father who punishes his son. A wise son will not turn away to escape, or look for help or even for someone to intercede with his father, who is compassionate, righteous, and merciful. Instead, he will look straight at his father, face to face, and endure his blows with love, "for his benefit always."[53] . . .

The recommendation to accept suffering with love is the counsel of God as given us by our Sages, of blessed memory: "To examine one's conduct."[54] You will find that you have committed sins that must be

---

lated in English as "Lord") symbolizes Rahamim and love. By an act of loving mystical intuition ("thou shalt love"), man unifies the symbol of divine Judgment, and hence suffering and the body ("thy God").

The answer to the Besht's original question is now evident. God does not "need" our love. He is telling us how to react to the suffering that is our daily lot: by "unifying" suffering and joy in the overarching unity of the Ein-Sof, in which pain and misery—namely the body—disappear of themselves. By an act of loving meditation, suffering is diffused in the cosmic unity of the Ein-Sof.

52. Since God permeates the universe, it follows that all pain and suffering must be ascribed to Him, hence the theme of God's sympathy for man, discussed elsewhere in this chapter. But this raises an apparent conflict between God's immanence and His benevolence. The Besht solves the problem by positing the paradox that an awareness of God's inherence in suffering eliminates the suffering—a psychological answer to a theological problem. One is reminded of "A Dudelle," a Yiddish song celebrating the divine omnipresence that is ascribed to R. Levi Yitzhak of Berditchev: "If things are good, [I know they come from] You. If bad, from You; but if [from] You, why, then, it is good!"

53. Paraphrase of Deut. 6:24.

54. Berakhot 5a, Eruvin 13b.

cleansed by suffering.[55] Then you will clearly see His great love for you—love that causes a change in ordinary behavior,[56] as in the case of the great and awesome king who, out of his great love, personally washes the filth from his only son, as it is written: *When the Lord shall have washed away the filth of the daughters of Zion . . . by the spirit of judgment* (Isa. 4:4). And *as water reflects one's face, so the heart of man to man* (Prov. 27:19),[57] there will be an arousal of love in the heart of everyone who perceives and understands the preciousness of God's love for the beings below. It is dearer and better than all the life of all the worlds, as it is written: *How precious is Thy loving-kindness* (Ps. 36:8) . . . *For your loving-kindness, which is better than life* (ibid. 63:4) . . . For loving-kindness, which is an aspect of love, is the fountainhead of all life[58] in all the worlds, as it is written: "He sustains life through loving-kindness."[59]

And then God too will grant His goodness and make His face shine toward you with open love which at first was clothed and hidden in overt admonition.[60] Thus will harshness be sweetened in its source, and the judgments be nullified forever.[61]

11. NO EXCESSIVE ASCETICISM
Source: R. Shneur Zalman of Liady, Tanya, Iggeret ha-Teshuvah, chap. 1

The mitzvah of repentance (*teshuvah*) as required by the Torah is simply to abandon sin.[62] . . . It is not at all the common conception that repentance is synonymous with fasting. Even where suffering completes the process of atonement, as in the case of sins of excision or execution,[63] it is God Who brings the suffering on the sinner.[64] . . . When the *teshuvah* is acceptable before Him, as man lovingly returns

---

55. See Berakhot, loc. cit. Cf. Zohar III, 57b.
56. See Genesis Rabbah 55:11.
57. Meaning: Just as clear water truthfully reflects one's face, so the heart elicits a reciprocal response.
58. Lit. "the life of the life." Cf. Yoma 71a, *Tikkunei Zohar* 19.
59. From the second benediction of the Amidah.
60. Paraphrase of Prov. 27:5. If suffering is accepted as divine love in disguise, that love will now appear in its pure form.
61. See above, chap. 8, introduction and additional note 11.
62. Sanhedrin 25b; Maimonides, *Mishneh Torah*, Hilkhot Teshuvah 1–2.
63. See Yoma 86a. Without physical suffering, the atonement for certain grave sins is incomplete.
64. The afflictions are not self-imposed, but are brought on by God as part of the divine process of atonement. Man is not called upon to add to his own affliction.

to God with all his heart and soul, then following the initiative from below,[65] *as water reflects one's face* (Prov. 27:19), there is an awakening from Above,[66] arousing God's love and kindness to scour his sin through affliction in the physical world. *For whom the Lord loves He chastises* (Prov. 3:12).

That is why Maimonides and the author of *Sefer Mitzvot Gadol*[67] do not mention fasting in [connection with] the mitzvah of *teshuvah*, even for sins of excision or capital sins. They cite only confession and the plea for forgiveness; *They shall confess their sin* (Num. 5:7). What of the verse *Return to me with all your hearts, with fasting and weeping* (Joel 2:12)?[68] The answer is that this was meant to nullify the heavenly decree that had *already* been issued, to expunge the sin of the generation through the plague of locusts. It is the justification for all fasts undertaken when trouble of any kind threatens the community, as in the Book of Esther.[69]

There are many descriptions in the Musar literature, particularly the *Roke'ah*[70] and *Sefer Hasidim*,[71] of fasts and ascetic practices for one who transgresses sins for which the punishment is excision or execution. The same is true of sins punished by divinely ordained death, like wasteful emissions of semen, as the Torah recounts of Er and Onan (Gen. 38:7–10). In this sense, the judgment is identical. The fasts and mortifications are intended to preclude the punishment of suffering at the hand of heaven, God forbid, and also to urge on and expedite the conclusion of the soul's atonement. Also, perhaps he does not return to God with all his heart and soul out of love, but only out of fear.[72]

---

65. Human initiative.

66. The divine response. Cf. the excerpt from *Iggeret ha-Kodesh* 22 in selection 10 above.

67. R. Moshe b. Yaakov of Coucy (13th cent.), known as Semag, French tosafist scholar.

68. Doesn't this indicate that man must fast and undergo mortification as part of his penitence?

69. Fasting and mortification are appropriate in order to avoid far greater suffering that has already been decreed as punishment by heaven, but they are not a necessary part of the process of repentance.

70. *Sefer ha-Roke'ah* by R. Eleazar b. Judah of Worms (ca. 1165–ca. 1230), major teacher of the Hasidei Ashkenaz, a pietist movement in medieval Germany.

71. The "Book of the Pious," often ascribed to R. Yehudah he-Hasid (ca. 1150—1217), the teacher of R. Eleazar of Worms, is the foremost ethical work of Hasidei Ashkenaz.

72. The ascetic practices are not obligatory but are advisable for the three reasons implied in the last two sentences.

12. THE TWO WORLDS
Source: R. Shneur Zalman of Liady, Tanya, Likkutei Amarim, chap. 26

I offer this sound counsel as to how to cleanse one's heart of sadness and of every trace of worry about mundane things, even about "children, health, and sustenance."[73] Everyone is familiar with the statement of the Rabbis that "just as one must recite a blessing for the good, one must also recite a blessing for misfortune."[74] The Talmud explains that we should accept misfortune joyously, like the joy of a visible and obvious benefit, "for this too is for the good,"[75] except that [the good] is not apparent and visible to mortal eyes, because it stems from the hidden world which is higher than the revealed world. The latter emanates from the letters *vav* and *heh* of the Tetragrammaton, whereas the hidden world reflects the letters *yod* and *heh*. Hence the meaning of the verse *Happy is the man whom Thou, O God (Ya-H),*[76] *chasteneth* (Ps. 94:12).

Therefore, the Rabbis commented that the verse *But they that love Him shall be as the sun going forth in its might* (Judg. 5:31) refers to those who rejoice in their afflictions.[77] For this is the joy of desiring God's nearness more than anything in the life of this world, as it is written, *Because Thy loving-kindness is better than life*, etc. (Ps. 63:4). God's nearness is infinitely more real and more sublime in the hidden world. For *there is the hiding of His power* (Hab. 3:4), and *the Most High abides in secrecy* (Ps. 91:1).

The man who accepts affliction joyously merits to see *the sun going forth in its might* in the world-to-come, i.e., the sun emerging from the sheath in which it is enclosed in *this* world.[78] In the world-to-come it will appear without its covering, meaning that the hidden world will be revealed, and will shine and send forth light in a great and intense revelation to those who had taken refuge in Him in this world, and had taken shelter beneath His shadow—the shadow of wisdom.

---

73. The basic human needs, according to the Talmud (Mo'ed Katan 28a), frequently mentioned in the works of the hasidic masters, especially as regards petitionary prayer.
74. Berakhot 9:5.
75. Ta'anit 21a.
76. *Yod* and *heh*. Thus, the misfortunes are blessings in disguise, originating in the hidden worlds.
77. Yoma 23a.
78. Nedarim 8b.

13. MIND AND MISERY
Source: R. Nahman of Bratslav, Likkutei Etzot Moharan, Savlanut, nos. 1, 4

When we know that everything that happens to us is solely for our own good, our present state of existence is akin to the world-to-come. We can attain this by confessing our sins before a scholar of Torah (*talmid ḥakham*).[79] Then we will merit knowing that everything that happens to us during the course of our entire life is for our own good, for everything derives from the Holy One's great love for us. The essential perfection of the human mind lies in not remonstrating or being confused because of the ordeals we experience, but instead believing that everything is for the eternal good.

Basically, our pain from the anguish, suffering, and ordeals we experience, heaven forbid, is solely because we are diminished in mind,[80] so that we do not consider the ultimate purpose, which is wholly good. For if we considered the purpose, we would realize that our sufferings are not evils at all but great goods.

14. SUFFERANCE AND SUFFERING
Source: R. Nahman of Bratslav, Likkutei Etzot Moharan, Savlanut, no. 11

Everyone in the world experiences great suffering, adversity, and various and innumerable ordeals, whether in making a living or in matters of health or family. No one in the world can avoid suffering and vicissitudes, for *man is born unto toil* (Job 5:7). It is also written: *For all his days are pains, and his occupation vexation* (Eccl. 2:23). There is no way out except by fleeing to God and to the Torah. Therefore, we must all have great sufferance to suffer[81] whatever may befall us. So our Rabbis taught, "There is a tradition: the cure for suffering is silence."[82] As the wise man said, "Sufferance is the counsel for him who has no other counsel." All our Sages elaborate upon this, and they all declare that this world is full of immeasurable worries and ordeals,

---

79. Because the scholar will help us to understand this.
80. Referring to the perfection of the human mind mentioned in the preceding paragraph.
81. In Hebrew, as in English, there is a similarity between the words for "anguish" and for a patient, passive attitude toward it. The root s-v-l means both "suffering" and "sufferance" in the sense of enduring the suffering.
82. In the sense of sufferance or resignation. I have not been able to locate a source for the exact (Aramaic) quotation. The closest is Berakhot 62a.

for man was not created to enjoy the world, but to toil in it in order to merit the world-to-come. Therefore it is necessary to endure adversity and to believe that all that happens is for our good. "For all that the Merciful One does is for the good."[83]

15. ISRAEL'S SUFFERING IN EXILE
Source: R. Levi Yitzhak of Berdichev, Kedushat Levi, Kelalot ha-Nissim, no. 1

Nahmanides and Maimonides (in his *Sefer ha-Mada*)[84] ask why the wicked, such as Pharaoh and Nebuchadnezzar, who destroyed the Holy Temple, were punished. Did not God, through His prophets, command Nebuchadnezzar to destroy the Temple? And Pharaoh too, did not God say to Father Abraham, *Know of a surety that thy seed shall be a stranger in a land that is not theirs, and shall serve them; and they shall afflict them for four hundred years* (Gen. 15:13)?

The answer can be expressed by means of a parable. A man has an only son and wants him to follow the right path, to serve the Creator by studying Torah and practicing moral conduct. He tells the child's teacher that if the child does not want to study, the teacher may chastise him with a blow, discipline him, and guide him on the path of righteousness in Torah and moral conduct, to heed the instruction of parents and teachers.

Now, when the father sees the teacher striking his son, teaching him properly, then most certainly the father is pained. He is distressed when he sees his son hurting, suffering from blows. However, upon reflecting that because of the beating his son will follow the right path and obey his parents and teachers, the fathers finds the beating and chastisement of his son acceptable, gratifying, and pleasant.

However, if the teacher himself follows evil ways, such as stealing and killing, and beats and chastises the child, admonishing him to be gluttonous and sensual, to follow a crooked path, to steal from his father and from others in order to enrich the teacher, and to rob and kill as he does, punishing him if he goes in the ways of righteousness, because the teacher prefers immorality, idolatry, murder, and stealing—then the father is deeply troubled for two reasons: first, that his son has gone astray on an evil path, and second, that his son must

---

83. Berakhot 60b.
84. Nahmanides to Gen. 15:14; Maimonides, Hilkhot Teshuvah 6, end. The idea developed here, that the gentiles must educate Israel, is not found in the earlier writers.

endure the pain and suffering of being beaten by the teacher. . . . The father will therefore exact vengeance from the teacher who struck his son in order to detour him from the right way to the wrong way. The father's vengeance is twofold: for the suffering endured by his son, and for teaching him to be a scoundrel.

The same is true of the Jewish people. In the Prayerbook we confess that "because of our sins were we exiled from our land" for disobeying the words of the prophets. We were given over into the hands of our enemies. The Creator intended that we would return to Him with a whole heart as a result of suffering, as it is written in the Torah of Moses, *In your distress, when all these things are come upon you . . . you will return to the Lord your God* (Deut. 4:30). God loves us—*in their afflictions He is afflicted* (Isa. 63:9), and *I will be with* Israel *in trouble* (Ps. 91:15)—but nevertheless, in order to make us return to Him with whole-hearted repentance and fulfill the Torah of Moses and the prophets, God storms in all the worlds and all the heavens, trampling in all the heavens and shedding two tears into the Great Sea.[85] However, He consoles Himself, as it were, because as a result Israel will repent and attain *a pure heart* and *a steadfast spirit* (Ps. 51:12).

That is why, through the prophets, He permitted and commanded wicked Nebuchadnezzar to destroy the house of God, so that Israel would observe the Torah of Moses and the prophets. Indeed, this occurred in the instance of Darius, who sent Ezra to teach Israel the Torah and its commandments. But Nebuchadnezzar did not do so; instead he ordered the Israelites to worship idols and bow down to a statute. . . . Therefore God storms at the tribulations visited upon Israel by Nebuchadnezzar and other evil men. His intention that through these afflictions Israel would return to Him was not realized. . . . And God exacts vengeance from the nations of the world who oppress Israel for two reasons: one, for the tribulations and suffering they impose on Israel, which are unjustified because they do not allow Israel to repent. . . . And second, as a result of compulsion they transgress against His will.

---

85. Berakhot 59a: "When the Holy One recalls His children immersed in pain amongst the nations of the world, He sheds two tears into the Great Sea [i.e., the Mediterranean], and the sound is heard from one end of the world to the other."

Suffering Is for Man's Good

16. THE LORD IS GOOD TO ALL
Source: R. Elimelekh of Lizhensk, Noam Elimelekh to Miketz 24c, s.v. first o yomar

The Lord is good to all (Ps. 145:9); i.e., everything the Holy One does is for the good. Even when He punishes someone, it is for his good. Nevertheless, *His tender mercies are upon all His works* (ibid.): Even though the punishment is intended for man's good, to purify him so that he may merit the life of the world-to-come, still God has pity on him and removes the sufferings and punishment from him and pardons him if he shows remorse, as it is written: *whoso confesses and forsakes them* [the sins] *shall obtain mercy* (Prov. 28:13).

17. PAIN PURIFIES THE SOUL
Source: R. Shneur Zalman of Liady, Tanya, Iggeret ha-Teshuvah, chap. 12

The reason for happiness in bearing afflictions[86] of the body is that they are a great and mighty favor for the sinning soul, to cleanse it in this world and redeem it from purification in Gehenna. (This is particularly true in our generations, when it is impossible to fast, in accordance with all the prescriptions for penance by R. Isaac Luria, the fasts mandated for the cleansing of the soul to rescue it from the scouring in Gehenna.)[87]

Nahmanides, in the introduction to his commentary on Job,[88] writes that even the sufferings of Job for a seventy-year span cannot be compared in any way to the suffering of a soul only momentarily in Gehenna, for fire is a sixtieth part of the punishment in Gehenna.[89] It is only that *the world is built on kindness* (Ps. 89:3), and through mild suffering in this world, one is saved from severe judgments in the next.

---

86. One of several attitudes praised by the Talmud, to which it applies Judg. 5:31, "Those who love Him shall be like the sun rising in full strength" (Yoma 23a, Shabbat 88b).
87. The passage appears in parentheses in the text. Compare the limitation of ascetic practices in selection 11.
88. See *Kitvei Ramban*, I, 23. R. Shneur Zalman paraphrases Nahmanides, who refers to "a lifetime of Job's sufferings."
89. Berakhot 57b.

18. THE LONG-RANGE BENEFITS OF SUFFERING
Source: R. Nahman of Bratslav, Likkutei Etzot, Savlanut, nos. 2–3

Just as all medicines for healing the body consist of bitter drugs, so too must we accept bitterness as medicine for the soul. . . .

We must suffer in order to earn true healing of the spirit. . . . But when God, Who is full of mercy, discerns in us a true desire to return to Him but a lack of strength to suffer all the bitterness needed for our cure as a result of our many sins, then God ignores our sins, so that we will not have to suffer any more bitterness than we can take.

Thus, if you truly desire to return to God, know and believe that all the bitterness, suffering, and tribulation coming upon you is really a great kindness. For in view of your many sins, you should be suffering much more bitterness in order to be cured. . . .

Therefore, we must not be alarmed and confused by anything that may happen to us. For we should know and believe that everything that passes over us each day, whether good events or afflictions and troubles and worries and disasters, heaven forbid, is for our eternal benefit.[90]

Suffering as a Way to the Good

19. RECOGNIZING THE SOURCE OF SUFFERING
Source: Besht, cited in Oraḥ le-Ḥayyim to Ha'azinu

When a man is visited by suffering, he should reflect on the allegory of the father of a small son who disguises himself so as to frighten his son. If the son understands and sees that it is really his father, he cries out to him, "Father!" The father, in turn, responds tenderly, removing his strange garments and revealing his true identity to his son. Thus is the son's pain nullified.

So it is with man. When he experiences any form of grief, heaven forbid, if he understands that nothing exists except for God, and that it is He Who is causing him this pain to see if he will have the wisdom to call out to God, then the pain will be banished. But when man is not wise enough to know that everything comes from Him, and looks to medicines and other physical methods to be saved from this path, then, heaven forbid, he will remain as he was.

---

90. See above, selections 13 and 14, for more from the same work.

20. EVIL AS A MEANS TO THE GOOD
Source: R. Levi Yitzhak of Berdichev, Kedushat Levi to Shemot, s.v. lekhah va-eshlaḥekha

As is well known, evil does not issue from God;[91] only the good does. When our eyes are opened so that we can see the great benefit that accrues to the wicked as a result of the punishment that God inflicts upon them, then we will directly perceive the great benefit that suffering confers on all men.

The wicked of the nations lack understanding hearts, and do not yearn to accept affliction lovingly, to find refuge in the pleasantness of God by means of it.[92] For it is known that as a result of Egypt's punishment, God's great Name was magnified and sanctified in the world.[93] Until then the world had no knowledge of God; with Egypt's punishment, the truth of the Creator's existence and providence over the world was revealed. Then Israel began to seek His great Name, and drew closer to its Father in heaven with intense love, for it saw God as Master of all Who had the power to *make great and give strength to all* (1 Chron. 29:12).

---

91. Paraphrase of Lam. 3:38, "Out of the mouth of the Most High proceedeth not evil and good." The verse may be read either as a rhetorical question, indicating that God is the author of both good and evil, or as a declarative sentence supporting a monistic view (see Rashi and R. Joseph Kara ad loc.; Lamentations Rabbah 3:31 also interprets the verse as declarative). Hasidism, with its strong emphasis on God's presence in everything and on the goodness of the entire creation, found the existence of evil a thorny problem, and sought to resolve it by several strategies, such as the nonreality of evil (see the introduction to this chapter). Since the verse in Lamentations could not be read as expressing the idea that God created evil, Scripture was assumed to be proclaiming that the Most High was *not* the Source of good and evil as two separate and opposing elements, but was the Creator *only* of the good. See Additional Note *1, end.

92. For the purposes of the homily from which this selection is extracted, R. Levi Yitzhak differentiates Israelites from Egyptians ("the wicked of the nations"). The former understand the hasidic teaching, here propounded, that evil, taken by itself, seems evil, but in context and viewed from a long perspective is the indispensable means for bringing on a much greater good. The "wicked of the nations" rebel against their suffering because they lack this perspective. In the end of days, however, they too will realize that their anguish served a higher purpose which made their suffering worthwhile.

93. The greater good that justifies such blows is not the good of the sufferer, but his spiritual fulfillment as he becomes aware that he is an instrument of *kiddush ha-shem* ("sanctification of the Name"), i.e., the greater glory of God. The "magnification and sanctification of the Name," based upon a verse in Ezekiel (38:23), forms the beginning of the Kaddish prayer, which is recited, among other occasions, by mourners for eleven months after the death of a parent.

Similarly, when the wicked are punished, God's Name is magnified and sanctified, as is often mentioned by the prophets. Since God's Name is magnified and sanctified through His blows, how much must we yearn and long for the privilege that, because of us, His Name will be magnified. How delightful, how pleasant, how sweet and gratifying are all these blows and this suffering, for they are the means whereby His great Name is magnified and sanctified in the world. The nations, however, are callous-hearted; their eyes are sealed and their hearts too dull to understand all the good they might attain by means of these blows. But that is not so when it happens to us; for then, because of the wisdom granted us by the Master of all, and our true understanding of the purpose and effect of whatever happens, we accept all the punishment and suffering with great yearning and love, for by means of these blows the Name of our Creator is magnified and sanctified. Indeed, we eagerly await this all our lives. Our Sages tell us that when the students of R. Akiva observed how joyously he embraced martyrdom at the hands of the Romans, they asked him, "To such lengths?" He answered them, "Every day of my life I looked forward to observing the commandment of martyrdom."[94] For this is the very quest of our hearts and our souls, that we offer up our lives and souls and spirits for the love of our Creator. How dear and beloved and cherished are all the ordeals and blows we suffer, whether to go into fire or water, so that by means of them God's Name can be magnified and sanctified!

21. FAITH AND SUFFERING
Source: R. Gedaliah of Linitz, Teshuot Ḥen to Vayeishev, s.v. ve'al derekh zeh

I heard in the name of the Besht, of blessed memory, an interpretation of the dictum that "prayer is a need of heaven."[95]

He explained that prayer relates to the fulfillment of a need in the Holy One, as it were. For even when wicked Jews are in pain, the

---

94. Berakhot 61b.

95. That is, prayer fulfills a divine need, as it were. The text implies that this is a quotation from the Sages, but while it is widely repeated in Lurianic and later writings, especially in hasidic works, I have not been able to locate a talmudic or midrashic source for it. The idea, in less harshly anthropomorphic form, is contained in the talmudic saying that "the Holy One desires the prayers of the righteous" (Ḥullin 60b and elsewhere). It is related to the Lurianic-hasidic concept of petitionary prayer as deflected from the self onto God: prayer to relieve "the pain of the Shekhinah," discussed in this chapter and in chap. 6.

Shekhinah cries out, "My head hurts, My arm hurts."[96] His intention in creating the world was to bestow goodness upon His creatures, *for He desires kindness* (Mic. 7:18).[97]

This was the way of Nahum of Gamzu, who understood that some good was concealed in everything that happened to him, for no evil issues from God.[98] And if what happens seems hurtful, it is only because the good, at present, is concealed and in a state of *katnut*.[99] But by means of his faith in its essential goodness, saying, "This too is for the good," the concealed goodness is aroused and emerges into a state of *gadlut*.[100]

Reciprocal Sympathy

22. HUMAN AND DIVINE SUFFERING
Source: R. Yaakov Yosef of Polennoye, Toledot Yaakov Yosef to Va'eira, sec. 1

I heard from my teacher the Besht that the zaddikim are emissaries of the Matrona.[101] As a result of their own want, whether of food or of clothing, they recognize that there is a corresponding lack above. They pray solely for the lack above to be rectified.[102] They do not pray for their own benefit.[103]

---

96. Sanhedrin 46a—the Shekhinah commiserates with man.
97. Since God's purpose in the creation was to do good to His creatures, their suffering frustrates His design. Hence, prayer for relief from human pain is really a prayer for God, i.e., that He will fulfill His purposes and express His goodness unimpeded. See Additional Note *6.
98. Ta'anit 21a. See notes to selection 1 above.
99. Hasidism saw all phenomena as existing in two states, smallness and greatness. The minor state, *katnut*, or constriction, is one of passivity and lack of inspiration, in which ultimate fulfillment exists only *in potentia*. Greatness, or *gadlut*, is the state of fulfillment, of arousal and inspiration. Applied to the present thesis, it means that evil is illusory in the sense that it is merely the good in a state of smallness, "concealed" and present only potentially, but nonetheless very real. It requires human confidence and faith to flower into greatness and stand revealed, in this aroused state, as actual goodness. See above, chap. 12.
100. See Additional Note *7.
101. A kabbalistic synonym for the Shekhinah (Divine Presence).
102. R. Yaakov Yosef here repeats the theme, expressed in other selections in this chapter, that human needs are projected onto the Shekhinah and thus prayer is not self-serving, but for the purpose of removing the Shekhinah's need or suffering. In this passage, however, the projection is reserved for the zaddik in his role as a messenger of the Shekhinah.
103. This passage should be compared to the excerpts from the same work in selections 8, 9, and 22.

23. A REFLECTION OF THE SHEKHINAH'S PAIN
Source: R. Yaakov Yosef of Polennoye, Toledot Yaakov Yosef to Beshalla, sec. 4, s.v. u-neva'er

A wise and enlightened man will take heart to understand that the suffering that afflicts us is really the pain of the Shekhinah. As our Sages said, "When man suffers punishment, what does the Shekhinah say? 'My head hurts, My hand hurts.'"[104] The man will then pray to alleviate the Shekhinah's suffering, thereby banishing his own suffering. . . .

This explains the meaning of *Are not these evils come upon us because God is not among us?* (Deut. 31:17). That is, if we had only realized that the Shekhinah was suffering when we were in pain, the evil would not have afflicted us.[105]

24. BUT WITHOUT HYPOCRISY
Source: R. Yitzhak Yehudah Yehiel of Komarno, Hekhal ha-Berakhah to Beha'alotekha, p. 82a, on Num. 12:16

The heart knows its own predicament, and not all times are alike. Sometimes pain and depression overcome a man so that he is insensitive to the pain of the Shekhinah, and he prays instead for his own pain to be relieved. But the Holy One is merciful to all and will answer even such prayers. His prayers would be more likely to be answered if he prayed for *tikkun* in the supernal Root;[106] that is the preferred way. But if one is so troubled by his own pain that he does not feel the pain above, and yet pretends to pray for the Shekhinah so that his own prayers will be answered quickly, then He Who probes all hearts[107] knows that such a person is really praying for his own benefit, not for the Shekhinah. Hence it is possible that he will be rejected altogether.[108]

---

104. Sanhedrin 46a. See above, selection 21.
105. Cf. R. Yaakov Yosef's *Ben Porat Yosef*, p. 23a, citing the Besht's explanation of "Thou Who didst set me free when I was in distress" (Ps. 4:2) in accordance with the idea expressed here.
106. That is, for the alleviation of the divine pain.
107. God, Who is omniscient, cannot be fooled by pious hypocrisy.
108. Duplicity of this kind invalidates prayer and makes it much worse than ordinary, self-centered prayer.

Therefore, let him pray simply, according to his spiritual level at the time of prayer. If he feels the pain of the Shekhinah, but is especially conscious of his own pain because of his suffering, let him say, "Master of the world, my pain is very great, but nevertheless I feel in my heart the pain above, and I pray for the alleviation of both."

Sometimes a man is in great distress, but is most conscious of the pain above; if so, let him say so explicitly. But the fool who ignores this should only pray for himself, for *he who speaks falsely shall not be established before My eyes* (Ps. 101:7).[109] But even a completely righteous person (zaddik) should not trust in himself, but explicitly say he is praying for both his own pain and the pain of the Shekhinah.[110]

ADDITIONAL NOTES

*1   The difference between the two attitudes is not altogether clear. The way of "all that the Merciful One does is for the good" is apparently an expression of faith that a present *evil* can be reformed into something good. At bottom, it recognizes that despite its original goodness (before the permutations because of the accusers), and despite the possibility of being turned to good, it is now, functionally, an evil—and will remain so if man does not summon up the spiritual resources of repentance and faith to transform it. The second way, "this too is for the good," does not recognize the evil as evil, even temporarily. The evil merely *seems* to be evil, because we cannot now foresee the end of the chain of events of which it is a part. This attitude does not include the *sine qua non* conditions of repentance and faith. It accepts the event as unpleasant for the time being, but a necessary and *certain* precursor of some greater good. Because it does not grant evil even ephemeral existence, it is considered superior to the first way. There is a practical difference between the two attitudes. The first transforms the evil event to a good one. But the "vestment" in which the evil was enwrapped, i.e., the aftertaste of pain or unpleasantness while experiencing this real though transient evil, remains. In the second and superior attitude, that of Nahum of Gamzu, the seemingly evil event is, in reality, good; nothing evil ever existed, even temporarily, except in the eyes of an unfaithful observer deprived of the proper perspective—and hence no evil residue or impression remains. Both ways, however, conform to an ethical monism which denies the ontological reality of evil.

Alternatively, the first way may view evil as illusory until its goodness is revealed by an act of faith. The second way does not consider the real or illusory nature of evil, but looks at it instrumentally; evil, taken by itself, is evil, but it functions as the harbinger of a good far greater in its goodness than the evil in its evilness. In the end, the

---

109. Better unsophisticated prayer than dishonest presumption.
110. It is not easy to concentrate exclusively on the divine pain, as demanded by the Kabbalah and by Hasidism, because personal suffering is distracting. In order to avoid the danger of dishonesty, even the most righteous and spiritually sophisticated person should forthrightly state that he prays both for himself and for the relief of the divine suffering. Spiritual exercises must never be based on inauthenticity.

evil will be seen as the necessary precursor to a far more potent good. The Besht, in our text, favors the second of the two ways.

*2   All the notes to this passage, which appears in *Zava'at ha-Rivash, Or Torah* of the Maggid, and elsewhere, refer to Zohar I, 49b. I have not been able to find any reference to a symbolic interpretation of *mi-le'el* and *mi-le'ra*, which are grammatical terms indicating, respectively, the accents on the penultimate and ultimate syllables. The only explanation appears in R. Shneur Zalman's *Likkutei Torah* to Deuteronomy, p. 77a. There he quotes our passage in the name of R. Dov Ber, the great Maggid, but the Zohar passage is different; he refers to Zohar II, 163a, where the *yetzer ha-ra* is compared to a harlot hired by a king to test his son, who ingratiates himself with his father by rejecting her advances. The harlot's actions are commendable; she obeyed the king, and because of her the prince now merits his father's royal affections. Similarly, the evil urge is not intrinsically evil; on the contrary, it performs a necessary service. The reference to the grammatical terms comes at the end, when R. Shneur Zalman points out that they are used by the Aramaic translators (Onkelos and Jonathan b. Uziel) to Gen. 1:7 for, respectively, "over" the firmament and "under" it. The significance of the term, according to R. Shneur Zalman, is that the nethermost part is *mi-le'ra* (lit., "from to evil"), not *ra*, evil itself, indicating that it possesses evil only *in potentia* and after a long chain of development.

*3   In Luria's thought, however, they represent various manifestations of permutations of the divine Name (see *Shulḥan Arukh ha-Ari*, Hilkhot Netilat Yadayim, secs. 1 and 4, and Hilkhot Seudot Shabbat, sec. 2) and, as well, symbolize the sefirot Hesed, Tiferet, and Gevurah respectively. (See too *Kedushat Levi*, Beshallah, s.v. "the Or ha-Ḥayyim questions.") Luria's basically theurgic doctrine is here ethicized by R. Levi Yitzhak, who subtly reinterprets the purely mystical interpretation of *netilat yadayim* to imply the concept of sublimation or elevation of the material to the spiritual via holy intention.

*4   There is a notable difference here between Luria and R. Levi Yitzhak. For Luria, the blessing is a mystical, theurgic performance implying the movement out of earth, which he identifies as the sefirah of Binah. (See *Shulḥan Arukh ha-Ari*, Hilkhot Seudot Ḥol, sec. V.)

*5   This passage confirms that R. Nahman of Bratslav stands fully in the mainstream of hasidic thought on this issue, in contradistinction to the thesis of the late Joseph Weiss (*Meḥkarim be-Ḥasidut Bratslav*, pp. 90–91), who purported to have discovered a parting of the ways between the mystical-panentheistic schools of the Great Maggid and Habad on one side, and R. Nahman on the other. The former, Weiss maintains, reinterpreted the dualism of Lurianic Kabbalah to yield a monistic theory which denies the reality of evil; the latter followed the Lurianic dualism and considered evil real and autonomous. The present passage, and others like it, refute Weiss's thesis both as to the Bratslaver view of evil and the conception of theism/panentheism. R. Nahman, as mentioned, stands clearly with other hasidic thinkers as a monist on the problem of evil and suffering.

*6   This is an interesting modification of the usual Lurianic and hasidic interpretation, espoused especially by the Great Maggid (see R. Shatz-Uffenheimer, *Hasidism as Mysticism*, chap. 6), that divine commiseration means that one must consciously intend the good of the Shekhinah even while articulating prayers which speak only of human grief and suffering. Our text, quoting the Besht, would seem to imply that one need not intend the pain of the Shekhinah, for every human affliction is *ipso facto* a divine affliction, and petitionary prayer is therefore a prayer for God even if the worshiper does not know it.

*7   The end of the passage, not translated here, is an ingenious numerological analysis of Ps. 136:1 ("Give thanks to the Lord, for He is good, His mercy endureth forever") in which the Besht recapitulates all the foregoing. He relates the major and minor phases, i.e., the states of *gadlut* and *katnut*, to the major and minor ways of calculating the numerical value of the proper divine Name, the Tetragrammaton. Because it is not crucial to the theme and rather abstruse for those uninterested in hasidic and kabbalistic writing, I have omitted this segment from the English text.

Ordinary gematria assigns a value to each letter depending upon its position in the alphabet. *Alef* = 1, *bet* = 2, *gimmel* = 3, and so on. The four letters of the Tetragrammaton yield the sum of 26 (*yod* = 10, *heh* = 5, *vav* = 6, *heh* = 5). Another form of gematria is that of the minor number (*mispar katan*), or condensed gematria, in which all zeroes are canceled out. Thus *yod* = 1 (not 10), and the other numbers remain the same, adding up to 17. At the other end is an expanded, or major, number (*milui*), in which the word includes the sum of each letter as it is written out. Here the name of the tenth letter of the alphabet, *yod*, is written as *yod-vav-dalet* and equals 20 (10 + 6 + 4). If the other three letters of the Name are treated similarly (spelling them with a *yod* instead of an *alef*, i.e., *h* = *heh-yod* and *v* = *vav-yod-vav*), the sum total is 72.

There are two key words in Ps. 136:1, *tov* ("good"), which amounts to 17 in ordinary gematria, the same number as the Name in its minor count, and *ḥesed* ("mercy"), which equals 72, the same as the Name in its major expansion. Like everything else, the Tetragrammaton has its minor and major phrases (*katnut* and *gadlut*), symbolized, respectively, by the numbers 17 and 72.

Hence: If in contemplating life you can penetrate through all its vicissitudes and discover the good (*tov*) in its minor phase, or state of *katnut*, and thank God (perceived as the Tetragrammaton in the minor phase, corresponding to *tov* in its minor form, both being equal to 17), then you will be privileged to have God and His mercy (*ḥesed*) revealed to you in their major state (*gadlut*), each symbolized by the number 72.

16

Life and Death

From the perspective of everyday biological reality, life and death are well-understood phenomena. The healthy organism values life and strives to conserve it; by the same token death is ordinarily something to be loathed. Religious thought both confirms these common attitudes and transcends them. The hasidic texts presented here recognize the ordinary man's outlook and affirm much of the morality based on it, e.g., the abhorrence of acts which destroy human life in this world (see selection 11).

At the same time, hasidic writers, no less than their predecessors, stressed that life and death are not to be interpreted as simple physical categories; true life is the life of the spirit, true death is alienation from the life of the spirit. Several of the selections below are devoted to the spiritual redefinition of life and death. This idea is frequently formulated in conventional religious terms: if life is good, then the kind of life that is not a blessing, because it is cut off from the good, partakes of death.

In addition to formulating the true value of life and death, hasidic texts also educate the reader's thinking about the consciousness and anticipation of pain connected with the prospect of death. Though pain is justified as a necessary means to atonement, it is also possible to overcome the consequences of sin by intensifying one's life, e.g., by studying Torah (see selection 8).

Given the nature of this world, death is necessary. Because death, in itself, need not be a punishment, but a transition to a more spiritual existence, it is not truly painful for one properly prepared. To the contrary, it can be viewed as the final act of a blessed life. This can be illustrated by reference to the custom of certain saintly individuals who calmly washed their hands before dying, as one would in preparation for any other religious ritual.[1] A more dramatic story tells of a Kotzker hasid on his deathbed, surrounded by his grieving family. He opened his eyes and asked for some spirits to drink le-ḥayyim. They thought he had taken leave of his senses, but he explained to them that whenever a hasid betakes himself to perform God's will, he does so with joy at the opportunity to do a mitzvah. "If God has willed my death," he said, "I am now performing His will. And it is proper to do so in a joyous spirit!" A similar story is recounted by R. Abraham Isaac Kook about his ancestor, R. Isaac Katz, who was one of the early hasidim to rally to the Besht. As he lay dying, R. Isaac reproached the disciples and relatives who surrounded his bed, their faces drawn and glum: "Is it not written, *and she laughs at the last day* (Prov. 31:25)? We must be happy when the soul departs from the body and rises upward." He requested that candles be lit in the Sabbath candelabrum, and that musicians play their instruments and sing to accompany his soul on its joyful journey.[2]

R. Zevi Elimelekh Shapiro of Dinov well expressed the "duty" of dying by way of a homiletic exegesis of God's injunction to Adam. The father of the human race was commanded not to eat of the tree of the knowledge of good and evil; furthermore, he was told that on the day he ate of the tree, he must surely die (Gen. 2:17). This was not merely a prediction; it was also a commandment. Mankind, having transgressed the prohibition, must now fulfill the positive injunction and die. If that is the case, then the Jew must invest his dying with a religious intent (*kavvanah*), even as one does in fulfilling any other positive commandment.[3]

The basic themes of life and death, the spiritually elevating character of the former and loving acquiescence in the latter, are common to Hasidism and "perennial" Jewish literature. Yet, as the examples

---

1. The custom is recorded in *Bet Leḥem Yehudah* to Yoreh De'ah 338:1, and attributed to *Sefer Terumot*. The explanation that death is treated as a mitzvah because it is the will of God was provided orally by R. Yehoshua Baumol.
2. Moshe Zevi Neriyah, *Mo'adei ha-Reiyah*, p. 523.
3. *Derekh Edotekhah* to Joshua, s.v. *ve-od yesh lomar*.

cited above and the selections in this chapter indicate, hasidic writing and tradition often bring to these ideas a special zest and profundity.

1. ATTAINING LIFE THROUGH THE ZADDIK
Source: R. Yaakov Yosef of Polennoye, Toledot Yaakov Yosef to Noah 2

I have taken heaven and earth as witness against you, life and death I have placed before you, the blessing and the curse; therefore choose life that you may live, you and your children (Deut. 30:19).

I have taken as witness; I warn you of the need for unity between *heaven,* [symbolizing] scholars, and *earth,* [symbolizing] the multitude of [ordinary] people, so that each can reciprocally influence the other, [as Scripture puts it,] *Mercy and truth are met together* (Ps. 85:11).

The *life and death* that *I have placed before you* are themselves *the blessing and the curse.* For if you cleave to a scholar who is a zaddik, who is called *ḥai* ("living"),[4] then you are actually connected with [the source of] life, which is God [Himself]. As it is written, *But you who cleave to the Lord your God are alive every one of you this day* (Deut. 4:4).

Conversely, if you cleave to the wicked, who are called dead,[5] you are joined with death. Just as life encompasses blessings of all kinds, as Maimonides writes in his *Commentary on the Mishnah* (Rosh ha-Shanah, chap. 1) . . . concerning the three books [of life and death] that are opened on Rosh Hashanah, similarly, death encompasses curses of all kinds. Consequently, *life and death* are themselves *the blessing and the curse. Therefore choose life,* by cleaving to the zaddik, *so that you may live, you and your children,* etc. [That is why the Talmud teaches:] "He who loves scholars will have children who are scholars" (Shabbat 23b); i.e., he will have scholarly children, zaddikim, who are called living. Thus, it properly follows that, *so that you may live, you and your children.*[6]

---

4. "The righteous (*zaddikim*) [even] in death are called living" (Berakhot 18a).
5. "The wicked [even] while living are called dead" (Berakhot 18b).
6. The exegetical argument proceeds by a series of equivalencies or correspondences. By cleaving to the zaddik, symbol of life, one joins the plenitude of blessings which are synonymous with life. And since one who loves the scholar-zaddik merits children who are scholars-zaddikim, the gift of life passes over to the second generation. The way to the gift of life for oneself and one's family, therefore, is through intimate association with a zaddik.

2. LIFE IN DEPTH
Source: R. Dov Ber of Mezeritch, Maggid Devarav le-Yaakov, no. 189

I shall not die, but live, and declare the works of the Lord (Ps. 118:17).

This can be understood in light of the Zohar's statement that "any prayer or word of Torah which is not issued in fear and love [of God], from the depth of the heart, [does not ascend heavenward]."[7] He who utters, heaven forbid, words of Torah or prayer without fear and love, meaning pure and refined thought with understanding of the heart, is called dead even during his lifetime.[8] The reason is that he has no part in the *Y-H* name of God, the two letters of which correspond, as we know, to the sefirot of Hokhmah and Binah; and it is written, *The dead praise not the Lord (Y-H)* (Ps. 115:17).[9]

This, then, is the prayer of David: *I will not die, but live,* meaning that I should not be considered dead, heaven forbid, but rather I [should] be [considered] amongst those who purify their thoughts and conceptions, and who speak from the depths of the heart. Then [I will] *declare (asapper) the works of the Lord.* The word *asapper* ("I will declare") is related to *sefirah* ("brightness"), implying, "I will illuminate the works of *Y-H*," the latter symbolizing Hokhmah and Binah, the sources of all divine grace (*shefa*), and through them I will brighten and illuminate all the worlds."[10]

3. WHY DESIRE LIFE?
Source: R. Ze'ev Wolf of Zhitomir, Or ha-Meir, sermon for Passover

Who is the man who desires life and loves days that he may see the good therein? (Ps. 34:13).

The intent of this verse is to refute our many fellow Jews whose sole goal in their quest for length of days and years is to fill their houses with gold and silver, and who deny themselves no pleasure. In truth, their days are brief, not lengthy. Of what use is [such a] life to

---

7. *Tikkunei Zohar* 10.
8. Berakhot 18b.
9. Those who do not praise the Lord with proper fear and love fail, in effect, to invoke Hokhmah and Binah, the sefirotic equivalents of these experiential dimensions, which are symbolized by the letters Y and H. The verse states that "the dead praise not Y-H"; hence those devoid of love and fear in their service of the Lord are considered dead.
10. The play on words, *a-s-p-r* to *s-p-r-h*, may be connected to the attempt of some kabbalists to connect *sefirah* to *sappir* ("sapphire").

them? Did God go to all the trouble of creating man and breathing *the breath of life* (Gen. 2:7) into him in order to bestow vain affluence upon him? It were better that they be as the stillborn, buried in the earth, and never having gazed upon the sun![11]

Such is the case with one who has been touched by the fear of God, whose entire purpose and desire in asking for length of days and years is in order to be privileged thereby to perceive and be sensible of the light of His goodness, which is revealed [progressively] every day, disclosing each day the spiritual uniqueness specific to it.

It is to this which King David alluded [in our verse]: *Who is the God-fearing man that desires life,* and for whom it is truly fitting that he desire life? He who *loves days that he may see goodness therein,* i.e., one who does not desire length of days [in themselves, for material pleasure and gratification,] but [seeks] by means [of longevity] to perceive the hidden goodness, as discussed above. This excludes those who walk in darkness, devoid of light; such people do not really desire [spiritual] life at all.

4. LIFE AND CHARACTER
Source: R. Yaakov Yosef of Polennoye, Toledot Yaakov Yosef to Bereshit, sec. 2

And Jacob lived, etc. *And the time drew near that Israel must die* (Gen. 47:28–29).

The name Israel is superior to the name Jacob, as stated in the Talmud on the verse *Declare unto My people their transgression, and to the house of Jacob their sins* (Isa. 58:1).[12] But if so, why was he called Jacob while still alive, but in death he was called Israel?[13] The other way around would seem reasonable.

The answer is that [Jacob] indicates lowliness and [the level of the] heel,[14] and it is for this very reason that [according to our verse] he is connected in life to Him, blessed be His Name. But this does not apply in the case of Israel, which implies high station, *For you have striven,*

---

11. Alluding to Pss. 58:9 and 16:3.
12. Bava Metzia 33b. The Talmud, in this passage, is actually addressing itself only to one of the two names, identifying "My people" with the scholars, and "Jacob" with the ignorant multitude. However, the superior connotation of "Israel" is well known and widely quoted in the commentaries.
13. This is implied in the text: "And *Jacob* lived. . . . *Israel must* die."
14. Yaakov, the Hebrew form of Jacob, includes the three letters that make up *ekev* ("heel"). This is the etymology Scripture gives for his name (see Gen. 25:26).

etc. (Gen. 32:28),[15] and this leads to haughtiness, as the Zohar states on the verse *When a ruler sinneth* (Lev. 4:22).[16] [Scripture says *when a ruler sinneth* as if it were certain that he would do so,] and does not use the [conditional word] "if," as is to be found in the other instances, for [in the case of a ruler] there is no doubt [but that he will succumb to haughtiness].[17] God does not abide with those who are arrogant, [for God says] "that I and he cannot abide in one world."[18] And one who is far from God is far from life and close to death.

5. LIFE AND DEATH ON FOUR LEVELS
Source: R. Levi Yitzhak of Berdichev, Kedushat Levi to Emor, s.v. emor

There are four worlds: Emanation, Creation, Formation, and Action.[19] Each of them possesses the quality of life and its opposite, heaven forbid. [Thus,] in the world of Action (*Asiyah*) we see that there is life and its opposite,[20] heaven forbid. Similarly, in the world of Formation (*Yetzirah*), which [corresponds to] speech, when a person speaks of vain matters, it is the opposite [of life], and when a man speaks suitable words, relating to Torah and the mitzvot and the service of the Creator, blessed be He, it is called the category of life. This is alluded to in the verse *Death and life are in the power of the tongue* (Prov. 18:21). It is a major principle in the service of God that man should be careful about what he says. In the world of Creation (*Beriah*), too, which [corresponds to the realm] of thought, there are categories of life, as when man thinks constantly about serving God; this is referred to as "life." And, heaven forbid, the opposite, etc. And the world above

---

15. The name *Yisrael* (Israel) is etymologically related, in this verse, to *sarita*, "you strived" with God. Hence it connotes lordship.

16. Zohar III, 23a.

17. Preceding the rules for the sin-offering of the *nasi*, or ruler, the Torah prescribes the sacrifices "*if* anyone shall sin" (Lev. 4:2), "*if* the whole congregation of Israel shall err (v. 13), and "*if* any one of the common people sin through error" (v. 27). Only the ruler's sin is introduced with *asher* ("when"), implying the probability or certainty that high station leads to the sin of pride.

18. Sotah 5a.

19. The Kabbalah posits a hierarchy of four worlds which mediate between the Ein-Sof and our mundane world (which, for R. Levi Yitzhak, is identical with *Asiyah* ["Action"]). In descending order they are Emanation, Creation, Formation, and Action. These four states correspond, respectively, to faith, in which man loses his sense of separate existence in the presence of God; thought; speech; and action.

20. Note the reluctance to use the word "death," and, instead, the euphemistic "the opposite [of life]."

these, [*Atzilut,*] which is the world of piety, wherein man experiences the nullification of his existence, life and its very opposite exist.

6. DEATH IN LIFE, AND LIFE IN DEATH
Source: R. Israel of Koznitz, Avodat Yisrael to Vayishlaḥ, s.v. va-yomer

"R. Simeon b. Abba declared: `Because You renew us every morning, we know that Your trustworthiness is great [and You will] resurrect the dead.'"[21]

R. Simeon's opinion can be explained in light of the opinion of the philosophers and the kabbalists on the resurrection of the dead, namely, that death does not mean that the individual dies completely and is later [at the resurrection] re-created as a new being, but that even when a man dies there remains within him some trace and impression of life upon which, in the time-to-come, the blessing of the resurrection can fall. The Midrash teaches that there is a bone in man called *luz* that never decays, and from which [at the time of resurrection] he will be re-created and restored as he was.[22]

We can bring further proof of this from the words of our Sages, who describe sleep as one-sixtieth of death.[23] Now, you may point out that at death all of a person's vital spirit departs from him, leaving nothing [of life], [and on this basis ask] how our Sages could compare sleep to death, estimating it about one part in sixty. In sleep at least some small measure of life remains [you might argue], whereas death is complete [in that there is no vitality whatsoever], in which case sleep and death are wholly different, and the analogy [between them] is invalid, asserting, as it does, that a living person [while asleep] is in a state that is one-sixtieth the condition of one completely dead. Therefore we are compelled to say, as above, that even in death there remains some measure of life enabling the deceased to rise again in the time-to-come when the Creator will wish to resurrect him. However, this vitality is very limited in quantity, and the Sages estimated the degree of diminished vitality to be one-sixtieth the measure of life possessed by one in a state of slumber, and inversely, the sleep of a living person is considered to be one-sixtieth of the state of death. Viewed in

---

21. Genesis Rabbah 78:1.
22. Genesis Rabbah 28:3. R. Israel takes the midrashic teaching about the bone as indicating that a trace of vitality continues after death and, like the *luz* bone, will be the source of man's resurrection.
23. Berakhot 57b.

this manner, the comparison is valid: in a sleeping person the ratio is sixty measures of life to one of death, and the reverse pertains to a dead person, for there the ratio is sixty measures of death to one of life. *The words of the wise are as our goads* (Eccl. 12:11) and contain hidden mysteries.

We can now understand the words of R. Simeon bar Abba cited above: "Because You renew us every morning," by virtue of our awakening from sleep [every day], we know "that Your trustworthiness is great, [and You will] resurrect the dead," for similarly in death there remains a trace of life, even as the bone called *luz* exists in [a corpse], as stated above.

7. HOW TO DIE ON FRIDAY
Source: R. Yitzhak Yehudah Yehiel of Komarno, Zohar Ḥai, p. 182

Our master R. Israel Baal Shem Tov commented on the passage, "He who passes away on the eve of the Sabbath is spared the body's tribulations in the grave (*ḥibbut ha-kever*)."[24] Although this is undoubtedly true, my master asked: Certainly the Talmud intends to advise us on how to be spared the body's tribulations in the grave. If so, what is this passage telling us, for it is not within a man's power to [ensure that he will] die on the eve of the Sabbath?

He answered that it contains a great ethical teaching: that a person should bring himself to death [lit. kill himself][25] in this world, which is [described as] "the eve of Sabbath,"[26] as is well known. He should [be willing to] endure failure, humiliation, distress, and suffering in love in order to prepare for the Sabbath (the world-to-come). Thus will he be rescued from the body's anguish in the grave. Such persons depart from this world during their lives, achieving *tikkun* by means of dust: "May my soul be lowly to all as the dust."[27] By virtue of eternal life,

---

24. Ketubbot 103b. The Talmud states of one who expires on the eve of the Sabbath, "it is good for him."

25. This term occurs, *inter alia*, in Berakhot 63b, "Resh Lakish said, '. . . the words of the Torah are firmly held by one who kills himself for it.'" It denotes willingness to suffer and sacrifice unto death for Torah, in the sense of expending one's vigor and strength on it. See *Torah Temimah* to Num. 19:14.

26. Avodah Zarah 3a, "He who has labored on the eve of Sabbath shall eat on the Sabbath," referring to labors in this world meriting reward in the next world.

27. By embracing suffering and meekness—in the words of Mar son of Ravina (Berakhot 17a, and universally recited at the end of the three daily Amidah prayers), "May my soul be silent to those who insult me; may my soul be lowly to all as the dust"—man achieves his *tikkun*. Even while physically alive, he is vicariously dead ("one who dwells in the dust") because he was "lowly to all as the dust."

[such a person] dies to this world, for he has "brought himself to death" in [his service of] Torah and prayer.

Afterwards, after his mortal span of days is completed, and he actually [physically] dies, his death is far more praiseworthy than the deaths of everyone else in the world. But you might say, won't they be judged in the world-to-come?[28] No [they won't], for it is written, *Trouble shall not rise up the second time* (Nah. 1:9) [so they will not be judged twice], because they have [already] endured punishment and suffering in this world.

Thus, [a person acting in this manner] has most certainly perished on the eve of the Sabbath, having brought himself to death in the study of Torah for its own sake, and his place is wholly prepared with surpassing praise.[29]

8. DEATH AS THE WAY TO LIFE
Source: R. Zadok ha-Kohen of Lublin, Zidkat ha-Zaddik, no. 123

Our Sages state of certain individuals that they have incurred the death penalty [for their transgressions].[30] The words of our Sages are most certainly motivated by mercy for all creatures and aim to bring goodness and life to the world. When they declare that a person deserves a certain punishment, they really mean to say that he achieves atonement thereby. As the Talmud says concerning those condemned to capital punishment by the court, their death is their atonement.[31] For our Sages saw that it was difficult to atone [for certain transgressions], so they derived the appropriate punishment from a biblical verse; consequently, this specific punishment is the means for atonement.[32] Were it not so, why should he be punished? For we

---

28. In which case, their willing sacrifice in this world was in vain.

29. Probably to be understood in a double sense: his physical remains will not experience the anguish of the grave, and the soul has a place in readiness in the world-to-come without having to undergo judgment.

30. The passage is addressed to the sin of spilling seed in vain. The Talmud declares that one who is guilty of wasting semen is deserving of death (Niddah 13b). R. Zadok is concerned with this and many similar statements wherein the Sages declare a variety of acts deserving of death, though there may be no explicit scriptural warrant for the harsh judgment.

31. Sanhedrin 47b.

32. That is, the Sages interpreted the Torah so as to derive, morally, not legally, the punishments appropriate to various specific sins, and these punishments (which, as we shall see, may be spiritualized) expiate the sins in question.

know that punishment is meant only as a means of atoning. Therefore, because of this sin,[33] it may be decreed that one will be childless, or any other of the four things considered equivalent to death as stated in the Talmud.[34]

However, by [studying] Torah, "bringing oneself to death" for the sake of Torah[35]—for this too is called death, as our Rabbis said in their comment on the verse *This is the law, when a man dieth in a tent* (Numbers 19:14)[36]—one's sin is forgiven, for this [vigorous study of Torah] is the equivalent of death.[37] (Therefore the Talmud says, "What shall man do that he may live? He should bring himself to death.")[38] Torah is called the Tree of Life, as our Sages taught,[39] and death is called *the way of the earth*, as it is written [that Joshua said just before he died]: *And, behold, this day I am going the way of all the earth* (Josh. 23:14). Therefore death is the way to reach eternal life.

9. DEATH WITH A KISS
Source: *R. Levi Yitzhak of Berdichev, Kedushat Levi, Likkutim, p. 107, s.v. leva'er*

Let us explain the concept of death by means of the [divine] kiss.[40]

Our Sages said: "R. Abbahu gazed upon thirteen rivers of fragrant scent."[41] That is, before his death he was shown the reward he would receive in the time-to-come for his service of the Lord. So it is with all the righteous: before death they are led [into the world-to-come], and their great reward is revealed to them. Then, because of their great love and yearning for this reward, they remain there alive, not desir-

---

33. In this case, the spilling of seed.
34. Avodah Zarah 5a. The other three are poverty, blindness, and leprosy.
35. See above, n. 25.
36. Berakhot 63a.
37. Readiness to sacrifice one's vigor and vitality for Torah—to bring oneself to death over Torah—is a symbolic equivalent of death sufficient to atone for those sins which the Rabbis (speaking hyperbolically) considered deserving of death.
38. Tamid 32a.
39. *Tanna de-bei Eliyahu Rabbah* 1.
40. The concept of death by a kiss is applied by the Talmud to Moses, Aaron, Miriam, and, by implication, the patriarchs (Bava Batra 17a and elsewhere). It was later expanded to include other deserving righteous people.
41. Genesis Rabbah 62:1; Midrash Tanhuma, Bereshit 1. The incident of R. Abbahu is a midrashic illustration of the general rule that "when the righteous are about to die, the Holy One shows them their [future] reward." When R. Abbahu was shown his unexpected reward, he could hardly believe it and yearned for death.

ing to return to the world. How right the Sages were when they said, "The righteous [even] in death are called living,"[42] by which they meant that when the righteous are about to die, they are called [to the other world] to be shown their great reward. Why is this so? In order to make them remain there while yet alive, as they are in this world.

This is what is meant by death by a kiss, for those who know the hidden wisdom in esoteric matters (i.e., initiates into Kabbalah). Therefore, it cannot be said of [the righteous] that they died in this world; their death is primarily in the world-to-come, when the magnitude of their reward is revealed to them [and they do not desire to return to the realm of human existence].[43]

10. THE NATURE OF REWARD IN THE AFTERLIFE
Source: R. Levi Yitzhak of Berdichev, Kedushat Levi, Likkutim, pp. 107a–b, s.v. leva'er

The Zohar and the Midrash ha-Ne'elam teach: What is the reward of the righteous? Certainly it is not what most people think, that in the world-to-come the righteous are placed upon an exalted and lofty throne. The zaddik derives neither entertainment nor pleasure from such things. For he desired no pleasures in this world, but instead chose to serve the Lord.[44] The Zohar and Midrash ha-Ne'elam cite the parable of the man who for a long time tried hard to understand some subject, its essence and nature. After [continuing to] investigate and research it, he succeeds in discovering the truth of the subject.[45] There is no greater pleasure than [what he feels when] God gives him the reason and intelligence to discover that for which he has expended so much time and effort.

So it is with the zaddik. All his life in the world is spent in the pursuit of learning the essence of how to serve the Lord. Daily his mind

---

42. Berakhot 18a. See Additional Note *1.

43. R. Levi Yitzhak offers a novel interpretation of death by a kiss. It is a death that blurs the discontinuity between life and afterlife. For most people, death is a sharp end to a this-worldly existence, after which the soul enters the afterlife. For the righteous, however, physical death occurs *after* they are introduced to the delights of the spiritual realm. Hence the startling statement that for a zaddik or righteous person, death takes place not in this world but in the next.

44. Since the zaddik abjures the pleasures of this world, we may deduce that he is equally uninterested in the spiritual pleasures of the other world. His service of the Lord is completely selfless.

45. See, for example, Midrash ha-Ne'elam in Zohar I 125b.

turns to it, but he is unable to comprehend it adequately in this world. In the world-to-come, however, he achieves a fundamental understanding of how to serve the Creator, as our Sages said: "In the world-to-come there is neither eating nor drinking; but the righteous sit with diadems upon their heads and derive pleasure from the radiance of the Shekhinah."[46] No pleasure is greater than this, and it is the primary reward in the future world. For the fundamental desire and heart's yearning of the zaddik is to apprehend now [in the other world] that which was inaccessible to him from the day of his birth till the present time.

11. THE CONSEQUENCES OF MURDER
Source: R. Zevi Elimelekh of Dinov, Derekh Pekudekha, negative commandment 34[47]

In refraining [from murder], be sure to bear in mind that you do so because of your Creator's commandment, and not because of fear of the government or of other people, as has been explained several times.

The Torah states, among the Noahide commandments: *For in the image of God made He man* (Gen. 9:6). There is a simple reason why God permitted the slaying of animals, beasts, and birds that man requires for his personal needs, whereas it is prohibited to shed human blood: *For in the image of God*, etc. It is unnecessary to elaborate reasons [for this commandment], because it is one of the rational commandments, to which reason obligates us because [on it] depends the survival of humankind. *For in the image of God made He man*—to be His servants and do His will; hence the murderer is one who kills a servant of the King, and prevents him from begetting other servants who will serve Him. Therefore "he is answerable for the blood [of the victim] and the blood of his [unborn] descendants."[48] Moreover, the soul has no peace when it leaves the body before its time, unable to come unto

---

46. Berakhot 17a. R. Levi Yitzhak's point is not merely that the rewards of the righteous are not material (that, after all, is a commonplace and is explicit in this talmudic passage), but that the zaddik's delight in the radiance of the Shekhinah is his sense of fulfillment, in the afterlife, of a profound, arduous, and lifelong spiritual quest in this world.
47. *Derekh Pekudekha* is a commentary on the 613 commandments. The book is divided into positive and negative commandments, and each mitzvah is treated on three planes, as action, speech, and thought. This selection is from the "thought" commentary on "Thou shalt not murder," secs. 1—3.
48. Mishnah Sanhedrin 4:5.

its proper place. That is why our Sages call [murder] "the spilling of bloods" (*shofekh damim*, plural), implying two [spillings of blood], the victim's and his descendants'.[49] The plural, *damim*, also refers to body and soul, for the soul [of the victim] has no peace.[50] *Damim* further implies that [the murderer] causes the shedding of his own blood, for it is inevitable that his own blood will be shed too, whether by human courts or by the heavenly Court.[51] *No expiation can be made for the land for the blood that is shed therein, but by the blood of him that shed it* (Num. 35:33). Although the four forms of capital punishment are no longer in effect,[52] the law concerning them still holds, as our Rabbis said.[53]

If you meditate upon the holy words of our master the Ari [= R. Isaac Luria], of blessed memory, you will understand, from the exalted heights from which his words issue, that *the blood is the life* (Deut. 12:23), [in the blood inheres the] man's vitality. The power of the Master (*Aluf*) of the World to sustain all life is vested in the blood, and when the letter *alef*, symbolizing the *Aluf* of the World, is connected to the blood (*dam*), man (*adam*) emerges.[54] The murderer [by shedding his victim's blood] separates out the *alef* (= *Aluf*). That is why *Thou shalt not murder* was placed on the second tablet [as the first of the second half of the Ten Commandments], corresponding to *I am the Lord thy God* on the first tablet, because the murderer removes, as it were, the vital power of *I am the Lord thy God*.[55]

12. LIFE AFTER DEATH THROUGH LOVE
Source: *R. Shneur Zalman of Liady, Tanya, Iggeret ha-Kodesh, chap. 27*

[An explanation of] the saying of our Sages that "he has bequeathed life unto all the living."[56] *The righteous liveth by his faith* (Hab. 2:4), and

---

49. Ibid.
50. As R. Zevi Elimelekh previously stated.
51. Every act of murder involves the shedding of the victim's blood and, eventually, the murderer's.
52. The four forms of execution, described in Mishnah Sanhedrin, fell into disuse shortly before the destruction of the Temple in 70 C.E. If a criminal is not executed by the courts, he will nevertheless not escape punishment at the hands of heaven, for his guilt is not diminished by the powerlessness of human agencies to punish him.
53. Ketubbot 30a.
54. The *alef* (a) plus the two Hebrew letters for blood, *d-m*, yields *a-d-m* (Adam), the word for "man."
55. By removing the *alef-Aluf* from man.
56. Berakhot 61b. A euphemism for death frequently found in the later rabbinic literature. This passage is part of a letter of consolation to the hasidim of R. Menahem

by *the fear of the Lord* [which] *tendeth to life* (Prov. 19:23), and by the flashes of the fire of the flame of his love [for God, which is] greater than life, to absorb therein the life of his *ruah*[57] for all the days of his existence.[58] And when it comes about that the Lord takes up his *ruah* and *neshamah*, gathering them unto Himself, and he ascends from one elevation to another to the peak of levels, he then bequeaths the life of his *ruah*, for which he had labored previously in Israel, the life that is the reward of the righteous,[59] to every living being. That is, [he leaves it to] the souls of every living being bound to his soul by a thick rope of an everlasting, irremovable, magnanimous, and eternal love.[60] For the man who loves life [and wishes] to be attached to the living Lord and have his soul cleave to the service [of God, his soul] will be *bound up in the bundle of life* with the Lord (1 Sam. 25:29) in the life of *the breath (ruah) of our nostrils . . . of whom we said: In his shadow (tzel) we shall live among the nations* (Lam. 4:20).[61] [This] he left unto us, in each and every one corresponding to the degree of his genuine involvement and pure love of truth from his very innards and from the depths of his heart. For *as in water face answereth to face* (Prov. 27:19), "spirit *(ruah)* rouses spirit, and brings forth spirit."[62] Thus his *ruah* remains truly in our midst, when he sees his children, the work of his hands,

---

Mendel of Vitebsk, who died in 1788. Both R. Menahem Mendel and R. Shneur Zalman were students of the Great Maggid, and after his death R. Shneur Zalman considered R. Menahem Mendel his master.

57. The Kabbalah posits five levels of the human soul: in ascending order, *nefesh* ("soul"), *ruah* ("spirit"), *neshamah* ("pneuma"), *hayah* ("anima"), and *yehidah* ("psyche"; often called "the pneuma of the pneuma"). *Nefesh* normally refers to physical vitality, *ruah* to emotional-intellectual existence, and *neshamah* to the spiritual dimension which links man with the transcendent. The other two are usually considered too esoteric for ordinary theological discourse. The souls are not completely separate entities, but are linked to each other.

58. During his lifetime on earth, the righteous man strives to merit the life of *ruah* (and, according to another version of the text, of *neshamah* as well), and not to remain on the level of *nefesh*.

59. Paraphrase of Prov. 10:16.

60. When a righteous person dies, he leaves some aspect of his *ruah* to those whom he loved. On *ahavah rabbah* ("magnanimous love") and *ahavat olam* ("eternal love"), see Zohar III, 263b and chap. 4 above, selections 23–24.

61. See Additional Note*2.

62. Zohar II, 162b. Genuine friendship and love create a relationship in which the *ruah* of one evokes the *ruah* of the other.

in his midst, sanctifying His blessed Name.[63] For [God's Name] is magnified and sanctified[64] when we walk in the right way that He has shown us of His ways, and we walk in His path forevermore.

The holy Zohar states that when the zaddik departs he is more present in all the worlds than in his lifetime.[65] . . . This has to be understood. Granted that he is to be found increasingly in the upper worlds, because he ascends there; but how can he be found more in this world?

The explanation is along the lines of what I heard about the saying of our Sages that "He has bequeathed life unto all the living."[66]

As is known, the life of a zaddik is not a physical life but a spiritual life, consisting of faith, awe, and love. Of faith it is written, *And the righteous (zaddik) liveth by his faith* (Hab. 2:4). Of awe it is written, *And the fear* [awe] *of the Lord tendeth to life* (Prov. 19:23). And of love it is written, *He that followeth after righteousness and mercy (ḥesed) findeth life* (Prov. 21:21), and ḥesed is synonymous with "love."

These three attributes are prevalent in every world up to the highest, all proportionate to the levels of the worlds—one higher than the other, by way of cause and effect, as it is known. While the zaddik was alive on earth, these three attributes were contained in their vessel and garment in the physical-spatial realm. This is the aspect of the *nefesh* bound to his body. All his disciples receive, by a glimmer of these attributes, a ray that illuminates beyond the vessel by means of his holy utterances and thoughts. That is why our Sages said that a person cannot comprehend his master [until forty years have passed], etc.[67] But after his passing, as the *nefesh* [which remains in the grave][68] is separated from the *ruaḥ*, which is in the Garden of Eden, whoever is close to him can receive a part of his *ruaḥ*, i.e., these three attributes,[69] which is in the Garden of Eden. [This is] because it is no [longer] in a vessel or in physical spatial realm. [In a similar way we may

---

63. Paraphrase of Isa. 29:23. Disciples are regarded as their master's children and the "work of his hand." See Sanhedrin 19b and 99b.
64. The language is that of the Kaddish, "May His great Name be magnified and sanctified."
65. Zohar III, 71b.
66. The verse expounded in the first half of this selection.
67. Rashi on Deut. 29:6; Avodah Zarah 5b. Only a radiation and a mere ray are apprehended.
68. The *nefesh*, as a vitalizing principle of the body, does not survive death.
69. The three attributes of faith, awe, and love survive in their *ruaḥ* form. This clause has been brought down from above in order to make the syntax clearer.

understand] the saying of our Sages with reference to our father Jacob, that "the Garden of Eden entered with him."[70] Likewise, it is stated in the book *Asarah Ma'amarot*[71] that the sphere of the Garden of Eden spreads itself around every person, and in it are recorded all his good thoughts and utterances of Torah and divine worship.[72] (And likewise to the contrary, heaven forbid, [impure thoughts and utterances] are recorded in the sphere of Gehenna, which spreads itself around everyone.) Thus it is very easy for his disciples to receive their part of the essential aspects of their master's *ruah*, i.e., his faith, his awe, and his love, wherewith he served the Lord, and not merely a glimmer thereof which radiates beyond the vessel. For the essential aspect of his *ruah* is raised, elevation upon elevation, to become absorbed in his *neshamah*, which is in the Upper Garden of Eden,[73] in the supreme world.

Something sacred is never wholly and totally uprooted from its place and original level, even after it has been elevated ever so high. Its original aspect—remaining below, in the Lower Garden of Eden, in its place and original level—extends itself among his disciples, each one according to the level of his involvement with and closeness to [the zaddik] during his lifetime and after his death, out of a magnanimous love.[74]

13. LIFE AND DEATH COMMINGLED
Source: R. Levi Yitzhak of Berdichev, Kedushat Levi to Shelah, s.v. ve-ulam

By means of our free will, choosing the good and abhorring evil, and fulfilling the will of God in the study of Torah, observing its com-

---

70. When he came to his father Isaac for the blessings. That is, Jacob entered his father's presence in a state of spiritual elation in which his *ruah* (his qualities of faith, awe, and love) was activated. Genesis Rabbah 65:22; Midrash Tanhuma, Toledot 10.
71. By the kabbalist and talmudic scholar R. Menahem Azariah da Fano (1548–1620), sec. *Hakor Din*, pt. II, chap. 12.
72. The Garden of Eden is a spiritual aura surrounding a person and corresponding with his level of moral and religious achievement.
73. The Upper Garden of Eden is the world of Beriah, and the locus of the zaddik's *neshamah*. His *ruah*, like the *neshamah* of an ordinary person, is generally on a lower level, called the Lower Garden of Eden. See *Tanya*, chap. 39.
74. Even though in one sense the zaddik's *ruah* is absorbed in his *neshamah* after his death and ascends from this mundane realm, in another sense its original presence is preserved and survives with his disciples and loved ones. (The former is the Upper Garden of Eden, the latter, the Lower Garden of Eden.)

mandments and performing good deeds, we connect ourselves to the Source of Life, the Creator, blessed be He and blessed be His Name, Who lives and exists forever. As our Sages declare: "Great are the righteous, for even in death they are called living"[75]—because they attach themselves to the Source of Life by means of their good deeds in Torah and mitzvot. Not so the wicked, who "even while living are called dead"[76]—because they attach themselves to the source of death by means of their evil deeds.

We can now understand what Moses meant when he declared [concerning Korah and his rebellious followers], *If these men died the common death of all men . . . then the Lord hath not sent me. But if the Lord make a new thing, and the ground open her mouth and swallow them up with all that appertain to them, and they go down alive into the grave, then ye shall understand that these men have despised the Lord* (Num. 16:29–30).

At first blush one may ask: Why the specific punishment of descending alive into the grave? The answer is that Korah's complaint concerned the priesthood [in that Korah desired the privileges of priesthood for himself, begrudging Aaron the honor of that exalted post]. He wanted to perform the commandments [related to the priesthood], and therefore attached himself to the Source of Life.[77] However, his intention was unwholesome; he aspired to what was not his,[78] for the Lord had already given the priesthood to Aaron. In effect, he wanted to transgress God's word, and thus [although unaware of his error] he attached himself to the source of death. [Paradoxically] Korah achieved two contradictory things at once: by striving to perform a mitzvah by means of a sin, he attached himself [simultaneously] to the Source of Life and the source of death.

The punishment meted out to Korah corresponded, measure for measure, to his sin; as is well known, "The way a person conducts himself, that is how God deals with him."[79] He descended while still *alive* into the *grave*, which is a punishment of life and death at one and the same time. This is what Moses meant when he said, *they* [shall] *go down alive into the grave*; specifically so, so that everyone would know that the priesthood was Aaron's by virtue of God's having chosen him. How would this come to be known? If they were to descend

---

75. Berakhot 18a.
76. Berakhot 18b.
77. Since the priesthood was a means of serving God, his ultimate goal was virtuous.
78. Lit. "he wanted to wrap himself in a tallit not his own."
79. Sotah 8b, Sanhedrin 100b.

alive into the grave, i.e., if their punishment commingled life and death, it would clearly show everyone that by striving for the priesthood, he had attached himself to the Source of Life; but since the priesthood had already been given by the Lord to Aaron, the performance of this mitzvah [i.e., the priesthood] entailed violating God's word, and thus Korah had attached himself to the source of death. Korah's punishment was set and measured according to his [and his accomplices'] deeds, combining both [opposite] elements. Specifically, *they descended alive into the grave.*

14. WHEN DEATH IS LIFE
Source: R. Levi Yitzhak of Berdichev, Kedushat Levi to Beshallah 38b., s.v. ha-or ha-hayyim

The Rabbis say that the Red Sea did not want to cast out [the Egyptians who had drowned in it] until God hinted to the Sea [to do so].[80] And the holy commentary, the *Or ha-Hayyim* asks: [Why was this necessary?] As commonly observed, the sea does not tolerate a corpse.[81] The reason is that death was [originally caused] by the eating from the Tree of Knowledge, and the sea had no [sinful] pleasure from the fruit [of the Tree of Knowledge]. The earth, however, was cursed because of Cain, as is mentioned in the Torah (Gen. 3:17). But the sea cannot tolerate anything dead [and casts it up to the surface]. A dead object is something that was alive before its death; this the sea will not tolerate. But in the case of the wicked, the opposite is true, because the wicked, even while alive, are called dead, as our Rabbis taught.[82] For them death is an ascent, for when they perish by means of an unnatural death [e.g., the drowning of the Egyptians in the Red Sea], the Name of heaven is sanctified before all mankind. Thus their death was their life.[83] Why shouldn't the sea tolerate them, then, since their death was their life? There can be no sanctification of God's Name greater than the death of the wicked, as in the case of Egypt, for in this way His great and holy Name was magnified, for all now knew that He is the Creator who constantly renews the world's existence [and that the world is constantly subject to divine providence].[84]

---

80. Mekhilta to Exod. 15:12.
81. *Or ha-Hayyim* to Exod. 15:12.
82. Berakhot 18b.
83. This paradoxical statement means that the wicked first find meaning in their lives by perishing, since their death is a sanctification of the Name.
84. The *Or ha-Hayyim's* question is now answered: were it not for the divine hint, the sea would not have cast up the corpses of the Egyptians.

15. DEATH AND DEFILEMENT
Source: R. Levi Yitzhak of Berdichev, Kedushat Levi to Hukkat, s.v. zot ḥukkat

Man's soul and vitality, hewn from under the divine Throne of Glory, always wish to serve the Creator without the slightest interruption. However, man's body does not permit this to happen, and soul and body are continually at war with each other. The individual who is worthy wins a victory over the body and follows the wishes of his soul.

Why is the body unwilling to observe the Torah and the mitzvot? Because the body does not understand the reasons for the Torah and the mitzvot (ta'amei ha-torah ve-ha-mitzvot).[85] For if the body knew the reasons for the Torah and the commandments, it too would willingly observe the mitzvot. The soul, however, hewn from under the divine Throne of Glory, understands the reasons for the commandments and therefore wishes to observe them without the slightest interruption. If a man is worthy, he makes his soul dominate his body, so that he can do and observe the Torah and its mitzvot.[86]

When a person dies and the soul rises upward and the body remains alone, the body defiles.[87] It is for this reason that the burial places of the zaddikim do not cause defilement, for the bodies of the righteous are wholly purified [during their lives], so that the body too desires to fulfill the Torah and its mitzvot. That is why even their bodies do not cause defilement [normally associated with death].[88]

---

85. As employed here, this must be understood in the mystical sense, referring to kabbalistic insights, not the usual rationales, which range from the pedagogical to the historical, and from the anthropological to the theological.

86. The passage, superficially, seems rather ordinary. The body-soul dichotomy is not original with R. Levi Yitzhak or even with Hasidism. In light of the preceding note, however, this passage is not just another pietistic preachment about the soul's superiority over the body, but a polemic for the kabbalistic and against the philosophic version of ta'amei ha-mitzvot.

87. The Halakhah considers corpses the major source of ritual defilement. This defilement had broad social and personal implications during the time of the Temple. For example, a person who had been defiled by physically having touched a corpse or having been under the same roof with one, had to undergo an elaborate ritual of purification before he could participate in any Temple or sacrificial ritual. In our times this law has specific consequences for kohanim (Jews of priestly descent), for they are still obliged to avoid occasions of defilement (e.g, approaching within four cubits of a grave or entering a house where there is a dead body).

88. This statement must be taken in a purely aggadic sense. I know of no instance in which this concept is the basis of a halakhic ruling; but see Tosafot Ketubbot 103b, s.v. oto.

16. A VISION AT THE MOMENT OF DEATH
Source: R. Israel of Koznitz, Avodat Yisrael to Parashat Parah, s.v. ve-shaḥat otah

And he shall slaughter it before him (Num. 19:3). Rashi explains that a *zar* [any non-kohen] slays the red heifer while Elazar [the son of Aaron, the high priest] looks on.

This passage can be interpreted by reference to the view that when the soul leaves the body, a man beholds the Shekhinah [divine countenance]. But only if he has lived righteously; then he is worthy to behold the countenance of the Shekhinah at the time of his demise, and his soul cleaves to it. Thus Scripture instructs, *And he shall slay it before him*, that the stranger slays; the stranger is the Angel of Death. But "Elazar looks on," i.e., the dying person looks on the Presence, symbolized by the name *El-azar* (lit. "God Who helps").

17. DEATH AS LIBERATION
Source: R. Zadok ha-Kohen of Lublin, Kedushat Shabbat, no. 4, pp. 11b–12a, s.v. ve-Yitzḥak yatza

In the same way did the seduction take place in this instance.[89] [The

---

89. This passage is part of a longer discourse in which R. Zadok analyzes Satan's seductive role. The darker forces ("Satan") appeal not to our lower appetites, but to our sense of morality and self-sacrifice for higher ideals. R. Zadok invokes the description in Genesis Rabbah 56:4 of the story of the Akedah—the binding of Isaac by Abraham, who was ready to offer him as a sacrifice (Gen. 22). The Midrash portrays Abraham's inner conflicts. "Samael [Satan] came to Father Abraham and said, 'Old man, old man, you are out of your mind! . . . By tomorrow [after you've killed Isaac] God will tell you that you deserve the punishment of one who sheds blood, for you have shed the blood of your son.' Answered Abraham, 'Nevertheless!'" Abraham, R. Zadok explains, is ready to surrender his life and reputation, but will not violate the divine word. Samael further argued, says R. Zadok, that Abraham was misinterpreting the situation: it was not his obedience to the special divine command that was being tried, but his obedience to the divine prohibition of murder, which as one of the seven Noahide commandments is universally obligatory. Here again Abraham answers, "Nevertheless," and prefers to violate a mitzvah for the sake of God (a concept of considerable importance in hasidic thought). The point is clear: to a moral man, temptation always appears in moral guise. This dynamic of high-minded temptation is now applied to Adam's primeval sin, with the significant difference that Abraham resisted but Adam did not. In the biblical story, the role of Satan-Samael is assumed by the serpent, who attempts to lure Adam and Eve into eating the forbidden fruit of the Tree of Knowledge of Good and Evil (Gen. 3).

serpent] told [Adam] that the intent of the divine command [not to eat of the Tree of Knowledge under pain of death] was to test whether he would choose the good even if he had to die as a result.[90] [The serpent told Adam that] after making this choice [to eat] he would not die. Thus, Adam's transgression was based upon an error.[91] For this reason Adam immediately thereafter heard the voice of *the Lord God walking in the Garden* (Gen. 3:8). God's speaking to him (ibid. 3:9 ff.) implies that Adam attained prophecy, something which could not have happened unless Adam had cleaved to Him with all the powers [of his soul]. Therefore, even after the transgression, he was still completely holy unto God with full depth of heart and mind, for he only possessed [an abstract and detached] *knowledge* of evil.[92] But this already marked the beginning of an opening for the *yetzer ha-ra*, who was later to become a man and then master of the house.[93] At this point it became impossible to separate [the Evil Urge] from him save by death.[94] That is why it was necessary for Adam to be expelled from the Garden of Eden, so that he would not stretch out his hand and partake of the Tree of Life, which would enable him to live forever. [Were he to live forever] he would never achieve the *tikkun* of uprooting the evil [from within him].[95]

---

90. That is, God actually wanted him to eat the forbidden fruit, because it would expand his moral awareness, but Adam's will to achieve this state had to be strong enough for him to risk death for it.

91. Because in yielding to the serpent's arguments, he thought he was performing God's will.

92. In his own mind, Adam had not done an evil act, he had merely obtained the knowledge of good and evil.

93. Referring to an earlier statement by R. Zadok, "This is the way of the Evil Urge: first he is a wayfarer, then he becomes a guest; then a man [i.e., member of the household], and finally master of the household" (based upon a similar passage in Genesis Rabbah 22:15). The *yetzer ha-ra* appears as a fleeting temptation and soon takes over a man's whole life. In the case of Adam, the entree for the Evil Urge was provided by his newfound knowledge of evil.

94. Adam did not die as a punishment for his sin of eating the fruit, for the act was done in error, as R. Zadok previously stated: the deed was wrong, but the intention was pure, and in Jewish law there is no corporal punishment for an unwitting transgression. Rather, death was the only way to save Adam, for it would separate him from the clutches of the Evil Urge.

95. Eternal life dominated by evil is simply an unredeemed life infinitely extended. Without *tikkun*—rectification, here signifying his liberation from the *yetzer ha-ra* and his restoration to his original blemishlessness—life is meaningless. Liberation from evil is achieved through death, making death an act of grace rather than vengeance.

18. THE UNREALITY OF DEATH
Source: R. Zadok ha-Kohen of Lublin, Kedushat Shabbat, no. 7, p. 29b, s.v. uve-Vavel

In truth, Father Jacob did not die, for death derives from the world of falsehood, which dissembles and does not endure.[96] But Jacob is the source of the quality of truth,[97] wherein death cannot exist; as the Talmud states, "In the realm of heaven, there is truth."[98] The knowledge of essential truth is [identical with] the knowledge that "nothing exists other than God."[99] Truth and faith are said to be identical,[100] as it is written, *And thy faith in the night-times* (Ps. 92:3).[101] The perception [of God] is found in this word [*night-times*] in a concealed form [and therefore can be attained only] by means of faith. For Israel are "the faithful, sons of the faithful" [i.e., descended from] Father Abraham, about whom it is written that *he believed in God* (Gen. 15:6). But concerning Jacob there was no need to write that he had faith, for [God's omnipresence] was already clear to him. In his heart, the oneness and perfect unity of God were unqualified, and Jacob cleaved to the living God with truly complete devotion. When the letter *alef*, which refers to God the *Aluf* ("Master") of the universe, is connected to the two-letter word *met* ("death"), there results the word *emet*,[102] which is the negation and nullification of death due to awareness of God's oneness and perfect unity, and that nothing at all exists except Him. Death really has no existence, for it applies only to a created being when it is separated from the Creator so as to become an entity in itself.[103]

---

96. "Father Jacob did not die" (Ta'anit 5b). Scripture says only that "the days [i.e., time] of Israel [Jacob] drew near to die" (Gen. 47:29).
97. In the aggadic tradition, Abraham represents *ḥesed* (love or grace), Isaac symbolized *paḥad* (awe and reverence), and Jacob is the paradigm of *emet* (truth). The Kabbalah took over this symbolism and identified Jacob with both *tiferet* (beauty) and *emet*.
98. And since heaven is deathless, so is truth. By the same token, Jacob = truth = deathless.
99. Habad Hasidism's interpretation of Deut. 4:35, *ein od mi-levado*.
100. *Ra'ya Mehemna*, Pinhas, Zohar III, 230a.
101. The prooftext from Psalms will become evident in the sentences following: truth is seen as faith at night; one who cannot perceive truth in its fullness takes it on faith, but the content remains the same.
102. *Met* is spelled *mem-tav; emet* ("truth") is spelled *alef-mem-tav*.
103. Since death occurs only to the ephemeral, it is really an illusion. When someone cleaves to God by acknowledging His absolute unity (in the sense of His allness), which is to say that he communes with truth, death is irrelevant to and powerless against him.

However, [Jacob's *devekut* with the Creator] could not be manifestly revealed in this world, and therefore, from the vantage point of this world [it seemed that] the gravediggers buried him. But in the future [world] it will be revealed that all this was only a dream and an illusion; it *appeared* as though Jacob had died and been buried, embalmed, and eulogized. But in reality he did not die, albeit within the bounds of this world, his [spiritual] level was not revealed.[104]

ADDITIONAL NOTES

*1   Normally this dictum is taken as a purely terminological statement; "living" and "dead," respectively, are meant to be no more than honorific and pejorative terms. R. Levi Yitzhak, however, reads at least half the passage literally.

*2   The context suggests that this is not a mere paraphrase. *Tzel* ("shadow") is a term associated with the soul and related to the sublime rank of *hayah* (see above, n. 57), which transcends not only *ruah* but *neshamah* as well. The phrase appears to mean: In the life (or essence) of the *ruah* (of the zaddik) of which we said, "In his *tzel* we shall live" . . . Thus the zaddik, who is in *devekut* with God, and because of whose exalted spiritual achievements (*tzel*) we survive, leaves us some aspect of his *ruah*.

---

104. The unreality of death is not readily apparent in this mundane world, the world of falsehood and night-time, and must be taken on faith. But in the bright light of the world-to-come, it will be obvious.

17

Exile and Redemption

Many characteristic features of hasidic writings on exile and redemption are rooted in mystical doctrines that permeate other chapters of this book. Thus the fundamental kabbalistic notion of the ten sefirot appears in the hasidic account of exile: Shekhinah (= Malkhut, the lowest of the sefirot) is tragically detached from the others. This means, in effect, that in some sense God Himself is in exile, together with His people—a notion prefigured in the Talmud. Similarly, the idea that redemption requires the descent of the righteous, who must interact with the profane and corrupted in order to recover the sparks of holiness from the fallen realm, an idea that we have encountered in connection with the zaddik, offers an explanation of the spiritual work accomplished through the exile of God's people among the nations. Thus, at one and the same time the imprisoned sparks are liberated from their exile among the gentiles, and converts are attracted to Judaism, in accordance with the talmudic teaching that conversions are one of the essential functions of the exile (Pesahim 87b).

At another level, the dialectic of exile and redemption both reflects and frames a philosophy of history marked by the interplay of shadow and light, in which the former is the necessary background from which the latter emerges. The phrase from Ecclesiastes, *yitron ha-or min ha-ḥoshekh* ("the superiority of light *over* darkness"), was interpreted to mean that the supremacy of the light derives *from* the darkness. Among the writers presented here, this approach is most consistently and dramatically pursued by R. Zadok of Lublin.[1] Some hasidic writers use a typology which equates each of the three Temples (the two that were destroyed, and the one to be restored in the messianic era) with one of the patriarchs. Our exile, the longest of Israel's four exiles, which will culminate with the third Temple, that of Jacob, the "most perfect of the patriarchs, all of whose children remained within the Jewish people."

Before we comment on different scholarly views on the nature of hasidic eschatology, it would be well to consider a basic ambiguity to which mystical categories are prone. For the political realist, the identification of redemption with the return to Israel is no more and no less than a prescription for action in the real, historical world. For the mystic, however, the return to Israel can be both more and less than the literal restoration of an individual and public Jewish presence in the Land. It is much more, because the difference between the Land of Israel and the countries of the exile is not merely halakhic and political, but spiritual and ontological; one's very being is qualitatively altered by being in Israel. At the same time, it is possible for the mystic to reinterpret Israel in spiritual terms, so that a properly redeemed existence in Eastern Europe can be regarded as almost equivalent to literal residence in the Holy Land. Thus a disciple of R. Yaakov Yitzhak of Przysucha (the "Holy Jew"), early in the nineteenth century, states that "whoever serves God has, in his home, an aspect of Eretz Israel."[2] For R. Zadok, building a synagogue or a study house is equivalent to the three mitzvot of building the Temple, appointing a king (i.e., a rabbi for the synagogue), and extirpating the forces of evil. On the other hand, for R. Shneur Zalman, the real exile is a personal one: our attention and our essence are diverted into worldly channels connected with physical survival; only during prayer may we be redeemed—but redeemed we are, if only for a short time. And of course, in accordance with classical Jewish teaching, prayer serves as a substitute for the sacrificial system in the Temple, a person's table serves as an altar, and so on.

1. See Y. Elman, "R. Zadok haKohen on the History of Halakha."
2. Cited by M. Pierkarz, *Hasidut Polin*, p. 205. See also R. Shatz-Uffenheimer, *Hasidism as Mysticism*, pp. 168–177. For the medieval roots of this idea in Kabbalah and in the Meiri to Ketubbot 111a, see I. Twersky, "Maimonides on Eretz Yisrael," p. 288, n. 46.

Hasidic thought thus accommodates, side by side, an emphasis on the literal realization of aliyah as a religious goal, together with a spiritualization of the Land of Israel. R. Gershon of Kutov, brother-in-law of the Besht, and R. Menahem Mendel of Vitebsk, a leading rebbe of the next generation, moved to Israel, despite the physical and economic dangers and difficulties this entailed. Groups of hasidim continued to immigrate during the nineteenth century, in the hope that they would be helping to usher in the expected messianic age.[3] Zionist historians like B. Z. Dinur have pointed to these settlers as precursors of their own political commitments.

At the same time we find the spiritual approach cited in the preceding paragraph, and even the suggestion that *galut* may, in certain respects, be more spiritual than life in the Holy Land. R. Shneur Zalman of Liady offers the following rationale for the spies in the era of the Exodus who deterred their fellow Jews from entering the Land:

> Therefore the root of the mitzvot is precisely in Eretz Yisrael, and the spies were then at a very high level and did not wish to lower themselves to the practical mitzvot, which is the aspect of drawing down the Infinite Light. And they said about Eretz Israel that it consumes its inhabitants, for it was their opinion that if the Infinite Light were revealed below as above, their being would be completely abrogated.[4]

The implication is clear: in a certain spiritual sense, Eretz Israel plays a lesser role than life outside it. Of course R. Shneur Zalman, himself a younger colleague and disciple of R. Menahem Mendel, knows very well that the attitude of the spies is rejected by the Torah. But what shall we say of the paradoxical behavior of the paradoxical R. Nahman of Bratslav? R. Nahman decided to go to Israel. He did so, although the Napoleonic expedition to the Middle East made his passage even more perilous than would ordinarily have been the case. Having arrived in Acre, however, he immediately turned around and returned to his Ukrainian place of origin. This deadly serious game of fascinated attraction and sudden withdrawal in the life of one individual reflects the collective hasidic experience we have outlined.

---

3. See A. Morgenstern, *Meshiḥiyut ve-Yishuv Eretz Yisrael ba-Maḥatzit ha-Rishonah shel ha-Me'ah ha-19.*
4. *Likkutei Torah*, Bamidbar Shelah 36b–37a. For a late-nineteenth-century discussion by the Gerer Rebbe, see *Sefat Emet, Shelah*, p. 92. This, and the following discussion, covers the same ground as S. Carmy, "A View from the Fleshpots," esp. pp. 51–53.

Scholars have debated whether the early appropriation of eschatological themes for spiritual purposes effectively "neutralized" messianic fervor among hasidim. Against Dinur, who held that Hasidism
maintained unabated the messianic momentum of Lurianic Kabbalah
that had led to the convulsive Sabbatean heresy, Gershom Scholem
argued that Hasidism succeeded in deflecting messianic speculation
from the political domain to the spiritual, thus averting despair even
while preventing a recurrence of the Sabbatean disaster.[5] Despite criticism by Tishby and others, his view is still widely accepted.[6]

In any event, the spiritualized eschatology remained popular
among later hasidic thinkers. The leading authority on later Polish
Hasidism maintains that the internalizing, pro-*galut* trend persisted
into our century, at least in part, as a negation of Zionist pessimism
about Jewish survival and authenticity outside of Israel.[7]

With the challenge of Zionism, much hasidic discussion of eschatology has focused on the nature of the historical redemption. The
interpretation of the well-known talmudic statement according to
which the Jews vowed not to rebel against the nations, implying a
prohibition of political independence prior to the Messiah's advent,
has, for example, taken on central importance, as has an occasional
tendency to demonize Zionism as a metaphysical evil rather than a
halakhic error. This position is most vigorously urged by certain
Hungarian writers, most notably the late Satmarer Rebbe, R. Yoel
Teitelbaum.[8]

Contemporary events have also precipitated a change in the traditional outlook of Habad Hasidism. Traditionally, this school avoided
explicit messianic speculation. In recent years, however, the late
Lubavitcher Rebbe and his followers have preached the imminence of
the messianic era. This emphasis is perhaps not unconnected to their
position on the State of Israel, which combines a rejection of the
Zionist movement with a hard line on the retention of territory taken
in the Six-Day War and even in the various incursions into Lebanon.[9]

---

5. G. Scholem, "Neutralization of the Messianic Element in Early Hasidism."
6. I. Tishby, "Ha-Ra'ayon ha-Meshiḥi veha-Megamot ha-Meshiḥiyot bi-Tzemiḥat ha-
Ḥasidut." Emanuel Etkes, in a recent state-of-the-field survey ("Ḥeker ha-Ḥasidut")
regards Scholem's position as the consensus.
7. Pierkarz, *Ḥasidut Polin*, p. 206, and the documentation in chaps. 8–9.
8. N. Lamm, "The Ideology of Neturei Karta." On the oath not to rebel, see more
recently A. Ravitzky, *Ha-Ketz ha-Megulleh u-Medinat ha-Yehudim*, pp. 277–306.
9. See A. Nadler, "Last Exit to Brooklyn," and Ravitzky, *Ha-Ketz ha-Megulleh*, pp.
249–276, for discussions of recent Habad writing.

The Land draws but also endangers. It provides an optimum locale for the holy life, but also presents a greater challenge and the chance for greater calamity in case of failure. This ambivalence cuts through hasidic discussions of the place of the Land in the life of piety. As R. Zevi Elimelekh of Dinov put it:

> During the time of exile (because of our many iniquities!) it is better to dwell outside the Land; this is equivalent to living in an inn or a shelter, where even the unworthy may become a host for the Shekhinah. Whereas in Eretz Israel one has to be an accomplished person [to do so].

The history of hasidic eschatology is still unfolding. The purpose of the present chapter is to uncover its theological sources.

A Story

When the Seer of Lublin died, his sons came to claim their shares of the inheritance. One son, who had traveled quite a distance, took his father's *bekesha* (formal Sabbath cloak) and a wall clock. On the way home, he stopped at an inn, and had to stay there for several days because of the heavy rain. When he was able to leave, he found that he did not have enough money, and so he left the wall clock in lieu of payment.

Many years later a famous rabbi stopped at the same inn and noticed the clock. He called the innkeeper and said, "Where did you get it?" The innkeeper told him that a rebbe's son had left it there. The rabbi told the innkeeper that he recognized it as the wall clock that had belonged to the saintly Seer of Lublin.

"How did you recognize it?" asked the innkeeper.

The rabbi replied, "Because every other clock, when it strikes the hour, has its own peculiar and characteristic message—'one hour closer to death.' But the clock of the Seer of Lublin has a different message from any other clock in the world. It sings out, 'one hour closer to the coming of the Redeemer.'"

The Nature of Exile and Redemption

1. WITHIN AND WITHOUT
Source: R. Shneur Zalman of Liady, Tanya, Iggeret ha-Kodesh, chap. 4

It is written, *In Thy behalf my heart hath said, "Seek ye My face (panai)"* (Ps. 27:8). [This may be interpreted to mean] "Seek the inwardness (*penimiut*) of the heart."[10] For in the heart (or, the element of the divine fire that is in the heart)[11] there are two aspects: the aspect of outwardness and the aspect of inwardness. The outwardness of the heart is the enthusiasm that flares up on account of its understanding (*binah*) and knowledge (*da'at*)[12] of the greatness of the Lord, the blessed Ein-Sof, by contemplating His greatness, and from this contemplation giving birth to a strong love like unto flashes of fire,[13] etc. The inwardness of the heart is that deep inner point of the heart which transcends the aspect of Da'at and the contemplation wherewith man can contemplate in his heart the greatness of the Lord. As it is written, *From the depths I called unto Thee, O Lord* (Ps. 130:1), i.e., from the depths of the heart.[14] It is similar to worldly affairs: sometimes there is an extremely important matter upon which a man's existence hinges, affecting him even to the innermost point of the heart, and it impels him to perform acts and say things without any reason whatever.[15] And [by the principle of] *the one corresponding to the*

---

10. "Inwardness," or "the innermost point of the heart," refers to the very essence of man's existence or soul. The concept is discovered in the verse from the Psalms by the phonetic similarity of the Hebrew words for "face" (*panim*) and "interiority" (*penim*). Cf. Maimonides, Hilkhot Yesodei ha-Torah 1:10.

11. The parentheses appear in the original text. The reference is to religious feeling or passion.

12. In the Habad system, the first three sefirot differ from the conventional listing. The accepted version is Keter ("Crown"), Hokhmah ("Wisdom"), Binah ("Understanding"), but the Habad system replaces them with Hokhmah, Binah, and Da'at ("Knowledge"), the components of the acronym HaBaD. R. Shneur Zalman regards Keter as too removed into the Ein-Sof to be one of the sefirot, which are, after all, the self-revelation and manifestation of the Ein-Sof. He begins with Hokhmah and introduces, as the third of the sefirot, Da'at, which serves the function of implementing the intellect, i.e., the intimate connection of the process of thought with its object. It is important for an understanding of this selection to recall that one of Habad's great achievements was the development of a kabbalistic psychology based on the ten sefirot. The ten sefirot are not only the self-manifestation of the Ein-Sof on a cosmic scale, but also describe the ten states of the soul, as the sparks of the divine within man manifest themselves in his psychic life. The first three sefirot, for instance, deal with man's intellectual faculties, and the other seven with his emotional or experiential dimensions. In this passage R. Shneur Zalman ascribes outwardness to Binah and Da'at, and inwardness to the more mysterious and esoteric Hokhmah.

13. Paraphrase of Song of Songs 8:6.

14. Zohar II, 63b.

15. Man's most vital and crucial decisions are suprarational. His judgments issue from an intuition that transcends reason.

other (Eccl. 7:14),[16] it is precisely so with the service of the heart.[17] This is because the faculty of the innermost point of the heart transcends the faculty of reason (*da'at*)[18]—which expands and vests itself in the attributes born of Hokhmah-Binah-Da'at (Habad), as is known.[19] [This inwardness] is, rather, an aspect of the illumination of the Supreme Hokhmah, which transcends Binah and Da'at, and in which is vested and concealed the actual light of God, as it is written, *The Lord by wisdom (hokhmah) founded the earth* (Prov. 3:19).[20] And this is precisely [what is meant by] the spark of divinity that exists in every Jewish soul.

The reason that not everyone merits this rank [of performing the service of the heart from the depths of its inwardness] is because this aspect within us is in a state of exile and captivity.[21] Actually it is the exile of the Shekhinah, for it is precisely the spark of divinity in our divine soul. The meaning of the exile is, as our Sages said, "They were exiled to Babylon, and the Shekhinah went with them,"[22] i.e., [man] has vested the aspect of the innermost point of his heart in the corresponding opposite,[23] namely, in the soiled garments of mundane matters and worldly desires which are referred to as Babylon. [These are symbolized by] the foreskin that covers the covenant[24] and the inner-

---

16. The verse reads, "God hath made even the one as well as the other," taken in kabbalistic writings as a principle of symmetry or correspondence that permeates all of existence. Hence, all phenomena in the realm of the sacred have analogues in the realm of the profane.
17. The worship of God, as with the pursuit of worldly matters.
18. Referring both to reason as such and to the sefirah of Da'at.
19. The seven character attributes identified as the lowest sefirot, the offspring of the intellectual faculties of Hokhmah, Binah, and Da'at (cf. *Tanya*, chap. 3). Da'at in particular exerts a determinative influence upon the lower attributes. See also *Tanya* 2:8.
20. Binah and Da'at are rooted in Hokhmah, the *hyle* ("formless matter") of the creation, which embodies divinity. Hence the soul contains a spark of divinity in its faculty of Hokhmah that ultimately originates in the Supreme Hokhmah. See *Tanya* 1:18.
21. Intellect and emotion are external to the soul; they are its expression and manifestation. Hokhmah, a state of potentiality rather than an external entity, is as close to the essence of soul as is attainable. It is in a state of exile, the spark of divinity within it prevented from manifesting itself, and remaining more potential than effective in ordering actual life.
22. Megillah 29a. By "psychologizing" the sefirot, the author derives a new and striking interpretation of the talmudic concept of the Shekhinah's exile.
23. In the corresponding opposite of the love and worship of God.
24. The male organ, on which is performed *berit milah*, the "circumcision of the covenant."

most point of the heart. Of this it was said, *And ye shall circumcise the foreskin of your heart* (Deut. 10:16).[25]

Circumcision has two stages: excision (*milah*) and retracting (*periah*),[26] which [apply respectively to] the coarse prepuce and the thin membrane. With respect to the "foreskin of the heart," there are likewise coarse and delicate desires. These require *milah* and *periah*; "circumcising and not retracting is tantamount to not having circumcised,"[27] because, after all, the innermost point of the heart is still covered by a garment of thin sackcloth: in a state of exile and captivity.[28] Now, concerning the excision of the foreskin, it is written, *And ye shall circumcise the foreskin of your heart*, i.e., *ye* by yourselves. But the removal of the thin membrane is difficult for man, and of this it was said that with the coming of the Messiah *the Lord thy God will circumcise thy heart and the heart of thy seed to love the Lord thy God with all thy heart and with all thy soul, that thou mayest live* (Deut. 30:6).[29] That is why this love[30] stems from the depths of the heart, from the truly innermost point, as mentioned above, and transcends the faculty of Da'at. Therefore, too, the Messiah will come when he is altogether unexpected by Israel,[31] which is the manifestation of the collective innermost point, and the emergence of the collective Shekhinah from the exile and captivity forevermore.

Similarly, every individual spark of the Shekhinah, inherent in the soul of every Jew, emerges temporarily from its exile and captivity

---

25. The same Hebrew word means "excise" and "circumcise." The author now takes the biblical idiom in its literal-symbolic sense, applying halakhic principles to the literal expression (that of circumcising the foreskin of the heart), in order to derive a spiritual conclusion.

26. As in Num. 5:18; see Ibn Ezra ad loc.

27. Shabbat 137b.

28. Merely ridding oneself of coarse desires, the symbolic equivalent of *milah*, is insufficient. As long as the more arduous and fundamental spiritual purification, equivalent to *periah*, has not been achieved, the Shekhinah remains in exile in oneself.

29. The advent of the Messiah will invite the divine initiative in completing man's spiritual fulfillment and purification.

30. The love spoken of in the verse quoted, which comes after the divine excision or uncovering of the heart's thin membrane.

31. Sanhedrin 97a. The term we have translated as "unexpected," or "in a state of distraction," literally reads, "the removal [or lack] of *da'at*." The lack of *da'at* results from a transcendence of Da'at (meaning both reason and the sefirah) rather than the more usual inference of forgetfulness or absent-mindedness.

during the momentary life—meaning prayer.[32] The service of the heart [emerges] from the depths of the heart, i.e., from the aspect of the innermost point. And this, too, is considered a state of distraction[33] of man. For this stage[34] transcends man's *da'at* and contemplation of the greatness of the Lord; it is, though, a type of gift given by the Lord from heaven through the illumination of the Supreme Face (*panim*), as is written, *The Lord make His face (panim) to shine upon thee* (Num. 6:25), and it is written, *And the Lord thy God will circumcise thy heart*, etc. (Deut. 30:6).[35]

2. THE PAIN OF THE SHEKHINAH
Source: R. Elimelekh of Lizhensk, Noam Elimelekh to Shemot, s.v. va-yashav mosheh

Because the Shekhinah is in exile with us, and suffers with us,[36] we who are in this bitter exile should only be concerned with and lament the exile of the Shekhinah, and not think about our personal distress. Were we truly preoccupied and distressed solely because of the Shekhinah's pain, and not our own suffering, we would most certainly merit immediate redemption.

We are but mortal, however, and it is almost impossible for us to endure our own pain and suffering; therefore, alas, the exile has been lengthened. This is so because we combine our pain with the Shekhinah's, and are distressed because of our own pain.[37]

---

32. Prayer is termed "momentary life" because it deals with requests for momentary needs (of one's ephemeral life on earth) in opposition to the study of Torah, "eternal life," the benefit of which is not solely for the moment but for all eternity; Shabbat 10a, and see commentary ad loc. of Rashi and R. Samuel Edeles (Maharsha).

33. Or absent-mindedness; see above, n. 25.

34. The revelation of the inmost spark, the Shekhinah residing within man in concealment.

35. The rest of the chapter is a discussion of *tzedakah* (charity). R. Shneur Zalman states that the divine action comes only as a response to human initiative; therefore man must first perform the circumcision of the foreskin of his heart spoken of earlier. This is achieved by giving charity, especially if it comes from a hard-earned living. One's occupation often requires total dedication, even of the innermost point of the heart, and by giving to charity in response to the divine commandment, one is redeeming the inwardness of his heart from its state of exile within him.

36. A concept prominent in both the Talmud (Mishnah Sanhedrin 6:5) and the Kabbalah, based on the verse, "In all their affliction, He was afflicted" (Isa. 63:9).

37. Rather than concentrating only on the pain of the Shekhinah.

Were there but one zaddik, he could save the whole world from exile.[38]

3. THE ETERNITY OF ISRAEL
Source: R. Zevi Elimelekh of Dinov, Benei Yisaskhar, Adar, Ma'amar 2, Shekel ha-kodesh, derush 4

Know and understand: each and every nation has a specific guardian angel that came into existence when God dispersed mankind into many nations (Gen. 11:1–9). Each of these angels is like a head in relation to his nation.[39]

[The angel's function] is similar to the function of a person's head, which directs the rest of his body. Just as life ceases when a human head is severed, so when the power of the guardian angel above is neutralized, his nation below is rendered powerless. As the prophet states, *The Lord will punish the host of the high heavens on high,* and only then, *the kings upon the earth* (Isa. 24:21). That is why other nations can cease to exist, because they are all sustained by their guardian angels, and these celestial beings are subject to destruction.

Israel is unique, though, in that it is the *portion of the Lord* (Deut. 32:9), chosen to be His inheritance, *borne* [by Him] *from birth* (Isa. 46:3). [Israel] has no particular guardian angel, but is wholly dependent upon the power of the Divine Presence. It is He Who is the head of the Jewish people, corresponding, though obviously wholly incomparable, to the guardian angels who are the heads of the other nations. (The Hebrew letters of *Yisrael* comprise the two words *li rosh,* "unto me is the head," the singular Head of the Kingdom of Heaven—*and His Kingdom ruleth over all* [Ps. 103:19].)

When Israel, because of its many transgressions, is oppressed by other nations, it is in a state of exile under the dominion of their guardian angels. But that is not in the least comparable to other instances of one nation conquering another, for then it is actually possible for the captive nation to cease to exist if its guardian angel is destroyed. Many of the famous nations mentioned in the Bible have vanished totally from history. This happened because their guardian angels were nullified. Surviving members of these peoples were either taken captive or assimilated into other nations. All memory of the

---

38. By praying exclusively for the Shekhinah, without allowing self-interest to distract him from his totally theocentric devotion.

39. The tower of Babel is described in Gen. 11:4 as having "its top [head] in heaven."

defeated nations was completely wiped off the face of the earth. However, Israel, *the nation near to Him* (Ps. 148:14), though subject to other nations and their guardian angels, can never be totally destroyed. Its guardian and head is the sacred Shekhinah, and just as it is impossible for the Almighty not to exist, so Israel's nonexistence is unthinkable. The Jewish people shall abide eternally and inherit the earth and its fullness.

Even in the time of their affliction and anguish, the Shekhinah has not departed from them, but protects and saves them. It is as though the radiance of the Shekhinah has vested itself within the guardian angel of the captor nation to protect the Jewish people and ensure its continued existence during the exile. (But this is accomplished by means of the concealment of the divine countenance, as it were, *He has withdrawn His right hand* [Lam. 2;3]. That is what is meant by "the exile of the Shekhinah" among the nations.)[40]

4. DURING AND AFTER THE TEMPLE PERIOD
Source: R. Zev Wolf of Zhitomir, Or ha-Meir, Rimzei Devarim, 159d, s.v. eikha yashevah badad.

By the rivers of Babylon, there we sat down, yea, we wept, when we remembered Zion (Ps. 137:1).

We, the children of Israel, are indeed destined and prepared at any moment and any time to restore the configuration of the Shekhinah, by means of all the minutiae of our service [of God], both before the time of the Temple and after its destruction.[41] The prayers on our lips take the place of the sacrifices,[42] and our table stands in place of the altar.[43] So states the holy Zohar: It is the purpose of man's table to purify him from all iniquities. But the study of Torah is a substitute for everything, as the Sages taught on the verse *This is the law (torah) of the burnt-offering . . . and of the guilt-offering* (Lev. 7:37).[44] They arrived

---

40. Note the novel definition of the Shekhinah's exile: a purposeful self-enclosure of the Shekhinah in the spiritual sources of the oppressing nations so as to prevent Israel's total destruction.

41. In Kabbalah and Hasidism, the service of God is said to restore the *komah*, or structure, of the Shekhinah—or the wholeness of God, as it were.

42. See Yoma 86b, based on Hos. 14:3, "We will render for bullocks the offering of our lips." Cf. Numbers Rabbah 18:17.

43. Cf. Hagigah 27a, "When the Temple was standing, the altar atoned for man's sins; now man's table brings him atonement."

44. Menahot 110a: "One who is engaged in the study of Torah, it is as if he brought a burnt-offering . . . and a guilt-offering."

at this idea by interpreting the verse *"This is the Torah, and if you study it, you will need neither a burnt-offering nor a guilt-offering."*[45] For studying [the portions of the] Torah that treat the laws of the burnt-offering [or the guilt-offering] brings atonement just as if there had been an actual sacrifice of a burnt-offering [or a guilt-offering]. Through the intermediacy of Torah study and prayer, and even of eating food and drinking water in faith, one is able to unify the limbs of the Shekhinah that were shattered [in *galut*].[46]

However, there is surely a great difference between one's deeds inside [the Sanctuary] and outside [i.e., after the destruction of the Temple], for as is well known from kabbalistic works, there is a difference between the unification [of the Shekhinah] while the Temple was in existence and now, when we are exiled from our Father's table. *"Woe to the children who were driven from their Father's table!"*[47] For the unifications one can accomplish through good deeds are small, both in quantity and in quality.

This, then, is the meaning of *By the rivers of Babylon*: after we were exiled from our Father's table, our holy Temple, *there we sat down*, i.e., even there God has granted us laws and statutes by means of which we are able to realign the limbs of the Shekhinah, as mentioned. Nothing in the world is diminished from our service of God, and wherever Israel is exiled, the Shekhinah is exiled with them,[48] so that we can restore the Shekhinah's configuration and repair its structure.

All this is good and kind and beneficial for us, so that even outside the holy Temple nothing is lacking in our service. Nevertheless, *we wept when we remembered Zion*, the city of our strength, where the unification was perfect, great in quantity and quality, with much greater light and scope than we now have by virtue of our service outside the Land.

From the foregoing we understand that even now, when the Temple is not in existence, if only we fulfill the dictum *In all thy ways*

---

45. This novel interpretation is based on the assertion in Nedarim 10b that a *lamed* voweled by a *pattaḥ* at the beginning of a word may indicate the negative: *lo*. Thus *la-olah . . . la-ḥattat* in the verse means: "no need for an *olah* or a *ḥattat*." Rashi, ad loc., gives a different interpretation.

46. The Shekhinah is shattered and must be restored by Israel's divine service. But since this service is usually understood to be the sacrifices, how can the *komah* of the Shekhinah be restored in exile and the absence of a Temple? The answer is that prayer, study of Torah, etc., are substitutes for the sacrificial rites.

47. See Berakhot 3a.

48. Megillah 29a. Cf. Zohar I, 120b; II, 2a.

acknowledge Him (Prov. 3:6), and do no deeds whatsoever other than those that entail some service to the Creator[49] [we can attain spiritual eminence]. This applies to all times and occasions, no matter how unalike they are, for there are times to laugh and times to weep.[50] Both [seasons] pertain to the study of Torah and the service of God. All these seasons and occurrences are nothing in themselves, for their vitality is derived from them by means of the quality of our deeds. One must serve God at every opportunity in accordance with its own value. This will perfect the soul and restore it to its full plenitude, even at *a time to weep.*

The Purpose of Exile

5. GALUT: A PRELIMINARY STAGE OF GE'ULAH
Source: R. Levi Yitzhak of Berdichev, Kedushat Levi ha-Shalem, Lamentations, pp. 142–143

a. This is the principle: That God destroyed His majestic house [the Temple], and we Jews were driven into exile, was surely meant for Israel's good. God will certainly have mercy on us evermore and will rebuild the holy Temple with greater dignity and greater strength. Hence the exile, which we now see as not good, [is only an illusion] because, in truth, God, to Whom all mysteries are revealed, knows that it is all good for Israel.   [ibid., s.v. *dor orev*]

b. The point of the suffering and the destruction of our Temple is that when God rebuilds [the holy Temple] in the abundance of His mercy and loving-kindness, it will be revealed that the pain and the destruction were [in reality] only loving-kindness. Hence it is the pain that begets the joy. . . .

c. "Weep for Zion and her cities as a woman in her birthpangs."[51] The general meaning [of this analogy is as follows]: When a woman kneels to deliver a baby, she has pain. After the baby is born, she feels great happiness. Those present at the time feel happy even while she is in pain, for they know that a baby will be born, a son or a daughter. This is truly [an occasion for] joy, and she too will be happy after she delivers. So indeed is it with Zion: Even though she is now in pain

---

49. This, of course, is a central theme of Hasidism.
50. Paraphrase of Eccl. 3:1 ff.
51. From the poem at the end of the Kinnot recited during the Shaharit service on Tisha be-Av.

because of her destruction, it is like a woman suffering birthpangs [which result in joy]. But God rejoices [even before], for He knows that the woman's agony is temporary [and so too that Zion's pain is temporary], because God will rebuild her with even greater dignity and greater strength. [ibid., *eli tziyyon*]

d. "There is none but Thee, O our Redeemer, for the days of the Messiah."[52] That is to say, when our righteous redeemer comes, soon and in our own time, then it will be known that everything that has happened to us during [the long years in] exile was in preparation for the redemption. Now, in *galut*, we are unable to perceive this, but at the time of the redemption it will be revealed that it was all a preparatory stage for our liberation. From all this we see the meaning of "There is none but Thee": today the fact [of our troubles being a preparation for redemption] is known only to God. [ibid., s.v. *efes*]

6. PROSELYTES AND ISRAEL
Source: R. Elimelekh of Lizhensk, Noam Elimelekh, Likkutei Shoshanah, p. 199

The Talmud states that he who dwells in Eretz Israel is like (*domeh*) one who has a God; and he who dwells in exile is like (*domeh*) one who has no God.[53]

I have heard that some find it difficult to reconcile the two [parts of the talmudic statement]. For the word *domeh* is related to the word *dimyon* ("imagination") [thus referring to an imagined similarity, not a reality]. This would seem to imply that one who dwells in Eretz Israel imagines [i.e., it is "as if"] he has a God, but in actuality, heaven forfend, he has no God. The second statement, then, would mean that he who dwells in the Diaspora imagines [i.e., it is "as if"] he has no God, when in actuality he has a God.

I suggest the following answer: The Talmud states that Israel was sent into *galut* only in order to gain converts.[54] This must be clarified: Is it a reason for those who are holy to be made to endure the yoke of exile and adversity? Wouldn't it have been far better for the gentiles to come to Eretz Israel and convert there? [The answer is] that when the zaddik wants to influence others, he must descend from his level.

52. From the Shaharit service for Shabbat.
53. Ketubbot 111a.
54. Pesahim 87b.

That is the only way he can affect others. For one can only be influenced by someone similar (*domeh*) and comparable to him.[55]

As is well known, the sanctity of Eretz Israel is very great. Consequently, because the sanctity of Israel is of so great and lofty a degree, and Jews are unique and separate from the other nations of the world, a Jew [living in Eretz Israel] would be unable to have any effect on prospective converts. He would have no [spiritual] relationship with or similarity to them, and would be unable to diminish their power [as pagans] and thereby bring about their conversion [to Judaism].

It was for this reason that Israel was exiled. In the Diaspora, which is of less sanctity [than Eretz Israel], they can bring about the addition of proselytes to Judaism. In exile, even if the zaddik possesses great sanctity, he can descend from his level somewhat, and achieve a limited degree of correspondence with the proselyte who wishes to convert. But in Eretz Israel, because of its extreme holiness, even if the zaddik should descend somewhat from his spiritual level, he would have no connection with the proselyte seeking to convert.

This is the interpretation of the aforementioned talmudic text: He who lives in Eretz Israel *domeh*—though at this moment the zaddik descends to a lower level, nonetheless it is "as if he has a God," i.e., he remains similar to one on the highest level of sanctity. Even those [ordinary] individuals who in general are on a lesser level, it is "as if" they had a God, i.e., they exist in the highest realms of sanctity. [The reverse is true of those who dwell outside Eretz Israel.][56]

7. REDEMPTION AND THE EXTRACTION OF THE HOLY SPARKS
Source: R. Zevi Elimelekh of Dinov, *Benei Yisaskhar, Nisan Ma'amar 4, Tiyyul ba-Pardes, derush 8, p. 60d*

The reason for all the exiles is to release the holy sparks from the *kelipot* through the servitude of captivity. The Egyptian exile was the

---

55. For one party to exercise spiritual influence over another, there must be some resemblance or point of contact between them. If they are so different and dissimilar that the gap is unbridgeable, no spiritual influence can flow from one to the other.
56. The Talmud means to establish the different levels of sanctity that apply to those who live in Eretz Israel and in the Diaspora. This, in turn, explains the other talmudic statement about Israel having to go into exile in order to win converts.

root of all exiles and all kingdoms,[57] and a multitude of holy sparks were submerged.[58] . . .

Through the enslavement of the Israelites by the nations, Israel extracts from their mouths that which they had swallowed up, i.e., the holy sparks,[59] and when the extrication [and return of the sparks] to their sacred source is wholly completed, all the *kelipot* will be annihilated, for the *kelipot*, have no vitality except for the holy sparks. . . . Idolatry derives from the *sitra aḥara*, which is called *other gods* (Exod. 20:3); and when the holy sparks are delivered from the *kelipot*, all idol worship will be annihilated, *and the idols shall utterly pass away* (Isa. 2:18); *and all the earth shall be filled with the glory of the Lord* (Num. 14:21).

The people of Israel will, of necessity, sift all the holy sparks from the four corners of the earth, *for the portion of the Lord is His people, Jacob the lot of His inheritance* (Deut. 32:9). . . . And just as it happened in Egypt that the holy sparks were separated from the *kelipot*, and the *kelipot* remained as mere dead corpses, so also it will be with all the kingdoms[60] until the final redemption. When the [universal] separation is completed, then *all the earth shall be filled with the glory of the Lord*, and all the nations will revert to a pure language[61] so that they can together call upon the unified Name.

8. THE LONG EXILE AND THE GREAT REDEMPTION
Source: R. Israel of Koznitz, Avodat Yisrael to Vayetzei, s.v. vayetzei

It is the way of the zaddik that when he is distressed or in exile, he is not preoccupied with his own soul's anguish but is concerned because the souls of Israel are the limbs of the Shekhinah, and in all likelihood His mighty Shekhinah is impaired. It is about this that the zaddik protests.

---

57. Referring to the four kingdoms that represent the four exiles Jews will suffer before the coming of the Messiah. See Dan. 2:37–40 and Ibn Ezra to v. 39. See Midrash Tanhuma *vayetzei* 2; *Pesikta de-Rav Kahana* 23. (The word *malkhut* in the source is a misprint and should be in the plural, *malkhuyot*.)
58. Although in Egypt the Israelites sank in "forty-nine gates of defilement" (see elsewhere in this chapter), the *kelipot* contained a multitude of holy sparks waiting to be redeemed.
59. Paraphrase of Jer. 51:44. Immanent in the nations, or *kelipot*, are the holy sparks that Israel retrieves from them.
60. See n. 57 above.
61. Paraphrase of Zeph. 3:9.

Thus, when Jacob was compelled to flee from his brother Esau in Beersheba, [we read] *and he went toward Haran* (Gen. 28:1). This means that he sensed the advent of wrath[62]—the attribute of judgment, heaven forbid. Our Sages already indicated that all four exiles were hinted to him in this dream, the severest of them being the last destruction [that of the Second Temple], of which we have no fore-knowledge as to the time of redemption [from the present exile].[63]

As is well known, the First Temple corresponds to Abraham, and the Second to Isaac. The Third Temple, may it be rebuilt speedily in our days, corresponds to Jacob, the most perfect of the patriarchs, whose "bed was complete,"[64] and it will never be destroyed. It was taught: "Neither like Abraham, who called [the site of the Temple] a mountain, nor like Isaac, who described [the site of his prayer] as a field, but like Jacob, who referred to it as a house."[65] This is alluded to in the verse *And Jacob awoke from his sleep . . . and he was afraid* (Gen. 28:16–17). When he foresaw the length of the last exile [following upon the destruction of the Second Temple], he was seized with fear, [wondering,] when will the final redemption occur? *And he said . . . This is none other than . . . the gate of heaven* (Gen. 28:17), meaning that he consoled himself [with the thought] that in all probability this destruction was a prelude to the [Third] Temple, which is called the fixed abode [of the Lord] for all eternity; and proportional to the mag-nitude of the light of redemption is the magnitude of the destruction [and exile which precedes it].

That is why this [last] exile is so long and endless, to teach us that the future redemption will be of boundless and unlimited radiance.

This is the meaning of the verse *And behold the angels of God ascend-ing and descending on it* (the celestial ladder) (Gen. 28:12). The problem of the ascent preceding the descent is commented upon by Rashi.

---

62. The rabbinic commentators relate Haran, a place-name, to *ḥaron* (*af*), "anger" or "wrath." The play on words is meant to convey the deeper sense that Jacob prophet-ically intuited the future tribulations of his descendants.

63. Genesis Rabbah 68, end, referring to the exiles in Egypt and Babylon, and the per-secutions by Greece and Rome. On our ignorance of the end of the present exile, see Yoma 9b.

64. A rabbinic euphemism for the completeness of his family. Unlike Abraham and Isaac, all his children remained loyal to his faith in God. See Leviticus Rabbah 36 and Pesahim 56a. For the correspondence between patriarchs and periods of Jewish histo-ry, see Sforno in his introduction to his commentary on Genesis.

65. Pesahim 88a. For Abraham, see Gen. 22:14, for Isaac, Gen. 24:16, and for Jacob, Gen. 28:19. "House" is here taken to symbolize the third and permanent Temple.

Another answer is that when the Children of Israel dwell in their land, fulfilling the will of their Creator, then the celestial Chariot (*merkavah*) [a realm in the mystical spheres] is conducted in accordance with their actions, and all the worlds receive their divine grace in the proper order through the Children of Israel, who become the conduit [for this divine grace]. When Israel is in a lowly state, however, heaven forbid, the reverse occurs, and it is the nations of the world that receive the primary divine grace (*shefa*), while we receive the remnant.

It is for this reason that our Sages state, "Israel in exile worship idols in purity."[66] This means that when Israel has to obtain *shefa* by means of the [guardian] angels [of the other nations], it is regarded as comparable to idolatry, for the Children [of Israel] should derive sustenance [directly] from their Father's table [i.e., God Himself]. The nations of the world, upon receiving [divine grace directly as a result of Israel's lowly plight], imagine that they are in the ascent, but actually [it is a descent], for the order [of the flow of grace] should only be evoked by those who perform God's will.[67]

Eretz Israel and the People of Israel

9. LAND AND TORAH
Source: R. Levi Yitzhak of Berdichev, Kedushat Levi to Shelah, s.v. o yevo'ar

Send thou men, that they may spy out the land of Canaan, which I give unto the children of Israel (Num. 13:2).

---

66. Avodah Zarah 8a.
67. R. Israel's answer to the question of ascent prior to descent requires some explanation. Scripture states (Gen. 28:12) that Jacob perceived the angels ascending and descending in his dream. The problem raised by Rashi, the eminent medieval commentator, is that since the angels are heavenly beings, Scripture should have stated that they first descended and then ascended. He resolves this by saying that the angels who protected Jacob in Eretz Israel were not the same as those who watched over him when he left the Land. Since Jacob was departing from Eretz Israel, those angels ascended, leaving him, while the angels of the lands outside Eretz Israel descended to guard him. The answer proffered by R. Israel is that the angels in the dream are the guardian angels of the nations of the world. Since Jacob is going into exile, they seem to be ascending and gaining eminence over him, and over the children of Israel, his descendants. In reality, however, they are *descending*, because it is specifically by means of the Jewish people, acting as the divine conduit, that God desires to bestow His heavenly blessing upon the world. The terms "ascending" and "descending" apply not to two different sets of angels but to one—the angels of the pagan nations. When Israel goes into exile, they take this as a token of their own spiritual ascent, whereas it is really a descent.

The primary intent of the Creator was to send God-fearing and morally perfect men whose whole purpose was to serve the Lord and not, heaven forbid, [merely] to spy out Eretz Israel in the physical sense. The Creator commanded Moses to dispatch servants of the Lord in advance [of the conquest of Canaan] so as to make a spiritual impression in the land by means of their divine service of Torah study and prayer, and thereby to draw down spiritual vitality and grace from the [spiritual] land above to the [material] land below, so that the land itself would long for the children of Abraham, Isaac, and Jacob.

That is the meaning [of our verse]: they were to *send* out, or expel from themselves, their quality as *men*, or mere corporeality, so that they might attain to *thou*, the spiritual level of you, Moses. They were to come unto the land of Canaan not to spy it out materially, heaven forbid, but so as immediately to occupy themselves with Torah and prayer. The word *ve-yaturu* ("that they may spy out") is related to the word *torah*.[68] Thus, when the Jewish people occupy themselves with Torah and mitzvot, they acquire [their own] share in Eretz Israel over and above what is theirs by inheritance from the patriarchs; hence [the end of the verse], *which I give unto the Children of Israel* in the present tense, implying that whenever Jews engage in Torah and the commandments, I (i.e., God) constantly give the Holy Land to the Jewish people. But this was not what the spies counseled, for they acted in a foolhardy manner. They thought that Moses had dispatched them to spy out Eretz Israel only for worldly reasons. This is the significance of Moses' prayer [on behalf of his student Joshua]: "May God rescue you from the counsel of the spies,"[69] so that he would not be at one with them in their counsel to spy out Eretz Israel materially, but would be conscious that *ve-yaturu* derives from *torah* (i.e., that their sole task was the divine service of Torah).

10. THE ANATOMY OF ISRAEL
Source: R. Levi Yitzhak of Berdichev, Kedushat Levi to Shelah, s.v. va-yikra mosheh

The Midrash states that just as man has 248 organs [or bones] and 365 arteries [or sinews], so the Land [of Israel] has similar qualities. That

68. The connection is homiletical rather than etymological; *torah* derives from *y-r-h*, "to teach," not from *tur*.
69. The talmudic interpretation of the change of name from Hosea to Joshua; see Sotah 34b.

is why we find [anthropomorphic terms in the Bible, such as] *the nakedness of the land* (Gen. 42:9), *the heart of the land* [this expression is not biblical], *the navel of the land* (Judg. 9:37), *the eye of the land* (Exod. 10:5). Man's 248 organs correspond to the 248 positive biblical commandments, and the 365 arteries correspond to the negative commandments. [Man must take care that] no part [of his body] violates the specific transgression corresponding to it. Similarly, the "organs" and "arteries" of the land are obligated to observe the 613 commandments. When [the people of] Israel observe the mitzvot in the Land [of Israel], they make the Land yearn and desire for Israel to abide in it and observe the Torah's 613 mitzvot. That is why Moses sent the twelve spies (Num. 14:2) with the task of *ve-yaturu* (lit. "to spy and seek out"), related to the word *torah*:[70] they were to study the Torah there, thus making the Land more susceptible to conquest by the Israelites who would observe the Torah's mitzvot in the Land. Israel would thus be [active] bestowers, and the Land would be in the category of [passive] receiver.[71]

11. THE LAND'S LONGING FOR THE PEOPLE
Source: R. Levi Yitzhak of Berdichev, *Kedushat Levi to Lamentations*, s.v. *attah ha-Shem*

And your enemies that dwell therein shall be astonished (Lev. 26:32). Nahmanides interprets this verse as meaning that many nations repeatedly attempted to make Eretz Israel into a place of flourishing habitation, similar to other lands, but they never succeeded.[72]

Why? Because the Holy One created the whole world, and decreed that certain areas would be places of habitation, and others would remain desolate. When a settled area is destroyed, it is transformed into a desert where wild beasts are normally found. When it is later resettled, no wild beast will be found there, as would normally be the case in the desert. As for Eretz Israel, however, when the people of Israel live there securely, it is an inhabited region. But when the Jewish

---

70. A play on words; see the preceding selection.
71. Another occurrence of the kabbalistic/hasidic male-female metaphor symbolizing, respectively, active and passive agents. If the Israelites put themselves in the active category spiritually, a task which can be achieved by virtue of the correspondence of the mitzvot to the Land's "anatomy," the Land becomes a receiver, i.e., passive, and yearns to be conquered by the Israelites.
72. Commentary to Lev. 26:16.

people are exiled, even though other nations reside there, it remains a wasteland. Why? Because whenever Jews do not reside in Eretz Israel, it remains a desert, inhabited by wild beasts, even though other nations may be there. This is so specifically because Israel is not present there. So we find in the case of Sennacherib, who settled the people of Cuthin (i.e., the Samaritans) in Eretz Israel, and wild bears and lions came upon them and slew them as though they were in a desert.[73] The operative principle is that so long as the people of Israel do not dwell [in Eretz Israel], it remains a wasteland, even though other nations abide there. This proves that Eretz Israel is specifically ours and does not accept the habitation of any other nation.

12. REDEMPTION—IN THE DIASPORA
Source: R. Zadok ha-Kohen of Lublin, Zidkat ha-Zaddik, no. 176

Immediately after the [chapter in the Torah concerning the] destruction of Amalek there follows [the law of] the sanctity of the Temple site. So our Sages declare, "The people of Israel were instructed in the performance of three mitzvot upon their entering Israel: to appoint a king over them, to destroy the seed of Amalek, and [immediately afterward] to build the holy Temple."[74] That was why our Sages placed the chapter of "The People of the City," dealing with the halakhot of the sanctity of a synagogue and house of study, in tractate Megillah [which deals with the commemoration of the downfall of the Amalekite Haman]. Thus [too the sequence in the verse] *All the horns of the wicked will I cut off; but the horns of the righteous shall be lifted up* (Ps. 75:11). The Sages state: "Wherein is their horn uplifted? In Jerusalem."[75] This means that the uplifting of the horn of Israel (i.e., the redemption) is limited to a sanctified locale in Eretz Israel and cannot be diffused, lest it be nullified. Now, synagogues and houses of study have the sanctity of Eretz Israel, for our Sages state that these sacred edifices [in the Diaspora] will all be transposed to Eretz Israel at the time of the redemption.[76]

The three [aforementioned] mitzvot are linked together. When one person is somewhat exalted [above others] in the building of a new

---

73. See 2 Kings 17:25 and *Pirkei de-R. Eliezer*, chap. 38.
74. Sanhedrin 20b, referring to Deut. 12:10 ff.
75. Megillah 17b.
76. Megillah 29a.

synagogue or house of study, which our Sages considered a miniature Temple,[77] it is like the appointment of a king.[78]

13. PIETY IS GREATER IN ERETZ ISRAEL
Source: R. Shelomoh of Lutzk, Divrat Shelomoh to Shelah, s.v. od efshar lomar

Israel, the holy people, were endowed with great faith, but even [more so when they reside] in the Holy Land, Eretz Israel. [Living in the Land] is the basis and foundation of faith, the fear of the Kingdom of the Creator. [This is because] through faith that He created [everything] . . . and [that] everything is in His hand like clay [in the hands of the potter] . . . comes great fear and awe and acceptance of the yoke of the heavenly Kingdom, as it is written: *And God hath so made it, that man should fear before Him* (Eccl. 3:14).

The Creation of the world began with the holy Land of Israel, as the Rabbis stated [based on] the verse, *Out of Zion the perfection of beauty [God hath shined forth]* (Ps. 50:2).[79] The Foundation Rock (*even shetiyah*)[80] was so called because it was the cornerstone of the world.[81] Thus the glory of His Kingdom dwells mainly in the holy Land of Israel, and there is the root of His fear and awe, which are said to be a consuming fire destined to destroy and vomit out the seven [pagan] nations.[82]

14. FAITH AND THE SANCTITY OF THE LAND
Source: R. Nahman of Bratslav, Likkutei Etzot, Eretz Israel, nos. 1, 2, 3, 14, 15, 17

1. The main expression of faith in terms of prayer and miracles can only take place in Eretz Israel. It is where the main ascent of prayers

---

77. Ibid.
78. Therefore, the three mitzvot are fulfilled in the construction of a new synagogue or house of study, for it is a miniature sanctuary, corresponding to the Temple in Jerusalem; the appointment of a rabbi or spiritual leader is equivalent to the coronation of a king; and the extirpation of evil that will take place in such a place corresponds to the destruction of Amalek. By transposing the process of redemption, as adumbrated by the Talmud, from the Land of Israel to the Diaspora, this passage is saying that spiritual redemption can take place, "in miniature," even in exile.
79. Yoma 54b.
80. The Rock which, according to tradition, was beneath the ark in the Holy of Holies.
81. Yoma, loc. cit.
82. Thus, R. Shelomoh argues, since religious faith and piety are based on God's creation of the world, and the Creation began with Eretz Israel, faith and piety flourish more in Eretz Israel than elsewhere.

occurs. An individual's prayers [in the Land of Israel] can effect the miracles and true wonders [that are necessary] for the world.

2. When one impairs Eretz Israel, which is in the category of faith and prayer, a descent into exile occurs, primarily in the sense that prayer descends into exile, and it is impossible to pray and perform miracles in the world.

3. He who desires to be a true Jew, i.e., to ascend from level to level, can only achieve this by means of the sanctity of Eretz Israel. The ascents needed in order to advance to sanctity can only occur by means of Eretz Israel. Similarly, any ascent of prayer can only take place in Eretz Israel.

14. By means of the sanctity of Eretz Israel you can attain faith and, through it, the attribute of forbearance, i.e., [the ability] to shatter the traits of anger, sadness, and the sense of being oppressed. As long as you are very diligent in your service of the Lord, no obstacle will confuse you, for you will be so forebearing that you will be able to endure anything.

15. Entreat God [to let] you experience great yearning and longing for Eretz Israel until you actually merit going there, and also long for the zaddikim to [reach] Eretz Israel, for the sanctity of Eretz Israel has the unique power to banish anger and sadness, as mentioned above.

17. Eretz Israel [represents] the comprehensive [quality of] sanctity of all sanctities. There, we merit to emerge from the confines of Nature and to know and believe that everything [happens] because of divine providence, for this is the comprehensive quality of sanctity; and thereby we can imitate Him and distinguish between light and darkness.

15. ISRAEL AND THE DIASPORA
Source: R. Menahem Mendel of Lubavitch, Derekh Mitzvotekha, Ta'amei ha-Mitzvot, p. 114

All the festivals are observed for two days in the diaspora, whereas in Eretz Israel each holiday is observed for only one day. Thus they keep the first and last days of Passover and Sukkot, and Shavuot for only one day. In the galut, however, we observe two days [for each, instead of only one].

This can be understood on the basis of what is written in Or Ne'erav by [the kabbalist] R. Moses Cordovero, of blessed memory: The Diaspora is [so] material that it is incapable of receiving the radiance [of spirituality] in but one day, as it is received by Eretz Israel, [and can only receive it if the festival is] divided into two days. This is because every festival represents the evocation and revelation of exalted sanctity from beyond the realm of time. That is why the day is designated as a holiday.

Now, Eretz Israel, which *the Lord cares for* (Deut. 11:12), is closer to Godliness, and refined in level and degree [of sanctity]. The revealed and luminous radiance can be absorbed there in one day, whereas in the Diaspora it cannot be encompassed in one day because of the extreme remoteness of exile from Godliness. That is why two days are observed, so that during the course of the two days [of a festival in the Diaspora] the radiance can be absorbed, as occurs in Eretz Israel during the span of only one day.

This can be understood by comparison to light, which radiates from a luminary, the source of the light, like the radiance of the sun, or the sparkle of a precious stone. In such instances we perceive that when the light is close to its luminous source, it appears to be of limited magnitude, so that it can be contained in a small area. As it extends farther from the source, it seems larger and of greater magnitude, so that the small area can no longer contain it. In actuality, of course, there has been no increase or augmentation of the substance of the light as it extends farther out. Quite obviously, the radiation itself, as it moves farther from the source, *appears* to be greater in size because of the greater distance over which it stretches and illuminates.

The same holds in the case of the spiritual light that illuminates and is revealed [specifically within the temporal realm] on the occasion of a holiday. When the light is revealed in a land closer to Godliness, it does not seem to be of such great magnitude, and a shorter span of time can contain it.[83] That is why the festivals are observed for only one day in Eretz Israel. However, when it shines from afar, as it does in the lands of the Diaspora, it cannot be contained within limited confines, and two days are necessary [for its full manifestation].[84]

16. THE GATE OF HEAVEN
Source: R. Zevi Elimelekh of Dinov, *Agra de-Kallah* to Vayishlah, s.v. va-ya'al

Jacob was the most perfect of the patriarchs. He attained divine prophecy, and the divine word was revealed to him repeatedly outside

---

83. Comparable to the smaller *space* needed to encompass the light in the analogy.
84. See R. Meir Simhah of Dvinsk, *Meshekh Hokhmah*, Bo, s.v. *u-va-zeh*, and J. Katz, "Second Day of Festival."

Eretz Israel. When he reached the Land [of Israel] and God assured him that he would possess the Holy Land, God appeared and showed him, in sacred love, the difference between the revelation of prophecy outside Eretz Israel and prophecy as manifested in the Land. Prophetic revelation outside the Land must, of necessity, come through the *gate of heaven* (Gen. 28:17) in Eretz Israel.[85] The divine grace then proceeds indirectly to the lands outside Israel. In Eretz Israel, however, the divine grace comes without any mediation, descending directly from the *gate of heaven*. This is what God revealed to Jacob when He assured him that he would possess Eretz Israel. Thus, *and God went up from him*, when the divine word was concluded, *in the* [very] *place where he spoke with him* (Gen. 35:13). The gift of prophecy did not have to issue obliquely, for the *gate of heaven* is there [in Eretz Israel]. Understand this.

Settling Eretz Israel

17. THE EXALTED SANCTITY OF ERETZ ISRAEL
Source: R. Nahman of Bratslav, Likkutei Etzot, Eretz Israel, 13, 18, 19, 8

13. Eretz Israel will certainly prove most helpful to one whose intentions are truly for the sake of heaven, and who travels to Eretz Israel in order to return to God. By the very act of entering Eretz Israel, he is absorbed in it and [becomes part of its] sacred nature. It is for this reason that one who merely walks four cubits in Eretz Israel merits the world-to-come,[86] but if he is not motivated by the desire to serve God and to eradicate the evil within himself, then of what avail is dwelling in Eretz Israel? It shall cast him out as it *vomited out* [the pagan nations that dwelt there before Israel conquered it] (Lev. 18:28). 18. The essence of intelligence and wisdom exists only in Eretz Israel. Even Jews in the Diaspora receive and derive all their intelligence and wisdom from Eretz Israel. Every Jew has a share in Eretz Israel, and commensurate with his share, he derives and receives his wisdom from Eretz Israel. But when someone impairs the honor of God, heaven forbid, this causes a fall from the *moḥin*[87] of Eretz Israel to the *moḥin*

---

85. Referring to Jacob's first revelation in the Holy Land.
86. Ketubbot 111a.
87. Literally "brains," but used so variously in hasidic writings that it defies accurate translation; it can imply mind, cognitive capacity, level of inspiration, or the esoteric source of wisdom, and is often identified with the sefirah of Hokhmah.

of exile, and this brings about dispute and controversy. For the *moḥin* of exile comes under the category of controversy.[88]

19. The *moḥin* of Eretz Israel is in the category of pleasantness, the category of the pleasantness of Torah, and the category of peace. By means of charity, particularly for Eretz Israel, there is created within one the capacity to receive the flow of this pleasantness. At that time the aforementioned *moḥin* of exile can also be set aright. But when, heaven forbid, the *moḥin* of exile is greatly impaired, resulting from offenses to the Glory of God, the impairment cannot be rectified. On the contrary, the *moḥin* of exile then impairs the *moḥin* of Eretz Israel, which belongs to the category of peace, and then controversy occurs also in Eretz Israel. This explains the controversies that exist at present both in Eretz Israel and in the Diaspora.

8. Eretz Israel is a spiritual facilitator (*segullah*) for the bearing of children,[89] and it shields [us] from conflict and controversy. Also, by means of the sanctity of Eretz Israel, one merits to recognize those who increase truth in the generation, truth is revealed in the world, and all return to God, even the nations of the world—*to serve Him with one consent* (Zeph. 3:9).

18. THE PARADOX OF THE SHEKHINAH ABROAD
Source: R. Zevi Elimelekh of Dinov, Agra de-Pirka, sec. 19

It is stated in *Tikkunim*: A *ḥasid* ("pious person") is someone who conducts himself with loving-kindness toward his Creator, i.e., he builds a nest for Him;[90] he [personally] becomes a lodging for the Shekhinah—Her shelter, Her house, Her palace, Her inn. The Holy Land, however, is Hers alone—Her private home, and not merely an inn or a shelter. [Therefore, if a man in the Land of Israel wishes to become a lodging-place for the Shekhinah, it can be] only commensurate with the [quality of] the person who hosts it.

See too *Kissei Melekh* ("The Royal Throne"), where this is understood to mean that outside of the Land, by means of Torah study and good deeds, it is only possible to establish a nest and a shelter for the Shekhinah, while in the Holy Land it becomes a home, and in the Holy Temple it becomes a palace.

---

88. Cf. Sanhedrin 24a.
89. Cf. Yevamot 64a.
90. Wordplay on *kono* ("his Creator") and *kano* ("his nest").

The statement that the Holy Land is the special place and home [for the Shekhinah] and not merely an inn or a shelter, and that this is so only commensurate with the person who establishes it, implies that outside of the Land it is *not* commensurate with the person— meaning, even if he is not worthy. This is puzzling!

It can be explained in accordance with what was taught by the disciples of the Besht: that spiritual perception is attained more easily outside the Land, even by the unworthy. It may be compared to a king who, when traveling, may stay overnight in a shelter unfit for someone so important; he does so out of necessity. When he is home, however, he stays only in his beautiful, magnificent palace. This parable is clearly indicated in the Midrash in the allegory of a king who traveled in the desert, and when a man brought him a basket of figs, he enjoyed it.[91] . . .

From this you will understand that [the distinction between Eretz Israel and other lands] is valid indeed. Outside the Land, [where the Shekhinah is transient, as] in an inn or a shelter, one can host the Shekhinah even in greater measure than one deserves, and even if one is unworthy [to be host], since the situation requires it. However, in the Land of Israel proper, where the Shekhinah's abode is not as in a shelter but as in a home, the person [who offers himself as Her host] must be worthy. Understand this.

The foregoing is a possible explanation for the opinion of R. Yehudah, who said that one who ascends from Babylonia to Eretz Israel transgresses a positive commandment, for it is written: *They shall be carried to Babylon [and there they shall be]* (Jer. 27:22).[92] R. Yehudah holds that during the time of exile (because of our many iniquities!) it is better to dwell outside the Land; it is equivalent to living in an inn or a shelter, where even the unworthy may become a host for the Shekhinah, whereas in Eretz Israel one has to be an accomplished person [to do so]. This also explains why R. Ze'ira tried to avoid meeting with R. Yehudah, because he intended to ascend to Eretz Israel.[93] He did not want to give the impression that he was so confident of his merits that he might become a palace [for the Shekhinah] even in Eretz Israel.

---

91. Leviticus Rabbah 7:2. A king was traveling in the desert; when his friend brought him a basket of figs and a jug of wine, the king said, "This is a great treat!"
92. Ketubbot 110b—111a.
93. Ibid. It is difficult to avoid the contemporary relevance of this interpretation, which makes it easier to be religiously observant in the Diaspora than in Israel.

19. THE SECOND TRIP TO ERETZ ISRAEL
Source: R. Zevi Elimelekh of Dinov, *Agra de-Pirka 108*

I heard in the name of a certain zaddik that there is special significance in dwelling in Eretz Israel when one returns to it after having
temporarily gone to the diaspora. A person who returns to settle in
the Land tastes (i.e., experiences) in it a sanctity the second time that
far surpasses the first.

In my opinion, we learn this from Father Abraham. For
[Abraham's] truly significant attainment and [spiritual] ascent
occurred the second time (upon his return): *And Abraham ascended* [to
a higher level] *from Egypt* (Gen. 13:1).

20. THE INDIVIDUAL'S DUTY TO EXPAND THE LAND OF ISRAEL
Source: R. Zevi Elimelekh of Dinov, *Maggid Ta'alumah to Berakhot 51*

R. Yehudah holds that he who ascends from Babylon to the Land of
Israel transgresses a positive commandment, for it is written: *They
shall be carried to Babylon, and there shall they be* [*until the day that I
remember them, saith the Lord*] (Jer. 27:22).[94] Even though this verse
refers to the vessel(s) [of the Temple],[95] R. Yehudah utilizes it as added
scriptural support for his opinion. His real argument is for the sake of
the love of Eretz Israel: It would be improper to go up to the Land of
Israel knowing that one will see it in its desolation.[96] For [Eretz Israel]
keeps herself ugly while in captivity until God remembers her,[97] when
she will appear to us *as a bride adorned with her jewels* (Isa. 61:10).

As you can see, praising Eretz Israel was so dearly valued in the
eyes of R. Yehudah that he forbade seeing her except in her glory and

---

94. Ketubbot 110b—111a.
95. As pointed out by R. Ze'ira, who disagrees with R. Yehudah (ibid.).
96. An original interpretation of R. Yehudah's famous and controversial statement.
97. Alluding to the Talmud's observation that a dignified woman in captivity deliberately makes herself ugly in the presence of her captor (Kiddushin 12b). The Sifra
makes a similar observation on "And I will bring the land into desolation; and your
enemies that dwell therein shall remain desolate in it" (Lev. 26:32). Unlike the standard translation of *ve-shamemu aleha oyveikhem*, "your enemies shall be astonished by
its desolation," the Sifra interprets *ve-shamemu* as "they will remain desolate," implying that the Land of Israel will not produce for its captors and will deliberately keep
itself ugly and desolate until the return of her true sons (see Sifra, sec. 38, and the
comment of Rabbenu Bahya, ad loc.).

adorned with her ornaments. However, his opinion is not accepted as halakhah, and we do not follow his ruling.[98] . . .

It was taught: R. Eliezer says, one who did not say "the desired, good, and broad land" [in the recitation of grace after a meal] did not fulfill his duty.[99] [By "broad" is meant that] the Land expands through its settlers; the greater the multitude of Israelites who settle there, the more expansive she becomes. The same is true in reverse, etc., for it is called "the deer land."[100] . . .

For God gives the Land anew in all times and eras to each individual Jew. Anyone who does not state that it is a "good and broad land" does not fulfill his duty, for it is written: *And thou shalt . . . bless [the Lord for the good land] which He hath given thee* (Deut. 8:10).

21. SUFFERING FOR ERETZ ISRAEL
Source: R. Nahman of Bratslav, Likkutei Etzot, Eretz Israel

5. It is impossible to attain Eretz Israel without suffering. Most of the suffering is [caused by] wicked people who spread evil reports about the Land.[101] By drawing upon (i.e., expanding) Torah, we merit to overcome all the hindrances and suffering. In accordance with the wholeness of Torah [that we merit] to draw the greatest possible *tikkun* [into this world], to that degree do we succeed in overcoming all the obstacles and arriving in Eretz Israel.

Messianism

The Letter of the Besht to R. Gershon of Kutov

INTRODUCTION

Of the hundreds of sayings, interpretations, and homilies that have come down to us from R. Israel Besht, not one word issues directly

---

98. Thus we do have a duty to ascend to Eretz Israel even before the end of her captivity and to rebuild her from her state of desolation.
99. Berakhot 48b.
100. Rosh Hashanah 13a. Cf. Ketubbot 112a and Gittin 57a. The scriptural reference is to Jer. 3:19 or Dan. 11:41 (or possibly Ezek. 20:6, 15). Scripture uses the word *tzevi* to describe Eretz Israel, an adjective which denotes "beauty, glory." As a noun, however, it also means "deer," and the Talmud utilizes this meaning, stating that Eretz Israel, like a deer, can stretch and contract its body. It expands when settled by masses of Jews, and contracts when not inhabited by Jews (Gittin, loc. cit.).
101. The same term used to describe the majority report of the spies sent into Canaan (Num. 13:32).

from his pen. His entire teaching is an oral tradition, transmitted by students and by students of students. But while the Besht wrote no books, he did write other things, such as amulets and letters. His correspondence was generally carried on by means of two scribes; the present letter may have been written by his son-in-law, R. Yehiel Mikhel, of whom not much is known.

Four letters attributed to the Besht are extant today in a number of versions. Of these, the one that has attracted the attention of historians of Hasidism is the one here translated. Its authenticity is unquestioned by scholars, and in recent years a lively literature has grown up about it.[102] While some investigators have considerably overstated its significance—Dubnow erroneously declares it a "manifesto" of the new hasidic movement—such hyperbole does not diminish from its value as a singularly important document which tells us much about the Besht: his personal life, his pneumatic experiences, his goals and ambitions.

The epistle first appears in *Ben Porat Yosef*, the second volume by R. Yaakov Yosef of Polennoye, one of the two most important disciples of the Besht. The book was published in Korecz in 1781. Another version of the letter was published in Lemberg in 1923 by David Frenkel, as part of a collection of early Hasidiana owned by R. Israel Friedman, the hasidic rabbi of Husiatin. Two writers on Hasidism, Abraham Rubinstein and Mordecai S. Bauminger, are of different opinions as to these variants, Rubinstein insisting on the superior authenticity of the Korecz edition, and Bauminger preferring the Frenkel version.[103] We are here translating the Korecz text, noting only those deviations in the Frenkel edition which are significant.

The letter is a personal recommendation of the bearer, R. Yaakov Yosef, to R. Abraham Gershon Ashkenazi of Kutov, brother-in-law of the Besht, who was then in Palestine. It was written in 1750 or 1751, perhaps 1752.[104] The colophon indicates that R. Yaakov Yosef's trip never took place, and that after the Besht's death R. Yaakov Yosef decided to publish the letter in order "to benefit our people, the Children of Israel."

---

102. See Ben Zion Dinur, *Be-Mifneh ha-Dorot* (Jerusalem, 1954), pp. 181 ff.; Isaiah Tishby, "Ha-Ra'yon ha-Meshiḥi, pp. 29ff; Abraham Rubinstein, "Iggeret ha-Besht," pp. 120–139; Gedaliah Nigal, "Moro ve-Rabbo shel R. Yisrael Baal Shem Tov," pp. 150–159; Mordecai Shraga Bauminger, in "Od le-Iggerot ha-Besht," pp. 270-283.
103. See Rubinstein, op. cit., and Bauminger, op. cit.
104. See Bauminger, op. cit., nn. 52, 65.

It consists of three parts, all interwoven. One deals with personal and familial matters. The Besht speaks of his longing for his correspondent. This same R. Gershon, a devoted follower of the Besht who recognizes in him undisputed spiritual excellence, is the one who first rejected him off-hand as an ignoramus unworthy of marrying his sister. A strong factual core underlies the legendary material that accumulated about the fascinating relationship between the brothers-in-law, and was later compiled and published in the hagiographical *Shivḥei ha-Besht*.[105] In this letter the Besht apologizes for not being able to send funds for the support of R. Gershon in Palestine, and he asks R. Gershon to look after his student, R. Yaakov Yosef. He speaks of letters never delivered because of the hectic conditions of the day; of his young, brilliant grandson, later to achieve eminence in his own right; of his own financial distress in the face of his family's needs and his charitable disbursements.

The second aspect of the letter is a reflection of the era—the anti-Semitic excesses of the Haidamak uprisings in the Ukraine, the forced conversions to Christianity, the epidemics that took a dreadful toll, and the strengths and weaknesses of the Jewish victims—as Poland was crumbling in the mid-eighteenth century, beset by incursions from without and rebellions from within.

Most significant for hasidic scholarship is the main part of the letter—the Besht's revelation to his brother-in-law of his most intimate religious experience. Two such events are related by the Besht in this remarkable autobiographical disclosure, both characterized by *aliyot neshamah*, "ascents of the soul," and both taking place on Rosh Hashanah.

This phenomenon of "ascent" takes place during *devekut*, the ecstatic contemplative communion which Hasidism—beginning with the circle of pneumatics to which the Besht belonged[106]—cherished as the goal of all religious activity. The psychological manifestations of this experience are hardly mentioned by the Besht—another instance of the reticence of Jewish mystics and their reluctance to speak of their supreme religious experience[107]—but there is an abundance of description of the content of the vision.

Both visions, separated by three years, have a clear purpose: to negate and void anti-Semitic decrees. The Besht takes it upon himself

---

105. Translated into English by Dan Ben-Amos and Jerome R. Mintz as *In Praise of the Baal Shem Tov*.
106. See in detail in the article by Joseph G. Weiss, "Reishit Tzemiḥatah shel ha-Derekh ha-Ḥasidit," in *Zion* 16 (1951).
107. Gershom Scholem, *Major Trends in Jewish Mysticism*, pp. 15–17

to risk his life—for the ecstatic ascent threatens to sever the vision-ary's link with mundane existence—in order to plead in heaven for his people.

In the second vision, much less elaborately described than the first, the Besht appears as almost petulantly tenacious. The arguments that "they" in heaven present, in an effort to dissuade the Besht from addi-tional pressure to ease the burdens of Israel, certainly seem reasonable. An agreement is an agreement, and the Besht had agreed that an epi-demic is better than a pogrom. Yet he will not desist, but seeks all kinds of schemes for circumventing the decree.

The first vision, in the fall of 1746, is by far more detailed, and is the major part of the document that has given rise to conflicting his-toriographic interpretations. The Besht himself testifies to the unusu-al nature of the experience. He speaks (if we are to accept the Korecz text which includes this remarkable passage; see below) of recogniz-ing some of the multitude of souls he encountered—he assures R. Gershon that he, too, knows some of them—and is amazed at the willingness of heaven to accept the repentance of certain sinners. The latter probably refers to Jews who submitted to baptism out of fear of death. The souls plead with him for his assistance, and the reader is struck by the self-awareness of the Besht as a superior charismatic (to use Rudolf Otto's term)—a self-image that is clearly defined but unself-conscious. The Besht appeals to his "teacher," Ahijah the prophet of Shiloh, for assistance.[108] He engages Samael, the chief demon, in a dialogue about the evil decree.

But most important is the personality upon whom the Besht focus-es all his intercessionary efforts: the Messiah. The Besht enters the "Palace of the Messiah," and finds the latter studying Torah. He asks the Messiah when he is coming—a question laden with pathos—and is told: when the Besht's teachings will have spread throughout the world, and when what the Messiah had taught the Besht (presumably in a previous encounter) will have been learned by others. Suddenly the unprecedented joy is dissipated, and a sense of brooding sadness sets in. Nevertheless, the Besht relates that he learned three *segulot* (generally "remedies," or occult techniques for assisting the distressed) and three Holy Names which, however, he is not permitted to reveal to R. Gershon.

It is this brief passage which has so tantalized the historians. Why the Messiah? And what kind of "Torah" was the Messiah studying?

---

108. See Nigal, op. cit., on the significance of this discipleship of the Besht.

What was the mysterious teaching that the Messiah transmitted to the Besht supposed to accomplish? Answers to these questions cover the full range of opinion on the role of Messianism in primitive Hasidism.

Dinur, following S. A. Horodetsky but in much greater detail, sees in these lines a confirmation of his thesis that Hasidism continues unabated the messianic momentum of Lurianic Kabbalah that had led to such convulsive results in the Sabbatean heresy. The "Torah" studied and taught by the Messiah in the Beshtian vision is *torat ha-ge'ulah*, "the teaching of redemption," the national liberation by the Messiah.

At the other end of the spectrum, Dubnow reads this passage as proof that personal salvation has displaced national redemption for Hasidism.[109] It is for this reason that he dubs the letter a "manifesto" of Hasidism, quite ignoring the pertinent fact that a personal letter to a relative not intended for publication can hardly be considered a manifesto.

Tishby quite rightly fails to find any such radical substitutions of personal for national redemption in this brief passage. But in opposition to Dinur, Tishby holds that it can tell us nothing about the role of Messianism in Hasidism after the Besht, for what we have here is the last manifestation of the kabbalistic effort to accelerate the coming of the Messiah by means of sacred magic—Holy Names and the like.[110]

Scholem sees in this letter additional evidence for Hasidism's "neutralization" of the messianic element. The Besht's sadness at the length of time it will take the Messiah to come—although the Messiah set no date, stipulating only that it would depend on the success of the hasidic movement—is itself sufficient proof that the explosive Messianism is no longer a real element in the Beshtian view, but that neither has Messianism as such been abandoned. The Besht's belief in the eventual messianic redemption is no different from that which prevails in normative traditional Judaism.[111]

An unprejudiced reading of the letter fails to yield any highly charged attempt to precipitate the messianic redemption. The answer

109. Simon Dubnow, *Toledot ha-Ḥasidut*, p. 62.
110. Tishby, loc. cit.
111. Scholem, "Neutralization of the Messianic Element in Early Hasidism." *Journal of Jewish Studies*, Fall 1970, reprinted in Scholem, *The Messianic Idea in Judaism* (New York: Schocken, 1971), pp. 176–203.

the Messiah gives is not substantially different from the classical formula that the redemption depends on repentance and good deeds,[112]
except that it here receives a hasidic reformulation. The dialogue
between the two is decidedly non-eschatological.

Indeed, what emerges is the figure of the Messiah as simply the
most appropriate historical or metahistorical personality whom the
pneumatic can choose to invoke as a possible source of assistance in
seeking to intercede with God on behalf of persecuted Israel. It might
just as well have been any one of a number of other traditional personalities whom Jewish visionaries over the ages have discoursed
with—Elijah, Moses, and Jacob amongst others. The Messiah, as the
one destined to usher in the *final* redemption, is an obviously appropriate accomplice in any effort to relieve Jewish suffering. But the
Besht learns, to his great displeasure, that the Messiah's activity is
limited to that ultimate redemption, which is still far off, and if he
wants to accomplish something now, he must look elsewhere. The
mystical techniques he learned appease him—but he does not at all
say that these were taught to him by the Messiah. On the contrary,
the context, though the style is somewhat rambling, would lead us to
think otherwise. So certain is the Besht that the Messiah cannot help
in the present predicament that he undertakes a direct confrontation
with the personification of evil itself, Samael.

It is, therefore, not Messianism that stamps this letter as an important religious document, but rather the incessant and spiritually hero-
ic efforts of the founder of Hasidism to "nullify the accusations," to
act as the defender of his people. This activity, which was assumed by
the successors to the Besht, notably R. Dov Ber, the Great Maggid, is
known in hasidic thought as *hamtakat ha-dinim*, "the sweetening of
the judgments."

Interestingly, as Rubinstein has pointed out, the two visions
recorded in this letter take place on Rosh Hashanah, when judgment
is the theme of the day. In a parallel report in *Shivḥei ha-Besht*, the
ecstatic vision and attempted intercession take place on the eve and
day of Yom Kippur, culminating in the Neilah service, climax of the
day.[113] In a report by R. Yaakov Yosef, at the very end of his *Toledot
Yaakov Yosef*, we read that in an "ascent of the soul," the Besht saw
Michael, the guardian archangel of Israel, defending the people against
the diabolical accusers.

---

112. Sanhedrin 96b; Rubinstein, op. cit., p. 134.
113. Ben-Amos and Mintz, op. cit., no. 41.

It is, thus, *hamtakat ha-dinim* that seems to be the purpose not only of the visions recorded in this letter, but of all Beshtian "ascents of the soul."[114] Conversely, *hamtakat ha-dinim* is a pneumatic activity, performed during the high ecstasy of *devekut* by means of the "ascents of the soul" of the zaddik.

TEXT

This is the letter which the rabbi, Rabbi Israel Besht, may his memory be a blessing for eternal life, gave to our rabbi and master, the author, Yaakov Yosef Hakohen, that it be delivered to his brother-in-law, R. Gershon Kutover, who was in the Holy Land. But because of an impediment which came from the blessed Lord, [R. Yaakov Yosef] did not journey to the Land of Israel, and it remained in his hands so as to benefit our people, the Children of Israel.

To the honor of my beloved brother-in-law, my friend who is as dear to me as my [own] soul and heart, who is the distinguished rabbinic scholar, the saint (*hasid*)[115] famous in [the study of] Torah and in piety, the honor of our master, Rabbi Abraham Gershon, may his lamp shine, and peace be unto all that is unto him and unto his modest wife Bluma and all their children, may they all receive the blessing of life,[116] Amen selah!

I received your holy letter, which you sent along with the emissary who went from Jerusalem,[117] at the fair in Loka in 1750 [5510].[118] It is written with extreme brevity, and in it is said that you had already written at length to each and every one through the man who traveled to Egypt.[119] However, those letters which were written at length did not reach me, and it caused me great anguish that I did not see your holy handwriting which you wrote in detail. Certainly this is because of the havoc of the countries, because of our many sins, the

---

114. Nigal, op. cit., p. 156, considers the role of Ahijah, "teacher and master" of the Besht, as primarily one of *hamtakat ha-dinim*. In our letter, too, the Besht seeks Ahijah's assistance specifically in executing the function of *hamtakat ha-dinim*.

115. At the time the Besht was writing, the term *hasid* had not yet acquired the meaning that it later did, of a member of the hasidic movement.

116. "May they all stand upon . . . the blessing," referring to Deut. 27:12—13.

117. One of the fundraisers who visited Jews in the Diaspora to gather money for schools and other public institutions in Palestine.

118. The Loka fair was held in Elul or Nisan each year; Bauminger, op. cit. p. 65.

119. Another fundraising emissary.

plague having spread in all the countries.¹²⁰ For the plague came close to our areas, in the holy community of Mohilov, and the countries of Walachia and Turkey.

Also, [in your letter] it is said that those new interpretations and secrets which I wrote to you, through the scribe, the rabbi and preacher of the holy community of Polennoye,¹²¹ did not reach you. This too caused me great anguish, for certainly you would have derived great satisfaction [from them]. However, I have now forgotten a number of them. But I will write to you, in great brevity, some details of what I remember.

For in the beginning of the [Hebrew] year, 5507¹²² I performed the oath of the ascent of the soul,¹²³ as you know.¹²⁴ I saw wondrous things in a vision,¹²⁵ [what I had not seen heretofore, from the day that I reached maturity]. It is impossible to state, even to *speak mouth to mouth* (Num. 12:8), of what I saw and learned when I ascended there.

When I returned¹²⁶ to the lower Garden of Eden, I saw the souls of many living and dead, both those known to me and those unknown to me, without limit and number, *running and returning* (Ezek. 1:14)¹²⁷ to ascend from world to world throughout the "column" which is known to those initiated into the Kabbalah, in great and extensive joy, such that the mouth is too weary to tell of it and the physical *ear heavy that it cannot hear* (Isa. 59:1). Also [there were present] many wicked people who had repented, and their sins were forgiven, so it

120. Severe epidemics spread across much of Eastern Europe in 1750, interrupting the massacres of many Jewish communities in the Ukraine by the Haidamaks.
121. Yehudah Leib, the *mokhiah* of Polennoye.
122. Rosh Hashanah (the Jewish New Year) of 1746.
123. Ascents of the soul are mystical experiences of the soul rising, level beyond level, toward God. This spiritual adventure is initiated by a *hasbaah*, or oath, invoking the Divine Names in their various configurations and permutations.
124. Rubinstein deduces from this that R. Gershon was already aware of this particular vision. Bauminger prefers to interpret it as a reference to the techniques employed by the Besht, which were known to R. Gershon.
125. The remainder of this paragraph, all the next paragraph, and the beginning of the one following are found only in the Korets edition and not in Frenkel's version. Bauminger (p. 84) argues rather unconvincingly that this passage is inauthentic because the Besht later is perplexed by the reason for all the joy.
126. From the upper worlds.
127. A term, from Ezekiel's vision of the Chariot, referring to the angels rushing in both directions, and used in Kabbalah for the principle of alternation, of recoil and advance, as a feature of the pneumatic experience.

was a time of great acceptability,[128] such that in my eyes too it was exceedingly amazing that so many were accepted [by God] in their repentance—and you, too, know them. There was amongst them, too, very great joy, and they too rose up in the above-mentioned ascents. And they all as one beseeched me and implored me until I was embarrassed, saying, "To the exalted excellency of the honor of thy Torah! The Lord hath graced thee with a special understanding to perceive and know these matters." Because of the great joy which I beheld amongst them, I decided to ascend with them.

And I saw in a vision[129] that the Samael[130] had arisen to accuse, in the midst of this great and unprecedented joy. He executed his deeds—decrees of forced conversion against a number of souls, that they be killed [and die] unnatural deaths.[131] I was seized with terror, and I actually offered my life to save them.[132] I beseeched my master and teacher[133] to go with me, for it is exceedingly dangerous to go [on such a mission] and ascend to the upper worlds; for since I arrived at my station[134] I had not risen in such ascents. I went up, level after level, until I entered the palace of the Messiah,[135] where the Messiah studies Torah with all the tannaim[136] and the righteous people, and also with the seven shepherds.[137] I beheld very great joy there, but I do not know *of mirth, what doth it accomplish?* (Eccles. 2:2).[138]

---

128. Based on Ps. 69:14; a time when God is most accessible to human prayer, a time of divine compassion.

129. This is the end of the passage that appears only in the Korecz version.

130. The chief demon, head of the Satanic forces.

131. The reference is undoubtedly to the Haidamaks, who decimated many Ukrainian Jewish communities, giving the inhabitants the choice of baptism or death; in some cases, where Jews submitted to forced conversion to Christianity, they were killed anyway.

132. The experience of ascent of the soul and intercession on behalf of Israel is fraught with great physical and spiritual danger. See Ben-Amos and Mintz, op. cit., no. 41.

133. The Besht regarded the prophet Ahijah of Shiloh as his teacher. See Nigal, op. cit.

134. The text is unclear. It may refer to the time he attained general intellectual maturity, or the time he achieved spiritual-mystical eminence.

135. In pre-medieval Kabbalah, the pneumatic ascends through spiritual phrases known as *hekhalot*, or "palaces."

136. Palestinian teachers of the Oral Law, who flourished during the first two centuries C.E., and whose teachings form the substance of the Mishnah, the core of the Talmud.

137. Adam, Seth, Methuselah, Abraham, Jacob, Moses, and David. See Sukkah 52b and Rashi, ad loc.

138. That is, he does not know the reason for the happiness in the palace of the Messiah.

I thought this joy was, heaven forbid, because of my departure from this world.[139] But they notified me afterward that I had not yet departed, but that they derived pleasure up above when I performed contemplative unifications (*yiḥudim*)[140] below by means of their holy Torah. But the nature of this happiness I do not know to this day.

I asked the Messiah, "When are you coming, sir?" He answered me,[141] "*By this shalt thou know it* (Exod. 7:17): when your teaching has become renowned and revealed throughout the world, and when *thy springs* [have been] *dispersed abroad* (Prov. 5:16), [imparting to others] what I have taught you and you apprehended, [so that] they too will be able to perform contemplative unifications and ascents [of the soul] as you do. Then will all the shells (*kelipot*)[142] perish and it will be a time of acceptability[143] and salvation." I was bewildered at this [response]. I had great anguish because of the length of time [he implied it would take until he came, and I wondered] when it would be possible for this to occur.

However, while I was there I learned three remedies (*segulot*)[144] and three Holy Names,[145] which are easy to learn and to explain [to others]. So I was assuaged, and I thought that perhaps, in this manner, my associates (*anshei gili*)[146] might also be able to attain my level and category, that is, they will be able to practice ascents of the soul, and learn and apprehend supernal mysteries as I do.[147] But all my life I have

---

139. The righteous in the upper worlds take delight in welcoming the souls of other righteous who enter their realm after death in their world.

140. Kabbalistic meditations performed on Divine Names, revealing the underlying unity of God.

141. What follows comes from the Korecz version. The Frenkel text records only the response, "until your teaching is spread in the whole world," and then omits all of this and the next two paragraphs.

142. The kabbalistic term for the nondivine and hence the powers of evil; also translated as "husks."

143. See above, n. 27.

144. Various kind of cures employed by folk healers, ranging from herbs to incantations to magical practices as a means of assisting the distressed.

145. Holy Names were similarly used by *ba'alei shem* in applying the "practical Kabbalah" to such diverse matters as healing the sick, enabling barren women to give birth, initiating mystical experiences, etc.

146. Two interpretations are possible: either it refers to all his contemporaries, or to his associates and disciples in his immediate circle. In the first case, the Besht would be referring to the popularization of Hasidism among all Jews. In the second, he would be intending the disclosure of the three *segulot* and Holy Names to his closest disciples in an attempt to have them achieve as rich a charismatic life as his own. The context clearly favors the second interpretation. So for Dinur, op. cit., p. 182, n. 6, and Rubinstein, op. cit., p. 135.

147. That is, by using the Holy Names he learned in heaven, he hoped to enhance the

not been granted permission to do this.[148] I pleaded on your behalf that
I be permitted to teach [it to] you, but I was not at all granted [such]
permission, and I am under oath [not to do so].[149]

But this I can tell you, and may the Lord be thy help:[150] *before the
Lord is thy way* (Judg. 18:6), and do not depart [from it],[151] especially in
the Holy Land. [With] every single utterance, and all that comes out
of your mouth, during the time of your prayer and your study, intend
to unify a Name.[152] For in every single letter there are worlds and souls
and divinity. And [these] ascend and bind up with each other and
unite with each other. Afterwards, the letters bind up and unite with
each other and a word is formed, and they unite in a true unity with
divinity. Include your soul with them in every single step of the above.
[Then] all the worlds unite as one and rise up, and there is [thus] great
joy and pleasure without limit, as you mediate on the joy of bride and
groom,[153] in smallness[154] and corporeality,[155] and certainly in a high

---

spiritual lives of his students and help them to achieve ascents of the soul.
148. Hence, despite his desire to have others achieve his rank, the Besht remains spiritually preeminent.
149. This may be an oblique reference to the Besht's desire to entrust R. Gershon with
the future leadership of the group, but the refusal of heaven to endorse his choice. Cf.
Ben-Amos and Mintz, op. cit., no. 46. Rubinstein, op. cit., p. 136, suggests that these
secrets, and hence the authority of spiritual leadership of the movement, were given
to R. Dov Ber, the Great Maggid.
150. The expression is partly based on Deut. 33:26.
151. The Hebrew is unclear, and the plural form of "depart" does not accord with the
singular in the first half of the sentence. The use of the particular plural form is probably a reference to Prov. 3:21 or 4:21. The import of the sentence seems to be to
encourage R. Gershon to continue in his (hasidic) way, and to pay special attention
to what follows.
152. The *kavvanah*, or sacred intention, behind every utterance of prayer or study of
Torah must be another *yiḥud*, or "unification." See above, n. 39.
153. "Bride" refers to the Shekhinah, or Malkhut (the lowest of the ten sefirot), and
"groom" to the upper sefirot, especially as represented by the sixth, Tiferet. The mystical unification effected by the meditation on the Names is that of the male principle—the nine upper sefirot—with the female, Shekhinah or Malkhut.
154. "Greatness" and "smallness" are regarded by the Besht as two modes that characterize all things, especially in relation to the Creator. When man is "in greatness,"
he is fully inspired, acts out of selfless love, is in direct *devekut* (communion) with
God, and his contemplation is clear and uninterrupted. When he cannot summon up
such inspiration; when his concentration in *devekut* is broken, especially when he is
disturbed by mundane thoughts, he is in a state of "smallness." The Besht taught that
man must serve God in smallness as well, and use the very obstacles to *devekut* as a
way of reaching Him.
155. "Corporeality" is the collective term for all mundane impediments to sustained
contemplation of and communion with God. It is that which determines the state of
smallness. The Besht held that we must "elevate," or sanctify," the alien or distract-

level such as this.[156] Certainly the Lord will "be thy help,"[157] and wherever you turn you will prosper and succeed.[158] *Give to a wise man, and he will be yet wiser!* (Prov. 9:9). Also, pray for me with this intention [in mind], that I be privileged *to cleave unto the inheritance of the Lord* (1 Sam. 26:19) whilst yet alive; and also [pray for] the remnant [of Israel] that is outside the Land of Israel.

And I also prayed there:[159] "*Wherefore hath the Lord done thus; what meaneth the heat of this great anger?* (Deut. 29:23), that so many Jewish souls were given over to Samael to be killed—and of them a number who were baptized and then killed!" They gave me permission to ask Samael himself. And [so] I asked Samael: "Wherefore hast thou seen concerning this matter,[160] and what is your thinking about this, that they should become apostates and then be killed?"[161] He answered me, "My intention is for the sake of heaven,"[162] [for if they remained alive after their apostasy, then when other decrees and libels occurred, they would not sanctify the Name of Heaven but all would convert in order to save their lives. Therefore his action was such that those who converted were killed afterward. Thus, no Jew would convert, but would sanctify the Name of Heaven.]

And so it happened afterward, because of our many sins, that in the holy community of Zaslav there was a blood libel against several souls; two of them converted and were later killed, and the rest sanctified the Name of Heaven with great sanctity and died unnatural

---

ing thoughts, and serve God by transforming the corporeal into a mode of worship.
156. That is, in the state of greatness.
157. Above, n. 49.
158. Based on Prov. 17:8.
159. In the palace of the Messiah. The Besht now resumes the narrative concerning his mystical experience.
160. Based on Esther 9:26.
161. Apparently Jews who refused baptism and chose martyrdom were tortured to death, while those who converted were killed without being tormented. The Besht seems resigned to the death of the martyrs and prays that at least the weak ones, who submitted to apostasy, should be spared. Rubinstein, op. cit., pp. 137 ff.
162. Based on Avot 2:12. The Korecz text ends the sentence here. The meaning is not entirely clear. Rubinstein (loc. cit.) takes this as a reflection of the historical fact that many Jews, seeing that apostasy did not help them escape death, "sanctified the Name" by reaffirming their Judaism. This is partially confirmed by the passage that follows, but the meaning is still vague. The bracketed passage that follows, which does not appear in the Korecz version, comes from the Frenkel text, where it appears in parentheses (perhaps to indicate the omission in Korecz).

deaths.[163] Then there were blood libels in the holy communities of Sibatuvka and Dunawitz, and there no one converted after they had seen what happened in Zaslav.[164] Rather, all of them laid down their lives for the sanctification of the Name. They sanctified the Name of Heaven and withstood the trial. In the merit of this [martyrdom] may our Messiah come and avenge us: may he make expiation for his land and for his people.[165]

And on Rosh Hashanah of 1749 [5510] I performed an ascent of the soul, as you know, and I saw a great accusation [against Israel], until Samael was almost given permission to destroy entire countries and communities, and I offered up my life and prayed, "Let us fall now into the hand of the Lord, and let us not fall into the hand of man."[166] And they granted me permission that instead of [the anti-Semitic persecutions] there shall be great weaknesses, something the likes of which had not occurred in all the lands of Poland and other countries close to us. And that is what happened, that the weakness spread exceedingly, such that it cannot be related, and the plague too [spread] in other countries. I indulged in intense discussion with my group (*havurah*)[167] [and we decided] to recite the Ketoret[168] early in the morning in order to nullify the judgments mentioned above. Then they revealed to me in a vision of the night, "But did not you yourself choose [the plague, by saying,] 'Let us fall now into the hand of the Lord,'" as mentioned above. "Why then do you wish to nullify [the

---

163. A pogrom occurred in Zaslov in 1747. See Dubnow, *Toledot ha-Ḥasidut*, p. 61, n. 1.

164. Dunawitz, or Dunaigrod, in Podolia, experienced a pogrom in 1748. Dubnow (loc. cit.) believes that Sibatuvka or Subatuvka is an error, and probably the author meant Shepetovka.

165. Deut. 32:43, according to Onkelos.

166. Paraphrase of 2 Sam 24:14, in which David, responding to the prophet Gad, who had offered him the choice between pestilence and the enemy's sword, chose the former, preferring death by natural means ("the hand of the Lord") to decimation by the foe ("the hand of man"). The Besht is asserting that he prayed for a plague in preference to the Haidamak pogroms. See above, n. 19.

167. The intimate circle of the Besht's disciples.

168. The scriptural portion concerning the incense to be offered in the Tabernacle (Exod. 30:34—37) and a series of talmudic passages concerning the incense. These are normally recited as preliminaries to the regular morning service, and are considered a special means of nullifying evil decrees. See Num. 17:8—15, where Aaron burns the incense as a means of atoning for Israel's sins and staying the plague. See Shabbat 98a and Rashi to Num. 17:11.

decree of plague]? Surely an accuser [does not become a defender]!"[169] From then on I did not recite Ketoret, and I did not pray about this. But on Hoshanah Rabbah[170] I went to the synagogue with all the world [i.e., the entire community], [and I tried to intercede on behalf of Israel] by means of several oaths,[171] because of [my] great fear [for the safety of the people], and I recited Ketoret once so that we were successful with the help of the Lord.

I wanted to elaborate and speak at length, but because of my tears when I recall your departure from me, I am not able to speak. But I do beseech you to review all my words of admonition which I told you several times. Let them always be in your thoughts, to meditate on them and ponder them scrupulously. Surely you will find in every word all kinds of sweetness, for what I told you *is no vain thing* (Deut. 32:47). For the Lord knows that I do not despair of journeying to the Land of Israel, if that be the will of the Lord, to be with you together; but the time is not ripe for it. Also, do note be aggrieved that I have not sent you money, for it is because of the treachery of fate (*zeman*) that befell me, because of the plague and the famine and the many young children of our family who are dependent upon me to support them and provide for them, in addition to other poor Jews. *Our money is all spent . . . there is naught left but our bodies!* (Gen. 47:18). But the Lord willing, when the Lord shall enlarge, etc., then certainly, etc.[172]

Also, my grandson, the worthy young man, the honorable Ephraim,[173] is a great prodigy in the essence of study (*be-takhlit ha-lim-mud*).[174] Surely if the time is opportune for it, how fitting would it be

---

169. Berakhot 59a, Rosh Hashanah 26a, et passim. That is, you cannot change roles and seek to void that which you chose.

170. The seventh day of the festival of Sukkot (Tabernacles). Thus the spiritual intercession of the Besht lasted for twenty-two days, from Rosh Hashanah (the first of Tishri) to Hoshanah Rabbah (the twenty-second of Tishri). The latter is considered the very last day of judgment, following that of Yom Kippur. See Zohar III:31b.

171. See above, n. 22.

172. That is, when I am able to afford it I will send you money. The brevity of the style is an act of delicacy toward R. Gershon's feelings and a general aversion to elaborate on material things.

173. Mosheh Hayyim Ephraim, later rabbi of Sudlikov and author of *Deggel Mahaneh Ephraim*.

174. This is probably a simple hyperbolic flourish. Rubinstein (op. cit., p. 126) takes this phrase as connoting the specifically Beshtian conception of study *lishmah*, which means for the purpose of *devekut*. However, this is reading too much into the text.

[for you] to come here by yourself so that we may see each other face to face and to be happy in our happiness, as you promised me.[175]

I also very much beseech you concerning the renowned rabbi, the saint (hasid), our master Yosef Katz,[176] a servant of the Lord, that you draw him close with both hands [i.e., befriend him] and [offer him] all kinds of benefit, for his deeds are acceptable before the blessed Lord, and "all his deeds are for the sake of heaven."[177] [I also request of you] to write on his behalf to the wealthy people to provide adequate support and arrange for proper maintenance for him (lit. a seat with a back against which to lean),[178] for certainly he will be [a source of] satisfaction to you if he will be in your company.

Such are the words of your brother-in-law who looks forward to seeing you face to face and prays for length of days for you and your wife and your children, and seeks your welfare all day and also nights for length of good days, Amen, selah.

> Israel Besht
> of the holy community of
> Medzhibozh

22. REDEMPTION, RESURRECTION, AND REVELATION
Source: R. Shneur Zalman of Liady, Tanya, Likkutei Amarim, chap. 36

As is well known, the messianic era and, even more, the time of the resurrection of the dead, are the culmination and fulfillment of the creation of the world; [they are] the purpose for which it was originally created.

Something of this reward was already experienced on earth long ago, at the time of the giving of the Torah. Thus is it written, *Unto thee it was shown, that thou mightest know that the Lord He is God; there is naught else beside Him* (Deut. 4:35); *it was shown,* verily with physical vision, as is written, *And all the people saw the thunderings* (Exod.

---

175. Apparently inviting R. Gershon to return from Palestine to Europe to visit the Besht. According to *Shivḥei ha-Besht* he did indeed do so. Ben-Amos and Mintz, op. cit., no. 46, and editors' notes, n. 1.

176. An acronym for *kohen zedek* ("priest of righteousness"), an honorific for a *kohen* (member of the priestly family). Note the Besht's tendency to use only the last name of one who has a compound name. Similarly, he refers to his grandson, Mosheh Hayyim Ephraim, as Ephraim.

177. Avot 2:12.

178. See Ketubbot 111a–b.

20:15); "they saw what is [normally] heard."[179] The Rabbis explained, "They looked eastward and heard the speech issuing forth: *I am the Lord thy God*, etc., and so [turning] in all four directions, and upward and downward." It is also explained in the *Tikkunim* that "there was no place from which He did not speak unto them," etc. This was because of the revelation of His will in the Decalogue, which constitutes the epitome of the whole Torah, and is [therefore] the inwardness [or very essence, core] of His will and wisdom, wherein there is no hiding of the face whatsoever,[180] as is written [in the liturgy for putting on Tefillin], "For in the light of Thy countenance hast Thou given us the law of life." In consequence, [the Israelites at Sinai] vanished out of existence [in the presence of God], for as the Rabbis taught, "at each [divine] utterance their souls took flight, etc., but the Holy One restored it to them with the dew wherewith He will revive the dead."[181] This is the dew of the Torah . . . as the Rabbis said, "Everyone who occupies himself with Torah is revived by the dew of the Torah," etc.[182] Later, however, the sin [of the Golden Calf] caused both them and the world to become gross again—until the end of days, when the dross of the body and of the world will be purified, and they will be able to apprehend the revealed divine light that will shine forth to Israel by means of the Torah.

As a result of the outpouring of illumination on Israel, the darkness of the gentiles will also be illuminated, as is written, *And the nations shall walk by Thy light* (Isa. 60:3); and *O house of Jacob, come ye and let us walk in the light of the Lord* (Isa. 2:5); again, *And the glory of the Lord shall be revealed, and all flesh shall see together* (Isa. 40:5); and *To go into the holes of the rocks, and into the clefts of the boulders, for fear of the Lord and for the glory of His majesty* (Isa. 2:21). And as we pray, "Shine forth in the splendor and excellence of Thy might upon all the inhabitants of the world," etc.[183]

---

179. Mekhilta on this verse.
180. In other words, God's revelation is not mediated or indirect.
181. Shabbat 88b. Confronted with the inwardness of Torah, in which there is no screen or impediment, the word of God came to them, as it were, from all sides.
182. Ketubbot 111b.
183. From the liturgy for Rosh Hashanah and Yom Kippur.

23. THE FINAL CLARIFICATION
Source: R. Zevi Elimelekh of Dinov, Benei Yisaskhar, Nisan 4, Tiyyul ba-Pardes, derash 8, al derekh remez, pp. 61a–b

"When the Messiah comes, the Holy One will accept gifts from all the kingdoms except Edom, because wicked Edom destroyed the holy Temple.[184] Although the Babylonians too destroyed [the First Temple], they did not uproot it [completely]. Of Edom, however, it is written: *[they said] raze it, raze it, even to the foundation thereof* (Ps. 137:7). So too was it said that in the time-to-come all nations are destined to bring gifts to the King-Messiah, and the Egyptians will be the first to do so."[185] . . .

Now, let us first explore what gifts the nations will bring to the King-Messiah. Will the King-Messiah need their silver and gold? If silver counted as nothing in the days of King Solomon,[186] it will surely be so in the days of the King-Messiah. What this really means, then, is that the gifts are the holy sparks that the Jews were unable to extract in the days of their exile.[187] This is evident from what happened in Egypt when many tens of thousands of Israelites perished during the three days of darkness;[188] for not all the sparks could be clarified, because they were embedded very deeply in the overpowering *kelipah*. But at the time of the final redemption, when the Messiah comes, God willing, they will be extracted, as it is written: *And they shall come who were lost in the land of Assyria; and they who were dispersed in the land of Egypt* (Isa. 27:13).

Everything in the world contains holy sparks. When food and drink permitted by the Torah are consumed, they become part of our body, turning into blood and human flesh. We, in turn, utilize the strength gained from this nourishment to study Torah and do mitzvot. As a result, the holy spark within the food is elevated and incorporated into the holiness [of Torah and mitzvot]. This is the mystery of the selection.

---

184. Edom is considered the ancestor, and hence the symbol, of Rome, which destroyed the Second Temple in 70 C.E.
185. Exodus Rabbah 35:5. The midrash goes on to describe Edom's attempt to do likewise, which is rejected.
186. See 1 Kings 10:2.
187. These Lurianic references are explained in the next paragraph. *Berur* can be translated as "selection," "extraction," "clarification," or "sifting," depending upon which nuance is more appropriate.
188. See Mekhilta to Exod. 13:18.

But what of the foods prohibited to us by the Torah, such as the forbidden species of cattle, beasts, and fowl? They too perforce possess some spark [of holiness], as it is written, *And thou preservest them all* (Neh. 9:6).[189] Then why did God forbid them to us? Is there no need for these too to be selected? [The answer is:] God knows that this extraction is beyond mankind's capability. The holy sparks in these species are too deeply embedded in the *sitra aḥara*, because their life-force is derived from the three impure *kelipot*, as is well known.[190] When a person eats of them, they will [not be elevated but instead will] overpower his soul, dulling his mind and intellect, and inciting him to lust. That is why God forbade them, and commanded us to select [the holy sparks] only from that which is permitted.

One may ask how the good will be selected from these material beings. The answer is that once we have done our duty and selected [those sparks] that we are obligated to extract, then, at the end of days, God will withdraw the sparks from their abodes and all the *kelipot* will be nullified. So it was in Egypt: When the end [of the exile] came *and they could not tarry* (Exod. 12:39), all those whose [sparks] could not be extracted died during the three days of darkness. God will select them at the time of the final [redemption] in the end of days. *And they shall come who were lost in the land of Assyria, and they who were dispersed in the land of Egypt, and they shall worship the Lord* (Isa. 27:13). . . . So too God forbade certain species, knowing that we could not complete the extraction, and He will do the selection at the end of days.

Likewise, in my humble opinion, all the selections that Jews are unable to complete, during all the years of their affliction and wretchedness, will be achieved at the end of days. Among them will be all the nations that come to attach themselves and join Israel to serve [the Lord] in various ways. And these precisely are the gifts that all nations will bring to the King-Messiah, achieving thereby their own deliverance. Not so with Edom, of whom it is written: *And there shall not be any remnant of the house of Esau* (Obad. 18). Whatever sparks that Israel extracted [from among the Edomites] during the years of affliction became true converts [to Judaism] before the coming of the

---

189. The sparks are the means by which God sustains the creation. To exist at all, nonkosher foods too must possess holy sparks.

190. The Kabbalah posits four *kelipot* ("shells"), or orders of the demonic, three of which are absolute, in different intensities. The fourth, *nogah*, is ambivalent or neutral. When combined with one or a combination of the other shells, it is an evil force; when it adheres to holiness, it enhances the benevolent forces.

Messiah. However, after the coming of the Messiah, as mentioned, there will no longer be any deliverance for the house of Esau.

Our Sages' statement [that God will not accept a gift from the Edomites] because they utterly destroyed the foundations of the Temple deserves an explanation: The Talmud in Zevahim [62a] asks, "From whence did the Men of the Great Assembly know the exact location of the altar? Granted they knew the location of the Temple because its form could be recognized, [but what of the altar]?" (Rashi comments: "The foundations of the walls," because the preceding destroyers left the foundations intact.)[191] It seems that the intention of the wicked kingdom [Edom], when they said, *Raze it, raze it, even to the foundation thereof* (Ps. 137:7), was to leave no trace of the location of the walls, so that Israel would be unable to rebuild the Temple. Just as they left no trace of the Temple's foundation, so shall there be no foundation remaining for them to attain deliverance by means of Israel.

Now, the Rabbis said: Jerusalem is destined to become a beacon for the whole world, as it is written, *And nations shall walk by thy light* (Isa. 60:3). . . . Through the illumination of Jerusalem and the holy Temple, all the holy sparks left among the nations will be drawn to it and delivered. They will say to Israel, *O house of Jacob, come ye, and let us walk in the light of the Lord* (Isa. 2:5), and the light of the holy Temple will be their remedy. Not so, however, with the wicked kingdom [Edom], which intended, by destroying the very foundations of the Temple, to make it impossible for Israel to rebuild it. Because of this they will derive no benefit from the light of Jerusalem and the Temple, and thus *there shall not be any remaining of the house of Esau* (Obad. 1:18).

24. TWO KINDS OF ZADDIK[192]
Source: R. Dov Ber, Maggid Devarav le-Yaakov, no. 68

And ye shall traffic in the land (Gen. 42:34).

There are two kinds of love. The first is that of a father who loves the deeds of his wise son. He prides himself on his son's wise acts or wise sayings. The second is the [father's] love for the son himself.[193] Everything that [his son] says is proper in his eyes because of his love for him.

---

191. Since only the walls were toppled, but the foundations remained intact, the Men of the Great Assembly were able to determine the location and ground plan of the Temple.

192. See also chap. 8, selections 9—10.

193. As opposed to love for what the son does.

Now, with regard to God's love for us, the first kind of love [is manifested] when the zaddik does mitzvot and good deeds with wondrous wisdom, elevating the holy sparks in the mineral, vegetable, animal, and human realms.[194] Then God has great love for his deeds. Thereby [the zaddik] binds even the external aspects of the worlds to God, for God abides in all his deeds. The complete *tikkun* will take place, God willing, at the time of the coming of the Messiah, speedily in our days, as it is written, *for the earth shall be full of the knowledge of the Lord as the waters cover the sea* (Isa. 11:9). Even animals and wild beasts will have knowledge of the Lord: *They shall not hurt nor destroy in all My holy mountain* (ibid.).[195]

The second love occurs when the zaddik himself is bound to God, and God loves him exceedingly. [The zaddik] does not perform his deeds in wisdom, as in the first case, but with great wholeheartedness, and is bound to God.[196] Therefore God loves him. This is called the ascent of the inner aspect of the worlds, for the zaddik is the inwardness of the world.

---

194. The fourfold division of existence usually found in medieval philosophy.

195. The first kind of zaddik achieves *tikkun* of the world and its contents by means of kabbalistic meditations. But the *tikkun* is incomplete and will be fulfilled only when the Messiah comes.

196. The first zaddik expresses *devekut* by mastering the mystical technology whereby *tikkun* is performed (the exercise of the *kavvanot*). Meditation requires great wisdom. The second zaddik transcends kabbalistic techniques, and is himself, in the inner core of his being, bound to God in great *devekut*. His way is not *hokhmah* ("wisdom") but *temimut*, which we have translated as "wholeheartedness," but which often has the implication of simplicity, of uncomplicated and total devotion. It is not his thoughts or words or acts that are wielded in order to perform *tikkun*, but his inner self, which is in communion with God. Interestingly, in this selection the Maggid, the great exponent of hasidic mysticism, asserts the superiority of simplicity in devotion—a theme which was to be much emphasized shortly thereafter in Hasidism. This interpretation is evident from the opening simile. God loves the first zaddik's wise *deeds*; the divine love is conditioned on the wisdom of the deed. But God loves the second zaddik for himself, and therefore "everything [the son] says is proper in the eyes [of the father]." No matter what form the divine service of the second zaddik takes, even if not "in wisdom," i.e., without the complex mystical meditations required by Lurianic Kabbalah, it is acceptable to God merely by virtue of the fact that the zaddik *himself* is beloved by God. The subsequent metaphor, "external" and "internal" aspects of existence, points in the same direction. The second zaddik's internality grants him the status of the internality or core of all creation. (This interpretation differs somewhat from that of R. Shatz-Uffenheimer in *Maggid Devarav le-Yaakov*, pp. 114–115.)

Therefore is it written, *And ye shall traffic in the land (ve-et ha-aretz tisharu)*: *ve-et* ["and," composed of the Hebrew letters *vav, alef, tav;* the *vav* is the conjunction, and] the letters *alef* [the first letter of the Hebrew alphabet] to *tav* [the last letter of the alphabet], which now abide in *the land,* or worldliness.[197] For all was created by means of the [Hebrew] letters, which constitute the Word of God, and they are [identical with] the holy sparks.[198] *Tisharu* ("ye shall traffic") from the word meaning "elevation," from the wheel, which turns [so that one side always goes up].

25. EVERY JEW IS PART OF THE MESSIAH
Source: R. Menahem Nahum of Chernobyl, Me'or Enayim to Pinhas

A teaching of the Baal Shem Tov: Every Jew must rectify and enhance the aspect of the full stature (*komah shelemah*) of the Messiah that is related to his own individual soul.[199] As is known, the name Adam (*a-d-m*) is the acronym of *Adam, David, Messiah.* This is so because Adam's full stature extended from one end of the world to the other.[200] All Jewish souls are encompassed within the full stature of Adam, the first man. Afterwards, because of the sin, his full stature was diminished. Similar, the Messiah will possess the full stature of all Jewish souls, encompassing six hundred thousand souls[201] as it was before Adam's sin.[202] Therefore every individual Jew must endeavor to enhance the aspect of the Messiah that is related to his soul, so that the entire stature is rectified and established. Then there will be an unending and general unity [of souls]. May it happen speedily and in our days.

---

197. The equivalent of the English "from A to Z." The second zaddik, in his simplicity but total and immediate communion, elevates not only the externalities of the world but corporeality (*artziut,* "worldliness," "earthliness") itself. It is a more radical transformation of existence.

198. A reference to traditional kabbalistic letter-mysticism. The Hebrew letters are manifestations of God's hidden powers (see Scholem, *Major Trends in Jewish Mysticism,* pp. 14, 17, et passim), and the alphabet from *alef* to *tav,* which is "in the land," symbolizes the fallen sparks awaiting redemption by the zaddik.

199. "Gestalt" would be a better translation of *komah shelemah.* The term implies the mystic configuration of the Messiah.

200. Hagigah 12a. The biblical Adam represented universal man.

201. The number of adult male Israelites present at the revelation at Sinai, and therefore representing the totality of the people of Israel.

202. Thus the Messiah will restore the universal fullness that was Adam's before the primeval sin.

26. THE GARDEN OF EDEN AND THE RESURRECTION
Source: R. Shneur Zalman of Liady, Iggeret ha-Kodesh, chap. 17

It is known that arousal from below—man arousing in his heart the traits of kindness and compassion for all who are in need of compassion—elicits arousal from above,[203] i.e., the arousal of great compassion for him from the Source of compassion, which causes the fruits to be emanated upon him in this world, while the principal abides for the world-to-come."[204] The fruits are the grace flowing from the Source of compassion and the Fountainhead of life. It proceeds downwards, descending from above to below, etc., until it vests itself in this world in [the blessing of] children, life, and sustenance, etc.[205]

The principal is [the mitzvah], as it is written, *Thy commandment (mitzvatekha) is very broad* (Ps. 119:96). It should say *mitzvotekha*—in the plural form! Furthermore, the term *broad* is unclear. However, *mitzvatekha* refers specifically to the precept of charity, which is truly the mitzvah of the Lord, which the Holy One Himself, in all His majesty, performs at all times by animating the world, and will do in the future with great power and force. And thus it is written, *That they may keep the way of the Lord to do righteousness (tzedakah) and justice* (Gen. 18:19). Metaphorically speaking, [tzedakah, "charity" or "righteousness"] is like a road from one city to another.[206] It is a capacity for the manifestation and radiation of the light of the blessed Ein-Sof, which encompasses all worlds. [This light] will in the future, at the resurrection of the dead, shine and become manifest even unto this world (with great power and force infinitely exceeding the state of manifestation of the illumination in the upper and lower Garden of Eden),[207] by means of arousal from below in the form of charity and gratuitous kindness. For in the time-to-come, the souls of all the zaddikim and tannaim and prophets who are now in the Upper Garden of

---

203. Arousal from below (*itaruta di-letata*) is an act undertaken by man, a human effort, while arousal from above (*itaruta di-le'ela*) refers to the divine grace, issuing from above. To elicit this heavenly emanation, the arousal must be initiated by an appropriate benevolent act on earth.
204. Referring to Mishnah Pe'ah 1:1, which says of certain good deeds that the fruits may be eaten in this world, while the principal remains for the world-to-come.
205. Mo'ed Katan 28b.
206. *Tzedakah* is called the "way of the Lord" because it is like a roadway that makes it possible to travel from one place to another.
207. On these terms, see above, chap. 1, selection 13.

Eden, at the ultimate level, will be vested in their bodies, and they will arise at the time of the resurrection to derive pleasure from the splendor of the Shekhinah.

That is, the manifestation and illumination as it is in the Garden of Eden is on the level of *memallei kol almin* ("permeating all worlds").[208] This is the level of the progression from one rung to another by means of immense contractions,[209] and as our Sages said, "The world-to-come was created by the *yod*,"[210] the sphere of the supreme Hokhmah,[211] referred to as the upper Eden, and evolving and vesting itself in all the worlds, as it is written, *In wisdom (hokhmah) hast Thou made them all* (Ps. 104:24), and *wisdom (hokhmah) preserves the life of him that has it* (Eccles. 7:12). In the Garden of Eden, [the sphere of Hokhmah] is in a state of being apprehended by each according to his own measure. For as is known, the delight of the souls in the Garden of Eden derives from their perception of the secrets of the Torah, [as a reward] for having occupied themselves in this world with the revealed [parts of Torah], as mentioned in the holy Zohar[212] and in the Talmud[213] with reference to Rabbah bar Nahmani.

The illumination at the time of the resurrection, however, will derive from the level of *sovev kol almin* ("encompassing all worlds"),[214] which is not in a state of contraction, measure, and limit, but is limitless and endless. The concept of *sovev kol almin*, as has been explained in *Tanya*, chapter 48, is not to be taken in its literal sense of [spatial] encirclement, heaven forfend, but rather that it is not in a state of investment [immanence]. Note this carefully.

---

208. The term denotes divine immanence: God as revealed or manifest in creation. *Sovev kol almin* denotes divine transcendence: God in His utter and undifferentiated beyondness. In terms of the sefirot, *sovev kol almin* corresponds to Keter, the supreme transcendent sphere, and *memallei kol almin* corresponds to Hokhmah, which is the immanent source of all subsequent emanations.

209. The illumination of divine immanence is an immensely screened derivative of the light of divine transcendence. As the world cascades from higher to lower, the light is contracted ever more.

210. Menahot 29b.

211. The *yod*, by its very form as a simple point, indicates the immense contraction of the divine light contained in it. Immanence is related to the sefirah of Hokhmah.

212. Zohar III, 169b.

213. Bava Metzia 86a.

214. R. Shneur Zalman now distinguishes between the Garden of Eden, the spiritual state of life after death and before the resurrection, in which souls bask in the *memallei kol almin*, or immanence, and the resurrection, when they will relate to God in the superior illumination of transcendence, *sovev kol almin*.

This is the meaning of what our Sages said, [that in the world-to-come the righteous will set] "their crowns upon their heads, and taking delight," etc.[215] A crown (*atarah*) is something that encompasses and encircles, and is called *keter*.[216] It is the aspect of the intermediary which joins the illumination of the Emanator, the blessed Ein-Sof, to the emanated, and in the time-to-come it will shine and will be revealed in this world to all the righteous who rise at the resurrection.

This explains what our Sages meant when they said: "In the time-to-come the righteous will be addressed as holy."[217] Holiness is the rank of being separated; it is not subject to apperception and knowledge, because it transcends the rank of wisdom and knowledge that applies to the Garden of Eden.[218] Thus Scripture states, *Wisdom (ḥokhmah) shall be found from nothingness (ayin)* (Job 28:12)[219]—i.e., from the rank of the Supreme Keter, which, in the holy Zohar, is called *Ayin*.[220] [Keter's] abundance and illumination are manifested only when [after the resurrection] the soul is vested in a pure and clear body. For "their beginning is intertwined, expressly, in their end,"[221] and "last in deed, first in thought," etc.,[222] as is known. But it is impossible to reach this level until one has first been in the Garden of Eden, to perceive the aspect of the Supreme Hokhmah in accordance with one's measure.[223] . . .

This explains the meaning of *Thy commandment is very broad*, i.e., the precept of charity, which is a vessel and lid, is very broad so that there may be invested in it the illumination from the light of the

---

215. Berakhot 17a.
216. Hence the sefirah by that name, beyond Hokhmah, and transcending the illumination of the Garden of Eden (immanence).
217. Bava Batra 75b.
218. Holiness implies transcendence, and is superior to the Garden of Eden, which derives from divine immanence.
219. The standard English translation is, "but wisdom, where shall it be found?" The translation in the text is the characteristic hasidic reading. *Ayin* ("nothingness") is a euphemism for Keter, which, as intermediary to the Ein-Sof, is too far beyond human ken to be dealt with as a definable and identifiable substance.
220. Zohar III, 256b end.
221. *Sefer Yetzirah* 1:7.
222. Siddur, Lekhah Dodi hymn. The final act was no accident, but part of the divine plan from the very beginning.
223. Before the supreme gift of the illumination of divine transcendence can be attained at the resurrection, one must first have experienced the illumination of immanence, symbolized by Hokhmah.

blessed Ein-Sof which, in the time-to-come, will shine without limit and end, because of the gratuitous kindness and the arousal from below, called *the way of the Lord*. The term *very broad* means without limit and end. But *I have seen an end to every purpose* [*tikhlah*] (Ps. 119:96).[224] *Tikhlah* is [etymologically] related to *kelot ha-nefesh*, the yearning of the soul in the Garden of Eden, for there it is in a mode of end, limit, and contraction, as mentioned above. And [the reason it says] *to every tikhlah* is because the Garden of Eden has innumerable levels and rungs, one higher than the other, to the highest level, as is mentioned in *Likkutei ha-Shas* by Rabbi Isaac Luria, explaining the saying of our Sages, "Scholars [of Torah] have no rest," etc.,[225] because they rise constantly—from level to level—in understanding of the Torah, which has no end, etc., until after the resurrection, when they will have rest, etc.

27. THE PHYSICAL FORM OF RESURRECTION
Source: *R. Levi Yitzhak of Berdichev, Kedushat Levi to Va'ethanan*

There is a well-known debate between the kabbalists and the philosophers concerning one [whose soul] has undergone many transmigrations:[226] in which body will he be resurrected? The kabbalists hold that the soul will be vested in the first body, the philosophers, that it will be vested in the last body.[227] I maintain a middle position. It is well known that the 248 positive commandments correspond to the 248 organs of the body, and the 365 negative commandments correspond to its 365 sinews. Each part of the body corresponds to a specific mitzvah. [Thus we may understand] the dictum of the rabbis[228] that patriarch Abraham fulfilled [the whole Torah], including *eruv*

---

224. The beginning of the verse the author is expounding, "Thy commandment is very broad . . ."

225. Berakhot 64a. In the present world, governed by immanence, differentiation in value and substance predominates, necessitating a constant struggle, climbing, and the aspiration for improvement and betterment; there is no rest for the spiritually ambitious. But at the resurrection, when the divine transcendence, which is uniform and unlimited, will prevail, rest will be granted to all.

226. The idea of *gilgul* (metempsychosis, or the transmigration of souls) was widely accepted by mystics. Most Jewish philosophers, being of a rationalistic bent, opposed it. Hasidism, profoundly influenced by the Kabbalah, accepted the belief in metempsychosis with questions. See G. Scholem, *On the Mystical Shape of the Godhead*.

227. The kabbalists believed that at the resurrection man's original body will be restored to him. See Additional Note *1.

228. Yoma 28b, Kiddushin 82a.

tavshilin,[229] even though this was before the giving of the Torah.[230] By
the sensibility of his organs he was able to grasp [the essence of] the
entire Torah. Consequently, when a man fulfills the entire Torah, he
sets aright and perfects the entire structure of his body by means of
the 248 organs and 365 sinews; and when he impairs a mitzvah he
impairs and weakens the organ [or sinew] that corresponds to it. [As
a consequence, he] lacks the limb that corresponds to the commandment he violated. His soul, therefore, must undergo many transmigrations until it has rectified all its earlier transgressions. In this way
all its organs are healed, and the structure of his body is rectified and
completed in utter perfection.[231]

At the time of the resurrection, when God gathers the dispersed of
Israel, every single Jew will be whole in the structure of his body and
soul, utterly perfect; and will be ready to enter into the sanctuary of
the King, wholly free of any defect. This will occur by means of the
joining of all the healthy limbs together, each limb having achieved
tikkun, made whole and healed as a result of many transmigrations.
Each separate organ, so rectified, will be joined to the others in the
structure of the body, which will be utterly perfect and without
defects.[232]

28. THE NATURAL AND THE SUPERNATURAL
Source: R. Levi Yitzhak of Berdichev, Kedushat Levi, Kedushah Sheniyah,
119b, s.v. ve-attah neva'er

Our Sages said that all of the holidays except Purim will be abrogated.[233]

---

229. A relatively minor commandment, for it is not biblical but an "ordinance of the
scribes."
230. R. Levi Yitzhak is seeking to resolve an apparent anachronism: how can Abraham
be said to have observed the Torah if it was not yet revealed? He answers that by dint
of the correspondence of parts of the body to the mitzvot, Abraham intuited the mystical essence of the commandments that were later to be revealed. See R. Hayyim of
Volozhin, *Nefesh ha-Hayyim,* 1:21.
231. The organs and sinews here are not the physical body, but the structure of the
body, i.e., the *Gestalt* which is man's spiritual self mystically related to his material
body.
232. The kabbalists anticipate the restoration of the original physical body, and the
philosophers, a new physical body. R. Levi Yitzhak differs with both positions. In his
view the old body is purified through the various transmigrations of its individual
parts and rejoined; it is neither the old body nor a new one, but a *renewed* body.
233. Yalkut Shemoni II:944. The discourse is based on a literal reading of this
midrashic statement. Most authorities, however, understand it as referring not to the
biblically mandated festivals but to the postbiblical celebrations recorded in Megillat
Ta'anit. See Rosh Hashanah 19b and Yerushalmi Ta'anit 2:13.

We know from the writings of Nahmanides and other Rishonim (medieval commentators) that at the time of the Messiah all natural creatures will be rectified[234]—*the cow and the bear shall feed* [together] (Isa. 11:7)—and all the creatures of nature will do the will of the people of Israel, and supernatural miracles will not be needed, for natural beings will be rectified at the time of the Messiah. All of them will have to obey the will of God and of His people Israel.

On the verse *I will cause evil beasts to cease from the land* (Lev. 26:6), Nahmanides writes, "When the mitzvot are observed, Eretz Israel will be as the world was in the beginning, before the sin of Adam; neither beast nor crawling thing killed a human." Later in the same passage he writes, "They will achieve their original nature, placed in them at the time of their creation." . . .

Now, all the festivals commemorate the Exodus from Egypt, as Nahmanides comments; for this reason, the *Tur* tells us, we recite in the Kiddush, "commemorating the Exodus from Egypt."[235] Passover is itself the anniversary of leaving Egypt; Sukkot too, as the verse states, *I made the children of Israel to dwell in booths* [*when I brought them out of the land of Egypt*] (Lev. 23:43); and Shavuot celebrates the giving of the Torah [at Mount Sinai], when [the first commandment of the Decalogue] was given, *I am the Lord thy God, Who brought thee out of the land of Egypt* (Exod. 20:2). Thus, all of the holidays commemorate the Exodus from Egypt, when [the Children of Israel] saw changes in nature itself, and signs and miracles clearly indicating that God created the world *ex nihilo*, as Nahmanides states.[236]

In the future, in the messianic time, all of nature will be compelled to act in accordance with the will of God's people, Israel. . . . the holidays will be abrogated because they are a sign to remind us of the Exodus, when supernatural miracles and wonders occurred. But in the

---

234. The kabbalistic idea of *tikkun*. In the messianic era, everything in nature and all creatures of nature will realize the original character they had at the time of their creation.

235. The *Tur* was written by R. Jacob b. Asher (Spain, 14th cent.), one of the most eminent medieval codifiers of the Halakhah. The point is that the Kiddush (the sanctification pronounced over wine on the eve of Sabbaths and festivals) for *every* occasion, and not only Passover, contains the words "in memory of the Exodus from Egypt."

236. The miracles were supernatural, to teach that God, who can suspend natural law, is the Creator of nature out of nothing.

days of the Messiah there will be no need for nature to be changed.[237] As a result, the holidays will all be abrogated, because the illumination that once occurred [at the Exodus] and which is commemorated by means of the sanctity of the festivals, will now be revealed (i.e., in the time of the Messiah), and God's grace, which appeared then, will be revealed again. . . . In the days of the Messiah, there will be no need for changes in nature, because all nature shall be set aright.

Purim, however, will not be abolished, for the [special] illumination of Purim was that nature had been rectified, for the miracles occurred within nature, even as will happen in the days of the Messiah. In the [messianic] future, therefore, Purim will not be abolished.[238]

29. THE MESSIAH'S ANCESTRY
Source: R. Elimelekh of Lizhensk, No'am Elimelekh, Likkutei Shoshanah, p. 101a

The Talmud states that a found object, the Messiah, and a serpent all come unexpectedly.[239] All of these are really one, for the Messiah was

---

237. Because the supernatural will have become natural. In effect, what we now call nature is corrupt. The world's original state was perfect, but was perverted by man's sin, so that nature and its objects no longer responded to the divine will. This necessitated the legislation of the festivals, but they will be superfluous when the Messiah comes and nature is restored to its pristine purity.

238. The miracle of Purim, unlike those of the Exodus, was a "hidden miracle," i.e., it occurred within nature as we know it and necessitated no suspension of natural law. The divine intervention was indirect, guiding historical forces and diplomatic processes rather than breaking the rules of nature. Purim is a paradigm of the messianic condition, when what we now call supernatural will become natural, and God's involvement in the world will require no change in the world order. Hence Purim will abide even if other holidays do not.

239. Sanhedrin 98a. This passage is part of a discourse on the verse "I have found David My servant; with My holy oil have I anointed him" (Ps. 89:21). The Midrash (Genesis Rabbah 41:5) asks, "Where did I find him?" and answers, "In Sodom." According to R. Elimelekh, this refers to David's ancestry, since his great-grandmother Ruth was a Moabite, and Moab was the son of one of the two daughters of Lot, who, concluding from the destruction of Sodom that the whole world had been devastated, committed incest with their father in order to continue the human race (Gen. 19:30—38). R. Elimelekh attributes immoral intentions to Lot (surprisingly, since he was intoxicated at the time), as opposed to the noble intentions of the daughters. Hence there are two contradictory elements in the ancestry of David and, by extension, of the Messiah, who will be a scion of David. The daughters provide the side of holiness, and Lot "the other side" (sitra aḥara), the euphemism for evil and the diabolical. The element of sanctity is a "find" in the sordid episode of incest, and it is this find which R. Elimelekh sees in the verse "I have found David," etc.

born as a result of the two others, the found object and the serpent. The two are also one, for the find came about by emerging from the *sitra aḥara*, [symbolized by] the serpent.[240] David was anointed with great sanctity. . . . Why did it happen first through the serpent, when he was anointed with such great sanctity and eminence?

I suggest the following good reason. From the very outset our Creator intended that there would be an exile [of the people of Israel]. Had the Messiah been born from a righteous person,[241] no enemy could possibly have prevailed against us, to exile us from our land. God ordained that it would be this way because *My thoughts are not your thoughts* (Isa. 55:8), and for reasons known [only to Him]. God caused the sequence of events to occur whereby the anointed of God was to be born specifically from the portion [of the realm of evil]. Afterwards, when David wanted to banish the [evil] side from which he had been born, eliminating it from the world, and thus becoming the true and eternal Messiah, so that there would no longer be an exile, he was unable to do so, for he had no power over [the reach of evil] because he had been born from it. Hence Rashi says that David wished to destroy [the pagan nations, embodying the *sitra aḥara*], but was prevented by heaven from doing so until our righteous Messiah comes, speedily and in our days, amen, and then *our horn shall be exalted* (Ps. 89:18).

And in order that we may have a remnant in the world, and that we may survive in this bitter exile amidst these wolves (the oppressor nations), David was anointed with the horn of oil and with great sanctity: *My horn is exalted*. Thus is he able to protect us during the exile so that we can survive. As our Sages tell us, "The Messiah sits at the gates of Rome and suffers for the people of Israel"[242]—scrutinize the text carefully—and when his splendorous horn flourishes, may it be speedily, then [the Messiah] will be established and enduring, powerful and mighty, forever and ever.[243]

---

240. Lot's daughters are the find. The serpent is a symbol of evil, the *sitra aḥara*, i.e., Lot's immoral intentions.

241. That is, had all his ancestors been righteous; had he not been descended from the incestuous Lot.

242. Sanhedrin 98a, according to the reading of the Gaon of Vilna.

243. Because of his descent from the *sitra aḥara*, the Messiah could not prevent the exile, but his descent from the side of holiness enabled him to keep Israel alive. When the Messiah finally arrives, good will triumph over evil, and Israel will endure forever in peace and without thought of exile.

30. THE PRECIOUS FROM THE VILE
Source: R. Zadok ha-Kohen of Lublin, Zidkat ha-Zaddik, no. 111

In the era ushering in the Messiah, the main [achievement will be] the extraction of the precious from the vile.[244] Specifically, from a place of the *yetzer ha-ra* (Evil Urge) and where sin prevails, from there will He take you, by means of *teshuvah*. As our Sages state, "The son of David (the Messiah) will come in a generation that is completely guilty."[245] A soul [that repents from a life full of sin, issues] from the portion of the Messiah. Similarly, King David [from whom the Messiah is descended] is described as "he who exalted the yoke of repentance."[246] And it is known of the congregation of Israel that *her feet go down to death* (Prov. 5:5), may God protect us![247] In the era ushering in the Messiah, the souls will be derived from the feet,[248] where wickedness and the Evil Urge prevail. Therefore, it is precisely a generation of such souls that will merit the Messiah. That is why our Sages said, "*And God saw everything that He had made, and behold, it was very good* (Gen. 1:31); this is the *yetzer ha-ra*."[249] Similarly, [the soul of] the Messiah himself is born from such a place, for it is stated in the Midrash ha-Ne'elam regarding the daughters of Lot and Lot himself that they are the source of the power of the Evil Urge;[250] and from there grew the root of the son of David [the Messiah].[251] But here is the essence of perfec-

---

244. See Jer. 15:19, "Therefore, thus saith the Lord: if thou return, and I bring thee back . . . and if thou bring forth the precious out of the vile, thou shalt be as My mouth."
245. Sanhedrin 98a.
246. Mo'ed Katan 16b, commenting on 2 Sam. 23:1.
247. That is, Israel has the capacity to descend, morally, to the very depths.
248. The feet, the very bottom of the body, symbolize spiritual lowliness. In the era before the Messiah's advent, spiritual degradation will prevail. There may be a pun here: the traditional term for this era is *ikveta di-meshiḥa* ("the heels of the Messiah," i.e., when the footsteps of the approaching Messiah can already be heard). R. Zadok may be interpreting "heels" as alluding to the spiritual level of "feet," which "go down to death." The underlying idea is that human history is symbolized by a comprehensive body from which individual human souls derive. By the time history reaches its end, the souls entering the world are those deriving from the heels of the cosmic body.
249. Genesis Rabbah 9:9.
250. Zohar I, 109a—112a.
251. Since we know that the Messiah is descended from David ("the son of David"), who, in turn, was descended from Ruth, and she comes from Moab, the child of Lot's incest with one of his daughters; and since the Zohar tells us that Lot and his daughters are the source of the *yetzer ha-ra*; hence the Messiah's origin is lowly indeed.

tion for them [in the messianic era]: the source of evil will be transformed into the good—what the Talmud describes as "the slaughter of the *yetzer ha-ra.*"[252] And the [Messiah's] soul is the nethermost of the body, and the closest to evil, possessing all manner of intensity. In this [material] world the generations progressively decline. But [in the messianic era], when the *tikkun* is performed, it will [emerge] as the good—"last in action, first in thought."[253]

That is the mystery of *And the living creatures ran and returned as the appearance of a flash of lightning* (Ezek. 1:14), for where [the light] stops, from thence it returns and begins to illuminate and becomes the head [of the beam].[254] As the Rabbis said, "an inverted world have I seen."[255]

31. THORNS AND LILIES
Source: R. Zadok ha-Kohen of Lublin, Zidkat ha-Zaddik, no. 52

Do not be astonished if you see the wicked increasing in the world, and growing ever stronger. Keep in mind that God is the Master of the

---

252. Sukkah 52a, "In the time-to-come, the Holy One will bring the evil urge and slaughter it in the presence of the righteous and the wicked."

253. A well-known principle: all that happens at the end was deliberately planned by the Creator at the very beginning; everything was providentially ordained, nothing is an accident. So too the emergence of the Messiah, the essence of goodness, out of the depths of evil; the transformation of evil into its very opposite is part of the divine plan.

254. This verse from Ezekiel is widely quoted in the kabbalistic literature, usually to illustrate the principle of alternation in the mystic's psyche—the exaltation and depression, the surging toward God in love, and the retreat in awe. For R. Zadok it alludes to the dialectical transmutation of evil into good. The tip of the light beam is the first to be reflected back; hence the Messiah's soul, which reaches farthest into the realm of evil, is reflected back (transmuted) into the realm of righteousness, and reaches farthest into this domain.

255. Pesahim 50a. When R. Joseph was deathly ill, he saw a vision of an upside-down world. When he was saved from death's door and told this to his father, the latter replied that the world he had perceived (the spiritual world, or the redeemed world of the Messiah) was the normal one, and ours is the inverted one. Thus the messianic world will be the reverse of ours, and the souls that issue from evil will be transformed into virtuous ones. The source of this radical transformation is repentance. R. Zadok is predicting a profound turnaround in mankind's spiritual condition based on the power of repentance, and he sees this as the distinguishing mark of the messianic age as it emerges abruptly from the premessianic period of "the heels of the Messiah."

Vineyard, as the Rabbis said,[256] "and He knows the vineyard far better than we do, and constantly attends to its needs."[257] Our Rabbis said that the son of David may come to a generation that is wholly guilty,[258] for God will place a king as cruel as Haman over them, thereby inducing them to repent. Moreover, they said: Which generation [of Israel] is the most beloved of all? The generation [that wandered] in the desert, for they were privileged to receive the Torah. The same is said about the generation of King Solomon: they were informed that they merited the world-to-come because they were privileged to build the [First] Temple.[259] Certainly the generation of the Messiah will be beloved, even if it should be a completely guilty generation. It will be transformed into a generation that is beloved [in the eyes of God] by means of God's bringing them to repentance.[260] We must assume, therefore, that the root of their souls comes from a source far loftier than any other generation.[261] For Israel's sins are truly not part of its essence. The Sages compared them to the "myrtle amidst reeds."[262] Therefore their punishment is by means of these [very] sins, for the thorn pricks [the flower].[263] But when the surrounding thorns are burned, the lily remains whole. Moreover, a lily among thorns stands out more [than a lily by itself], as has been said.[264] (This agrees

---

256. In Bava Metzia 83b, R. Yehoshua b. Korha says, in reference to God, "Let the Master of the Vineyard Himself come and weed out the thorns."
257. The apparent triumph of the wicked should not disturb us; there are thorns in the vineyard only by leave of the Master, Who allows them to flourish because they form part of His plan.
258. Sanhedrin 98a.
259. Mo'ed Katan 9a.
260. By initiating a chain of events in which they will, of their own volition, repent and return to Him.
261. Cf. the same author's theory in the preceding selection, and see further in this one.
262. Sanhedrin 44a, "The myrtle, even though it stands among reeds, is still a myrtle and is called a myrtle." The sins of Israel are extraneous and not indigenous to their inner selves.
263. Two literary allusions are mixed here, but the intent is the same. In addition to the talmudic metaphor of a myrtle amidst the reeds, R. Zadok refers to the biblical verse, "As a lily among the thorns" (Songs of Songs 2:2). According to the Midrash (Leviticus Rabbah 23:5), whichever way the wind blows the lily, it is pricked by the thorns; nevertheless "its heart faces upward," and when the thorns are burned, the lily remains whole. R. Zadok is saying that the sins, like the thorns, are the source of punishment and suffering but, again like the thorns, they are extraneous to the lily-Israel and can be burned away.
264. *Zohar Ḥadash* II, 189b. To have overcome sin and lust is nobler than to be naturally without the propensity for evil.

with the opinion that a penitent is superior to a completely righteous person [who never sinned].) *Teshuvah* can occur in one brief instant, as the Talmud indicates.[265]

We pray, *Turn Thou us unto Thee, O Lord, and we shall be turned* (Lam. 5:21), but God cries out, *Return unto Me, and I will return unto you* (Mal. 3:7). See Lamentations Rabbah, end. We call upon God to initiate the reconciliation, and He calls upon us to take the first step. It is likely that "in a generation wholly guilty," Israel's request will prevail.[266] When God so desires, in one brief instant all of the surrounding thorns will be consumed. Everything will happen in accordance with God's will. At that time it will be manifest that whatever happened before had to be.[267]

32. THE MESSIAH'S ORIGIN: THE DESTRUCTION
Source: R. Zadok ha-Kohen of Lublin, Zidkat ha-Zaddik, no. 70

Man's excellence is to be found in, and achieved by means of, the very thing wherein he is blemished.

Thus, on the verse *And they sewed fig leaves together* (Gen. 3:7), the Sages commented, "The very thing which brought them ruin was the means for setting them aright."[268] Similarly, our Sages state that "on the very day that the Temple was destroyed, the Messiah was born."[269] In the same vein they said, "Where in the Torah is [the idea of] the resurrection of the dead to be derived from?"[270] (By this they mean to say that everything in the world has its root in the Torah, or, to put it another way, that all existence is connected with the Source of life, which is the authentic will of God.)

---

265. Kiddushin 49b.
266. If Israel is wholly guilty, how can it return to God? Hence He must turn to us first.
267. R. Zadok here returns to his first premise: the Creator, as Master of the Vineyard, knows His world and plans for it properly. If evil seems to reign supreme, it is only temporary, for the thorns will soon be consumed, and the lily will flourish.
268. Sanhedrin 70a. This follows the opinion that the tree of the knowledge of good and evil, from which Adam and Eve ate in defiance of the divine command, was a fig tree.
269. Yerushalmi Berakhot 2:4.
270. Sanhedrin 91b. The talmudic passage suggests several scriptural sources for the belief in resurrection. For the present purpose, they are irrelevant; it is the question which is illuminating, and it is this which R. Zadok's parenthetical statement in the text is meant to convey: the source of the resurrection is the Torah. The restoration of life to the dead is the archetypical instance of the paradoxical insight as to the close relationship of man's blemish and excellence: from death emerges life. This holds true because everything derives, via Torah, from the ultimate source, the will of God.

This also explains why the [red] heifer cleanses from the impurity caused by death.[271] Our Sages commented, "Let the mother come and cleanse her son's dirt."[272] (That is why Jeroboam set up idols of golden calves [1 Kings 12:28], for he was the source of Messiah son of Joseph, who will be descended from Abijah son of Jeroboam. Messiah son of Joseph is destined to be killed, for only Messiah son of David will survive, as it is written, *He asked life of You, and You gave it to him* [Ps. 21:5].)[273] The heifer is the mother [symbolizing the sefirah of Binah and identified with the heart], which gave birth to this; i.e., that all comes from God; from Him all things emerged. Thus [the red heifer] is the cleansing of the dirt, as stated above.[274]

---

271. Ritual impurity, contracted from contact with a corpse, can be lifted only by a rite which involves sprinkling with the ashes of a red heifer (Num. 19:1—22).

272. Numbers Rabbah 19:4. The heifer is the mother of the calf. The calf is reminiscent of the golden calf, the infamous sin of the biblical period. The heifer, whose ashes purify, is the antidote to the calf. Hence: "Let the mother cleanse the dirt of her son." The same animal is the source of both defilement and purification. R. Zadok presumably identifies the moral uncleanliness of the golden calf episode with death, and the purification with life.

273. Another biblical illustration of the author's principle, based upon kabbalistic tradition. Jeroboam was the idolatrous king who set up two golden calves for public worship. Yet the same Jeroboam is the ancestor of Messiah son of Joseph. Tradition has it that there will be two Messiahs. One, descended from Joseph, will fall in battle, where as the other, the scion of David, will survive and his kingdom will flourish. R. Zadok draws upon an interesting kabbalistic source (*Zohar Hadash* to Balak, s.v. *telat malkin*) which records a fascinating tradition. According to the biblical text (1 Kings 14:1–18), all of Jeroboam's children met unnatural deaths and were not buried. Only Abijah merited burial. His mother's attempts to save him via the intervention of the prophet Ahijah backfired; upon her return from the prophet she found that "the child died" (v. 17). But, the *Zohar Hadash* relates, the day Abijah died, a child was born unto him. The baby was snatched and raised in the desert by 170 Ephraimites (of the tribe of Jeroboam) who were not implicated in the king's idolatrous activities. This child became the ancestor of the Messiah son of Joseph (i.e., from the tribe of Ephraim, son of Joseph). Hence, once again, the Messiah issues from the king who set up the golden calves; the source of blemish is the source of excellence as well.

274. R. Zadok now suggests a kabbalistic exegesis of the heifer-calf illustration of his thesis. The heifer, as stated, is the mother. And in the kabbalistic doctrine, the third sefirah, Binah, is the Mother, the celestial womb, from which all existence flows. It is in this realm that we find the first signs of differentiation, as the Ein-Sof turns outward in self-revelation. Just as all existence issues from Binah, the Mother, so the heifer-mother (borrowing the metaphor of Numbers Rabbah, see above, n. 195) is the source of both the dirt and its cleansing: the calf-idols established by Jeroboam, and

33. THE MESSIAH'S UNIVERSAL SOUL
Source; R. Zadok ha-Kohen of Lublin, Zidkat ha-Zaddik, no. 159

When a person repents, forgiveness is granted both to him and to the whole world, as our Sages declared.[275]

How does [one person's repentance] bring about forgiveness [for the whole world]? This happens because the penitent awakens thoughts of *teshuvah* in the hearts of others. But not everyone has the capacity to be this one person [whose repentance can occasion forgiveness for the entire world]. Such a person has not yet existed, for that unique person will only be the Messiah, the son of David. [In order to perform this task] his soul must comprise all other souls. Otherwise a person's thoughts of *teshuvah* cannot evoke thoughts of *teshuvah* in others who are unrelated to his soul.[276] [Moreover,] it is necessary for the thought of repentance to affect *all* aspects of his soul. One who encompasses the entire world possesses [in his soul] the plenitude of powers of the entire world; and if he repents with only one power, he can arouse repentance only within those others who are dependent upon this one power.[277] King David possessed a soul that encompassed all other souls, for he was the "fourth leg of the *Merkavah*,"[278] and assumed the yoke of repentance solely for the transgression of desire.[279] That is why Jeroboam, who did not have this blemish, did not repent, and entered into conflict with the house of David. Except for the patriarchs and King David, no other soul has

the Messiah who will issue from his loins.

---

275. Yoma 86b, "R. Meir used to say, 'Great is repentance, because for the sake of a single person who repents, the entire world is forgiven.'"
276. Only the Messiah is that single person because only the Messiah's soul is universal; since it encompasses all human souls, his own repentance as a single person evokes repentance in everyone else.
277. Even if one possesses a universal soul, his repentance must touch every aspect of his personality for it to be effective for everyone. Should he limit his repentance to one trait (or potency), his influence will be restricted to those who relate to him in that trait.
278. Zohar III, 262b. As one of the legs of the Divine Chariot (*Merkavah*), his soul encompasses all others. For an explanation of this reference, see next note.
279. While King David, as the progenitor of the Messiah, possessed a universal soul, his repentance for his sin with Bathsheba concerned only one potency, or aspect of his personality, sexual desire. He succeeded in obtaining forgiveness for all who had succumbed to the same weakness (for they were, in this sense, related to his potency), but not for anyone else.

encompassed the world in its entirety.[280] (Moses' soul encompassed only the souls of scholars; [his far-ranging effect on his contemporaries came about because] his generation was wholly a generation of knowledge and scholarship.) Other individuals who repent have the ability to evoke *teshuvah* only in souls who are dependent upon them, and then only with the specific power concerning which they repent.

34. THE MESSIAH IN EACH OF US
Source: R. Zadok ha-Kohen of Lublin, Zidkat ha-Zaddik, no. 153

The grief (i.e., pangs of conscience) that we experience because of our sins takes the place of suffering.[281] This is what the Zohar teaches concerning the Messiah.[282]

As we know, the soul of the leader of the generation encompasses all the individual souls in his generation. The soul of the Messiah is a composite of the souls of *all* generations after they have completed their striving in this world (even as the patriarchs encompass the souls of all generations in their beginnings . . . in their roots and source).[283]

In every individual soul, the point of its striving to attain its true purpose is the point of the Messiah. It is in this point that [the Messiah] suffers pain over their sins—in the sense of *he was crushed by our iniquities* (Isa. 53:5)—and thereby eases their punishment of suf-

---

280. The Divine Chariot of Ezekiel's famous vision (Ezek. 1) was a *locus classicus* for a great deal of speculative mystical thought in the history of Kabbalah. See Additional Note *2. The most prevalent symbolic interpretation, and the one evidently alluded to by R. Zadok, has the *Merkavah* consisting of four sefirot: Hesed, Gevurah, Tiferet, and Malkhut. These, in turn, are personified by Abraham, Isaac, Jacob, and David, "the legs of the Chariot" (see Genesis Rabbah 47:8; Zohar I, 60b, 99a, 237a, 248b). As such, they have souls that were universal or microcosmic.
281. Since the psychological distress is punishment enough, there is no physical retribution for our sins.
282. Zohar II, 212a, "In the Garden of Eden there is a palace called the Palace of Sufferers. The Messiah goes up to this palace and calls to all who are in grief and in pain: 'Let all the suffering of Israel come upon me.' And it all comes upon him. If he did not lighten [Israel's burden of suffering] and take it upon himself, no human being would be able to bear the suffering of Israel because of the punishments [they deserve for disobeying] the Torah."
283. The patriarchs possessed universal souls made up of the roots of untarnished souls that have not experienced the vicissitudes of this-worldly life. The Messiah's is the collective of all souls after they undergo the earthly experience.

fering.[284] Study that [Zohar] passage well, for it describes how they are received in the Garden of Eden, which indicates that [the Messiah] is inspired to do this by virtue of words of Torah. We know this because of another passage in the Zohar, which tells us that the heaven [immediately] above the Garden of Eden is composed of words of Torah.[285] [A person] notices the severity of his sins, and so forth, and by means of the pain and grief he bears in the point of his heart because of them, there is aroused within him the mighty point of Messiah hidden within, and this illuminates him.

And see further [in the Zohar] that the light of Gehenna issues into the Garden of Eden;[286] this is a sign that God has accepted the grief [of contrition], for it is transformed into delight: the Garden of Eden.[287] This means that he is being illuminated by the point of Messiah, which is to say his ultimate perfection.[288]

35. FAITH AND THE TIME OF THE MESSIAH'S ARRIVAL
Source: R. Zevi Elimelekh of Dinov, Benei Yisaskhar, Sivan 5:19

Now I will reveal to you one of the things that are within my heart in

---

284. The point of contact or empathy between the Messiah and individual humans is in the striving for the soul's true purpose, and it is in regard to this *spiritual* quest that the Messiah suffers the anguish of sympathy that the Zohar discusses. (Note the difference between the idea of the Messiah voluntarily embracing the pain of others—focused on the pain of spiritual frustration—and the far different christological concept of the Messiah as a vicarious atonement for the sins of mankind.) Though talmudic and midrashic sources speak of vicarious atonement achieved through the death of the righteous, as in Mo'ed Katan 28a, these righteous individuals do not voluntarily take up that role.
285. Zohar II, 210a. This emphasizes the spiritual interpretation of the Messiah's sympathetic suffering.
286. Zohar II, 211b.
287. The Zohar passage discusses in some detail the manner in which the soul is purified of its sin in Gehenna before it is allowed to enter Paradise, or the Garden of Eden. Gods sends the healing rays of the sun to bring relief to the tormented soul, whereupon it is welcomed in Paradise. R. Zadok interprets this description in a strictly spiritual, nonmythological way: the anguished contrition of the soul is a source of divine illumination which warrants its entry into the Garden of Eden, the realm of spiritual felicity. This capacity for the travail of conscience is the Messiah aspect of every human being.
288. As opposed to the soul before its earthly adventure, for (as stated earlier) it is precisely in man's final resolution of his spiritual struggle on earth that he relates to the Messiah.

order to console grief-stricken souls and strengthen their faith.[289] The prophet Jeremiah states, *Behold, the days will come, saith the Lord, that the city shall be built to the Lord* (Jer. 31:38). The word "come" is *keri* and not *ketiv*.[290] And "I pondered how I might know this."[291] For behold, time [itself] is always being created, and yet, at the end of any given year, the year reverts to its sheath [or: source].[292] [And] then another year is emanated from the upper world which is above time into the temporal realm.

This is hinted to us in the prophet's statement by the word *come*, which is not expressed within the confines of the written letters.[293] This teaches us that the time fixed for the end [redemption] will not come within the temporal order from the upper world. But when [redemption] does [finally] come, you will readily understand that the years [specified for the redemption] of which the Sages spoke in their holy spirit [are valid], and that those times [although appearing to have long passed] will remain [hidden] in the celestial heights until their time has arrived [at the messianic redemption].[294]

At that time the word *come* will be written within the bounded confines [of the letters]: *Behold, the days* [of redemption] *come,* etc. And it will be revealed to all eyes that all the words of the prophets and Sages are valid.[295] Understand this matter well, for I have written obliquely of only one detail of that which appears correct to me on the basis of my limited understanding. [Only] God knows how it will all

289. This selection addresses a dilemma with regard to the messianic era. There is a long tradition of calculating the end of days, i.e., attempting, by various means, to predict the date when the Messiah will come. Such calculations, which began in pre-talmudic times, and are especially rife in the kabbalistic literature, often have distinguished authority behind them. See Additional Note *3.
290. In the Hebrew of the scriptural text, only the vowel signs appear but not the consonants. Hence the word *ba'im* ("coming") is read (*keri*) but not written (*ketiv*).
291. Paraphrase of Ps. 73:16.
292. All creations must return to their maker at the end of their allotted period. This is especially true of time, which, by its very elusiveness, is ephemeral. But time's transitory nature holds only for this mundane sphere.
293. Since the word "come," referring to days or years, is only pronounced but not written (see n. 213), this implies a lack of specificity and a suggestion of some higher meaning.
294. The specified years are not lost. Having returned to their celestial sheaths, they await the moment of redemption and then their truth will be miraculously revealed.
295. In other words, because time itself is of supratemporal origin, it remains impervious to human understanding, for man's comprehension cannot transcend it. At the redemption, however, we will have such understanding, and will appreciate the truth of calculations that now, in our limited view, seem denied by history.

come about, but we are obligated to believe with the faith of the faithful. *And the word of our God shall stand forever* (Isa. 40:8). Understand
[this] and meditate upon it.

36. ONE MAN'S HEAVEN IS ANOTHER'S HELL
Source: R. Yaakov Yosef of Polennoye, Tzafnat Pa'ane'ah, p. 118

Thy right hand, O Lord, is glorious in power, They right hand, O Lord, shat-
ters the enemy; and in the greatness of Thy excellency, Thou overthrowest
them that rise against Thee; Thou sendest forth Thy wrath, it consumeth them
as stubble (Exod. 15:6–7).

The following questions may be posed: First, why the redundancy,
mentioning *Thy right hand* twice? Second, [in Kabbalah] the right
hand always symbolizes mercy, and the left hand, judgment. How
then can Scripture say, *Thy right hand shatters the enemy* [an obvious
instance of judgment]? Third, how does *the greatness of Thy excellency*
overthrow His enemies?

I suggest that the answer agrees with the statement in the Talmud
that in the time-to-come [there will be no Gehenna; but] God will
remove the sun from its sheath, bringing healing to the righteous and
punishment to the wicked.[296] I have heard it said [in explanation of
this text] that instead of Gehenna, the wicked will be admitted to the
Garden of Eden—and it will be their Gehenna! For there they will see
the righteous praying joyously, dancing, and diligently learning Torah,
and in itself this will [cause them] suffering, for the wicked are unaccustomed to this. The very fact that the righteous find this gratifying
means that the wicked will experience it as punishment. *The words of*
a wise man's mouth are gracious! (Eccl. 10:12).[297]

Thus are our questions answered. The *right hand* [which rewards
the righteous] itself [as the attribute of mercy], by virtue of Torah and
prayer, *shatters the enemy*. In the same way, *the great of Thy excellency*
[by making the wicked uncomfortable] *overthrowest them that rise*
against Thee.

37. THE RIGHTEOUS AND THE WICKED IN THIS WORLD
Source: R. Yaakov Yosef of Polennoye, Toledot Yaakov Yosef to Ki Tavo, no. 1

The wicked and the righteous are essentially opposites [in this world]

---

296. Nedarim 8b.
297. The standard rabbinic formula of approval. See Additional Note *4.

and likewise in the world-to-come.[298] The way of the wicked in this world is all joy and [external] happiness—*slaying cattle and slaughtering sheep* (Isa. 22:13), and as the [same] prophet said, *Woe unto them that rise up early in the morning, that they may pursue strong drink* (Isa. 5:11).

The reason is stated in Midrash ha-Ne'elam to Vayera on the verse *Come, let us make our father drink wine* (Gen. 19:32).[299] The covetous soul entices the physical soul to become attached to the *yetzer ha-ra* (Evil Urge), saying, "What need do we have of the world-to-come? Let us follow the Evil Urge and the desire and lust of this world by means of food and drink." *And he knew not when she lay down, nor when she arose* (Gen. 19:33); that is to say, the wicked person ignores the fact that he will end up lying in a grave and then will rise to give account of himself on the day of judgment. And the Holy Spirit cries: *But these also reel through wine* (Isa. 28:7).[300]

But the righteous person knows no happiness in this world, for he is preoccupied by the struggle against *yetzer ha-ra*, day and night without rest, as the Sage said (to the returning warriors): "You have returned from a small war; now prepare yourselves for a great war."[301] ...

---

298. This selection's brooding statement on the pathos and existential suffering of the life of the righteous as they constantly struggle with their bodily drives (symbolized by the Evil Urge) is based on the kabbalistic interpretation of the biblical story of Lot's incest with his two daughters (Gen. 19:30—38).

For the Midrash ha-Ne'elam (Zohar I, 109—110), the story is a parable of two of man's three potencies: the ordinary drive to sustain his body, symbolized by the younger sister, and primarily sexual instincts, represented by the older sister (the third is man's spiritual potency—his "power of the holy soul"). Man is symbolized by Lot, intoxicated and victimized by his two instincts. The sexual instinct entices the normal instincts for food and drink, etc., to ravage their "father," because, in the words of the Zohar (and true to the spirit of the scriptural tale), "What else is there for us in the world?" Falling prey to both his corporeal appetites, man knows not "when she lay down" (its effects in this world) and "when she arose" (its consequences in the world-to-come).

299. Zohar I, 109b.

300. The Zohar, in this passage, describes three souls or dimensions of man: the rational soul; the covetous soul, repository of lust and passion; and the physical or vegetative soul, the source of the body's vitality. It is the latter two which, as mentioned above, n. 298, are identified with the two daughters of Lot who intoxicated their father in order to commit incest with him. The elder daughter symbolizes the covetous soul, and the younger represents the vegetative. Hence, "Come, let us make our father drink wine, and we will lie with him" (Gen. 19:32) is interpreted as man's emotions prevailing upon his body to succumb to temptation.

301. Ḥovot ha-Levavot, Sha'ar Yiḥud ha-Ma'aseh 5, referring to the more consequential war with one's own passions.

The Evil Urge overpowers man only when he indulges in [excessive] food and drink. Therefore our Sages counseled: "This is the way of [the study of] Torah: a morsel of bread with salt shall thou eat, and water by measure [shalt thou drink] . . . and live a life of hardship."[302] R. Moses Alshekh explains this at length [in his commentary to Num. 6:13],[303] and adds: "Joy had a proper place [in the life of the Jewish people when the Temple was standing and] when the altar was established in its place. . . . But now, however, our souls are bent to the earth, the idol worshipers are the kings and governors, and we His people are pained and persecuted." . . .

I heard from my teacher (the Besht) an allegorical explanation of the above-mentioned two groups (i.e., the wicked and the righteous). A road through a forest was inhabited by robbers and very dangerous to travelers. Once, two people took the road through the forest. One was totally inebriated—as drunk as Lot[304]—and the other was sober and clear-minded. The robbers attacked both [travelers], beating and wounding them; they were left barely alive. As they emerged [from the forest], some men met them. They asked the drunkard if [he and his companion] had crossed the forest without incident, and he replied: "We passed through safely; there is absolutely no danger." When asked to account for his bruises and wounds, he was unable to answer. They asked [the same question] of the sober one, and he said: "Heaven forbid [that you should go there]. There are robbers, and you must be very careful." And he elaborated on his warning to them. The difference [between the two] is this: the sober [person] knew [the danger from experience] and warned the others not to go there unless they were alert and armed, etc. The drunkard, however, did not even know to warn them.

Similarly, the righteous person who serves God is aware of the struggle with his yetzer ha-ra, and of the robbers who lurk on the road of those who serve the Lord. [He knows] how dangerous it is, how full of suffering life is, how one must always be on the alert to avoid ensnarement (by the Evil Urge). Thus he knows to warn others about this robber (i.e., the Evil Urge), for *he that increaseth knowledge*

---

302. Avot 6:4.

303. Alshekh (Safed, 16th cent.) describes the drinking habits in Israel during the era of the Temple, when wine was used liberally, especially when a sacrifice was offered. He then continues as quoted in the text.

304. In Halakhah, a state of intoxication in which one is unable to feel or perceive what is happening to oneself, as in the case of Lot with his daughters. See Eruvin 65b.

increaseth sorrow (Eccles. 1:18). Not so the wicked, who is happy with the joys always [provided] by the *yetzer ha-ra*, and says: all is peace, there is no danger whatsoever in this world.[305]

Likewise, there are two opposites in the world-to-come. The righteous man will consider it a joy to have rid himself of the [material] world. That is why the demise of the righteous one is defined as *petirah* [from the adjective *patur*, "acquitted"], for he has been freed from the pain of this world, the world of falsehood. He is happy to arrive in the next world. Not so the wicked one, who sees there an open ledger with his account prepared, [and is ordered] to stand in judgment and account [for his wicked deeds].

ADDITIONAL NOTES

*1   The great philosopher Hasdai Crescas (end of 14th cent.) held that the restoration of the original body led to too many contradictions and logical absurdities, and that resurrection involves the same identity in a similar body, but not one necessarily composed of the self-same substance (*Or Adonai* 3:2, chap. 4). Since in all probability it is Crescas to whom R. Levi Yitzhak is referring, his terminology must be understood in these terms: "first body" is the original body before death, and "last body" is a new one. If it is indeed Crescas whom he has in mind, then his ascription of the position is questionable, for Crescas was uncertain about the whole doctrine of metempsychosis. He held it to be rationally contraindicated, but was willing to accept it if it was confirmed as an authentic tradition (ibid. 4:6).

*2   See references in the index of G. Scholem's *Major Trends in Jewish Mysticism*.

*3   The contemporary period is not without its calculators; see my "United States of America," 1974, pp. 49–64. The Talmud was ambivalent about messianic speculations; it points out that according to tradition the Messiah should have come at the end of the fourth millennium (since Creation), i.e., some eighteen hundred years ago, but did not (Sanhedrin 97a–b). In the same passage other dates are offered as well, and then R. Yonatan is quoted as cursing all who indulge in such speculations, because reality has proved them wrong. This encouraged a countertendency to do away with detailed speculations of this kind. Yet even among the more rationalist thinkers, the penchant for identifying an end to oppression and misery breaks through now and then with hints as to the time of redemption.

During R. Zevi Elimelekh's lifetime, specific hopes were entertained with respect to 5600 (= 1840) by both hasidim and disciples of the Vilna Gaon. Hence the issue was far from academic; see A. Morgenstern, *Meshiḥiyut ve-Yishuv Eretz Yisrael*.

---

305. R. Yaakov Yosef does not recommend austerity and asceticism as an end in itself, but to underscore the existential suffering of the righteous as they face constant moral struggles. Those who are morally obtuse have no such problems; having yielded to temptation, they have no conscience with which to wrestle, and instead revel in their hedonistic exploits. The situation will be reversed in the world-to-come.

R. Zevi Elimelekh is clearly no rationalist. One of the most gifted and creative intellects that Galician Hasidism produced, he fought valiantly and vigorously against the
Haskalah, and uncompromisingly condemned philosophy, rationalism, and the study
of secular wisdom; he considered them the nemesis of true faith and a danger to
Judaism. For him, for his hasidim, indeed for all pious Jews, the failure of the redemption to materialize at the various times predicted by learned authorities was more
than a psychological threat of frustration and disappointment. It led to a crisis of confidence in these authorities. The rationalist's way out of the dilemma was not open
to him; his literalism and his faith in the infallibility of every dictum in the body of
talmudic, midrashic, and kabbalistic literature precluded such a solution. He found his
answer, instead, in an even more intense affirmation of faith, declaring that we are
bound to accept every aggadic statement even if it flies in the face of reason, and even
if fact has apparently belied a prediction.

The existence of God, prophecy, Torah—these can be accepted on faith. One can even,
in faith, affirm such apparent opposites as free will and predestination. But how can
one accept the coming of the Messiah at a date which has already passed, without
violating common sense and the most elementary principles of logic and reason? R.
Zevi Elimelekh's solution, of which this selection is part, uses a quirk in a verse in
Jeremiah to explain a theological point to buttress that mighty faith which, alone, can
confirm the words of various Sages despite history, and endow the believer with the
strength to wait for the redemption—at which time all these problems will be solved.

*4   The humor of this interpretation should not escape the reader. The pious
man's paradise is a hell for the scoffer. But there is more to this than the irony that
what is eternal bliss for the God-fearing is everlasting boredom for the sinner. R.
Yaakov Yosef is telling us, first, that there may well be no separate and identifiable
spiritual realm called Gehenna or hell. This fits in with Hasidism's denial of the reality of evil and its unwillingness to impute harsh judgments to God. And second, there
is the insight that heaven is the continuation, on a different plane, of creative spiritual activity in this world, and that the punishment of the wicked in the world-to-
come is their inability to enjoy and come to terms with a form of existence which
they ignored or denigrated in their earthly existence, and which it is too late to learn
in the afterlife.

*5   Sodom having been destroyed, the two sisters thought that the entire world
had been devastated, and that they and their father were the only survivors. "And the
firstborn [daughter] said unto the younger, 'Our father is old, and there is not a man
in the earth to come in unto us after the manner of all the earth. Come, let us make
our father drink wine, and we will lie with him, that we may preserve seed of our
father.' And they made their father drink wine that night. And the firstborn went in
and lay with her father; and he knew not when she lay down nor when she arose. And
it came to pass on the morrow that the firstborn said unto the younger: 'Behold, I lay
yesternight with my father, let us make him drink wine this night also, and go thou
in and lie with him, that we may preserve seed of our father.' And they made their
father drink wine that night also. And the younger arose and lay with him, and he
knew not when she lay down nor when she arose."

18

Women

INTRODUCTION

Jacob Katz astutely notes that the rise of Hasidism weakened family ties and lowered the status of women.[1] Women did not play a role in hasidic leadership, though they did act as receivers of prophetic dreams and as intercessors who could accept a *kvitl*, or amulet, a prerogative normally reserved for the zaddik/rebbe. The famous case of Hannah Rachel, "the maid of Ludmir," was the exception that proved the rule; essentially, she had to renounce her feminine identity in order to function as a full rebbe.

Women in hasidic homilies are idealized projections made by men for other men; nevertheless, some of them are important for understanding the hasidic worldview and the role that women played in it.

Maimonides and Maharal each viewed corruptible matter (*homer*) as essentially female, and form (*tzurah*) as male.[2] Form, of course, imposes itself on matter, as the superior male, with his intellect or Torah, subdues the wanton impulses of the female.

In many early hasidic texts man is the embodiment of culture, while women represent Nature untamed, unbridled, and dangerous. Thus, hasidic statements regarding Nature reflect their authors' fear

---

1. Katz, *Tradition and Crisis*, p. 243.
2. See Maimonides, *Guide of the Perplexed* III:8; Maharal, *Gevurot Hashem*, p. 244; *Or Ḥadash*, p. 104.

of the unknown—a realm without Torah, the physicality that limits and impedes Torah observance. Women's lives are determined by their role, and are thus identified with the necessary realms of food preparation, family life, and physical needs. Home and hearth, which occur steadily without apparent need for divine intervention in the natural order, nevertheless are warrantors of God's Presence. Eastern European *tekhines* (women's prayer manuals in Yiddish) attributed supernal consequences to mundane domestic activities, and viewed them as essential for providing God's blessings.

R. Levi Yitzhak of Berdichev portrays women's lives as demonstrating the passive influx of divine blessings within the natural realm. Conventional Jewish religiousness and the ultimate redemption both take place within the here and now of ordinary activities. The miracles of Hanukkah and Purim occurred through women, without explicit divine aid, and thus allow us to ponder the wonder of God's presence in the simple and commonplace (see selection 2). They serve as reminders for us to refresh our understanding of the importance of these mundane activities. Thus, in the end, the feminine is an autonomous realm, without the need for male completion, and itself independently capable of offering divine grace to its inhabitants.

Nevertheless, R. Levi Yitzhak presents a tension between this accessible sanctification of the everyday, which serves in its own way to "raise the sparks," and the temporary suspension of Torah law that occurs, often through the agency of a woman, at crucial points in humanity's confrontation with Nature. Yael's yielding to Sisera, and Esther's to Ahasuerus, represent this violation, as their ultimate victories represent the ultimate redemption, when the divisiveness of evil and the separation of the spiritual from the material will be overcome by the unification effected by means of proper intention and purity of heart. Thus, in the end, Deborah's single-mindedness resolves the tension.

R. Zadok too associates women with secular activities and transgressions for the sake of heaven (see selection 4). These are actions performed out of great love, and accompanied by the willingness to accept punishment for violating the Torah's strictures for the greater goal of preserving the Torah and Israel, the nation which observes the Torah. These women, Yael and Esther in particular, but also Tamar, serve as models for the need to integrate emotional drives, generated in the course of one's ordinary activities, within the greater realm of a mature religious life. Because of Eve's role in bringing sin to the world, and the foulness (*zuhama*) she received from the Serpent, women are more highly motivated to destroy the evil of physicality through intentional transgresssions, and it is for this reason that "transgression for the sake of Heaven" is associated primarily with them. Great piety is associated with greater power of imagination, and thus a greater struggle with the evil inclination.[3] Again, since a repentent sinner stands higher than a saint without sin,[4] R. Zadok connects these talmudic statements with the story of Eve's sin; in the end, her struggle against the Serpent symbolizes the eternal principle that failure, a "fall," allows for greater subsequent spiritual growth.

The Maggid of Mezeritch and many of his disciples portray women as a personification of the physical realm (see selection 5). In an ideal state, God is represented as a male, for whom the natural realm of the female is a source of satisfaction. Simultaneously, however, the Maggid holds the converse as well: women also represent the evil inherent in the unredeemed natural realm—in particular, their physical beauty poses a constant temptation. Beauty must therefore be viewed with visceral revulsion as a source of evil thoughts and sin. Nevertheless, paradoxically, the Divine Presence is to be found in all physical beauty, and the pious person must focus on the source of the beauty in the Holy One.[5] God wishes the multifarious mundane manifestations of His creation to be raised to their supernal root.

Human virtues are thus seen as pale reflections of their source in the higher realms. The pious man must restore all beauty to its empyrean root by himself cleaving to that supernal source.

Thus, a strongly puritanical view of pleasure and beauty serves as a prerequisite for the mature acceptance of the legitimate role of beauty in the world. But this negative view of pleasure is absolutely indispensable; sexuality, both masculine and feminine, is to be feared. The female body, not excepting the nurturing female breast, is abhorrent. Virtue involves the suppression of physical desire and pleasure; the ideal male understands the putridness of the physical world. Moral

---

3. See Sukkah 52a.
4. Berakhot 34b.
5. Thus, the opponents of Hasidism castigated some hasidim for gazing on non-Jewish women as a religious act; see M. L. Wilensky, *Hasidim u-Mitnaggedim*, II, pp. 239–250; Jacobs, *Hasidic Prayer*, p. 111. On the spiritual root of physical beauty, see my "Matter and Spirit."

values, for the hasid, trump esthetic judgments—indeed, determine them. The visceral revulsion which carnal appetites arouse in the hasid are a tribute to his training.

Despite all this, women—especially biblical figures—serve as role models for male behavior. The hasidic ethos placed a premium on the virtue of humility. The story of Jacob's marriage to Leah and Rachel was paradigmatic. Jacob was misled by Laban into marrying Leah instead of Rachel, with the connivance of both sisters; Leah came to him in the darkness with the "code word" which he had given to Rachel to foil just such an attempt on Laban's part (see Gen. 29). Leah therefore represents hiddenness and submissiveness. Jacob's long-desired marriage to Rachel followed after he had worked several more years for Laban. Like Rachel herself, it symbolizes the explicit revelation of the divine (see selection 7).

Esther's self-sacrifice is also exemplary, as is Sarah's purity. Hasidism demands of men, without a trace of self-consciousness, the assumption of these "womanly" virtues. However, contemporary women are not mentioned at all, either as exemplars or as beings called upon to follow their ancestresses.

Nevertheless, women are portrayed positively in some late texts. Based on the midrashic statement that Sarah was a greater prophet than Abraham,[6] hasidic texts portray Sarah as a prophetess in her own right. Maimonides' portrayal of Miriam as Moses' equal,[7] and the extension of this teaching to other prophetesses, led Hasidism to describe Miriam as having achieved an eschatological level beyond the limits of the feminine, natural realm.

However, here again the positive is accompanied by a negative. Following kabbalistic tradition, the feminine is associated with the attribute of judgment (*din*). Women are stern, unflinching, and without the mercy represented by the Torah. *Shem mi-Shmuel* portrays Sarah as a strict interpreter of Torah who rejects sinners. Isaac inherited Abraham's attribute of mercy in order to counteract the attribute of strictness he received from his mother (selection 3).

The selections which follow offer a range of texts that manifest the role of gender in hasidic texts. They culminate in an acceptance of the autonomous woman in some parts of the hasidic community of the early nineteenth century (selection 9), and, especially, in the twentieth century (selection 10).

---

6. See Tanhuma Shemot 1, and see Rashi to Gen. 21:12.
7. *Guide of the Perplexed* III:51.

1. AWAKENING FROM BELOW BY YEARNING FOR GOD
Source: R. Moshe Hayyim Ephraim, Degel Maḥaneh Ephraim to Tazria, s.v
o yomar.

It may be said that the [lower] worlds in relation to the Holy One are
as a female in relation to a male—that is, they receive their vitality
from the Holy One Who in turn is the male element in all the worlds,
He showers them with vitality and loving-kindness. . . .

Therefore, when a person yearns to cleave to the Holy One, he elevates the Female Waters,[8] arousing from Above the Male Waters–and
thus shefa (grace) and vitality are born for him and for all the worlds.
This is not so when one desires the pleasures of this world, which
themselves represent the Female Waters, for all things must receive
their vitality from God.

As is known, "a person does not commit a transgression unless the
spirit of folly enters him first,"[9] and thus his soul departs from him,
God forbid. However, when the person's soul rests with him, he
yearns for its root, for the Holy One. This is hinted at in the verse a
woman who conceives (Lev. 12:1); that is, the soul, which is compared to
a woman and a female in relation to the Holy One, when she conceives,
that is, when she yearns for the Holy One, and in this way she conceives, that is, [she arouses] the Female Waters,[10] an awakening from
Below to Above, then, she gives birth to a son (Lev. 12:1), as mentioned
above, in that loving-kindness, vitality, and shefa proceed from Above
to Below, as represented by the Male Waters.

2. WOMAN AND THE MIRACLES OF PURIM AND HANUKKAH
Source: R. Levi Yitzhak of Berdichev, Kedushat Levi, Derushim le-
Ḥanukkah, s.v. ha-taam, 24a–b.

We recite the blessing "Who performed miracles for our forefathers,
etc." on Hanukkah and Purim, but we do not do so on Passover, even
though the Exodus too was accompanied by miracles. The reason for
this seems to be because the miracles of Hanukkah and Purim were
accomplished through the activities of women. Moreover, these miracles were performed by natural means, unlike those accompanying

---

8. See Glossary.
9. Sotah 3a.
10. R. Moshe Hayyim Ephraim here refers to the talmudic teaching which states that
when a woman attains climax first, the ensuing offspring will be male (Niddah 25b).

the Exodus, when the Egyptians were struck by the Ten Plagues, and the [Red] Sea was split [in order to allow the fleeing Israelites to pass]—all miracles beyond natural means. In contrast, the miracles of Hanukkah and Purim were accomplished naturally. In the case of Hanukkah, Judith fed the Syrian governor milk, and killed him while he lay sleeping; as to Purim, at first Ahasuerus loved Haman and then transferred that love to Esther. These miracles were thus performed *in time*, a natural phenomenon,[11] and we therefore recite the blessing "Who performed miracles for our forefathers in those days *at this time*.[12] The miracles of Passover were supernatural, and thus we do not recite the blessing.

The miracles of Hanukkah and Purim were thus accomplished through the activities of women, who represent the world which is the passive recipient of God's *shefa*. . . .

The incident involving Judith during the miracle of Hanukkah [can be explained as follows]. When the righteous wish to raise the sparks [of holiness], they must at times transgress the words of the Torah. For example, in the case of Gideon, as the Talmud records (Temurah 28b–29a), seven laws were violated[13] in regard to the altar [on which he sacrificed his father's young bull (Jud. 6:23–27)]. The reason [for these violations] is that the Israelites at that time were guilty of idolatry, and so the righteous among them who wished to ascend to God had first to perform some act which was parallel to an idolatrous one, thereby to break [the power of] the "shells" (*kelipot*). So too in the case of the miracle of Deborah, which involved the [relationship] of Yael, the wife of Heber the Kenite, with Sisera, the Canaanite general, as Scripture states, *[Between her legs] he knelt, he fell dead* (Jud. 5:27). [However, since,] in truth, at that time the Israelites were not acting idolatrously, so their redemption did not come through any action forbidden by the Torah....Now, the Israelites of that generation were not, God forbid, idolators, as the Talmud states [on the verse] *"[Deborah] sat under the palm of Deborah* (Jud. 4:5—just as the palm tree has but

---

11. Time was, of course, the first of God's creations; the first word of Genesis is *bereshit*, "in the beginning," thus indicating that time had been created.

12. *Ba-zeman ha-zeh* means literally, "at this time," but the *bet* can be interpreted as "by means of." The blessing would then mean: "Who performed miracles for our forefathers in those days by means of time."

13. Literally, "permitted." Actually, there were eight prohibitions that were suspended; among these were sacrificing at night by a non-priest without priestly vessels an animal designated for idolatry and actually worshiped idolatrously by the use of vessels and firewood designated for pagan rites.

one heart, so too the Israelites of that generation had only one heart—
[turned] to their Father in Heaven."[14]   But they were in need of
redemption.   In the time of the Hanukkah miracle, too, the Jews were
not idolatrous; the intention of that wicked man was to initiate illicit relations with Judith, so she served him cheese [and killed him in his
sleep, as Yael did Sisera], because the Jews of that time required
redemption [which occurred without the violation of the Torah].

3. SARAH AS PROPHETESS
A. Source: R. Shemuel of Sochotchov, Shem mi-Shemuel to Vaeira, 175a–b,
s.v. va-titzhak.

Sarah laughed within herself, saying, After I have grown old shall I have
pleasure, my lord (referring to Abraham) too being old? (Gen. 18:12). We
must understand [how Sarah could come to think such a thing] when
she had certainly heard God's promise from Abraham.   Nahmanides
[in his commentary] had difficulty with this passage.   Why did she
laugh at the angel's announcement? After all, she saw a decisive proof
of this, inasmuch as her menses returned. . . .
    We must understand the purpose of this special announcement to
Sarah: what need was there of this, given her own status as a
prophetess in her own right? It would have been simpler for her to
have received such a prophecy [directly]. The answer may be inferred
from [the Sages'] statement (Genesis Rabba 76) regarding Benayahu
ben Yehoyadah's response to King David: "Amen, so may God
promise. . ."—even though the monarchy had already been promised
to Solomon prophetically. Nevertheless, [David] was concerned that
various obstacles [of sin would prevent his objective from becoming
fulfilled].   We see from this that even a prophet's vision may be
changed, as Nahmanides states in his commentary, "Know that every
heavenly decree in order to become actualized in all events [must be
accompanied by] a symbolic action."[15] So too regarding this prophecy
of Abraham's: it required a concrete act [in order to ensure its fulfill-
ment].   Thus, another announcement was made by an angel embodied in human form, eating at Abraham's house—this all was a symbolic act which prefigured the great feast which Abraham would
make when Isaac was weaned.[16]

---

14. Megillah 14a.
15. Nahmanides to Gen. 12:6.
16. As described in Gen. 21:8.

B. Source: R. Shemuel of Sochotchov, Shem mi-Shemuel to Vaeira, 190af., s.v. ve-hineh Avraham ve-Sarah.

Now, Abraham and Sarah were themselves [embodiments] of Hesed (Loving-kindness) and Din (Judgment); Hesed relates to the male [side of the World of Emanation] and Din to the female [side]. We therefore find that Abraham never rejected any one, even the greatest sinner. We find that he invited the three angels to dine even though they appeared to be Arabs who bow to the dust of their feet (a particularly degrading form of idolatry), and so too he prayed on behalf of the inhabitants of Sodom and Gomorrah, even though they were notorious for their wicked ways, [as Scripture itself testifies,] *they were evil and exceedingly sinful against God* (Gen. 13:13). Nevertheless Abraham sought to attract them with bonds of love. . . thus bringing them beneath the wings of the Divine Presence. Even his war with the Kings of the East (Gen. 14) was only to save [his nephew] Lot, and not to reject the kings. . . .

But we find that Sarah, as the embodiment of Din, representing the Left Side of the World of Emanation, did reject [sinners]. Even though, as the Midrash notes, she would convert women to God's worship, as Isaac converted males [just as did Abraham],[17] nevertheless, when she observed Ishmael "playing"[18]—that is, indulging in idolatry, sexual transgressions, and murder, as Rashi comments[19]—she told Abraham, *Cast out this maidservant and her son [from your household], for the son of this maidservant must not be heir with my son* (Gen. 21:10), thus distancing the one deserving of being distanced, not for [Ishamael's] good, [but for the good of others]. The reason for this, is, as mentioned, that the quality of Din relates to the female.

Therefore, just as Abraham had to be informed of the impending conception of Isaac from the perspective of Din, so contrariwise Sarah had to be informed [independently, even though Abraham had most likely informed her of God's statement in Gen. 17:19, and she too was a prophetess] from the perspective of Hesed, so that both would contribute to Isaac [as the embodiment of Gevurah]; moreover, it is for this reason that the second announcement [i.e., the one by the angels] had to occur by means of the hospitality extended to her guests, which is completely [an act of] Hesed.

---

17. See Rashi to Gen. 12:5.
18. Gen. 21:9.
19. See Rashi to Gen. 21:9.

4. LOVE AND SACRIFICE
Source: R. Zadok ha-Kohen of Lublin, Takkanat ha-Shavin, no. 5, s.v. umi-tzad ha-ahavah.

Through love [of God] one may enter into matters such as this (i.e., to fulfill God's will even to the detriment of one's own spiritual wellbeing) by means of a "transgression for its own sake" as did Yael [who, according to the Talmud, had a physical relationship with Sisera], though we do not find any explicit dispensation in the Torah for this action. Rather, it is from this incident that we derive this [teaching that "a transgression for its own sake is greater than a mitzvah done not for its own sake"].[20] That is, because of her own great desire and love for the salvation of Israel, and in order to destroy such a great enemy of God as Sisera, she did not take into consideration the [gravity of the] transgression, and the foulness that he cast into her although, as the Sages say, she regarded [the act] as wrong.[21] Nevertheless, she sacrificed her own spiritual wellbeing[22] for this, for she thought that although there was no way in which such an action could be permitted, and she would be punished for it, nevertheless, better that she should go down to perdition so long as an enemy of God be removed from the world thereby.

Esther acted in the same way, as we find when she stated to Mordecai, *and if I perish, I perish* (Esther 4:16).[23] That is, [she was willing to risk] even the destruction of her soul, God forbid, in that she transgressed [in marrying Ahaseurus], with the intent of saving the Jewish people.

---

20. That is, this principle is derived not from the Torah itself, but from this incident in the Book of Judges, which describes the part Yael played in the ultimate salvation of the Israelites from Sisera. According to the Talmud in Nazir 23b, Jud. 5:24, "Let Yael, the wife of Heber the Kenite, be blessed above all women," refers to the superiority of Yael's action, in engaging in such relations, over the Matriarchs Sarah, Rachel, and Leah, who each urged their respective husbands to take a concubine out of jealousy (so Rashi there). Their actions thus constitute "mitzvot [done] not for their own sake," and are inferior to Yael's, which was a technical transgression done for the sake of bringing about the salvation of Israel.
21. That is, the pleasure derived from physical relations with the wicked is unpleasant in an extreme degree for the righteous. The word *zuhama*, translated here as "foulness," refers to the sin of Eve and the serpent in the Garden of Eden; the serpent cast his foulness into Eve, and this foulness was not cleansed until the time of the Sinaitic Covenant.
22. Literally, "her soul."
23. This midrash seems to be an amalgam of one on the Esther verse in Megillah 15a, and one on *hikaret tikaret* in Sanhedrin 64b.

5. A WOMAN'S BEAUTY
Source: R. Zev Wolf of Zhitomir, Or ha-Meir, Hayyei Sarah, s.v. va-yihyu.

The life of Sarah was one hundred years,[24] *and twenty years, and seven years*[25] (Gen. 23:1). The Zohar questions the change [from singular to plural in this verse, especially in respect to the paradox that the expression for] the longer spans of time [is coupled with the singular "year" while the expression] for the shorter one ("seven years") takes the plural. [While] the Zohar explained this anomaly in its own way, I heard another interpretation from the Maggid [of Mezeritch], who explained [the matter as follows]. [As the Talmud states], "a woman's *raison d' être* is beauty,"[26] which he interprets to mean that all the worlds [represented by "woman"] were created only for the purpose of providing the Holy One with delight from the lower regions [of the created universe] known as "woman," in order that the latter should receive enlightenment from Him.[27] Our Sages were given this insight in accordance [with the verse] *there they dwelt, occupied with the king's work* (I Chron. 4:23)—with whom did the Holy One consult when He created the world? With the souls of the righteous, for it was His pre-existent Will that He obtain delight from the righteous.[28] This, in turn, is the cause of the creation of [all] the worlds, and causes the lights of supernal clarity (*orot behirim*) to be diminished, fitting the capacity of the lower orders. And the enlightened ones who take it upon themselves to obtain a hint of true wisdom are the ones who ensure the continued existence of the world which was created for their sake. [From this perspective] I will explain the talmudic passage which states that when R. Akiva saw the wife of the evil Tyranus Rufus, he spat, wept, and laughed.[29] In order to understand the symbolism of these three actions, [we must remember] that when a person observes a woman unexpectedly, without prior intention and with great surprise, he expectorates and considers the incident odious

---

24. In Hebrew, singular *shanah*; see below.
25. Plural in the Hebrew: *shanim*.
26. Literally, "a woman is only for beauty," as those maidens possessing beauty and looking for a husband called out in the dances described in Ta'anit 31a.
27. The kabbalistic theme of the unity of God is often expressed as the vision of "the Holy One" and His Shekhinah. This, in turn, is frequently formulated in human terms—the union of man and woman. The Maggid, as cited by R. Zev Wolf, finds allusions to this in this homily.
28. See Genesis Rabbah 8:7.
29. Avodah Zarah 20a.

because of the consequent danger—that the sight of her might arouse evil thoughts and desires in him, God forbid.

Indeed, I heard from the Maggid that when he was a teacher in a certain small town, sitting in a corner, a certain lord came with a beautiful woman immodestly dressed—whose breasts were exposed to the nipples, as was their manner. When the Maggid espied her without forewarning, it pained him greatly, and he then began to find this evil disgusting, realizing that the origin of this beauty was the seed of her father and mother, which in turn arose from the disgusting foods that they consumed, and which produced the red and white humors [which went into her creation], realizing from which came this putrid and vile seed, like serpents and the empty-headed and the like—the most abhorrent matters. It [occured to him] that the vanity of her beauty[30] issued from such an abominable thing, [so that he therefore vomited] in their presence, at which point the lord ordered him expelled.

This, then, is the reason for which R. Akiva too spat. He then wept because of the beauty that would be consumed in the dust[31] (i.e., that such a beauty would eventually die). Now, it is not at all understandable why [R. Akiva] would lament the return of the pagan beauty to the dust, even though our Sages stated that R. Akiva foresaw with divine inspiration that she would ultimately convert to Judaism and that he would marry her. This truly requires consideration. However, this may be explained according to what we have said, for R. Akiva, observed her stunning beauty and perceived the origin of this beauty in the [upper] worlds—that is, the Shekhinah [Divine Presence], which is called *the most beautiful of women* (Song of Songs 1:8, 5:9, 6:1), and which is the ideal pattern (*demut*) of all visible representations . . . which clothe the Shekhinah in their multiform varieties. Now, if some purpose is served by this outburst of colors (or: varieties), the Creator derives pleasure from this, for He raises them to their Roots.

However, when He observes this expansion of these aspects in an unclean place and an abhorrent body, in the dust of the pagans—the descent of these aspects from their high and exalted locus to a lowly place of these *kelipot*[32] and materiality—for this does R. Akiva weep, for this beauty which proceeded from an exalted place . . . and which

---

30. Alluding to Prov. 31:30.
31. Of the grave; see Berakhot 5b.
32. "Shells," referring to demonic and unclean forces; see Glossary, s.v. *kelipot*.

is now being consumed in the dust of an unclean body, dust with no spiritual purpose, and whose beauty is of no pleasure to the Creator.

After this, R. Akiva observed by divine inspiration that [Tyranus Rufus' wife] would convert and that he would marry her and rejoice in her (for which reason he laughed), as already noted—that the proselytes are sparks of holiness[33] which have fallen from the *kelipot*, and one who is a complete sage (*he-ḥakham ha-kolel*) and is able to obtain some degree of wisdom, may raise them to their root. Now, R. Akiva, because of the profundity of his comprehension and the clarity of his thought, rejecting the evil and choosing the good,[34] that [he perceived] in the wife of the evil Tyrranus Rufus, was touched by wisdom so that he could weep for the beauty which would be consumed in the dust— and raised the holy sparks which were enclothed within her, from which her beauty originated. Thus, she was forced to convert [by the power of] the holiness of the raised sparks—for the entire goal and soul's desire of a Jewish person in his divine service and his Torah study and his performance of the mitzvot—all is for the sake of [the One] on High, to please the Creator, and repair the seven days of Creation which is the essential purpose of man's divine service in this world . . . ,as is written, *She established seven pillars* (Prov. 9:1), [since] the Torah is divided into seven "pillars," as the Sages explained [when they interpreted the verses] *When the Ark traveled* (Num. 10:35-36) as a "book unto itself."[35] From these seven pillars[36] of our Holy Torah the enlightened one may rectify them to raise them to their source and origin, as we have already mentioned many times. It is with respect to this that the Torah states that "the life of Sarah was one hundred years, and twenty years, and seven years." The intent of the first [phrase which contains the singular of the word "year"] refers to the time before the embodiment; the life of Sarah up to that point represented the early characterstics (*middot ha-rishoniyyot*) of a man's life, when his essence is hidden and when he is still unified in a simple way. For this reason the singular is employed in the phrase "a hundred years"—to indicate the unity of his origin, an indivisible unity.

---

33. See Glossary.

34. Alluding to Is. 7:15-16.

35. Soferim 6:1; that is, the words contained within the reversed *nuns* of Num. 7:15 and Num. 7:16 constitute a "book unto themselves." From this the Sages derive the teaching that a segment of Scripture containing 85 letters, as are contained herein, must be treated with all the respect and care accorded a Torah Scroll.

36. Since these verses all occur in it, the book of Numbers consists of three sections (one before, one after, and the section of "When the Ark"), thus producing a "Pentateuch" of seven sections—or a Septateuch.

In the phrase *seven years*, the plural is used to teach [us] that since the life of Sarah—that is, the vitality of the Shekhinah (Divine Presence), which is called "Sarah"—received its divine *shefa* from the time that man is enclosed within the material world, it is referred to in the plural, implying that this is in the World of Fragmentation (*alma de-Peruda*).

If you wish to know why He did this, Rashi explains [this verse as hinting] that [Sarah] was at age one hundred as a twenty year old—without sin; and when she was twenty, she was as beautiful as a seven-year old. At first glance this presents difficulties, but in light of what has been said, [we may understand that] it was for this purpose that the Holy One did thus in His world: He caused the general, absolute unity of the [Hebrew] alphabet (indicated by the number 100) to undergo transformations to a lower level, that of 20, in which (the divine potencies) were still unified and not disassociated from each other. All these [spiritual] qualities were then further enclosed in that of 7—that is, the material world, which experienced the [break-up of the unity and its] dispersal into a mixture of good and evil.[37] Why did the Creator do this? For the purpose of "beauty"—in the light of the statement we mentioned earlier, that "a woman is only for beauty"—so that the Creator might receive from His people Israel, so close to Him,[38] an increased portion of delight and pleasure, since they have the sense to reject evil and choose the good, and to raise all the sparks which dwell in the lower regions to their [supernal] roots. For this reason Rashi ends his explanation with the statement that all Sarah's days were "for the good." This hints at the foregoing—that although they are as yet enclothed in the seven days of the week—symbolized by the phrase "the years of Sarah's life," expressed in the plural—they are equally for good of the knowledge of the enlightened one, the inspired man whose entire being and goal is to raise the dis-

---

37. The author here alludes to the Kabbalah's letter-mysticism, in which God formed the world via the creative potencies inherent in the letters of the Hebrew alphabet. His main point, however, refers to numbers rather than letters: the number 100 is a high-level rounded number, thus symbolizing the most sublime level of divine unity, and therefore taking the singular, "year." Thereafter, the divine power "descends" as it is transformed into and enclosed in a lower level of unity, that of 20—which is still a rounded number but of a lower degree of unity. In the last stage, the unity implied by rounded numbers is broken, and we emerge with the integer 7—an odd number, that of the seven days of the week, symbolizing disunity and fragmentation, and therefore taking the plural, "years," unlike the numbers 100 or 20.
38. Alluding to Ps. 148:14.

persed sparks to their original root and source, to the surpernal good, equally in absolute unity with Him. Consider this carefully, and understand.

6. CLEAVING TO THE SUPERNAL BEAUTY
Source: R. Dov Ber, Maggid of Mezeritch, Maggid Devarav le-Yaakov, no. 5

And Rachel was coming with the sheep (Gen. 29:9). The Midrash states that this was "in order to attract [Jacob] with her beauty."[39] At first blush this is not understandable. [How could our Mother Rachel hope to attract our Father Jacob with mere physical beauty?] However, the true explanation is that [the Midrash] speaks of the supernal Rachel, that is, that by seeing the earthy Rachel, Jacob would cleave to the supernal Rachel, for all of Rachel's earthy beauty is a projection of the beauty of the supernal Rachel.

This is similar [to the true explanation of the verse] Joseph entered to do his work (Gen. 39:11) [with the intent of submitting to the blandishments of Potiphar's wife] but, as our Sages noted, "he saw the countenance of his father [Jacob, and resisted]."[40] The explanation of this is that Potiphar's wife displayed her beauty before him (mit-pa'eret), as the Midrash says, "the clothes she wore in the morning she did not wear in the evening, in order to entice him." The righteous Joseph did not want any part of this [earthly] display of beauty, but [through it] he was filled with desire and passion for the supernal beauty, which was the countenance of his father [Jacob, which is engraved on the Heavenly Throne] and represents Tiferet. This then is the interpretation of the verse, "he fled and went outside," that is to say, from this earthly display—bodily lust—he became impassioned to flee outside, i.e., outside this-world[ly matters and desires], and to cleave to the supernal Tiferet.

This is the meaning of the verse, Go out and see, O daughters of Zion, [King Solomon]. . . (Song of Songs 3:11), namely, leave your earthly desires, look at the inner meaning of things and not their outward appearance—for example, the outer beauty of a woman; the material substance of beauty [is] termed daughters of Zion, which is only a symbol of the Supernal Beauty, for there rests upon her a spark of the beauty of the World of Tiferet within the Community of Israel. No one

---

39. Yalkut Shimoni I, 824.
40. Sotah 36b.

is permitted to cleave to this Lower Beauty, but if he encounters it suddenly he may cleave through it to the Supernal Beauty. And this is why the verse mentions King Solomon, who [in the Song of Songs] represents the Holy One. Thus, a woman's beauty is only the symbol and manifestation of King Solomon, viz., the Holy One.[41]

And this is the meaning of the verse, *When you go out to war, [and you see among the captives a beautiful woman and you desire her,]*. . . (Deut. 20:1)—when you, a man, go out of your [state of] cleaving to God, you must certainly enter a war, that is, when you leave off your cleaving to God, you enter the World of Fragmentation, which is where the War [against one's evil inclination is waged], as is known. *And you see among the captives a beautiful woman*—that is, the "beauty of a woman," the material world, which is called "captivity," for it all comes from the Breaking [of the Vessels], which is the mystery of captivity. *And you desire her*—that is, lest your desire be only for the physical [manifestation of this] beauty. This is why the verse contines with, *and you take her for yourself,* i.e., you may not attribute your "taking" for yourself, that is, for your pleasure; rather, if she appears to you suddenly, you must do all for *isheh,* a burnt-offering sacrificed entirely to God, [and not *ishah,* a woman,][42] as it is written, "a burnt-offering of sweet savor to God" (Num. 29:13). In other words, [the intent must be] to raise the sparks, that is, that your thoughts cleave to the root of the supernal emotion, as is known.

7. LEAH AND RACHEL, THE HIDDEN AND REVEALED WORLDS
Source: R. Kalonymos Kalman Epstein, *Maor va-Shemesh* to Vayetzei, 31a, s.v. *ve-einei.*

Leah's eyes were weak, but Rachel was beautiful of figure and beautiful of appearance (Gen. 29:17). Targum Onkelos renders this verse as "Leah's eyes were lovely (*ya'ayan*), and Rachel was beautiful of form and of lovely appearance." This translation seems difficult, since Targum employs the same Aramaic root, *ya'aya,* "lovely," for two distinct Hebrew words, *rakot,* "weak," and *yefat mar'eh,* "beautiful appearance." Moreover, the *alef* of the the Aramaic *ya'ayah* seems superfluous, since it could have been spelled *ya'ey* without the *alef.*

---

41. See Genesis Rabbah 12:4.
42. A play on words: the Hebrew *ishah,* "woman," has the same letters as *isheh,* "a burnt-offering," which implies the destruction of physicality in favor of the spiritual element.

It seems to me that this all is a hint, for it is known from the holy books that Rachel is called *alma de-itgalya*, "the world that is revealed," while Leah is called *alma de-itkasya*, "the world that is concealed." Now, to understand this matter we must appreciate what these terms mean. Submission (*avdut*) involves at first acceptance of the yoke of the Kingdom of Heaven, to know that the Creator is Master and Ruler, and that His Kingship extends to all things. This is called "that which is revealed," since it is apparent and well-known to all that the universe cannot exist without a Ruler. After a person truly accepts the yoke of His Kingdom upon himself, and wishes to serve Him in all sorts of ways as a slave does his master, as befits the Glorious King,[43] God then brings [the servant] close to Him and allows him to enter the Innermost Palace of Palaces.[44] There the servant may better understand the greatness of God so that a spirit of shame and great submission falls upon him, and his heart is broken. From the worship with which he began, that is, the acceptance of the yoke of the Kingdom of Heaven . . . he comes to submission and complete repentance, with a broken heart, and that is called "the world that is concealed." This is because this stage of worship is essentially one which involves the heart and mind, and is totally hidden from the eyes of all.

This is what the Targum hints at by employing the Aramaic word *ya'ayan*, whose letters form the anacronym *yod-alef-heh-nun*—that is "the Lord our God, the Lord is *nun*," i.e., the Tetragrammaton, by which our God is called, is the Being of the world of repentance, the world of Binah, from which issue the fifty (*nun*) Gates of Understanding.

[In contrast,] the Targum employs the Aramaic word *ya'aya* in connection with Rachel, for she represents "the world that is revealed," the world of [God's] Kingdom, which is also an anacronym: *yod-alef-yod-alef, the Lord our God, the Lord is One.*[45] [This is] the world which the worshipper must unify and tie to the upper world, in the light of the Tetragrammaton, for this is the purpose of our [divine] service.

We may say that this is what the following verses hint at. *I will serve you seven years for your younger daughter, Rachel,* for the essential unification is accomplished by a person's acceptance on himself of the yoke of His Kingdom in the reading of the Shema morning and evening,

---

43. An allusion to Ps. 24:8-9.
44. Literally, "the palace of the inner palaces."
45. The words of the Shema.

with the unification [implicit in] *Shema Yisrael,* which contains twenty-five letters in the morning, along with twenty-five letters in the evening, making a total of fifty—in order to tie it to "the world that is concealed," which is hinted at by the *nun* [of *ya'ayan*]. The worshipper must also recite seven blessings—two before the Shema and one after it during the morning prayer, and two before and two after it during the evening prayer—and that is what Jacob hinted at when he offered to serve Laban for seven years for Rachel, his younger daughter—thus accepting upon himself the yoke of the Heavenly Kingdom symbolized by Rachel. Through this acceptance comes the clarity of understanding of "the world that is concealed," which is symbolized by Leah.

[When Jacob asks Laban,] *Why have you cheated me?* (Gen. 29:25), he means to say: Why have you raised me greatly to the world which is hidden from this one [by giving me Leah instead of Rachel]? Laban then answers him, "Fulfill the week of this one, and we will give you this one also by the work which you do for another seven years" (Gen. 29:27). The meaning of this is that you must struggle with great effort in order to rectify the seven gates of the soul, as is noted in *Sefer Yetzirah,* and then you will attain the upper worlds, and you will have the strength and understanding to unify the upper and lower worlds, as we may well understand.

8. THE SONG OF LOVE
Source: R. Kalonymos Kalman Epstein, Maor va-Shemesh to Beshallah, s.v. ki va sus.

[The ability] to sing songs and praises to Him comes from love; because of great love [the Israelites'] hearts were inspired to offer song. However, with fear alone it is impossible to offer song. Only if the fear of God is derived from love . . . when one comprehends His exaltedness, [and] one manifests fear before Him—if the fear is of this nature, then one may sing before Him at all times, despite that fear. [For] this fear stems from love.

As long as one does not [progress from the greatness of] love to the fear of exaltation, one's heart is not inspired to offer song, even though one is joyful. . . .[46]

---

46. There are three levels of religious emotion: fear or reverence for God; love for God; and "fear of exaltation." Neither fear alone nor even love is sufficient to inspire song; only "fear of exaltation" leads to the ecstasy of "song."

Although Miriam was a prophetess, she was in the state of *nukva* [feminine], and did not attain the state of fear of exaltation. Had she waited for Moses [to begin singing], she would have been able to sing the entire Song [of the Sea, Exod. 15], but she did not wait. Instead, as soon as she saw the Egyptians enter the Sea and the waters return over them, and *the Israelites went on dry land in the midst of the Sea* (Exod. 14:29), she took the timbrel in her hand and uttered song. That is why she was only privileged to say the first verse. . . . That is, she grasped only the quality of love. . . .

9. THE END OF HIERARCHY
Source: *R. Kalonymos Kalman Epstein, Maor va-Shemesh to Beshallah, s.v. od al pasuk hana"l and s.v. ve-zot kavvanat Miriam.*

All the worlds and all creatures may be contegorized as masculine or feminine, that is, as aspects of their bestowal (= masculine) and receptivity (= feminine). This means that a higher world bestows [the *shefa*] to the world below it. Similarly, a person who is on a lower spiritual level requires someone greater to learn from. This is because anything bounded has both upper and lower ends, and the distance between the two is vast. Whoever is above the lower end is closer to the upper; so too, whoever is much above the Lower World is closer to the Ein Sof.

For this reason, one who is on a lower spiritual level requires someone greater from whom to learn the ways of God's worship, for the latter apprehends more and thus bestows on the one who is below him.

However, in the messianic age, each one will perfect his soul [back] to its Root, and the holy sparks will ascend, and the "husks" will become entirely null. The clear light of His divinity will illuminate all the worlds, and the line and the circle will be equal. There will no longer be categories of masculine and feminine, for all will come to realize equally His divine light. This is just like a round object which has no beginning and end; then no one will need to learn from his fellow.

This is like a circle dance, where every part of the circle's circumference is equidistant from the center. So all will absorb the clear light of His divinity in equal measure, as is written, *They shall teach no more every man his neighbor, and every man his brother, saying, "Know the Lord," for they shall know Me, from the least of them to the greatest of them, says God* (Jer. 31:33). This is the [correct] interpretation of the Talmudic passage which states that "the Holy One will make a circle dance for the righteous, and the Holy One will sit in their midst. . . ."[47]

This was the intention of Miriam the Prophetess. She had all the women follow her and performed circle dances (hakafot) with them, in accordance with the mystery of *a woman shall encircle a man* (Jer. 31:21), in order to draw upon the supernal light from the place where the categories of masculine and feminine do not exist.

Now, Moses said, *I will sing unto the Lord* (Exod 15:1). This is because Moses spoke while still under the categories of masculine and feminine, before the light of supernal clarity had been manifested....It is for this reason that he employed the future tense—I *will* sing when I attain this. But Miriam [through her circle dance] drew down the supernal light and attained then the highest apprehension [of divinity] that was possible, and therefore she said [to the women], "sing [now] to the Lord," now that you have attained the highest possible level. . . . By making a circle-dance, she drew down the supernal light [from the source] where the categories of masculine and feminine do not exist.

10. WOMEN'S OWN EFFORT
Source: R. Kalonymos Kalmish Shapiro, Esh Kodesh, Hukkat, 5702.

When a woman becomes a *zaddeket* (righteous), studies Torah, and fulfills the commandments—that is her own accomplishment, since she is not under any obligation to do so; Heaven has not really aroused her to do what she did.[48] . . . That she reached such a high spiritual level is not attributable to divine arousal, but rather to her own self-generated effort. . . . The source of her service is within her; it flows from her. That is why the well [of Miriam], the source flowing with living water, holy water, existed by virtue of her merit.

---

47. Taanit 31a.
48. That is, to take upon herself the mitzvah of Torah study or other mitzvot that are not obligatory upon women.

Biographies

R. Aharon of Zhitomir (d. 1817), a disciple of R. Levi Yitzhak of Berdichev, was a hasidic preacher in Zhitomir and other communities in Russia, and perhaps as far as Hungary. He emphasized practical ethics and the service of God, with particular emphasis on *devekut*.

R. Avraham Katz of Kalisk (1741–1810), a disciple of the Maggid of Mezeritch, joined the group of hasidim who emigrated to Eretz Israel in 1777 under the leadership of R. Menahem Mendel of Vitebsk, and succeeded him as leader of the hasidim in Eretz Israel. He broke with R. Shneur Zalman of Liady after the *Tanya* was published in 1796, because of his profound disagreement with R. Shneur Zalman's system of thought.

R. Dov Ber, the Maggid of Mezeritch (1710–1772), known as the Great Maggid, succeeded the Besht, despite the seniority of R. Yaakov Yosef of Polennoye, and attracted a great number of brilliant, creative disciples who became the leaders of the next generation. Because of physical infirmities brought on by his earlier ascetic practices, he did not travel much, but his disciples spread Hasidism far and wide over eastern Europe. His influence was incalculable; among other innovations, he introduced the systematic study of Kabbalah into the hasidic system; his *Maggid Devarav le-Yaakov* appeared in 1781. The members of the Rizhiner dynasty trace their descent from him.

R. Elimelekh of Lizhensk (1717–1787) was a disciple of the Maggid of Mezeritch, after whose death he settled in Lizhensk. He is thought to have been the innovator of "practical zaddikism." He and his brother, R. Zusya of Hanipol, helped establish Hasidism in Galicia, and both founded dynasties. His *Noam Elimelekh* remains a popular hasidic work. Among his disciples was R. Yaakov Yitzhak, the "Seer of Lublin."

R. Gedaliah of Linitz (d. 1814), a popular preacher, was a disciple of the Maggid of Mezeritch and R. Yaakov Yosef of Polennoye, and founded a dynasty.

R. Hayyim Halberstam of Sanz (1793–1876), renowned as a *posek* and scholar, was converted to Hasidism by R. Yaakov Yitzhak, the Seer of Lublin. He studied under R. Naftali of Ropshitz, R. Zevi Hirsch of Zhidachov, and others, and founded a dynasty prominent in Poland and Hungary.

R. Israel Baal Shem Tov (1700–1760), the founder of Hasidism, is known most commonly as the Besht, sometimes as Rivash. He gained fame as a miracle-worker and wandering visionary teacher, but left no systematic exposition of his teachings. Hundreds of his sayings and lessons are scattered through the writings of his disciples, and it is sometimes difficult to disentangle his opinions from those of his followers, though the general outlines and many specific details can be extracted with some assurance. Many of his teachings have been assembled into separate collections, such as the *Keter Shem Tov*.

R. Israel Hapstein, the Maggid of Koznitz (1733–1814), a disciple of R. Dov Ber, the Maggid of Mezeritch and R. Elimelekh of Lizhensk, and a close associate of R. Levi Yitzhak of Berdichev, was an enormously popular preacher and propagator of Hasidism in central Poland. He wrote on Kabbalah and Halakhah, but his most influential work is his homiletical *Avodat Israel*.

R. Kalonymos Kalman Epstein (d. 1823), a disciple of R. Elimelekh of Lizhensk, was the leader of a hasidic group in Cracow, where he came under severe criticism for his hasidic views and especially for his fervent mode of worship. His *Ma'or va-Shemesh* is one of the most popular of all hasidic books.

Rabbi Kalonymos Kalmish Shapiro, the Piaseczner Rebbe (1889–1943), a descendant of R. Kalonymos Kalman Epstein (q.v). The talks on the weekly Torah portions that he gave in the Warsaw Ghetto were collected in *Esh Kodesh*, and discovered after the war.

R. Levi Yitzhak of Berdichev (1740–1810), who was introduced to Hasidism by R. Shmelke of Nikolsburg, became an intimate disciple of the Maggid of Mezeritch, and furthered the movement in central Poland and Ukraine, and even in Lithuania, the center of mitnaggedic oppposition. His *Kedushat Levi* remains one of the most popular hasidic works, and stories of his spirited defense of Jews in his debates with God still circulate. The Maggid's *Maggid Devarav le-Yaakov* owes much to his notes.

Maggid of Mezeritch. *See* R. Dov Ber

R. Menahem Mendel of Lubavitch (1789–1866) was the grandson of R. Shneur Zalman of Liady and the son-in-law of the R. Dov Ber, the second Rebbe, whom he succeeded. He is generally known as the *Zemah Zedek*, after his highly esteemed halakhic work; many of his other writings remain in manuscript.

R. Menahem Mendel of Vitebsk (1730–1788), oldest disciple of the Maggid of Mezeritch, was active in Belarus, Lithuania, and later in Eretz Israel. When the first organized opposition to Hasidism erupted in 1772, he tried to meet with the Vilna Gaon, its leader, to make peace, but the Gaon refused to see him.

R. Menahem Nahum of Chernobyl (1730–1787), a disciple of both the Besht and the Maggid of Mezeritch, became an itinerant preacher in Ukraine, eventually settling in Chernobyl. His son R. Mordechai founded the Chernobyl dynasty, continued by his many grandsons. His *Me'or Einayim* became a popular hasidic text.

R. Moshe Elyakim of Koznitz (1757–1828) was the son of the Maggid of Koznitz (1733–1814), one of the founders of Hasidism in Poland. R. Moshe became a rebbe by direction of his father's close friend and associate, the Seer of Lublin, R. Yaakov Yitzhak, and authored many hasidic works.

R. Moshe Hayyim Ephraim of Sudlikov (1740–1800) was a grandson of the Besht on his mother's side, and was praised by the Besht in a letter to R. Avraham Gershon of Kutov. He also studied with the Maggid of Mezeritch and with R. Yaakov Yosef of Polennoye. Though he did not establish a dynasty, R. Moshe Hayyim Ephraim was the author of the highly influential *Degel Maḥaneh Ephraim*.

R. Nahman of Bratslav (1772–1811) was a great-grandson of the Besht on his mother's side, and on his father's side was the grandson of R. Nahman of Horodenka, who was prominent in the Besht's circle. In 1798 he visited Eretz Israel, but was forced to leave by Napoleon's invasion, after a stay of only a few months. Returning to Ukraine, he came into conflict with several other hasidic leaders, eventually settling in Bratslav and later Uman, where he died; his grave is still an object of pilgrimage by Bratslaver hasidim. His teachings were recorded in numerous volumes by his disciple, R. Nathan Sternhartz, who led the group after R. Nahman's death.

R. Pinhas of Koretz (1726–1791) met the Besht but was primarily a disciple of the Maggid of Mezeritch. He left Mezeritch in 1770 because of differences with the Maggid's followers and went his own way in hasidic thought. His disciples included R. Zev Wolf of Zhitomir and R. Yaakov Shimshon of Shepetovka. He too founded a dynasty.

R. Shelomoh of Lutzk (d. 1813) was an intimate disciple of the Maggid of Mezeritch and the publisher of his *Maggid Devarav le-Yaakov*. R. Shelomoh was himself the author of *Dibrat Shelomoh*.

R. Shemuel of Sochotchov (1856–1926), son of R. Abraham Borenstein, who was the son-in-law of the Kotzker Rebbe. R. Shemuel edited his father's halakhic works, *Eglei Tal* and *Avnei Nezer*, which quickly became standards, and himself authored the influential *Shem mi-Shemuel*, in which he sets forth many of his father's hasidic ideas.

R. Shneur Zalman of Liady (1745–1813), a disciple of the Maggid of Mezeritch, founded Habad Hasidism, which remains one of the most influential hasidic groups to this day. He was both a prominent *posek* and a systematic mystical thinker. His *Tanya* wields great influence even among Habad's opponents. Because of the systematic nature of his thought, he deals with many topics and issues which do not receive full treatment in other works.

R. Yaakov Yosef of Polennoye (d. ca. 1782) was Hasidism's first theoretician. His *Toledot Yaakov Yosef*, published in 1780, was the very first hasidic book printed, and it, along with his other works (*Ben Porat Yosef, Tzafnat Pa'ane'ah, Ketonet Pasim*), is a major source of the Besht's teachings, which R. Yaakov Yosef carefully labeled as such.

R. Yehudah Aryeh Leib of Gur (1847–1905) was a grandson of R. Yitzhak Meir (1789–1866), the founder of the Gur dynasty. He had great influence during his thirty-five years of leadership and after his death through his *Sefat Emet*, which remains highly popular.

R. Yitzhak Meir of Gur (1799-1866), a disciple of the Kotkzer Rebbe, was the founder of the Gur dynasty, and a noted talmudic scholar, known for his work, *Hiddushei ha-Rim*.

R. Yitzhak Yehudah Yehiel of Komarno (1806–1874) was a son of R. Alexander Sender of Komarno and thus a nephew of R. Zevi Hirsch of Zhidachov. He left many important works, among them *Zohar Hai* on the Zohar, *Asirit ha-Efah* on Sifra, *Otzar Hayyim*, a kabbalistic commentary on the mitzvot, and *Notzer Hesed* on Avot.

R. Zadok ha-Kohen of Lublin (1823–1900) was born to a rabbinic/mitnaggedic family in Latvia. A child prodigy, he became a hasid as a young man, and a follower of R. Mordecai Joseph Leiner of Izbica, known as the Izhbitzer, one of whose successors he eventually became. He was an incredibly prolific writer, and some ten volumes of his writings were published in the decades after his death, though many of his works seem to have been lost in the destruction of the Lublin ghetto during World War II.

R. Zev Wolf of Zhitomir (d. 1800) was a disciple of the Maggid of Mezeritch. His *Or ha-Meir* contains much of importance on the history of Hasidism and the teachings of the Besht and the Maggid.

R. Zevi Elimelekh of Dinov (1783–1841) was a nephew of R. Elimelekh of Lizhensk, after whom he was named. He studied with the Seer of Lublin, the Kozhnitzer Maggid, and R. Menahem Mendel of Rimanov. Aside from establishing a dynasty, he was the author of a number of influential works, among them *Benei Yisaskhar, Agra de'Kalla*, and *Agra de'Pirka*.

R. Zevi Hirsch of Zhidachov (d. 1831) was one of the four sons of R. Yitzhak Isaac of Safrin. He studied with R. Elimelekh of Lizhensk and R. Yaakov Yitzhak, the Seer of Lublin. Well known as a kabbalist, he produced a commentary on the Zohar as well as other important works.

Select Bibliography

PRIMARY SOURCES

The following bibliography is primarily intended to aid those researching the original sources of the selections. Standard rabbinic works in standard editions are not listed, nor are works cited only once or twice in the notes.

Agra de-Kallah. R. Zevi Elimelekh Shapiro of Dinov. Jerusalem, 1964.

Agra de-Pirka. R. Zevi Elimelekh Shapiro of Dinov. Brooklyn, 1984/5.

Asarah Ma'amarot. R. Menahem Azariah da Fano. Repr. Israel, n.d.

Avodat Yisrael. R. Israel of Kozhnitz. Bnei Brak, 1973.

Bahya b. Asher, *Commentary on Leviticus*. Ed. Chavel. Jerusalem, 1973/4.

Benei Yisaskhar. R. Zevi Elimelekh Shapiro of Dinov. New York, 1975.

Ben Porat Yosef. R. Yaakov Yosef of Polennoye. Pietrkow, 1887/8, Repr. Jerusalem, 1970/1.

Derashot ha-Ran. Ed. Feldman. Jerusalem, 1977.

Degel Mahaneh Ephraim. R. Mosheh Hayyim Ephraim. Jerusalem, 1963. New York: Baer, 1946/7. Bnei Brak, 1968/9.

Derekh Edotekah. R. Zevi Elimelekh Shapiro of Dinov. Jerusalem, 1986/7.

Derekh Mitzvotekha. R. Menahem Mendel of Lubavitch. Brooklyn, 1955/6.

Derekh Pikkudekha al Taryag Mitzvot ha-Torah. R. Zevi Elimelekh Shapiro of Dinov. Lemberg, 1914.

Divrat Shelomoh. R. Shelomoh of Lutzk. Jerusalem, 1955.

Emet va-Tzeddek; Emunah. R. Nahman of Bratslav. Jerusalem, 1980.

Esh Kodesh. R. Kalonymos Kalmish Shapiro. Jerusalem, 1960.

Hekhal ha-Berakhah. R. Yitzhak Yehudah Yehiel Safrin of Komarno.

Imrei Pinhas. R. Pinhas of Koretz. Ed. Yehezkel Shrage Frankel. 1987/8.

Kedushat Levi ha-Shalem. R. Levi Yitzhak of Berdichev. Munkacz, 1939. Repr, New York, 1962.

Kedushat Shabbat. R. Zadok ha-Kohen of Lublin. Lublin, 5691. Repr. Bnei Brak, 1971/2.

Kehillat Moshe. R. Moshe Elyakim Beri'ah, son of the Maggid of Kozhnitz. Repr. Brooklyn, 1965.

Ketav Yosher Divrei Emet. R. Zevi Elimelekh Shapiro of Dinov. Lublin, 1922.

Keter Shem Tov. Lemberg, 1865. Repr. Brooklyn, 1972.

Ketonet Passim. R. Yaakov Yosef of Polennoye. Lemberg, 1876. Repr. Brooklyn, 1976.

Likkutei Amarim. R. Pinhas of Koretz. Lemberg, 1792.

Likkutei Etzot. R. Nahman of Bratslav. Jerusalem, 1994/5.

Likkutei Moharan. R. Nahman of Bratslav. New York, 1957/8.

Likkutei Torah. R. Shneur Zalman of Liady. Repr. Brooklyn, 1965.

Likkutim Yekarim. Jerusalem, 1974.

Likkutim Yekarim. R. Pinhas of Koretz. Lemberg, 1792.

Maor va-Shemesh al ha-Torah ve-al ha-Moadim. R. Kalonymos Kalman Epstein. Jerusalem, 1990.

Ma'ayan Gannim to *Or ha-Ḥayyim*. R. Zevi Elimelekh Shapiro of Dinov. Lemberg, 1863. Lublin, 1926.

Maggid Devarav le-Yaakov. R. Dov Ber, Maggid of Mezeritch. Ed. Shatz-Uffenheimer. 2nd ed., Jerusalem, 1990.

Maggid Ta'alumah. R. Zevi Elimelekh Shapiro of Dinov. Jerusalem, 5747.

Ma'or va-Shemesh al ha-Torah u-Mo'adim. R. Kalonymos Kalman Epstein. 2nd ed., Jerusalem, 1985/6.

Me'or Einayim. R. Menahem Nahum of Chernobyl. Repr. Jerusalem, 1985/6.

Meshekh Ḥokhmah. R. Meir Simhah of Dvinsk. Ed. Cooperman. Jerusalem, 1974.

Meirat Einayim. R. Isaac of Acre. Jerusalem, 1981.

Midrash Pinḥas. R. Pinhas of Koretz. Ashdod, 1989/9.

Mishneh Torah. R. Moses Maimonides. Standard eds.

Moreh Nevukhim. R. Moses Maimonides. Standard eds.

Netiv Mitzvotekha. R. Yitzhak Yehudah Yehiel Safrin of Komarno. Jerusalem, 1982/3.

No'am Elimelekh. R. Elimelekh of Lizhensk. Ed. Gedaliah Nigal. Jerusalem, 1978.

Or Hashem. R. Hasdai Crescas. Ferrara, 1555. Repr. Jerusalem, 1970.

Or ha-Emet. R. Dov Ber of Mezeritch. Berdichev, 1899.

Or ha-Ḥayyim. R. Yosef Ya'avetz. Lublin, 1926.

Or Ne'erav. R. Moses Cordovero. Brooklyn, 1965.

Or Torah. R. Menahem Mendel of Lubavitch. Brooklyn, 1965.

Otzar ha-Ḥayyim. R. Yitzhak Yehudah Yehiel Safrin of Komarno. Brooklyn, 1969–70.

Or ha-Meir. R. Ze'ev Wolf of Zhitomir. Ashdod, 1994.

Pardes Rimonim. R. Moses Cordovero. Jerusalem, 1961/2.

Peri ha-Etz. R. Menahem Mendel of Vitebsk. Jerusalem, 1987.

Peri ha-Aretz. R. Menahem Mendel of Vitebsk. Jerusalem, 1987.

Pitgamin Kaddishin: Likkutim. Warsaw, 1886.

Reshit Ḥokhmah. R. Elijah de Vidas. Repr. Tel Aviv, 1962/3.

Sefer ha-Baal Shem Tov. Jerusalem, 1991/2.

Sefat Emet. R. Yehudah Aryeh Leib of Gur. Repr. Jerusalem, 1970/1.

Sha'ar ha-Kavvanot. R. Hayyim Vital. Repr. Tel Aviv, 1961/2.

Shem mi-Shemuel. R. Shmuel Borenstein of Sochachev. Jerusalem, 1991/2.

Shenei Luḥot ha-Berit. R. Isaiah Horowitz. Jerusalem, 1959.

Shivḥei ha-Besht. Ed. Horodetzki, Berlin, 1922.

Siḥot ha-Ran. R. Nahman of Bratslav. Jerusalem, 1976/7.

Sur Me'ra va-Aseh Tov im Hosafot MaHaRatzA [= Zevi Elimelekh Shapiro of Dinov] *Hashalem*. R. Zevi Hirsch of Zhidachov. Tel Aviv, n.d.

Takkanat ha-Shavin. R. Zadok ha-Kohen of Lublin. Repr. Bnei Brak, 19767/8.

Tanya, Likkutei Amarim. R. Shneur Zalman of Liady. Repr. Brooklyn, 1948/9.

Teshuot Ḥen. R. Gedaliah of Linitz. Jerusalem ed.

Toledot Yaakov Yosef. R. Yaakov Yosef of Polennoye. Jerusalem, 1962.

Tomer Devorah. R. Moses Cordovero. New York, 1942.

Torah Or. R. Shneur Zalman of Liady. Kopust, 1837.

Tzafnat Pa'ane'aḥ. R. Yaakov Yosef of Polennoye. Repr. Jerusalem, 1989.

Zava'at ha-Rivash. Besht. Ed. Kehos, Brooklyn, 1975/6.

Zidkat ha-Zaddik. R. Zadok ha-Kohen. Bnei Brak, 1973/4.

Zohar Ḥai. R. Yitzhak Yehudah Yehiel Safrin of Komarno.

SECONDARY SOURCES

Arendt, H. *The Life of the Mind*. New York, 1978.

Bauminger, Mordecai Shraga. "Od le-Iggerot ha-Besht ve-Hotno R. Avraham Gershon Kutov," *Sinai* 72 (1973), 270–283.

Ben-Amos, B., and J. Mintz, eds. *In Praise of the Baal Shem Tov: The Earliest Collection of Legends About the Founder of Hasidism*. Bloomington, 1972.

Blidstein, Gerald. *Honor Thy Father and Thy Mother: Filial Responsibility in Jewish Law and Ethics*. Hoboken, 1975.

Brill, A., *Intellectual Mysticism of R. Zadok ha-Kohen of Lublin*. New York, forthcoming.

Carmy, S. "Destiny, Freedom and the Logic of Petition." *Tradition* 24, no. 2 (1989): 17–37.

——. "A View from the Fleshpots: Exploratory Remarks on Gilded Galut Existence." *Tradition* 26, no. 4 (1992): 39–66.

Dienstag, J. "*Guide to the Perplexed* and *Sefer ha-Madda* in Hasidic Literature." In *Abraham Weiss Jubilee Volume*. New York, 1964, pp. 307–330.

Donner, M. M. *Sefer Baal Shem Tov*. Cleveland, 1948.

Dresner, Samuel H. *The Zaddik*. Northvale, N.J., 1994.

Dubnow, S. *Toledot ha-Ḥasidut*. Tel Aviv, 1960.

Elman, Yaakov. "R. Zadok haKohen on the History of Halakha." *Tradition* 21, no. 4 (Fall 1985): 1–26.

Etkes, E. "Heker ha-Ḥasidut: Megammot ve-Kivvunim." In *Madda'ei ha-Yahadut* 31. Jerusalem, 1991, pp. 5–21.

Finn, S. J. *Ha-Otzar*. Warsaw, 1921.

Green, Arthur. *Tormented Master: A Life of Rabbi Nahman of Bratslav*. University, Ala., 1979. Repr. New York, 1981.

Gries, Ze'ev. "Kuntras Hanhagot Ne'elam le-R. Nahman mi-Bratslav." *Kiryat Sefer* 53, no. 4 (September 1978).

——. *Sifrut ha-Hanhagot: Toledoteha, u-Meqomah be-Ḥayyei R. Yisrael Baal Shem Tov*. Jerusalem, 1989.

Hallamish, Moses. "The Attitude of the Kabbalists to Non-Jews" (Heb.). In *Philosophia Yisraelit*. Ed. Moshe Halamish and Assa Kasher. Tel Aviv, 1983.

———. *Mavo la-Kabbalah*. Jerusalem, 1992.

———. "Alim Rishonim mi-Perush ha-Tanya," *Da'at* 13 (Summer 1984): 67–76.

Hanokh, Hayyim. *Ha-Ramban ke-Hoqer u-Mequbbal*. Jerusalem, 1978.

Hertz, J. H. *The Pentateuch and Haftorahs*. 2nd ed. London, 1965.

Heschel, Abraham J. *The Circle of the Baal Shem Tov: Studies in Hasidism*. Chicago, 1985.

———. *A Passion for Truth: Reflections on the Founder of Hasidism, the Kotzker and Kierkegaard*. New York, 1973.

Hillmann, David Tzvi. *Iggerot Baal ha-Tanya*. Jerusalem, 1953.

Jacobs, Louis. *The Doctrine of the Zaddik in the Thought of Elimelekh of Lizhensk*. Rabbi Louis Feinberg Memorial Lecture in Judaic Studies. Cincinnati, 1978.

———. *Hasidic Prayer*. London, 1993.

———. *Seeker of Unity: The Life and Works of Aaron of Starosselje*. New York, 1967.

Jacobson, Yoram. *Toratah shel ha-Hasidut*. Tel Aviv, 1985.

Katz, Jacob. *Tradition and Crisis: Jewish Society at the End of the Middle Ages*. New York: 1977.

———. "Yom Tov Sheni shel Galuyot." In idem, *Ha-Halakhah be-Metzar*. Jerusalem, 1992, pp. 73–122.

Lamm, Norman. *Faith and Doubt*. New York, 1971.

———. *Halakhot ve-Halikhot*. Jerusalem, 1990.

———. "The Ideology of Neturei Karta—According to the Satmarer Version." *Tradition* 12, no. 2 (Fall 1971): 38–53.

——. "The Letter of the Besht to R. Gershon of Kutov." *Tradition* 14/4 (Fall 1974), pp. 110–125.

——. "Loving and Hating Jews as Halakhic Categories." *Tradition* 24, no. 2 (1989): 98–122.

——. "Matter and Spirit: Hasidic Doctrine According to Rabbi Solomon of Lutzk." *Gesher* 7 (5741): 7–13.

——. "Peace and Truth: Strategies for the Reconciliation—A Meditation." In *Reverence, Righteousness and Rahamanut: Essays in Memory of Rabbi Dr. Leo Jung*, ed. Jacob J. Schachter, Northvale, N.J., 1992, pp. 193–199.

——. *The Shema: Spirituality and Law in Judaism*. Philadelphia, 1998.

——. "Study and Prayer: Their Relative Value in Hasidism and Mitnagdism." In *Sefer Zikaron li-Shmuel K. Mirsky: Meḥkarim be-Halakhah uve-Aggadah be-Safrutha-Dorot uve-Maḥshevet Yisrael*. Ed. Gersion Appel, et al. New York, 1970, pp. 37–52.

——. "Teshuvah: Maḥshavah u-Ma'aseh." *Bet Yitzhak* 26 (1994), pp. 115–128.

——. *Torah Lishmah: Torah for Torah's Sake in the Works of Rabbi Hayyim of Volozhin and His Contemporaries*. New York, 1989.

——. *Torah u-Madda: The Encounter of Religious Learning and Worldly Knowledge in the Jewish Tradition*. Northvale, N.J., 1991.

——. "The Unity of God and the Unity of the World: Saadia and Maimonides." In Ruth Link-Salinger, ed., *Torah and Wisdom: Studies in Jewish Philosophy, Kabbalah, and Halacha; Essays in Honor of Arthur Hyman*. New York, 1992, pp. 113–120.

——. "United States of America: Perspectives," in *The Yom Kippur War: Israel and the Jewish People*, ed. Moshe Davis. New York, 1974, pp. 49–64.

Levinger, Y. "Amarot Otentiyot shel ha-Rabbi mi-Kotzk." *Tarbits* 55 (1986): 109–135.

————. "Torato shel ha-Rebbe mi-Kotzk le-Or ha-Amarot ha-Meyuhasot lo al yedei Nikhdo R. Shmuel mi-Sokhochov." *Tarbits* 55 (1986): 413–431.

Lysander, T. *Studien zum Beschtschen Hasidismus.* Uppsala, 1933.

Morgenstern, A. *Meshihiyut ve-Yishuv Eretz Yisrael ba-Mahazit ha-Rishonah shel ha-Me'ah ha-19.* Jerusalem, 1985.

Naor, B. "Two Types of Prayer." *Tradition* 25, no. 3 (1991): 26–34.

Neriyah, Moshe Zevi. *Mo'adei ha-Reiyah.* Tel Aviv, 1980.

Nigal, Gedaliah. "Al Demut ha-Zaddik be-Hasidut." *Molad* 30, n.s. 7(1975).

————. "Hashpa'ato ha-Filosofit shel R. Yosef Yaavetz," *Kiryat Sefer* 51 (5736): 289–299.

————. "Mishnat ha-Hasidut be-Kitvei R. Elimelekh mi-Lizhensk u-Veit Midrasho." Ph.D. diss. Yeshiva University, 1972.

————. "Moro re-Rabbo shel Yisrael Baal Shem Tov," *Sinai* 71 (1972), 150-159.

————. "Mishnat ha-Hasidut be-*Sefer Maor va-Shemesh.*" *Sinai* 75 (1974).

————. "De'otav shel R. Y. Yaavetz al Filosofia u-Mitpalsefim, Torah u-Mitzvot." *Eshel Beer Sheva* 1 (5736): 258–287.

————. Ed. *Noam Elimelekh.* Jerusalem, 1978.

Otto, Rudolf. *The Idea of the Holy.* Trans. John N. Harvey, New York, 1923.

Pierkarz, Mendel. *Hasidut Polin: Magganamot Ra'ayoniyot bein Shtei ha-Milhamot uvi-Gezerot Tash-Tashah ("Ha-Shoah").* Jerusalem, 1990.

————. "'Al Mah Avedah Galut Sefarad?'—ke-Leqah kelapei ha-Haskalah be-Mizrah Eiropa ha-Hasidit be-Einei R. Zevi Elimelekh Shapira mi-Dinov." *Da'at* 28 (5752): 87–115.

Ravitzky, Aviezer. *Al Da'at ha-Makom*. Jerusalem, 1991.

———. "Paradigms of Peace in Jewish Thought." In idem, *Ha-Ketz ha-Megulleh u-Medinat ha-Yehudim*. Tel Aviv, 1993.

Rubinstein, Avraham. "Iggeret ha-Besht le-R. Gerson mi-Kutov," *Sinai* 67 (1970), 120–139.

Saperstein, Marc. Ed. *Jewish Preaching, 1200–1800: An Anthology*. New Haven, 1989.

———. "Jews and Christians: Some Positive Images." *Harvard Theological Review* 79 (1986): 236–246.

Schindler, Pesach. *Responses of Hassidic Leaders and Hasidim During the Holocaust in Europe, 1939–1945, and a Correlation Between Such Responses and Selected Concepts in Hassidic Thought*. Hoboken, N.J., 1990.

Schochet, Ezriel. "Al ha-Simḥah be-Ḥasidut." *Zion* 16 (1951): 30–43.

Scholem, Gershom. "Demuto ha-Historit shel R. Yisrael Baal Shem Tov." *Molad* 18 (1960): 335–356. Also in idem, *Devarim Bego*. Tel Aviv, 1975.

———. "Devekut, or Communion with God." *Review of Religion* 14 (1950): 115—139. Also in idem, *The Messianic Idea in Judaism and Other Essays in Jewish Spirituality*. New York, 1971, pp. 203–227.

———. "Redemption Through Sin." In *The Messianic Idea in Judaism and Other Essays in Jewish Spirituality*. New York, 1971, pp. 78–141.

———. *Major Trends in Jewish Mysticism*. New York, 1961.

———. *The Messianic Idea in Judaism and Other Essays in Jewish Spirituality*. New York, 1971.

———. "Neutralization of the Messianic Element in Early Hasidism." In *The Messianic Idea in Judaism and Other Essays in Jewish Spirituality*. New York, 1971, pp. 176–203.

——. *On the Kabbalah and Its Symbolism*. New York, 1975.

——. *On the Mystical Shape of the Godhead*. New York, 1991.

——. *Von der Mistischen Gestalt der Gottheit*, Zurich, 1962.

Shatz, Rivka. "Le-Mahuto shel-ha-Zaddik be-Hasidut." *Molad* 18 (1960): 365–377.

Shatz-Uffenheimer, Rivka. *Hasidism as Mysticism: Quietistic Elements in Eighteenth Century Hasidic Thought*. Princeton, 1993.

——. *Maggid Devarav le-Yaakov*. See Primary Sources.

Shmueli, E. *Ba-Dor ha-Yehudi ha-Aharon be-Polin*. Tel Aviv: Alef, 1986.

Sperling, A. I. *Ta'amei ha-Minhagim*. Jerusalem, 1957.

Teitelbaum, M. *Ha-Rav mi Ladi u-Mifleget HaBaD*. Warsaw. 1913.

Tishby, I. "Ha-Ra'yon ha-Meshihi veha-Magamot ha-Meshihiyyot bi-Tzemihat ha-Hasidut," [Heb.]. *Zion* 32 (1967), pp. 1–45.

——. *Mishnat ha-Zohar*. Jerusalem, 1961.

——. "'Kudsha Berikh Hu', Oraita ve-Yisrael Kula Had Hu'—Mekor ha-Imrah be-Ferush *Idra Rabba* le-Ramhal." *Kiryat Sefer* 50 (Sivan 5735 [1975]): 480–492.

Twersky, I. "Maimonides on Eretz Yisrael: Halakhic Philosophic and Historical Perspectives." In *Perspectives on Maimonides: Philosophical and Historical Studies*. Ed. J. Kraemer. Oxford, 1991.

Underhill, Evelyn. *Mysticism: A Study in the Nature and Development of Man's Spiritual Consciousness*. New York, 1955.

Urbach, E. E. *The Sages: Their Beliefs and Opinions*. Trans. Israel Abrahams. Jerusalem, 1979.

van der Heide, Albert. "PARDES: Methodological Reflections on the Theory of the Four Senses." *Journal of Jewish Studies* 34 (1983): 147–159.

Weiss, David Yoel. *Megadim Ḥadashim*. Jerusalem, 5749.

Weiss, Joseph G. "A Circle of Pneumatics in pre-Hasidism." *Journal of Jewish Studies* 8 (1956): 199–213. Also in idem, *Studies in Eastern European Jewish Mysticism*. Ed. David Goldstein. Oxford, 1985, pp. 27—46.

———. "The Great Maggid's Theory of Contemplative Magic." *Hebrew Union College Annual* 31 (1960): 137–147. Also in idem, *Studies in Eastern European Jewish Mysticism*. Ed. David Goldstein. London, 1985, pp. 126–130.

———. "The Kavvanoth of Prayer in Early Hasidism." *Journal of Jewish Studies* 9 (1958): 163–192. Also in idem, *Studies in Eastern European Jewish Mysticism*. Ed. David Goldstein. London, 1985.

———. *Meḥkarim be-Ḥasidut Bratslav*. Jerusalem, 1974.

——— "Petitionary Prayer in Early Hasidism." In *Studies in Eastern European Jewish Mysticism*. Ed. David Goldstein. London, 1985, pp. 126–130.

———. "Reshit Tzemiḥatah shel ha-Derekh ha-Ḥasidit." *Zion* 17, nos. 3–4 (1951). Also in *Perakim be-Torat ha-Ḥasidut*. Ed. A. Rubenstein. Jerusalem, 1977, pp. 122–181.

———. "Talmud Torah be-Reshit ha-Ḥasidut." *Hadoar* 45, no. 3 (1965–66): 615–617.

———. "Talmud Torah le-Shitat R. Yisrael Besht." In H.J. Zimmels, *Tiferet Yisrael* (the *Brodie Feshtschrift*). London, 1967.

Werblowsky, R. J. Zwi. *Joseph Karo: Lawyer and Mystic*. Philadelphia, 1977.

Wertheim, A. *Law and Custom in Hasidism*. Hoboken, 1992.

Wiesel, Elie. *Four Hasidic Masters and Their Struggle Against Melancholy*. Notre Dame, 1978.

——. *Souls on Fire: Portraits and Legends of Hasidic Masters.* New York: Random House, 1972.

Wilensky, M. L. *Ḥasidim u-Mitnaggedim* (2 vols.). Jerusalem, 1970.

Glossary

ABBA. In the Zohar, Abba ("Father") usually refers to the sefirah of Hokhmah; in Lurianic Kabbalah, Hokhmah is the *partzuf* ("physiognomy") of Abba, and Binah that of Imma ("Mother"). In both systems Father is superior to Mother, in that Hokhmah precedes Binah in the emanation of the sefirot. For R. Elimelekh of Lizhensk, Father is clearly on a lower level than Higher Mother. *See* chap. 4, selection 10.

ACOSMISM. The doctrine that God is not only one and not only unique but utterly alone; that *nothing* exists other than God, and everything else is illusion; that there is, in reality, no cosmos, no world, nothing at all but God.

ADAM KADMON. "Primordial Man," the first configuration of divine light, which flows into the primeval space created by the initial act of *tzimtzum*, God's withdrawal into Himself. A ray of the Ein-Sof, called the "line" or "thread," penetrates through the first zone, Adam Kadmon, and then through the four worlds beginning with Atzilut and ending with Asiyah. This emanation suffers diminution and constriction as it descends through the worlds, and is identified with *memallei*, or immanence.

ADNUT. The Name *Adonay*, lit., "my Lord," not to be confused with the Tetragrammaton. *Adon* is a "master" or "lord," and Adnut represents that aspect of God; *see also* Malkhut.

ANIMAL SOUL. (1) the soul (*nefesh ha-bahamit*) that animates the physical functioning of the human organism; (2) the source of all lust, arrogance, and anger. According to R. Shneur Zalman, it is located in the left ventricle of the heart, whereas the divine soul (*nefesh ha-elohit*) dwells in the right one, and in the head. The two souls are in conflict over control of the body and its limbs. *See* Divine Soul.

AROUSAL FROM ABOVE. *See* Itaruta di-Le'ela.

ASIYAH. The lowest of the four worlds (Atzilut, Beri'ah, Yetzirah, Asiyah) which mediate between the Ein-Sof and the mundane world, the scene of human, profane activity. The spiritual dimension or essence of the world of Asiyah is called the lower Garden of Eden.

ATZILUT. The highest of the four worlds (Atzilut, Beri'ah, Yetzirah, Asiyah) that mediate between the Ein-Sof and the phenomenal world.

ATTRIBUTE, DIVINE. A divine quality, an aspect of God's relation to the world, usually hinting at one of the sefirot, the ten emanations of God's Being which mediate between the Ein-Sof and the worlds accessible to humankind. The sefirot are the "vessels," or channels, through which the Infinite Light or grace of the Ein-Sof issues forth and is contracted so as to create and act in the universe.

BENONI. A person who has only attained an intermediate spiritual level, i.e., though he may lead an entirely blameless life, he has not yet subdued his entire nature to God's Will, and therefore is motivated by both his good and evil inclinations.

BERI'AH. The second of the four worlds (Atzilut, Beri'ah, Yetzirah, Asiyah) which mediate between the Ein-Sof and the mundane world.

BERUR. A term that can be translated as "selection," "extraction," "clarification," or "sifting," depending upon the context. It refers to the liberation of the sparks of holiness in the husks (*kelippot*); *see* Breaking of the Vessels.

BITTUL, HITBATLUT. Self-nullification of one's identity or selfhood, as in the Habad school, or of the totality of one's evil qualities, such as avarice, lust, etc.

BREAKING OF THE VESSELS. After *tzimtzum*, God's "contraction," a *halal*, or vacuum, was left in the divine Being. Into this vacuum He radiated a "line" or "thread" of Light, which turned into ten vessels (the ten sefirot), which were inactive, merely the potential for divine self-revelation but not yet a reality. The Ein-Sof then poured of His own essence into the vessels, vitalizing them. The encounter between the infinitude of the Ein-Sof's Light and the limited nature of the ten sefirot resulted in a cosmic accident or catastrophe, the Breaking of the Vessels, which were unable to contain the infinite plenitude of the Ein-Sof. The overflow of sparks fell into a variety of *kelipot* ("shells")— symbols of mundane denseness, the nondivine, the potential for evil—where they were captured and await redemption, or liberation, by man by means of his service of the Lord, especially the performance of the mitzvot, the study of Torah, and kabbalistic meditations. When the divine sparks resulting from the Breaking of the Vessels have been completely redeemed from their servitude to base matter, they will have been elevated to their Source; then the Messiah will come, and Israel and the world will be redeemed. This final process is referred to as *berur* or *tikkun*.

DEVEKUT. The contemplation of God at all times, even when engaged in mundane occupations. According to the Besht, it is a state of heightened emotion, rhapsodic and ecstatic, in which *devekut* and social or physical activity must be simultaneous, and must relate to each other and interpenetrate. *Devekut* acts to raise the sparks of the mundane activity.

DIVINE SOUL. The source of elevated drives and desires, such as love of God, the divine soul (*nefesh ha-elohit*) abides in the head and the right ventricle of the heart. It is in conflict with the animal soul (*nefesh ha-bahamit*) which is located in the left ventricle, and is the source of physical lust, arrogance, and anger.

EIN-SOF. The absolute, self-contained Godhead, from which all comes, totally without distinction or differentiation in His absolute perfection, unknowable and indescribable, and devoid of all attribut- es—even of volition. The turning outward of the Ein-Sof takes place by means of the emanation of the ten sefirot, which are the self- expression of the Ein-Sof. The problem, however, is that the Ein-Sof, by virtue of His very absoluteness, leaves no space for that-which-is- not-Ein-Sof; the existence of anything that is other than Ein-Sof constitutes an infringement of His infinity. Hence, according to the Ari, the emanation of the sefirot was preceded by an act of *tzimtzum* ("constriction," or self-limitation), whereby the Ein-Sof entered into Himself, leaving room, as it were, for the creative process to take place by the emanation of the sefirot into the *halal* (primordial space) which thus emerged.

FATHER. *See* Abba.

FEMALE WATERS. *Mayyin Nukvin,* the kabbalistic term for the below-to-above motion, equivalent to another term widely used, "the awakening from below." The converse is Male Waters or "the awakening from above." The former denotes human initiative and endeavors, the latter, divine grace or effluence (*shefa*).

GEVURAH. *See* Sefirot.

HALAL. The primordial space which opened up after the *tzimtzum*. *See* Breaking of the Vessels; Ein-Sof.

HAMTAKAT HA-DINIM BE-SHORASHAM. "The sweetening of judgments in their source," i.e., the regression via contemplation of what is apparently evil and harsh to its roots in the sefirot, where it undergoes a metamorphosis to the good and beneficent.

HESED. *See* Sefirot.

HOMER. Unformed matter, which requires *tzurah* ("form") to give it shape and direction. Similarly, the body too requires the direction of the soul—its form; a complete human being requires both.

IMMA. In the Zohar, "Lower Mother" refers to Malkhut and "Higher Mother" to Binah. *See* Abba.

IMMANENCE, DIVINE. God's closeness to man or, more accurately, His "withinness" in the world. His inherence in the cosmos ensures that He is close enough to relate to, experience, love and fear, assume the aspects of personality. The Aramaic phrase *memallei kol almin*, "permeating all worlds," corresponds to Hokhmah, the basic sphere which embodies Keter and is the immanent source of all subsequent emanation. Compare Transcendence.

IMMANENTISM. The doctrine of divine immanence.

ITARUTA DI-LE'ELA. *See* Itaruta di-Letata.

ITARUTA DI-LETATA. "Arousal from below"; an act undertaken by man, a human effort. Arousal from above (*itaruta di-le'ela*) refers to the divine *shefa*, issuing from above. Generally, to elicit this heavenly emanation, the arousal has to be initiated by an appropriate benevolent act on earth.

KELIPAT NOGAH. "Translucent shell," one of the four classes of shells (*see* Kelipot), the only one that is not entirely evil. It is the "skin" most directly in touch with the holy spark that gives it existence, and thus good and evil "serve in confusion." Man's function is to purify the good from its contamination by evil.

KELIPOT. "Shells." Symbols of mundane denseness, the nondivine, the potential for evil, parts of the broken vessels (*see* Breaking of the Vessels). They would be unable to survive if not for the spark of holiness they enclose.

LOWER UNITY. *See* Upper Unity, Lower Unity.

MALKHUT. The lowest sefirah; it represents God's kingdom or kingship in this world, and is identified with the Shekhinah, and with the Jewish people, *Kelal Yisrael*. In the Zohar, Lower Mother refers to Malkhut.

Malkhut also represents the culmination of the divine will to be revealed. In the diagramming of the sefirot according to the pattern of Adam Kadmon, the primordial man, it is represented by the mouth, which is the climax of the process that begins with the initial thought and devolves into speech. Hence it is also identified with the Oral Torah—Mishnah, Talmud, and the related literature—which in Hebrew is literally "Torah of the mouth."

MAYYIN NUKVIN. *See* Female Waters.

MICROCOSM (*olam katan*, "small world"). Every human being is a miniature world, each of his limbs corresponding to an aspect of the universe. This is the general understanding of the term; R. Yaakov Yosef of Polennoye and R. Yitzhak Isaac of Komarno apply it to the people of Israel as a whole.

MIDDOT. Moral/emotional attributes of the human soul, corresponding to the seven lower sefirot, which are their root: love of God, dread and awe of Him, glorification of Him, etc.

MOHIN. Lit. "brains," but used variously in hasidic literature. The term defies accurate translation; it can imply mind, cognitive capacity, level of inspiration, or the esoteric source of wisdom, and is often identified with the sefirah of Hokhmah.

MOTHER. *See* Imma.

NEFESH. *See* Soul.

NEFESH HA-BAHAMIT. *See* Animal Soul.

NEFESH HA-ELOHIT. *See* Divine Soul.

NESHAMAH. *See* Soul.

PANTHEISM. The belief that all is God, i.e., that He is the principle of Nature, identified with the world itself, and coextensive with it.

PARTZUF. "Countenance." Term used in Lurianic Kabbalah to denote one aspect of the deity. The *partzuf* is a whole entity in its own right, merging its constituent parts into one unity. R. Yaakov Yosef uses the term in its general sense to show how the zaddikim and the masses relate to each as parts of one whole organism.

RAHAMIM. Another name for the sefirah of Tiferet; *see* Sefirot.

RATZON HA-ELYON. "The Supernal Will." Identical with the sefirah of Keter, which is one level higher than Hokhmah. In R. Shneur Zalman's system of Habad, in which Hokhmah is the first of the ten sefirot, Keter is assigned to the intermediate region between the absolute, self-contained Ein-Sof and the realm of the sefirot, His self-revelation. By relating mitzvah (the observance of the commandments) to Keter, and (the study of) Torah to Hokhmah, he relates the observance of the commandments to transcendence, and hence a higher spiritual level than Torah, which expresses divine immanence.

REDEMPTION. *See* Tikkun.

RUAH. *See* Soul.

SEFER YETZIRAH. One of the classic early texts of Kabbalah.

SEFIROT (sing. SEFIRAH). The ten emanations of God's Being which mediate between the Ein-Sof and the worlds accessible to humankind. The sefirot are "vessels," or channels, through which the Infinite Light from the Ein-Sof issues forth and is contracted to create and act in the universe.

The ten sefirot are Hokhmah ("Wisdom"), Binah ("Understanding"), Da'at ("Knowledge"), Hesed ("Kindness"), Gevurah ("Might"), Tiferet ("Beauty, Majesty")—sometimes called Rahamim ("Mercy")—Netzah ("Eternity, Victory"), Hod ("Majesty"), Yesod ("Foundation"), Malkhut ("Kingdom"). They interact in various ways in order to transmit God's grace to the the world; for example, Tiferet dialectically reconciles Hesed and Gevurah. The triad Hesed-Gevurah-Tiferet represents the patriarchs (Abraham, Isaac, and Jacob).

The sefirot also serve to categorize different aspects of man's experience of God and to generate a complex network of correspondences between the divine sphere and the world (e.g., the lower seven sefirot correspond to the three patriarchs, David and Solomon, Moses and Aaron), thus providing a focus for man's contemplation of God. Particularly in Habad, the ten sefirot are internalized and become a paradigm for character traits.

SHAHARIT. Morning prayers, texts from which are often used as sources for essential mystical doctrines.

SHEFA. Often translated as "abundance," "grace," "effluence"; the beneficient outpouring of God's benevolence in the world and on human beings.

SHEKHINAH. Lit. "the Indwelling," used in rabbinic literature to designate the Divine Presence; in Kabbalah it is identified with the sefirah of Malkhut.

SHEVIRAT HAKELIM. *See* Breaking of the Vessels.

SITRA AHARA. Lit. "the other side." There are ten sefirot in the world of *tum'ah* ("impurity"), just as there are ten sefirot in the world of *kedushah* ("holiness"). These latter are called *sitra de-yamina,* ("the right side") or *sitra da* ("this side"), while the others are called *sitra di-semala* ("the left side") or *sitra ahara* ("the other side"). The last phrase also designates the demonic forces.

SOUL. In Kabbalah and Hasidism, the soul comprises several parts or layers. The three most basic of its five elements are, in ascending order, *nefesh,* the quality of biological vitality; *ruah,* the power of speech and intellect, or emotional-intellectual existence; and *neshamah,* the most spiritual and partly transcendent aspect of the soul that links man, ultimately, to God. The next two, *hayah* and *yehidah,* are much less frequently discussed because of their superior degree of transcendence.

Classical Kabbalah tended to describe the divine structures in human terms. R. Shneur Zalman reversed the order and describes man's personality in terms of divine sefirot. Thus, the Kabbalah largely elaborated an anthropological theology, whereas R. Shneur Zalman offered a theological anthropology, or kabbalistic psychology. By asserting the equivalents of the ten sefirot in each level of the soul, R. Shneur Zalman opens up the possibility of attaining knowledge of God by probing the human soul.

SPARKS. *See* Breaking of the Vessels.

SUPERNAL WILL. *See* Keter.

TETRAGRAMMATON. The ineffable four-letter Hebrew "proper" Name of God, representing the divine quality of Hesed, in the sense of the generation of existence.

TIFERET. One of the sefirot, sometimes called Rahamim; *see* Sefirot.

TIKKUN. After the Breaking of the Vessels, the overflow of sparks fell into a variety of *kelipot* ("shells"), where they were captured and await redemption, or liberation, by means of man's service of the Lord, especially the performance of the mitzvot, the study of Torah, and kabbalistic meditations. When the divine sparks resulting from the Breaking of the Vessels have been completely redeemed from their servitude to base matter, they will have been elevated to their Source, the Messiah will come, and Israel and the world will be redeemed.

TRANSCENDENCE. The doctrine that God is Other, different ("far") from the created order in essence, substance, and nature. One possible consequence of this view is belief in a personal God, so that we are aware of a Presence to which or Whom we can attempt to relate. Another consequence, if it is carried too far, is deism, the doctrine that God is so removed from the world that He is indifferent to it, and to humankind. The Hebrew-Aramaic phrase *sovev kol almin*, "surrounding the worlds," denotes divine transcendence: God in His utter and undifferentiated beyondness. In terms of the sefirot, *sovev kol almin* corresponds to Keter, the supreme transcendent sphere. Compare Immanentism.

TZIMTZUM. The Ein-Sof's self-limitation in order to allow room for creation. The Ein-Sof, by virtue of His very absoluteness, leaves no "space" for that which-is-not-Ein-Sof; the existence of any object that is other than Ein-Sof constitutes an infringement of His infinity. Hence, according to the Ari, the emanation of the sefirot was preceded by an act of *tzimtzum* ("constriction" or self-limitation), whereby the Ein-Sof entered into Himself, leaving "room," as it were, for the creative process to take place by the emanation of the sefirot into the *halal* (primordial space) which thus emerged. *See* Ein-Sof; Sefirot.

TZURAH. Form, *see* Homer.

UPPER UNITY, LOWER UNITY. The Upper Unity is the vision of God and the world in which the Divine Presence overwhelms and hence nullifies the world: only God exists, all else is mere illusion. This is the aspect of the Tetragrammaton. The Lower Unity, represented by the various other divine names, depicts a relationship between king and subjects, i.e., between God and world, and hence confirms both. It is in this dimension that man's life is lived, his emotions felt, his environment experienced.

YETZIRAH. Formation, the third of the four worlds (Atzilut, Beri'ah, Yetzirah, Asiyah), the abode of the angels.

ZOHAR. The central text of Jewish mysticism, attributed to the tanna, R. Simon b. Yohai (2nd cent. C.E.).

Index of Scriptural Citations

(Hebrew Bible and Apocrypha)

130:1	520
136:1	488
136:4	312
137:1	525
137:7	559, 561
139:12	42
139:21	422
139:22–23	273
145	214
145:9	97, 480
145:18	20, 453
145:19	189, 203, 286
145:20	190
147:8	45
147:20	428
148:14	525, 599

Proverbs

1:5	381
1:6	471
1:8	240
3:6	337, 380, 526–527
3:12	342, 474, 476
3:16	234
3:18	236, 245
3:19	46, 521
3:21	553
3:35	212
4:21	553
4:23	236, 423
5:5	572
5:16	552
9:1	91, 598
9:9	554
10:6	504
10:12	439
12:8	212
12:19	122
14:23	394, 397
14:28	12
16:7	66
16:15	470
17:8	554
17:16	236

18:2	210
18:21	496
19:9	236
19:11	352
19:23	504, 505
21:3	349
21:21	505
22:17	471
23:16	181
25:2	26
26:11	357
27:5	128, 475
27:6	307
27:10	432
27:19	126, 146, 434, 475, 504
28:13	480
28:14	241, 242
31:10	65–66
31:25	492
31:30	123, 385, 597

Job

2:4	349
5:7	478
11:7	162
11:9	451
19:20	288
19:26	207, 248, 374
22:14	87
22:28	287
23:9	194
25:3	147
28:12	45, 286, 446, 566
28:28	85
31:2	57
34:19	46
35:17	36

Song of Songs

1:2	144, 153
1:8	597
2:2	574
2:6	144
3:11	600

5:2	195
5:8	161
5:9	597
6:1	409, 597
7:7	121, 131
8:1	467
8:6	467, 520
8:7	129

Ruth
2:4	125, 433

Lamentations
2:3	525
2:19	403
3:23	95, 412
3:38	462, 464, 483
4:20	504
5:21	353, 575
5:22	341

Ecclesiastes
1:14	63
1:18	584
2:2	399, 551
2:13	89
2:14	357
2:23	478
3:1	317
3:1 ff.	527
3:2–8	317
3:14	115, 536
3:21	420
7:11	71
7:12	565
7:14	62, 117, 472, 520–521
7:19	241
7:24	86
7:29	87, 471
8:15	399
9:11	85
9:14–15	274
10:7	378

10:12	21, 31, 159, 311, 449, 581
12:11	498
12:13	91

Esther
3:8	437
4:16	437, 595
9:26	554

Daniel
2:37	530
4:24	344
7:10	147

Nehemiah
9:6	29, 117, 559–560

1 Chronicles
4:23	76, 596
16:27	397, 470
28:9	72, 78, 79, 162
29:12	483

2 Chronicles
6:18	281
17:6	356
32:31	470

Judith
4:5	592
5:24	595
5:27	592
6:23–27	592

Commentaries on the Torah and Nakh

Index of Rabbinic Citations

Deuteronomy
11:22 — 150
14:21 Re'eh — 169
21:10 — 158
46 — 421

Sifrei
Va-Ethanan 32 — 276

Song of Songs Rabbah
1:2 — 44
5:2 — 214, 430
5:3 — 358, 418

Tana de-vei Eliyahu Rabbah
1 — 498
3 — 129

Tanhuma
Nitzavim 5 — 421
Shemini 3 — 470
Shemot 1 — 588
23 — 64, 83, 93

Tosafot
Ketubbot 103b — 507
Pesahim 113b — 126, 432
Yom Tov to Avot 5:5 — 190

Tosefta Berakhot
6:13 — 417

Yalkut Shimoni I
824 — 598

Yalkut Shimoni II
944 — 567

Yalkut Shimoni
sec. 604 — 181
1 Kings 5:11 — 77
Ps. 89:1 — 77
Jonah 3:8 — 217
Va-Ethanan 9 — 835

Zohar I
4b — 230
11 — 108
11b — 111, 114, 115, 120
12a — 111, 129
18b — 11, 18
23b — 191
24a — 229
24b, Pekudei — 128
25a — 468
31b — 17
35b — 469
49b — 486
54a — 241
58a — 289
60b — 576
83a, — 317
99a — 576
109–110, Midrash ha-Ne'elam — 580
109a–112a — 571
109b — 580
111b — 102
120 — 524
125b, Midrash ha-Ne'elam — 499
137b — 293
138a — 126, 431
153b — 304
167b — 293
170b — 228
179a — 209
180b — 395
181a — 467
197a — 210
206a — 58
216b — 427
237a — 576
245b — 304
248b — 576
254b — 128

Index of Post-Talmudic Citations

Index of Names and Subjects

"Demuto ha-Historit shel R.
  Yisrael" (Scholem), 254
"De'otav shel R. Y. Ya'avetz al
  Filosofiya" (Nigal), 69
Depression. *See* Sadness
Derekh Pekudekha, 500
Derekh Tevunot (Luzzatto), 40
Derush, 20
Descent for purpose of ascent, 337
"Destiny, Freedom and the Logic
  of Petition" (Carmy), 174, 217
Determinism and predestination,
  89
Devekut
  Abraham, 261
  Adam, 509
  Aharon of Zhitomir, 605
  alien thoughts, 376
  and halakhah, 24, 194
  and bodily needs, 327
  antinomian aspect, 166
  ascent, 19, 543
  ascent to God, 134
  atomization of, 377
  avodah be-gashmiyut, 137
  basis for *yihud*, 143
  Besht, 136, 138, 141, 150, 163,
    323, 406, 443, 452
  Buber, xlvii
  challenge posed by, 324
  common man, 136
  constant, 26, 140, 181
  cosmic, 26
  d-b-k etymological root, 133
  defined, 26, 133–139
  descent from, 189, 270
  divrei reshut, 323
  dualistic view, 137
  during mundane activity, 151
  elevating worlds, 26
  Elimelekh of Lizhensk, 318
  equated with *talmud torah
    lishmah*, 171
  greatness and smallness, 324,

    378, 404, 406, 551
  hasidic emphasis on, 3
  Hayyim of Volozhin, 164
  hishtavut, 443
  in religiously "neutral" realm, 24
  in Bible, 133
  irrelevance of death, 510
  Israel with God, 283
  Jacob, 510, 511
  Jacob and Rachel, 143
  joy, 3
  kabbalah, 141
  letters of Hebrew alphabet, 183
  Luria, 183
  Maimonides, 135
  Menahem Mendel, 163
  mitzvot, 148, 194, 247
  monistic view, 137, 323
  mundane activities, 324
  mystical view, 134
  Nahman of Kossov, 136–137,
    150, 157, 163, 249, 328
  Nahmanides, 135
  observing mitzvot, 104, 121
  prayer, 288
  pre-hasidic pneumatics, 135,
    136, 150, 543
  pride in, 452
  Scholem, xlvii, 135, 139
  seclusion, 157
  sefirot, 135
  self-annihilation, 217
  sexual aspects, 246, 261
  Shatz-Uffenheimer, 139, 142
  Shulhan Arukh, 141
  Talmud, 134
  Torah study, 148, 172, 220–221,
    240, 243, 245–247, 249, 554
  weeping on Sabbath, 389
  Weiss, 249, 377
  wholehearted, 560
  Yaakov Yitzhak of Polennoye,
    327
  yihud, 137, 145

disciples, 607
dying vision of Shekhinah, 508
exile and redemption, 528–529
life and death, 495
mentioned, 120
resurrection, 495–496
selections, 495, 508, 528
Israel of Riszhin, xlix
Isserles, Moses, 160
It'hapkha, 381, 457
Itkafia, 380, 457
Izhbitzer Rebbe, xlvi, 609

Jacob
attribute of everlasting love, 128
called Israel, 318, 469–470, 493
corresponds to Third Temple,
529
death, 493
devekut, 143, 511
did not really die, 510, 511
dream of angels, 530
Emet, 510
Ephraim and Manasseh, 278
equated with Third Temple, 514
Esau, 469–470, 529
evening prayer, 129
faith and trust, 466
Garden of Eden, 504
great love, 129
indicates lowliness, 493
Joseph, 137, 598
Laban, 601
Leah, 588, 601
mentioned, 546
most perfect of patriarchs, 536
observed 613 commandments
before Sinai, 383
Rachel, 143, 189, 383, 588, 598,
601
Rahamim, 45, 142, 144
represents divine soul, 122
root of all good, 469
symbolizing type of religious
leader, 303

tam, 87, 383
Tiferet, 56, 330, 349, 383, 510,
576
tikkun, 470
took note of beauty, 383, 598
went his own way, 206
yihud, 143
Jacob b. Asher, 567
Jacob Emden of Altona, xl
Jacob of Lissa, 460
Jacob of Orleans, 78
Jacobs, Louis
cited, 5, 13, 51, 176, 183, 186,
188, 215, 216, 218, 252, 257, 259,
261, 262, 319, 321, 322, 587
Jacobson, Yoram
cited, 454, 457
Jealousy, 416
Jeroboam, 574, 575–576
"Jewish devils," 248, 303–305
Jewish people, as microcosm, 308
Jewish Preaching (Saperstein), 438
"Jews and Christians" (Saperstein),
424
Job, 479
Joel, 340
Jonah, 279, 280
Joseph
Ephraim and Manasseh, 277, 278
Jacob, 137, 169, 598
Potiphar's wife, 598
Yesod, 56
Joshua, 158, 531
Joy
and freedom, 400
attained by wicked in this world,
580
basic hasidic tenet, 191
Besht, 389, 408
continual, 389, 399, 468
displays of, 387, 388
frivolity, 400–402, 408
God's immanence, 390
in Temple era, 581
in *katnut*, 404

Upper Garden of Eden, 563
Urbach, Ephraim E.
  cited, 141
U-Vikkashtem mi-Sham
  (Soloveitchik), 221
Vadnick, Shimon Mendel, 433
Van der Heide, Albert
  cited, 236
Vernacular prayer, 198
"A View from the Fleshpots"
  (Carmy), 515
Vilna Gaon
  calculating end of days, 583
  Kabbalah, 6
  Menahem Mendel of Vitebsk,
    607
  mentioned, 570
  mitnaggedism, xxxi–xxxii
  opposition to Hasidism, 6,
    xxxi–xxxii, xliv
  Shneur Zalman, xliv, 40
  tzimtzum, 40
Visualization, 158
Vital, Hayyim
  Etz Hayyim, 103
  heart and mind, 103
  Torah lishmah, 242
  two souls, 57, 328
Volozhiner, Hayyim. *See* Hayyim
  of Volozhin
*Von der Mistischen Gestalt der
  Gottheit* (Scholem), 248

Warsaw Ghetto, 459, 607
Wasting semen, 497
Water, 103, 465
Weddings, 400
Weeping, 389
Weiss, David Yoel, 223
Weiss, Joseph G.
  descent of zaddik, 267–268
  devekut, 137, 163, 249, 328, 377
  Dov Ber, 49, 53
  dualism, 454, 486

evil, 454–455
Habad vs. Bratslav prayer, 217
hasidic conceptions of God,
  49–50, 53
maggidim, xliii
mystic religion vs. faith religion,
  49–50, 53, 319
Nahman of Bratslav, 49, 53,
  216–217, 455
pre-hasidic pneumatic circle,
  135, 253, 267
raising of sparks, 374
Shneur Zalman, 53, 216–217
Torah study, 249
zaddik, 265, 268, 319
cited, 49, 53, 69, 135, 150, 162,
  164, 175, 183, 216, 249, 250,
  252, 253, 254, 255, 283, 319,
  320, 327, 328, 454, 543
Werblowsky, R. J. Zwi
  cited, 153, 249
Wertheim, A.
  cited, 252, 322
Wicked Son (Passover Haggadah),
  30
Wiesel, Elie, xlvi, 459
  cited, 49, 388
Wilensky, M. L.
  cited, 40, 216, 299, 587
Wolfson, Harry A., 67
Women
  and rise of Hasidism, 585
  associated with Din, 588
  compared with men, 585
  conversation with, 281
  Dov Ber, 587
  evil inherent in natural realm,
    587
  faith based on tradition, 73, 85
  Levi Yitzhak of Berdichev, 586,
    589
  Maharal, 585
  Maimonides, 585
  miracles, 586, 590

locus of *neshamah*, 504
lofty soul, 258
love for, 309
Lower and Higher Zaddiks, 321
lowering of, 318
magic, 284, 320
Man of Form, 162, 255, 275
merit, 273
mesirat ha-mahshavot la-zaddik,
    299, 312
Shekhinah, 483
messianic aspects, 254, 319
metempsychosis, 257
miracles, 284, 294–295
mitnaggedic criticisms of, 299,
    312
mitzvot, 193, 321
Moses, 294
Moshe Hayyim Ephraim,
    280–281
mystical aspects, 255, 266
Nahman of Bratslav, 252,
    254–255, 258, 261–262,
    273–275, 292–296, 300–303,
    312, 319
neshamah, 504
no prophetic powers, 262
nullifies divine decrees, 261, 285,
    286, 291–292, 321
parental endowment, xliv, 257
perfection of, 302
piety and good deeds, 272
powers, 261, 285
prayer, 187, 255, 260–262, 264,
    283, 291–292, 320–321, 363,
    401
pre-hasidic, 253
prophecy, 262, 275, 319
protests, 528
redemption money, 401
redemptive role, 267, 513
relations with followers, 175,
    194, 266–267, 280–281, 299,
    300–306, 312, 318, 363

relegating thoughts to, 299, 312
repentance, 313, 348, 353, 356,
    357
retreat and self-constriction, 311
righteousness, 26
role of, xliii, xliv, 26, 267, 513
ruah ha-kodesh, 262, 275, 319, 504
sadness, 303
sanctifies self through physical,
    330
scholarship, 272, 300
secular knowledge, 91, 296
self-confidence, 295
"self-made," 319
selflessness, 316–317, 499
shefa, 261, 262, 264, 266, 308,
    310–311
Shekhinah, 308, 321
Shneur Zalman, 258–259, 320,
    503
sin, 314
sitra ahara, 122
solitude, 282
source of authority, 274
spiritual powers, 287
stories, 398
strange conduct, 301
studying the seven sciences, 91
sweetening the judgments, 263,
    283, 320–321
talking to God in Yiddish, 199
talmid hakham, 252–254, 300
Torah study, 228, 238, 247,
    305–306, 321
Torah discourse, 186
"totality of Israel," 257
traditional sense term, 26
understanding him through his
    followers, 273
Upper Garden of Eden, 563
Upper and Lower Zaddiks, 321
vernacular prayer, 199
Weiss, 319
when distressed or in exile, 528

Zev Wolf of Zhitomir
  biography, 608, 609
  exile and redemption, 523, 524
  life and death, 492–493
  upper and lower zaddik, 321
  women, 594–597
  selections, 492, 523, 594
Zidkat ha-Zaddik, 64

Zionism, 515–516
Zohar, 115
  fear of God, 99
  love, 127
  alefbet, 11
Zusya of Hanipol, 606
Zweifel, Eliezer, 21